Simulation Foundations, Methods and Applications

For further volumes:
www.springer.com/series/10128

Murilo G. Coutinho

Guide to Dynamic Simulations of Rigid Bodies and Particle Systems

Springer

Murilo G. Coutinho
Sony Pictures Imageworks
Los Angeles, CA, USA

Series Editor
Prof. Louis G. Birta
School of Information Technology and Engineering
University of Ottawa
Ottawa, ON, Canada

ISSN 2195-2817　　　　　　　　　　ISSN 2195-2825 (electronic)
Simulation Foundations, Methods and Applications
ISBN 978-1-4471-6116-5　　　　　　ISBN 978-1-4471-4417-5 (eBook)
DOI 10.1007/978-1-4471-4417-5
Springer London Heidelberg New York Dordrecht

To my family
Izabella, Leticia and Nicholas

Preface

Physically based modeling is widely used within the computer graphics and mechanical engineering industries as a way of achieving realistic animations and accurate simulations of complex systems. Such complex systems are usually hard to animate using scripts, and difficult to analyze using conventional mechanics theory, which makes them perfect candidates for physically based modeling and simulation techniques.

The field of physically based modeling is broad. It includes everything from modeling a ball rolling on the floor, to a car engine working, to clothing a virtual character. The theory varies from precise mathematical methods to purpose-specific approximated solutions that are mathematically incorrect, but produce realistic animations for the particular situation being considered. Depending on the case, an approximated solution might serve the purpose, however, there are times when approximations are not admissible, and the use of accurate simulation engines is a requirement. Developing and implementing physically based dynamic-simulation engines that are robust is difficult. The main reason is that it requires a breadth of knowledge in a diverse set of subjects, each of them standing alone as a broad and complex topic.

Instead of attempting to address all types of simulation engines available in the broad area of physically based modeling, this book provides in-depth coverage of the most common simulation engines. These simulation engines restrict the general case of physically based modeling to the particular case wherein the objects interacting are either particles or rigid bodies.

This book is a comprehensive introduction to the techniques needed to produce realistic simulations and animations of particle and rigid-body systems. It focuses on both the theoretical and practical aspects of developing and implementing physically based dynamic-simulation engines that can be used to generate convincing animations of physical events involving particles and rigid bodies, such as the demolition of a bridge or building with debris falling all over. It can also be used to produce accurate simulations of mechanical systems, such as a robotic parts feeder where parts are dropped on a conveyor belt and then positioned and aligned as they hit fences strategically placed on the conveyor and used to align the parts at a specific orientation.

Guide to Dynamic Simulations of Rigid Bodies and Particle Systems was written for computer graphics, computer animation, computer-aided mechanical design and modeling software developers who want to learn to incorporate physically based dynamic-simulation features into their own systems. The goal of this book is to make the principles and methods of physically based modeling of particle and rigid-body systems accessible to a broader audience of software developers who are familiar with mainstream computer-graphics techniques, and the associated mathematics.

The book is organized into three main topics: particle systems, rigid-body systems, and articulated rigid-body systems. The first chapter is an overview of how all techniques covered in this book fit together as independent modules constituting a simulation engine. The following chapters and appendices go into more detailed explanations for each technique. The techniques developed can be used to create simulation engines capable of combining particles, rigid bodies and articulated rigid bodies into a single system. Each chapter presents many algorithms and covers them in considerable depth, yet makes their design and analysis accessible to all levels of readers. We have tried to keep explanations elementary without sacrificing depth or mathematical rigor.

The most complex mathematical algorithms are described in detail in the appendices. Our goal here is to focus the reader's attention to the details of the topic being covered, and not be distracted by mathematical issues that can be viewed as "black box" modules having specific functionality (such as a numerical integrator or a rigid-body-mass-properties computation module). Readers should be able to develop their own software implementation of a simulation engine using the techniques covered in-depth in this book, or shorten their software development effort by taking advantage of the several resources available on the Web.

Acknowledgments

I wish to thank my wife, Izabella, and my children Leticia and Nicholas for all their support, encouragement and love.

Los Angeles, CA, USA   Murilo G. Coutinho

Contents

Part I
Dynamic Simulation

The following five chapters will guide the readers through both theory and practical aspects of implementing a real-time dynamic simulation engine for rigid body and particle systems. These chapters will cover in details all components needed for the robust software implementation of a simulator.

Dynamic Simulations

1

1.1   Introduction

The quest for realism and precision in computer-graphics simulations of complex systems started decades ago, when engineers realized the importance and cost effectiveness of having reliable computer models for their products. The ability to study the inner workings of a system according to several different scenarios long before the beginning of the manufacture cycle was compelling enough to lead to an impressive amount of work on physically-based simulation and modeling.

The physically based modeling of the interactions between parts in such systems is particularly attractive because they are not limited to a single-domain analysis. On the contrary, the simulations are extremely useful because they can be extended to multiple-domain analysis of the system, such as the combination of thermal and stress-test analysis of the materials used to manufacture the parts, with the forces exerted on them obtained from the mechanical-contact analysis. In this case, the combination can be used to predict the maximum force that can be exerted on each part before it cracks. The set of applications with the potential of benefiting from such work is diverse, ranging from aircraft and automobile design, to structural analysis of buildings, to weather simulations and toxic-plume-spread analyzers, and even to video games.

The challenge in combining multi-domain simulations is that usually each domain of interest being simulated requires the development of specialized mathematical models capable of expressing subtle interactions that match the correct theoretical physical behavior of the system. In many cases, such specialized mathematical models are implemented using different numerical methods that may or may not be compatible with one another. When the numerical methods are compatible, the models can be easily merged and the coupling effects between the different domains can be quickly evaluated. However, there are cases when the numerical methods are incompatible and a direct merge is infeasible. In these cases, the models are usually combined in an interleaved fashion. The interleaved approach consists of solving one method at a time, with their coupling being represented by a set of external forces and constraints that are applied from the system that was just solved to the

M.G. Coutinho, *Guide to Dynamic Simulations of Rigid Bodies and Particle Systems*,
Simulation Foundations, Methods and Applications,
DOI 10.1007/978-1-4471-4417-5_1, © Springer-Verlag London 2013

system that will be solved next. By so doing, each system interacts with the others using its own specialized techniques.

The generation of reliable models for each domain also turns out to be of great interest, since the results that can be drawn from the simulation experiments directly depend on the accuracy of the models used. The models can range from simple first-order approximations for a quick evaluation of the system, to highly complex and accurate models of the theoretical physical behavior, capable of capturing several aspects of the system more realistically. The choice of the model to be used depends on the simulation goals that need to be met, as well as on the computational efficiency required. For example, the dynamic simulation of a wall being blown out by an explosive in a video game does not need to use a highly accurate model of the internal structure of the wall. It suffices to use a simple model that gives a sufficiently accurate feeling of authenticity to the scene. Nevertheless, the same simulation in the context of a miliary operation may need a more accurate model of the wall so that the appropriate weapon can be chosen for the task.

Even though the number of models and specialized mathematical methods that can be used in a physically based simulation is significant, there are two types of multi-domain simulations that represent the most commonly used simulation engines. These simulation engines restrict the general case of physically based modeling to the particular case wherein things interacting are either particles or rigid bodies.

1.2   Particle and Rigid-Body Systems

Arguably, particle and rigid-body systems are the most important and commonly used models in physically based dynamic simulations. They represent a very good trade-off between mathematical complexity and accuracy of the models used to capture the observed real-world behavior of the system.

Particle systems can range from basic implementations of point-mass systems that use discrete particles to represent gaseous or fluid motion,[1] to specialized systems that use computational fluid mechanics to simulate turbulent gases and liquids such as swirling steam, gusts of wind, and flooding, to name a few. The former applies standard Newtonian physics to each particle in the system to determine the dynamics of motion, whereas the latter uses sophisticated numerical methods to solve the Navier–Stokes volumetric differential equations of motion.

Rigid-body systems, on the other hand, take into account the shape and mass distribution of the objects being simulated. They are especially suitable to simulate systems where the internal bending, extension or compression of the object can be neglected, meaning, the object does not change its shape during the entire simulation. The rigidity assumption also simplifies the computations, since it makes forces

---

[1]In this book, we shall focus the study of particle systems to the case in which particles are approximated by point-mass objects.

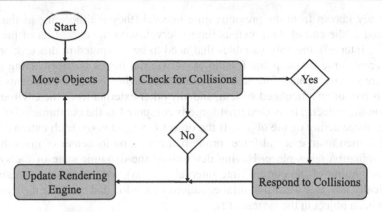

Fig. 1.1 Block diagram illustrating the general structure of a dynamic-simulation engine

being applied at any point on the object equivalent to a force-torque pair being applied at its center of mass, which can be easily computed.

Rigid bodies can also be combined into systems of articulated rigid bodies, where bodies are attached to each other using joints. There are several types of joints that can be used to connect bodies, and they differ from each other by the degree of freedom of relative motion allowed. An unconstrained rigid body has six degrees of freedom, three degrees to translate and another three degrees to rotate along and about the coordinate axis, respectively.

1.3 Simulation Overview

In this section, we shall discuss the general structure of a dynamic-simulation engine for non-penetrating particle and rigid-body systems. A more detailed explanation of each step will be provided in the next section. Figure 1.1 shows a block diagram representation of the main loop of a dynamic-simulation engine. The engine starts at some time t_0 and advances by some time interval value Δt, to reach a new dynamic state at $t_1 = t_0 + \Delta t$. There are four high-level steps that need to be executed to determine this new dynamic state of the system.

The first step moves all objects from the beginning to the end of the current time interval, ignoring any possible collisions that might happen during the motion. This consists of determining the dynamic state of the system at the beginning of the current time interval, and using this information to solve the ordinary differential equations (ODEs) of motion for each object. The dynamic state of the system is given by all linear and angular positions, velocities and accelerations, as well as by the net external force-torque pair acting on each object[2] in the system. Since the positions, velocities and accelerations at the beginning of the current time interval

---

[2]In this book, we shall sometimes refer to object as a synonym to particle or rigid body.

are already known from the previous time interval (they are the same as the ones computed at the end of the previous time interval, with the exception of the very first time interval), the only variables that need to be computed in this task are the net external force-torque pairs. Examples of external forces possibly acting on an object are gravity, contact forces, constraint forces owing to joint attachments if the object is part of an articulated system, and any other external force the environment exerts on the object. The net external force is computed as the combination of each external force acting on the object. If the object is a rigid body, each external force is transformed to an external force-torque pair acting on its center of mass, before the combination takes place. Having determined the dynamic state of the system at the beginning of the current time interval (i.e., t_0), we use this information to numerically integrate the differential equations of motion and compute the dynamic state of each object in the system at t_1.

The second step checks for collisions that may occur between one or more objects during their motion. Collisions are usually detected by checking for geometric intersections between the objects' boundary representations at t_1, that is, at the end of the current time interval. The collision check can be a very time-consuming task, especially if every object is checked against all others for collisions. In practice, the simulation engine uses auxiliary structures to speed the collision checking.

The first auxiliary structure considered in this book is used to speed the determination of which pairs of objects should be checked for collisions. It consists of some sort of cell decomposition of the simulated world that is guaranteed to contain all objects for the entire simulation. As objects move around the world, the simulation engine keeps track of which of the cells intersect their boundary representations, and checks for collision only between objects that share a common cell at t_1.

The second auxiliary structure also covered in this book is used to speed the collision detection between pairs of objects. It consists of decomposing each object in a hierarchical tree of simple structures that can be quickly checked for intersections, such as boxes, spheres or convex polygons. The tree is constructed in a pre-processing step before the simulation engine starts, in such a way that the structure associated with each parent node in the tree bounds the structures of all its children. For example, a hierarchical bounding-box representation of an object would consist of one top-level bounding box that contains the entire object, several intermediate levels of possibly overlapping bounding boxes that contain sub-parts of the object, down to leaf bounding boxes that contain one or more faces of the object. The goal is to postpone the more expensive check for collisions between the object's faces as long as possible, substituting them for inexpensive collision checks between their hierarchical representations.

Whenever a pair of objects shares a common cell of the world-cell decomposition at t_1, their hierarchical structures are checked for intersections, starting with their top-level structures, and moving down to their intermediate structures until reaching a leaf. Objects that are farther apart, yet in the same cell of the world decomposition, are quickly discarded after checking for intersections between their top-most level representation. Objects that are closer together may require checking for intersections between several intermediate levels of their hierarchical tree representation. Objects that are really close will probably require the more expensive

Fig. 1.2 The nonlinear trajectory of two colliding objects obtained from their numerical integration

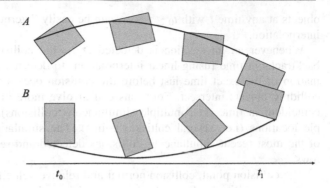

Fig. 1.3 The collision detection module replaces the nonlinear trajectory of the colliding objects by a linear trajectory with constant translation and rotation. The position of the objects at any time $t \in [t_0, t_1]$ can be obtained by simple linear interpolation (see Sect. 6.8 of Appendix A (Chap. 6) for more details)

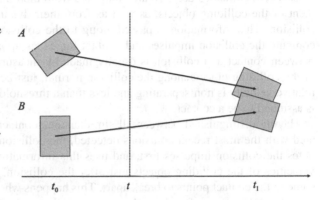

check for collisions between the faces associated with the intersecting leaf nodes. As Fig. 1.1 illustrates, if no collisions are detected, then the movement of the objects for the current time step is valid and their new positions and orientations are sent to the rendering engine, which is in charge of updating the display showing the simulation. However, if a collision is detected, the simulation engine moves on to the third step.

The third and most difficult step is to establish the non-penetrating constraints for all collisions and contacts detected in the second step. This consists of responding to collisions that may occur between two or more objects during their motion. Because collisions introduce discontinuities into the velocities of the colliding objects, it is necessary to stop the numerical integration of the ODEs of motion just before the collision, resolve the collision to determine the new velocities of the objects just after the collision, and re-start the numerical integration for the remaining time using the updated position and velocity values.

In practice, the collision detection dependency on the numerical integration can be simplified by approximating the nonlinear motion of the colliding objects from t_0 to t_1, by a linear motion with constant translation and rotation, as illustrated in Figs. 1.2 and 1.3. The total change in translation and rotation for the colliding objects can be computed from their known positions and orientations at t_0 and t_1. If we assume this change takes place at a constant rate then the position of the colliding objects at any time t with $t_0 \leq t \leq t_1$, can be easily determined by a simple linear interpolation.

Whenever an intersection is detected at t_1, the collision-detection algorithm backtracks in time (using linear interpolation) to determine an adequate approximation of the exact time just before the collision occurs, that is, just before the colliding objects intersect. Collisions can involve more than two objects, can be coincident in time (i.e., multiple simultaneous collisions), and can be at multiple locations (i.e., several collision points). The simulation engine keeps track of the most recent simultaneous collisions detected and responds to them as follows.

The collision point, collision normal and relative velocities associated with the most recent collisions detected are computed from the relative geometric displacement of the colliding objects, as well as from their dynamic state just before the collision. This information is passed along to the collision-response algorithm to compute the collision impulses and contact forces, as appropriate. The distinction between contact and collision is usually made by measuring the relative velocity of the colliding objects along the collision normal, just before the collision. If the relative velocity is non-separating and less than a threshold value then the collision is assumed to be a contact.

Having distinguished between all simultaneous contacts and collisions associated with the most recent collisions detected, the collision-response module computes the collision impulses first, and uses this information to update the relative velocities of the colliding objects just after the collision. This update may cause some of the contact points to break apart. This happens whenever the relative velocities at contact points after the update are separating and greater than a user-defined threshold value. In this case, after the collision impulses are resolved, the relative velocities of the objects at the contact point indicate that the objects are now moving away from each other, meaning the contact will break apart and there is no need to take into account the contact force associated with this contact. For the remaining contacts, a contact force is computed to prevent the contacting objects from interpenetrating.

Because resolving collisions requires backtracking the colliding objects in time to place them just before the collision was detected, the simulation engine needs to recompute the dynamic state of the colliding objects for the remaining time until the end of the current time interval. This is done by restarting the numerical integration using the new dynamic state of the colliding objects just after the collision. The final position and orientation of the colliding objects is then updated to reflect the changes introduced by the collision. Because these changes affect the path of the objects for the time-interval, the simulation engine needs to check again for new collisions. This loop continues until there are no collisions within the current time-interval.

The forth and final step consists of communicating the final position and orientation of each object in the system to the rendering engine being used. Here, we assume the actual display of the simulation is carried out by the rendering engine, which communicates with the simulation engine through a well defined interface.

1.4   A Computationally Efficient Implementation

Even though the general structure of a dynamic simulation engine is relatively easy to understand, its implementation is usually an involved task. Despite the fact that a naive implementation works, its operation can be frustrating and disappointing, even for a small number of simple rigid bodies and particles being simulated. Naive implementations carry out unnecessary time-consuming computations, since they tend to ignore coherence between time intervals, as well as the spatial distribution of the rigid bodies and particles in the scene when computing their interactions. This can negatively affect the allocation of important computer resources such as memory and CPU run-time. As it happens, the use of computationally efficient algorithms in dynamic-simulation engines is a necessity rather than a luxury.

In this section, we discuss in detail a possible architectural design of a computationally efficient implementation of a dynamic-simulation engine for non-penetrating particle and rigid-body systems. In doing so, we are mostly interested in studying algorithms that can produce real-time or near real-time performance. The actual description of the algorithms used in each step of the simulation engine proposed in this book, as well as reference software implementations of several modules that make up the entire simulation, are provided in the remaining chapters and appendices. The main goal of this section is to justify the book's organization, and describe the high-level steps necessary to implement an efficient dynamic-simulation engine.

1.4.1   Interface with the Rendering Engine

The portability of the simulation engine across a multitude of computer platforms is the first important issue that needs to be addressed. Usually, the results of a dynamic simulation are rendered in a computer display using one of the several sophisticated rendering engines available in the market. Such rendering engines have an internal representation of the scene being rendered, which contains lots of information that is also necessary for the dynamic-simulation engine. At first, the temptation to use the same internal representation of the rendering engine is almost irresistible, since a considerable amount of source-code development can be forgone. However, the fact that there exists a diverse set of internal representations, each tailored to capitalize upon the underlying hardware capabilities, makes it critical to have our own internal representation of objects in the scene that is independent of the specifics of the rendering engine being used. The way this can be done in a dynamic-simulation engine, without sacrificing portability, is to create an interface between the rendering engine and the simulation engine. The number of methods implemented by the interface should be kept small, to avoid unnecessary redundancies.

In an efficient implementation, the interface between the rendering and simulation engines should contain at least three basic features. The first feature lets the rendering engine register objects with the simulation engine, and update their status as appropriate. The registration process consists of passing to the simulation engine some basic information about the object being registered, and receiving back a handle to the internal representation of the object in the simulation engine. This handle (a unique identification number) is used to map the internal representation of objects in the simulation engine to their counterparts in the rendering engine.

The basic information the rendering engine passes to the simulation engine when registering an object should include the geometry defining its boundary representation[3] as well as user-adjustable physical properties such as density (or total mass), coefficients of friction and restitution, and the object's initial dynamic state (it may be already in motion at the start of the simulation). Depending on the application, significant performance improvements can be achieved if the geometry used by the rendering engine can be simplified before it is registered with the simulation engine. This simplification consists of either creating a lower resolution geometry representation of the object or approximating the object's shape by a small set of simple bounding volumes.

Upon registering an object, either on its original or simplified version, the simulation engine computes the object's extended representation, which includes the following information in addition to the geometry and physical properties information already obtained from the rendering engine:

1. Center of mass and inertia tensor. This is used to compute the object's local-coordinate frame with origin at the center of mass and coordinate axes aligned with the principal axes of inertia. The symmetric matrix representation of the inertia tensor becomes a diagonal matrix in this local-coordinate frame, further simplifying rotation matrix computations.
2. Geometry converted from world-coordinate to local-coordinate frame.
3. Face list specifying which vertices and edges belong to a face.
4. Face normal vectors pointing outwards the object. The vertices defining a face should be given in counter-clockwise order such that the right-hand rule can be applied to determine the outwards normal direction.
5. Edge list specifying which vertices belong to an edge, as well as which faces share the edge. The edge vertices are labeled *from* and *to*, defining the correct edge direction with respect to the face on its left side. The left-side face is chosen as the first face found in the list of faces that contains the edge.
6. Hierarchical representation of the object in its local-coordinate frame.
7. Bounding rotation sphere. This is used to replace the object's geometry by a sphere that bounds any possible rotation of the object around its center of mass. The radius of the sphere is defined as the maximum distance between a vertex and the object's center of mass (i.e., the rotation sphere's center). The easiest way to compute the rotation sphere's radius is to first compute a regular bounding sphere for the object in the local-coordinate frame, and then translate its center to the origin. In this case, the rotation sphere's radius is given by the sum of the

---

[3]In this book, we assume the object's geometry is defined by its boundary representation, that is, by its vertices, edges and faces.

bounding sphere's radius and the distance between its center and the local-frame origin.

8. Optional convex decomposition of the (non-convex) object.

All this information is computed only once, when an object is registered, with respect to the object's local-coordinate frame. This information is then used in several modules throughout the simulation engine to speed computations and optimize the overall efficacy, as the object moves within the world-coordinate frame.

At the end of each time interval, the simulation engine returns to the rendering engine a list of object handles and their updated positions and orientations. The object handles can be used by the rendering engine to quickly get a pointer to the internal representations of the objects, and apply the necessary transformations to position and orient them in the scene. Not all objects registered with the simulation engine are on this list, just those that changed position or orientation since the last time interval. As far as efficacy is concerned, it is very important to implement a fast mechanism to retrieve the object structure from its handle (such as a hash table) in both rendering and simulation engines.

The rendering engine should also be capable of updating the status of objects registered with the simulation engine. This consists of carrying out operations ranging from removing the object from the simulation engine, to changing its current position, orientation and velocities, to adjusting its physical properties and simulation status. Possible values for the simulation status are *inactive*, *static*, *dynamic* and *animated*. By default, all registered objects can be initially set to the inactive state. In this state, even though the objects exist in the simulation engine, they are ignored during the run-time execution. Static objects, on the other hand, are taken into account during the simulation execution, but are considered fixed objects in the scene. Only dynamic objects have their positions and orientations determined using the physically based computations of the dynamic-simulation engine.

The distinction between animated and dynamic objects makes it possible to interface script-based motion with the simulation engine. This can be done by setting the dynamic state of all objects that have a predefined script-based motion to animated, and updating their positions and velocities between each time interval following the script. We just need to be careful when updating the position of each animated object following the script so as not to overlap and completely block any other dynamic object. The dynamic-simulation engine enforces the non-penetration constraints on all registered objects for every time interval, and if the script-based objects are forced to move on top of another dynamic object completely blocking its motion, then the simulation engine will not work properly and will yield an abnormal result for the subsequent time intervals.

The second feature to be implemented in the interface between the rendering and simulation engines lets the rendering engine specify the dimensions of the scene to which the dynamic-simulation engine is constrained. The goal is to impose bounds on the distance an object can move inside the simulation engine. Objects that fall outside these bounds have their status automatically set to inactive, and are left out of the simulation execution for the rest of the simulation. Optionally, the bounds can be represented as static objects in the simulation engine. In this case, dynamic

objects can collide and bounce off these static bounds and remain active for the rest
of the simulation.

In order to simplify things, the dimensions of the scene can be given by the coordinates of a bounding box containing the entire simulated world. Once the bounding
box is defined, the simulation engine decomposes it into subregions (or cells) that
are used to speed the collision-detection phase. The decomposition can be single-
or multi-level. In the single-level case, a coarse uniform grid is constructed from the
bounding box that contains the entire simulated world. The size of each cell in the
grid is determined as a combination of the size of the objects being simulated. In the
multi-level case, several uniform grids with cells of different sizes are constructed,
forming a coarse-to-fine decomposition of the simulated world. Objects are then assigned to the grids with cells that can completely contain them. The techniques to
decompose the simulated world will be explained in more detail in Sect. 2.4.1.

Last, but not least, the third desired feature of the interface between the rendering
and simulation engines should let the rendering engine specify the *time interval* to
be used, that is, the amount of time the dynamic-simulation engine needs to be
executed between two consecutive frames. Usually, the time interval is set to be the
inverse of the desired frame rate,[4] so that the dynamic simulation returns the state
of the system after each frame, and the rendering engine can update the computer
display accordingly. The state of the system can be returned as a list of objects that
moved since the last time interval, with their new positions and orientations given
by a translation vector and a rotation matrix, respectively.

It is important to notice that the actual time step used in the simulation engine
to numerically integrate the differential equations of motion of each dynamic object
may be different from the time interval. This is most often the case when the numerical method uses adaptive time steps to automatically adjust the current time step
used, depending on the value of the estimated integration error.

1.4.2 Moving the Objects

At the start of each simulation cycle, the first step to be executed consists of moving all dynamic objects from the beginning to the end of the current time interval,
ignoring any collisions that may happen during the motion (see Fig. 1.1). Initially,
the current time-step used by the numerical integration

$$\Delta t = t_1 - t_0$$

is set to match the current time interval. However, depending on the size of the current time-step Δt and the desired error tolerance on the calculations, the numerical
integration process may need to subdivide Δt into smaller sub-steps Δt_s to increase
the computation accuracy. For each dynamic object in the system, the simulation
engine undertakes the following actions to complete each sub-step Δt_s.

---

[4]A value of $\Delta t = 1/24$ corresponds to 24 frames per second of simulation.

1. Computes the net force-torque pair acting on the object at the beginning of the sub-step. The net force at each sub-step is obtained from the addition of all external forces the environment exerts on the object, such as gravity, contact forces and joint forces, if applicable. If the object is a rigid body or an articulated rigid body, then each external force is transformed to an external force-torque pair acting on its center of mass before they are added to form one net force-torque pair.
2. Numerically integrates the ODEs of motion associated with the object for Δt_s, assuming no collisions occur during the entire motion.

The time subdivision of the current time-step Δt into smaller sub-steps Δt_s can be either fixed or adaptive. In a fixed time stepping scheme, the integrator divides the current time step Δt into N sub-steps, where N is a user-adjustable parameter of the system. The objects are then moved forward in time using N sub-steps of size $\Delta t_s = \Delta t / N$ each. This scheme works well for simple simulation setups using a small number of objects with limited inter-connectivity. However, it scales poorly as the number of objects increase and their interactions become more complex (i.e., multiple simultaneous contacts and collisions). In such complex cases, the number of sub-steps N might not be big enough to satisfy the desired error tolerance on the calculations and the numerical integration can become unstable and fail to produce a satisfactory result. The workaround for fixed time stepping is to reset the system to its dynamic state at the beginning of the simulation (i.e., restore the state to the start frame) and re-run it using larger N values on a trial-and-error basis, until the numerical integration succeeds for all simulated frames. Clearly, this approach considerably limits the range of applications that can rely on a fixed time stepping scheme.

Due to this limitation, the adaptive time stepping scheme is the preferred choice for most simulations. Similar to the fixed time stepping scheme, the integrator also divides the current time step Δt into N sub-steps. The difference is that the value of N is automatically adjusted during the simulation to accommodate the complexity of the system. This is done as follows. At the end of each sub-step, the integrator estimates the error in the calculations and compares it to the user-adjustable error tolerance value. If the estimated error is less than the error tolerance value for all N sub-steps, then the integration result for Δt is accepted. An internal counter is used to keep track of the number of consecutive times the integration result is accepted. When this internal counter reaches a user-adjustable limit,[5] the number of sub-steps N is halved[6] and the internal counter is reset to zero. However, if the estimated error is greater than the error tolerance value while processing a sub-step, the integration result for Δt is rejected. The number of sub-steps N is doubled to improve accuracy and the internal counter is reset to zero. Likewise, the dynamic state of the system is also reset to what it was at t_0, and the integrator starts again the integration of Δt using what is now twice as many sub-steps. This process continues until the

---

[5] A value of 4 is a common choice.

[6] The value of N should be clamped at a minimum value of one, otherwise the system will end up moving forward in time by more than Δt.

estimated error is reduced to less than the user-adjustable error tolerance, and the integration succeeds for Δt.

Clearly, in an adaptive time stepping scheme, the number of sub-steps N used for each simulated object varies over time, increasing when the object is subjected to complex collision scenarios and gradually decreasing as the system resolves itself. At any given time interval, simulated objects will likely need a different number of time-steps to have their integration results accepted. Since the goal of the simulation engine is to move the system forward in time as efficiently as possible, each simulated object should have its own numerical integrator to process its motion.

Finally, upon completion of the numerical integration, the cell decomposition of the simulated world is updated to account for the objects' new positions at t_1. This update consists of removing an object from cells it no longer intersects and adding it to the new intersecting cells. The simulation engine uses the updated world-cell decomposition to construct a list of potential collisions. This list contains pairs of objects that are within the same cell or group of cells, and therefore may be colliding with each other at t_1.

1.4.3 Detecting Collisions

The collision check is undertaken only for the pairs of objects that are in the list of potential collisions. Here, the simulation engine goes through each element in this list, checking whether the pair of objects are actually colliding. Concurrently, a global-collision list for the entire world is built with information about all collisions sorted by increasing order of collision time. This process is best described as follows.

1. Checks whether the objects' hierarchical representations do intersect at t_1. The pair is discarded if no intersections are found.
2. If an intersection is indeed detected, the approximate collision time is determined by backtracking in time the colliding objects' motion (using linear interpolation) to just before the collision occurs, that is, just before the colliding objects intersect.
3. The collision information obtained from the objects' positions and orientations at that collision time (i.e., closest features[7] and distance) is added to the global-collision list (sorted by increasing collision time).

At the end of this process, the list of potential collisions is empty and the global-collision list may or may not have entries. If no collisions were detected, then the dynamic state of the system computed in Sect. 1.4.2 is accepted, and the simulation engine returns to the rendering engine the new positions and orientations of the objects that were moved during the current time interval. Otherwise, the simulation engine uses the global-collision list information to process all valid collisions in the system. This consists of identifying the earliest collision or simultaneous collisions

---

[7]The closest features between two objects are vertex–face, face–vertex or edge–edge.

for each colliding object. Notice that any other collision detected at a later time involving an already collided object should be discarded, since the earliest collision will change the dynamic state of the colliding object for the remainder of the time interval. In other words, the update on the object's motion after its earliest collision is resolved invalidates any of its other collisions detected at a later time.

Starting with the first element in the global-collision list, the simulation engine goes through the following steps to determine the earliest collisions for each object. In particular, multiple simultaneous collisions are discovered one entry at a time, and are added to a collision group. We keep postponing the processing of the collision group until the next valid collision-pair in the list happens at a different (i.e., later) time.

1. Checks if any of the objects in the current collision-pair were involved in an earlier collision. If so, discard this collision-pair and move on to the next element in the global-collision list.
2. If the collision group is empty, then initialize it with the current collision-pair. Move on to the next element in the global-collision list.
3. If there is already one or more collision-pairs in the current collision group, then compare the current collision-pair time with the one associated with the group.
   (a) If they are the same up to a user-adjustable tolerance, then assume this is a simultaneous collision and add the current collision-pair to the collision group. Move on to the next element in the global-collision list.
   (b) If the collision times for the current collision-pair and the collision group are different, then resolve the simultaneous collisions in the collision group. When done, reset the group to contain only the current collision-pair. Move on to the next element in the global-collision list.
4. Upon reaching the end of the global-collision list, resolve the collisions in the collision group, if it is not empty.

At the end, the earliest collision or simultaneous collisions for each colliding object is resolved (see Sect. 1.4.8 for an overview of resolving collisions). The final position and orientation of each object is updated to reflect the change in its dynamic state due to collisions. This is done by restarting the numerical integration for the remaining time between the collision time and the end of the current time interval. Because the changes introduced by collisions affect the trajectories of the objects, the simulation engine needs to check again for new collisions. In theory, this loop continues until there are no more collisions within the current time interval. In practice, the simulation engine needs to have a mechanism to account for the special cases in which the number of collision iterations may grow indefinitely. For instance, consider a system with a large number of simulated objects surrounded by many other objects moving in close proximity. At each iteration, as collisions are resolved, the objects' new trajectories will most likely intersect the trajectory of other nearby objects, introducing new collisions for the next iteration. This can create a "bounce off" effect between the objects, which continually feeds new collisions into future collision checks. Clearly, a significantly high number of collision iterations will be needed to resolve all collisions in these cases.

In order to deal with these unstable cases, we propose creating a user-defined parameter to limit the maximum number of collision iterations performed. After this number is reached, the simulation engine overrides the objects' physical parameters to use only inelastic collisions (i.e., zero coefficient of restitution) on all future collision iterations. By doing so, the relative motion of the colliding objects after each inelastic collision becomes zero, and they no longer bounce off of each other. This simple change can significantly improve the overall performance and stability of the system, because the number of new collisions introduced in the following iterations is drastically reduced.

In general, the determination of the collision time between two objects relies on techniques capable of keeping track of the distance between their closest points when they are not intersecting, or their penetration depth when they are intersecting. Usually, the objects start at a non-intersecting position at t_0 and are known to be intersecting at t_1. As they move forward in time from t_0 to t_1, the distance between their closest point decreases until it becomes zero at the collision time t_c, with $t_0 < t_c \leq t_1$. Alternatively, as the objects move backwards in time from t_1 to t_0, their penetration distance decreases until it becomes zero at the collision time. Either way, the determination of the collision time is an iterative process where we incrementally move a step forward from t_0 or backward from t_1 until we reach the collision time, up to a user-defined threshold value. Efficiency is gained when the closest point information at a new iteration can be quickly obtained from the closest point information already computed at the previous iteration. The actual algorithm used in the computations depend on the colliding objects' shape and relative velocity. The more generic non-convex object shapes require computationally demanding algorithms to process their collision times, whereas convex objects enjoy efficient and specialized algorithms that rely on their convexity properties to execute properly. Fast motion and thin objects are handled using continuous collision detection that takes into account their trajectories from t_0 to t_1, as opposed to only their position and orientation at t_1. All of these methods are discussed in details in the following sections.

1.4.4 Determining Collision Time for Non-convex Objects

In the specific case of non-convex objects, the main difficulty to determine the collision time using the distance of the closest points when the objects are not intersecting is that the closest point information can change in a non-monotonic way between consecutive iterations. This is exemplified in Figs. 1.4 and 1.5.

As the objects move from t_i to t_{i+1}, their closest points change from vertices $(\vec{a}_1, \vec{b}_1)$ to vertices $(\vec{a}_5, \vec{b}_7)$. In order to reach vertex $\vec{a}_5$ from vertex $\vec{a}_1$ using a geometric search algorithm, we would have to pass through vertices $\vec{a}_2$, $\vec{a}_3$ and $\vec{a}_4$, which are farther away from object B than vertex $\vec{a}_1$, before reaching vertex $\vec{a}_5$, which is closest to object B at t_{i+1}. In other words, starting from the closest points determined at t_i, the geometric search would have to move along directions that increase the closest distance value between the objects, before a new minimum value

Fig. 1.4 Two non-convex objects A and B moving for the time interval $[t_0, t_1]$, and intersecting at t_1. The simulation engine backtracks in time using the bisection method to determine their collision time

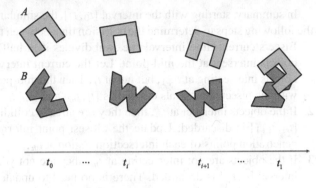

Fig. 1.5 Intermediate iterations t_i and t_{i+1} of the bisection method used in Fig. 1.4. There is a non-monotonic change in distance to move from closest points $(\vec{a}_1, \vec{b}_1)$ at t_i to closest points $(\vec{a}_5, \vec{b}_7)$ at t_{i+1}

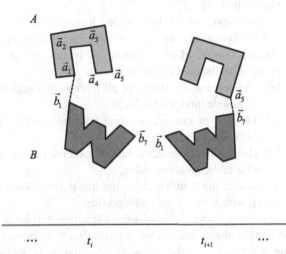

is reached at vertex $\vec{a}_5$. This increase followed by a decrease in the closest distance makes it impractical to use an effective search direction criteria that is guaranteed to find the closest points at t_{i+1} from the ones already known at t_i.

Because of the possibility of having non-monotonic changes in distance to move between closest points of consecutive iterations, the simulation engine relies instead on the penetration depth calculations to obtain the collision time for non-convex objects. The penetration depth is computed for each intersection region between the objects. This computation consists of determining the deepest inside point on each object with respect to the other (i.e., there are two deepest inside points per region, one on each object). The deepest points are set as the collision points and their distance is set as the closest distance for their corresponding intersection region. The collision time is reached when the penetration depths of all intersection regions become less than a user-adjustable threshold. Section 2.5.14 of Chap. 2 presents an efficient algorithm to find the deepest penetration point associated with an intersection region. This algorithm is applied once for each object to determine its deepest point inside the other object.

In summary, starting with the interval $[t_0, t_1]$, the simulation engine goes through the following steps to determine the collision time between two non-convex objects.

1. Bisects current time interval (i.e., subdivides it in half), checking whether the objects intersect at the mid-point. Let the current interval be $[t_i, t_{i+1}]$, with the objects intersecting at t_{i+1}, but not at t_i. Then the mid-point is $t_m = (t_i + t_{i+1})/2$, with the bisected intervals defined as $[t_i, t_m]$ and $[t_m, t_{i+1}]$.

2. If the objects intersect at t_m, then they are already colliding at t_m and the interval $[t_m, t_{i+1}]$ is discarded. Update the closest point information from the deepest penetration points of each intersection region at t_m.

3. If the objects are not intersecting at t_m, they are not yet colliding at t_m and the interval $[t_i, t_m]$ is discarded. There is no need to update the closest point information in this case.

4. At this point, one of the bisected intervals has been discarded and the closest point information is up-to-date. There are three termination conditions to be considered. If none of these conditions is satisfied, then the backtracking in time proceeds to the next iteration.

   (a) The penetration depths of all intersection regions become less than a user-adjustable threshold value.

   (b) The size of the current time interval becomes less than a user-adjustable threshold value.

   (c) The number of bisect iterations executed so far becomes greater than a user-adjustable threshold value.

At the end, the simulation engine has narrow down the current time interval to $[t_c, t_{c+1}]$, with t_c being the collision time.

Lastly, the above collision-time algorithm still holds for the cases in which the non-convex objects are already intersecting at t_0. In such special cases, the collision time is set to t_0 and the collision information is obtained from their intersection regions.

1.4.5 Determining Collision Time for Thin or Fast Moving Non-convex Objects

In the case of thin or fast moving objects, checking for intersections at t_1 is usually not enough to determine whether the objects are colliding for the entire time interval. In many situations, the objects are not intersecting at t_1, but their trajectories have crossed each other during their motion from t_0 to t_1, indicating that the objects could have collided. One possible approach to minimize this problem is to subdivide the time interval $[t_0, t_1]$ into several smaller intervals, and check for intersections at the end of each sub-interval. Figure 1.6 illustrates this approach. Though effective in many cases, this approach is not efficient because the computation cost to detect collisions increases linearly with the number of subdivisions. Besides, the number of subdivisions need to grow bigger as the objects get thinner and the motion becomes faster.

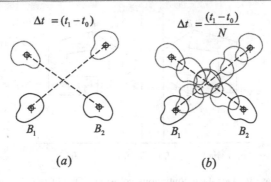

Fig. 1.6 (a) Two non-convex objects moving from t_0 to t_1. The objects do not intersect at t_1, but their trajectories overlap during their motion, indicating a collision might have occurred; (b) The initial time interval used to check for collisions is subdivided into N smaller intervals, and the objects are tested for intersections at the end of each sub-interval

A viable approach to address this problem is to consider the intersection between the continuous trajectories of the objects for the entire time interval, as opposed to just performing discrete intersections tests at the end of the time interval. This *continuous collision detection* approach requires several modifications to the data structures used to represent the simulated world and their objects. The first important modification is on the way the objects' hierarchical tree representations are constructed. In the case of continuous collision detection, the hierarchies need to be built to bound the entire motion of the objects from t_0 to t_1, instead of just their poses at t_1.

The second modification is related to the way the simulated world is represented. Unfortunately, the grid-based representation of the simulated world becomes less efficient when the entire motion of the objects is considered. This is due to fast moving objects being able to pass through several grid cells during their motion, creating a lot of redundant entries in the list of potential collisions obtained from the pairs of objects that share a cell. A better way of representing the simulated world for continuous collision detection is to use a hierarchical tree instead of a grid. The leaf nodes of this hierarchical tree are built to bound the entire motion of their corresponding objects (see Sect. 2.4.3 for details). Hence, the list of potentially colliding objects can be obtained by self-intersecting this world tree hierarchy. The result of the self-intersection is a list of pairs of objects that have intersecting bounded motions. We still need to check if their actual trajectories intersect. As will be shown in Sect. 4.6, the trajectories of the non-convex objects will intersect whenever the trajectories of one or more of their primitives (i.e., faces) intersect. That is, the continuous collision time between non-convex objects can be computed as the earliest detected collision between their faces.

Even though the continuous collision detection between faces is quite effective in practice, it does not give an exact collision time between the rigid bodies. The problem is that the continuous collision detection for faces replaces their transla-

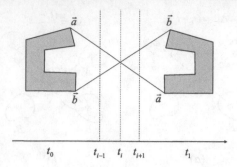

Fig. 1.7 Extreme case for face–face continuous collisions. One of the objects being tested for collisions undergo a 180° rotation. The in-between motion is continuous but not rigid, as the object compresses at t_{i-1}, almost collapses to a flat shape at t_i, and starts expanding back at t_{i+1}, until it returns to its correct shape at t_1. Collisions detected in such cases are inaccurate because the shape has undergone extreme deformations

tion and rotation by a simple translation defined by straight lines connecting their vertices' positions at t_0 and t_1. Clearly, the in-between motion of the faces is continuous but not necessary rigid, because the faces can deform at intermediate time values $t \in [t_0, t_1]$, depending on the amount of rotation experienced by them. Figure 1.7 shows an extreme case in which a rigid body rotates by 180° during its motion in the time interval. In such cases, the linearized trajectory does not completely bound the original trajectory of the rigid body and thus collisions can be inaccurate.

In summary, the simulation engine goes through the following steps in order to detect collisions between thin or fast moving non-convex objects.

1. Replaces the geometry of each object by its bounding rotation sphere, precomputed when the objects are registered with the simulation engine.
2. Uses a world hierarchy tree to represent the simulated world. Each leaf node is represented by an axis-aligned bounding box bounding the object's bounding rotation spheres at t_0 and t_1. Notice that this is a conservative bound on the object's trajectory. Intermediate tree nodes are built as usual bounding their children's volumes (see Sect. 2.2 for details on building hierarchies).
3. Self-intersects world tree to find pairs of potential collisions (see Sect. 2.5.2 for details on self-intersecting hierarchies).
4. For each pair of potential collisions, perform a continuous sphere–sphere intersection test to check if the bounding rotation spheres intersect. This intersection test is covered in Sect. 2.5.16.
5. If the bounding rotation spheres do intersect then perform a continuous collision detection between the objects' faces (see Sect. 2.5.15 for details on continuous triangle–triangle intersections). The earliest face–face collision time between zero and one is set as the collision time between the objects.

1.4.6 Determining Collision Time for Convex Objects

In the convex case, the determination of the collision time is still an iterative process. A simplified one however, since the distance to move between closest points of consecutive iterations varies monotonically. This is very important because when a geometric search algorithm moves along the objects' boundary representation trying to find their closest points at iteration t_{i+1}, it can discard all search directions that correspond to an increase in the current value it has for the closest distance at iteration t_i. Starting from the closest point information at t_i, the geometric search can then quickly converge to the actual closest points between the convex objects at t_{i+1}. Therefore, it is feasible for the simulation engine to keep track of the closest points between the convex objects when they are *not* intersecting, instead of having to compute the deepest penetration points for each intersection region and use them as an approximation to the collision points, as required in the non-convex case.

Another significant optimization possible in the case of convex objects is to replace the bisection method with a conservative time advancement algorithm. Instead of halving the time interval at each iteration and testing whether the objects intersect (i.e., collide) at the middle point, the conservative time advancement let us estimate a lower-bound on the amount of time Δt we can move forward from t_i, such that the objects are guaranteed to not be intersecting at $t_m = t_i + \Delta t$. Fortunately, the number of iterations it takes for the conservative time advancement method to converge to the collision time is much less than the number of iterations it takes using the bisection method. In fact, all intermediate t_m values computed using the conservative time advancement method are always associated with non-intersecting (i.e., non-colliding) states and are used to update the closest point information between the convex objects.

The main idea behind the conservative time advancement algorithm is that an upper bound on the maximum distance traveled by any point of a convex object along a direction vector $\vec{n}$ can always be computed, provided the convex object is moving at constant translation and rotation for the time interval. The simulation engine uses the conservative time advancement algorithm to compute an upper-bound on the maximum distance traveled by any point on each convex object along their closest direction,[8] for the time interval $[t_i, t_{i+1}]$. These upper-bounds together with the closest distance between the convex objects at t_i, are used to estimate a lower-bound on the collision time. This lower-bound is conservative, that is, it is guaranteed to give a time t_m with $t_i < t_m < t_{i+1}$ such that the objects are closer but not yet intersecting at t_m. Details on the conservative time advancement algorithm and how these upper-bounds are computed can be found in Appendix H (Chap. 13).

Starting with the interval $[t_0, t_1]$, the simulation engine goes through the following steps to determine the collision time between two convex objects.

---

[8]The direction defined by the line connecting the closest points at t_i.

1. Computes the closest points between the convex objects at t_0 and use their distance to initialize the closest distance value. Efficient geometric search algorithms for computing the closest points between convex objects are covered in details in Chap. 4.

2. Uses the conservative time advancement algorithm to compute the intermediate time t_m that corresponds to an intersection-free state. Computes the closest point information at t_m. The efficient geometric search algorithms covered in Chap. 4 use the closest point information at t_i as their starting point for the search of the closest points at t_m. The time coherence of the motion between t_i and t_m increases the chance that the closest points at t_m are topologically near the closest points at t_i. The monotonic property of the closest distance allows the search algorithm to focus only in directions that reduce the closest distance value.

3. At this point, the time interval has been reduced to $[t_m, t_1]$, and the closest point information is up-to-date. There are three termination conditions to be considered. The algorithm continues to the next iteration if none of the following conditions are satisfied.

    (a) The distance between the closest points becomes less than a user-adjustable threshold value.

    (b) The size of the current time interval becomes less than a user-adjustable threshold value.

    (c) The number of iterations executed so far becomes greater than a user-adjustable threshold value.

At the end, the simulation engine has narrow down the current time interval to $[t_c, t_1]$, with t_c being the collision time.

1.4.7 Determining Collision Time for Thin or Fast Moving Convex Objects

The auxiliary data structures used for determining the collision time for thin or fast moving convex objects are analogous to the ones used for the non-convex case. Here, the simulated world is also represented by a hierarchical tree (instead of a grid), with leaf nodes bounding its associated object's motion from t_0 to t_1. Self-intersecting the simulated world tree provides all pairs of objects that are potentially colliding. For each of those pairs, the simulation engine does sphere–sphere continuous collision detection tests to determine whether the objects' bounding rotation spheres intersect during their motion.

It is only at the final stage when the object–object intersection tests are performed that the convex and non-convex algorithms differ. In the non-convex case, the simulation engine computes an approximation to the collision time between the objects by simplifying the continuous object–object intersection problem to a continuous face–face intersection problem that does not enforce the rigidity property during the motion. As for the convex case, the simulation engine computes the exact collision time between the objects by using the same conservative time advancement algorithm discussed in the previous section. The idea is to compute a lower-bound to the collision time based on the closest distance between the objects and their dynamic state at t_0. If this lower-bound Δt is such that the new "safe" time $t_m = t_0 + \Delta t$ ends up being greater than t_1 (i.e., the end of the time interval) then the objects are guaranteed to not be intersecting. Otherwise, the time interval is updated to $[t_m, t_1]$, and the algorithm iterates until one of the following termination conditions is satisfied:

1. The distance between the closest points becomes less than a user-adjustable threshold value.
2. The distance between the closest points starts to increase. Since we don't know whether the objects intersect or not, it is possible that their closest distance starts to increase at some iteration. This situation corresponds to the case in which the objects pass by each other during their motion, without intersecting. That is, their closest distance is reduced during their approach, but increases again as soon as they start to move away from each other, without colliding.
3. The size of the current time interval becomes less than a user-adjustable threshold value.
4. The number of iterations executed so far becomes greater than a user-adjustable threshold value.

Clearly, the use of the conservative time advancement algorithm discussed in Appendix H (Chap. 13) provides a key performance advantage of collision detection between convex rigid-bodies over their non-convex counter-parts. It is therefore recommended to use convex objects as much as possible in practical implementations of dynamic simulation engines, even at the expense of requiring an additional convex decomposition step of the non-convex objects in a pre-processing stage.

1.4.8 Resolving Collisions

As explained in Sect. 1.4.3, the collision detection module goes through the global-collision list, detecting the most recent single or multiple collisions in the system. These collisions are passed to the collision response module to compute the collision impulses and contact forces required to prevent interpenetration.

Here, the simulation engine creates yet another auxiliary list that contains the collisions that are in fact contacts. This distinction is necessary because collisions should be resolved before contacts are resolved. In other words, only after the dynamic state of the system is updated with the collision impulses can we compute the contact forces that will enforce the non-penetration constraints between objects.

The simulation engine executes the following steps while resolving each single or multiple collision.

1. Backtracks in time (using linear interpolation) all colliding objects to the moment just before their collisions.
2. Checks whether the collisions are in fact contacts. This check is carried out for each collision and consists of testing whether the module of the relative velocity of the colliding objects at the collision point, along the collision normal, is less than a threshold value. If this is the case, the collision is said to be a contact and is moved to the auxiliary list of contacts.

3. Computes the collision impulses associated with each collision. As we shall see later in the chapters to come, this step consists of solving a sparse linear system.

4. Updates the dynamic state of the system with the collision impulses computed in the previous step. This will update the linear and angular velocities of all colliding objects.

5. Checks whether the contacts, if any, are still valid. This check is carried out for each contact associated with an object that was also involved in a collision. This consists of testing one more time whether the module of the relative velocity along the contact normal at the contact point is still non-separating the objects. Since the dynamic state of the colliding objects has changed, the contacts that involve any of them will have their relative velocity at the contact point changed as well. In some cases, the contact may beak apart just after the collision impulses are applied, making it unnecessary to process the contact.

6. Computes the contact forces at each contact point that prevent the objects from interpenetrating. The contact-force computation involves solving a Linear Complementarity Problem (LCP) that is obtained from the current contact configuration of the system. The general LCP problem formulation, as well as efficient techniques to solve such systems, are addressed in details in Appendix I (Chap. 14).

7. Adds the contact forces (and associated torques) to the net external force-torque pair acting on the object. This will enforce the non-penetration constraints for the remaining time necessary to reach the end of this time interval.

After resolving all collisions and contacts, the simulation engine computes the remaining time to reach the end of the current time interval, and numerically integrates the ODEs of motion *only* for the objects involved in a collision or contact. Again, the simulation engine will move these objects ignoring any collisions that may occur during the movement. Objects that remain in contact for the rest of the current time interval will not interpenetrate owing to the updated net force and torque.

The final position and orientation associated with each colliding object is updated to reflect the effects of the collision or contact, and a new list of potential collisions is created after the simulated world representation is updated. The simulation engine then continues detecting and resolving collisions until it reaches the end of the current time interval.

At the end of the current time interval, the simulation engine sends to the rendering engine the list of objects that had their positions or orientations changed since the last update. It then continues moving the objects, detecting and responding to collisions, and updating the display until it receives a stop command from the rendering engine.

1.5 Guide to Readers

The book's organization is justified according to the structure of the efficient dynamic-simulation engine presented in Sect. 1.4, and the techniques needed to implement it. The book contains five chapters and nine appendices. Each chapter presents many algorithms and covers them in considerable depth, yet makes their design and analysis accessible to all levels of readers, keeping the explanations as elementary as possible without sacrificing depth of coverage or mathematical rigor. The more complex mathematical algorithms and associated implementations are described in details in the appendices. The goal of doing so is to focus the reader's attention to the details of the topic being covered, and not get distracted with mathematical issues that can be viewed as "black box" modules that have specific functionality, such as a numerical integrator or a rigid-body mass-properties-computation module. A set of exercises is presented at the end of each chapter, with questions ranging from algorithm enhancements to alternate approaches that complement the algorithms presented in this book. We highly recommend readers to study the list of exercises.

Chapter 1 introduces the computational-dynamics topic to readers, describing the general structure of a dynamic-simulation engine for non penetrating particle and rigid-body systems. It sets the stage for the remaining chapters of the book by explaining what it takes to design and implement a computationally efficient simulation engine. The following chapters and appendices address the specialized tools and techniques mentioned in this chapter.

Chapter 2 focuses on the problem of computing a hierarchical representation of the geometric description of each simulated object, as well as the simulated world. This representation is used to speed collision-detection checks by taking advantage of the geometric arrangement of the objects in the simulated world, such that collision tests are only carried out on objects that are "close enough" to collide. The hierarchical decomposition of the colliding objects is used to prune unnecessary intersection tests and quickly specify the collision points, or discard the collision if no intersections are found.

Chapter 3 covers the design and implementation of particle systems as a collection of point mass objects that can collide with each other and other rigid-body objects in the simulation. Even though this is one of the simplest models of particle systems that can be used, the computational efficiency and degree of realism that can be attained with these systems is highly attractive. This chapter also discusses in details the use of spatially dependent interaction forces to model particle-based fluid simulations.

Chapter 4 presents the theoretical and practical aspects of designing and implementing dynamic-simulation engines for rigid-body systems. In this chapter, special attention is given to one of the most difficult and least understood topics in physically based modeling, namely, the computational techniques needed for determining all impulsive and contact forces between bodies with multiple simultaneous collisions and contacts.

Chapter 5 extends the techniques for rigid bodies to include articulated rigid bodies. Here, we shall focus on linking rigid bodies with joints. The goal is to demonstrate and implement techniques that can be used to dynamically simulate articulated rigid bodies. These techniques can be easily applied to include other types of joints suitable to the reader's interests, but not covered here.

The remaining part of the book is devoted to a set of appendices describing the mathematical algorithms used throughout the entire book, each of these standing alone as a broad and complex topic in itself. The appendices focus on the tools being used in the simulation engine. Nonetheless, they provide pointers to the literature, wherein interested readers can get more information about the topic.

Appendix A (Chap. 6) briefly covers some of the geometric constructions used as building blocks to implement the several intersection tests that are part of the particle–particle, particle–rigid body and rigid body–rigid body collision-detection algorithms. It also discusses how the tangent plane of a collision or contact can be determined given the collision or contact point and normal vector.

Appendix B (Chap. 7) discusses some of the most common methods used to integrate the differential equations of motion in dynamic simulations. These methods range from simple explicit-Euler, to more sophisticated Runge–Kutta methods, with adaptive time step sizing.

Appendix C (Chap. 8) presents an alternate representation of rotation matrices using quaternions. This representation is extremely useful in reducing rounding-error problems found when combining rotation matrices. Also, the interpolation between two quaternions representing the orientation of an object is easier than using rotation matrices. This is especially useful when backtracking in time the object's motion to determine the instant just before a collision.

Appendix D (Chap. 9) shows an efficient algorithm to compute the mass properties of 3D polyhedra. The mass properties include the total volume, total mass, center of mass, and inertia tensor. These quantities are used in the physically based modeling of the dynamics and interactions of objects in the simulated world.

Appendix E (Chap. 10) presents a detailed description of how the time derivatives of a normal vector, a rotation matrix and a quaternion are computed. These time derivatives are extensively used in Chaps. 4 and 5 to describe the dynamics of a rigid-body system.

Appendix F (Chap. 11) addresses the technical barriers to using non-convex polyhedra in a dynamic simulation. Most interesting objects to be simulated are usually non-convex. However, most of the more efficient algorithms presented in this book are especially tailored for convex objects. Therefore, it is often necessary to preprocess all objects in the simulation with a convex decomposition module that decomposes the objects into a set of non-overlapping convex parts. The algorithms can then be applied to the convex parts of each object.

Appendix G (Chap. 12) describes the use of signed distance fields to create a simplified, lower-resolution version of the objects registered with the simulation engine. The memory efficient algorithm presented in this book is capable of handling grid-resolutions for the signed fields on the order of 10^3 cells along each coordinate axis. A collision detection and response algorithm based on signed distance fields is also discussed.

Appendix H (Chap. 13) discusses the Conservative Time Advancement (CTA) algorithm used to compute the exact collision time between convex objects. This algorithm can be applied to both standard and continuous collision detection.

Last, but not least, Appendix I (Chap. 14) presents the Linear Complementarity Problem (LCP) in the context of impulse and contact-force computation of multiple simultaneous collisions. This appendix also presents an extension of the original algorithm to cope with static and dynamic friction at the collision or contact point.

1.6 Exercises

1. How constraint forces between objects are handled when their integrators use a different number of sub-steps?
2. Suppose we want to design a simulation engine that does not backtrack in time. We want to use the intersection information at the end of each simulation interval as the actual collision information and resolve for that.
   (a) What is the main disadvantage of not backtracking in time the motion? What is the main advantage?
   (b) What changes to the collision detection and response algorithms need to be made to accommodate this new method? (*Hint:* penalty-based methods.)
3. An alternate approach to improve the quality in the linearization of the motion for continuous collision detection is to subdivide the time interval into smaller sub-steps and check for continuous collisions on each one of them. Let N be the number of sub-steps to be used.
   (a) Derive an expression to compute N as a function of the object's linear and angular velocities, and shape?
   (b) Design an algorithm to efficiently check for collisions for the N intervals. (*Hint:* collision time is the earliest of all valid collisions.)
4. Assume we are using an adaptive time-stepping scheme for the objects in the previous exercise. Design an algorithm to update the integrator time step such that at most one sub-step will be redone each time the numerical error becomes greater than the user-definable error tolerance (as opposed to going back to the beginning of the simulation interval and redo all sub-steps).

Hierarchical Representation of 3D Polyhedra

2

2.1 Introduction

Collision detection is undoubtedly the most time-consuming step in a dynamic-simulation engine. In theory, as the simulation evolves, every object needs to be checked for collisions against all other objects in the simulation. Whenever a collision is detected, the simulation engine needs to backtrack in time to the instant before the collision, and determine the collision point and collision normal from the relative geometric displacement of the colliding objects.

Usually, collisions are checked by looking for geometric intersections between the objects. When objects are given by their boundary representations, this check can be done by looking for geometric intersections between the primitives of each object, that is, between the polygonal faces defining the boundary of each object. Clearly, checking for collisions between objects this way is a laborious task, and the use of intermediate representations to speed collision checking is critical to achieve real-time performance, especially for simulations involving several thousand objects, each described by several hundred primitives.

In this chapter, we study the use of hierarchical representations to speed the collision-detection phase. Our aim is to compute in a preprocessing stage the hierarchical volumetric decomposition of each object with respect to its local-coordinate frame. This usually consists of a tree hierarchy of bounding volumes where the topmost bounding volume bounds the entire object, the intermediate nodes of the tree bound sub-parts of the volume bounded by their parent, and the leaf nodes of the tree bound one or more primitives that lie inside the bounding volume of their parent. Collision checks are then carried out using the objects' hierarchical representations to quickly determine that the objects do not intersect (i.e., are not colliding), or to reduce the number of pair-wise primitive intersection tests needed to check for collision. For example, if the top-most bounding volumes of each object do not intersect, then we can safely conclude that the objects are not colliding. However, if the top-most bounding volumes do intersect, then we have to move down one level in the tree hierarchy to check whether their children intersect. If not, then the objects are not colliding. Otherwise, we move down one more level in the tree hierarchy to the children of the intersecting parents. This process continues until we either reach the leaf nodes of the trees, or detect that the objects do not intersect. Should we reach the leaf nodes of the trees, the collision check proceeds by computing the pair-wise primitive intersections of the primitives bounded by each intersecting leaf.

In practice, there are two important points to consider when using hierarchical representations in a simulation engine. The first is that the intersection test of the bounding volumes must be considerably faster than the intersection test of the primitives. Otherwise, the collision check will take longer using the hierarchical representation than using the original objects' boundary representations. Therefore, our choice of bounding volumes is restricted to simple geometric shapes such as boxes and spheres, which can be quickly tested for intersection against each other. The primitives can also be restricted to convex polygons, or even triangles, to further speed the primitive–primitive intersection tests.

The second point addresses how the hierarchical representation is updated as the object translates and rotates with respect to the world-coordinate frame. As mentioned before, the hierarchical decomposition is computed with respect to the object's local-coordinate frame. However, all intersection tests should be carried out with respect to the world-coordinate frame, thus requiring a coordinate transformation from the object's local-coordinate frame to its position and orientation in the world-coordinate frame. One solution to this problem would be to transform the entire tree hierarchy of all objects to the world-coordinate frame, just before testing for intersection. The drawback of so doing is the substantial waste of time transforming entire tree hierarchies that have only their top-most, or even some of their internal nodes checked for intersection. All other internal nodes that were transformed but not used in the intersection tests were unnecessary transformed to the world-coordinate frame, and the time spent applying the transformation could have been saved. The idea is then to transform only what is absolutely necessary. We can do this as follows.

The simulation engine represents each object in the world-coordinate frame by its top-most bounding volume only, and keeps the entire tree hierarchy, as well as the object's boundary representation, in the object's local-coordinate frame. At each time step, *only* the top-most bounding volume of each object is moved in the world-coordinate frame. The movement consists of updating the position and orientation of the object according to the numerical method being used,[1] applying it to the top-most bounding volume of the object.

The collision-detection phase then checks for geometric intersections between the top-most bounding volumes that can potentially collide. Potentially colliding objects are determined from the world-cell decomposition structure, as explained in Sect. 2.4, or from the world-tree hierarchy in the case of continuous collision detection, as explained in Sect. 2.4.3. Whenever the top-most bounding volumes intersect, the simulation engine transforms only their next-level children from their local-coordinate frame to the world-coordinate frame. If their next-level children do not intersect, the objects are not colliding and no further transformations are

---

[1] This is discussed in detail in Appendix B (Chap. 7).

required. Otherwise, the simulation engine keeps transforming only the next-level children of the intersecting bounding volumes until it concludes that the objects are not intersecting, or have intersecting leaf nodes. In that case, each primitive associated with the intersecting leaf node pair is then transformed from its local-coordinate frame to the world-coordinate frame before the more expensive primitive–primitive test is carried out. Using this scheme, the simulation engine is guaranteed to transform only the parts of the objects that are absolutely necessary for the collision check, thereby saving substantially on execution time.

Another interesting observation about this scheme is that, because the simulation engine presented in this book is decoupled from the rendering engine, it does not need to position and orient the objects' primitives in the world-coordinate frame throughout the simulation. After each time step, the simulation engine just needs to position and orient the top-most bounding volume of each object. Of course, it also needs to communicate to the rendering engine the new positions and orientations of the objects that moved since the last simulation time step, so that the rendering engine can itself place and render the objects' primitives at the correct position and orientation. Therefore, as far as the simulation engine is concerned, the cost of moving an object containing several hundred faces, and that does not intersect any other objects in the scene, is the same as moving the top-most bounding volume associated with the object. This in turn reduces even more the simulation engine's execution time.

2.2   Hierarchical Representation of Objects

The hierarchical representations considered in this book are limited to the case when the bounding volumes are either boxes or spheres. Moreover, the object's primitives are assumed to be triangles. This assumption is used not only to speed the primitive–primitive intersection tests, as discussed in Sect. 2.5, but also to simplify building Oriented Bounding Boxes (OBB) trees, as explained in Sect. 2.2.2. The Axis-Aligned Bounding Boxes (AABB) and the Bounding Spheres (BS) representations are not affected by this assumption. These representations are covered in detail in Sects. 2.2.1 and 2.2.3, respectively.

In general, it is not clear which hierarchical representation is best, since collision detection is highly dependent on the relative displacement of the objects being considered. For example, if the objects are close enough to each other, the OBB representation usually function better than the others, in the sense that it considerably reduces the number of primitive–primitive intersection tests owing to its tight fit. On the other hand, if the objects are farther apart, the less expensive bounding volume intersection tests of the AABB and BS representations offer a better choice of hierarchical representation. Modern approaches use hybrid hierarchies with differing representations for its internal nodes based on their proximity to leaf nodes. For example, a hybrid representation can use AABB bounding volumes for its top-most internal nodes providing inexpensive culling of no-colliding regions, and OBB bounding volumes for its leaf and bottom-most internal nodes for improved and more accurate culling.

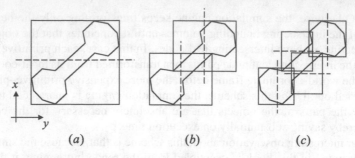

Fig. 2.1 A 2D example of a binary AABB tree. The boxes at each intermediate level are aligned with the axis of the object's local-coordinate frame. The *broken lines* show the partition plane used at each level

Independent of the hierarchical representation used, the tree hierarchy can be constructed in a top-down or bottom-up fashion. In the top-down case, the object's primitives are initially assigned to the top-most bounding volume, which in turn is recursively decomposed into sub-volumes according to some partitioning rule until there is only one primitive or group of primitives assigned to each sub-volume. In the latter case, the sub-division ends with the group of primitives if and only if they can no longer be subdivided according to the partitioning rule. Examples of the top-down approach will be discussed in Sects. 2.2.1 and 2.2.2. In the bottom-up case, the primitives are individually assigned to an initial bounding volume. These bounding volumes are then merged according to some merging rule, until there is only one top-most bounding volume in the tree containing all primitives.

There are several techniques to partition (or merge) bounding volumes into (or from) two or more sub-volumes to form a tree hierarchy. Examples of such partitions are the binary tree (parent has two children), the quad-tree (parent has four children) and the oct-tree (parent has eight children). In this book we limit our analysis to the most common case of building binary tree hierarchies using the top-down approach. Section 2.6 has references to the literature wherein the other possible partitions are covered in detail.

2.2.1 Axis-Aligned Bounding Boxes

In the Axis-Aligned Bounding Box (AABB) representation, the tree hierarchy is constructed from boxes bounding the primitives associated with them, such that the boxes' axes are aligned to the axis of the object's local-coordinate frame. Figure 2.1 illustrates the top-down construction of a binary AABB tree for a simple 2D object.

Initially, the top-most bounding box is constructed by looping through the vertices of all primitives, keeping track of the minimum and maximum values along each axis of the object's local-coordinate frame. The minimum and maximum values will define the lower-left and upper-right corners of the top-most bounding box, respectively.

A partition plane is then selected such that it splits the top-most bounding box into two regions along its longest axis. The intersection point between the partition plane and the longest axis is chosen such that the two regions will be as balanced as possible, that is, with more or less the same number of primitives assigned to each region of the subdivision. The subdivision rule used here is to pass the partition plane through the mean point of all vertices of all primitives associated with the top-most bounding box. The primitives are then assigned to the region in which their midpoint falls.

At each subsequent level, intermediate bounding boxes are constructed from the primitives associated with them, and new partition planes are created to divide the boxes into two regions. The primitives are then assigned to each region and the process recursively continues until there is only one primitive assigned to each region of the subdivision.

In the event all primitives are assigned to just one region (or the subdivision is unbalanced), another partition plane is chosen such that it divides the second longest axis into two regions, passing through the mean point. If this new partition plane still assigns all primitives to just one region, then a last attempt is made with the partition plane dividing the last axis. In the rare case that the group of primitives is assigned to just one region for all three choices of partition plane, the group is said to be indivisible and the current box containing the group becomes a leaf node of the tree. However, in the most common case when the primitives are equally split into both subdivisions, the leaves of the hierarchical tree end up having just one primitive.

2.2.2 Oriented Bounding Boxes

In the Oriented Bounding Box (OBB) representation, the tree hierarchy is constructed from bounding boxes forming a tight fit around the primitives associated with them. In this case, each intermediate bounding box has a different alignment with respect to the object's local-coordinate frame, since their orientation depends on the geometric displacement of their primitives. Figure 2.2 illustrates the top-down construction of a binary OBB tree for the same 2D object considered in the AABB case.

The fact that OBB trees provide a tighter hierarchical representation if compared with AABB trees clearly gives them an advantage over AABB trees when testing for collisions between objects that are close together, since this tightness generally reduces the number of primitive tests to be carried out. However, this comes at the price of having to carry out a more costly overlap test at each intermediate level of the OBB tree, as explained in Sect. 2.5.

The OBB tree construction is much more complex than the simple AABB tree construction, since the orientation of each intermediate bounding box needs to be computed from the set of primitives associated with it. The OBB tree construction algorithm described in this section assumes that the object's primitives are all triangles, that is, that the object's boundary representation is given by triangular faces.

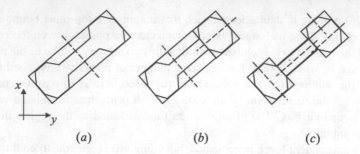

Fig. 2.2 A 2D example of a binary OBB tree. The boxes at each intermediate level provide a tight fit around their primitives. The *broken lines* show the partition plane used at each level

This assumption is especially suited to implementing a simulation engine as described in Chap. 1, since by the time a non-convex object is registered with the simulation engine its convex decomposition is computed (see Appendix F (Chap. 11)) and the faces of each convex polyhedron that make up the object are triangulated. The final internal representation of objects in the simulation engine is therefore made up of triangular faces only.

The main difficulty when computing OBB bounding boxes is the determination of the direction of their axes such that the box provides a tight fit around the vertices of the triangle primitives associated with it. This can be done by considering the mean vector and the covariance matrix of the triangle primitives. The mean vector for each triangle primitive T_k is given by

$$\vec{\mu}_k = \frac{1}{3}(\vec{v}_1 + \vec{v}_2 + \vec{v}_3),$$

where $\vec{v}_1$, $\vec{v}_2$ and $\vec{v}_3$ are the vertices defining the triangle. Each vector $\vec{v}_r$ is described by its components $(v_r)_x$, $(v_r)_y$ and $(v_r)_z$. The mean vector of the vertex set is then

$$\vec{\mu} = \frac{1}{n}\sum_{k=1}^{n}\vec{\mu}_k,$$

with n being the total number of triangles being considered when computing the OBB bounding box.

The elements of the 3×3 covariance matrix of each triangle T_k can be computed as

$$C_{ij} = \frac{1}{3}\left((\bar{p}_1)_i(\bar{p}_1)_j + (\bar{p}_2)_i(\bar{p}_2)_j + (\bar{p}_3)_i(\bar{p}_3)_j\right),$$

Fig. 2.3 A 2D example of how interior points can degrade the quality of OBB bounding boxes; (**a**) The initial set of points; (**b**) The OBB bounding box created taking all points into account; (**c**) The OBB bounding box created taking into account only the convex hull points

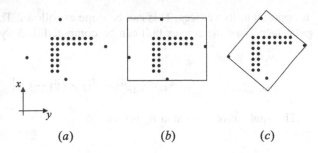

(a) (b) (c)

where $i, j \in \{x, y, z\}$ and $\bar{p}_i = (\vec{p}_i - \vec{\mu})$ for $i \in 1, 2, 3$. The covariance matrix of the vertex set is then

$$C_{ij} = \frac{1}{n} \sum_{k=1}^{n} (C_k)_{ij},$$

with $(C_k)_{ij}$ being the $\{ij\}$ element of the covariance matrix associated with the kth triangle.

Since the covariance matrix is a real symmetric matrix, its eigenvectors are guaranteed to be mutually orthogonal. Moreover, two of its three eigenvectors are the axes corresponding to the maximum and minimum variance of the vertices' coordinates. Therefore, if we use the eigenvectors of the covariance matrix as a base, we can determine a tight-fitting bounding box by transforming all vertices to this base and computing the AABB box of the transformed vertices. In other words, the OBB bounding box has the orientation of the eigenvector base and a size that bounds the maximum and minimum coordinates of the transformed vertices.

It is important to notice that the direction of the eigenvectors of the covariance matrix is influenced, not only by the vertices that define the maximum and minimum coordinates, but by *all* vertices being considered. This may cause problems because interior vertices, which should not affect the bounding-box computation, can influence the direction of the eigenvectors. For example, a large number of interior vertices concentrated in a small area can cause the eigenvectors to align with them, instead of aligning with the boundary vertices, thereby creating a low-quality OBB bounding box. This is illustrated in Fig. 2.3.

The computation of the covariance matrix should therefore take into account *only* the boundary vertices of the vertex set. It should also be immune to clusters of boundary vertices, since they will tend to influence the direction of the eigenvectors in the same manner clusters of interior vertices do.

Interior vertices can be avoided if we consider only the vertices that are in the convex hull of the vertex set.[2] Clusters of boundary vertices can be ignored if we compute the mean vector and covariance matrix over the surface of the convex hull,

---

[2]The computation of the convex hull of a vertex set is described in Sect. 2.2.4.

as opposed to its vertices. This can be done as follows. The area A_k of each triangular face T_k of the convex hull can be computed directly from its vertices, given by

$$A_k = \frac{1}{2} |(\vec{v}_2 - \vec{v}_1) \times (\vec{v}_3 - \vec{v}_2)|.$$

The total convex hull area A_t is then

$$A_t = \sum_{k=1}^{n_k} A_k,$$

where n_k is the total number of triangular faces in the convex hull.

The mean vector $\vec{\mu}_t$ associated with the convex hull, weighted by the total convex hull area, is obtained from

$$\vec{\mu}_t = \frac{\sum_{k=1}^{n_k} A_k \vec{\mu}_k}{\sum_{k=1}^{n_k} A_k} = \frac{\sum_{k=1}^{n_k} A_k \vec{\mu}_k}{A_t}.$$

The elements $(C_k)_{ij}$ of the 3×3 covariance matrix of each triangular face T_k, also weighted by the total convex hull area, are given by

$$(C_k)_{ij} = \frac{A_k}{12 A_t} \left(9(\mu_k)_i (\mu_k)_j + (v_1)_i (v_1)_j + (v_2)_i (v_2)_j + (v_3)_i (v_3)_j \right).$$

Finally, the elements $(C_t)_{ij}$ of the 3×3 covariance matrix associated with the convex hull are computed from the elements $(C_k)_{ij}$ of the covariance matrix of each of its triangular faces as

$$(C_t)_{ij} = \left(\sum_{k=1}^{n_k} (C_k)_{ij} \right) - (\mu_t)_i (\mu_t)_j.$$

Having determined the covariance matrix, we proceed by computing its associated eigenvectors using one of several methods available for computing eigenvalues and eigenvectors of real symmetric matrices. Section 2.6 has pointers to the literature describing such methods. The OBB axis will be aligned with the direction of the eigenvectors and its dimensions will be given by the extremal vertices along each axis.

2.2.3 Bounding Spheres

In the Bounding Sphere (BS) representation, the tree hierarchy is constructed from minimum-radius bounding spheres encapsulating the primitives associated with them. Figure 2.4 illustrates the top-down construction of a binary BS tree for the same 2D object considered in the AABB and OBB cases.

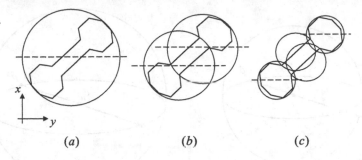

Fig. 2.4 A 2D example of a binary BS tree. The *broken lines* represent the partition plane used at each level

The BS hierarchical tree is usually of poorer quality than its OBB and AABB counterparts, with respect to the tightness of the decomposition. However, its overlap test is undoubtedly the easiest and fastest to carry out (see Sect. 2.5), thus giving this representation an advantage over the others for quick rejection tests.

In this section, we present a method for finding a near-optimal bounding sphere from the set of primitives associated with it. The sphere calculated using this method is usually slightly larger than the minimum-radius sphere, but this inaccuracy is offset by the efficiency of the method.

The bounding sphere computation is carried out in two passes through the list of vertices of all primitives associated with it. The first pass is used to estimate the initial center and radius of the sphere. The second pass goes through each vertex in the list and checks whether it is included in the sphere. If it is not included, then the sphere is enlarged to include it. At the end, the center and radius of the near-optimal bounding sphere are determined.

In the first pass, we loop through the list of all vertices to obtain the following six points.

1. The point with maximum x.
2. The point with minimum x.
3. The point with maximum y.
4. The point with minimum y.
5. The point with maximum z.
6. The point with minimum z.

From these six points, we select the two that are farthest apart. These two points will define the first approximation of the diameter of the bounding sphere. The center of the sphere is assumed to be at their midpoint.

In the second pass, we loop again through the list of all vertices, and for each vertex, we compare the square of its distance to the center with the square of the current radius of the bounding sphere. If the distance is smaller than the radius, then the vertex is inside the sphere and we proceed to the next vertex in the list. Otherwise, we adjust the sphere's radius and center as follows.

Let $\vec{v}_i$ be the current vertex being tested against the bounding sphere, and falling outside it. Let $\vec{c}$ be the center of the bounding sphere, r be its radius and $\vec{p}$ be the point in the sphere diametrically opposed to $\vec{v}_i$ (see Fig. 2.5(a)).

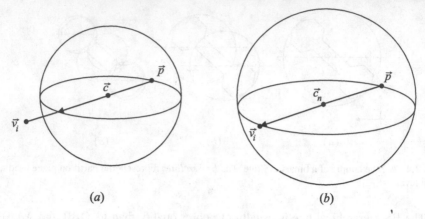

$$(a) \hspace{6cm} (b)$$

Fig. 2.5 Efficient, incremental computation of a bounding sphere for a given vertex set; (**a**) Vertex $\vec{v}_i$ falls outside the sphere, and therefore the sphere needs to be enlarged to bound it as well; (**b**) The sphere is augmented such that $\vec{v}_i$ and $\vec{p}$ define its new diameter

Let d be the distance between $\vec{v}_i$ and $\vec{c}$, that is

$$d = \sqrt{\left((v_i)_x - c_x\right)^2 + \left((v_i)_y - c_y\right)^2 + \left((v_i)_z - c_z\right)^2}.$$

The enlarged sphere is then computed from the current sphere such that $\vec{v}_i$ and $\vec{p}$ become the new diameter, as shown in Fig. 2.5(b). The new center $\vec{c}_n$ and radius r_n of the enlarged sphere are given by

$$r_n = \frac{r + d}{2}$$

$$\vec{c}_n = \frac{r\vec{c} + (d - r)\vec{v}_i}{d}.$$

This process continues until all vertices are checked for inclusion against the bounding sphere.

Having determined the top-most bounding sphere, a partition plane is chosen such that it passes through the median point of all vertices of all primitives associated with the bounding sphere. The partition plane subdivides the bounding sphere into two regions, and the primitives are assigned to each region following the same rules used on the AABB and OBB cases, namely, the primitive is associated with the region that contains its midpoint. The subdivision continues until there is only one primitive assigned to each bounding sphere, or the primitives cannot be split, in which case the group of primitives is assigned to the bounding sphere.

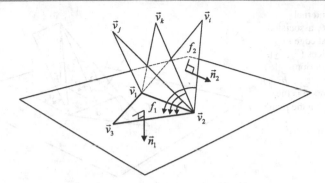

Fig. 2.6 Determining the neighbor face that shares edge e_1 with f_1. The selected vertex $\vec{v}_i$ will define a face f_2 that forms the largest convex dihedral angle with f_1. The ordering of the vertices defining the new face should be chosen so that the normal vector of the new face always points towards the outside of the object. Because we are using the right-hand coordinate system, the correct order is $(\vec{v}_1, \vec{v}_i, \vec{v}_2)$

2.2.4 Convex Hull

The convex hull can be used not only to provide a hierarchical representation of the object's primitives as a tree of convex polyhedra, but also as an intermediate step for computing other types of representations, such as the OBB trees already covered in Sect. 2.2.2.

The convex hull of a given vertex set S is defined as being the smallest convex set containing S. There are several algorithms and methods that can be used to compute the convex hull in 2D, 3D, or even higher dimensions. In this section, we focus on the *gift wrapping* method, which is intuitive, easy to visualize in 3D, simple to implement, and applicable to higher-dimensional spaces.

The basic idea of the gift-wrapping method consists of imagining folding a piece of paper around the primitives being considered. We start with a face that is guaranteed to be in the convex hull, and loop through its edges determining its neighbor faces that are also part of the convex hull. The algorithm then proceeds looping through the edges of the new neighbor faces until all faces are discovered and the convex hull is completely determined. All faces will be discovered whenever the list of edges to be checked is empty.

Given a set of vertices $S = \{\vec{v}_1, \dots, \vec{v}_n\}$, let's assume that the triangular face f_1 defined by vertices $(\vec{v}_1, \vec{v}_2, \vec{v}_3)$ is the starting face guaranteed to be in the convex hull. According to the high-level description of the algorithm presented in the previous paragraph, we need to loop through the edges of face f_1 and determine its associated neighbor faces that are also in the convex hull. A face is said to be in the convex hull if all vertices of S that are not vertices of the face lie on the same side of the plane defined by the face. Since we are using the right-hand coordinate system in our simulation engine, we want all vertices of S to lie on the inside region of the plane. More specifically, we want to construct each face of the convex hull such that its normal is always pointing outwards, as illustrated in Fig. 2.6.

Fig. 2.7 The internal
dihedral angle θ_i associated
with vertex $\vec{v}_i$ at edge e_1
defined by vertices $(\vec{v}_1, \vec{v}_2)$,
shown as the exterior angle at
vertex $\vec{a}$ of triangle $(\vec{a}, \vec{b}, \vec{v}_i)$.
Notice that vertex $\vec{b}$ is the
projection of $\vec{v}_i$ on the plane
of face f_1

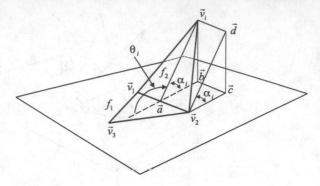

Fig. 2.8 The interior angle
α_i at vertex $\vec{a}$ can be obtained
from the dot product of the
face normals $\vec{n}_1$ and $\vec{n}_2$
associated with faces f_1
and f_2, respectively

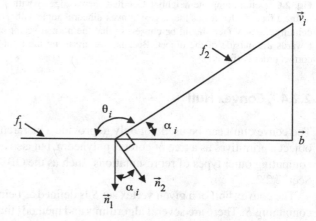

Let's consider, for example, the determination of the neighbor face f_2 that shares
edge $e_1 = (\vec{v}_1, \vec{v}_2)$ with f_1. We want to find the vertex $\vec{v}_i \in S$, with $i \neq 1, 2$, such
that the triangular face f_2 defined by $(\vec{v}_1, \vec{v}_i, \vec{v}_2)$ forms the largest convex internal
dihedral angle at edge e_1. Figure 2.7 shows how the internal dihedral angle can be
computed.

Let θ_i be the internal dihedral angle associated with vertex $\vec{v}_i$ at edge e_1. Let $\vec{n}_1$
and $\vec{n}_2$ be the normal vectors of faces f_1 and f_2, respectively. By construction, since
the normals at each face are pointing outwards, their dot product gives the cosine of
$(\pi - \theta_i)$ (see Fig. 2.8). The dihedral angle can then be computed directly from

$$\theta_i = \pi - \arccos(\vec{n}_1 \cdot \vec{n}_2).$$

We select the vertex $\vec{v}_i$ corresponding to the maximum θ_i, and add face f_2 to the
list of convex hull faces. The ordering of the vertices defining the new face should be
chosen so that the normal vector of the new face always points towards the outside
of the object. Because we are using the right-hand coordinate system, the correct
order is $(\vec{v}_1, \vec{v}_i, \vec{v}_2)$. The edges of f_2 are then added to the list of edges that need
to be checked, so that the algorithm can compute the convex hull faces that share
these edges with f_2. It is important to notice that the algorithm assumes each edge

Fig. 2.9 The first edge of the starting face is computed using the projection of the vertices on the xy-plane. Here the problem is reduced to its 2D counterpart

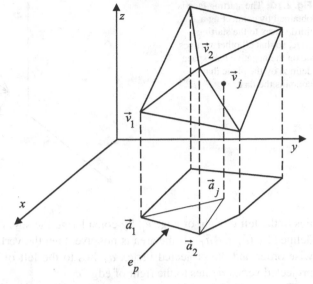

is shared by exactly two faces. Therefore, every time a new edge is added to the list of edges that need to be checked, we should first check whether the edge is already in the list. If the edge is already in the list, then one of the faces that contains this edge was already discovered in some previous step, and the other face that contains this edge has just being discovered. In this case, there is no need to check for this edge because both faces that share the edge are already included in the convex hull. Therefore, the edge can be removed from the list. Otherwise, the edge should be added to the list.

Up till now we have assumed the existence of a starting face that is guaranteed to be in the convex hull, and have determined all other faces from it. The only step we still have to describe is how the first face of the convex hull is computed. The computation of the vertices of the first face is incremental, in the sense that we compute one of them at a time. We start with one vertex that is guaranteed to be in the convex hull, then use it to determine the second vertex, thus forming an edge of the starting face. We then use the edge to determine the third vertex that makes up the first face. Having the first face, we proceed as explained before and determine all other convex hull faces.

The first face of the convex hull is computed as follows. Consider the projection of all points on the xy-plane, as shown in Fig. 2.9. Let $\vec{a}_1$ be the vertex with the lowest projected y-coordinate value. This vertex is guaranteed to be in the convex hull, since all other points of the vertex set will lie on the same half-space defined by a plane orthogonal to the y-axis (i.e., parallel to the xz-plane), passing through vertex $\vec{v}_1$. Therefore, vertex $\vec{v}_1$ is one of the vertices of the starting face.

The second vertex of the starting face can be found by looping through the projected vertices and selecting a vertex $\vec{a}_2$ such that all other projected vertices lie to the left of the edge $e_p = (\vec{a}_1, \vec{a}_2)$. We can determine whether the projected vertex $\vec{a}_j$

Fig. 2.10 The starting face is obtained by connecting a third vertex to the starting edge, so that all other vertices lie on the negative half-space defined by the plane that contains the face

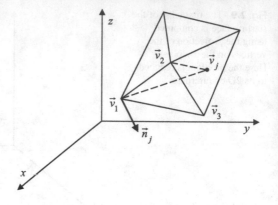

lies to the left or right of edge e_p by considering the sign of the area of the triangle defined by $(\vec{a}_1, \vec{a}_2, \vec{a}_j)$. If the area is positive, then the vertices are in counterclockwise order and the projected vertex $\vec{a}_j$ lies to the left of edge e_1. Otherwise, the projected vertex $\vec{a}_j$ lies to the right of edge e_p.

The area A of the projected triangle $(\vec{a}_1, \vec{a}_2, \vec{a}_j)$ can be quickly computed from the vertices' coordinates

$$A = \frac{1}{2} \begin{vmatrix} (\vec{a}_1)_x & (\vec{a}_2)_x & (\vec{a}_j)_x \\ (\vec{a}_1)_y & (\vec{a}_2)_y & (\vec{a}_j)_y \\ 1 & 1 & 1 \end{vmatrix}.$$

Finally, the third vertex of the starting face can be obtained by considering the triangular faces f_j defined by vertices $(\vec{v}_1, \vec{v}_j, \vec{v}_2)$ in 3D space. The order of the vertices defining the triangular face f_j is such that the normal points to the outside of the convex hull.[3] Here, the third vertex $\vec{v}_3$ is selected such that all other vertices lie in the negative half-space defined by the plane that contains the triangular face $(\vec{v}_1, \vec{v}_3, \vec{v}_2)$ (see Fig. 2.10).

Let $\vec{n}_j$ be the normal of the plane defined by the triangular face $(\vec{v}_1, \vec{v}_j, \vec{v}_2)$, and let d_j be the plane constant computed as

$$d_j = \vec{n}_j \cdot \vec{v}_1.$$

Vertex $\vec{v}_p$ will lie on the negative half-space of the plane provided

$$(\vec{n}_j \cdot \vec{v}_p) < d_j.$$

Having the first face, we proceed as explained and compute all other convex hull faces of the polyhedron.

---

[3]Recall that we are using the right-hand coordinate system.

Fig. 2.11 (a) Two fast moving objects at t_0; (b) Even though they do not collide at t_1, they do pass through each other during their motion from t_0 to t_1

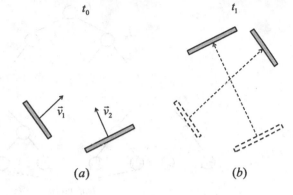

t_0 t_1

$\vec{v}_1$ $\vec{v}_2$

(a)   (b)

2.3 Hierarchical Representation for Continuous Collision Detection

In general, the collision detection between objects moving for a time interval $[t_0, t_1]$ is performed by a pairwise intersection test of the objects at t_1. Depending on the objects' shape and velocity, it is possible that some pairs of objects end up not intersecting at t_1 even though their paths crossed each other during their motion. This is usually the case for thin or fast moving objects, as illustrated in Fig. 2.11.

The continuous collision detection is suitable to handle these special cases because it takes into account the motion of the objects from t_0 to t_1, not just their position and orientation at t_1. It still uses the hierarchical representations of the objects to speed computations, but they need to be modified to bound the entire motion from t_0 to t_1 in *world-coordinate frame*. Notice that the standard procedure is to construct the hierarchies once in their local-coordinate frame at the time the objects are registered with the simulation engine, and incrementally transform their nodes from local- to world-coordinate frame as they are checked for intersections in world space. In the continuous collision case, the hierarchies need to be constructed in the world-coordinate frame to take into account the objects' motion in world space. Theoretically, we need to re-build the hierarchies at the end of each time interval using the top-down approach already explained in Sect. 2.1, but replacing each primitive with a bounding volume that contains its world-coordinate positions at both t_0 and t_1. However, the significant performance hit it takes on the simulation to rebuild the hierarchical trees at every time interval deems this approach impractical, especially when the number of objects being simulated in large (i.e., in the thousands).

A more efficient approach adopted in this book is to *refit* the hierarchical trees originally built in their local-coordinate frames, but with the motion information in world space. The efficiency comes from the fact that the process of refitting a hierarchical tree retains the parent–children relationship obtained when the tree was initially built, so all intermediate computations to determine the bounding volumes of internal nodes in a top-down fashion are forgone. When refitting a tree, the leaf nodes are updated first to bound their primitive's motion from t_0 to t_1, and then their parent (internal) nodes are updated to bound the volume of their children. It

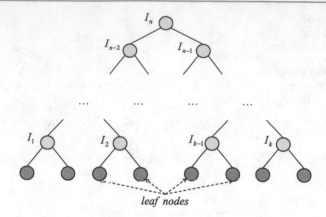

Fig. 2.12 Hierarchical tree representation of an object

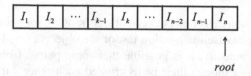

Fig. 2.13 Array representation of the internal nodes in Fig. 2.12, sorted by decreasing depth (i.e., distance to the root node). The root node is positioned at the last entry because it is the only node that does not have a parent

is important that an internal node is updated only after its children are updated. This requires special attention when building the hierarchical tree for the first time, to make sure the internal nodes are stored in decreasing order with respect to their depth (i.e., their distance to the root node). Figure 2.13 shows an array representation of all internal nodes of the hierarchical tree shown in Fig. 2.12, sorted by decreasing depths. A node located at the k-th entry is guaranteed to have its parent node located at an entry j with $j > k$, that is, by updating the internal nodes using their order in the sorted array, we can guarantee the children nodes will always be updated before their parents.

As far as performance is concerned, refitting a tree is about an order of magnitude faster than rebuilding it. A more detailed discussion on the advantages and disadvantages of refitting a hierarchical tree can be found in the references provided in Sect. 2.6.

2.4   Hierarchical Representation of the Simulated World

Even though the use of hierarchical representations does speed the collision-detection phase, they themselves do not provide mechanisms to take advantage of the time coherence between consecutive frames in a simulation. For instance, the fact that two or more objects are farther apart, such that their top-most bounding volumes do not intersect, should be exploited in the following simulation time steps to avoid unnecessary collision checks between these objects. The hierarchical representation does minimize the time spent on such unnecessary collision checks, since they are usually dismissed after the top-most bounding volumes are checked against each other. However, the time expended on these unnecessary checks can be significant, especially when the simulation contains several thousand objects.

The idea is then to create a partition of the simulated world into cells, and assign objects to the cells in which their top-most bounding volume intersects. Objects that are assigned to the same cell can be potentially colliding and therefore should be checked for geometric intersections between their hierarchical representations. On the other hand, objects that have no cells in common are clearly distant from each other and should not be checked for collisions at all.

The simulated world considered in this book is assumed to be bounded by a box that defines the maximum and minimum spans along each coordinate axis. The cell decomposition is then a partition of the box into sub-volumes that may or may not contain objects during the simulation.

There are two important issues that should be taken into account when decomposing the simulated world into cells. First, the cell decomposition should be simple, that is, should have simple geometry such that the cost of updating the cells that intersect each moved object is negligible compared with the cost of checking for collisions between their hierarchical representations. This issue is addressed in Sect. 2.4.1, where the simulated world is subdivided into boxes of uniform size. Second, the size of each cell directly affects the efficacy of the decomposition. For instance, a too-small size will assign several cells to each object, making it more expensive to update the list of occupied cells after each simulation time step. On the other hand, a too-large size will assign several objects to the same cell and a large number of unnecessary collision checks between their hierarchical representations may be carried out. This issue is addressed in Sect. 2.4.2, where the uniform-grid approach presented in Sect. 2.4.1 is extended to a multi-level grid that better fits the different sizes of objects being simulated.

2.4.1 Uniform Grid

Uniform-grid decomposition, as its name implies, subdivides the bounding box of the simulated world into cubic cells of same size along each axis of the world-coordinate frame. A simple uniform-grid decomposition of an hypothetical world is shown in Fig. 2.14.

In the uniform-grid decomposition, the dimension of the cubic cells plays an important role in minimizing the number of unnecessary objects to cell assignments, and in maximizing the overall efficacy of the simulation. Intuitively, the size of each cell should be:

- Large enough to allow objects to rotate and translate for a while without leaving the cell, thus minimizing the number of dynamic updates of objects assigned to each cell;

Fig. 2.14 A simple uniform-grid decomposition of an hypothetical simulated world with a resolution of fourteen boxes along each dimension. Each cell is identified by the index on its lower-left corner vertex. For example, the first cell is indexed as cell $(0, 0, 0)$. The shaded cell is indexed as cell $(2, 5, 13)$

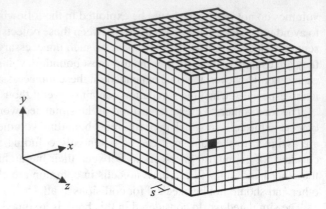

- Small enough to have as many objects as possible assigned to different cells, thus minimizing the pair-wise collision checks between the object's hierarchical representations.

Let d_i be the maximum diameter of the top-most bounding volume of object i. For example, if the bounding volume is a box, then the maximum diameter is the distance between the two diagonally opposing vertices defining box. If the bounding volume is a sphere, then the maximum diameter is equal to the diameter of the sphere. The average maximum diameter of the objects being simulated is then

$$\bar{d} = \frac{1}{n} \sum_{i=0}^{n} d_i,$$

where n is the total number of objects.[4] The size b of each cell in the uniform-grid decomposition is also given by the cell's maximum diameter, and can be related to the average maximum diameter of the objects being simulated as

$$\frac{\bar{d}}{b} = k, \tag{2.1}$$

with $k \geq 1$. The variable k is used to adjust the size of the cell with respect to the average maximum diameter of the objects being simulated. As a rule, we suggest using $k = 2$, that is, the size of each cell in the uniform grid is twice the average maximum diameter. The rationale behind this choice is as follows. If all objects had the average size, then we could have up to eight objects in each cell (two objects touching each other along each dimension), giving some room to an object to move within the same cell. Also, objects that are farther apart by more than twice their average size are guaranteed not to be in the same cell. On average, this choice gives us a reasonable trade-off between the number of objects assigned to each cell and

---

[4]The size of particles in a particle system is not taken into account during this computation because particles are usually considered as point mass, as explained in detail in Chap. 3.

the number of pair-wise collision checks carried out at each time step if the objects' sizes are close to the average. However, if the objects' sizes vary by orders of magnitude, then a more sophisticated approach, such as the one presented in Sect. 2.4.2, should be used.

Having selected the size of the boxes in the decomposition, the next step is to provide an efficient mechanism to keep track only of cells that have at least one object assigned to them, as opposed to allocating memory to all cells. Clearly, the latter approach is not advisable for cases when the size of each cell is orders of magnitude smaller than the size of the simulated world, since the number of cells along each axis would be huge, and the memory needed for a subdivision containing n cells is n^3. The idea here is to use a hash table to keep track of the occupied cells. There are many ways this hash table of cells can be constructed, and some may be more effective than others, depending on the specifics of the simulation being considered. However, as a rule, we suggest using a hash table of size n, where the key is the sum of the indexes of the cell along each axis. This will have the effect of assigning one slice (plane) of the grid decomposition to each hash-table entry.

The update mechanism using the hash table is used to efficiently detect pairs of potentially colliding objects. Initially, the top-most bounding volume of each object is checked against the cell decomposition. Each cell that intersects the object's bounding volume is added to the hash table of cells. If the cell was already added to the hash table, then there are at least two objects assigned to this cell, and a pointer to this cell is added to a list of cells that need to be checked for collisions. At the end, after all objects are checked against the cell decomposition, another list of potentially colliding objects is created from the list of cells that needs to be checked for collisions. The former list contains pairs of objects that occupy the same cell. For each of these pairs, the more expensive collision check using their hierarchical representation is carried out.

The cells of the uniform-grid decomposition that intersect an object's bounding volume can be efficiently determined if we consider an AABB bounding box of the object's bounding volume in the world-coordinate frame. Notice that this selection is independent of the hierarchical tree representation of the objects. The AABB bounding box is aligned with the world coordinate frame, as are all cubic cells in the uniform-grid decomposition. The box–box intersection test between boxes that have their axes aligned is extremely fast and can be used to determine the actual cubic cells in the decomposition that need to be checked for intersection with the object's bounding volume. Figure 2.15 illustrates this situation for an object using the bounding-sphere representation. The AABB bounding box of the bounding sphere is used to efficiently locate the cells in the decomposition that need to be checked for intersection with the object's bounding sphere, as opposed to checking the intersection of every cell with the object's bounding sphere.

As objects translate and rotate during the simulation, their top-most bounding volume will move. This movement may cause the bounding volume to no longer intersect some of the cells the object is assigned to, and may also intersect new cells that did not have the object on their list. Therefore, the list of objects assigned to each cell needs to be updated after each simulation time step to reflect these changes.

Fig. 2.15 The AABB
bounding box of the object's
bounding sphere is used to
quickly determine which cells
of the decomposition need to
be checked for intersection
with the bounding sphere. In
this case, the bounding sphere
will be checked further for
intersections with cells
$(2, 5, 4), (2, 6, 4), (3, 5, 4),$
$(3, 6, 4), (2, 5, 5), (2, 6, 5),$
$(3, 5, 5)$ and $(3, 6, 5)$

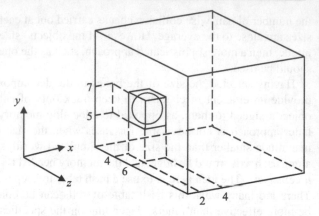

This update can be efficiently implemented using coherence between simulation time steps, as follows.

Throughout the simulation, each object keeps track of the indexes of the cells that intersect its bounding volume. At each time step, a new list of indexes of cells that intersect the object's bounding volume is generated. This new list is then compared with the old list. If the new list is the same as the old list, then the object's cell assignment remains the same as in the previous time step, and nothing else needs to be done. If there are cells on the new list that are not on the old list, then we search for these cells in the hash table of cells. If we find the cell in the hash table, then we add a reference to this object and raise the cell's internal counter. Otherwise, we create an entry for the cell in the hash table and set its internal counter to one. Finally, if there are boxes on the old list that are no longer on the new list, then the reference to this object should be removed from the cell's entry in the hash table, and its internal counter is subtracted by one.

The cell's internal counter is used to keep track of the number of objects currently intersecting the cell. The first time the counter is set to two, a reference to this cell is added to the list of cells that contain potentially colliding objects. The counter can be set to values greater than two, but as long as it has at least two, the reference to this cell will be kept in the list. The reference to this cell is removed from the list when the counter first is reduced from two to one. The cell is removed from the hash table of cells when the counter is set to zero.

2.4.2 Multi-level Grid

If the size of the objects being simulated differs by orders of magnitude, the efficiency of the uniform-grid approach can be improved by extending it to a multi-level grid. The idea is to group at the same level, objects with sizes of the same order of magnitude such that each level can be treated as an uniform grid in itself. The advantage is that each level attempts to maximize the efficiency of its uniform grid, since it is guaranteed to have objects of similar size. There are three important issues that need to be addressed when using this method.

- How many levels should be chosen for a given set of objects?
- What should be the size of the cells at each level?
- How the levels are related so that collisions between objects assigned to different levels can be efficiently detected?

In the uniform-grid case, since we have a single level, the size of the cell is determined from Eq. (2.1) as a multiple of the average size of the maximum diameter of the objects in the simulation. In the multiple-level case, object i is assigned to level j if

$$k_{min} \le \frac{d_i}{L_j} \le k_{max}, \tag{2.2}$$

where d_i is the maximum diameter of the top-most bounding volume of object i, k_{min} and k_{max} are user-definable constants, and L_j is the size of the cells at level j, such that

$$0 < L_1 < L_2 < \cdots < L_j < \cdots < L_m$$

for $1 \le j \le m$. The idea is to assign object i to the largest level j such that Eq. (2.2) is satisfied. In other words, the largest objects are assigned to the largest boxes (largest levels), so that objects at level $(j + 1)$ have diameters greater than objects at level j. The constants k_{min} and k_{max} are used to relate the size of the cells at different levels. They must satisfy

$$0 < k_{min} < 1$$

$$k_{max} \ge 1.$$

Let d_{min} and d_{max} be the minimum and maximum diameters of all objects in the simulation. Clearly, the objects associated with d_{min} (the smallest objects) should be assigned to level 1 (the lowest level). This is done by substituting d_{min} and L_1 into Eq. (2.2), that is

$$k_{min} \le \frac{d_{min}}{L_1} \le k_{max}.$$

If we make

$$k_{min} = \frac{d_{min}}{L_1},$$

then we have that the size of the cells at the lowest level is given by

$$L_1 = \frac{d_{min}}{k_{min}}. \tag{2.3}$$

The objects associated with d_{max} should be assigned to the largest level m. This is done by substituting d_{max} and L_m into Eq. (2.2), and making

$$\frac{d_{max}}{L_m} = k_{max},$$

that is

$$L_m = \frac{d_{max}}{k_{max}}. \tag{2.4}$$

Because we want the level assignment to be continuous, we need to make sure the maximum value at level j is equal to the minimum value at level $(j+1)$, that is

$$k_{max}L_j = k_{min}L_{j+1}. \tag{2.5}$$

Equation (2.5) relates the size of the cells at two consecutive levels. We can use this equation to recursively compute the size of the cells at level j as a function of the size of the cells at level 1, as follows:

$$L_2 = \frac{k_{max}}{k_{min}}L_1$$

$$L_3 = \frac{k_{max}}{k_{min}}L_2 = \left(\frac{k_{max}}{k_{min}}\right)^2 L_1 \tag{2.6}$$

$$\dots$$

$$L_j = \left(\frac{k_{max}}{k_{min}}\right)^{j-1} L_1.$$

Because we have the size of the boxes at the first level L_1 and the largest level L_m given by Eqs. (2.4) and (2.5), respectively, we can substitute these equations into (2.6) and compute the number of levels m needed as a function of k_{min}, k_{max}, d_{min} and d_{max}. We have

$$\frac{d_{max}}{k_{max}} = \left(\frac{k_{max}}{k_{min}}\right)^{m-1} \frac{d_{min}}{k_{min}},$$

which gives

$$m = \left\lceil \log_{\left(\frac{k_{max}}{k_{min}}\right)}\left(\frac{d_{max}}{d_{min}}\right) \right\rceil. \tag{2.7}$$

Figure 2.16 shows an example of a multi-level grid assignment. At each level j, the simulated world is subdivided in a uniform grid with boxes of size L_j.

Fig. 2.16 An example of a multi-level grid assignment for $k_{max} = 1$, $k_{min} = 0.5$, $d_{max} = 16$ and $d_{min} = 2$. The maximum number of levels to be used and their sizes can be directly computed from Eqs. (2.7) and (2.6), respectively. In this case, $m = 3$, $L_1 = 4$, $L_2 = 8$ and $L_3 = 16$

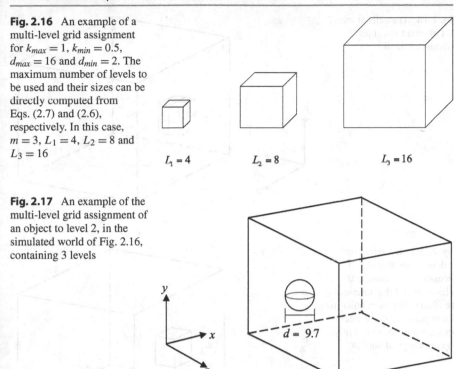

$L_1 = 4$ $L_2 = 8$ $L_3 = 16$

Fig. 2.17 An example of the multi-level grid assignment of an object to level 2, in the simulated world of Fig. 2.16, containing 3 levels

$d = 9.7$

Therefore, the multi-level grid has one hash table of cells for each level, and the sizes of their cells are given by Eq. (2.6). The update mechanism for each hash table is the same as that used in the uniform grid, since we do have a uniform grid at each level. Consider, for example, the bounding sphere of an object with center at $(5, 5, 5)$ and maximum diameter $d = 9.7$ (see Fig. 2.17). For the multi-level grid of the simulated world shown in Fig. 2.16, according to Eq. (2.2), the object should be assigned to level 2. Within level 2, the cells that intersect the object's bounding volume are computed the same way as shown in Fig. 2.15 for the uniform-grid case.

The only remaining issue is how this scheme can be used to efficiently detect potential collisions between objects assigned to different levels of the grid decomposition. We address this issue by adding a reference to the object, not only to the cells that intersect the object at its level, but also to all other cells that intersect the object at levels greater than its level. For example, an object assigned to level j will have its reference added to all cells that intersect its bounding volume at levels j, $(j + 1)$, ..., m. In the case shown in Fig. 2.17, the cells at levels 2 and 3 that intersect the object's bounding volume will keep a reference to this object (see Figs. 2.18 and 2.19). Using this scheme, two objects b_1 and b_2 assigned to levels L_{b_1} and L_{b_2} can potentially collide if and only if there exist at least one cell at level $\max(L_{b_1}, L_{b_2})$ that has a reference to both of them. This situation is illustrated in the one-dimensional case shown in Fig. 2.20.

Fig. 2.18 The cells at level 2 that intersect the object's bounding sphere

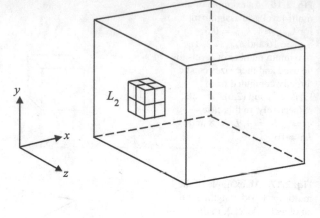

Fig. 2.19 The multi-level grid assignment makes it necessary to determine the cells at level 3 that intersect the object. This is in order to detect potential collisions between this object and other objects assigned only to level 3

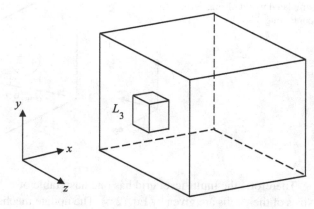

In this example, objects b_1 and b_2 are assigned to levels L_1 and L_3, respectively. Since there is a box at level $m = \max(L_1, L_3) = L_3$ that contains a reference to both of them, the objects are added to the list of potentially colliding objects. On the other hand, objects b_3 and b_4 are assigned to levels L_1 and L_2, respectively. Since there are no boxes at level $m = \max(L_1, L_2) = L_2$ that contain a reference to both of them, they are not considered to be on the list of potentially colliding objects, even though there is a cell at level L_3 referring to both of them.

As a rule, we suggest choosing k_{min} and k_{max} such that

$$\frac{k_{max}}{k_{min}} = 2.$$

This choice means the size of the cells will be a power of two times the minimum diameter d_{min}. With this choice, given an object assigned to level j, it is straightforward to ascertain which cells intersect the object at levels $(j + 1), \ldots, m$.

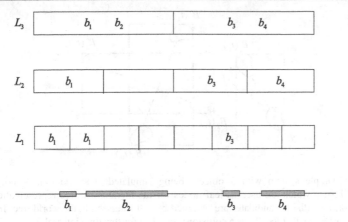

Fig. 2.20 A one-dimensional example of how potential collisions are detected between objects assigned to different levels

2.4.3   Bounding Volume for Continuous Collision Detection

The grid-based representation of the simulated world becomes less efficient for continuous collision detection, where the entire motion of the objects is considered. This is because objects may pass through several grid cells during their motion thus creating a lot of redundant entries in the list of potential collisions obtained from the pairs of objects that share a cell. A better way of representing the simulated world for continuous collision detection is to use a hierarchical tree representation with leaf nodes bounding the objects' entire motion. This is very similar to the hierarchical representation of objects discussed in Sect. 2.3, where leaf nodes contain the motion of their primitives for the entire time interval.

Figure 2.21 shows an example of a system with 3 objects. Their motion for the current time interval is bounded by axis-aligned boxes that are used as leaf nodes in the simulated-world tree representation of this system. The list of potential collision pairs is obtained by self-intersecting the tree, that is, by detecting all pairs of objects that cross each other's paths during their motion.

2.5   Collision Detection Between Hierarchical Representations

Up till now, we have described several types of hierarchical representations that can be used to speed collision detection between objects in a simulation engine, as well as how we can build them using simple primitives. In this section, we shall present efficient algorithms to quickly determine whether two hierarchies or two of their primitives are intersecting.

The primitives of the representations covered in this book are boxes and spheres for the tree hierarchies, and triangles for the faces of the objects. Therefore, we need algorithms for checking the intersection of each possible pair-wise combination of

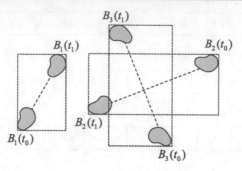

Fig. 2.21 A simple system with 3 objects being simulated. Their motion is bounded by axis-aligned boxes, which are used as leaf nodes for the hierarchical tree representation of the simulated world. Collision candidates are obtained by self-intersecting the world tree. In this example, the pair of objects (B_2, B_3) is a collision candidate for this time interval

such primitives. Moreover, for the triangle–triangle intersection test, we need to go one step further and save pointers to the intersecting triangles. This information will be used by the collision-response module to estimate the collision (or contact) point between the objects, and determine the collision impulses (or contact forces) needed to prevent their interpenetration.

2.5.1   Computing Hierarchy–Hierarchy Intersections

Let H_1 and H_2 be two hierarchical representations of objects that are currently being checked for collisions. Here, the hierarchies are used to help speed the detection of all primitive–primitive pairs that are potentially colliding, without incurring the $O(n^2)$ cost of testing every primitive of one object against all primitives of the other object.

The hierarchy–hierarchy intersection test is carried out in a top-down manner doing pair-wise intersection tests between their internal nodes as needed. A priority queue Q is used to keep track of all internal node pairs that still need to be tested for intersection. This queue is initialized with the pair containing the root nodes of each hierarchy. At each iteration of the intersection test, we remove the front element of Q and check if its corresponding pair of nodes are intersecting. If no intersections are found, then we proceed to the next iteration, that is, the next element in the queue. Otherwise, the pair-wise combination of the intersecting nodes' children are added to the back of Q, so that they too can be checked for intersections. In the special case in which the intersecting nodes have no children, that is, they are leaf nodes of their hierarchies, then their corresponding primitives are added to a list of potentially colliding candidates. The following summarizes this recursive process.

1. Get (and remove) the first element in Q. Let $n_1 \in H_1$ and $n_2 \in H_2$ be the nodes corresponding to this element.

2. Check if the nodes intersect. If they don't intersect, discard this pair and move on to the next element in the queue.
3. The nodes do intersect at this point. Now, check if both nodes are leaves of their trees. If both of them are leaves, then add their primitives to the list of collision candidates. Discard this pair and move on to the next element in the queue.
4. Check if at least one of the nodes is a leaf. If one of the nodes is in fact a leaf, say n_1, then do the following:
   (a) Add the pair $(n_1, (n_2)_{left})$ to the priority queue, where $(n_2)_{left}$ is the child to the left of the node n_2.
   (b) Add the pair $(n_1, (n_2)_{right})$ to the priority queue, where $(n_2)_{right}$ is the child to the right of the node n_2.
5. At this point, both nodes n_1 and n_2 are internal nodes of their hierarchies. The following pairs are added to the priority queue for further intersection tests:
   - $((n_1)_{left}, (n_2)_{left})$,
   - $((n_1)_{left}, (n_2)_{right})$,
   - $((n_1)_{right}, (n_2)_{left})$,
   - $((n_1)_{right}, (n_2)_{right})$.

At the end of this process, we have a list of collision candidates containing pairs of primitives that need to be tested for intersections. The usually more expensive primitive–primitive intersection tests are carried out for all elements in this list. The hierarchies do not intersect if the list of collision candidates is empty, or no pairs of collision candidate primitives end up intersecting.

The fact that the hierarchies are not intersecting at the end of the current time interval does not guarantee that the objects are not colliding. Depending on the dynamic state of the objects and the size of the time interval used, it is possible that one object has moved completely inside the other object. In order to detect such cases, we need to perform an additional point-in-object test for one vertex of each object against the other. This test is explained in details in Sect. 2.5.13.

2.5.2   Computing Hierarchy-Self Intersections

The algorithm for self-intersecting a hierarchy is very similar to the one presented in Sect. 2.5.1 for intersecting different hierarchies. We still maintain a priority queue of node pairs, but in this case the nodes belong to the same hierarchy. The priority queue is initialized with the root node testing against itself. The following summarizes the recursive process used to self-intersect a hierarchy.

1. Get (and remove) the first element in the queue. Let $n_1 \in H_1$ and $n_2 \in H_1$ be the nodes corresponding to this element.
2. If $n_1 \neq n_2$, then check if the nodes intersect. If they don't intersect, then discard this pair and move on to the next element in the queue.
3. Check if both nodes are leaves of the tree. If they are leaves, then add their primitives to the list of collision candidates. Discard this pair and move on to the next element in the queue.
4. Check if at least one of the nodes is a leaf. If one of the nodes is in fact a leaf, say n_1, then do the following:

(a) Add the pair $(n_1, (n_2)_{left})$ to the priority queue, where $(n_2)_{left}$ is the child to the left of the node n_2.

(b) Add the pair $(n_1, (n_2)_{right})$ to the priority queue, where $(n_2)_{right}$ is the child to the right of the node n_2.

5. At this point, both n_1 and n_2 are internal nodes. The following pairs are added to the priority queue for further intersection tests:

- $((n_1)_{left}, (n_2)_{left})$,
- $((n_1)_{left}, (n_2)_{right})$,
- $((n_1)_{right}, (n_2)_{right})$,
- if $n_1 \neq n_2$ then add the pair $((n_1)_{right}, (n_2)_{left})$.

The main difference between this algorithm and the one presented in Sect. 2.5.1 is the avoidance of redundant calculations by making sure the children nodes are different before adding them to the priority queue. Notice that

$$\left((n_1)_{left}, (n_2)_{right}\right) = \left((n_1)_{right}, (n_2)_{left}\right)$$

whenever $n_1 = n_2$. At the end, we have a list of collision candidates containing pairs of primitives that need to be tested for intersections. The hierarchy doesn't self-intersect if this list is empty, or no pairs of primitives intersect.

2.5.3 Computing Box–Box Intersections

The intersection test between two boxes is based on the separating-axis theorem. This theorem states that two boxes A and B are disjoint if and only if there exists a separating plane such that the boxes are located on different sides of the plane.

Let $\vec{n}$ be the normal of a plane P, and let d be its nonnegative distance to the origin. The plane P is a separating plane of boxes A and B if

$$\vec{n} \cdot \vec{a} + d \leq 0, \quad \forall \vec{a} \in A \tag{2.8}$$

and

$$\vec{n} \cdot \vec{b} + d > 0, \quad \forall \vec{b} \in B, \tag{2.9}$$

that is, if the projections of A and B along the normal fall on opposite sides of the plane. Equations (2.8) and (2.9) can then be combined into the single equation

$$\vec{n} \cdot \vec{a} < \vec{n} \cdot \vec{b}, \quad \forall \vec{a} \in A, \forall \vec{b} \in B. \tag{2.10}$$

Equation (2.10) states that, if P is a separating plane of boxes A and B, then their images are disjoint under axial projection along an axis parallel to the plane normal $\vec{n}$. In other words, $\vec{n}$ is a separating axis of A and B. It can be shown that the separating-axis candidates are the normals to the faces of A and B, and the normals to the planes defined by one edge of A and one edge of B. This results in

Fig. 2.22 Axis-aligned box–box intersection test. Each box is defined by its minimum and maximum vertices. The intersection test is then carried out by checking whether their projections along each coordinate axis overlap. In this case, the z-axis is a separating axis and the objects do not overlap

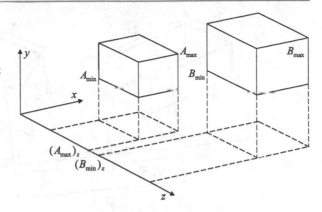

15 potential cases to be tested: 3 different face normals for each box plus 9 pair-wise combinations of edges. If none of the potential separating axes actually separates the boxes, then the boxes are guaranteed to be overlapping.

Let us first consider the simple intersection case, where the boxes are aligned with each other and are parallel to the world-coordinate frame's axis. This case occurs in the hierarchical representation of the simulated world, where all boxes in the uniform or multi-level grids have the same orientation with respect to the world-coordinate frame. In such situations, the 15 potential cases are reduced to just 3, since the face normals of each box are the same and the pair-wise combination of their edges always gives another edge. Therefore, the three separating-axis candidates are the axes of the world-coordinate frame.

Let each box be represented by its minimum and maximum vertices, as indicated in Fig. 2.22.

Let $[(A_{min})_i, (A_{max})_i]$ and $[(B_{min})_i, (B_{max})_i]$ be the projections of boxes A and B along the coordinate axis i, for $i = \{x, y, z\}$. The boxes A and B will *not* overlap if and only if

$$\big((A_{max})_i < (B_{min})_i\big) \cup \big((B_{max})_i < (A_{min})_i\big) \tag{2.11}$$

for at least one projection axis $i \in \{x, y, z\}$. This projection axis is then the separating axis for the boxes. On the other hand, if Eq. (2.11) is not satisfied for all projection axes, then the boxes are guaranteed to be overlapping.

Having considered the simple axis-aligned case, let's move on to the more complex case wherein the boxes are arbitrarily oriented with respect to each other. This happens when checking for intersections between boxes in the AABB or OBB hierarchical representations, since they usually have different orientations in the world-coordinate frame.

Let $\vec{T}_A$ and $\mathbf{R}_A$ be the translation vector and rotation matrix from A's local-coordinate frame to the world-coordinate frame. The axis of A in the world-coordinate frame will then be given by the columns of $\mathbf{R}_A$, namely $(\vec{R}_A)_x$, $(\vec{R}_A)_y$ and $(\vec{R}_A)_z$, that is

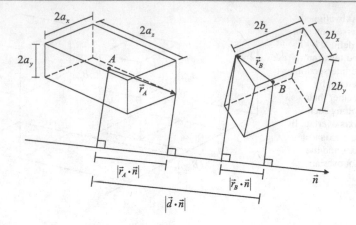

Fig. 2.23 Arbitrarily oriented box–box test. The boxes will not intersect if the axial projection of the distance between their centers is greater than the sum of the axial projection of their half-sides. There are 15 possible axial directions to be tested

$$\mathbf{R_A} = \left((\vec{R}_A)_x \mid (\vec{R}_A)_y \mid (\vec{R}_A)_z \right)$$

$$= \begin{pmatrix} (R_A)_{xx} & R_A)_{yx} & (R_A)_{zx} \\ (R_A)_{xy} & (R_A)_{yy} & (R_A)_{zy} \\ (R_A)_{xz} & (R_A)_{yz} & (R_A)_{zz} \end{pmatrix}$$

Similarly, let $\vec{T}_B$ and $\mathbf{R_B}$ be the translation vector and rotation matrix from B's local-coordinate frame to the world-coordinate frame, and the axis of B in the world-coordinate frame be $(\vec{R}_B)_x$, $(\vec{R}_B)_y$ and $(\vec{R}_B)_z$. Let $\vec{d}$ be the distance vector between the center of the boxes in the world-coordinate frame. The boxes A and B will be disjoint if and only if the sum of the projections of their half-sides along the candidate separating axis $\vec{n}$ is less than the projection of their distance vector $\vec{d}$ along $\vec{n}$, that is

$$|\vec{r}_A \cdot \vec{n}| + |\vec{r}_B \cdot \vec{n}| < |\vec{d} \cdot \vec{n}|, \tag{2.12}$$

where $\vec{r}_A$ and $\vec{r}_B$ are the sum of the projections of the half-sides of A and B, respectively. Figure 2.23 illustrates this.

The distances between boxes A and B to the origin of the world-coordinate frame are given by $\vec{T}_A$ and $\vec{T}_B$. Therefore, their distance vector can be directly obtained from

$$\vec{d} = \vec{T}_B - \vec{T}_A. \tag{2.13}$$

The half-sides of each box can be computed from the boxes' minimum and maximum vertices transformed to the world-coordinate frame. Let a_x, a_y and a_z be the half-sides of box A along its axes $(\vec{R}_A)_x$, $(\vec{R}_A)_y$ and $(\vec{R}_A)_z$. Similarly, let b_x, b_y and

b_z be the half-sides of box B along its axes $(\vec{R}_B)_x$, $(\vec{R}_B)_y$ and $(\vec{R}_B)_z$. The sum of the projections of the half-sides of A and B along $\vec{n}$ are then

$$\vec{r}_A \cdot \vec{n} = a_x |(\vec{R}_A)_x \cdot \vec{n}| + a_y |(\vec{R}_A)_y \cdot \vec{n}| + a_z |(\vec{R}_A)_z \cdot \vec{n}|$$
$$\vec{r}_B \cdot \vec{n} = b_x |(\vec{R}_B)_x \cdot \vec{n}| + b_y |(\vec{R}_B)_y \cdot \vec{n}| + b_z |(\vec{R}_B)_z \cdot \vec{n}|. \tag{2.14}$$

Substituting Eqs. (2.14) and (2.13) into (2.12), we have that $\vec{n}$ is a separating axis if and only if

$$\begin{aligned}
|(\vec{T}_B - \vec{T}_A) \cdot \vec{n}| > (&a_x |(\vec{R}_A)_x \cdot \vec{n}| \\
&+ a_y |(\vec{R}_A)_y \cdot \vec{n}| \\
&+ a_z |(\vec{R}_A)_z \cdot \vec{n}| \\
&+ b_x |(\vec{R}_B)_x \cdot \vec{n}| \\
&+ b_y |(\vec{R}_B)_y \cdot \vec{n}| \\
&+ b_z |(\vec{R}_B)_z \cdot \vec{n}|)
\end{aligned} \tag{2.15}$$

is satisfied for the 15 possible combinations of $\vec{n}$, namely $\vec{n} = (\vec{R}_A)_i$, $\vec{n} = (\vec{R}_B)_i$ or $\vec{n} = (\vec{R}_A)_i \times (\vec{R}_B)_j$ for $i, j \in \{x, y, z\}$ and $i \neq j$.

Equation (2.15) can be simplified if we carry out the computations in A's local-coordinate frame, as opposed to the world-coordinate frame. This can be done by translating all points by $-\vec{T}_A$ and rotating them by $\mathbf{R_A}^{-1} = \mathbf{R_A}^t$. This yields

$$\begin{aligned}
\vec{T}_A &= (\vec{T}_A - \vec{T}_A) = (0, 0, 0) \\
\mathbf{R_A} &= \mathbf{R_A}^t \mathbf{R_A} = \mathbf{I_3} \\
\vec{T}_D &= \mathbf{R_A}^t (\vec{T}_B - \vec{T}_A) \\
\mathbf{R_B} &= \mathbf{R_A}^t \mathbf{R_B},
\end{aligned} \tag{2.16}$$

where $\mathbf{I_3}$ is the 3×3 identity matrix. Substituting Eq. (2.16) into (2.15), we can explicitly derive the equations for all 15 possible tests for finding a separating axis for boxes A and B with respect to A's local-coordinate frame. These results are summarized in Table 2.1.

2.5.4 Computing Sphere–Sphere Intersections

The sphere–sphere intersection test is by far the simplest in this chapter. Two spheres are *not* intersecting if and only if the distance between their centers is greater than the sum of their radii. This is illustrated by Fig. 2.24.

Let r_A and $\vec{c}_A$ be the radius and center of sphere A, respectively. Similarly, let r_B and $\vec{c}_B$ be the radius and center of sphere B. The spheres will not overlap if and only if

$$|\vec{c}_A - \vec{c}_B| > (r_A + r_B).$$

Table 2.1 The 15 candidate separating axes and their associated tests with respect to A's local-coordinate frame. The boxes are overlapping if and only if all tests fail

Separating axis $\vec{n}$	Simplified overlap test
$(\vec{R}_A)_x$	$\lvert (T_B)_x \rvert > (a_x + b_x \lvert (R_B)_{xx} \rvert + b_y \lvert (R_B)_{xy} \rvert + b_z \lvert (R_B)_{xz} \rvert)$
$(\vec{R}_A)_y$	$\lvert (T_B)_y \rvert > (a_y + b_x \lvert (R_B)_{yx} \rvert + b_y \lvert (R_B)_{yy} \rvert + b_z \lvert (R_B)_{yz} \rvert)$
$(\vec{R}_A)_z$	$\lvert (T_B)_z \rvert > (a_z + b_x \lvert (R_B)_{zx} \rvert + b_y \lvert (R_B)_{zy} \rvert + b_z \lvert (R_B)_{zz} \rvert)$
$(\vec{R}_B)_x$	$\lvert (T_B)_x (R_B)_{xx} + (T_B)_y (R_B)_{yx} + (T_B)_z (R_B)_{zx} \rvert$ $\quad > (b_x + a_x \lvert (R_B)_{xx} \rvert + a_y \lvert (R_B)_{yx} \rvert + a_z \lvert (R_B)_{zx} \rvert)$
$(\vec{R}_B)_y$	$\lvert (T_B)_x (R_B)_{xy} + (T_B)_y (R_B)_{yy} + (T_B)_z (R_B)_{zy} \rvert$ $\quad > (b_y + a_x \lvert (R_B)_{xy} \rvert + a_y \lvert (R_B)_{yy} \rvert + a_z \lvert (R_B)_{zy} \rvert)$
$(\vec{R}_B)_z$	$\lvert (T_B)_x (R_B)_{xz} + (T_B)_y (R_B)_{yz} + (T_B)_z (R_B)_{zz} \rvert$ $\quad > (b_z + a_x \lvert (R_B)_{xz} \rvert + a_y \lvert (R_B)_{yz} \rvert + a_z \lvert (R_B)_{zz} \rvert)$
$(\vec{R}_A)_x \times (\vec{R}_B)_x$	$\lvert (T_B)_z (R_B)_{yx} - (T_B)_y (R_B)_{zx} \rvert$ $\quad > (a_y \lvert (R_B)_{zx} \rvert + a_z \lvert (R_B)_{yx} \rvert + b_y \lvert (R_B)_{xz} \rvert + b_z \lvert (R_B)_{xy} \rvert)$
$(\vec{R}_A)_x \times (\vec{R}_B)_y$	$\lvert (T_B)_z (R_B)_{yy} - (T_B)_y (R_B)_{zy} \rvert$ $\quad > (a_y \lvert (R_B)_{zy} \rvert + a_z \lvert (R_B)_{yy} \rvert + b_x \lvert (R_B)_{xz} \rvert + b_z \lvert (R_B)_{xx} \rvert)$
$(\vec{R}_A)_x \times (\vec{R}_B)_z$	$\lvert (T_B)_z (R_B)_{yz} - (T_B)_y (R_B)_{zz} \rvert$ $\quad > (a_y \lvert (R_B)_{zz} \rvert + a_z \lvert (R_B)_{yz} \rvert + b_x \lvert (R_B)_{xy} \rvert + b_y \lvert (R_B)_{xx} \rvert)$
$(\vec{R}_A)_y \times (\vec{R}_B)_x$	$\lvert (T_B)_x (R_B)_{zx} - (T_B)_z (R_B)_{xx} \rvert$ $\quad > (a_x \lvert (R_B)_{zx} \rvert + a_z \lvert (R_B)_{xx} \rvert + b_y \lvert (R_B)_{yz} \rvert + b_z \lvert (R_B)_{yy} \rvert)$
$(\vec{R}_A)_y \times (\vec{R}_B)_y$	$\lvert (T_B)_x (R_B)_{zy} - (T_B)_z (R_B)_{xy} \rvert$ $\quad > (a_x \lvert (R_B)_{zy} \rvert + a_z \lvert (R_B)_{xy} \rvert + b_x \lvert (R_B)_{yz} \rvert + b_z \lvert (R_B)_{yx} \rvert)$
$(\vec{R}_A)_y \times (\vec{R}_B)_z$	$\lvert (T_B)_x (R_B)_{zz} - (T_B)_z (R_B)_{xz} \rvert$ $\quad > (a_x \lvert (R_B)_{zz} \rvert + a_z \lvert (R_B)_{xz} \rvert + b_x \lvert (R_B)_{yy} \rvert + b_y \lvert (R_B)_{yx} \rvert)$
$(\vec{R}_A)_z \times (\vec{R}_B)_x$	$\lvert (T_B)_y (R_B)_{xx} - (T_B)_x (R_B)_{yx} \rvert$ $\quad > (a_x \lvert (R_B)_{yx} \rvert + a_y \lvert (R_B)_{xx} \rvert + b_y \lvert (R_B)_{zz} \rvert + b_z \lvert (R_B)_{zy} \rvert)$
$(\vec{R}_A)_z \times (\vec{R}_B)_y$	$\lvert (T_B)_y (R_B)_{xy} - (T_B)_x (R_B)_{yy} \rvert$ $\quad > (a_x \lvert (R_B)_{yy} \rvert + a_y \lvert (R_B)_{xy} \rvert + b_x \lvert (R_B)_{zz} \rvert + b_z \lvert (R_B)_{zx} \rvert)$
$(\vec{R}_A)_z \times (\vec{R}_B)_z$	$\lvert (T_B)_y (R_B)_{xz} - (T_B)_x (R_B)_{yz} \rvert$ $\quad > (a_x \lvert (R_B)_{yz} \rvert + a_y \lvert (R_B)_{xz} \rvert + b_x \lvert (R_B)_{zy} \rvert + b_y \lvert (R_B)_{zx} \rvert)$

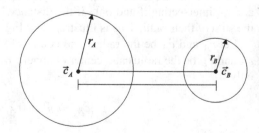

Fig. 2.24 The sphere–sphere intersection test can be quickly conducted by comparing the distance between the centers of the sphere with the sum of their radii

Fig. 2.25 Case where just
one vertex of triangle B
touches the plane P_a
containing triangle A. As
shown, $\vec{b}_2$ lies outside A and
the triangles do not intersect

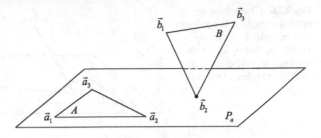

2.5.5   Computing Triangle–Triangle Intersections

The triangle–triangle intersection test is considered a primitive–primitive intersection test, since the triangles are in fact faces of the objects in the simulation. Let
triangles A and B be defined by vertices $\vec{a}_1, \vec{a}_2, \vec{a}_3$ and $\vec{b}_1, \vec{b}_2$ and $\vec{b}_3$, respectively.
The first step of the intersection test is to conduct a quick rejection test. This test
consists of determining whether all vertices of one triangle lie on the same side of
the plane defined by the other triangle. Let P_a and P_b be the planes defined by triangles A and B, respectively. Let $\vec{n}_a$ and $\vec{n}_b$ be the normal vectors of P_a and P_b. The
normals can be directly computed from the vertex list as

$$\vec{n}_a = (\vec{a}_2 - \vec{a}_1) \times (\vec{a}_3 - \vec{a}_2)$$
$$\vec{n}_b = (\vec{b}_2 - \vec{b}_1) \times (\vec{b}_3 - \vec{b}_2).$$

The vertices of triangle B will lie on the same side of P_a if and only if

$$\vec{n}_a \cdot (\vec{b}_1 - \vec{a}_1)$$
$$\vec{n}_a \cdot (\vec{b}_2 - \vec{a}_1) \qquad (2.17)$$
$$\vec{n}_a \cdot (\vec{b}_3 - \vec{a}_1)$$

are not zero and have the same sign. If they do not have the same sign, then the
following cases can occur.

Case 1   Two of the three equations defined in (2.17) have the same sign and the
third evaluates to zero, say that corresponding to $\vec{b}_2$. In this case, the intersection
between triangle B and plane P_a is single point, that is, vertex $\vec{b}_2$ (see Fig. 2.25).
The triangle–triangle intersection test is then reduced to check whether $\vec{b}_2$ lies inside
triangle A. This point-in-triangle test can be quickly done by considering the line
segment connecting $\vec{b}_2$ to the barycenter of A. If this line segment intersects one of
the edges of triangle A, then $\vec{b}_2$ lies outside the triangle. Otherwise, $\vec{b}_2$ lies inside
triangle A, and triangle B intersects triangle A. More details on how to implement
the point-in-triangle test are given in Sect. 2.5.12.

Fig. 2.26 Case where an edge of triangle B is coplanar with triangle A. As shown, vertices $\vec{b}_1$ and $\vec{b}_2$ lie inside and outside A, respectively, and the triangles intersect

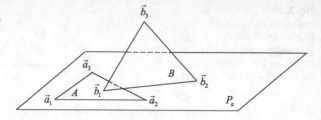

Fig. 2.27 Case where the triangles A and B are coplanar. As shown, the vertices of B lie outside A, and the triangles do not intersect

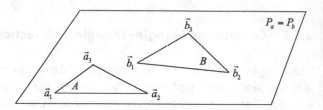

Case 2   Two of the three equations defined in (2.17) evaluate to zero, say those corresponding to $\vec{b}_1$ and $\vec{b}_2$. In this case, the intersection between triangle B and plane P_a is the line segment defined by $(\vec{b}_1, \vec{b}_2)$ (see Fig. 2.26). We can then apply the edge–edge intersection test given in Sect. 2.5.12, to check for intersections between line segment $(\vec{b}_1, \vec{b}_2)$ and each one of the triangle edges $(\vec{a}_1, \vec{a}_2)$, $(\vec{a}_2, \vec{a}_3)$ and $(\vec{a}_3, \vec{a}_1)$. An intersection is detected whenever $\vec{b}_1$ or $\vec{b}_2$ lie inside triangle A. If no intersections are detected, then we still need to check if segment $(\vec{b}_1, \vec{b}_2)$ lies completely inside triangle A. This requires an additional point-in-triangle test for $\vec{b}_1$ or $\vec{b}_2$.

Case 3   All three equations defined in (2.17) evaluate to zero. In this case, triangles A and B are coplanar (see Fig. 2.27). The intersection test can then be reduced to nine edge–edge tests by considering the three edges of triangle B checked against the three edges of triangle A. If at least one of the B edges intersect an edge of A, then the triangles intersect. However, if all edge–edge intersection tests fail, then there is still the possibility that A is completely inside B, or vice-versa. Therefore, an extra two point-in-triangle tests are performed: one for a vertex of A against B, and another for a vertex of B against A.

Case 4   None of the three equations defined in (2.17) evaluates to zero. In this case, we shall have two vertices of B on one side of plane P_a, and the third vertex on the other side of P_a. This is illustrated by Fig. 2.28.

Let $\vec{b}_2$ be the vertex that lies on the opposite side of plane P_a. Triangle B will then intersect plane P_a in two points $\vec{p}_1$ and $\vec{p}_2$ defining a line segment on the plane of A. These points can be computed as follows. Consider edge $e_1 = (\vec{b}_1, \vec{b}_2)$ given by its parameterized equation

$$\vec{p} = \vec{b}_1 + t(\vec{b}_2 - \vec{b}_1), \tag{2.18}$$

Fig. 2.28 Triangle–triangle intersection test for the case where no vertices of triangle *B* are coplanar with triangle *A*. One vertex of *B* will lie on the opposite side of the other two vertices, with respect to the plane defined by triangle *A*

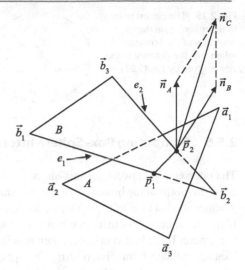

where $0 \leq t \leq 1$ and $\vec{p}$ is a point on the edge. The plane equation of P_a is given by

$$\vec{n}_a \cdot \vec{p} = d, \tag{2.19}$$

where $\vec{p}$ is any point on the plane and d is the plane constant given by

$$d = \vec{n}_a \cdot \vec{a}_1 = \vec{n}_a \cdot \vec{a}_2 = \vec{n}_a \cdot \vec{a}_3.$$

Edge e_1 intersects plane P_a at a point $\vec{p}_1$ that satisfies both Eqs. (2.18) and (2.19). Substituting Eq. (2.18) into (2.19), we can compute the value of t corresponding to the intersection point $\vec{p}_1$, that is

$$t_p = \frac{d - \vec{n}_a \cdot \vec{b}_1}{\vec{n}_a \cdot (\vec{b}_2 - \vec{b}_1)}. \tag{2.20}$$

Substituting Eq. (2.20) back into (2.18), we can immediately find the intersection point $\vec{p}_1$. A similar computation can be done to find the intersection point $\vec{p}_2$ between edge $e_2 = (\vec{b}_2, \vec{b}_3)$ and plane P_a.

The line segment $(\vec{p}_1, \vec{p}_2)$ can then be checked for intersection with triangle *A*. We can apply the edge–edge intersection test between $(\vec{p}_1, \vec{p}_2)$ and the edges of triangle *A*. If an intersection is detected, then triangle *B* intersects triangle *A*. Otherwise, we still need to test if edge $(\vec{p}_1, \vec{p}_2)$ lies completely inside triangle *A*. This requires an additional point-in-triangle test for $\vec{p}_1$ or $\vec{p}_2$.

Fig. 2.29 The closest point to the sphere is on the boundary of the box and minimizes the distance to the center given by Eq. (2.21)

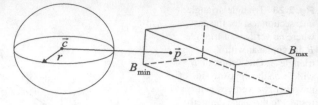

2.5.6 Computing Box–Sphere Intersections

The intersection between an axis-aligned box and a sphere is carried out by considering the point in the boundary of the box that is closest to the sphere, and checking whether its distance to the center of the sphere is greater than the sphere's radius. If the distance is less than or equal to the sphere's radius, then the box intersects the sphere. If the box is oriented, then this intersection test can be carried out on its local-coordinate frame, intersecting the sphere transformed to local space with the local-space axis-aligned box representation of the oriented box.

Let $\vec{p}$ be a point in the box, and let $\vec{c}$ and r be the sphere's center and radius, respectively. Let $x_{min}, x_{max}, y_{min}, y_{max}, z_{min}$ and z_{max} define the minimum and maximum values of the boundary of the box along each of the coordinated axes, as shown in Fig. 2.29.

The square of the distance from $\vec{p}$ to $\vec{c}$ is then given by

$$d^2 = (c_x - p_x)^2 + (c_y - p_y)^2 + (c_z - p_z)^2. \tag{2.21}$$

The point $\vec{p}$ that is closest to the sphere is that which minimizes Eq. (2.21), subject to the following constraints:

$$x_{min} \leq p_x \leq x_{max}$$
$$y_{min} \leq p_y \leq y_{max}$$
$$z_{min} \leq p_z \leq z_{max}.$$

Notice that each term of Eq. (2.21) is nonnegative and can be independently minimized. For example, if $x_{min} \leq c_x \leq x_{max}$, then $p_x = c_x$ minimizes the term $(c_x - p_x)^2$. However, if $c_x < x_{min}$ or $c_x > x_{max}$, then $p_x = x_{min}$ or $p_x = x_{max}$ minimizes the term, respectively. We do a similar analysis for finding the value of p_y and p_z that minimizes their corresponding quadratic terms.

Having determined the coordinates of the closest point to the sphere, we just need to compare its distance to the center of the sphere with the sphere's radius by substituting the coordinates of $\vec{p}$ into Eq. (2.21), and checking whether

$$d^2 \leq r^2. \tag{2.22}$$

The box will intersect the sphere if and only if Eq. (2.22) is satisfied.

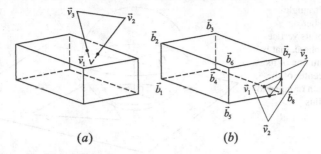

Fig. 2.30 (a) The triangle intersects the box whenever one of its vertices lies inside the box; (b) The plane containing the triangle intersects the box. Edges of the box that have vertices at opposite sides of the plane, in this case edges $\bar{b}_5\bar{b}_8$, $\bar{b}_4\bar{b}_8$ and $\bar{b}_7\bar{b}_8$, need to be checked for intersection with the triangle

2.5.7 Computing Box–Triangle Intersections

The box–triangle intersection test can be quickly carried out in at most three steps. In the first step, we check whether the vertices of the triangle are inside the box. If at least one of the vertices is inside the box, then the triangle intersects the box.

Let the box be defined by its minimum and maximum vertices, and let $\vec{v}_1$, $\vec{v}_2$ and $\vec{v}_3$ be the vertices of the triangle (see Fig. 2.30(a)). Vertex $\vec{v}_i$ is inside the box if and only if

$$x_{min} \leq (v_i)_x \leq x_{max}$$
$$y_{min} \leq (v_i)_y \leq y_{max} \qquad (2.23)$$
$$z_{min} \leq (v_i)_z \leq z_{max}.$$

If at least one of the vertices $\vec{v}_1$, $\vec{v}_2$ or $\vec{v}_3$ satisfies Eq. (2.23), then the triangle intersects the box. Otherwise, we proceed to the second step.

In the second step, we check whether the plane containing the triangle intersects the box. This can be done by checking whether the eight vertices of the box lie on the same side of the plane (see Fig. 2.30(b)). Let $\vec{n}$ be the normal of the triangle and d the plane constant determined from

$$d = \vec{n} \cdot \vec{v}_i, \quad \text{for } i \in \{1, 2, 3\}.$$

A point $\vec{p}$ is classified with respect to the plane containing the triangle as follows:

$$\begin{aligned}
\text{If } \vec{n} \cdot \vec{p} - d > 0 &\Rightarrow \vec{p} \text{ is on positive half-plane} \\
\text{If } \vec{n} \cdot \vec{p} - d = 0 &\Rightarrow \vec{p} \text{ lies on the plane} \qquad (2.24) \\
\text{If } \vec{n} \cdot \vec{p} - d < 0 &\Rightarrow \vec{p} \text{ is on negative half-plane.}
\end{aligned}$$

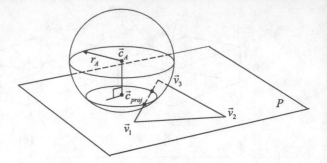

Fig. 2.31 The triangle intersects the sphere whenever one of its vertices lies inside the sphere, that is, the distance from one of its vertices to the center of the sphere is less than or equal to the sphere's radius

Using Eq. (2.24), we classify each vertex of the box according to its relative position with respect to the plane. If all vertices lie on the same half-space, then we can immediately conclude that the box does not intersect the triangle. Otherwise, we need to consider the edges of the box that intersect the plane, that is, the edges that have vertices at opposite sides of the plane, or one vertex on the plane and another on either side. These edges define line segments and a line segment–triangle intersection test is done for each of them, as explained in detail in Sect. 2.5.10.

2.5.8 Computing Sphere–Triangle Intersections

The sphere–triangle test is more complex than the box–triangle test, in the sense that it has more steps to be carried out before we can determine whether the sphere is intersecting the triangle.

The first step is to check whether the plane that contains the triangle intersects the sphere. This can be done by comparing the distance of the plane to the center of the sphere with the radius of the sphere. Let r_A and $\vec{c}_A$ be the sphere's radius and center. Let $\vec{v}_1$, $\vec{v}_2$ and $\vec{v}_3$ be the vertices of the triangle defining plane P (see Fig. 2.31). Let $\vec{n}$ and d_n be the plane normal and plane constant. The distance between the plane P and the sphere's center is then

$$d_A = |\vec{n} \cdot \vec{c}_A - d_n|.$$

The plane containing the triangle intersects the sphere whenever

$$d_A \leq r_A.$$

If this is the case, then we proceed with the sphere–triangle intersection test by checking whether the vertices of the triangle are inside the sphere. If at least one of the vertices is inside the sphere, then the triangle intersects the sphere. Let d_i be the distance between vertex $\vec{v}_i$ and the sphere's center, that is

$$d_i = |\vec{v}_i - \vec{c}_A|.$$

Fig. 2.32 Intersection test
between a sphere and a line
segment. We only need
consider the intersection of
the line segment with the
circle resulting from the
intersection of the sphere and
the plane defined by the
center of the sphere, and the
end points of the line segment

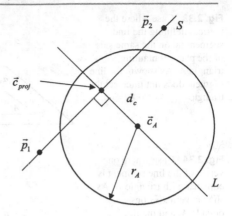

The sphere will intersect the triangle if

$$d_i \leq r_A \tag{2.25}$$

for at least one vertex $\vec{v}_i$ (see Fig. 2.31). If this is not the case, then we proceed to the third step of the sphere–triangle intersection test. In this step, we project the sphere onto the plane containing the triangle, and check whether the projected center lies inside the triangle. The projected center $\vec{c}_{proj}$ is determined from

$$\vec{c}_{proj} = \vec{c}_A - d_n \vec{n}.$$

We can use the point-in-triangle test already explained in Sect. 2.5.12 to see whether the projected center lies inside the triangle. If the projected center $\vec{c}_{proj}$ lies inside the triangle, then the sphere intersects the triangle (see Fig. 2.31). Otherwise, we need to do one more test to check whether the triangle edges intersect the sphere, as explained in the next section.

2.5.9   Computing Line Segment–Sphere Intersections

Let $\vec{p}_1$ and $\vec{p}_2$ define a line segment S, and $\vec{c}_A$ and r_A be the sphere's center and radius, respectively. Consider the line L passing through $\vec{c}_A$ and perpendicular to the line segment S (see Fig. 2.32).

Line L will intersect the line segment S at a point $\vec{c}_{proj}$ such that

$$\vec{c}_{proj} = \vec{p}_1 + t(\vec{p}_2 - \vec{p}_1)$$

for t, given by

$$t = \frac{(\vec{p}_2 - \vec{p}_1) \cdot \vec{c}_A - (\vec{p}_2 - \vec{p}_1) \cdot \vec{p}_1}{(\vec{p}_2 - \vec{p}_1) \cdot (\vec{p}_2 - \vec{p}_1)},$$

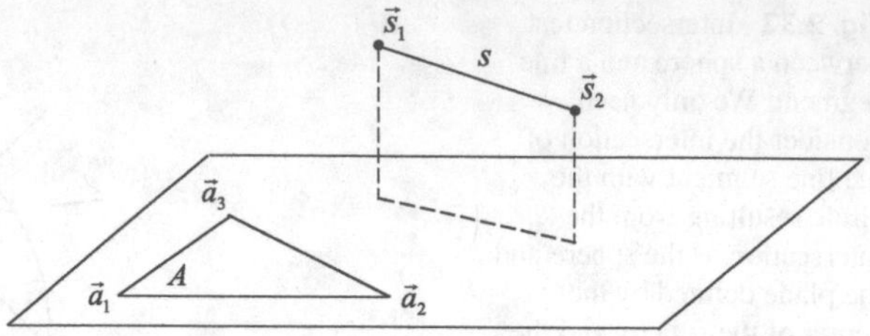

Fig. 2.33 Case where the vertices defining the line segment lie on the same side of the plane containing triangle A. As shown, the line segment does not intersect the triangle

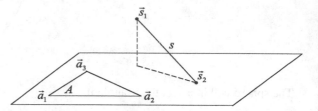

Fig. 2.34 Case where one vertex of the line segment is coplanar with triangle A. As shown, vertex $\vec{s}_2$ lies outside A, and the line segment does not intersect the triangle

that is, $\vec{c}_{proj}$ is the projection of the center of the sphere onto the line segment's supporting line. The distance between the projection point $\vec{c}_{proj}$ and the center of the sphere is directly obtained from

$$d_c^2 = (\vec{c}_{proj} - \vec{c}_A) \cdot (\vec{c}_{proj} - \vec{c}_A).$$

Having determined the projection point $\vec{c}_{proj}$ and its (squared) distance d_c^2 to the center of the sphere, one of the following three cases occurs.

1. If $d_c^2 > r_A^2$, then the sphere does not intersect the triangle.
2. If $d_c^2 = r_A^2$, then the supporting line is tangential to the sphere. If the projection point $\vec{c}_{proj}$ is inside the segment, that is, if $0 \leq t \leq 1$, then the line segment intersects the sphere.
3. If $d_c^2 < r_A^2$, then the supporting line intersects the sphere. The segment intersects the sphere if the projection point $\vec{c}_{proj}$ is inside the segment. Otherwise, an intersection occurs if the closest end point to $\vec{c}_{proj}$ is inside the sphere. The closest end point is $\vec{p}_1$ if $t \leq 0$, or $\vec{p}_2$ if $t \geq 1$.

2.5.10 Computing Line Segment–Triangle Intersections

The intersection of a line segment S with a triangle A can be viewed as a subset of the intersection test between two triangles. Let the line segment be defined by vertices $\vec{s}_1$ and $\vec{s}_2$, and the triangle be defined by vertices $\vec{a}_1$, $\vec{a}_2$ and $\vec{a}_3$.

First, we check whether the vertices defining the line segment lie on the same side of the plane containing the triangle (see Fig. 2.33). If this is so, then we can quickly conclude that the segment does not intersect the triangle. Otherwise, we can have one of the following three cases.

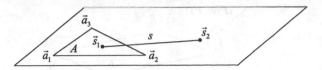

Fig. 2.35 Case where the line segment is coplanar with triangle A. In the situation shown, vertices $\vec{s}_1$ and $\vec{s}_2$ lie inside and outside A, respectively, and the line segment does intersect the triangle

Fig. 2.36 Case where the vertices defining the line segment lie on opposite sides of the plane containing triangle A. As shown, the intersection point $\vec{p}_1$ between the line segment and the plane lies outside A, and the line segment does not intersect the triangle

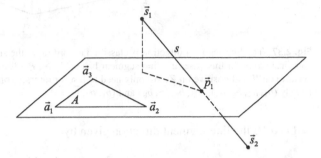

Case 1   One vertex of the line segment, say vertex $\vec{s}_2$, lies on the plane that contains the triangle, and the other lies on either side (see Fig. 2.34). In this case, we use the point-in-triangle test for checking whether $\vec{s}_2$ lies inside A. The line segment intersects the triangle only if $\vec{s}_2$ lies inside A.

Case 2   Both vertices of the line segment lie on the plane containing A (see Fig. 2.35). Again, we use the edge–edge test for checking for intersections between the line segment and the edges of A. The line segment intersects the triangle only if it crosses one of its edges, or if both vertices lie inside the triangle.

Case 3   The vertices of the line segment lie on opposite sides of the plane containing the triangle (see Fig. 2.36). Let $\vec{p}_1$ be the intersection between the line segment and the plane containing the triangle. Using the point-in-triangle test, we can check whether $\vec{p}_1$ lies inside the triangle.

2.5.11 Computing Line Segment–Box Intersections

A line segment intersects an axis-aligned box if either one of its vertices lie inside the box, or if it crosses one of the faces defining the box. In the case of oriented box, this same test can be carried out in its local-coordinate frame.

Let the box be defined by its minimum and maximum vertices $\vec{b}_{lower}$ and $\vec{b}_{upper}$, respectively. Let $(\vec{s}_1, \vec{s}_2)$ define the line segment being tested for intersection. As explained in Sect. 2.5.7, the line points $\vec{s}_i$ with $i \in 1, 2$, lie inside the box if they satisfy Eq. (2.23). If this is the case, then the line segment does intersect the box. Otherwise, we need to test whether it intersects one of the box's faces. This intersection test can be optimized if the direction of the line segment is taken into account to identify which three out of the six faces need to be considered. Figure 2.37 illustrates this.

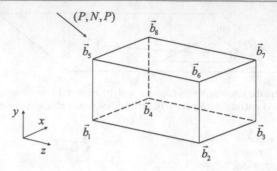

Fig. 2.37 The line segment direction is classified according to the sign of its projections on each coordinate axis. In this case, the line segment has a (P, N, P) direction, that is, positive on X, negative on Y and positive on Z. We only need to test for intersections with three out of six faces, namely $(\vec{b}_1, \vec{b}_4, \vec{b}_8, \vec{b}_5)$, $(\vec{b}_5, \vec{b}_6, \vec{b}_7, \vec{b}_8)$ and $(\vec{b}_1, \vec{b}_2, \vec{b}_6, \vec{b}_5)$

Let $\vec{d}$ be the line segment direction given by

$$\vec{d} = \vec{s}_2 - \vec{s}_1 = (d_x, d_y, d_z).$$

The direction is classified according to the sign of its components d_i as follows:

$$(d_x < 0), (d_y < 0), (d_z < 0) \rightarrow (N, N, N)$$
$$(d_x < 0), (d_y < 0), (d_z \geq 0) \rightarrow (N, N, P)$$
$$(d_x < 0), (d_y \geq 0), (d_z < 0) \rightarrow (N, P, N)$$
$$(d_x < 0), (d_y \geq 0), (d_z \geq 0) \rightarrow (N, P, P)$$
$$(d_x \geq 0), (d_y < 0), (d_z < 0) \rightarrow (P, N, N)$$
$$(d_x \geq 0), (d_y < 0), (d_z \geq 0) \rightarrow (P, N, P)$$
$$(d_x \geq 0), (d_y \geq 0), (d_z < 0) \rightarrow (P, P, N)$$
$$(d_x \geq 0), (d_y \geq 0), (d_z \geq 0) \rightarrow (P, P, P),$$

with N and P standing for negative and positive, respectively. A set of three faces is pre-assigned to each different classification, and the line needs to be tested for intersection with each one of them. Following the notation of Fig. 2.37 for the box–vertex assignment, the set of three faces associated with each classification is shown in Table 2.2. The corresponding vertex assignment of each face is summarized in Table 2.3.

The performance of the algorithm can be further improved if we do a quick rejection test before computing the actual intersections between the line segment and the box faces. This quick rejection test considers the silhouette formed by the set of three faces when viewing the box along the line direction, as shown in Fig. 2.38.

If we replace the line segment with a ray, with origin at $\vec{s}_1$ and direction $\vec{d}$, we can test whether the ray passes through the inside region of the silhouette. If the ray fails to pass through the inside of the silhouette, then the line segment does not intersect

Table 2.2 The set of three faces that need to be tested for intersection with the line segment depending on the classification of its direction

Classification	Set of faces
(N, N, N)	Top, Front, Right
(N, N, P)	Top, Back, Right
(N, P, N)	Bottom, Front, Right
(N, P, P)	Bottom, Back, Right
(P, N, N)	Top, Front, Left
(P, N, P)	Top, Back, Left
(P, P, N)	Bottom, Front, Left
(P, P, P)	Bottom, Back, Left

Table 2.3 Face–vertex assignment with face normals pointing outwards

Face label	Face vertices
Top	$(\vec{b}_5, \vec{b}_6, \vec{b}_7, \vec{b}_8)$
Bottom	$(\vec{b}_1, \vec{b}_4, \vec{b}_3, \vec{b}_2)$
Front	$(\vec{b}_2, \vec{b}_3, \vec{b}_7, \vec{b}_6)$
Back	$(\vec{b}_1, \vec{b}_5, \vec{b}_8, \vec{b}_4)$
Left	$(\vec{b}_1, \vec{b}_2, \vec{b}_6, \vec{b}_5)$
Right	$(\vec{b}_3, \vec{b}_4, \vec{b}_8, \vec{b}_7)$

Fig. 2.38 The silhouette of the box is highlighted for the case in which the line direction has a (P, N, P) classification. Notice that the silhouette will always contain exactly six edges of the box

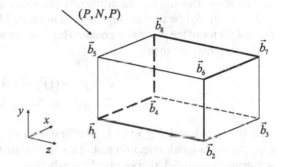

the box. Notice that the silhouette is always made of six edges. If we consider the relative position of the ray with respect to each of these edges, the ray will pass through the silhouette only if it lies on the inside side of each of its edges. The relative orientation of the ray with respect to an edge of the box is obtained from

$$side(ray, edge) = -(\vec{d} \cdot \vec{n}),$$

where $\vec{n}$ is the normal vector of the plane defined by $\vec{s}_1$ (i.e., the ray's origin) and the edge $(\vec{b}_i, \vec{b}_j)$, that is

$$\vec{n} = (\vec{b}_i - \vec{s}_1) \times (\vec{b}_j - \vec{s}_1),$$

as illustrated in Fig. 2.39.

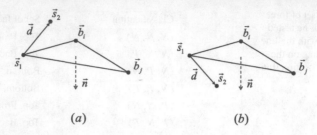

(a) (b)

Fig. 2.39 The relative orientation of the ray and the box's edge is determined from the sign of the scalar product between the ray direction $\vec{d}$ and the plane normal $\vec{n}$, defined by points $\vec{s}_1$, $\vec{b}_i$ and $\vec{b}_j$; (a) Case in which $\vec{d}$ points away from the normal, resulting in $side(ray, edge) > 0$; (b) $\vec{d}$ points along the normal giving $side(ray, edge) < 0$

Table 2.4 shows the side tests that need to be done for each ray classification. The fact that the box is axis-aligned considerably simplifies the final expressions obtained for the $side(ray, edge)$ relation, as shown in Table 2.5.

2.5.12 Point-in-Triangle and Edge–Edge Intersection Tests

All point-in-triangle tests can be transformed into coplanar segment–segment intersection tests. This test can be efficiently implemented as follows. Let $s_1 = (\vec{p}_1, \vec{p}_2)$ and $s_2 = (\vec{q}_1, \vec{q}_2)$ be the line segments being tested for intersection, and let $\vec{n}$ be the normal vector of the plane that contains both segments. The parameterized equations of the segments are then

$$\vec{p} = \vec{p}_1 + t(\vec{p}_2 - \vec{p}_1)$$
$$\vec{q} = \vec{q}_1 + m(\vec{q}_2 - \vec{q}_1),$$

with $0 \leq t \leq 1$ and $0 \leq m \leq 1$. The first step of the intersection test consists of carrying out a quick rejection test. This test consists of checking whether the line segments are parallel, that is, checking whether

$$(\vec{p}_2 - \vec{p}_1) \times (\vec{q}_2 - \vec{q}_1) = \vec{0}.$$

If the line segments are not parallel, they will intersect if and only if there exist $t = t_p$ and $m = m_q$ such that

$$\vec{p}_1 + t_p(\vec{p}_2 - \vec{p}_1) = \vec{q}_1 + m_q(\vec{q}_2 - \vec{q}_1), \tag{2.26}$$

with $0 \leq t_p \leq 1$ and $0 \leq m_q \leq 1$. Equation (2.26) can be solved for t_p and m_q if we consider two auxiliary vectors $\vec{k}_p$ and $\vec{k}_q$ given by

$$\vec{k}_p = \vec{n} \times (\vec{p}_2 - \vec{p}_1)$$
$$\vec{k}_q = \vec{n} \times (\vec{q}_2 - \vec{q}_1), \tag{2.27}$$

Table 2.4 Sign of side relations for each classification. The intersection is discarded if any of the relations is true

Classification	Quick rejection test
(N, N, N)	$(\vec{s}_1)_x < (\vec{b}_{lower})_x \cup (\vec{s}_1)_y < (\vec{b}_{lower})_y \cup (\vec{s}_1)_z < (\vec{b}_{lower})_z$
	$\cup\, side(\vec{b}_3, \vec{b}_4) < 0 \cup side(\vec{b}_6, \vec{b}_5) > 0 \cup side(\vec{b}_2, \vec{b}_6) > 0$
	$\cup\, side(\vec{b}_4, \vec{b}_8) < 0 \cup side(\vec{b}_8, \vec{b}_5) < 0 \cup side(\vec{b}_3, \vec{b}_2) > 0$
(N, N, P)	$(\vec{s}_1)_x < (\vec{b}_{lower})_x \cup (\vec{s}_1)_y < (\vec{b}_{lower})_y \cup (\vec{s}_1)_z > (\vec{b}_{upper})_z$
	$\cup\, side(\vec{b}_3, \vec{b}_4) < 0 \cup side(\vec{b}_6, \vec{b}_5) > 0 \cup side(\vec{b}_3, \vec{b}_7) > 0$
	$\cup\, side(\vec{b}_1, \vec{b}_5) < 0 \cup side(\vec{b}_4, \vec{b}_1) < 0 \cup side(\vec{b}_7, \vec{b}_6) > 0$
(N, P, N)	$(\vec{s}_1)_x < (\vec{b}_{lower})_x \cup (\vec{s}_1)_y > (\vec{b}_{upper})_y \cup (\vec{s}_1)_z < (\vec{b}_{lower})_z$
	$\cup\, side(\vec{b}_2, \vec{b}_1) < 0 \cup side(\vec{b}_7, \vec{b}_8) > 0 \cup side(\vec{b}_2, \vec{b}_6) > 0$
	$\cup\, side(\vec{b}_4, \vec{b}_8) < 0 \cup side(\vec{b}_7, \vec{b}_6) < 0 \cup side(\vec{b}_4, \vec{b}_1) > 0$
(N, P, P)	$(\vec{s}_1)_x < (\vec{b}_{lower})_x \cup (\vec{s}_1)_y > (\vec{b}_{upper})_y \cup (\vec{s}_1)_z > (\vec{b}_{upper})_z$
	$\cup\, side(\vec{b}_2, \vec{b}_1) < 0 \cup side(\vec{b}_7, \vec{b}_8) > 0 \cup side(\vec{b}_3, \vec{b}_7) > 0$
	$\cup\, side(\vec{b}_1, \vec{b}_5) < 0 \cup side(\vec{b}_3, \vec{b}_2) < 0 \cup side(\vec{b}_8, \vec{b}_5) > 0$
(P, N, N)	$(\vec{s}_1)_x > (\vec{b}_{upper})_x \cup (\vec{s}_1)_y < (\vec{b}_{lower})_y \cup (\vec{s}_1)_z < (\vec{b}_{lower})_z$
	$\cup\, side(\vec{b}_7, \vec{b}_8) < 0 \cup side(\vec{b}_2, \vec{b}_1) > 0 \cup side(\vec{b}_1, \vec{b}_5) > 0$
	$\cup\, side(\vec{b}_3, \vec{b}_7) < 0 \cup side(\vec{b}_8, \vec{b}_5) < 0 \cup side(\vec{b}_3, \vec{b}_2) > 0$
(P, N, P)	$(\vec{s}_1)_x > (\vec{b}_{upper})_x \cup (\vec{s}_1)_y < (\vec{b}_{lower})_y \cup (\vec{s}_1)_z > (\vec{b}_{upper})_z$
	$\cup\, side(\vec{b}_7, \vec{b}_8) < 0 \cup side(\vec{b}_2, \vec{b}_1) > 0 \cup side(\vec{b}_4, \vec{b}_8) > 0$
	$\cup\, side(\vec{b}_2, \vec{b}_6) < 0 \cup side(\vec{b}_4, \vec{b}_1) < 0 \cup side(\vec{b}_7, \vec{b}_6) > 0$
(P, P, N)	$(\vec{s}_1)_x > (\vec{b}_{upper})_x \cup (\vec{s}_1)_y > (\vec{b}_{upper})_y \cup (\vec{s}_1)_z < (\vec{b}_{lower})_z$
	$\cup\, side(\vec{b}_6, \vec{b}_5) < 0 \cup side(\vec{b}_3, \vec{b}_4) > 0 \cup side(\vec{b}_1, \vec{b}_5) > 0$
	$\cup\, side(\vec{b}_3, \vec{b}_7) < 0 \cup side(\vec{b}_7, \vec{b}_6) < 0 \cup side(\vec{b}_4, \vec{b}_1) > 0$
(P, P, P)	$(\vec{s}_1)_x > (\vec{b}_{upper})_x \cup (\vec{s}_1)_y > (\vec{b}_{upper})_y \cup (\vec{s}_1)_z > (\vec{b}_{upper})_z$
	$\cup\, side(\vec{b}_6, \vec{b}_5) < 0 \cup side(\vec{b}_3, \vec{b}_4) > 0 \cup side(\vec{b}_4, \vec{b}_8) > 0$
	$\cup\, side(\vec{b}_2, \vec{b}_6) < 0 \cup side(\vec{b}_3, \vec{b}_2) < 0 \cup side(\vec{b}_8, \vec{b}_5) > 0$

that is, $\vec{k}_p$ and $\vec{k}_q$ are nonzero vectors perpendicular to $(\vec{p}_2 - \vec{p}_1)$ and $(\vec{q}_2 - \vec{q}_1)$, respectively. If we apply a dot product by $\vec{k}_p$ on both sides of Eq. (2.26), then the term multiplying t_p evaluates to zero, and we can therefore determine m_q as

$$m_q = \frac{\vec{k}_p \cdot (\vec{p}_1 - \vec{q}_1)}{\vec{k}_p \cdot (\vec{q}_2 - \vec{q}_1)}.$$

If $m_q < 0$ or $m_q > 1$, then the intersection point lies outside the line segment s_2, and the segments do not intersect. Otherwise, we apply a dot product by $\vec{k}_q$ on both sides of Eq. (2.26), and obtain t_p as

$$t_p = \frac{\vec{k}_p \cdot (\vec{q}_1 - \vec{p}_1)}{\vec{k}_q \cdot (\vec{p}_2 - \vec{p}_1)}.$$

Table 2.5 Simplified expressions for each $side(ray, edge)$ relation when the box is axis-aligned with the coordinate frame. The ray direction is given by $\vec{d} = (\vec{s}_2 - \vec{s}_1)$ and the auxiliary variables are computed as $\vec{b}_l = (\vec{b}_{lower} - \vec{s}_1)$ and $\vec{b}_u = (\vec{b}_{upper} - \vec{s}_1)$

$side$ relation	Simplified test
$side(ray, (\vec{b}_3, \vec{b}_4))$	$d_x(\vec{b}_l)_y - d_y(\vec{b}_u)_x$
$side(ray, (\vec{b}_6, \vec{b}_5))$	$d_x(\vec{b}_u)_y - d_y(\vec{b}_l)_x$
$side(ray, (\vec{b}_2, \vec{b}_6))$	$d_x(\vec{b}_u)_z - d_z(\vec{b}_l)_x$
$side(ray, (\vec{b}_4, \vec{b}_8))$	$d_x(\vec{b}_l)_z - d_z(\vec{b}_u)_x$
$side(ray, (\vec{b}_8, \vec{b}_5))$	$d_y(\vec{b}_l)_z - d_z(\vec{b}_u)_y$
$side(ray, (\vec{b}_3, \vec{b}_2))$	$d_y(\vec{b}_u)_z - d_z(\vec{b}_l)_y$
$side(ray, (\vec{b}_3, \vec{b}_7))$	$d_x(\vec{b}_u)_z - d_z(\vec{b}_u)_x$
$side(ray, (\vec{b}_1, \vec{b}_5))$	$d_x(\vec{b}_l)_z - d_z(\vec{b}_l)_x$
$side(ray, (\vec{b}_4, \vec{b}_1))$	$d_y(\vec{b}_l)_z - d_z(\vec{b}_l)_y$
$side(ray, (\vec{b}_7, \vec{b}_6))$	$d_y(\vec{b}_u)_z - d_z(\vec{b}_u)_y$
$side(ray, (\vec{b}_2, \vec{b}_1))$	$d_x(\vec{b}_l)_y - d_y(\vec{b}_l)_x$
$side(ray, (\vec{b}_7, \vec{b}_8))$	$d_x(\vec{b}_u)_y - d_y(\vec{b}_u)_x$

Again, if $t_p < 0$ or $t_p > 1$, then the intersection lies outside the line segment s_1, and the segments do not intersect. Otherwise, the segments intersect at the intersection point computed by substituting either t_p or m_q into Eq. (2.26).

2.5.13 Point-in-Object Test

The determination of whether a point lies inside an object[5] can be efficiently done with the use of six auxiliary rays with origin at the point and directions parallel to the positive and negative axis of the world-coordinate frame, respectively. The point is inside the object if and only if all six rays intersect the object from the inside, as shown in Fig. 2.40.

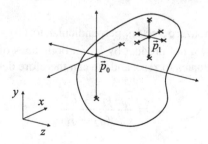

Fig. 2.40 Six auxiliary rays are used to detect whether a point is inside or outside the object. In this example, all rays shot from point $\vec{p}_1$ intersect the object's geometry from the inside, and the point is determined to be inside the object. If any of the rays miss the object or intersect it from the outside, like some shot from point $\vec{p}_0$, then the point is determined to be outside the object

---

[5]In this book we assume objects are represented by closed meshes.

Fig. 2.41 (a) Convex objects overlap in only one region; (b) Non-convex objects can overlap in multiple disjoint regions. The penetration depth of each region is approximated by the distance between their deepest points

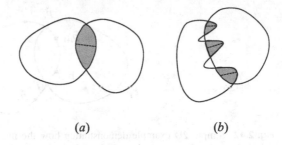

(a) (b)

The ray–object intersection tests can be efficiently implemented using the object's hierarchical representation. In a top-down recursion, we start intersecting the ray with the root bounding volume of the hierarchy. If the ray misses the root bounding volume then the point is guaranteed to be outside the object. Otherwise, we recursively check for intersections between the ray and its children node, until the ray misses all children nodes or hits a leaf node. When a leaf node is reached, we perform the appropriate ray–primitive intersection test to determine the intersection point. We also need to check if the ray is hitting the primitive from the inside, that is, the ray is coming out of the object from the intersection point. This can be quickly done by making sure the scalar product between the ray direction and the primitive normal is positive, before computing the intersection point.

2.5.14 Vertex-in-Object Test

Whenever two non-convex objects intersect, we need to determine which vertices of the first object are inside the second object, and vice-versa. This information is used to compute the penetration depth for each disjoint intersection region, as exemplified in Fig. 2.41.

The penetration depth of an intersection region is approximated by the distance between its deepest vertices. In order to determine the deepest vertex of one object inside the other object, we first need to compute all inside vertices associated with the intersection region and then choose the deepest one from this set. This can be done as follows.

Each intersection region has a corresponding intersection curve. The intersection curve is made up of line segments computed from the primitive–primitive intersections. Therefore, each intersection curve can be associated with a set of primitive pairs that intersect at some of the curve's line segments. Moreover, each intersection curve partitions one object into two disjoint regions with respect to the other object. The first region is inside the other object and the second region is outside. So, the vertices of the primitive pairs associated with the intersection curve can be partitioned into two groups as well, namely, the inside and outside groups with respect to the other object. This partition is obtained by executing the point-in-object test described in Sect. 2.5.13, for each vertex of the intersecting primitive pairs to determine the ones that are inside the other object. A simple 2D example of this partition is shown in Fig. 2.42.

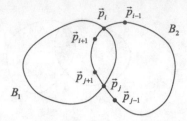

Fig. 2.42 Simple 2D example demonstrating how the intersection information can be used to quickly identify all inside vertices. Objects B_1 and B_2 are intersecting at points $\vec{p}_i$ and $\vec{p}_j$, and we need to determine the vertices of B_2 that are inside B_1. Using the edge connectivity information from B_2's mesh, we can run point-in-object tests for all $\vec{p}_i$'s neighbor vertices. In this example, vertex $\vec{p}_{i-1}$ is determined to be outside B_1, whereas vertex $\vec{p}_{i+1}$ is inside. We recursively inside-test all neighbor vertices of $\vec{p}_{i+1}$ that have not been tested yet until all inside vertices are found

Starting with the list L_1 of vertices of the first object that are inside the second object, we continue searching for neighbor vertices that are also inside the second object until all inside vertices have been found. The easiest way to perform this search is to maintain an auxiliary list L_a of neighbor vertices that were found but still need to be inside-tested against the second object. This auxiliary list is initialized by looping through L_1's vertices and adding all of their neighbor vertices that haven't been tested yet. Then, for each vertex in L_a, we use the point-in-object test to check if the vertex is inside the second object. The vertex is discarded if it lies outside the object. Otherwise, the vertex is added to L_1 and its neighbor vertices that haven't been tested yet are added to L_a. We repeat this process until the auxiliary list L_a is empty, at which point we have determined in L_1 all vertices of the first object that are inside the second object. We go through the same steps to build the list L_2 with all vertices of the second object that are inside the first one. The penetration depth is computed as the distance between the deepest vertices in L_1 and L_2.

2.5.15 Computing Continuous Triangle–Triangle Intersections

The continuous triangle–triangle intersection test takes into account the motion of the triangles for the entire time interval $[t_0, t_1]$. This requires that the actual non-linear motion of the triangles obtained from the numerical integration module be linearized by assuming the triangles move with constant velocity for the time interval. That is, the trajectories of each triangle vertex are approximated by straight-line segments connecting their positions at t_0 and t_1. Even though this simplification is quite effective in practice, there is a theoretical drawback to it. As illustrated in Fig. 2.43, the in-between motion of the triangles is continuous but not necessary rigid, depending on the amount of rotation experienced by the triangles. Hence, it is possible that the linearized trajectory does not completely bound the original trajectory and thus collisions can still be missed.

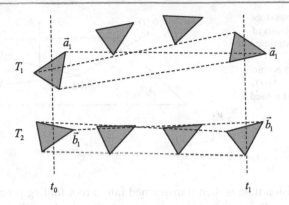

Fig. 2.43 The non-linear motion of triangles T_1 and T_2 obtained from their numerical integration is linearized for continuous collision detection. The vertices are assumed to have moved along a straight line connecting their initial and final positions at t_0 and t_1, respectively. Notice the quality of the linearization degrades as the amount of rotation experienced by the triangles increases. For instance, the linear motion for T_2 better approximates its real motion when compared to the results obtained for triangle T_1, which has a significant rotation component to its motion

Let T_1 and T_2 be the triangles being checked for continuous intersection. For simplicity, let the time parameter be normalized from $[t_0, t_1]$ to $[0, 1]$, with 0 corresponding to the positions at t_0 and 1 at t_1. The triangles will collide during their motion if there is a time $t_c \in [0, 1]$ at which one of the following two cases happen:

1. A vertex of one triangle moves from the front side to the back side of the plane defined by the other triangle at t_c, and the intersection point on the plane lies inside the triangle. This is commonly referred to as the *vertex–face* intersection test.

2. An edge of one triangle crosses an edge of the other triangle at t_c, and their intersection point is inside the end points of both edges. This is known as the *edge–edge* intersection test.

In the vertex–face case, we need to test each vertex of T_1 against T_2, and vice-versa. Since each triangle has three vertices, we have a total of six vertex–face intersection tests to be made. As for the edge–edge case, we need to test an edge of T_1 against all other edges of T_2, and vice-versa. Since each triangle has three edges, we have a total of nine edge–edge tests to be made. Therefore, the continuous triangle–triangle intersection requires a total of fifteen tests, each of them comprising four vertices at a time. These tests are carried out in different ways depending on whether:

1. The triangles' motion is not coplanar.
2. The triangles' motion is coplanar, but the motion of the vertices being tested is not collinear.
3. The triangles' motion is coplanar and the motion of the vertices being tested is collinear.

In each of the above cases, the positions of the four vertices being considered are described by a linear function of time. The geometric relationship needed for the vertices to collide can be rewritten as a polynomial in t. The problem of deter-

Fig. 2.44 The vertex–face intersection test consists of checking if there is a time t in which the triangle $(\vec{a}_1(t), \vec{a}_2(t), \vec{a}_3(t))$ becomes coplanar with vertex $\vec{b}_1(t)$. The triangle normal is used as the plane normal

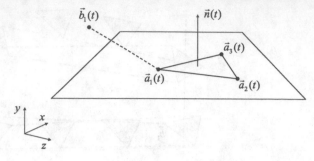

mining the collision time is then transformed into a root finding problem for such polynomial. The collision time t_c is set as the smallest real root between zero and one for all fifteen tests. If no real roots between zero and one are found, then the triangles do not intersect.

Case 1: Motion Not Coplanar   A necessary intersection condition when the motion of the triangles is not coplanar is that the four vertices being tested for intersections become coplanar at t_c. Otherwise, there can't be an intersection between them in the first place. Hence, their coplanarity is a key geometric condition to determine the collision time t_c in this case.

Let triangles T_1 and T_2 be defined by their vertices $\vec{a}_i(t)$ and $\vec{b}_i(t)$, with $i \in 1, 2, 3$ and $t \in [0, 1]$, such that

$$\vec{a}_i(t) = \vec{a}_i(0) + t\left(\vec{a}_i(1) - \vec{a}_i(0)\right)$$
$$\vec{b}_i(t) = \vec{b}_i(0) + t\left(\vec{b}_i(1) - \vec{b}_i(0)\right). \qquad (2.28)$$

Lets first consider the vertex–face intersection test shown in Fig. 2.44. In this case, the face normal is used as the normal of the plane containing all four vertices, that is

$$\vec{n}(t) = \left(\vec{a}_2(t) - \vec{a}_1(t)\right) \times \left(\vec{a}_3(t) - \vec{a}_2(t)\right).$$

Consider the vector connecting vertices $\vec{a}_1(t)$ and $\vec{b}_1(t)$, and notice that it must be perpendicular to the plane normal for the four vertices to be coplanar, that is

$$\vec{n}(t) \cdot \left(\vec{b}_1(t) - \vec{a}_1(t)\right) = 0. \qquad (2.29)$$

Expanding the terms in Eq. (2.29) as a function of the vertex positions given in Eq. (2.28), we obtain a 3rd degree polynomial on t of the form:

$$f_3 t^3 + f_2 t^2 + f_1 t + f_0 = 0, \qquad (2.30)$$

with the polynomial coefficients f_i given by:

$$f_3 = \vec{k}_1 \cdot \vec{k}_2$$

$$f_2 = \vec{k}_3 \cdot \vec{k}_2 + \vec{k}_1 \cdot \vec{k}_4$$

$$f_1 = \vec{k}_3 \cdot \vec{k}_4 + \vec{k}_1 \cdot \vec{k}_5 \tag{2.31}$$

$$f_0 = \vec{k}_3 \cdot \vec{k}_5,$$

and the auxiliary variables $\vec{k}_i$ obtained from the vertex positions at 0 and 1, namely:

$$\vec{k}_1 = \left(\vec{b}_1(1) - \vec{b}_1(0)\right) - \left(\vec{a}_1(1) - \vec{a}_1(0)\right)$$

$$\vec{k}_2 = \left(\left(\vec{a}_2(1) - \vec{a}_2(0)\right) - \left(\vec{a}_1(1) - \vec{a}_1(0)\right)\right)$$
$$\times \left(\left(\vec{a}_3(1) - \vec{a}_3(0)\right) - \left(\vec{a}_2(1) - \vec{a}_2(0)\right)\right)$$

$$\vec{k}_3 = \vec{b}_1(0) - \vec{a}_1(0)$$

$$\vec{k}_4 = \left(\vec{a}_2(0) - \vec{a}_1(0)\right) \times \left(\left(\vec{a}_3(1) - \vec{a}_3(0)\right) - \left(\vec{a}_2(1) - \vec{a}_2(0)\right)\right)$$
$$+ \left(\left(\vec{a}_2(1) - \vec{a}_2(0)\right) - \left(\vec{a}_1(1) - \vec{a}_1(0)\right)\right) \times \left(\vec{a}_3(0) - \vec{a}_2(0)\right)$$

$$\vec{k}_5 = \left(\vec{a}_2(0) - \vec{a}_1(0)\right) \times \left(\vec{a}_3(0) - \vec{a}_2(0)\right).$$

There are a few different ways for computing the roots of the polynomial in Eq. (2.30), varying from closed formulas to advanced iterative methods. We refer the reader to Sect. 2.6 for references to the literature where these different solution methods can be found. Here, we assume the roots were computed using one of such methods.

For each real root t_r found in the [0, 1] interval, we need to verify that an actual intersection does take place. This is done by positioning the four vertices at t_r and performing a point-in-triangle test to make sure vertex $\vec{b}_1(t_r)$ is inside triangle $(\vec{a}_1(t_r), \vec{a}_2(t_r), \vec{a}_3(t_r))$. If the vertex lies outside the triangle, then the points are coplanar but do not intersect at t_r and this root is discarded. Otherwise, the current collision time t_c is updated to t_r if $t_r \le t_c$. The collision point and normal are set as $\vec{b}_1(t_r)$ and $\vec{n}(t_r)$, respectively.

Now, lets consider the edge–edge intersection test shown in Fig. 2.45. The main difference between this case and the vertex–face case is in the way the plane normal is computed. Since we no longer have an actual face to use its normal vector as the plane normal, and the plane normal needs to be perpendicular to both edges, we use the cross-product of the edges as the plane normal instead, that is

$$\vec{n}(t) = \left(\vec{a}_2(t) - \vec{a}_1(t)\right) \times \left(\vec{b}_2(t) - \vec{b}_1(t)\right).$$

Again, the vector connecting vertices $\vec{a}_1(t)$ and $\vec{b}_1(t)$ must be perpendicular to the plane normal in order to have all four vertices coplanar, that is

$$\vec{n}(t) \cdot \left(\vec{b}_1(t) - \vec{a}_1(t)\right) = 0. \tag{2.32}$$

Fig. 2.45 In the edge–edge intersection test, the edges $(\vec{a}_1(t), \vec{a}_2(t))$ and $(\vec{b}_1(t), \vec{b}_2(t))$ are checked for coplanarity as well. The plane normal must be perpendicular to both edges and is obtained from their cross-product

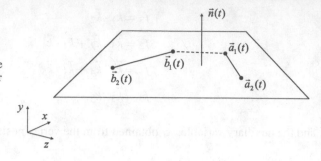

The polynomial coefficients f_i in the edge–edge case remain the same as in Eq. (2.31), but the auxiliary variables $\vec{k}_i$ are updated to:

$$\vec{k}_1 = \left(\vec{b}_1(1) - \vec{b}_1(0)\right) - \left(\vec{a}_1(1) - \vec{a}_1(0)\right)$$

$$\vec{k}_2 = \left(\left(\vec{a}_2(1) - \vec{a}_2(0)\right) - \left(\vec{a}_1(1) - \vec{a}_1(0)\right)\right) \times \left(\left(\vec{b}_2(1) - \vec{b}_2(0)\right) - \left(\vec{b}_1(1) - \vec{b}_1(0)\right)\right)$$

$$\vec{k}_3 = \vec{b}_1(0) - \vec{a}_1(0)$$

$$\vec{k}_4 = \left(\vec{a}_2(0) - \vec{a}_1(0)\right) \times \left(\left(\vec{b}_2(1) - \vec{b}_2(0)\right) - \left(\vec{b}_1(1) - \vec{b}_1(0)\right)\right)$$
$$\quad + \left(\left(\vec{a}_2(1) - \vec{a}_2(0)\right) - \left(\vec{a}_1(1) - \vec{a}_1(0)\right)\right) \times \left(\vec{b}_2(0) - \vec{b}_{21}(0)\right)$$

$$\vec{k}_5 = \left(\vec{a}_2(0) - \vec{a}_1(0)\right) \times \left(\vec{b}_2(0) - \vec{b}_1(0)\right).$$

Again, for each real root t_r found in the $[0, 1]$ interval, we need to position the two edges at that time and do an edge–edge intersection test to make sure the edges $(\vec{a}_1(t_r), \vec{a}_2(t_r))$ and $(\vec{b}_1(t_r), \vec{b}_2(t_r))$ do intersect. If the edges are parallel or intersect outside their end points, then they are coplanar but do not intersect and the root t_r is discarded. Otherwise, the current collision time t_c is updated to t_r if $t_r < t_c$. The collision point and normal are set as the intersection point between the edges at t_r and $\vec{n}(t_r)$, respectively.

As far as robustness is concerned, the collision normal obtained in the vertex–face intersection test tends to be more stable than the one obtained in the edge–edge intersection test. In the first case, the collision normal is the face normal itself whereas in the latter case the collision normal comes from the cross-product of the edges. If the edges are parallel or almost aligned, then the cross-product will be zero or very close to it and the computed normal vector becomes less reliable. Therefore, the collision information for the vertex–face case always takes precedence over the one for the edge–edge case when both collision times are the same. That's why we used the condition $t_r \le t_c$ to update the collision time for the vertex–face case, and $t_r < t_c$ to update it for the edge–edge case.

Case 2: Motion Coplanar but Not Collinear   In the special case in which the triangles' motion is coplanar for the entire time interval, the polynomial Eq. (2.30) degenerates because all of its coefficients f_i evaluate to zero. However, the triangles can still intersect while moving on the plane. This coplanar case is illustrated in Fig. 2.46.

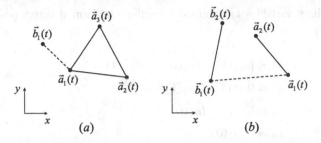

Fig. 2.46 (a) The vertex–face coplanar test consists of checking whether there is a time t in which vertex $\vec{b}_1(t)$ and one of the triangle edges become collinear; (b) In the edge–edge case, we need to test if the vertices of one edge become collinear with the other edge, and vice-versa. Notice that in both cases, the plane normal is aligned with the positive z-axis (pointing towards the reader)

Each coplanar vertex–face intersection test is replaced by three vertex–edge intersection tests in which a vertex of one triangle and an edge of the other triangle are tested for collinearity. Since we have six vertex–face tests to be made, we end up with a total of eighteen vertex–edge collinearity tests instead. Similarly, each coplanar edge–edge intersection test is replaced by four vertex–edge tests, in which a vertex of one edge is checked for collinearity with the other edge. Fortunately, all vertex–edge collinearity tests for the edge–edge case are a subset of the ones used in the vertex–face case, so they don't add up to the total of eighteen tests needed.

The collinearity tests are best carried out in a local-coordinate frame with the plane normal aligned with one of the coordinate axis, for example, the positive local z-axis. Consider a world-to-local transformation matrix with origin at $\vec{b}_1(0)$ and a rotation component that makes the plane normal in world-frame be the positive z-axis in local-frame. Let the vertices $\vec{a}_i(t)$ and $\vec{b}_i(t)$ in world-frame become vertices $\vec{la}_i(t)$ and $\vec{lb}_i(t)$ in local-frame under this world-to-local transformation. Since both vertex–face and edge–edge tests are replaced by a combination of vertex–edge tests, let's assume vertex $\vec{lb}_1(t)$ is being tested for collinearity with edge $(\vec{la}_1(t), \vec{la}_2(t))$. The vertices will be collinear whenever

$$\left(\vec{la}_2(t) - \vec{la}_1(t)\right) \times \left(\vec{lb}_1(t) - \vec{la}_2(t)\right) = 0. \tag{2.33}$$

Expanding the terms in Eq. (2.33) as a function of the transformed vertex positions, we obtain the following 2nd degree polynomial on t

$$f_2 t^2 + f_1 t + f_0 = 0, \tag{2.34}$$

with the polynomial coefficients f_i given by:

$$f_2 = \vec{k}_1 \times \vec{k}_2$$
$$f_1 = \vec{k}_3 \times \vec{k}_2 + \vec{k}_1 \times \vec{k}_4 \tag{2.35}$$
$$f_0 = \vec{k}_3 \times \vec{k}_4,$$

and the auxiliary variables $\vec{k}_i$ obtained from the transformed vertex positions at 0 and 1, namely:

$$\vec{k}_1 = \left(\vec{la}_2(1) - \vec{la}_2(0)\right) - \left(\vec{la}_1(1) - \vec{la}_1(0)\right)$$
$$\vec{k}_2 = \vec{lb}_1(1) - \left(\vec{la}_2(1) - \vec{la}_2(0)\right)$$
$$\vec{k}_3 = \vec{la}_2(0) - \vec{la}_1(0)$$
$$\vec{k}_4 = -\vec{la}_2(0).$$

The roots of the polynomial in Eq. (2.34) can be found analytically. For each real root $t_r \in [0, 1]$, we need to position both vertex and edge at that time and do a point-in-edge intersection test to make sure the vertex is inside the end points of the edge. If the vertex is outside, then the vertex and the edge are collinear but do not intersect and the root t_r is discarded. Otherwise, the current collision time t_c is updated to t_r if $t_r \le t_c$, and the collision point and normal is obtained from the current vertex–edge position.

Case 3: Motion Coplanar and Collinear   In the rare but still feasible situation in which the vertex and the edge in the above case are collinear for their entire motion, all coefficients of the polynomial Eq. (2.34) evaluate to zero. In this case, vertex $\vec{lb}_1(t)$ will intersect edge $(\vec{la}_1(t), \vec{la}_2(t))$ only if it passes through one of the edge's end points during its motion. This condition equates to the following two 1st degree polynomial equations on t

$$\vec{lb}_1(t) = \vec{la}_1(t)$$
$$\vec{lb}_1(t) = \vec{la}_2(t). \tag{2.36}$$

Expanding the terms in Eq. (2.36) as a function of the transformed vertex positions, we obtain the following two possible intersection times

$$t_r = \frac{\left(\vec{lb}_1(0) - \vec{la}_i(0)\right)}{\left(\vec{la}_i(1) - \vec{la}_i(0)\right) - \left(\vec{lb}_1(1) - \vec{lb}_1(0)\right)}$$

with $i \in 1, 2$. Any of these roots are discarded if they are below zero or above one. The current collision time t_c is updated to the smallest remaining root t_r if $t_r \le t_c$, and the collision point and normal is obtained from the current vertex–edge position.

2.5.16 Computing Continuous Sphere–Sphere Intersections

The continuous sphere–sphere intersection test consists of determining the earliest time $t \in [0, 1]$ at which the distance between the center of the spheres becomes less than the sum of their radiuses. Let the spheres be defined by their center points $\vec{a}(t)$

Fig. 2.47 Two spheres being
tested for continuous
collision. We need to find the
earliest time t at which their
centers are distant by less
than the sum of their radiuses

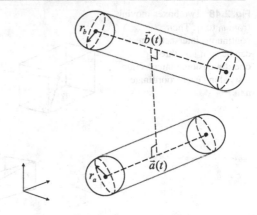

and $\vec{b}(t)$ and radiuses r_a and r_b, as shown in Fig. 2.47. The position of the centers
at time t is given by

$$\vec{a}(t) = \vec{a}(0) - t(\vec{a}(1) - \vec{a}(0))$$
$$\vec{b}(t) = \vec{b}(0) - t(\vec{b}(1) - \vec{b}(0)). \tag{2.37}$$

We begin by testing if the spheres are already intersecting at $t = 0$, that is, checking if

$$(\vec{a}(0) - \vec{b}(0)) \cdot (\vec{a}(0) - \vec{b}(0)) \leq (r_a + r_b)^2. \tag{2.38}$$

If Eq. (2.38) is satisfied, then the intersection time is set to t_0 and the collision
normal is taken as the line connecting the spheres' center points. Otherwise, we
need to find the smallest $t \in [0, 1]$, if any, that satisfies the condition

$$(\vec{a}(t) - \vec{b}(t)) \cdot (\vec{a}(t) - \vec{b}(t)) \leq (r_a + r_b)^2. \tag{2.39}$$

Substituting Eq. (2.37) into Eq. (2.39) and regrouping terms, we obtain the following 2nd degree polynomial on t

$$f_2 t^2 + f_1 t + f_0 = 0, \tag{2.40}$$

with the polynomial coefficients f_i given by:

$$f_2 = ((\vec{a}(1) - \vec{a}(0)) - (\vec{b}(1) - \vec{b}(0)))$$
$$\times ((\vec{a}(1) - \vec{a}(0)) - (\vec{b}(1) - \vec{b}(0)))$$
$$f_1 = 2(\vec{a}(0) - \vec{b}(0)) \cdot ((\vec{a}(1) - \vec{a}(0)) - (\vec{b}(1) - \vec{b}(0)))$$
$$f_0 = (\vec{a}(0) - \vec{b}(0)) \cdot (\vec{a}(0) - \vec{b}(0)) - (r_a + r_b)^2. \tag{2.41}$$

Fig. 2.48 Two boxes moving
from t_0 to t_1. Their
continuous intersection test
can be split into three
one-dimensional intersection
tests along each coordinate
axis

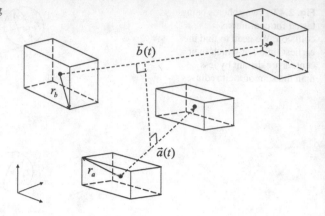

The roots of the polynomial in Eq. (2.40) can be found analytically. The spheres
will intersect only if there are roots between 0 and 1. The smallest of such roots is
set as the collision time for the spheres, and the collision normal is set as the line
connecting the current position of their center points.

2.5.17 Computing Continuous Box–Box Intersections

The continuous box–box intersection test is very similar to the continuous sphere–
sphere intersection test described in the previous section. The boxes will intersect
at the earliest time $t \in [0, 1]$ in which the distance between their centers is less than
the sum of their half-radiuses along each axis. Since this condition can be enforced
independently along each axis, the continuous box–box intersection test can be split
into three one-dimensional tests.

Let the boxes be defined by their center points $\vec{a}(t)$ and $\vec{b}(t)$ and half radiuses $\vec{r}_a$
and $\vec{r}_b$, respectively, as shown in Fig. 2.48. The position of the centers at time t is
given by

$$\vec{a}(t) = \vec{a}(0) - t\big(\vec{a}(1) - \vec{a}(0)\big)$$
$$\vec{b}(t) = \vec{b}(0) - t\big(\vec{b}(1) - \vec{b}(0)\big).$$

(2.42)

We begin by testing whether the boxes are already intersecting at $t = 0$, that is,
if the following three conditions are simultaneously satisfied:

$$\big(\vec{a}(0) - \vec{b}(0)\big)_x \leq (\vec{r}_a + \vec{r}_b)_x$$
$$\big(\vec{a}(0) - \vec{b}(0)\big)_y \leq (\vec{r}_a + \vec{r}_b)_y$$
$$\big(\vec{a}(0) - \vec{b}(0)\big)_z \leq (\vec{r}_a + \vec{r}_b)_z.$$

If this is the case, then the intersection time is set to t_0, and the collision normal is computed from the line connecting the boxes' center points. Otherwise, we need to find the smallest $t \in [0, 1]$, if any, that concurrently satisfies the conditions:

$$\left(\vec{a}(t) - \vec{b}(t)\right)_x \le (\vec{r}_a + \vec{r}_b)_x$$
$$\left(\vec{a}(t) - \vec{b}(t)\right)_y \le (\vec{r}_a + \vec{r}_b)_y \qquad (2.43)$$
$$\left(\vec{a}(t) - \vec{b}(t)\right)_z \le (\vec{r}_a + \vec{r}_b)_z.$$

Substituting Eq. (2.42) into Eq. (2.43), we obtain three 2nd degree polynomial equations on t that must be simultaneously satisfied, namely:

$$(f_2)_x t^2 + (f_1)_x t + (f_0)_x = 0$$
$$(f_2)_y t^2 + (f_1)_y t + (f_0)_y = 0$$
$$(f_2)_z t^2 + (f_1)_z t + (f_0)_z = 0,$$

where the polynomial coefficients are given by:

$$(f_2)_i = \left((\vec{a}(1) - \vec{a}(0))_i - (\vec{b}(1) - \vec{b}(0))_i\right)^2$$
$$(f_1)_i = 2(\vec{a}(0) - \vec{b}(0))_i \left((\vec{a}(1) - \vec{a}(0))_i - (\vec{b}(1) - \vec{b}(0))_i\right)$$
$$(f_0)_i = (\vec{a}(0) - \vec{b}(0))_i^2 - (r_a + r_b)_i^2,$$

with $i \in \{x, y, z\}$ specifying the axis along which the intersection is being checked. For each root between 0 and 1 of each polynomial, we position the boxes at the root time and verify that the objects are in fact intersecting, that is, that their center distance is less than the sum of their half radiuses. The smallest time t_c that satisfy these conditions is set as the intersection time between the boxes.

2.6 Notes and Comments

The literature on hierarchical decompositions is extensive, with related publications on several research areas such as computational geometry, computer graphics, robotics and molecular simulations. There are several other representations and variants of the techniques presented in this chapter, specially with respect to implementation.

The OBB tree representation became an option since Gottschalk et al. [GLM96, Got96] introduced the separating-axis theorem for carrying out fast interference detection between arbitrarily oriented boxes. Bergen [vdB97] presented a modified interference-detection test using AABB tree representations in which the search for a separating axis considered only the normals of the faces of the boxes. The pairwise edge-direction tests were ignored, thus reducing the complexity of the test, but consequently being about 6 % less accurate.

The use of bounding spheres, instead of bounding boxes, is also popular, owing to the simplicity of its implementation. The efficiency of bounding-sphere representations can be further improved if we use quad-trees or oct-trees instead of binary trees. Samet [Sam89] gives a good introduction to both quad-tree and oct-tree representations. The difficulty in using bounding-sphere representations is to come up with a partition that best approximates the original polyhedra. Hubbard [Hub96] developed a collision-detection algorithm that approximates 3D polyhedra with an oct-tree representation of bounding spheres, using a sophisticated technique based on 3D Voronoi diagrams to construct the spheres at each intermediate level of the decomposition.

The 3D convex-hull computation can be found in Preparata et al. [PS85], Edelsbrunner [Ede87], and in several other books on computational geometry. In the OBB case, there is also the need to determine the eigenvectors of the covariance matrix of the vertices of the convex hull. Eigenvectors and their associated eigenvalues are covered in detail in Strang [Str91], Golub [GL96], Horn [HJ91] and Press et al. [PTVF96].

The multi-level grid-structure analysis presented in Sect. 2.4.2 was derived from Mirtich [Mir96b]. Some primitive–primitive tests presented in Sect. 2.5 were obtained from Gottschalk [Got96] (box–box), Arvo [Arv90] and Larsson et al. [LML07] (box–sphere), Ritter [Rit90] (sphere–sphere), Karabassi et al. [KPTB99] (sphere–triangle) and Mahovsky et al. [MW04] (ray–box). The triangle–triangle intersection test presented in Sect. 2.5.5 is a combination of the different intersection tests found in Held [Hel97], Möller [Möl97] and Glaeser [Gla94]. Other interesting primitive–primitive tests can be found in Held [Hel97] and Ericson [Eri05].

The continuous time triangle–triangle intersection was originally introduced by Provot [Pro97] in the context of cloth simulations. Redon et al. [RKC02, RL06] used the concept of a screw motion to linearize the translation and rotation for the time interval being checked for collisions. They also present an interval-arithmetic approach to compute the roots of a 3rd degree polynomial which takes rounding errors into account. A closed form calculation of the roots can be found in Schwarze [Sch93].

2.7   Exercises

1. How can we improve the culling efficiency in the hierarchy–hierarchy intersection tests if we have information about the volume of its internal nodes?
2. Derive an algorithm to parallelize the hierarchy-self intersection algorithm presented in Sect. 2.5.2. What is the expected execution time of the algorithm?
3. Consider a set of points in world-space and a world-to-local transformation with origin at their mean point and local-coordinate axis aligned with the eigenvectors of the covariance matrix associated with the points. Consider two bounding spheres, one computed in world-space and the other in local-space using the above world-to-local transformation. Which bounding sphere has a tighter fit around the points? Explain.

4. The continuous triangle–triangle intersection test presented in Sect. 2.5.15 can be optimized in many ways.
   (a) Derive an equation for the vertex–face case to perform a rejection test if the vertex motion is on the same side of the plane containing the triangle. Derive an equivalent equation for the edge–edge case.
   (b) In a triangulated mesh, an edge is shared by two faces, whereas a vertex is shared by an average of six faces. Whenever a collision occurs at an edge or vertex, the collision detection will report multiple face–face collision candidates for the same collision. In particular, it will report two face–face collision candidates if the collision occurs at an edge, and as many face–face candidates as there are faces incident on a vertex, if the collision occurs at the vertex. Each of these multiple face–face collision candidates will be tested for intersection, reporting back the same intersection result. Devise a memory efficient data structure that is smart enough to process collisions at a vertex or edge just once, avoiding unnecessary, time-consuming, duplicate work.
5. We can use Sturm's theorem to find the number of real roots in the [0, 1] interval for the polynomials obtained in the continuous collisions described in Sects. 2.5.15, 2.5.16 and 2.5.17. The idea is to perform a quick rejection test and avoid solving the polynomial equations if there are no real roots in this interval.
   (a) Derive the equations for the Sturm chain for quadratic and cubic polynomials.
   (b) Is the quick rejection test still valid if an element of the chain evaluates to zero?
6. In the context of computing polynomial roots, consider the special case in which we have a double real root in the [0, 1] interval. Assume that the root was *not* found due to numerical rounding errors in the calculations. How can we improve the robustness of the root finding process to not miss such intersection cases? (*Hint*: saddle points.)

References

[Arv90] Arvo, J.: A simple method for box-sphere intersection testing. In: Graphics Gems I, pp. 335–339 (1990)

[Ede87] Edelsbrunner, H.: Algorithms in Combinatorial Geometry. Springer, Berlin (1987)

[Eri05] Ericson, C.: Real-Time Collision Detection. Kaufmann, Los Altos (2005)

[GL96] Golub, G.H., Van Loan, C.F.: Matrix Computations. Johns Hopkins University Press, Baltimore (1996)

[Gla94] Glaeser, G.: Fast Algorithms for 3D-Graphics. Springer, Berlin (1994)

[GLM96] Gottschalk, S., Lin, M.C., Manocha, D.: Obbtree: a hierarchical structure for rapid interference detection. Comput. Graph. (Proc. SIGGRAPH) **30**, 171–180 (1996)

[Got96] Gottschalk, S.: The separating axis test. Technical Report TR-96-24, University of North Carolina, Chapel Hill (1996)

[Hel97] Held, M.: Erit—a collection of efficient and reliable intersection tests. J. Graph. Tools **2**(4), 25–44 (1997)

[HJ91] Horn, R.A., Johnson, C.R.: Matrix Analysis. Cambridge University Press, Cambridge (1991)

[Hub96]   Hubbard, P.M.: Approximating polyhedra with spheres for time-critical collision detection. ACM Trans. Graph. **15**(3), 179–210 (1996)

[KPTB99] Karabassi, E.-A., Papaioannou, G., Theoharis, T., Boehm, A.: Intersection test for collision detection in particle systems. J. Graph. Tools **4**(1), 25–37 (1999)

[LML07]   Larsson, T., Möller, T., Lengyel, E.: On faster sphere-box overlap testing. J. Graph. Tools **12**(1), 3–8 (2007)

[Mir96b] Mirtich, B.V.: Impulse-based dynamic simulation of rigid body systems. PhD Thesis, University of California, Berkeley (1996)

[Möl97]   Möller, T.: A fast triangle–triangle intersection test. J. Graph. Tools **2**(2), 25–30 (1997)

[MW04]   Mahovsky, J., Wyvill, B.: Fast ray-axis aligned bounding box overlap tests with Plücker coordinates. J. Graph. Tools **9**(1), 35–46 (2004)

[Pro97]   Provot, X.: Collision and self-collision handling in cloth model dedicated to design garments. In: Proceedings Graphics Interface, pp. 177–189 (1997)

[PS85]   Preparata, F.P., Shamos, M.I.: Computational Geometry: An Introduction. Springer, Berlin (1985)

[PTVF96] Press, W.H., Teukolsky, S.A., Vetterling, W.T., Flannery, B.P.: Numerical Recipes in C: The Art of Scientific Computing. Cambridge University Press, Cambridge (1996)

[Rit90]   Ritter, J.: An efficient bounding sphere. In: Graphics Gems I, pp. 301–303 (1990)

[RKC02]   Redon, S., Kheddar, A., Coquillart, S.: Fast continuous collision detection between rigid bodies. Proc. EUROGRAPHICS **21** (2002)

[RL06]   Redon, S., Lin, M.C.: A fast method for local penetration depth computation. J. Graph. Tools **11**(2), 37–50 (2006)

[Sam89]   Samet, H.: Spatial Data Structures: Quadtree, Octrees and Other Hierarchical Methods. Addison-Wesley, Reading (1989)

[Sch93]   Schwarze, J.: Cubic and quartic roots. In: Graphics Gems I, pp. 404–407 (1993)

[Str91]   Strang, G.: Linear Algebra and Its Applications. Academic Press, San Diego (1991)

[vdB97]   van den Bergen, G.: Efficient collision detection of complex deformable models using AABB trees. J. Graph. Tools **2**(4), 1–13 (1997)

Particle Systems

3

3.1   Introduction

Particles are among the simplest and most versatile objects used in dynamic simulations. The fact that their mass is concentrated on a point (i.e., center of mass) considerably simplifies the dynamic equations governing their motion. All interaction forces among themselves and with other objects in the simulation are applied to the points representing each particle, and the rotational motion of a point is undefined, and therefore ignored. The reduced complexity in the dynamic equations allows for an increased number of particles being simulated without significantly impairing operation of the simulation engine. These simplifications make particle systems an extremely attractive option to simulate systems requiring a large number of objects that can be approximated as a collection of point-mass objects. Examples of such systems range from molecules, to smoke, fire, clouds, liquids, and even cloth and hair.

The main difference between the diverse set of particle systems in use nowadays resides in the types of interaction forces considered and the numerical-integration methods used to solve their equations of motion. Since particle systems usually need a large number of particles to achieve their desired effects, the complexity of the computation of the interaction forces between particles, other objects and the simulated environment plays a key role in overall simulation efficiency. Expensive interaction forces such as those that are spatially dependent, that is, their intensity varies with respect to the distance between the particles, can severely impair the efficiency, specially in naive implementations. For example, consider a molecular-dynamics simulation where the spatially dependent Lennard-Jones potential force acts between pairs of particles representing atoms. The computational cost of determining the potential forces between all pairs of particles is therefore $\mathcal{O}(n^2)$ for a particle system containing n particles. Clearly, a naive implementation of the potential-force computation becomes prohibitively expensive, even for a moderate number of particles.

M.G. Coutinho, *Guide to Dynamic Simulations of Rigid Bodies and Particle Systems*,   89
Simulation Foundations, Methods and Applications,
DOI 10.1007/978-1-4471-4417-5_3, © Springer-Verlag London 2013

The numerical-integration methods also play an important role in the overall simulation accuracy and robustness. Recall that the actual motion of the particles is determined from the numerical results obtained from the numerical-integration module. A fast but inaccurate method can produce unsatisfactory results that do not reflect the desired behavior of the particles in the system. On the other hand, an accurate numerical method can generate an unsatisfactory performance hit that deems useless any attempts to deliver interactive simulation speeds. In most cases, there is a trade-off between the computational accuracy of the models used to numerically integrate the evolution of particle systems over time, and the simulation's efficiency. Attaining interactive speeds using precise models of the particles' motion often requires computational power that is available only in high-performance computers, such as multi-core or multi-GPU computers, or a network of parallel computers.

In this book, we focus primarily on particle systems that can be analyzed as classical multibody systems, meaning, the motion of the center of mass of each particle follows the laws of classical mechanics. Such particle systems provide a reasonably good approximation of a wide variety of point-mass systems, such as dust, snow and rain. However, there are yet other types of point-mass systems that are widely used in dynamic simulations and animations that require specialized forms of equations of motion and force interactions to capture the precise physical behavior of the system. Examples of such particle systems include the simulation of turbulent gases (requires solving the volumetric differential Navier–Stokes equations), the simulation of light atoms or molecules (may need to take the quantum effects into account if the translational, vibrational and rotational motions are considered), and the detonation of explosives (requires using the Chapman–Jouget theory, possibly with the equations of the state for the detonated particles derived from laboratory experiments). The detailed explanation of the theoretical framework needed to capture the precise behavior of such specialized systems is beyond the scope of this book. The interested reader is referred to Sect. 3.9 for pointers to the literature wherein in-depth explanations of such techniques can be found.

Our approach to such particle systems as these, is the same as that commonly used in most animation environments. These software packages usually implement specialized particle systems having a set of user-adjustable parameters used to capture phenomena not otherwise considered in the standard particle-system model derived from classical mechanics. The idea is then to mimic the behavior of the system without having to solve the sophisticated (and computationally demanding) equations of motion associated with it. Section 3.7 presents some specialized particle systems commonly found in animation packages. It is important to notice that this is the *only* section in this book with examples that *do not* consider the mathematically accurate modeling of the dynamics. It was included here to demonstrate the versatility and modeling power that particle systems can have on dynamic simulations and animations.

From the users' perspective, a particle system is defined by both a particle emitter and the particles themselves. The particle emitter, as its name implies, is the source from which particles are created and released in the simulation environment. It can be either attached to other objects in the simulation, or be seem as an object in itself, in which case, the emitter is displayed with its default cubic shape (see Sect. 3.7.1). The particle emitter settings are used to control the dynamic behavior of the particles being emitted. These settings define the particle's size, mass, initial velocity and direction of movement, and many other user-adjustable parameters as explained in Sect. 3.7.2. As soon as the particles are released, their motion is governed by the dynamic equations derived from classical mechanical theory. The particle's parameters give an extra degree of flexibility in governing their motion, providing the added functionality needed to implement the specialized systems covered in this book. Examples of such parameters include the particle's split age, lifespan, color attributes and collision-detection options.

3.2 Particle Dynamics

The dynamic equations that govern the motion of a particle in our standard implementation of a particle system are the same as those governing the motion of a point-mass object in classical mechanics. Let the point-mass be represented by its mass m located at position $\vec{p}(t)$, which varies as a function of time. The velocity of the point is obtained by computing the derivative of its position with respect to time, namely

$$\vec{v}(t) = \frac{d\vec{p}(t)}{dt}.$$

Its acceleration is then given by

$$\vec{a}(t) = \frac{d\vec{v}(t)}{dt}. \tag{3.1}$$

Let $\vec{F}(t)$ be the net external force acting on the particle at the time instant t. Using Newton's law, we have

$$\vec{F}(t) = \frac{d\vec{L}(t)}{dt}, \tag{3.2}$$

where $\vec{L}(t)$ is the linear momentum of the particle computed as

$$\vec{L}(t) = m\vec{v}(t). \tag{3.3}$$

Substituting Eq. (3.3) into (3.2) and using Eq. (3.1), we obtain

$$\vec{F}(t) = \frac{d(m\vec{v}(t))}{dt} = m\frac{d\vec{v}(t)}{dt} = m\vec{a}(t). \tag{3.4}$$

Let $\vec{y}(t)$ denote the dynamic state of the particle at time t, that is, the vector comprising all variables necessary to define the dynamics of the particle at any instant during the simulation. Here, we shall pick the position and linear momentum of the particle to define its dynamic state, namely

$$\vec{y}(t) = \begin{pmatrix} \vec{p}(t) \\ \vec{L}(t) \end{pmatrix}.$$

The dynamic state of the particle at time $t = t_0$ is defined by the particle's position $\vec{p}(t_0)$ and its linear momentum $\vec{L}(t_0)$ computed as $m\vec{v}(t_0)$.

The time derivative of the dynamic state defines how the dynamic state of the particle changes over time, and is given by

$$\frac{d\vec{y}(t)}{dt} = \begin{pmatrix} d\vec{p}(t)/dt \\ d\vec{L}(t)/dt \end{pmatrix} = \begin{pmatrix} \vec{v}(t) \\ \vec{F}(t) \end{pmatrix}.$$

So, the time derivative of the dynamic state at time $t = t_0$ is defined by the particle's velocity $\vec{v}(t_0)$ computed as $(\vec{L}(t_0)/m)$ and the net force $\vec{F}(t_0)$ acting on it.

For a system with N particles, we can combine their individual dynamic states into a single system-wide dynamic-state vector

$$\vec{Y}(t) = \begin{pmatrix} \vec{p}_1(t) \\ \vec{L}_1(t) \\ \ldots \\ \vec{p}_N(t) \\ \vec{L}_N(t) \end{pmatrix}$$

with its corresponding time derivative

$$\frac{d\vec{Y}(t)}{dt} = \begin{pmatrix} \vec{v}_1(t) \\ \vec{F}_1(t) \\ \ldots \\ \vec{v}_N(t) \\ \vec{F}_N(t) \end{pmatrix}. \tag{3.5}$$

The dynamic simulation of a particle system works as follows. At the beginning of the simulation, we have the dynamic state of every particle, namely their positions and linear momenta defined with respect to the world reference frame. Each simulation time interval will then consist of numerically integrating Eq. (3.5), using the dynamic state of the particles at the beginning of the time interval as the initial condition for the numerical integration. There are several numerical methods that can be used to integrate Eq. (3.5). For example, the Euler method computes a quick (and less accurate) approximation of the time derivative by using only the information about the dynamic state at the beginning of the time interval to predict the dynamic state of the system at the end of that time interval. Others, such as the several variations of the Runge–Kutta method, use a more sophisticated approach in which the dynamic state at the end of the time interval is computed as a weighted sum of the dynamic state of the system at several intermediate positions within it. These and other popular methods are discussed in Appendix B (Chap. 7).

The computation of the net external force acting on each particle at each intermediate step of the numerical integrator is determined by summing all external forces acting on the particles. The types of external forces considered in this book range from simple global forces (such as gravity), to point-to-point forces (such as springs), to more computationally demanding spatially dependent forces (such as windy regions). The detailed discussion on how to determine the contribution of each of these forces to the net external force of each particle is presented in Sect. 3.3.

Initially, the determination of the dynamic state of each particle at the end of the current time interval is done without taking into account any possible collisions between particles and other objects in the simulation environment. The information about the initial and final dynamic state of each particle is then used to check for collisions between the particles themselves and with other rigid bodies in the simulation (see Sect. 3.4). Whenever a collision is detected, the colliding particles have their trajectories backtracked in time to the moment just before the collision. The collision point and collision normal are then computed from the relative displacement of the colliding particles. Only then the collision-response module is activated to compute the appropriate impulsive or contact forces that will be applied to change the direction of motion of the colliding particles. This is done slightly differently if we have a particle–particle collision or a particle–rigid body collision (see Sects. 3.5 and 3.6 for more details).

The dynamic equations of all particles involved in a collision are then numerically integrated for the remaining period of time, that is, from the collision time to the end of the current time interval. This new numerical integration will update the current particles' trajectories to account for all collision forces. Notice that this also requires the numerical integration of the dynamic state of all other particles connected to one or more particles involved in a collision, since the connection usually implies the existence of a force component between the particles. For example, consider a simple particle system consisting of four particles O_1, O_2, O_3 and O_4, and suppose particles O_1 and O_2 are connected by a spring.

Initially, the dynamic state of the system is numerically integrated from t_0 (the beginning of the current time interval) to t_1 (the end of the current time interval). Now, assume the collision-detection module detected a collision between particles O_2 and O_3 at time t_c such that $t_0 < t_c < t_1$ (see Fig. 3.1). The colliding particles are then backtracked in time to the moment before their collision (i.e., backtracked to t_c) and the collision impulses are computed so as to prevent their interpenetration. Having applied the collision impulses to both particles, their trajectories are numerically integrated for the remaining period of time, that is, from t_c to t_1. Notice that, if we just backtrack in time the trajectories of O_2 and O_3, the spring-force computation between particles O_1 and O_2 will be incorrect in the numerical integration for the remaining period of time. The problem is that, since particle O_1 was not involved in any collision, its dynamic state corresponds to time t_1, whereas the dynamic state

Fig. 3.1 A simple particle
system containing four
particles. The dynamic state
of the system is numerically
integrated from t_0 to t_1.
A collision between particles
O_2 and O_3 is detected at
time t_c

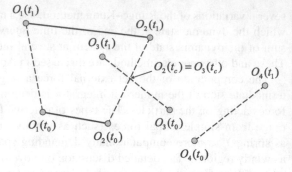

Fig. 3.2 Particles O_2 and O_3
are backtracked in time to the
moment just before their
collision

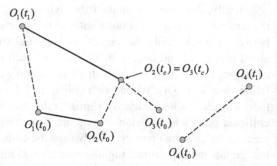

of particle O_2 corresponds to time t_c. So, if we do not backtrack in time O_1 too,
the spring-force computation will use O_1's position at time t_1 when it should use
it at the same simulation time of O_2, namely time t_c (see Fig. 3.2). In other words,
the numerical integration of the dynamic state of all interconnected particles should
be synchronized to provide the correct system behavior (see Fig. 3.3). On the other
hand, particles that are not connected can be asynchronously moved within the same
simulation time interval. This is the case of particle O_4 as shown in Fig. 3.3, since
the numerical integration of O_2 and O_3 for the remaining period of time does not
affect its dynamic state, already computed.

As far as implementation is concerned, this approach requires some bookkeeping
mechanism to efficiently determine which particles are connected to other particles
and rigid bodies. The payoff is the significant efficiency gain over the alternative approach of backtracking in time all particles, even those not involved in any collision,
to the moment before the most recent collision.

The information about the initial and final dynamic state of each particle along
the updated part of its trajectory is used to check again for collisions between all
other particles and rigid bodies in the simulation. In theory, this process repeats until all particle–particle and particle–rigid body collisions detected within the current
time interval have been resolved. In practice, a user-adjustable parameter is used to
limit the maximum number of iterations. When this number is reached, the simulation engine overrides the physical parameters of all particles, forcing all collisions
to be inelastic (i.e., coefficient of restitution set to zero). Doing so, the colliding

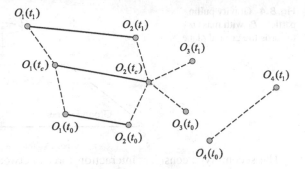

Fig. 3.3 Particle O_1 is also backtracked back in time to t_c before the numerical integrator is used to recompute the trajectories of particles O_1, O_2 and O_3. Notice that particle O_4 was not affected by the collision, and therefore remained unchanged throughout the collision-detection and response phases

particles will stick together after their collision is processed, thus significantly reducing the number of new collisions introduced in the next iterations.

Clearly, the collision check is an intense process that can consume much computational time, especially in a naive implementation. We suggest using a hierarchical bounding volume representation of the particle system to speed the continuous collision detection for particle–particle collisions. As the system evolves, the hierarchical representation of the particle system is updated to bound the entire motion of each particle. Self-intersecting the hierarchy provides information about all pairs of particles with intersecting trajectories. These pairs define the collision candidates for which the more expensive sphere-sphere continuous collision check is performed, as explained in Sect. 2.5.16.

Particle–rigid body collisions are checked for collisions by intersecting the hierarchical representation of the particle system with the one used for the rigid body. Usually these collisions do not require the extra precision of continuous collision for the rigid body motion and as such, the hierarchical representation of the rigid body can be updated to reflect its position and orientation at the end of the current time interval, instead of bounding its entire motion for the interval. The intersection results provide information about all pairs of particle and triangle face (assuming the rigid body is represented by a triangulated mesh) that have the particle's trajectory intersecting the triangle face positioned at the end of the time interval. A line segment–triangle intersection test is performed to check if the particle is actually intersecting the triangle.

3.3 Basic Interaction Forces

The interaction forces used in most particle-system simulations can be categorized into three different types of forces. The first type considers global interaction forces, that is, forces that are independently applied to all particles in the system. Examples of such forces include gravity and viscous drag (used to simulate air resistance). They are the least expensive interaction forces available in the simulation environment, since their required computational cost is negligible compared with the other types of interaction forces presented in this book.

Fig. 3.4 Gravity pulling
particle P_1 with mass m_1
towards the ground plane

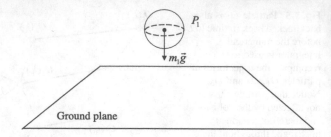

The second type considers interaction forces between a specific number of particles. Damped springs are a good example of such interaction forces between two given particles. Notice, however, that particles can be attached to more than one particle, and each attachment may use a different interaction force. For example, multiple attachments of springs to pairs of particles can be used to create a mesh of particles (i.e., a spring–mass system) that models cloth.

Interactive-user manipulation is also modeled as a point-to-point force between the current mouse position and the selected particle. The goal of using a fictitious interaction force between the mouse and the selected particle is to prevent the introduction of unstable configurations resulting from abrupt mouse movements, as explained in Sect. 3.3.5.

Finally, the third type of interaction forces considered in this book for particle-system simulations is the spatially dependent force. This comprises forces that depend on the position of the particles, either relative to each other or to the simulated environment. For instance, a gravitational force field depends on the relative positioning of the particles, in the sense that it will have a stronger influence on the motion of nearby particles than on the motion of those farther away. Another example is the interaction force created by defining a windy region on the simulated environment. Particles located on the windy region or passing through it will have to take the wind force into account when computing their net external force, whereas particles that are not in the windy region can ignore that force.

The spatially dependent forces are the most expensive interaction forces considered in particle-system simulations. Approximation methods are generally used to truncate the influence of the force field on particles that are more than one threshold value distant. This truncation technique is discussed in detail in Sect. 3.3.4.

3.3.1   Gravity

The force contribution of the gravitational force acting on each particle owing to its attraction to the ground (i.e., Earth) is directly obtained as

$$\vec{F} = m\vec{g},$$

where $\vec{g}$ is the gravity acceleration and m is the mass of the particle (see Fig. 3.4). The gravity acceleration is in most cases assumed to have constant magnitude of 9.81 m/s^2 and direction pointing downwards (i.e., towards the ground).

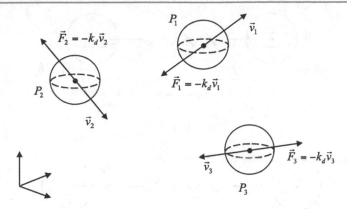

Fig. 3.5 A set of particles P_i moving in random directions and experiencing air resistance modeled as viscous drag $\vec{F}_i$

3.3.2 Viscous Drag

The most common use of viscous drag in dynamic simulations of particle systems is to model the air resistance to the particle's movement. The goal is to ensure that particles will eventually come to a rest if there are no other external forces acting on them. Figure 3.5 illustrates this. The force component of the viscous drag is computed as

$$\vec{F} = -k_d\vec{v},$$

where $\vec{v}$ is the velocity vector of the particle and k_d is the coefficient of drag.

Besides preventing particles from gaining excessive speeds that may introduce instabilities into the numerical-integration method being used, viscous drag can also be used to control the rate at which particles accelerate. For example, a particle system simulating smoke may use a coefficient of drag much greater than that used in a particle system simulating rain. This in turn has the effect of making the smoke particles slowly rise and spread over nearby regions, whereas the rain drops will be allowed to fall at a reasonable speed.

3.3.3 Damped Springs

Springs are mostly used to keep the distance between pairs of particles at a known value. Whenever the particles are pushed apart or pulled together, a spring force is applied to both particles with the same magnitude but opposing direction.

Let P_1 and P_2 be two particles connected by a spring of resting length r_0. Let $\vec{r}_1$, $\vec{v}_1$, $\vec{r}_2$ and $\vec{v}_2$ be the linear position and velocity of particles P_1 and P_2, respectively.

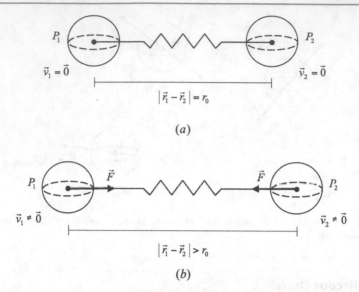

Fig. 3.6 Particles P_1 and P_2 are connected by a damped spring. (**a**) Particles at resting position; (**b**) Spring forces exerted on the particles when they are pulled away from each other

The spring-force component acting on both particles is then obtained from

$$\vec{F}_2 = -\left[k_s\left(|\vec{r}_2 - \vec{r}_1| - r_0\right) + k_d(\vec{v}_2 - \vec{v}_1) \cdot \frac{(\vec{r}_2 - \vec{r}_1)}{|\vec{r}_2 - \vec{r}_1|} \right] \frac{(\vec{r}_2 - \vec{r}_1)}{|\vec{r}_2 - \vec{r}_1|}$$
$$\vec{F}_1 = -\vec{F}_2,$$
(3.6)

with $\vec{F}_i$ being the spring force acting on particle P_i for $i \in \{1, 2\}$, k_s being the spring constant and k_d being the damping constant (see Fig. 3.6). The damping term of Eq. (3.6) is used to prevent oscillation, and does not affect the motion of the center of mass of the connected particles.

The spring system can be under, over or critically damped, depending on the value of k_d being used. Oscillations occur only when the system is under damped. The interested reader is referred to Sect. 3.9 for pointers to the literature wherein techniques to compute the value of k_d for under, over and critically damped spring systems can be found.

3.3.4 Spatially Dependent Forces

There are two types of spatially dependent forces considered in this book. The first type, referred to as *constrained force field*, deals with force fields defined over a region of the simulated environment. Such forces interact only with particles located within their region of influence. The second type, referred to as *unconstrained force*

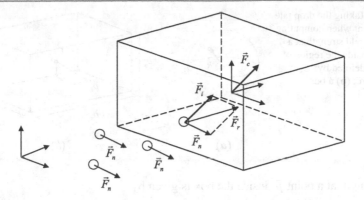

Fig. 3.7 A windy region defined as a box in the simulated environment. Particles that lie outside the box are not affected by the wind, whereas those inside the box have their net-force vector $\vec{F}_n$ adjusted to $\vec{F}_r$, as the result of taking into account the wind force $\vec{F}_i$ given by Eq. (3.7)

field, deals with interaction forces between all particles, which depend on the particles' relative positioning.

Constrained Force Fields   Constrained force fields are defined by their region of influence, force field strength and the drop rate. The region of influence, as its name implies, defines a region of the simulated world to which the force field is constrained. The boundary of the region of influence can be described by a polyhedron in the simulated environment (see Fig. 3.7). Particles that are located inside the polyhedron have their trajectories affected by the force-field strength. For efficiency reasons, the region of influence should be represented as a simple polyhedron such as a box or sphere, so that particle-inclusion tests can be efficiently implemented using the algorithms presented in Sect. 2.5.

The force-field strength is defined at the center of the region of influence. As we move away from the center, the strength of the force field is reduced according to its distance to the center. Therefore, particles closer to the center of the region of influence are more affected by the force field than those near the boundary of the region of influence. This is used to provide a smooth transition (i.e., avoid discontinuities) on the dynamics for particles entering and leaving the region of influence.

The drop rate is computed as follows. If the region of influence is a sphere, then the force-field strength at a point $\vec{p}_i$ inside the sphere is

$$\vec{F}_i = \left(1 - \frac{|\vec{r}_i|}{R}\right)\vec{F}_c,$$

where R is the radius of the sphere, $\vec{r}_i$ is the distance vector from point $\vec{p}_i$ to the center of the sphere $\vec{c}$, and $\vec{F}_c$ is the force-field strength at $\vec{c}$ (see Fig. 3.8(a)). When the region of influence is a box centered at $\vec{c}$ with dimensions $B = (b_x, b_y, b_z)$, the

Fig. 3.8 Taking the drop rate
into account when computing
the force-field strength at a
point $\vec{p}_i$ inside the region of
influence defined by:
(**a**) a sphere; (**b**) a box

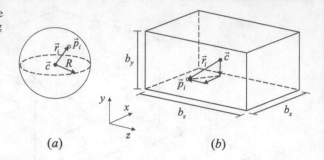

(a) (b)

field strength at a point $\vec{p}_i$ inside the box is given by

$$(\vec{F}_i)_x = \left(1 - \frac{|(r_i)_x|}{b_x}\right)(\vec{F}_c)_x$$

$$(\vec{F}_i)_y = \left(1 - \frac{|(r_i)_y|}{b_x}\right)(\vec{F}_c)_y \qquad (3.7)$$

$$(\vec{F}_i)_z = \left(1 - \frac{|(r_i)_z|}{b_x}\right)(\vec{F}_c)_z,$$

with $\vec{r}_i$ being the distance vector from point $\vec{p}_i$ to the center of the box. This situation
is illustrated in Fig. 3.8(b).

At a preprocessing stage, the region of influence of each constrained force field
is intersected with the cell decomposition of the simulated world. By so doing, the
simulation engine will know which cells are completely inside, partially covered,
or outside the region of influence. This greatly speeds run-time particle-inclusion
tests, since such tests are only necessary for particles associated with cells that are
partially covered by the region of influence.

Unconstrained Force Fields   Unconstrained force fields are used to specify long-
range force interactions between all particles in the system. Each particle influences
all others in the system, which in most cases depend on their relative displacement.
The farther the particles are apart, the weaker the force interaction affecting their
motion. Examples of such force fields include:

- The gravitational potential between two particles P_1 and P_2, computed as

$$\vec{F}_1 = G\frac{m_1 m_2}{|\vec{r}_1 - \vec{r}_2|^2}\frac{(\vec{r}_1 - \vec{r}_2)}{|\vec{r}_1 - \vec{r}_2|}$$

$$\vec{F}_2 = -\vec{F}_1,$$

where $m_1, \vec{r}_1, m_2$ and $\vec{r}_2$ are the mass and position of particles P_1 and P_2, respectively, and $G = 6.672 \times 10^{-11}\ \mathrm{N\,m^2\,kg^{-2}}$ is the universal gravitational constant.
- The Lennard-Jones potential, commonly used for computing non-bounding po-
tentials in molecular-dynamics simulators, and given by

$$\vec{F}_1 = \frac{48}{|\vec{r}_1 - \vec{r}_2|^2} \left(\frac{1}{|\vec{r}_1 - \vec{r}_2|^{12}} - \frac{0.5}{|\vec{r}_1 - \vec{r}_2|^6} \right)$$

$$\vec{F}_2 = -\vec{F}_1.$$

- The Coulomb potential, which is the equivalent of the gravitational potential when the particles have electrical charges

$$\vec{F}_1 = K \frac{q_1 q_2}{|\vec{r}_1 - \vec{r}_2|^2} \frac{(\vec{r}_1 - \vec{r}_2)}{|\vec{r}_1 - \vec{r}_2|}$$

$$\vec{F}_2 = -\vec{F}_1,$$

with q_1 and q_2 being the electrical charges of the particles, and K the Coulomb constant equal to $8.9875 \times 10^9 \, \mathrm{N\,m^2\,C^{-2}}$. In this case, the particles can either repel or attract each other, depending on whether their electrical charges are of the same or opposite signs.

Clearly, the computation of unconstrained forces for a particle system containing n particles has a $\mathcal{O}(n^2)$ computation time complexity, which makes it impractical for interactive simulations, even for a moderate number of particles (i.e., $n \geq 1000$). Fortunately, there is a workaround to this limitation that reduces the computational complexity to $\mathcal{O}(n)$. It is based on truncating the computation of the interaction forces to particles that are within a cut-off distance from the particle being considered. This can be efficiently implemented if we use the underlying cell subdivision of the simulated world.

As explained in Sect. 3.2, the simulation engine dynamically assigns particles to the cells in which they are included. Each particle will then interact with other particles in that same cell, and those in neighboring cells that are within a cut-off distance from the cell that contains the particle. Figure 3.9 shows how the neighboring cells are determined for a 2D cell decomposition.

The actual number of neighboring cells to be used depends on the size of each cell and the cut-off distance. Let s be the dimension of each cell along each axis of the world-coordinate frame,[1] and let s_c be the desired cut-off distance. Assume we are computing the force interactions for particles contained in cell $C = (c_x, c_y, c_z)$. Now, imagine a cut-off box with its center coincident with the center of cell C, and with sides of length equal to the cut-off distance. This situation is illustrated in Fig. 3.10.

The cut-off box will therefore intersect

$$p = \left\lceil \frac{s_c}{s} \right\rceil \quad \text{with } p \in \mathbb{N}$$

cells of the subdivision. The particles in $C = (c_x, c_y, c_z)$ will then interact with the particles assigned to cells $C = (i, j, k)$ satisfying

---

[1] Recall from Sect. 2.4 that the cell decomposition defines a uniform subdivision of the simulated world.

Fig. 3.9 Particles in cell C will only interact with other particles in C and in neighboring cells that are within the cut-off distance s_c from C

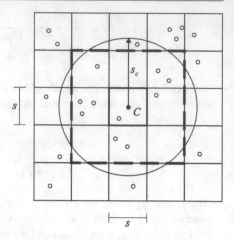

Fig. 3.10 The computation of the force interactions for particles in cell $C = (c_x, c_y, c_z)$ is limited to the cells with indexes within $\lfloor \frac{p}{2} \rfloor$ from it

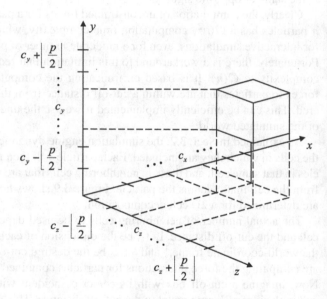

$$0 \le \left(c_x - \left\lfloor \frac{p}{2} \right\rfloor \right) \le i \le \left(c_x - \left\lfloor \frac{p}{2} \right\rfloor \right) \le c_n$$

$$0 \le \left(c_y - \left\lfloor \frac{p}{2} \right\rfloor \right) \le j \le \left(c_y - \left\lfloor \frac{p}{2} \right\rfloor \right) \le c_n$$

$$0 \le \left(c_z - \left\lfloor \frac{p}{2} \right\rfloor \right) \le k \le \left(c_z - \left\lfloor \frac{p}{2} \right\rfloor \right) \le c_n,$$

where c_n is the maximum cell-index value, as discussed in Sect. 2.4.

3.3.5   User Interaction

The user-interaction force is modeled as a damped spring connecting the current mouse position to the position of the particle being dragged. The goal of using this fictitious spring is to avoid the introduction of unrealistically large external forces acting on the selected particle because of abrupt mouse movements. These large external forces can make the dynamic equations describing the motion of the particle stiff. Stiff systems are more sensible to round-off errors and usually require the use of more elaborated and time-consuming numerical-integration methods, such as the implicit Euler method described in Appendix B (Chap. 7).

The main difference between the damped spring described in Sect. 3.3.3 and the fictitious spring used here is that the resting length of the fictitious spring should be zero. A zero resting length means that the selected particle will only stabilize its motion when its position is coincident with the mouse position. Therefore, as the user drags the particle around, the current mouse position is used to update the actual distance between the particle and the mouse. This distance is then used in Eq. (3.6) to compute the appropriate spring force to be applied.

3.4   Collision Detection

Even though particles are modeled as point-mass objects, they are usually represented by simple geometric shapes such as cubes or spheres that can be rendered in large numbers without affecting too much the overall performance of the rendering engine. The particle's shape can then be used to detect collisions between particles and other objects in the simulated environment.

We say the particle system has *internal collisions* whenever the collisions between its particles are taken into account. The particle system will have *external collisions* if the collisions between its particles and other particles defined by other particle systems are also taken into account. Collisions between rigid bodies and particles will be referred to as *complex collisions*.

In this book, we focus on particle systems that can have internal, external and complex collisions. Also, we assume all particles in the system have a *spherical* shape, possibly with different radii. The main reason for this assumption is efficiency. Since particles are point-mass objects, their trajectories between two consecutive time steps define a straight line segment. When their shape is taken into account, their trajectories will span a volume in 3D space. In this context, collision detection between particles and other objects in the simulated environment can be determined using quick and efficient continuous collision tests.

The relative displacement of the colliding particles or rigid bodies is used to determine the collision normal and tangent plane at the collision point. The actual computation of the collision normal is slightly different depending on whether we are considering particle–particle or particle–rigid body collisions. This is explained in detail in the following sections. The computation of the tangent plane, on the other hand, is done after the collision normal is determined, and depends strictly

Fig. 3.11 An example of a
particle system containing
four particles moving from t_0
to t_1

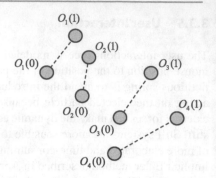

on it. Sect. 6.6 of Appendix A (Chap. 6) presents a thorough derivation of how the
tangent plane is obtained given the collision-normal vector $\vec{n}$. Henceforth, we shall
take for granted the computation of vectors $\vec{t}$ and $\vec{k}$ that, together with vector $\vec{n}$, form
the local frame used to compute the collision and contact forces.

3.4.1 Particle–Particle Collision

The collision detection between particles is usually undertaken by checking whether
the particles' trajectories intersect. These intersection tests can be efficiently performed if we consider a hierarchical representation for the particle system, with
each leaf node corresponding to a single particle. Depending on how large is the expected number of particles in the system (i.e., several hundred thousand particles),
it is possible to associate a small group of particles to each leaf node instead of
just a single one. A user-adjustable parameter is recommended to specify how many
particles per leaf node should be used when building the hierarchy.

The construction of the hierarchical representation of a particle system is best illustrated using the example shown in Fig. 3.11. In this example, the particle system
contains four particles moving from t_0 to t_1. Initially, the hierarchical representation
of the particle system is built using the particles' position at t_1 only, that is, using
their positions at the end of the current time interval. As previously explained in
Chap. 2, the hierarchical tree can be built in a top-down fashion with the root node
enclosing all particles, which in turn is recursively decomposed into internal nodes
according to some partitioning rule until there is only one particle or group of particles assigned to each leaf node. This recursive process is illustrated in Fig. 3.12.
The equivalent tree representation is shown in Fig. 3.13.

Having built the hierarchical tree from the particles positioned at t_1, the next
step consists of updating the tree to take into account the particles' entire motion
from t_0 to t_1. The idea is to refit the tree to also contain the particles' position
at t_0. The refit process maintains the current parent–child relationship in the tree,
and updates the bounding volumes of its nodes to encompass the entire motion of
the particles. First, the bounding volumes of all leaf nodes are updated to include
their particle's position at t_0 and t_1. Then, the next level up of internal nodes is
updated to bound the volume of its children leaf nodes, and the process continues

Fig. 3.12 A hierarchical axis-aligned bounding box representation of the particle system in Fig. 3.11 at time t_1. The splitting axis at each one of the three levels of the hierarchy are shown in *dotted lines*

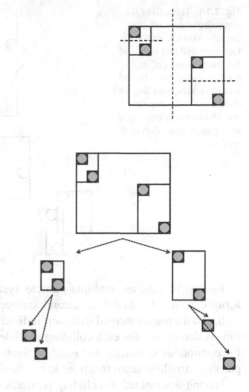

Fig. 3.13 The actual tree representation of the axis-aligned box hierarchy shown in Fig. 3.12, with each leaf node bounding its corresponding particle at t_1, and internal nodes bounding its children

until the root node is reached (see Fig. 3.14). The refit process is explained in more details in Sect. 2.3. We can use either sphere hierarchies (covered in Sect. 2.2.3) or axis-aligned box hierarchies (discussed in Sect. 2.2.1) to represent the continuous motion of the particle system. Notice that it is not recommended to use oriented box hierarchies for particle systems because the refit of the hierarchy still requires the computationally expensive rebuild of the oriented boxes at each node.

The collision detection between particles can be determined by self-intersecting the hierarchical tree representation of the particle system. This algorithm is discussed in details in Sect. 2.5.2. The self-intersection results in all pairs of particles with overlapping bounded motions. These define the list of collision candidate pairs that need to be further checked for intersections using the continuous sphere-sphere collision detection algorithm presented is Sect. 2.5.16. The algorithm transforms the sphere-sphere intersection test into a root finding problem for a 2nd degree polynomial in t. The smallest root between zero and one is taken as the collision time t_c between the particles. The collision information is obtained by positioning the colliding particles at t_c and using their closest point as the collision point, and the line connecting their centers as the collision normal. The simulation engine uses a global-collision list sorted by earliest collision times to detect all valid single and multiple simultaneous collisions for the colliding particles. This process was described in Sect. 1.4.3.

Fig. 3.14 The refit of the hierarchy of axis-aligned bounding boxes, with each leaf node updated to bound the entire motion of its corresponding particle, and internal nodes bounding its children. Notice that the parent–child relationship is maintained intact during the refit

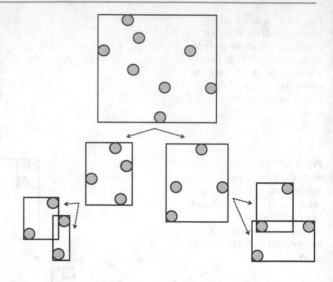

Finally, if there are multiple particle systems being simulated and their interactions are sought, then their hierarchical representations need to be intersected as well, and the results merged with their individual self-intersections before a collision time is determined for each colliding particle. The simulation world representation for continuous collisions discussed in Sect. 2.4.3 can help provide the candidate pairs of particle systems that need to be checked for collisions.

Having determined all colliding particles, either with another particle or a rigid body (discussed in the next section), the collision response impulses are computed and applied to each particle. The new particle trajectories are computed by numerically integrating their equations of motion for the remainder time between their collision and the end of the time interval. Once the integration is complete, the hierarchical tree representation of the particle system is refit one more time to reflect the changes in position of all colliding particles. A new round of collision detection starts at this point. In theory, this iterative process continues until all particle collisions are resolved. In practice, the simulation engine relies on a user-adjustable parameter to limit the maximum number of collision iterations to be used, after which, the coefficient of restitution for all particle collisions is overridden to zero (i.e., inelastic collisions) such that the colliding particles will stick together or with their colliding rigid bodies on future iterations. This adjustment considerably reduces the number of new collisions introduced in the following iterations and expedite the system resolution of all collisions.

3.4.2 Particle–Rigid Body Collision

The collision detection between particles and rigid bodies is more complicated than that involving only particles, owing to the use of hierarchical representations for rigid bodies, as discussed in Chap. 2. Here, we have to consider two possible

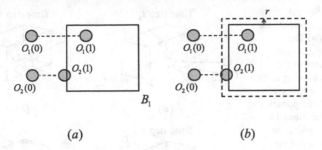

Fig. 3.15 (a) Two particles moving towards rigid body B_1. The collision detection module does not return particle O_2 as intersecting B_1 because its center point is not inside the object, as is the case for O_1; (b) This collision miss can be fixed by expanding the geometry representation of the object by the particle's radius

approaches for particle–rigid body collision detection, namely, the simple and the complex approaches. The choice of the appropriate approach to be used depends on the application.

In the simple approach, the rigid body's trajectory during the current simulation time interval is ignored, and the collision tests are carried out with the rigid body already positioned at the end of the current time interval. However, the particle system hierarchy is still built based on the particles' trajectories for the entire time interval. Hence, the intersection between these two hierarchical trees results in a list of particle–triangle pairs with the particle's trajectory crossing the triangle's plane at some point in time. This list defines the collision candidates that need further collision checks. The collision detection for each particle–triangle pair is carried out the same way as the vertex–face continuous collision test presented in Sect. 2.5.15, in the context of continuous triangle–triangle intersections. Here, the particle's geometry is ignored for a moment, and the particle's motion is approximated by the trajectory of its center point. This situation is illustrated in Fig. 3.15(a).

In this example, the trajectories of both particles O_1 and O_2 do intersect rigid body B_1. However, if we rely solely on the results of the vertex–face continuous collision tests, only particle O_1 is reported back as colliding with B_1. This is because the center point of the trajectory of particle O_2 does not pass through B_1's surface, and the vertex–face collision detection returns a no-collide state for O_2, even though its geometric representation does intersect the object's surface. Clearly, this approximation for the particle's trajectory results in a trade-off between using a fast vertex–face collision detection algorithm and letting the particles penetrate the rigid body by a distance up to their radius. Depending on the application, this trade-off between speed and accuracy is acceptable. However, if this is not the case, the accuracy of the algorithm can be further improved if we consider extending the object's geometry by the average particles' radius (see Fig. 3.15(b)). This extension can be done in a preprocessing step before the simulation begins, since we usually know the particle system's radius at that point.

Fig. 3.16 (**a**) Several
particles hitting a box at rest
at time $t = t_k$; (**b**) The
particles' trajectories are
updated according to the
impulsive forces owing to the
collision; (**c**) The reaction
forces owing to the particles'
collisions are substituted for a
net force-torque pair acting
on the box's center of mass;
(**d**) The net force-torque pair
is then used in the subsequent
simulation time interval
$t = (t_k + \Delta t)$ to update the
position and orientation of the
box

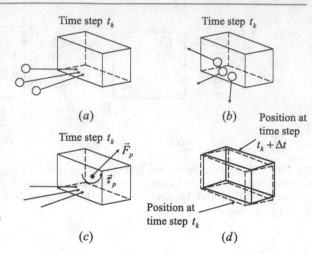

As for the complex collision detection approach, the rigid body's hierarchical
representation is built based on its entire motion for the time interval, similar to the
way the particle system's hierarchy was built. The intersection between these hierarchical trees results in a list of particle–triangle pairs with the particle's trajectory
crossing the triangle's trajectory at some point in time. Again, the particle–triangle
intersection test is undertaking using the same vertex–face collision test for continuous triangle–triangle intersections. The difference here is that there will be many
more particle–triangle collision candidates to be tested compared to the number of
pairs obtained using the simple approach. The extra number of collision candidates
is due to the triangle moving through space as opposed to being "fixed" at the end
of the time interval.

Independent of which approach is used, the particles can intersect with multiple triangles at different collision times. For each particle, we must keep track of
all single or multiple simultaneous collisions associated with the earliest collision
time between zero and one. The collision information is obtained from the relative
position of the particle and the triangle at the collision time. More specifically, the
collision point is set as the center of the sphere representing the particle, and the
collision normal can be either a vertex normal, an edge normal or a face normal
depending on the particle being closer to a vertex, an edge or an interior point of the
triangle, respectively.

The reaction on the rigid body's motion owing to the impulsive or contact forces
of the particles colliding with it will only be applied to the rigid body on the subsequent simulation time interval. In other words, even though the rigid body is modeled as a "fixed" object for the current time interval, the forces and impulses exerted
by particles colliding with it are accumulated as an external force and impulse that
will affect the rigid body's motion the next time its dynamic equations are integrated.
For instance, consider the situation shown in Fig. 3.16, where several particles are
moving toward a box at rest.

The collision-detection module will check for geometric intersections between the particles' trajectories and the box (see Fig. 3.16(a)). The collision-response module is then activated to resolve any detected collisions (more details in Sect. 3.6). The colliding particles have their trajectories updated according to the impulsive forces computed by the collision-response module, so as to prevent interpenetration with the box, as well as other particles during their movement (see Fig. 3.16(b)). The reaction impulsive force to the collision of each particle is summed and saved as an external impulsive force-torque pair acting on the box (see Fig. 3.16(c)). This external impulsive force-torque pair will then be used to update the box's motion during the next simulation time interval (see Fig. 3.16(d)).

The main drawback to using the above-mentioned simplification is that all rigid body–rigid body collisions must be processed *before* any particle–particle and particle–rigid body collisions. This is necessary because rigid body–rigid body collisions require that the colliding rigid bodies be backtracked in time to the moment just before their collision. Moreover, the impulses and contact forces are immediately applied and their trajectories are updated through the remaining period of time. So, if we compute all particle–particle and particle–rigid body collisions before the rigid body–rigid body collisions are dealt with, there is a chance that some rigid bodies will have their positions at the end of the current time interval modified because of some collisions with other rigid bodies. This would require recomputation of all particle–rigid body collisions and particle–particle collisions involving the particles that collided with those rigid bodies that had their trajectories modified by the rigid body–rigid body collisions.

Lastly, we still need to consider the case in which the particle finds itself inside the rigid body at t_0, that is, it starts already inside the rigid body at the beginning of the current time interval. This situation can happen in a couple of different ways. For instance, a rigid body can be laying on top of an emitter surface and newly created particles are placed inside the rigid body. Also, implementation problems in the collision detection software being used can introduce execution pitfalls that allow particles to move to the inside of rigid bodies with their collisions going undetected. In either case, we want to devise a strategy to cope with these unphysical situations.

In our view, the best way to cope with this particle-inside problem is to remove the particle from the simulation altogether. This has no side effects with respect to all other collisions already processed, it is easy and fast to implement, it does not affect the efficacy of the simulation, and may even pass unnoticed if there is a large number of particles nearby the one being removed. However, removing the particle from the system might not be a feasible option for the application at hand, and in such cases, we suggest the following approach to robustly handle particles inside rigid bodies.

Immediately before the beginning of a new simulation time interval, the simulation engine does an inside test for all particle systems against all rigid bodies they collided with in the previous time step. In the special case of the start frame that does not have a previous frame to look up to, the hierarchical representation of the simulated world can be used to determine the candidate particle system and rigid body pairs that have their hierarchies intersecting at their root nodes and thus need

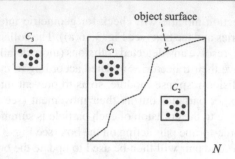

Fig. 3.17 An internal node N of the rigid–body hierarchy being tested for intersections against internal nodes C_1, C_2 and C_3 of the particle system's hierarchy. The nodes do not intersect, but an extra box–box inclusion test is performed. Node C_3 is located outside N and is discarded. Nodes C_1 and C_2 are inside N and their particles are added to the list of candidate particles that need to be further tested using the point-in-object algorithm discussed in Chap. 2. In this example, only the particles associated with C_2 will be detected inside the rigid body. They will be moved to their closest points on the object's surface at the beginning of the next time interval

to have the inside test performed on them. For each particle detected to be inside a rigid body at the beginning of the time interval, we move the particle to its closest point on the rigid body's surface, but keep the particle's dynamic state as is. In other words, the particle's position is instantaneously moved to match that of its closest point on the rigid body's surface, but its velocity, external and constraint forces are kept intact. Again, we use the hierarchical representation of both particle system and rigid body to speed the determination of which particles are inside the rigid body. First, we need to have both hierarchies built to reflect the position of their corresponding objects at the beginning of the new time interval. Notice that the position at the beginning of a new time interval matches the position at the end of the previous time interval, after all collisions have been processed. This very important observation is the main reason why we *always* build the hierarchies in the collision detection module using the objects' positions at t_1 instead of t_0. This is the case even for continuous collision detection where we build the hierarchies with the positions at t_1 and then refit them with the positions at t_0. So, instead of rebuilding the hierarchies at the beginning of the new time interval, we just need to refit them to reflect the changes in position due to the collisions resolved in the previous time interval. This approach is much more efficient than having to rebuild the hierarchies from scratch at the beginning of each simulation time interval.

Having the hierarchies updated with their objects' positions at the beginning of the new time interval, we can efficiently determine the particles that are inside the rigid body by executing a modified version of the hierarchical tree intersection algorithm presented in Sect. 2.5.1. The modification consists of the following. Whenever two internal nodes are found to be not intersecting, instead of discarding them as we do in the algorithm of Sect. 2.5.1, we perform one extra inclusion to check if the internal node corresponding to the particle system hierarchy is completely inside the internal node corresponding to the rigid body hierarchy (see Fig. 3.17). If the internal node is not completely inside the other node, then it must be outside and

Fig. 3.18 Particles O_1 and O_2 are traced back in time to the moment before their collision. The collision normal $\vec{n}$ is defined by the line connecting the center of the spheres. Its direction should be the opposite of the relative velocity $(\vec{v}_1 - \vec{v}_2)$ of the particles along the normal

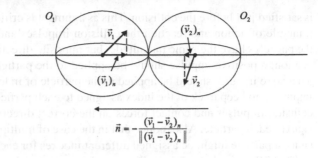

$$\vec{n} = -\frac{(\vec{v}_1 - \vec{v}_2)_n}{\left\|(\vec{v}_1 - \vec{v}_2)_n\right\|}$$

all particles associated with it are also outside the rigid body. The node is discarded in this case. However, if the internal node is in fact inside the other node, then all particles associated with it are added to a list of candidate particles that need to be further checked for inclusion in the rigid body. The particles associated with an internal node can be retrieved by following the links of its children nodes until all of its descendant leaf nodes are reached. As mentioned in Sect. 3.4.1, each leaf node is associated with a user-definable number of particles. Upon completion of the intersection algorithm, we have a list of candidate particles that are most likely inside the rigid body. Now, for each one of these particles, we perform a point-in-object test as described in Sect. 2.5.13 to detect whether the particle is actually inside the rigid body. If this is the case, we compute the closest point on the object's surface to which the particle will be moved to at the beginning of the next time interval.

3.5   Particle–Particle Collision Response

Whenever a particle–particle collision is detected, the collision-response module is invoked to compute the appropriate collision impulses or contact forces that will prevent interpenetration between the colliding particles. As explained in Sect. 3.4, the trajectories of the colliding particles are backtracked in time to the moment before their collision. The collision point and normal are then determined from their geometric displacement.

In the case of particle–particle collisions, the collision point is the mid-point between the actual particles' position, since the particles are treated as point-mass objects and all collision forces are directly applied to the center of the sphere representing each particle. The particles' shape is used to compute the normal direction of the collision. As indicated in Fig. 3.18, the collision normal is determined by connecting the center of the particles' spheres.

The colliding particles are arbitrarily assigned indexes 1 and 2, and the normal direction is selected such that the relative velocity $(\vec{v}_1 - \vec{v}_2)$ of the particles along the normal is negative just before the collision, that is, we choose $\vec{n}$ such that

$$(\vec{v}_1 - \vec{v}_2) \cdot \vec{n} < 0 \tag{3.8}$$

is satisfied just before the collision. This assignment is critical, since from Newton's principle of action and reaction the collision impulses and contact forces between the particles have the same magnitude, but opposite directions. Following our convention, a positive impulse should be applied to the particle with index 1, whereas a negative impulse should be applied to the particle of index 2. Therefore, it is very important to keep track of the index assigned to each particle so as to later apply the collision impulses and contact forces on the correct direction (i.e., with the correct sign) to each particle. Also, notice that in the case of multiple particle–particle collisions, a particle might be assigned different indexes for each collision it is involved.

The difference between a collision and a contact is determined from the module of the relative velocity along the collision normal, at the collision point. If the relative velocity of the particles along the normal, at the moment before the collision, is less than a threshold value, then the particles are said to be in contact and a contact force is computed to prevent their interpenetration. Otherwise, the particles are said to be in collision and an impulsive force is applied to instantaneously change the direction of motion of the particles to avoid the imminent interpenetration.

It may happen that several particles are involved in multiple collisions and contacts. If so, the collision-response module should first resolve all collisions by simultaneously computing all impulsive forces. Having determined all impulsive forces, the collision-response module proceeds by applying the impulses to the appropriate particles. By the time the impulses are applied, some of the contacts may break, depending on whether the relative velocity of the particles at their contact point, along the contact normal, is positive, zero or negative. A contact force is then simultaneously computed for all contacts that have a negative relative velocity along their contact normal.

3.5.1   Computing Impulsive Forces for a Single Collision

Let's start by examining the case where we have one or more simultaneous collisions, each involving two different particles. Here, each collision can be dealt with independently of the others, since they do not have particles in common.

Let collision C, involving particles O_1 and O_2, be defined by its collision normal $\vec{n}$ and tangent axes $\vec{t}$ and $\vec{k}$, as indicated in Fig. 3.19. Let $\vec{v}_1 = ((v_1)_n, (v_1)_t, (v_1)_k)$ and $\vec{v}_2 = ((v_2)_n, (v_2)_t, (v_2)_k)$ be the particles' velocities just before the collision, and $\vec{V}_1 = ((V_1)_n, (V_1)_t, (V_1)_k)$ and $\vec{V}_2 = ((V_2)_n, (V_2)_t, (V_2)_k)$ be their velocities just after the collision. We need to compute their velocities just after the collision, along with the impulsive force $\vec{P} = (P_n, P_t, P_k)$. This yields a total of nine unknowns ($\vec{P}$, $\vec{V}_1$ and $\vec{V}_2$), thus requiring the solution of a system with nine equations.

Applying the principle of impulse and momentum for each particle along the three collision axes, we obtain six out of the nine equations needed:

$$m_1(V_1)_n - m_1(v_1)_n = P_n \tag{3.9}$$

$$m_1(V_1)_t - m_1(v_1)_t = P_t \tag{3.10}$$

Fig. 3.19 Particles O_1 and O_2 just before their collision. The impulsive force is applied to each particle, with same magnitude, but opposite direction

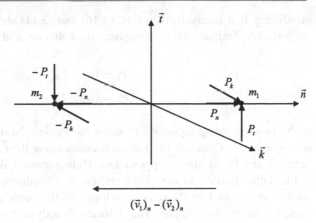

$$m_1(V_1)_k - m_1(v_1)_k = P_k \tag{3.11}$$

$$m_2(V_2)_n - m_2(v_2)_n = -P_n \tag{3.12}$$

$$m_2(V_2)_t - m_2(v_2)_t = -P_t \tag{3.13}$$

$$m_2(V_2)_k - m_2(v_2)_k = -P_k. \tag{3.14}$$

The next equation is obtained by the empirical relation involving the coefficient of restitution and the relative velocity of the particles along the normal direction of collision. Let e denote the coefficient of restitution along the normal direction. We have

$$(V_1)_n - (V_2)_n = -e\big((v_1)_n - (v_2)_n\big). \tag{3.15}$$

The remaining two equations are obtained from the Coulomb friction relations at the collision point. If the relative motion of the particles along $\vec{t}$ and $\vec{k}$ is zero just before the collision, that is, if

$$(v_1)_t - (v_2)_t = 0$$

$$(v_1)_k - (v_2)_k = 0,$$

then their relative motion will remain zero after the collision. More specifically, we use

$$(V_1)_t = (V_2)_t \tag{3.16}$$

$$(V_1)_k = (V_2)_k \tag{3.17}$$

as the two remaining equations to solve the system. However, if the relative motion is not zero, then the particles are sliding along $\vec{t}$ and $\vec{k}$ at the collision point. The collision impulse will then act on the opposite direction of motion, trying to prevent the sliding. If it succeeds, then Eqs. (3.16) and (3.17) should be used. Otherwise, the particles continue sliding throughout the collision, and we use

$$P_t = (\mu_d)_t P_n \tag{3.18}$$

$$P_k = (\mu_d)_k P_n \tag{3.19}$$

as the two remaining equations to solve the system. Notice that $(\mu_d)_t$ and $(\mu_d)_k$ are the dynamic Coulomb friction coefficients along the $\vec{t}$ and $\vec{k}$ axes, respectively. Since P_t and P_k are always opposing the sliding motion, the coefficients of friction can be either positive or negative to reflect that condition. The actual signs of the coefficients depend on the relative velocity of the particles along their associated axes, just before the collision. The signs are directly computed from

$$\text{sign}\big((\mu_d)_t\big) = \frac{(v_2)_t - (v_1)_t}{(v_2)_n - (v_1)_n} \tag{3.20}$$

$$\text{sign}\big((\mu_d)_k\big) = \frac{(v_2)_k - (v_1)_k}{(v_2)_n - (v_1)_n}. \tag{3.21}$$

This directional-friction model is a generalization of the widely used model of relating the tangential and normal impulses using just one omnidirectional coefficient of friction μ_d, as in

$$P_{tk} = \mu_d P_n, \tag{3.22}$$

where P_{tk} is the impulse on the tangent plane given by

$$P_{tk} = \sqrt{P_t^2 + P_k^2}.$$

For example, if friction is isotropic, that is, independent of direction, then we can write

$$(\mu_d)_t = \mu_d \cos\phi$$

$$(\mu_d)_k = \mu_d \sin\phi$$

for some angle ϕ, so

$$P_{tk} = \sqrt{P_t^2 + P_k^2}$$
$$= \sqrt{(\mu_d)^2 P_n^2 \cos\phi^2 + (\mu_d)^2 P_n^2 \sin\phi^2}$$
$$= \mu_d P_n,$$

which is the same result obtained using the omnidirectional-friction model of Eq. (3.22). The main advantage of using the directional-friction model is that the nonlinear equation

$$|P_{tk}| = \sqrt{P_t^2 + P_k^2} \leq \mu_d P_n,$$

which needs to be enforced when the particles are not sliding at the collision point, can be substituted for two linear equations

$$|P_t| \leq \mu_t P_n$$
$$|P_k| \leq \mu_k P_n$$

which are equivalent to the non-linear equation if friction is isotropic, and, most important, are easier to handle in matrix form, as we shall see shortly.

So, as far as friction is concerned, we have to consider two possible cases. In the first case, we assume the particles continue sliding on the tangent plane after collision, and we use Eqs. (3.9) to (3.15) with Eqs. (3.18) and (3.19) to compute the collision impulse and velocities after the collision. In the second case, the particles are not sliding on the tangent plane after collision, and we use Eqs. (3.9) to (3.15) with Eqs. (3.16) and (3.17) instead. For now, let's focus on the solution corresponding to the first case. Later, we consider the required modifications needed to address the second case.

Summing Eqs. (3.9) and (3.12), (3.10) and (3.13), (3.11) and (3.14), we get

$$m_1(V_1)_n + m_2(V_2)_n = m_1(v_1)_n + m_2(v_2)_n \tag{3.23}$$
$$m_1(V_1)_t + m_2(V_2)_t = m_1(v_1)_t + m_2(v_2)_t \tag{3.24}$$
$$m_1(V_1)_k + m_2(V_2)_k = m_1(v_1)_k + m_2(v_2)_k. \tag{3.25}$$

Subtracting the same equations pair-wise, we obtain

$$P_n = \frac{(m_1(V_1)_n - m_2(V_2)_n) - (m_1(v_1)_n - m_2(v_2)_n)}{2} \tag{3.26}$$
$$P_t = \frac{(m_1(V_1)_t - m_2(V_2)_t) - (m_1(v_1)_t - m_2(v_2)_t)}{2} \tag{3.27}$$
$$P_k = \frac{(m_1(V_1)_k - m_2(V_2)_k) - (m_1(v_1)_k - m_2(v_2)_k)}{2}. \tag{3.28}$$

Substituting Eqs. (3.26) to (3.28) into (3.18) and (3.19) gives

$$(\mu_d)_t m_1(V_1)_n - m_1(V_1)_t - (\mu_d)_t m_2(V_2)_n + m_2(V_2)_t$$
$$= (\mu_d)_t m_1(v_1)_n - m_1(v_1)_t - (\mu_d)_t m_2(v_2)_n + m_2(v_2)_t \tag{3.29}$$
$$(\mu_d)_k m_1(V_1)_n - m_1(V_1)_k - (\mu_d)_k m_2(V_2)_n + m_2(V_2)_k$$
$$= (\mu_d)_k m_1(v_1)_n - m_1(v_1)_k - (\mu_d)_k m_2(v_2)_n + m_2(v_2)_k. \tag{3.30}$$

Making a change of variables such that

$$(U_i)_j = m_i((V_i)_j - (v_i)_j), \quad \text{for } i = \{1, 2\}, \ j = \{n, t, k\},$$

the system defined by Eqs. (3.23) to (3.25), (3.15), (3.29) and (3.30) can then be written as

$$(U_1)_n + (U_2)_n = 0$$
$$(U_1)_t + (U_2)_t = 0$$
$$(U_1)_k + (U_2)_k = 0$$
$$\frac{(U_1)_n}{m_1} - \frac{(U_2)_n}{m_2} = -(1+e)((v_1)_n - (v_2)_n)$$
$$(\mu_d)_t (U_1)_n - (U_1)_t - (\mu_d)_t (U_2)_n + (U_2)_t = 0$$
$$(\mu_d)_k (U_1)_n - (U_1)_k - (\mu_d)_k (U_2)_n + (U_2)_k = 0.$$

Solving for the $(U_i)_j$, we obtain

$$(U_1)_n = m_1((V_1)_n - (v_1)_n)$$
$$= m_{12}(1+e)((v_2)_n - (v_1)_n) \tag{3.31}$$
$$(U_1)_t = m_1((V_1)_t - (v_1)_t)$$
$$= (\mu_d)_t m_{12}(1+e)((v_2)_n - (v_1)_n) \tag{3.32}$$
$$(U_1)_k = m_1((V_1)_k - (v_1)_k)$$
$$= (\mu_d)_k m_{12}(1+e)((v_2)_n - (v_1)_n) \tag{3.33}$$
$$(U_2)_n = m_2((V_2)_n - (v_2)_n)$$
$$= -m_{12}(1+e)((v_2)_n - (v_1)_n) \tag{3.34}$$
$$(U_2)_t = m_2((V_2)_t - (v_2)_t)$$
$$= -(\mu_d)_t m_{12}(1+e)((v_2)_n - (v_1)_n) \tag{3.35}$$
$$(U_2)_k = m_2((V_2)_k - (v_2)_k)$$
$$= -(\mu_d)_k m_{12}(1+e)((v_2)_n - (v_1)_n), \tag{3.36}$$

where

$$m_{12} = \frac{m_1 m_2}{(m_1 + m_2)}.$$

The particle velocities $\vec{V}_1$ and $\vec{V}_2$ just after the collision are directly obtained from Eqs. (3.31) to (3.36). Substituting their values into Eqs. (3.26) to (3.28), we immediately get the impulse $\vec{P}$.

All derivations up till now considered the case wherein the colliding particles continue sliding throughout the collision. If the particles are not sliding after collision, either because they were not sliding before the collision or the sliding motion stopped during the collision, then Eqs. (3.16) and (3.17) should be used instead of Eqs. (3.18) and (3.19), which are repeated here for convenience:

$$(V_1)_t = (V_2)_t$$
$$(V_1)_k = (V_2)_k.$$

Notice that the sliding motion on the tangent plane is directly affected by the coefficients of restitution and friction, as well as by the relative velocities of the particles just before the collision. Intuitively, for a given coefficient of restitution and relative velocities, the sliding motion will continue if the coefficient of friction is small, or will stop if the coefficient of friction is sufficiently large. Therefore, there exists a critical coefficient of friction value associated with a given coefficient of restitution and relative velocity of the particles. If the actual coefficient of friction is less than the critical coefficient of friction, then slide continues throughout the collision and the system equations associated with the first case should be considered. However, if the actual coefficient of friction is greater than or equal to the critical coefficient of friction, then slide stops somewhere during the collision and the system equations associated with the second case should be considered instead.

Let's derive an expression for computing the critical coefficient of friction. If we substitute back $(V_1)_t$, $(V_1)_k$, $(V_2)_t$ and $(V_2)_k$ obtained from Eqs. (3.32), (3.33), (3.35) and (3.36), respectively, into Eqs. (3.18) and (3.19), we get

$$\frac{(v_1)_t + (\mu_d)_t m_{12}(1+e)((v_2)_n - (v_1)_n)}{m_1}$$
$$= \frac{(v_2)_t - (\mu_d)_t m_{12}(1+e)((v_2)_n - (v_1)_n)}{m_2}$$
$$\frac{(v_1)_k + (\mu_d)_k m_{12}(1+e)((v_2)_n - (v_1)_n)}{m_1}$$
$$= \frac{(v_2)_k - (\mu_d)_k m_{12}(1+e)((v_2)_n - (v_1)_n)}{m_2}.$$

Solving for $(\mu_d)_t$ and $(\mu_d)_k$, we obtain

$$(\mu_d)_t = (\mu_d)_t^c = \frac{1}{(1+e)} \frac{((v_2)_t - (v_1)_t)}{((v_2)_n - (v_1)_n)} \tag{3.37}$$

$$(\mu_d)_k = (\mu_d)_k^c = \frac{1}{(1+e)} \frac{((v_2)_k - (v_1)_k)}{((v_2)_n - (v_1)_n)}, \tag{3.38}$$

where $(\mu_d)_t^c$ and $(\mu_d)_k^c$ are the critical values of the coefficient of friction such that the sliding motion stops exactly at the end of the collision.

We do the following in practice. First, compute the critical coefficient of friction using Eqs. (3.37) and (3.38). Then, compare the actual coefficient of friction $(\mu_d)_t$ and $(\mu_d)_k$ to their associated critical values. If $(\mu_d)_t < (\mu_d)_t^c$, then sliding continues along $\vec{t}$ and we use Eq. (3.18). Else, if $(\mu_d)_t \geq (\mu_d)_t^c$, then sliding along $\vec{t}$ stops during the collision and we use Eq. (3.16). The same analysis is used for comparing $(\mu_d)_k$ with $(\mu_d)_k^c$ and selecting the appropriate system equation.

Also, notice that there is no need to derive a new set of solutions to the system equations for the case in which sliding stops during the collision; we just need to use the critical value of the coefficient of friction instead of the actual friction value in the solution equations already obtained. Recall that, if we set $(\mu_d)_t = (\mu_d)_t^c$, then we immediately obtain the desired condition $(V_1)_t = (V_2)_t$. By analogy, if we set $(\mu_d)_k = (\mu_d)_k^c$, we get $(V_1)_k = (V_2)_k$.

An alternate representation of the system equations for computing the collision impulses commonly found in the literature is the partitioned-matrix representation. Even though this representation is not particularly useful for the singe-collision case because we were able to compute the impulse and final velocities, it proves to be extremely useful when dealing with multiple simultaneous collisions. Here, we shall focus on the partitioned-matrix representation of a single collision. In Sect. 3.5.2, we extend it to the multiple-collision case.

As previously explained, we use Eqs. (3.9) to (3.15) with Eqs. (3.18) and (3.19) whenever the particles continue sliding on the tangent plane after collision. In this case, the system equations can be put into the following matrix format:

$$
\begin{pmatrix}
0 & 0 & 0 & 1 & 0 & 0 & -1 & 0 & 0 \\
-(\mu_d)_t & 1 & 0 & 0 & 0 & 0 & 0 & 0 & 0 \\
-(\mu_d)_k & 1 & 0 & 0 & 0 & 0 & 0 & 0 & 0 \\
-1 & 0 & 0 & m_1 & 0 & 0 & 0 & 0 & 0 \\
0 & -1 & 0 & 0 & m_1 & 0 & 0 & 0 & 0 \\
0 & 0 & -1 & 0 & 0 & m_1 & 0 & 0 & 0 \\
1 & 0 & 0 & m_2 & 0 & 0 & 0 & 0 & 0 \\
0 & 1 & 0 & 0 & m_2 & 0 & 0 & 0 & 0 \\
0 & 0 & 1 & 0 & 0 & m_2 & 0 & 0 & 0
\end{pmatrix}
\begin{pmatrix}
(P_{1,2})_n \\
(P_{1,2})_t \\
(P_{1,2})_k \\
(V_1)_n \\
(V_1)_t \\
(V_1)_k \\
(V_2)_n \\
(V_2)_t \\
(V_2)_k
\end{pmatrix}
$$

$$
=
\begin{pmatrix}
-e((v_1)_n - (v_2)_n) \\
0 \\
0 \\
m_1(v_1)_n \\
m_1(v_1)_t \\
m_1(v_1)_k \\
m_2(v_2)_n \\
m_2(v_2)_t \\
m_2(v_2)_k
\end{pmatrix}
\tag{3.39}
$$

where $\vec{P}_{1,2} = ((P_{1,2})_n, (P_{1,2})_t, (P_{1,2})_k)$ is the collision impulse between particles O_1 and O_2.

If sliding along the $\vec{t}$ direction stops by the end of the collision, then we need to use Eq. (3.16) instead of Eq. (3.18). This in turn has the effect of substituting the second row of the system matrix for

$$
\begin{pmatrix} 0 & 0 & 0 & 0 & 1 & 0 & 0 & -1 & 0 \end{pmatrix}.
$$

Conversely, if sliding along the $\vec{k}$ directions stops by the end of the collision, then we need to substitute the third row of the system matrix for

$$\begin{pmatrix} 0 & 0 & 0 & 0 & 0 & 1 & 0 & 0 & -1 \end{pmatrix}.$$

The partitioned-matrix representation of the system can be directly obtained from Eq. (3.39), and is given by

$$\begin{pmatrix} \mathbf{A}_{1,2} & \mathbf{B}_{1,2} & -\mathbf{B}_{1,2} \\ -\mathbf{I} & m_1\mathbf{I} & \mathbf{0} \\ \mathbf{I} & \mathbf{0} & m_2\mathbf{I} \end{pmatrix} \begin{pmatrix} \vec{P}_{1,2} \\ \vec{V}_1 \\ \vec{V}_2 \end{pmatrix} = \begin{pmatrix} \vec{d}_{1,2} \\ m_1\vec{v}_1 \\ m_2\vec{v}_2 \end{pmatrix}, \tag{3.40}$$

where $\mathbf{I}$ is the 3×3 identity matrix, $\mathbf{0}$ is the 3×3 zero matrix, and

$$\vec{d}_{1,2} = \begin{pmatrix} -e((v_1)_n - (v_2)_n) \\ 0 \\ 0 \end{pmatrix}.$$

The matrices $\mathbf{A}_{1,2}$ and $\mathbf{B}_{1,2}$ are chosen depending on whether sliding continues along the tangent plane after the collision ends. We have four possible cases to consider.

1. If $(\mu_d)_t < (\mu_d)_t^c$ and $(\mu_d)_k < (\mu_d)_k^c$, then:

$$\mathbf{A}_{1,2} = \begin{pmatrix} 0 & 0 & 0 \\ -(\mu_d)_t & 1 & 0 \\ -(\mu_d)_k & 1 & 0 \end{pmatrix} \quad \text{and} \quad \mathbf{B}_{1,2} = \begin{pmatrix} 1 & 0 & 0 \\ 0 & 0 & 0 \\ 0 & 0 & 0 \end{pmatrix}.$$

2. If $(\mu_d)_t \geq (\mu_d)_t^c$ and $(\mu_d)_k < (\mu_d)_k^c$, then:

$$\mathbf{A}_{1,2} = \begin{pmatrix} 0 & 0 & 0 \\ 0 & 0 & 0 \\ -(\mu_d)_k & 1 & 0 \end{pmatrix} \quad \text{and} \quad \mathbf{B}_{1,2} = \begin{pmatrix} 1 & 0 & 0 \\ 0 & 1 & 0 \\ 0 & 0 & 0 \end{pmatrix}.$$

3. If $(\mu_d)_t < (\mu_d)_t^c$ and $(\mu_d)_k \geq (\mu_d)_k^c$, then:

$$\mathbf{A}_{1,2} = \begin{pmatrix} 0 & 0 & 0 \\ -(\mu_d)_t & 1 & 0 \\ 0 & 0 & 0 \end{pmatrix} \quad \text{and} \quad \mathbf{B}_{1,2} = \begin{pmatrix} 1 & 0 & 0 \\ 0 & 0 & 0 \\ 0 & 0 & 1 \end{pmatrix}.$$

4. If $(\mu_d)_t \geq (\mu_d)_t^c$ and $(\mu_d)_k \geq (\mu_d)_k^c$ then $\mathbf{A}_{1,2} = \mathbf{0}$ and $\mathbf{B}_{1,2} = \mathbf{I}$.

Notice that the first row of the partitioned matrix shown in (3.40) contains the coefficient of restitution and friction equations, and it is associated with the state variable $\vec{P}_{1,2}$. The second and third rows contain the conservation-of-linear-momentum equations associated with the final velocities $\vec{V}_1$ and $\vec{V}_2$, respectively. This ordering is extremely important because it can significantly simplify the updates required for the multiple-collision case.

Fig. 3.20 Multiple particle collisions separated into three clusters. Particle O_i is added to cluster G_j if it is colliding with at least one particle already in G_j. The collision-response module resolves each cluster in parallel, since they have no collisions in common and therefore can be viewed as independent groups of collisions

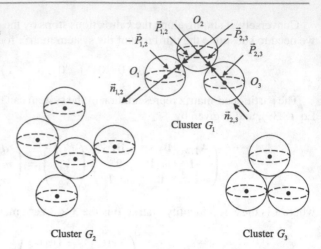

Cluster G_2 Cluster G_3

3.5.2 Computing Impulsive Forces for Multiple Simultaneous Collisions

During a simulation, there might be situations in which three or more particles are simultaneously colliding with each other. In these cases, instead of resolving one collision at a time not taking into account the presence of the others, the simulation engine needs to group the particles into clusters that share at least one collision. The collisions within each cluster can then be simultaneously resolved independent of all other clusters (see Fig. 3.20).

Consider the computation of the collision impulses associated with cluster G_1, as shown in Fig. 3.20. Let collisions C_1 and C_2 be the collisions $(O_1 - O_2)$ and $(O_2 - O_3)$, respectively. As far as particle O_2 is concerned, the linear momentum equation owing to both collisions becomes

$$m_2(\vec{V}_2 - \vec{v}_2) = -\vec{P}_{1,2} + \vec{P}_{2 \mapsto 1, 3 \mapsto 2}, \tag{3.41}$$

where $P_{2 \mapsto 1, 3 \mapsto 2}$ is the impulse $\vec{P}_{2,3}$ of collision C_2 expressed in the local coordinate frame[2] associated with collision C_1. The minus sign on $\vec{P}_{1,2}$ shows that particle O_2 has index 2 with respect to collision C_1.

Clearly, the impulse owing to collision C_2 will also affect the computation of the impulse owing to collision C_1, and vice-versa. Therefore, the correct way to compute the collision impulses is to take both collisions into account when solving the system of equations. Recall from Sect. 3.5.1 that we adopted the convention that a positive impulse is applied to the particle with index 1, and a negative impulse is applied to the particle with index 2. The choice of indexes is related to the relative velocities of the particles along the collision normal, such that Eq. (3.8) is satisfied at the moment just before the collision.

---

[2]The local-coordinate frame is defined by the collision normal and tangent plane.

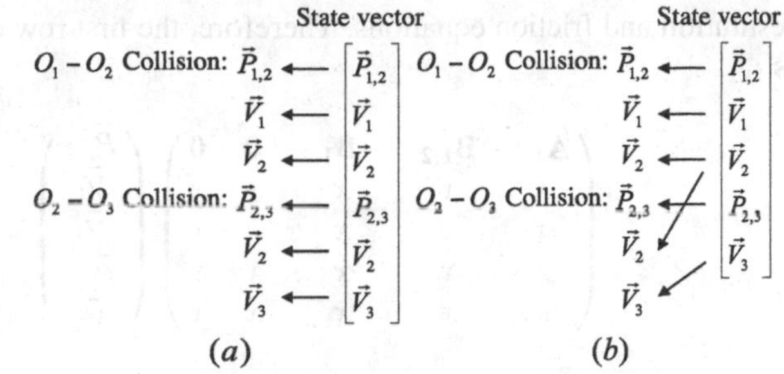

Fig. 3.21 (a) A naive concatenation creates multiple entries for the final velocities of particles that are involved in more than one collision; (b) The state-vector variables should have a link back to their collisions. More than one link is used for multiple collisions, as in the case of $\vec{V}_2$

$$O_1 - O_2 \text{ Collision: } \vec{P}_{1,2} \longleftarrow \begin{bmatrix} \vec{P}_{1,2} \\ \vec{V}_1 \\ \vec{V}_2 \\ \vec{P}_{2,3} \\ \vec{V}_2 \\ \vec{V}_3 \end{bmatrix}$$

$$\begin{aligned} \vec{V}_1 &\longleftarrow \vec{V}_1 \\ \vec{V}_2 &\longleftarrow \vec{V}_2 \end{aligned}$$

$$O_2 - O_3 \text{ Collision: } \vec{P}_{2,3} \longleftarrow$$

(a)

$$O_1 - O_2 \text{ Collision: } \vec{P}_{1,2} \longleftarrow \begin{bmatrix} \vec{P}_{1,2} \\ \vec{V}_1 \\ \vec{V}_2 \\ \vec{P}_{2,3} \\ \vec{V}_3 \end{bmatrix}$$

$$\begin{aligned} \vec{V}_1 &\longleftarrow \vec{V}_1 \\ \vec{V}_2 &\longleftarrow \vec{V}_2 \end{aligned}$$

$$O_2 - O_3 \text{ Collision: } \vec{P}_{2,3} \not\longleftarrow$$

(b)

If a particle is involved in multiple collisions, it is possible to have it assigned to different indexes for each collision. For the particular situation of cluster G_1, particle O_2 has index 2 with respect to its collision with particle O_1, and index 1 with respect to its collision with particle O_3. This in turn affects the choice of sign when combining the multiple-collision impulses in the system equations (i.e., the minus sign of $\vec{P}_{1,2}$ and the plus sign of $P_{2\mapsto1,3\mapsto2}$ in Eq. (3.41)). Moreover, the collision normal and tangent plane are different for each collision. So, we also need to implement a change of base between the collision impulses before combining them (i.e., the vector $P_{2\mapsto1,3\mapsto2}$ used in Eq. (3.41)).

The best way to deal with multiple collisions is to represent the system equations associated with each cluster in its partitioned matrix form

$$A\vec{x} = \vec{b},$$

where $\vec{x}$ is the state vector containing the variables that need to be determined. In the case of a single collision, the state vector is defined by the collision impulse and final velocities of the colliding particles. However, when dealing with multiple collisions, the state vector can be viewed as the concatenation of several single-collision state vectors, with the added complexity that no variables should be accounted for more than once. For instance, Fig. 3.21(a) shows the result of a naive concatenation of state vectors for the multiple collisions associated with cluster G_1 of Fig. 3.20.

Since particle O_2 is involved in both collisions, its final velocity $\vec{V}_2$ is counted twice. The correct way to create the state vector is then to keep track of the variables already added, and mark as "common" those added more than once. This is illustrated in Fig. 3.21(b).

Having determined the state vector associated with a cluster, the next step is to fill in the rows of matrix $\mathbf{A}$ and vector $\vec{b}$. This can be done by considering the equation associated with the first link of each variable in the state vector. For example, for the cluster G_1 of Fig. 3.20, the first variable of the state vector is $\vec{P}_{1,2}$. This variable is linked to the $(O_1 - O_2)$ collision. Its associated equations are the coefficient of restitution and friction equations. Therefore, the first row of matrix $\mathbf{A}$ and vector $\vec{b}$ is

$$
\begin{pmatrix}
\mathbf{A}_{1,2} & \mathbf{B}_{1,2} & -\mathbf{B}_{1,2} & 0 & 0 \\
x & x & x & x & x \\
x & x & x & x & x \\
x & x & x & x & x \\
x & x & x & x & x
\end{pmatrix}
\begin{pmatrix}
\vec{P}_{1,2} \\
\vec{V}_1 \\
\vec{V}_2 \\
\vec{P}_{2,3} \\
\vec{V}_3
\end{pmatrix}
=
\begin{pmatrix}
\vec{d}_{1,2} \\
x \\
x \\
x \\
x
\end{pmatrix}.
$$

The second variable of the state vector is $\vec{V}_1$. This variable is also linked to the $(O_1 - O_2)$ collision. Its associated equations are the conservation of linear momentum for particle O_1. So, the second row of matrix $\mathbf{A}$ and vector $\vec{b}$ is

$$
\begin{pmatrix}
\mathbf{A}_{1,2} & \mathbf{B}_{1,2} & -\mathbf{B}_{1,2} & 0 & 0 \\
-\mathbf{I} & m_1\mathbf{I} & 0 & 0 & 0 \\
x & x & x & x & x \\
x & x & x & x & x \\
x & x & x & x & x
\end{pmatrix}
\begin{pmatrix}
\vec{P}_{1,2} \\
\vec{V}_1 \\
\vec{V}_2 \\
\vec{P}_{2,3} \\
\vec{V}_3
\end{pmatrix}
=
\begin{pmatrix}
\vec{d}_{1,2} \\
m_1\vec{v}_1 \\
x \\
x \\
x
\end{pmatrix}.
$$

Doing the same for all other state variables, we obtain

$$
\begin{pmatrix}
\mathbf{A}_{1,2} & \mathbf{B}_{1,2} & -\mathbf{B}_{1,2} & 0 & 0 \\
-\mathbf{I} & m_1\mathbf{I} & 0 & 0 & 0 \\
\mathbf{I} & 0 & m_2\mathbf{I} & 0 & 0 \\
0 & 0 & \mathbf{B}_{2,3} & \mathbf{A}_{2,3} & -\mathbf{B}_{2,3} \\
0 & 0 & 0 & \mathbf{I} & m_3\mathbf{I}
\end{pmatrix}
\begin{pmatrix}
\vec{P}_{1,2} \\
\vec{V}_1 \\
\vec{V}_2 \\
\vec{P}_{2,3} \\
\vec{V}_3
\end{pmatrix}
=
\begin{pmatrix}
\vec{d}_{1,2} \\
m_1\vec{v}_1 \\
m_2\vec{v}_2 \\
\vec{d}_{2,3} \\
m_3\vec{v}_3
\end{pmatrix}. \qquad (3.42)
$$

Notice the difference between rows 1 and 4 of the system matrix shown in Eq. (3.42). Since $\vec{V}_2$ is common to both $(O_1 - O_2)$ and $(O_2 - O_3)$ collisions, the matrices $\mathbf{A}_{2,3}$ and $\mathbf{B}_{2,3}$ were rearranged to correctly multiply their associated state-vector variables. The correct order is $\mathbf{B}_{2,3}$ multiplying the linear velocity of the particle with index 1, $\mathbf{A}_{2,3}$ multiplying the impulse associated with collision $(O_2 - O_3)$ and $(-\mathbf{B}_{2,3})$ multiplying the linear velocity of the particle with index 2. Because for collision $O_2 - O_3$ particle O_2 is associated with index 1 and particle O_3 with index 2, the arrangement of these block matrices in row 4 of Eq. (3.42) is different from the one obtained for row 1.

Also, notice that Eq. (3.42) was built following *only* the first link of each state-vector variable. Now, we need to update Eq. (3.42) with the multiple-collision terms. This can be done by considering the state variables that have more than one associated link. The first link was used to define the row. The following links are used to update some elements of the row with the multiple-collision terms.

In general, if particle O_i is involved in more than one collision, then the row associated with $\vec{V}_i$, that is, the row associated with its final velocity, needs to be updated. Say for example that particle O_i has a second link to particle O_j. Let $\vec{P}_{i,j}$

designate the state-vector variable corresponding to the impulse associated with this collision. So, the index of $\vec{V}_i$ in the state vector defines the row of the system matrix to be updated, and the index of $\vec{P}_{i,j}$ in the state vector defines the column of the system matrix that needs to be updated. Therefore, we need to update the element

$$[\text{index of } \vec{V}_i][\text{index of } \vec{P}_{i,j}]$$

of the system matrix given in Eq. (3.42).

The actual update consists of accounting for $\vec{P}_{i,j}$ in the linear momentum equations associated with particle O_i. This can be done by expressing $\vec{P}_{i,j}$ with respect to the local-coordinate frame of the collision corresponding to the first link of the state variable $\vec{V}_i$.

Say for example that the first link of the state variable $\vec{V}_i$ is associated with collision C_m involving particles O_i and O_m. Let the local-coordinate frame $\mathcal{F}_{m,i}$ of collision $(O_m - O_i)$ be defined by vectors $\vec{n}_{m,i}$, $\vec{t}_{m,i}$ and $\vec{k}_{m,i}$.

The second link of the state variable $\vec{V}_i$ is associated with collision C_j involving particles O_i and O_j. Let the local-coordinate frame $\mathcal{F}_{i,j}$ of collision $(O_i - O_j)$ be defined by vectors $\vec{n}_{i,j}$, $\vec{t}_{i,j}$ and $\vec{k}_{i,j}$. The collision impulse $\vec{P}_{i,j}$ defined in the local frame $\mathcal{F}_{i,j}$ is expressed in the local frame $\mathcal{F}_{m,i}$ as

$$\vec{P}_{i\mapsto m,j\mapsto i} = \mathbf{M}_{i\mapsto m,j\mapsto i} \vec{P}_{i,j},$$

with

$$\mathbf{M}_{i\mapsto m,j\mapsto i} = \lambda \begin{pmatrix} \vec{n}_{i,j}\cdot\vec{n}_{m,i} & \vec{n}_{i,j}\cdot\vec{t}_{m,i} & \vec{n}_{i,j}\cdot\vec{k}_{m,i} \\ \vec{t}_{i,j}\cdot\vec{n}_{m,i} & \vec{t}_{i,j}\cdot\vec{t}_{m,i} & \vec{t}_{i,j}\cdot\vec{k}_{m,i} \\ \vec{k}_{i,j}\cdot\vec{n}_{m,i} & \vec{k}_{i,j}\cdot\vec{t}_{m,i} & \vec{k}_{i,j}\cdot\vec{k}_{m,i} \end{pmatrix}.$$

The variable λ can be either 1 or -1, depending whether particle O_i is assigned to index 2 or 1 in collision O_j. The necessary multiple-collision term update is then

$$[\text{index of } \vec{V}_i][\text{index of } \vec{P}_{i,j}] = \vec{P}_{i\mapsto j,i\mapsto m}.$$

As an example, let's apply this multiple-collision term update to the cluster G_1 of Fig. 3.21. In this example, the second link of $\vec{V}_2$ points to the collision of particle O_2 with particle O_3. Therefore, we need to update the element at

$$[\text{index of } \vec{V}_2][\text{index of } \vec{P}_{2,3}] = [3,4]$$

in the system matrix of Eq. (3.42). The actual update will be to substitute the current 0 element at position $[3, 4]$ for

$$\mathbf{M}_{2\mapsto 1,3\mapsto 2} = \lambda \begin{pmatrix} \vec{n}_{2,3}\cdot\vec{n}_{1,2} & \vec{n}_{2,3}\cdot\vec{t}_{1,2} & \vec{n}_{2,3}\cdot\vec{k}_{1,2} \\ \vec{t}_{2,3}\cdot\vec{n}_{1,2} & \vec{t}_{2,3}\cdot\vec{t}_{1,2} & \vec{t}_{2,3}\cdot\vec{k}_{1,2} \\ \vec{k}_{2,3}\cdot\vec{n}_{1,2} & \vec{k}_{2,3}\cdot\vec{t}_{1,2} & \vec{k}_{2,3}\cdot\vec{k}_{1,2} \end{pmatrix}, \tag{3.43}$$

where frame $\mathcal{F}_{1,2}$ is defined by vectors $\vec{n}_{1,2}$, $\vec{t}_{1,2}$ and $\vec{k}_{1,2}$, and frame $\mathcal{F}_{2,3}$ is defined by vectors $\vec{n}_{2,3}$, $\vec{t}_{2,3}$ and $\vec{k}_{2,3}$. Also, since particle O_2 is assigned to index 1 in its collision with particle O_3 (see Fig. 3.20), we should use $\lambda = +1$ in Eq. (3.43). That is, we need to set

$$\text{element } [3,4] = M_{2\mapsto 1,\, 3\mapsto 2}.$$

The final system matrix for this particular example is then:

$$\begin{pmatrix} \mathbf{A}_{1,2} & \mathbf{B}_{1,2} & -\mathbf{B}_{1,2} & 0 & 0 \\ -\mathbf{I} & m_1\mathbf{I} & 0 & 0 & 0 \\ \mathbf{I} & 0 & m_2\mathbf{I} & \mathbf{M}_{2\mapsto 1,\, 3\mapsto 2} & 0 \\ 0 & 0 & \mathbf{B}_{2,3} & \mathbf{A}_{2,3} & -\mathbf{B}_{2,3} \\ 0 & 0 & 0 & \mathbf{I} & m_3\mathbf{I} \end{pmatrix} \begin{pmatrix} \vec{P}_{1,2} \\ \vec{V}_1 \\ \vec{V}_2 \\ \vec{P}_{2,3} \\ \vec{V}_3 \end{pmatrix} = \begin{pmatrix} \vec{d}_{1,2} \\ m_1\vec{v}_1 \\ m_2\vec{v}_2 \\ \vec{d}_{2,3} \\ m_3\vec{v}_3 \end{pmatrix}.$$

In summary, for each state-vector variable with more than one link, we need to update the elements of the system matrix corresponding to each of these collisions. When all elements are updated, we solve the resulting linear system using, for example, the Gaussian elimination method. Another option would be to use specialized methods to solve sparse linear systems, since the system matrix is often sparse. The solution would then give the correct values of the state-vector variables to be used by the collision-response module.

3.5.3 Computing Contact Forces for a Single Contact

Two particles are said to be in contact whenever their relative velocities along the collision normal are either zero, or less than an user-adjustable threshold value. In these cases, a contact force should be applied, instead of the impulsive force described in Sect. 3.5.1.

The contact-force computation is considerably different from the impulsive-force computation. In the latter case, we have the equations of conservation of linear momentum and the coefficients of friction and restitution defining the system equations. Here, we need to derive other conditions to compute the contact forces, based on the contact geometry[3] and dynamic state of each particle.

The first condition states that the relative acceleration of the particles at the contact point, along the contact normal, should be greater than or equal to zero, assuming that a negative value indicates that the particles are accelerating towards each other. In this case, if the computed contact force is such that the relative acceleration at the contact point along the contact normal is zero, then the particles remain in contact. However, if their relative acceleration is greater than zero, then contact is about to break.

---

[3]When collision becomes a contact, the collision normal will also be referred to as the contact normal.

Fig. 3.22 (a) Particles O_1 and O_2 are about to make contact with other at points $\vec{p}_1$ and $\vec{p}_2$; (b) Contact is established whenever $\vec{p}_1 = \vec{p}_2$; (c) Interpenetration occurs if $(\vec{p}_1 - \vec{p}_2) \cdot \vec{n} < 0$, where $\vec{n}$ is the contact normal

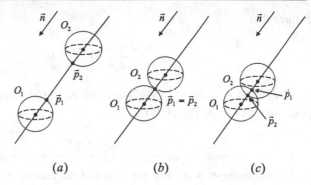

$(a) \qquad\qquad (b) \qquad\qquad (c)$

The second condition implies that the contact-force component along the contact normal should be greater than or equal to zero, indicating that the particles are being pushed away from each other. The contact force is not allowed to have a negative value, that is, is not allowed to keep the particles connected to each other, preventing their separation.

The third and final condition states that the contact force should be set to zero if the contact between the particles is about to break. In other words, if the relative acceleration at the contact point, along the contact normal, is greater than zero, then contact is about to break and the contact force should be set to zero.

Let's translate these three conditions into meaningful equations that can be used to compute the contact force. Figure 3.22 illustrates a typical situation in which particles O_1 and O_2 are shown at the moment before contact, in contact, and inter-penetrating each other in case the contact force is not applied.

Let $\vec{p}_1(t)$ and $\vec{p}_2(t)$ be the position of particles O_1 and O_2 that are about to be in contact. Consider the vector $\vec{q}(t)$ defined as

$$\vec{q}(t) = \begin{pmatrix} q_n(t) \\ q_t(t) \\ q_k(t) \end{pmatrix} = \begin{pmatrix} (\vec{p}_1(t) - \vec{p}_2(t)) \cdot \vec{n}(t) \\ (\vec{p}_1(t) - \vec{p}_2(t)) \cdot \vec{t}(t) \\ (\vec{p}_1(t) - \vec{p}_2(t)) \cdot \vec{k}(t) \end{pmatrix}, \qquad (3.44)$$

where $\vec{n}(t)$ is the contact normal, pointing from particle O_2 to particle O_1, and $\vec{t}(t)$ and $\vec{k}(t)$ are vectors defining the tangent plane at the contact. Clearly, $q_n(t)$ defines a distance measure between points $\vec{p}_1(t)$ and $\vec{p}_2(t)$, along the contact normal, as a function of time. We have $q_n(t) > 0$ if the particles are separated, $q_n(t) = 0$ if the particles are in contact, and $q_n(t) < 0$ if the particles are interpenetrating (see Fig. 3.22). Let t_c be the instant at which contact is established, that is

$$\vec{q}(t_c) = \vec{0}.$$

The first condition states that the relative acceleration at the contact point, along the contact normal, should be greater than or equal to zero. This is equivalent to enforce that

$$\left.\frac{d^2 q_n(t)}{dt^2}\right|_{t=t_c} \geq 0. \tag{3.45}$$

If we let $\vec{a}(t) = (a_n(t), a_t(t), a_k(t))$ be the relative acceleration at the contact point, we can rewrite Eq. (3.45) as

$$a_n(t_c) \geq 0. \tag{3.46}$$

The components $a_t(t)$ and $a_k(t)$ define the relative acceleration at the contact point on the tangent plane of the contact. They are only used if static or dynamic friction is considered at the contact point, as will be explained later in this section.

The second condition states that the contact-force component along the contact normal should be nonnegative, that is

$$F_n \geq 0, \tag{3.47}$$

where $\vec{F} = (F_n, F_t, F_k)$ is the contact force to be determined. If friction is taken into account, then the tangent components F_t and F_k of the contact force are computed following the Coulomb friction model. To elaborate, if the relative velocity of the points $\vec{p}_1$ and $\vec{p}_2$ along $\vec{t}$ is zero or less than a threshold value, then there is no sliding at the contact point. In this case, the component F_t will assume values in the range of

$$-(\mu_s)_t F_n \leq F_t \leq (\mu_s)_t F_n,$$

depending on the relative-acceleration component $a_t(t)$ being positive or negative. In other words, F_t will do its best to prevent the particles from sliding at the contact point by always opposing the relative acceleration $a_t(t)$.[4] On the other hand, if the relative velocity along $\vec{t}$ is greater than the threshold value, then the particles are sliding at the contact point and

$$F_t = +(\mu_d)_t F_n \quad \text{or} \quad F_t = -(\mu_d)_t F_n,$$

depending on the relative acceleration $a_t(t)$ being negative or positive. Here, $(\mu_d)_t$ is the dynamic coefficient of friction along the $\vec{t}$ direction. A similar analysis holds for $\vec{k}$.

The third and last condition states that the contact force is zero if the contact is breaking away, that is, if the relative acceleration along the contact normal is positive. Equivalently, we have

$$F_n a_n(t_c) = 0, \tag{3.48}$$

---

[4]Notice that F_t is zero if $a_t(t)$ is zero.

meaning that, if F_n is greater than zero, then the particles are in contact and the relative acceleration is zero. Otherwise, if a_n is greater than zero, then the contact is about to break and the contact force should be zero. Putting it all together, we see that the computation of the contact force involves solving the following system of equations:

$$a_n(t_c) \geq 0$$

$$F_n \geq 0 \qquad (3.49)$$

$$F_n a_n(t_c) = 0.$$

Here, we adopt the convention that a positive contact force $+\vec{F}$ is applied to particle O_1 (i.e., the particle with index 1) and a negative contact force $-\vec{F}$ is applied to particle O_2 (i.e., the particle with index 2).

According to Eq. (3.45), the relative acceleration $a_n(t)$, along the contact normal, can be obtained by differentiating Eq. (3.44) twice with respect to time. By so doing, we see that the first time derivative of Eq. (3.44) gives

$$\frac{dq_n(t)}{dt} = \left(\frac{d\vec{p}_1(t)}{dt} - \frac{d\vec{p}_2(t)}{dt} \right) \cdot \vec{n}(t) + (\vec{p}_1 - \vec{p}_2) \cdot \frac{d\vec{n}(t)}{dt}, \qquad (3.50)$$

or equivalently

$$v_n(t) = \left(\vec{v}_1(t) - \vec{v}_2(t) \right) \cdot \vec{n}(t) + (\vec{p}_1 - \vec{p}_2) \cdot \frac{d\vec{n}(t)}{dt}, \qquad (3.51)$$

where $\vec{v}_1(t)$ and $\vec{v}_2(t)$ are the velocity vectors of points $\vec{p}_1(t)$ and $\vec{p}_2(t)$. This gives us an expression for the relative velocity $v_n(t) = dq(t)/dt$ of points $\vec{p}_1(t)$ and $\vec{p}_2(t)$ along the contact normal, as a function of their velocities and collision normal. The time derivative of the collision normal indicates its rate of change in direction as a function of time.

Differentiating Eq. (3.50) once again with respect to time

$$\frac{d^2 q(t)}{dt^2} = \left(\frac{d^2 \vec{p}_1(t)}{dt^2} - \frac{d^2 \vec{p}_2(t)}{dt^2} \right) \cdot \vec{n}(t)$$

$$+ 2 \left(\frac{d\vec{p}_1(t)}{dt} - \frac{d\vec{p}_2(t)}{dt} \right) \cdot \frac{d\vec{n}(t)}{dt} + (\vec{p}_1 - \vec{p}_2) \cdot \frac{d^2 \vec{n}(t)}{dt^2}, \qquad (3.52)$$

or equivalently

$$a_n(t) = \left(\vec{a}_1(t) - \vec{a}_2(t) \right) \cdot \vec{n}(t) + 2 \left(\vec{v}_1(t) - \vec{v}_2(t) \right) \cdot \frac{d\vec{n}(t)}{dt}$$

$$+ (\vec{p}_1 - \vec{p}_2) \cdot \frac{d^2 \vec{n}(t)}{dt^2}, \qquad (3.53)$$

where $\vec{a}_1(t)$ and $\vec{a}_2(t)$ are the acceleration vectors of points $\vec{p}_1(t)$ and $\vec{p}_2(t)$, respectively. This gives us an expression for the relative acceleration $a_n(t) = d^2q(t)/dt^2$ of points $\vec{p}_1(t)$ and $\vec{p}_2(t)$ along the contact normal, as a function of their accelerations, velocities, contact normal and rate of change in direction of the contact normal.

At the instant of contact $t = t_c$, points $\vec{p}_1(t)$ and $\vec{p}_2(t)$ are coincident, that is

$$\vec{p}_1(t_c) = \vec{p}_2(t_c). \tag{3.54}$$

Substituting Eq. (3.54) into (3.53), we obtain an expression of the relative acceleration along the contact normal at the instant of contact:

$$a_n(t_c) = \big(\vec{a}_1(t_c) - \vec{a}_2(t_c)\big) \cdot \vec{n}(t_c) + 2\big(\vec{v}_1(t_c) - \vec{v}_2(t_c)\big) \cdot \frac{d\vec{n}(t_c)}{dt}. \tag{3.55}$$

According to Eq. (3.55), the relative acceleration at the instant of contact has two terms. The first term depends on the accelerations of the contact points, which in turn are related to the contact force using Newton's law. The second term depends on the velocities of the contact points and the rate of change in direction of the collision normal.

For now, let's assume the contact to be frictionless,[5] that is

$$\vec{F} = F_n\vec{n}.$$

If we separate the terms that depend on the contact force from those that do not, we can rewrite Eq. (3.55) as

$$a_n(t_c) = (a_{11})_n F_n + b_1. \tag{3.56}$$

Substituting Eq. (3.56) in (3.49), we obtain:

$$\big((a_{11})_n F_n + b_1\big) \geq 0$$

$$F_n \geq 0 \tag{3.57}$$

$$F_n\big((a_{11})_n F_n + b_1\big) = 0.$$

Thus, the computation of the contact force for the frictionless case involves solving the system of equations defined in (3.57), which is quadratic on F_n. One way of solving this system is to use quadratic programming. However, such techniques are difficult to implement, often requiring the use of sophisticated numerical software packages.

---

[5]Later in this section, we shall relax this assumption to show how the system of equations used in the frictionless case can be expanded to handle friction.

Fortunately, the system of equations defined in (3.57) is also of the same form of a renowned numerical programming technique called *linear complementarity*. The implementation using linear-complementarity techniques is significantly easier than the implementation of a quadratic program, and is discussed in detail in Appendix I (Chap. 14). There, we start presenting solution methods for the frictionless case, and show how to modify them to deal with static and dynamic friction at the contacts. These modifications on the solution method require that Eq. (3.56) be extended to also consider the relation between the relative-acceleration and contact-force components on the tangent plane of the contact.

Where friction is taken into account, the system of equations become

$$
\begin{pmatrix} a_n(t_c) \\ a_t(t_c) \\ a_k(t_c) \end{pmatrix} = \begin{pmatrix} (a_{11})_n & (a_{12})_t & (a_{13})_k \\ (a_{21})_n & (a_{22})_t & (a_{23})_k \\ (a_{31})_n & (a_{32})_t & (a_{33})_k \end{pmatrix} \begin{pmatrix} F_n \\ F_t \\ F_k \end{pmatrix} + \begin{pmatrix} (b_1)_n \\ (b_1)_t \\ (b_1)_k \end{pmatrix}
$$

$$
= \mathbf{A}\vec{F} + \vec{b}, \tag{3.58}
$$

where

$$
a_t(t_c) = \left(\vec{a}_1(t_c) - \vec{a}_2(t_c) \right) \cdot \vec{t}(t_c)
$$

$$
+ 2\left(\vec{v}_1(t_c) - \vec{v}_2(t_c) \right) \cdot \frac{d\vec{t}(t_c)}{dt} \tag{3.59}
$$

$$
a_k(t_c) = \left(\vec{a}_1(t_c) - \vec{a}_2(t_c) \right) \cdot \vec{k}(t_c)
$$

$$
+ 2\left(\vec{v}_1(t_c) - \vec{v}_2(t_c) \right) \cdot \frac{d\vec{k}(t_c)}{dt}. \tag{3.60}
$$

The solution method presented in Appendix I (Chap. 14) assumes both matrix $\mathbf{A}$ and vector $\vec{b}$ to be known constants computed from the geometric displacement and dynamic state of the particles at the instant of contact. Therefore, we need to determine the coefficients of matrix $\mathbf{A}$ and vector $\vec{b}$ before we can safely apply the linear-complementarity techniques of Appendix I (Chap. 14).

The first row of matrix $\mathbf{A}$ and vector $\vec{b}$ is obtained by expressing the normal relative acceleration $a_n(t_c)$ at the instant of contact as a function of the contact-force components F_n, F_t and F_k. This can be done using Eq. (3.55).

Let's start by examining its first term of Eq. (3.55), namely the term

$$
\left(\vec{a}_1(t_c) - \vec{a}_2(t_c) \right) \cdot \vec{n}(t_c).
$$

The acceleration $\vec{a}_1$ of point $\vec{p}_1$ is obtained directly from Eq. (3.4) as

$$
\vec{a}_1 = \frac{\vec{F} + (\vec{F}_1)_{ext}}{m_1}, \tag{3.61}
$$

where $(\vec{F}_1)_{ext}$ is the net external force (such as gravity, spring forces, spatially dependent forces, etc.) acting on particle O_1 and $\vec{F}$ is the contact force to be determined. Similarly, the acceleration $\vec{a}_2$ of point $\vec{p}_2$ is given by

$$\vec{a}_2 = \frac{-\vec{F} + (\vec{F}_2)_{ext}}{m_2}. \tag{3.62}$$

Substituting Eqs. (3.61) and (3.62) into the first term of Eq. (3.55) gives

$$
\begin{aligned}
\left(\vec{a}_1(t_c) - \vec{a}_2(t_c)\right) \cdot \vec{n}(t_c) &= \left(\frac{1}{m_1} + \frac{1}{m_2}\right) \vec{F} \cdot \vec{n}(t_c) \\
&\quad + \left(\frac{(\vec{F}_1)_{ext}}{m_1} + \frac{(\vec{F}_2)_{ext}}{m_2}\right) \cdot \vec{n}(t_c) \\
&= \left(\frac{1}{m_1} + \frac{1}{m_2}\right) F_n \\
&\quad + \left(\frac{(\vec{F}_1)_{ext}}{m_1} + \frac{(\vec{F}_2)_{ext}}{m_2}\right) \cdot \vec{n}(t_c).
\end{aligned}
$$

So, the total contribution to the coefficients of the first row of matrix $\mathbf{A}$ and vector $\vec{b}$ from the first term of Eq. (3.55) is

$$
\begin{aligned}
(a_{11})_n &= \left(\frac{1}{m_1} + \frac{1}{m_2}\right) \\
(a_{12})_t &= 0 \\
(a_{13})_k &= 0 \\
(b_1)_n &= \left(\frac{(\vec{F}_1)_{ext}}{m_1} + \frac{(\vec{F}_2)_{ext}}{m_2}\right) \cdot \vec{n}(t_c).
\end{aligned}
\tag{3.63}
$$

Notice that $(a_{12})_t$ and $(a_{13})_k$ are zero because the first term does not depend on F_t and F_k, respectively. Now, let's examine the second term of Eq. (3.55), namely

$$2\left(\vec{v}_1(t_c) - \vec{v}_2(t_c)\right) \cdot \frac{d\vec{n}(t_c)}{dt}.$$

The velocities of points $\vec{p}_1$ and $\vec{p}_2$ are known quantities independent of the contact force. So, the contribution to the first row of matrix $\mathbf{A}$ from the velocity components is zero. However, we still need to compute the rate of change in direction of the contact normal as a function of time and check whether it depends on the contact force.

Section 10.3.1 presents a detailed description of how the time derivative of the contact normal for the particle–particle case can be computed. For convenience, the result is reproduced here:

$$\frac{d\vec{n}(t)}{dt} = \frac{(\vec{v}_1 - \vec{v}_2)}{|\vec{v}_1 - \vec{v}_2|},$$

which is independent of the contact force as well. So, the contribution of the second term of Eq. (3.55) to the coefficients of matrix $\mathbf{A}$ and vector $\vec{b}$ is

$$(a_{11})_n = 0$$

$$(a_{12})_t = 0$$

$$(a_{13})_k = 0 \tag{3.64}$$

$$(b_1)_n = 2(\vec{v}_1 - \vec{v}_2) \cdot \frac{(\vec{v}_1 - \vec{v}_2)}{|\vec{v}_1 - \vec{v}_2|} = 2|\vec{v}_1 - \vec{v}_2|.$$

Combining Eqs. (3.63) and (3.64), we obtain the coefficients associated with the first row of matrix $\mathbf{A}$ and vector $\vec{b}$ as

$$(a_{11})_n = \left(\frac{1}{m_1} + \frac{1}{m_2}\right)$$

$$(a_{12})_t = 0$$

$$(a_{13})_k = 0$$

$$(b_1)_n = \left(\frac{(\vec{F}_1)_{ext}}{m_1} + \frac{(\vec{F}_2)_{ext}}{m_2}\right) \cdot \vec{n}$$

$$+ 2|\vec{v}_1 - \vec{v}_2|.$$

The computation of the coefficients associated with the second and third rows[6] of matrix $\mathbf{A}$ and vector $\vec{b}$ is similar to the derivations already obtained for the coefficients of the first row. The main difference is that, instead of computing the dot product with $\vec{n}$, we compute it with $\vec{t}$ for the second row, and with $\vec{k}$ for the third row, as shown in Eqs. (3.59). After some manipulation, we obtain

$$(a_{21})_n = 0$$

$$(a_{22})_t = \left(\frac{1}{m_1} + \frac{1}{m_2}\right)$$

$$(a_{23})_k = 0$$

and

---

[6]These coefficients need only be computed if friction is taken into account. In the frictionless case, both F_t and F_k are zero.

$$(b_1)_t = \left(\frac{(\vec{F_1})_{ext}}{m_1} + \frac{(\vec{F_2})_{ext}}{m_2} \right) \cdot \vec{t}(t_c)$$

$$+ 2(\vec{v}_1(t_c) - \vec{v}_2(t_c)) \cdot \frac{d\vec{t}(t_c)}{dt} \qquad (3.65)$$

for the second row, and

$$(a_{31})_n = 0$$

$$(a_{32})_t = 0$$

$$(a_{33})_k = \left(\frac{1}{m_1} + \frac{1}{m_2} \right)$$

and

$$(b_1)_k = \left(\frac{(\vec{F_1})_{ext}}{m_1} + \frac{(\vec{F_2})_{ext}}{m_2} \right) \cdot \vec{k}(t_c)$$

$$+ 2(\vec{v}_1(t_c) - \vec{v}_2(t_c)) \cdot \frac{d\vec{k}(t_c)}{dt} \qquad (3.66)$$

for the third row of matrix $\mathbf{A}$ and vector $\vec{b}$.

The actual determination of the coefficients $(b_1)_t$ and $(b_1)_k$ as shown in Eqs. (3.65) and (3.66) is more involved than that for $(b_1)_n$ because they require computing the rate of change in direction of the vectors $\vec{t}(t)$ and $\vec{k}(t)$ on the tangent plane of the contact. The computation of the time derivative of the tangent-plane vectors is discussed in detail in Sect. 10.4 of Appendix E (Chap. 10).

Lastly, having determined the elements of matrix $\mathbf{A}$ and vector $\vec{b}$, we can apply the LCP techniques of Appendix I (Chap. 14) to compute the contact-force components. We then update the dynamic state of each particle by applying $+\vec{F}$ on particle O_1 and $-\vec{F}$ on particle O_2.

3.5.4 Computing Contact Forces for Multiple Contacts

The principle behind the computation of multiple particle–particle contact forces is the same as the computation of multiple particle–particle collision impulses. Again, the simulation engine needs to group the particles into clusters that share at least one contact. The contacts within each cluster can then be simultaneously resolved independent of all other clusters (see Fig. 3.23).

When a particle is involved in multiple contacts, it is possible to have it assigned to different indexes for each contact. For the particular situation of cluster G_2 in Fig. 3.23, particle O_2 has index 2 with respect to its contact with particle O_1, and index 1 with respect to its contact with particle O_3. This in turn affects the choice of sign when combining the multiple-contact forces in the system equations. Moreover,

Fig. 3.23 A multiple
particle–particle contact-force
computation. In this case, the
particles are grouped into
three clusters that can be
solved in parallel

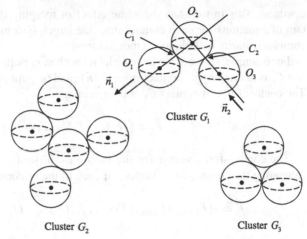

the contact normal and tangent plane are different for each contact. So, we also need
to carry out a change of base between the contact forces before combining them.

In the single particle–particle contact, the contact-force computation taking friction into account was done using linear-complementarity techniques to solve a system of equations of the form

$$a_n(t_c) \geq 0$$
$$F_n \geq 0$$
$$\vec{F}^t(\mathbf{A}\vec{F} + \vec{b}) = 0,$$

where[7]

$$\mathbf{A} = \begin{pmatrix} (a_{11})_n & 0 & 0 \\ 0 & (a_{22})_t & 0 \\ 0 & 0 & (a_{33})_k \end{pmatrix}$$
$$\vec{F} = (F_n, F_t, F_k)^t$$
$$\vec{b} = ((b_1)_n, (b_1)_t, (b_1)_k)^t.$$

This solution method can be extended to the case of multiple-contact-force computations. The main difference between multiple- and single-contact-force computations involving a given particle is that the contact force at contact C_i can affect
the computation of the contact force at contact C_j. So, instead of solving one contact at a time, we need to simultaneously solve all contacts having a particle in

[7]Here, we are already using the result of Sect. 3.5.3 that the matrix $\mathbf{A}$ is all zero, save for its
diagonal elements.

common. This in turn has the same effect of merging the several individual system of equations for each contact into one larger system, and applying the linear-complementarity techniques to merged system.

For example, suppose we have a cluster with m simultaneous contacts. Each contact C_i is defined by its contact-normal $(\vec{n})_i$ and tangent-plane vectors $(\vec{t})_i$ and $(\vec{k})_i$. The contact force at contact C_i is then expressed as

$$\vec{F}_i = \left((F_i)_{n_i}, (F_i)_{t_i}, (F_i)_{k_i}\right)^t.$$

The contact-force vector for the multiple-collision system is obtained by concatenating the contact-force vectors of each of the m contacts, that is

$$\vec{F} = \left((F_1)_{n_1}, (F_1)_{t_1}, (F_1)_{k_1}, \ldots, (F_m)_{n_m}, (F_m)_{t_m}, (F_m)_{k_m}\right)^t.$$

The vector $\vec{b}$ becomes

$$\vec{b} = \left((b_1)_n, (b_1)_t, (b_1)_k, \ldots, (b_m)_n, (b_m)_t, (b_m)_k\right)^t$$

and the matrix $\mathbf{A}$ is enlarged to accommodate all contact forces. Its partitioned representation is given by

$$\mathbf{A} = \begin{pmatrix} \mathbf{A_{11}} & \mathbf{A_{12}} & \ldots & \mathbf{A_{1m}} \\ \mathbf{A_{21}} & \mathbf{A_{22}} & \ldots & \mathbf{A_{2m}} \\ & \ldots & & \ldots \\ \mathbf{A_{m1}} & \mathbf{A_{m2}} & \ldots & \mathbf{A_{mm}} \end{pmatrix},$$

where each sub-matrix is given by

$$\mathbf{A_{ij}} = \begin{pmatrix} (a_{ij})_{n_i} & (a_{i(j+1)})_{t_i} & (a_{i(j+2)})_{k_i} \\ (a_{(i+1)j})_{n_i} & (a_{(i+1)(j+1)})_{t_i} & (a_{(i+1)(j+2)})_{k_i} \\ (a_{(i+2)j})_{n_i} & (a_{(i+2)(j+1)})_{t_i} & (a_{(i+2)(j+2)})_{k_i} \end{pmatrix}.$$

If contacts C_i and C_j have no particles in common, then the sub-matrix $\mathbf{A_{ij}}$ is set to zero, indicating that their contact forces do not affect each other. However, if contacts C_i and C_j do have a particle in common, then the coefficients a_{ij} are the contribution of the contact force of contact C_j to the relative acceleration at contact C_i. More specifically, the coefficient $(a_{ij})_{n_i}$ is the contribution of the contact-force component $(F_j)_{n_j}$ to the relative normal acceleration at the contact C_i. Analogously, the coefficients $(a_{ij})_{t_i}$ and $(a_{ij})_{k_i}$ are the contribution of the contact-force components $(F_j)_{t_j}$ and $(F_j)_{k_j}$ to the relative normal acceleration at the contact C_i.

Also, notice that the contact force $\vec{F}_j$ is given with respect to the contact frame of C_j, whereas the relative acceleration $\vec{a}_i$ is given with respect to the contact frame of C_i. Therefore, a change of base is required when computing the coefficients of matrix $\mathbf{A_{ij}}$ and vector $\vec{b}_i$.

Suppose contact C_i involves particles O_1 and O_2, and contact C_j involves particles O_2 and O_3, that is, they have particle O_2 in common. We want to determine the contribution of the contact force $\vec{F}_j$ acting on particle O_2 of contact C_j to the relative acceleration of contact C_i. This in turn involves determining the coefficients of the sub-matrix $\mathbf{A_{ij}}$ and the components $(b_i)_{n_i}$, $(b_i)_{t_i}$ and $(b_i)_{k_i}$ of vector $\vec{b}$. The relative acceleration at contact C_i between particles O_1 and O_2 is given by

$$(a_i)_{n_i} = (\vec{a}_1 - \vec{a}_2) \cdot \vec{n}_i + 2(\vec{v}_1 - \vec{v}_2) \cdot \frac{d\vec{n}_i}{dt}$$

$$(a_i)_{t_i} = (\vec{a}_1 - \vec{a}_2) \cdot \vec{t}_i + 2(\vec{v}_1 - \vec{v}_2) \cdot \frac{d\vec{t}_i}{dt} \qquad (3.67)$$

$$(a_i)_{k_i} = (\vec{a}_1 - \vec{a}_2) \cdot \vec{k}_i + 2(\vec{v}_1 - \vec{v}_2) \cdot \frac{d\vec{k}_i}{dt}.$$

As explained in the single-contact case, only the first term of Eqs. (3.67) depends on the forces exerted at contact C_i. The second term depends on the velocities and is added to $(b_i)_{n_i}$, $(b_i)_{t_i}$ and $(b_i)_{k_i}$, as appropriate. Thus, the contribution of the contact force $\vec{F}_j$ acting on particle O_2 of contact C_j does not affect the components of vector $\vec{b}$. In other words, the expressions used to compute the vector $\vec{b}$ for the single-contact case are still valid for the multiple-contact case, that is, the components $(b_i)_{n_i}$, $(b_i)_{t_i}$ and $(b_i)_{k_i}$ of vector $\vec{b}$ are given by

$$(b_i)_{n_i} = \left(\frac{(\vec{F}_1)_{ext}}{m_1} + \frac{(\vec{F}_2)_{ext}}{m_2} \right) \cdot \vec{n}_i + 2(\vec{v}_1 - \vec{v}_2) \cdot (\vec{v}_1 - \vec{v}_2)$$

$$(b_i)_{t_i} = \left(\frac{(\vec{F}_1)_{ext}}{m_1} + \frac{(\vec{F}_2)_{ext}}{m_2} \right) \cdot \vec{t}_i + 2(\vec{v}_1 - \vec{v}_2) \cdot \frac{d\vec{t}_i}{dt}$$

$$(b_i)_{k_i} = \left(\frac{(\vec{F}_1)_{ext}}{m_1} + \frac{(\vec{F}_2)_{ext}}{m_2} \right) \cdot \vec{k}_i + 2(\vec{v}_1 - \vec{v}_2) \cdot \frac{d\vec{k}_i}{dt},$$

where $(\vec{F}_1)_{ext}$ and $(\vec{F}_2)_{ext}$ are the net external forces (such as gravity, spring forces, spatially dependent forces, etc.) acting on particles O_1 and O_2, respectively.

Using Eq. (3.4), the contribution of the contact force $\vec{F}_j$ acting on particle O_2 of contact C_j to the acceleration $\vec{a}_1$ of particle O_1 involved in collision C_i is[8]

$$\frac{\vec{F}_j}{m_1}.$$

---

[8]Notice that the contact force acting on particle O_2 because of contact C_j can be $+\vec{F}_j$ or $-\vec{F}_j$, depending on particle O_2 having index 1 or 2 with respect to contact C_j. The following derivations assume the contact force is $+\vec{F}_j$.

Conversely, the contribution of $\vec{F}_j$ to $\vec{a}_2$ is

$$-\frac{\vec{F}_j}{m_2}.$$

The net contribution of $\vec{F}_j$ to the relative acceleration at the contact C_i is then

$$\left(\frac{1}{m_1} + \frac{1}{m_2}\right)\vec{F}_j.$$

Substituting this into the first terms of Eqs. (3.67), we obtain the contributions of $\vec{F}_j$ to each relative-acceleration component at contact C_i:

$$\text{contribution to } (a_i)_{n_i} = \left(\frac{1}{m_1} + \frac{1}{m_2}\right)\vec{F}_j \cdot \vec{n}_i$$

$$\text{contribution to } (a_i)_{t_i} = \left(\frac{1}{m_1} + \frac{1}{m_2}\right)\vec{F}_j \cdot \vec{t}_i$$

$$\text{contribution to } (a_i)_{k_i} = \left(\frac{1}{m_1} + \frac{1}{m_2}\right)\vec{F}_j \cdot \vec{k}_i.$$

Using the fact that

$$\vec{F}_j = (F_j)_{n_j}\vec{n}_j + (F_j)_{t_j}\vec{t}_j + (F_j)_{k_j}\vec{k}_j,$$

we immediately obtain the coefficients of the sub-matrix $\mathbf{A_{ij}}$ as

$$(a_{ij})_{n_i} = \left(\frac{1}{m_1} + \frac{1}{m_2}\right)\vec{n}_j \cdot \vec{n}_i \tag{3.68}$$

$$(a_{i(j+1)})_{n_i} = \left(\frac{1}{m_1} + \frac{1}{m_2}\right)\vec{t}_j \cdot \vec{n}_i \tag{3.69}$$

$$(a_{i(j+2)})_{n_i} = \left(\frac{1}{m_1} + \frac{1}{m_2}\right)\vec{k}_j \cdot \vec{n}_i \tag{3.70}$$

$$(a_{(i+1)j})_{t_i} = \left(\frac{1}{m_1} + \frac{1}{m_2}\right)\vec{n}_j \cdot \vec{t}_i \tag{3.71}$$

$$(a_{(i+1)(j+1)})_{t_i} = \left(\frac{1}{m_1} + \frac{1}{m_2}\right)\vec{t}_j \cdot \vec{t}_i \tag{3.72}$$

$$(a_{(i+1)(j+2)})_{t_i} = \left(\frac{1}{m_1} + \frac{1}{m_2}\right)\vec{k}_j \cdot \vec{t}_i \tag{3.73}$$

$$(a_{(i+2)j})_{k_i} = \left(\frac{1}{m_1} + \frac{1}{m_2}\right)\vec{n}_j \cdot \vec{k}_i \tag{3.74}$$

$$(a_{(i+2)(j+1)})_{k_i} = \left(\frac{1}{m_1} + \frac{1}{m_2}\right)\vec{t}_j \cdot \vec{k}_i \tag{3.75}$$

$$(a_{(i+2)(j+2)})_{k_i} = \left(\frac{1}{m_1} + \frac{1}{m_2}\right)\vec{k}_j \cdot \vec{k}_i. \qquad (3.76)$$

Notice that, if $i = j$, then the sub-matrix $\mathbf{A_{ii}}$ is reduced to

$$\mathbf{A_{ii}} = \begin{pmatrix} (a_{ii})_{n_i} & 0 & 0 \\ 0 & (a_{(i+1)(i+1)})_{t_i} & 0 \\ 0 & 0 & (a_{(i+2)(i+2)})_{k_i} \end{pmatrix},$$

which is the same expression obtained in Eq. (3.58) for the single-contact case.

When friction is not taken into account, the sub-matrix $\mathbf{A_{ij}}$ is reduced to

$$\mathbf{A_{ij}} = (a_{ij})_{n_i},$$

since the contact-force components $(F_j)_{t_j}$ and $(F_j)_{k_j}$ are zero in the frictionless case. This result is also compatible with that obtained for the frictionless single-contact-force computation explained in Sect. 3.5.3.

Having computed the contact force $\vec{F}_i$ for each contact C_i, $1 \le i \le m$, we update the dynamic state of each particle involved on contact C_i by applying $+\vec{F}_i$ to the particle O_1 (i.e., the particle with index 1) and $-\vec{F}$ to the particle O_2 (i.e., the particle with index 2).

When a particle is involved in multiple contacts, it is possible to have it assigned to different indexes for each contact. For the particular situation of cluster G_2 in Fig. 3.23, particle O_2 has index 2 with respect to its contact C_1 with particle O_1, and index 1 with respect to its contact C_2 with particle O_3. So, the net contact force actually applied to particle O_2 after all contact forces have been computed is

$$(\vec{F}_2 - \vec{F}_1),$$

where $\vec{F}_1$ and $\vec{F}_2$ are the contact forces associated with contacts C_1 and C_2.

3.6 Particle–Rigid Body Collision Response

Whenever a particle–rigid body collision is detected, the collision-response module is invoked to compute the appropriate collision impulses and contact forces that will prevent interpenetration. As explained in Sect. 3.4, the trajectories of the colliding particles are backtracked in time to the moment before the collision. The rigid body is usually not moved from its current position, which happens to be its position at the end of the current time step after any and all rigid body–rigid body collisions were resolved.

In this book, we model the particle–rigid body collision as the particle colliding with another particle on the rigid body's surface. The advantage of doing so is that we can reuse most of the results obtained for the particle–particle single or multiple collisions or contacts developed in Sect. 3.5. More specifically, there are only three main modifications that we need to make before we can reuse the equations already derived for the particle–particle collision and contact cases.

The first modification consists of making the mass of the particle on the rigid body's surface be the same as the rigid body's mass. For example, if particle O_1 is colliding, or comes in contact with, particle O_2 on the rigid body's surface, then we make m_2 be the rigid body's mass. Clearly, this modification induces no changes on the equations already derived for the particle–particle cases.

The second modification requires that both velocity and acceleration of the particle on the rigid body's surface be computed using the rigid body's dynamic equations covered in Sect. 4.2 of Chap. 4. Unlike the particle's dynamics, the rigid–body motion has to take into account rotational motion, making its dynamic equations much more complex than those derived for particles in Sect. 3.2. Therefore, this modification will cause some changes on the particle–particle collision and contact equations, as will be explained in Sects. 3.6.1 and 3.6.2.

The third and last modification involves the way the collision or contact normal is computed. Even though the particle is colliding with another particle on the rigid body's surface, the normal is defined by the rigid body's geometry, as opposed to being the line connecting both particles. This is done as follows.

Let O_1 be the particle colliding or in contact with rigid body B_1. The particle O_2 on the rigid body's surface can be an interior point, a point on an edge, or a vertex of the rigid body's triangle primitive being intersected by O_1's trajectory. So, if O_2 is in the interior of the triangle, then the triangle's normal is taken as the collision or contact normal. If O_2 lies on an edge of the triangle, then the edge's normal is taken as the collision normal. Notice that the edge normal is computed as the average of the normals of the triangle faces that share the edge. Lastly, if O_2 lies on a vertex of the triangle, then the vertex's normal is selected as the collision or contact normal. The vertex's normal is computed as the average of the normals of all triangles that contain the vertex.

If the particles are colliding, then the normal direction is selected such that

$$(\vec{v}_1 - \vec{v}_2) \cdot \vec{n} < 0,$$

that is, the particles are moving towards each other before the collision. Notice that this may require changing the direction of the normal computed from the triangle normal, edge normal or vertex normal if $\vec{v}_2 > \vec{v}_1$, that is, if the rigid body is moving faster towards the particle, as opposed to the particle moving faster towards the rigid body. On the other hand, if the particles are in contact, we have

$$(\vec{v}_1 - \vec{v}_2) \cdot \vec{n} = 0$$

and the normal direction remains unchanged (i.e., pointing outwards the rigid body's surface).

Fig. 3.24 Particle O_1 is colliding with rigid body B_1 at O_2. The velocity $\vec{v}_2$ and acceleration $\vec{a}_2$ of point $\vec{p}_2$ are computed using the rigid body's dynamic equations

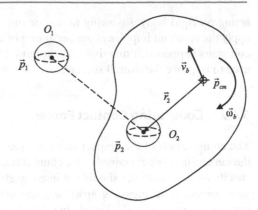

3.6.1 Computing Impulsive Forces

The computation of impulsive forces for the particle–rigid body collision is very nearly the same as that described for the single or multiple particle–particle collision. As mentioned, the main modifications are on the computation of the velocity of particle O_2 located on the rigid body's surface, and the collision normal.

Consider the situation illustrated in Fig. 3.24. Particle O_1 is about to collide with particle O_2 on the rigid body's surface.

Let M_b be the mass of the rigid body, and $\vec{v}_b$ and $\vec{w}_b$ be the linear and angular velocities of the rigid body just before the collision. The mass m_2 of the particle O_2 is then set to

$$m_2 = M_b. \tag{3.77}$$

Its velocity before the collision is computed as the velocity of a point on the rigid body (see Sect. 4.2 for more details), that is

$$\vec{v}_2 = \vec{v}_b + \vec{w}_b \times \vec{r}_2, \tag{3.78}$$

where $\vec{r}_2$ is the distance between particle O_2 and the rigid body's center of mass given by

$$\vec{r}_2 = \vec{p}_2 - \vec{p}_{cm}.$$

So, using Eqs. (3.77) and (3.78) as the mass and velocity of particle O_2 just before the collision, we can directly apply the single- or multiple-collision equations and compute the collision impulse $\vec{P}_{1,2}$ associated with the collision of particles O_1 and O_2.

The dynamic state of particle O_1 is then updated with the application of the collision impulse $\vec{P}_{1,2}$. However, recall that the update on the dynamic state of the rigid body owing to the impulse $\vec{P}_{1,2}$ is postponed to the next simulation time step. Therefore, for each simulation time step, we need to sum all collision impulses acting on rigid body B_1 owing to one or more particle–rigid body collisions, and apply the resultant impulse at the beginning of the next simulation time step, as if all collisions happened at that time. As explained in Sect. 3.4, this is an approximation used to improve the overall simulation efficacy.

3.6.2 Computing Contact Forces

The computation of the contact force between a particle and a rigid body follows the same principles explained in the computation of a particle–particle contact. More specifically, the particles should not interpenetrate, the contact force should not prevent contact from breaking apart, and the contact force should be set to zero if contact is about to break. Translating these conditions into equations, we have that the relative acceleration of the particles at the contact point should be greater than or equal to zero, the contact force should be greater than or equal to zero, and the contact force should be zero if the relative acceleration is positive, or it should be positive if the relative acceleration is zero.

Again, we use the vector $\vec{q}(t) = (\vec{p}_1 - \vec{p}_2) \cdot \vec{n}$ to compute the relative acceleration of the particles at the contact point, given by

$$a_n(t_c) = \left(\vec{a}_1(t_c) - \vec{a}_2(t_c)\right) \cdot \vec{n}(t_c) + 2\left(\vec{v}_1(t_c) - \vec{v}_2(t_c)\right) \cdot \frac{d\vec{n}(t_c)}{dt}, \qquad (3.79)$$

where t_c is the instant when contact was established. Equation (3.79) is the same as Eq. (3.55) rewritten here for convenience.

Clearly, the velocity $\vec{v}_2$ and acceleration $\vec{a}_2$ of particle O_2 should be computed using the rigid–body dynamics equations covered in Sect. 4.2. Moreover, since the contact normal is either a triangle normal, an edge normal or a vertex normal, the time derivative of the normal vector should also take into account the dynamics of the rigid–body motion. In other words, the rate of change in direction of the normal vector is a function of the linear and angular velocities of the rigid body.

Unfortunately, the derivation of these relations requires a significant knowledge of rigid–body dynamics, which is only covered in Chap. 4. Therefore, for the sake of clarity, we shall postpone the computation of the contact forces between a particle and a rigid body until Sect. 4.12. By so doing, the reader will have a chance to assimilate the concepts of rigid–body dynamics necessary to understand the contact-force computations.

3.7 Specialized Particle Systems

In this section, we shall discuss some specialized particle systems commonly found in animation packages. The idea behind such systems is to swap accuracy of the physical modeling of the particles' interactions for overall system efficiency without sacrificing the look of the simulation. For example, instead of using the Navier–Stokes equations to simulate vapor leaving a cup of hot water as a turbulent gas, we obtain the same effect by using a set of user-definable parameters to adjust some properties of the particle system representing the vapor. The result is a simulation that has a behavior similar to the hot turbulent gas modeled by the actual physics-based equations, but using a simpler mathematical framework.

There are two main reasons to include this section in this book, despite some of the methods used *not* being based on the accurate physical modeling of the particles' interactions. First of all, these specialized systems are very popular among computer graphics practitioners and animators, and we feel that this chapter would be incomplete without mentioning such systems. Besides, discussing in detail the mathematical framework needed to precisely model these systems, which require specialized forms of equations of motion and force interactions, is beyond the scope of this book.

Secondly, we want to make the point that the physics-based particle-dynamics and collision-detection and response modules developed here can be used in these systems as a fast and reliable way to evolve the particles' trajectories over time. The benefit of doing so from the object-oriented point of view is that particles and rigid bodies can use the same underlying simulation engine. This includes using the same numerical methods, collision-detection algorithms and collision-response-force computations. Particles and rigid–body objects can then be derived from a common parent class, and the shared functionality can be implemented as virtual methods of the parent class. So, as far as the simulation engine is concerned, virtual methods on the parent class are invoked and the appropriate particle or rigid–body behavior is obtained. In other words, the simulation engine makes no distinction between particles and rigid bodies when advancing the system by one more time interval because it only manipulates their parent class's objects.

3.7.1 Particle Emitter

The particle emitter is used to create and release particles in the simulated environment. Usually, particle emitters are implemented as an invisible planar quadrangular surface that can be attached to other objects in the simulation, or be used as a stand-alone object, in which case it can be displayed attached to a default cube (see Fig. 3.25). Sometimes an entire object or parts of it are selected as a particle emitter, in which case the object's faces are used as the emitting surface.

The actual emission of particles in the simulated environment is not as straightforward as it may seem. Some precautionary measures should be taken to avoid unnecessary implementation problems. For example, the particle–particle collision-detection module checks for geometric intersections of the particles' trajectories as the system evolves. It works best when the particles are not intersecting at the beginning of the current time interval, that is, at the starting point of their trajectories, so that the continuous collision can always detect a state wherein the particles are not intersecting. So, if the particles are created in such a manner that they overlap each other right from the start, then any particle–particle collisions detected immediately after they are released can introduce unrealistic spikes in their beginning movement

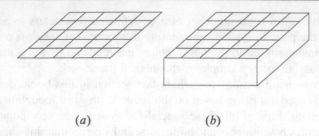

(a) (b)

Fig. 3.25 (a) In most cases, particle emitters are represented by a planar quadrangular face. The grid is created from the size of each particle and the total number of particles to be released at a time; (b) In the stand-alone version, a default cubic object can be created, and the particle emitter is attached to its top face

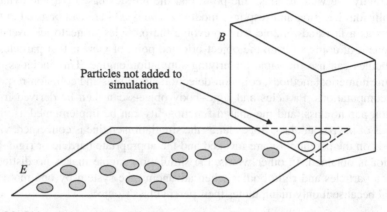

Fig. 3.26 Object B is partially obstructing the emitter surface E. Particles created on the obstructed area are not added to the simulation

as collision impulses are applied to resolve the intersections. Therefore, it is best to assure that particles not be overlapping each other at the time they are released.

Also, it is a good idea to establish a clearance region around the emitter surface to prevent situations in which an object is placed on top of the emitter and the particles either jam immediately after they are released, or simply cannot be released at all. This is illustrated in Fig. 3.26.

Our approach to these practical problems is as follows. Every time a new round of particles is released, the particles just created are checked for intersections with other particles already released, as well as rigid bodies that are in the same world-cell decomposition as the emitter. Whenever an intersection is detected, the particles just created are immediately removed from the simulation. In other words, the emitter will only add new particles to the system if there is enough room for them.

Clearly, this approach requires that we know the position on the emitter surface at which each particle is released. In order to do so, we consider a grid decomposition of the emitter surface such that a single particle is released at the center of each cell of the decomposition.

Let d be the desired diameter of the spheres representing the particles being emitted, and let n_t be the number of particles simultaneously released at a time. The dimension of each cell in the decomposition is then

$$f_s = 2d\sqrt{n_t} \qquad (3.80)$$

for a square emitter surface, where the factor of 2 is used to allow for some extra space between each particle positioned at the center of its associated cell.

Another practical problem that should be considered when emitting particles is that in most cases the particles should not behave exactly like each other. For instance, the introduction of some variations on size, speed and direction of movement of each particle often makes the particle system look and feel more real. In our approach, we define a set of user-adjustable parameters to control the dynamic behavior of the particles being emitted. For each parameter, we define its mean value and deviation. So, for example, a particle system with particles of size four and deviation two will have particles with size ranging from two to six, and average size of four. The actual size of each particle can be dynamically computed assuming a normal probability distribution for each parameter. Equation (3.80) should then be modified to accommodate this deviation on size.

Each time new particles are released, we need to compute their maximum diameter d_{max}. Notice that the value of d_{max} will probably vary from consecutive releases, that is, the emitter grid dynamically grows and shrinks to the appropriate size before each release. The dimensions of each cell in the decomposition is then dynamically obtained from

$$f_s = 2d_{max}\sqrt{n_t}. \qquad (3.81)$$

This in turn minimizes the risk of having particles just released intersecting each other.

3.7.2 User-Definable Parameters

The desired dynamic behavior of the particle system can usually be adjusted through a set of particle parameters. Each parameter is defined by its nominal (i.e., mean) value and an optional deviation value. Here, we provide a list of default parameters commonly found in animation packages to set up particle-emitter properties.

1. *Particle size*
   Defines the diameter of the spheres representing the emitted particles.
2. *Particle mass*
   Defines the mass of each particle.
3. *Particle age*
   Defines the age of a particle. This parameter is used to determine the maximum time interval the particle will exist in the simulation, in case the *particle resilience* parameter is set to true.

4. *Particle resilience*

   Regulates whether particles that exist for a time span longer than their age should be removed from the simulation.

5. *Emitter size*

   Limits the maximum size of the emitter surface. If the size computed using Eq. (3.81) turns out to be greater than this value, then the number of particles simultaneously released is reduced to

$$n_r = \left\lfloor \left(\frac{(f_s)_{max}}{2d_{max}} \right)^2 \right\rfloor ,$$

   where $(f_s)_{max}$ is the maximum size of the emitter surface and n_r is the actual number of particles being released.

6. *Emission velocity*

   Defines each particle's velocity at time of emission.

7. *Emission direction*

   Defines the direction in which the particles will move as soon as they are released.

8. *Emission delay*

   Controls the time elapsed between two consecutive emissions, as a multiple of the simulation time interval being used. For example, if the delay is set to three, then the emitter will skip two simulation time intervals, and will emit particles again only on the third time interval after the last emission.

9. *Emission rate*

   Defines the number of particles emitted at each emission. Notice that the maximum possible emission rate is constrained by the emitter size.

10. *Maximum emission*

    Defines the maximum number of particles emitted by this source. This is required not only to limit the overall number of particles being used in the simulation, but also to simulate effects such as smoke resulting from a fire being dissipated after the fire is out.

11. *Particle spawn*

    Regulates whether particles that were removed from the simulation should be reused by the emitter. If set to true, then the interpretation of the *maximum emission* parameter will be slightly different than its default interpenetration. In this case, the *maximum emission* parameter will regulate the total number of particles emitted by this source that are *active* in the simulation. (Active here means that the particle's lifespan has not yet reached its age.)

12. *Collision detection*

    This flag is used to indicate whether particle collisions should be taken into account during the simulation. The flag can turn on and off internal, external and complex collisions. Recall from Sect. 3.4 that internal collisions refer to collisions between particles emitted by the same particle system. External collisions indicate that collisions between particles emitted by different particle systems should be taken into account, whereas complex collisions refers to collisions between particles and rigid bodies. Notice that there is no deviation value associated with this parameter.

13. *Particle static friction*

Defines the static-friction coefficient of the particle when in contact with other particles and rigid bodies. The actual static-friction coefficient used in the computations is the average value of the static friction assigned to each of the contacting particles and rigid bodies.

14. *Particle dynamic friction*

Defines the dynamic-friction coefficient of the particle when in contact with other particles and rigid bodies. The actual dynamic-friction coefficient used in the computations is the average value of the dynamic friction assigned to each of the contacting particles and rigid bodies.

15. *External forces*

Defines a list of external forces globally applied to all (and only) particles emitted from this source. For example, this listing can be used to define a viscous drag force to simulate air resistance, add gravity to pull the particles towards the ground, or to force all particles to have a default movement along a specific direction, as happens when modeling rain falling diagonally to the ground.

16. *Particle split*

Indicates whether particles can generate new child particles. This parameter, combined with the age parameter, lets users create several interesting effects, such as air being burned by a rocket launcher and the smoke getting first more dense, then dispersed in air a few seconds later.

17. *Particle-split number*

Defines the total number of child particles that will be created by their parent after each split.

18. *Particle-split age*

Defines the age of the particle at which it will start to create its children. This age should be less than the particle age.

19. *Particle-split delay*

Defines the time elapsed between two consecutive splits, as a multiple of the simulation time interval. For example, a split delay of two indicates that, after the particle-split age has been reached, the particle will create new child particles every other simulation time interval.

20. *Particle-split depth*

Defines the maximum number of splits a particle may have.

21. *Particle-split velocity*

Defines the percentage value of the parent's velocity inherited by its children at the time of the split.

22. *Particle-split direction*

Defines a maximum deviation from the parent's direction inherited by its children at the time of the split. The deviation is used to spread the children round their parents, along the direction of movement.

23. *Particle-split size*

Defines the percentage value of the parent's size inherited by its children at the time of the split.

24. *Particle-split lifespan*
Defines a maximum deviation from the parent's age inherited by its children at
the time of the split.

25. *Motion trail*
Regulates whether particles should leave a motion trail behind them.

26. *Motion-trail age*
Defines the amount of time the motion trail remains visible. The "motion trail"
particles are then removed from the simulation as soon as this time expires.

27. *Color evolution*
Defines a sequence of RGB color intensities of the particle over its lifetime.
A time value is associated with each element of the color sequence, such that the
color changes as soon as its corresponding time has been reached. For example,
a color evolution of the form (R, G, B, t) with the values

$$\{(1.0, 1.0, 1.0, 0.0), (0.6, 0.6, 0.6, 2.0),$$
$$(0.3, 0.3, 0.3, 4.0), (0.0, 0.0, 0.0, 7.0)\}$$

assigns an initial white to the particle, then changes it to gray after two seconds,
changes it again to light gray at four seconds from the previous change, and
lastly sets it to black when seven seconds have passed from the last change.

28. *Particle electrical charge*
Defines the electrical charge of the particle; useful when electrical force fields
are used as external forces acting on the particle system.

There are several ways to create the visual effect of smoke using the particle
system parameters described so far. We can define a large number of particles with
small mass and size, and set up an external force that makes the particles flow from
the emitter in the desired direction to form the column of smoke. Notice that there is
no need to define gravity in these systems; only a viscous-drag force to compensate
for the acceleration increase owing to the external force being applied.

Particles should be assigned a large value for their age, such that the column of
smoke can rise slowly over time without disappearing too soon as it rises. On the
other hand, the split age should be set fairly soon compared with the particle's age
so that the smoke starts dense near the emitter. The dissipation is regulated by the
deviations in size, velocity and direction of the split. These deviations should be
set to small values such that the column of smoke remains concentrated along the
direction of movement near the emitter and opens up like a cone as the particles
move away from it, that is, as their deviation values accumulate to significant values
after a certain number of splits.

When we are creating the visual effect of smoke from a fire, the particles can be
set to an initial RGB color intensity of yellow, then change to orange, then to dark
gray and finally to black. The time span used for each color depends on the desired
visual effect for the intensity of the fire and the material being burned. The material
generally determines how quickly the smoke turns black or dark gray.

The type of visual effects involving liquids that can be created using the specialized particle-system framework described in this book is limited to liquids that can be effectively represented by their drops. This includes rain, sprinklers and jet flows of water. Large bodies of liquid such as lakes, rivers and the ocean are represented by other techniques not covered in this book.

In the case of rain, the emitter surface should be set as large as necessary to cover the area where the rain will fall. The size of the particles (i.e., rain drops) should be kept small, unless you want to create the effect of a summer thunderstorm or hailstorm. The number of particles used combined with the particle's velocities defines the intensity of the rain. A small number falling slowly characterizes a light rain, whereas a large number falling fast resembles a tropical rain. The direction of the rain can be set using an appropriate external force to pull the particles down, as opposed to using gravity. Again, viscous drag should be used to counter balance the acceleration increase owing to the external force and give the impression the rain is falling at constant speed. Also, there is no need to split the particles or change their color.

In the case of sprinklers, the mass of the particles and their initial velocity defines the maximum height the particles will reach along their entire trajectories. Notice that the trajectory will be parabolic if we consider only gravity as the external force. The deviation is used to control the "aperture" of the sprinkler. Small deviations force the particles to be concentrated near the emitter, whereas large deviations make the particles disperse all around the emitter. Particles may or may not be split, depending on the desired volume of liquid being simulated.

Jet flows are similar to sprinklers. The main difference is that the initial velocity on jet flows is usually considerably higher than the velocity used to model sprinklers. Also, the deviation is maintained as small as possible to force the particles to stay close together during their motion. When we use jet flows to push rigid bodies through the simulated environment, we should use a moderate number of particles with increased mass values so that the net reaction force to the impact of the particles on the rigid body is large enough to move it.

The visual effect of explosions can use either a planar or spherical emitter surface, depending on what is being exploded. For instance, if we are simulating the explosion of a grenade, then we can safely use the planar emitter with a large number of particles of small size, short lifespan and large deviation. The splitting of particles is usually over used in these explosions, since we want to form a dense cloud immediately after the explosion. The particle's age is then used to control how fast the cloud will dissipate. There is no need to use external forces in these effects.

The spherical emitter is useful if we are creating the visual effect of fireworks, or the explosion of an artifact in a game environment. The idea is the same as that presented for planar emitters. The sphere's surface is decomposed into a grid where each cell releases one particle at a time along its radial direction. The direction deviation is then used to vary the emission direction with respect to the nominal radial direction. Also, the initial velocity deviation can be used to obtain an uneven cloud of particles.

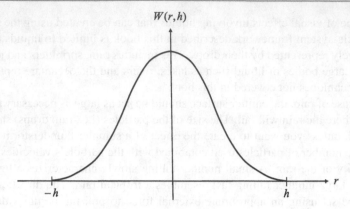

Fig. 3.27 The generic shape of a smoothing kernel function $W(r, h)$. The kernel has finite support h (i.e., goes to zero for $|r| \geq h$), is radially symmetric (i.e., $W(r, h) = W(-r, h)$) and the volume under its surface representation is normalized to one

3.8 Overview of Smoothed Particle Hydrodynamics

A popular way of simulating particle-based fluids is to use the mathematical framework based on Smoothed Particle Hydrodynamics (SPH). The SPH framework represents the fluid volume by a discrete set of particles, each carrying local information about the fluid such as its mass, velocity and viscosity. Radially symmetric smoothing kernels are used to specify how each particle affects its surroundings as a function of a user-adjustable interaction radius. Usually, the kernel value peaks at the particle position and decays as we move away from the particle, reaching zero when we are distant by interaction radius from it. This is best illustrated in the example of Fig. 3.27.

The determination of a fluid property at a given position in space consists of first finding all fluid particles that are within interaction radius from it, and then interpolating their contributions at the given position using the kernel functions to weight each contribution based on its distance to the given point. In other words, the SPH framework is used as an interpolation method that relies on the interaction radius and the kernel functions to determine the contribution of each particle to the fluid properties at a given location. According to this framework, the value of a scalar property A at a given location $\vec{r}$ is obtained from the interpolation

$$A(\vec{r}) = \sum_{i=1}^{n} m_i \frac{A_i}{\rho_i} W(\vec{r} - \vec{r}_i, h), \tag{3.82}$$

where h is the interaction radius, n is the total number of neighbor particles distant by less than h from position $\vec{r}$ and m_i, ρ_i and A_i are the fluid mass, density and scalar property value at particle i's location. The other two important quantities used in the SPH framework are the gradient and the Laplacian of the scalar property A at location $\vec{r}$. The gradient is computed using

$$\nabla A(\vec{r}) = \sum_{i=1}^{n} m_i \frac{A_i}{\rho_i} \nabla W(\vec{r} - \vec{r}_i, h), \tag{3.83}$$

and the Laplacian is given by

$$\nabla^2 A(\vec{r}) = \sum_{i=1}^{n} m_i \frac{A_i}{\rho_i} \nabla^2 W(\vec{r} - \vec{r}_i, h). \tag{3.84}$$

The particle-based fluid equations using the SPH framework can be derived from the Navier–Stokes equation. The details of such derivation is beyond the scope of this book. The interested reader is referred to Sect. 3.9 for pointers to the literature wherein in-depth explanations of such derivations can be found. Here, we will present an overview of the results needed for simulating particle-based fluids using the SPH framework.

The motion of a fluid particle j is affected by three main force components, namely

$$(\vec{F}_j)_{net} = (\vec{F}_j)_{pressure} + (\vec{F}_j)_{viscosity} + (\vec{F}_j)_{external}. \tag{3.85}$$

Both pressure and viscosity forces in Eq. (3.85) are obtained from the interpolation of their values at neighbor fluid particles distant up to interaction radius from the given particle. As for the external force, it is computed from forces that are directly applied to the particle, such as gravity, constraint and contact forces.

The acceleration of particle j owing to its net force is then

$$\vec{a}_j = \frac{(\vec{F}_j)_{net}}{\rho_j}, \tag{3.86}$$

with ρ_j being the fluid density at particle j. Using Eq. (3.82), the fluid density at particle j can be computed as

$$\rho_j = \sum_{i=1}^{n} m_i \frac{\rho_i}{\rho_i} W(\vec{r}_j - \vec{r}_i, h)$$

$$= \sum_{i=1}^{n} m_i W(\vec{r}_j - \vec{r}_i, h). \tag{3.87}$$

Now, let's examine in more details the terms in the right-hand side of Eq. (3.85). The first term comes from the fluid pressure exerted on particle j. The pressure force at particle j can be computed as

$$(\vec{F}_j)_{pressure} = -\sum_{i=1}^{n} m_i \frac{(p_i + p_j)}{\rho_i \rho_j} \nabla W(\vec{r}_j - \vec{r}_i, h), \qquad (3.88)$$

where p_i and p_j are the fluid pressure at particles i and j, respectively, and n is the number of neighbor particles i that are within distance h from particle j.

The computation of the pressure p_i used in Eq. (3.88) depends on whether the fluid being simulated is gas or liquid. If the fluid is gas then we use the pressure equation

$$p_i = k_p(\rho_i - \rho_0), \qquad (3.89)$$

with k_p and ρ_0 being user-definable values for pressure stiffness and rest density, respectively. For liquids, the pressure equation becomes

$$p_i = k_b\left(\left(\frac{\rho_i}{\rho_0}\right)^7 - 1\right), \qquad (3.90)$$

with the constant k_b used to control the compressibility of the fluid. Assuming the fluid is allowed to compress by c_p percent, the estimated value for the constant k_b is obtained from

$$k_b = \frac{\rho_0 |\vec{v}_{max}|^2}{7(c_f/100.0)},$$

where $\vec{v}_{max}$ is the maximum expected velocity a particle will have during the simulation.

According to Eqs. (3.89) and (3.90), the pressure force will constantly work on changing the particle density to match that of the equilibrium state, namely ρ_0. For instance, if the current particle density is greater than the desired rest density, then the pressure force will push away its neighbor particles in a attempt to reduce their contributions to the density calculations in Eq. (3.87). On the other hand, if the particle density is smaller than the rest density, then the pressure force will pull closer its neighbor particles to increase the particle's density. The pressure stiffness k_p controls how aggressive the push and pull of neighbor particles is performed during simulation. A lower stiffness value can prevent the fluid from achieving its desired rest density, reducing the overall fluid volume represented by the particles in the simulation. Conversely, a high stiffness value can make the fluid react too fast to small changes in density values, and will probably introduce instabilities in the system such as having particles being projected out of the fluid volume with high velocities, or having vibrations along the fluid surface. The appropriate choice of

Table 3.1 Most common smoothing kernels and their derivatives for particle j with respect to its neighbor particle i. Their distance $\vec{r} = \vec{r}_j - \vec{r}_i$ should be within the valid range of $0 \leq r \leq h$, where $r = |\vec{r}|$ and h is the interaction radius. The kernels are zero for all neighbor particles outside the valid range

Kernel	$\frac{315}{64\pi h^9}(h^2 - r^2)^3$
Gradient	$-\frac{945}{32\pi h^9}(h^2 - r^2)^2 \vec{r}$
Laplacian	$-\frac{945}{32\pi h^9}(h^2 - r^2)(h^2 - 5r)$
Kernel	$\frac{15}{\pi h^6}(h - r)^3$
Gradient	$-\frac{45}{\pi h^6}(h - r)^2 (\vec{r}/r)$
Laplacian	$\frac{90}{\pi h^6}(h - r)$
Kernel	$\frac{15}{2\pi h^3}(-\frac{r^3}{2h^3} + \frac{r^2}{h^2} + \frac{h}{2r} - 1)$
Gradient	$\frac{15}{2\pi h^3}(-\frac{3r^2}{2h^3} + \frac{2r}{h^2} - \frac{h}{2r^2})(\vec{r}/r)$
Laplacian	$\frac{15}{2\pi h^3}(-\frac{3r}{h^3} + \frac{2}{h^2} + \frac{h}{r^3})$

pressure stiffness and rest density depends on the application and the total number of particles used in the system.

The second term in the right-hand side of Eq. (3.85) comes from the fluid viscosity. The viscosity force at particle j can be computed as

$$(\vec{F}_j)_{viscosity} = \mu \sum_{i=1}^{n} m_i \frac{(\vec{v}_i - \vec{v}_j)}{\rho_i} \nabla^2 W(\vec{r}_j - \vec{r}_i, h), \qquad (3.91)$$

with $\vec{v}_i$ and $\vec{v}_j$ being the velocity of particles i and j, respectively. According to Eq. (3.91), the viscosity force will try to drag particle j along with its neighbor particles i in the direction of their relative motion. Notice that the viscosity force is zero whenever the particle and its neighbors are moving together at the same velocity.

Finally, the third term in the right-hand side of Eq. (3.85) accounts for all external forces acting on the particle. This include gravity, constraints, contact and any other user-definable forces that are directly applied to particle j. These external forces are accumulated into a single net external force before being applied to the particle.

Clearly, the behavior of the fluid system depends on the choice of smoothing kernel. We can use a single kernel for interpolating density, pressure and viscosity values, but the preferred approach is to use different kernels for each of these calculations. For each kernel, we need to derive expressions for its gradient and Laplacian derivatives. Table 3.1 summarizes the most common kernels used in practice.

The efficiency of the SPH framework comes from the quick determination of all neighbor particles to a given particle. This can be achieved using a grid cell decomposition of the simulated world (see Sect. 2.4.1), with grid spacing equal to the interaction radius h. Given a particle, we can quickly determine the grid cell it belongs to, and search its 27 neighbor cells for particles that are within interaction radius from it. A common optimization is to cache this search result at the beginning of each time interval, and reuse it during the density, pressure and viscosity calculations.

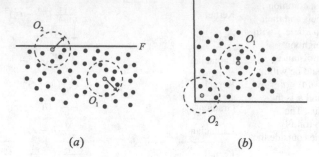

(a)   *(b)*

Fig. 3.28 Examples of the *edge effect* problem (also known as *boundary particle deficiency* problem) in the SPH framework; (**a**) Particle O_2 is closer to the fluid surface F by less than the interaction radius h, and it has significant less neighbors than particle O_1, which is farther inside the fluid; (**b**) Particle O_2 is closer to the collision object surface than particle O_1, and therefore has fewer neighbor particles that are within interaction radius from it

Notice that the simulation time interval can be sub-divided into several time steps, depending on how fast the particles are moving. Usually, we want to enforce that the particles will move by a distance no greater than their interaction radius along each world-coordinate axis in a single time step. This restriction is needed to keep the neighbor particles' information invariant during the computations for each time step. If the particles are allowed to move to another grid cell within a single time step, then their set of neighbor particles will likely change and their density, pressure and viscosity values will have to be updated to reflect this change. This stability condition on the time-step size is expressed by

$$\Delta t = \min\left\{ \frac{h}{|(\vec{v}_x)_{max}|}, \frac{h}{|(\vec{v}_y)_{max}|}, \frac{h}{|(\vec{v}_x)_{max}|} \right\}, \tag{3.92}$$

where $|(\vec{v}_i)_{max}|$ is the maximum component value of the particle velocity along the world-coordinate axis i. Depending on the application at hand, this stability condition can be relaxed by introducing a user-adjustable parameter k that scales the interaction radius used in Eq. (3.92) to kh, such that the particles can move by a distance greater (or smaller) than their interaction radius in a single time step.

As far as collisions are concerned, all particle–particle and particle–rigid body collision algorithms described in the previous sections can be used here. We just need to be careful when resolving collisions, to properly handle the cases in which one particle is moved on top of another particle, causing a "division-by-zero" exception on the kernel calculations. Another similar problem that arises in practice is when a particle finds itself completely isolated from all other fluid particles, that is, it has no neighbors within interaction radius distance from it. In these cases, the particle density obtained from Eq. (3.87) is zero, and we will have a "division-by-zero" exception when computing the particle's acceleration using Eq. (3.86). The workaround for these "division-by-zero" exceptions is to replace the zero-density values with the rest density of the fluid in the calculations.

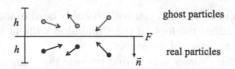

Fig. 3.29 A surface F possibly representing a fluid surface, a collision object geometry, or the interface between two different particle systems. Ghost particles are created as mirror images of their real-particle counterparts, but with inverted velocity component along the surface normal

Even though the SPH framework provides an efficient way of simulating particle-based fluids, it does have an intrinsic limitation regarding the kernel-based interpolation approach. Particles located near the fluid interface will always have less neighbor particles than other particles located in the inside region of the fluid. Figure 3.28 illustrates this particle-deficiency problem. These interfaces (i.e., fluid–air interface, collision objects, interface between different particle systems) act as clipping surfaces blocking the motion of the particles beyond them. This creates a bias on the fluid property calculations for particles near the fluid interfaces, potentially causing instabilities such as vibrations along the interfaces.

This limitation can be remedied if we use a set of *ghost* particles to fill-in for the missing ones. The best way to visualize this approach is to think of the clipping surfaces as mirrors where each ghost particle is a mirrored image of a real particle that is within interaction radius away from the surface. The mirrored (i.e., ghost) particles will have the same fluid attributes as their real-particle counterparts, but with inverted velocity component along the surface normal direction (see Fig. 3.29). The inversion on the velocity component along the normal direction is needed to make the interpolated velocity values at any position on the clipping surface have a zero component along the surface normal. This allows the particles to slide along the clipping surfaces without being pushed into or pulled away from them (i.e., without vibrations). Notice that the ghost particles are not being simulated. They are dynamically created at each time step and used in the kernel evaluations only. They do not participate in other modules of the system such as particle–particle collisions.

3.9 Notes and Comments

The idea of using particle systems as a modeling tool in computer graphics was originally introduced by Reeves [Ree83]. Nowadays, particle systems are so widely used to model diverse sets of systems that the large number of different techniques, implementations and parameter settings available makes it difficult to address this topic in depth.

From our experience, the selection of the particle system depends on the application at hand. For instance, if you are working on molecular dynamics, then you will probably be willing to trade efficiency for accuracy in your models, and so you need to use a particle system that models the details of particle interactions to a great extent. On the other hand, if your concern is to get a visually appealing simulation of smoke coming out of a fire, then you will probably need to use a flexible particle system that lets you adjust the look of the simulation without worrying too much about the underlying accuracy of the model.

Our approach in this chapter was to first provide the foundation needed to implement accurate models of particle interactions based on classical mechanics, then extend our model with some user-definable parameters commonly found in animation packages to support a diverse set of specialized particle systems. Frenkel et al. [FS96] also used the mathematical foundation of classical mechanics to model several molecular-dynamics systems. The types of force interactions described in Sect. 3.3 were inspired from the work of Frenkel and Baraff et al. [BW98]. A detailed discussion on under, over and critically damped spring systems can be found in Beer et al. [BJ77b].

The use of a critical-coefficient-of-friction value to determine whether the particles are sliding at their collision point was obtained from Brach [Bra91]. This in turn allows us to express the multiple particle–particle collision case in a concise block-partitioned matrix representation, which can be efficiently solved by Gaussian elimination, or by a specialized sparse-matrix solver routine. The mathematical foundation used to derive the single and multiple contact equations was adapted from Baraff et al. [BW98], which dealt with rigid body–rigid body contact-force computation.

Several parameters used in Sect. 3.7 were inspired from commercial software packages, such as Autodesk's Maya and SoftImage's Particle System. The suggested parameter settings for simulating smoke, liquids and explosions were obtained by trial and error.

The SPH model presented in Sect. 3.8 is a combination of the models proposed by Müller et al. [MC11, MCG03], Becker et al. [BM07] and Liu et al. [LL03]. More complex SPH models can be used to enforce fluid incompressibility, such as the ones presented in Adams et al. [APKG07], Solenthaler et al. [SBMG11, SP09], Kipfer et al. [KW06] and Borve et al. [BOT05].

Lastly, the mathematical theory of the Navier–Stokes equations and the physics of the conventional theory of turbulence can be found in Wilkins [Wil99], Stam et al. [SF95, Sta99], Foster et al. [FM96, FM97] and Bridson [Bri08]. An introduction to the Chapman–Jouget theory used to model detonation of explosives can also be found in Wilkins [Wil99].

3.10 Exercises

1. Equation (3.6) for damped springs presented in Sect. 3.3.3 can be improved in many ways.
   (a) The current form of the equation assumes the particles connected by the damped spring have the same mass. Derive a new formula for the case when the particles have different mass values.
   (b) The spring stiffness and damping coefficient are related by the *damping ratio*. A damping ratio of 1 is equivalent to a critically damped spring. Values greater than 1 result in an over-damped motion, whereas values between

0 and 1 makes the spring motion become under-damped. Given a stiffness value, we can use the damping ratio to compute the damping coefficient needed to get an under-, over- or critically-damped motion. Derive a new formula that uses the damping ratio as a user-adjustable parameter instead of the damping coefficient.

2. The particle–rigid body collision algorithm presented in Sect. 3.4.2 uses a vertex–face (i.e., ray–triangle) intersection test to detect continuous collision between them, ignoring the particle radius and treating it as a point mass.
   (a) Derive an intersection test between a continuously moving sphere and a static triangle.
   (b) Extend the previous intersection test to cope with a continuously moving triangle as well.

3. The approach used in this book to resolve the cases in which a particle finds itself inside a rigid body at the beginning of the current time interval is to move the particle to its closest point on the body's surface. An alternative approach would be to create a temporary spring connecting the particle to its closest point, and use it to pull the particle out of the rigid body.
   (a) How would you update the rest length of this spring to maximize stability and avoid over-shooting the particle?
   (b) Which modifications are needed in the continuous vertex–face collision algorithm to allow a particle to move from the inside to the outside of the object without getting stuck in the object's surface?

References

[APKG07] Adams, B., Pauly, M., Keiser, R., Guibas, L.J.: Adaptively sampled particle fluids. Comput. Graph. (Proc. SIGGRAPH) **26** (2007)

[BJ77b] Beer, F.P., Johnston, E.R.: Vector Mechanics for Engineers: vol. 2—Dynamics. McGraw-Hill, New York (1977)

[BM07] Becker, M., Müller, M.: Weakly compressible SPH for free surface flows. In: SIGGRAPH Symposium on Computer Animation, pp. 1–8 (2007)

[BOT05] Borve, S., Omang, M., Truslen, J.: Regularized smoothed particle hydrodynamics with improved multi-resolution handling. J. Comput. Phys. **208**, 345–367 (2005)

[Bra91] Brach, R.M. (ed.): Mechanical Impact Dynamics: Rigid Body Collisions. Wiley, New York (1991)

[Bri08] Bridson, R.: Fluid Simulation. AK Peters, Wellesley (2008)

[BW98] Baraff, D., Witkin, A.: Physically based modeling. SIGGRAPH Course Notes **13** (1998)

[FM96] Foster, N., Metaxas, D.: Realistic animation of liquids. In: Proceedings Graphics Interface, pp. 204–212 (1996)

[FM97] Foster, N., Metaxas, D.: Modeling the motion of a hot, turbulent gas. Comput. Graph. (Proc. SIGGRAPH) **31**, 181–188 (1997)

[FS96] Frenkel, D., Smit, B.: Understanding Molecular Simulation from Algorithms to Applications. Academic Press, San Diego (1996)

[KW06] Kipfer, P., Westermann, R.: Realistic and interactive simulation of rivers. In: Proceedings of Graphics Interface (2006)

[LL03] Liu, G.R., Liu, M.B.: Smoothed Particle Hydrodynamics. World Scientific, Singapore (2003)

[MC11]   Müller, M., Chentanez, N.: Solid simulation with oriented particles. Comput. Graph.
         (Proc. SIGGRAPH) **30** (2011)
[MCG03] Müller, M., Charypar, D., Gross, M.: Particle-based fluid simulation for interactive
         applications. In: SIGGRAPH Symposium on Computer Animation (2003)
[Ree83] Reeves, W.T.: Particle systems—a technique for modeling a class of fuzzy objects.
         Comput. Graph. (Proc. SIGGRAPH) **17**, 359–376 (1983)
[SBMG11] Solenthaler, B., Bucher, P., Müller, M., Gross, M.: SPH based shallow water simula-
         tion. In: Proceedings of Virtual Reality Interaction and Physical Simulation, pp. 39–46
         (2011)
[SF95]   Stam, J., Fiume, E.: Depicting fire and other gaseous phenomena using diffusion pro-
         cesses. Comput. Graph. (Proc. SIGGRAPH) **29**, 129–136 (1995)
[SP09]   Solenthaler, B., Pajarola, R.: Predictive-corrective incompressible SPH. Comput.
         Graph. (Proc. SIGGRAPH) **28** (2009)
[Sta99] Stam, J.: Stable fluids. Comput. Graph. (Proc. SIGGRAPH) **33**, 121–127 (1999)
[Wil99] Wilkins, M.L.: Computer Simulation of Dynamic Phenomena. Springer, Berlin (1999)

Rigid-Body Systems

4

4.1 Introduction

Rigid-body dynamic simulations are by far the most interesting ones, with applications ranging from mechanical-systems design and prototyping, to robotic motion, to physics-based computer-graphics animations. A rigid body is modeled as a collection of particles that make up its geometric shape. During motion, the relative position of each particle forming the rigid body must remain constant so that its shape remains unchanged throughout the motion. This requires taking into account the rotational motion of the rigid body, which in turn considerably complicates the derivation of the equations of motion, the collision-detection techniques to be used, and the computation of all impulsive and contact forces that prevent their interpenetration during a simulation.

Here, we shall focus on both unconstrained and constrained motion of rigid bodies. The unconstrained motion deals with the dynamic equations that govern the free motion of a rigid body as a function of the net force and net torque acting on it. By free motion, we mean that the motion is determined without worrying about collision detection and response. The constrained motion, on the other hand, deals with the computation of all impulsive and contact forces resulting from single or multiple collisions, or contacts between two or more rigid bodies during a simulation. Notice that the constraints considered in this chapter are imposed solely to prevent interpenetration of the rigid bodies. In the next chapter, we shall study other types of constrained motion where two or more rigid bodies are inter-connected through joints that limit their relative degree of freedom, forcing them to stay "connected" throughout the entire simulation.

All algorithms presented in this book assume that a rigid body is given by its boundary representation, that is, by the faces defining its geometric shape. From the boundary representation, we can compute the rigid body's mass properties and convex decomposition, as explained in Appendices D and F (Chaps. 9 and 11), respectively. The mass properties of a rigid body are used in the dynamic-equations formulation presented in Sect. 4.2. The convex decomposition can be used to speed the collision-detection phase using specialized algorithms tailored for convex objects,

M.G. Coutinho, *Guide to Dynamic Simulations of Rigid Bodies and Particle Systems*,
Simulation Foundations, Methods and Applications,
DOI 10.1007/978-1-4471-4417-5_4, © Springer-Verlag London 2013

Fig. 4.1 (**a**) Rigid body positioned and oriented with respect to its body frame; (**b**) Same rigid body described with respect to the world frame

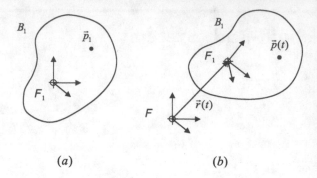

(*a*)   (*b*)

as discussed in Sect. 4.4. Also, we assume that the faces describing the rigid body geometry are all triangular. This is not a limitation, since the faces can be efficiently triangulated during the convex-decomposition computation (see Appendix F (Chap. 11) for details).

4.2 Rigid-Body Dynamics

The dynamic equations that govern the motion of a rigid body need to capture both translational and rotational effects owing to external forces acting on it. Moreover, the rigid body's motion is influenced not only by the external forces, but also by its shape and mass distribution. The former defines a set of variables known as the rigid body's *mass properties*.

The mass properties of a rigid body are its volume, total mass, center of mass and inertia tensor. The inertia tensor is the equivalent of the total mass for rotational motion. That is, in the same way that the mass is used to relate the linear acceleration with the net external force, the inertia tensor is used to relate the angular acceleration with the net external torque acting on the rigid body. The mass properties can be directly computed from the rigid body's boundary representation, as explained in detail in Appendix D (Chap. 9).

The boundary representation of a rigid body is usually given with respect to a local-reference frame known as the *body frame*. The mass properties of the rigid body are therefore computed with respect to this local frame. Scalar quantities, such as the rigid body's mass and volume, are independent of the reference frame being used. However, the position of the center of mass and the inertia tensor are affected by the choice of reference frame.

Let $\mathcal{F}_1$ be the body frame associated with the rigid body B_1, and let $\mathcal{F}$ be the world frame used in the simulation. Also, let the body frame be rotated by $\mathbf{R}(t)$ with respect to the world frame at time t. This is illustrated in Fig. 4.1.

As mentioned in Appendix D (Chap. 9), the inertia tensor is initially computed using a body frame that is parallel to the world frame, but has its origin at the rigid body's center of mass. Then the body frame is rotated to align with the principal axes of inertia transforming the symmetric inertia tensor matrix into a diagonal matrix, further simplifying rotation matrix computations. The main advantage of using such body frame is that the transformation between the inertia tensor from body-frame coordinates to world-frame coordinates is reduced to

$$\mathbf{I}(t) = \mathbf{R}(t)\mathbf{I_{body}}(t)\mathbf{R}^t(t),\qquad(4.1)$$

Given the position of a point $\vec{p}_1$ on the rigid body expressed in body-frame coordinates, its corresponding position $\vec{p}(t)$ with respect to the world frame is then computed as

$$\vec{p}(t) = \mathbf{R}(t)\vec{p}_1 + \vec{r}(t),\qquad(4.2)$$

where $\vec{r}(t)$ is the position of the center of mass of B_1 with respect to $\mathcal{F}$ at time instant t. Notice that $\vec{p}_1$ is computed with respect to the body frame $\mathcal{F}_1$, which moves with the body. Thus, $\vec{p}_1$ is a constant vector over time. The actual motion of the body with respect to $\mathcal{F}$ is encoded in the rotation matrix $\mathbf{R}(t)$ and the translation vector $\vec{r}(t)$.

The velocity of $\vec{p}(t)$ is obtained by computing the time derivative of its position vector, namely

$$\frac{d\vec{p}(t)}{dt} = \frac{d\mathbf{R}(t)}{dt}\vec{p}_1 + \mathbf{R}(t)\frac{d\vec{p}_1}{dt} + \frac{d\vec{r}(t)}{dt}.$$

Since $\vec{p}_1$ is a constant vector, we have

$$\frac{d\vec{p}(t)}{dt} = \frac{d\mathbf{R}(t)}{dt}\vec{p}_1 + \frac{d\vec{r}(t)}{dt}.\qquad(4.3)$$

Let $\vec{v}(t)$ be the linear velocity of the center of mass of body B_1 with respect to $\mathcal{F}$. Thus,

$$\frac{d\vec{r}(t)}{dt} = \vec{v}(t).\qquad(4.4)$$

Also, let $\vec{\omega}(t)$ be the angular velocity of body B_1 with respect to $\mathcal{F}$. According to Sect. 10.5 of Appendix E (Chap. 10), the time derivative of the rotation matrix is given by

$$\frac{d\mathbf{R}(t)}{dt} = \vec{\omega} \times \mathbf{R}(t) = \tilde{\omega}(t)\mathbf{R}(t),\qquad(4.5)$$

where $\tilde{\omega}(t)$ is the matrix–vector representation of a cross-product, described in Sect. 6.7 of Appendix A (Chap. 6). Substituting Eqs. (4.4) and (4.5) into (4.3), we obtain

$$\frac{d\vec{p}(t)}{dt} = \tilde{\omega}(t)\mathbf{R}(t)\vec{p}_1 + \vec{v}(t).$$

Using Eq. (4.2), we get

$$\frac{d\vec{p}(t)}{dt} = \tilde{\omega}(t)\mathbf{R}(t)\mathbf{R}(t)^{-1}\big(\vec{p}(t) - \vec{r}(t)\big) + \vec{v}(t)$$

$$= \tilde{\omega}(t)\big(\vec{p}(t) - \vec{r}(t)\big) + \vec{v}(t)$$

$$= \vec{\omega}(t) \times \big(\vec{p}(t) - \vec{r}(t)\big) + \vec{v}(t). \tag{4.6}$$

Equation (4.6) gives us a way of computing the velocity of any point $\vec{p}(t)$ in the rigid body. Finally, the acceleration of point $\vec{p}(t)$ is obtained by computing the time derivative of its velocity vector, namely

$$\frac{d^2\vec{p}(t)}{dt^2} = \frac{d\vec{\omega}(t)}{dt} \times \big(\vec{p}(t) - \vec{r}(t)\big)$$

$$+ \vec{\omega}(t) \times \left(\frac{d\vec{p}(t)}{dt} - \frac{d\vec{r}(t)}{dt}\right) + \frac{d\vec{v}(t)}{dt}. \tag{4.7}$$

Let $\vec{a}(t)$ be the linear acceleration of the rigid body's center of mass, that is

$$\vec{a}(t) = \frac{d\vec{v}(t)}{dt}$$

and let $\vec{\alpha}(t)$ be the angular acceleration of the rigid body defined as

$$\vec{\alpha}(t) = \frac{d\vec{\omega}(t)}{dt}.$$

Notice that both linear and angular accelerations are expressed in world-frame coordinates. Substituting these into Eq. (4.7), we obtain

$$\frac{d^2\vec{p}(t)}{dt^2} = \vec{\alpha}(t) \times \big(\vec{p}(t) - \vec{r}(t)\big)$$

$$+ \vec{\omega}(t) \times \big(\vec{\omega}(t) \times \big(\vec{p}(t) - \vec{r}(t)\big)\big) + \vec{a}(t). \tag{4.8}$$

Let $\vec{F}(t)$ be the net external force acting on the rigid body's center of mass at time instant t. Using Newton's law, we have

$$\vec{F}(t) = \frac{d\vec{L}(t)}{dt}, \tag{4.9}$$

where $\vec{L}(t)$ is the linear momentum of the rigid body computed from

$$\vec{L}(t) = m\vec{v}(t), \tag{4.10}$$

with m and $\vec{v}(t)$ being the rigid body's mass and linear velocity of its center of mass. Substituting Eq. (4.10) into (4.9), we have

$$\vec{F}(t) = \frac{d(m\vec{v}(t))}{dt} = m\frac{d\vec{v}(t)}{dt} = m\vec{a}(t). \tag{4.11}$$

A similar equation can be obtained relating the net torque $\vec{\tau}(t)$ acting on the rigid body's center of mass, with the angular acceleration $\vec{\alpha}(t)$. It is known as the Euler equation and is given by

$$\vec{\tau}(t) = \frac{d\vec{H}(t)}{dt}, \tag{4.12}$$

where $\vec{H}(t)$ is the rigid body's angular momentum computed as

$$\vec{H}(t) = \mathbf{I}(t)\vec{\omega}(t), \tag{4.13}$$

with $\mathbf{I}(t)$ being the inertia tensor expressed in *world frame* coordinates, obtained from Eq. (4.1).

The angular acceleration $\vec{\alpha}(t)$ is related to the angular momentum $\vec{H}(t)$, as follows. We already know that the angular acceleration is computed as the time derivative of the angular velocity. Since Eq. (4.13) relates the angular velocity and the angular momentum, we have

$$\vec{\alpha}(t) = \frac{d\vec{\omega}(t)}{dt} = \frac{d(\mathbf{I}^{-1}(t)\vec{H}(t))}{dt} = \frac{d\mathbf{I}^{-1}(t)}{dt}\vec{H}(t) + \mathbf{I}^{-1}(t)\frac{d\vec{H}(t)}{dt}.$$

Using Eq. (4.12),

$$\vec{\alpha}(t) = \frac{d\mathbf{I}^{-1}(t)}{dt}\vec{H}(t) + \mathbf{I}^{-1}(t)\vec{\tau}(t). \tag{4.14}$$

From Eq. (4.1), the inverse of the inertia tensor is given by

$$\mathbf{I}^{-1} = \mathbf{R}(t)(\mathbf{I_{body}})^{-1}(t)\mathbf{R}^t(t). \tag{4.15}$$

The time derivative of the inverse of the inertia tensor is then

$$\begin{aligned} d\mathbf{I}^{-1}(t)/dt &= \frac{d\mathbf{R}(t)}{dt}(\mathbf{I_{body}})^{-1}(t)\mathbf{R}^t(t) + \mathbf{R}(t)(\mathbf{I_{body}})^{-1}(t)\frac{d\mathbf{R}^t(t)}{dt} \\ &= \tilde{\omega}(t)\mathbf{R}(t)(\mathbf{I_{body}})^{-1}(t)\mathbf{R}^t(t) + \mathbf{R}(t)(\mathbf{I_{body}})^{-1}(t)(\tilde{\omega}(t)\mathbf{R}(t))^t \\ &= \tilde{\omega}(t)\mathbf{R}(t)(\mathbf{I_{body}})^{-1}(t)\mathbf{R}^t(t) + \mathbf{R}(t)(\mathbf{I_{body}})^{-1}(t)\mathbf{R}^t(t)\tilde{\omega}^t(t) \\ &= \tilde{\omega}(t)\mathbf{R}(t)(\mathbf{I_{body}})^{-1}(t)\mathbf{R}^t(t) - \mathbf{R}(t)(\mathbf{I_{body}})^{-1}(t)\mathbf{R}^t(t)\tilde{\omega}(t) \end{aligned}$$

because $\tilde{\omega}^t(t) = -\tilde{\omega}(t)$. Using Eq. (4.1) again, we can simplify the above expression to

$$\frac{d\mathbf{I}^{-1}(t)}{dt} = \tilde{\omega}(t)\overbrace{\mathbf{R}(t)(\mathbf{I_{body}})^{-1}(t)\mathbf{R}^t(t)}^{\mathbf{I}^{-1}(t)} - \overbrace{\mathbf{R}(t)(\mathbf{I_{body}})^{-1}(t)\mathbf{R}^t(t)}^{\mathbf{I}^{-1}(t)}\tilde{\omega}(t)$$

$$= \tilde{\omega}(t)\mathbf{I}^{-1}(t) - \mathbf{I}^{-1}(t)\tilde{\omega}(t). \tag{4.16}$$

Substituting Eq. (4.16) into (4.14), we obtain

$$\vec{\alpha}(t) = \left(\tilde{\omega}(t)\mathbf{I}^{-1}(t) - \mathbf{I}^{-1}(t)\tilde{\omega}(t)\right)\vec{H}(t) + \mathbf{I}^{-1}(t)\vec{\tau}(t)$$

$$= \tilde{\omega}(t)\mathbf{I}^{-1}(t)\vec{H}(t) - \mathbf{I}^{-1}(t)\tilde{\omega}(t)\vec{H}(t) + \mathbf{I}^{-1}(t)\vec{\tau}(t)$$

$$= \tilde{\omega}(t)\overbrace{\mathbf{I}^{-1}(t)\vec{H}(t)}^{\vec{\omega}(t)} - \mathbf{I}^{-1}(t)\tilde{\omega}(t)\vec{H}(t) + \mathbf{I}^{-1}(t)\vec{\tau}(t)$$

$$= \overbrace{\tilde{\omega}(t)\vec{\omega}(t)}^{\vec{\omega}(t)\times\vec{\omega}(t)=\vec{0}} - \mathbf{I}^{-1}(t)\tilde{\omega}(t)\vec{H}(t) + \mathbf{I}^{-1}(t)\vec{\tau}(t)$$

$$= -\mathbf{I}^{-1}(t)\vec{\omega}(t) \times \vec{H}(t) + \mathbf{I}^{-1}(t)\vec{\tau}(t)$$

$$= \mathbf{I}^{-1}(t)\vec{H}(t) \times \vec{\omega}(t) + \mathbf{I}^{-1}(t)\vec{\tau}(t). \tag{4.17}$$

So, the relation between the angular acceleration and angular momentum is expressed as

$$\vec{\alpha}(t) = \mathbf{I}^{-1}(t)\left(\vec{H}(t) \times \vec{\omega}(t) + \vec{\tau}(t)\right), \tag{4.18}$$

or alternatively

$$\vec{\tau}(t) = \mathbf{I}(t)\vec{\alpha}(t) - \vec{H}(t) \times \vec{\omega}(t)$$

$$= \mathbf{I}(t)\vec{\alpha}(t) + \vec{\omega}(t) \times \vec{H}(t). \tag{4.19}$$

Let $\vec{y}(t)$ denote the dynamic state of the rigid body at time t, that is, the vector comprising all variables necessary to define the dynamics of the rigid body at any instant during the simulation. Since the rigid body's motion can be sub-divided into translational and rotational components, we shall pick the center of mass's position, the rigid body's orientation, and its linear and angular momenta to define its dynamic state, namely

$$\vec{y}(t) = \begin{pmatrix} \vec{r}(t) \\ \mathbf{R}(t) \\ \vec{L}(t) \\ \vec{H}(t) \end{pmatrix}.$$

So, the dynamic state of the rigid body at time $t = t_0$ is defined by the center of mass's position $\vec{r}(t_0)$, the rigid body's orientation $\mathbf{R}(t_0)$, its linear momentum $\vec{L}(t_0)$ computed as $m\vec{v}(t_0)$, and its angular momentum $\vec{H}(t_0)$ computed as $\mathbf{I}(t_0)\vec{\omega}(t_0)$.

The time derivative of the dynamic state defines how the dynamic state of the rigid body changes over time, and is given by

$$
\frac{d\vec{y}(t)}{dt} = \begin{pmatrix} d\vec{r}(t)/dt \\ d\mathbf{R}(t)/dt \\ d\vec{L}(t)/dt \\ d\vec{H}(t)/dt \end{pmatrix} = \begin{pmatrix} \vec{v}(t) \\ \tilde{\omega}(t)\mathbf{R}(t) \\ \vec{F}(t) \\ \vec{\tau}(t) \end{pmatrix}.
$$

So, the time derivative of the dynamic state at time $t = t_0$ is defined by the center of mass's velocity $\vec{v}(t_0)$ computed as $(\vec{L}(t_0)/m)$, the updated orientation $\tilde{\omega}(t_0)\mathbf{R}(t_0)$ with $\vec{\omega}(t_0)$ being computed as $\mathbf{I}^{-1}(t_0)\vec{H}(t_0)$, and the net force $\vec{F}(t_0)$ and net torque $\vec{\tau}(t_0)$ acting on the center of mass.

For a system with N rigid bodies, we can combine their individual dynamic states into a single system-wide dynamic-state vector

$$
\vec{Y}(t) = \left(\vec{r}_1(t), \mathbf{R}_1(t), \vec{L}_1(t), \vec{H}_1(t), \ldots, \vec{r}_N(t), \mathbf{R}_N(t), \vec{L}_N(t), \vec{H}_N(t)\right)^t,
$$

with its corresponding time derivative being

$$
\frac{d\vec{Y}(t)}{dt} = \left(\vec{v}_1(t), \tilde{\omega}_1(t)\mathbf{R}_1(t), \vec{F}_1(t), \vec{\tau}_1(t), \ldots, \right.
$$
$$
\left. \vec{v}_N(t), \tilde{\omega}_N(t)\mathbf{R}_N(t), \vec{F}_N(t), \vec{\tau}_N(t)\right)^t. \tag{4.20}
$$

The general description of how the dynamic simulation of rigid-body systems work is very similar to the one already given in Chap. 3 for particle systems. At the beginning of the simulation, we have the dynamic state of each rigid body, namely its position, orientation and linear and angular momenta defined with respect to the world frame. Each simulation time interval consists of numerically integrating Eq. (4.20), using the dynamic state of the rigid bodies at the beginning of the time interval as the initial condition for the numerical integration. There are several numerical methods that can be used to integrate Eq. (4.20), and the most popular ones are discussed in detail in Appendix B (Chap. 7).

The computation of the net external force acting on each rigid body at each intermediate step of the numerical integrator is determined by summing all external forces acting on different points of the rigid body. These forces are then substituted for a force-torque pair acting on the rigid body's center of mass before they are used in the equations of motion. A force $\vec{F}_i(t)$ acting at point $\vec{p}_i(t)$ is substituted for a force-torque pair

$$
\vec{F}_{cm}(t) = \vec{F}_i(t)
$$
$$
\vec{\tau}_{cm}(t) = \left(\vec{p}_i(t) - \vec{r}(t)\right) \times \vec{F}_i(t),
$$

where the (cm) index stands for "center of mass." The types of external forces considered in this book for rigid-body simulations range from simple global forces (such as gravity) to point-to-point forces (such as springs), and are discussed in detail in Sect. 4.3.

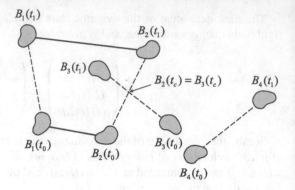

Fig. 4.2 A simple rigid-body system containing four objects. The dynamic state of the system is numerically integrated from t_0 to t_1. A collision between bodies B_2 and B_3 is detected at time t_c

In a first pass, the determination of the dynamic state of each rigid body at the end of the current time interval is done without taking into account any possible collisions between rigid bodies and other objects in the simulation environment. The information about the final dynamic state of each rigid body is then used on a second pass to check for collisions between themselves and other particles in the simulation. The collision detection consists of checking for geometric intersections between the bodies positioned at the end of the current simulation time interval with all other bodies and particles in the simulation. As explained in Sect. 3.4.2, the particular case of rigid body–particle collision is handled only after all rigid body–rigid body collisions have been detected and resolved. This is necessary because the rigid body–particle collision model used in this book is such that, when a particle collides with a rigid body, only the particle is backtracked in time to the moment before the collision.

Whenever a rigid body–rigid body collision is detected, the colliding rigid bodies have their positions and orientations backtracked in time to the moment before their collision. The collision point and collision normal are then computed from the relative displacement of the colliding bodies. Only after this information is obtained does the collision-response module engage to compute the appropriate impulsive or contact forces that will be applied to change the direction of motion of the colliding rigid bodies.

The dynamic equations of all rigid bodies involved in a collision are then numerically integrated for the remaining period of time, that is, from the collision time to the end of the current time interval. This new numerical integration will update the current rigid bodies' positions and orientations to account for all collision forces. Notice that this also requires the numerical integration of the dynamic state of all other rigid bodies connected to one or more rigid bodies involved in a collision, since the connection usually implies the existence of a force component between them. For example, consider a simple rigid-body system consisting of four rigid bodies, namely B_1, B_2, B_3 and B_4, and suppose rigid bodies B_1 and B_2 are connected by a spring.

Initially, the dynamic state of the system is numerically integrated from t_0 (the beginning of the current time interval) to t_1 (the end of the current time interval). Now, assume the collision-detection module detected a collision between bodies B_2

Fig. 4.3 Bodies B_2 and B_3 are backtracked in time to the moment just before their collision

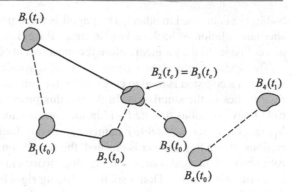

Fig. 4.4 Body B_1 is also backtracked in time to t_c before the numerical integrator is used to recompute the positions and orientations of bodies B_1, B_2 and B_3. Notice that body B_4 was not affected by the collision, and therefore remained unchanged throughout the collision-detection and response phase

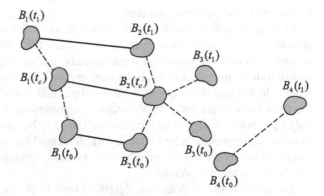

and B_3 at time t_c such that $t_0 < t_c < t_1$ (see Fig. 4.2). The colliding bodies are then backtracked in time to the moment just before their collision (i.e., backtracked to t_c) and the collision impulses are computed so as to prevent their interpenetration. Having applied the collision impulses to both bodies, their dynamic state is numerically integrated again save for the remaining period of time only, that is, from t_c to t_1. However, if we just backtrack in time bodies B_2 and B_3, the spring-force computation between bodies B_1 and B_2 will be incorrect in the numerical integration for the remaining period of time. The problem is that, since body B_1 was not involved in any collision, its dynamic state corresponds to time t_1, whereas the dynamic state of body B_2 corresponds to time t_c at the beginning of the integration. So, if we do not backtrack in time B_1 either, the spring-force computation will use B_1's position and orientation at time t_1 when it should use them at the same simulation time of B_2, namely time t_c (see Fig. 4.3). In other words, the numerical integration of the dynamic state of all interconnected bodies should be synchronized to provide the correct system behavior (see Fig. 4.4). On the other hand, bodies that are not involved in a collision can be asynchronously moved within the same simulation time interval. This is the case of rigid body B_4, as shown in Fig. 4.4, since the numerical integration of B_2 and B_3 for the remaining period of time did not affect its dynamic state already computed in the first pass. As far as implementation is concerned, this approach requires some bookkeeping mechanism to efficiently determine which rigid bodies are connected to others. The payoff is the significant efficiency gain over the alternate solution of backtracking in time all rigid bodies, even those not involved in a collision, to the moment before the most recent collision.

The updated information about the final dynamic state of each rigid body involved in a collision is used to check again for collisions between them and all other rigid bodies in the simulation. In theory, this process repeats until all rigid body–rigid body collisions detected within the current time interval have been resolved. In practice, a user-adjustable parameter is used to limit the maximum number of iterations. When this number is reached, the simulation engine overrides the physical parameters of all rigid bodies, forcing all collisions to be inelastic (i.e., coefficient of restitution set to zero). Doing so, the colliding rigid bodies will stick together after their collision is processed, thus significantly reducing the number of new collisions introduced in the following iterations.

Clearly, the collision check is an intense process that can take up a lot of computational time, especially in a naive implementation. We suggest using the cell decomposition of the simulated world already discussed in Sect. 2.4 to speed the collision-detection checks. As the system evolves, the position of each rigid body relative to the cell decomposition of the simulated world is tracked by assigning the rigid body to the cells its hierarchical representation intersects. By so doing, only rigid bodies assigned to the same cell need to be checked for collisions. This dynamic assignment can be efficiently implemented by observing that the cell decomposition defines a uniform subdivision of the simulated world into cubic cells (see Sect. 2.4 for more details).

The actual collision detection algorithm used to compute the collision time depends on the objects' shape and velocity. The most generic non-convex objects require more time consuming algorithms to process their collision times, whereas convex objects use fast and specialized algorithms that rely on their convexity properties to execute properly. Fast motion and thin objects are handled using continuous collision detection. All of these methods are discussed in details in the following sections.

4.3   Basic Interaction Forces

The interaction forces used in most rigid-body system simulations can be categorized into two different types of forces. The first type considers global interaction forces, that is, forces independently applied to all rigid bodies in the system. Examples include gravity and viscous drag (used to simulate air resistance). These are the least expensive interaction forces available and their required computational cost is often negligible compared with that of the second type of interaction forces discussed in this book.

The second type considers point-to-point forces between a specific number of rigid bodies. Damped springs are a good example of such interaction forces between two given bodies. Interactive-user manipulation is also modeled as a point-to-point force between the current mouse position and the selected rigid body. The idea of

Fig. 4.5 Gravity pulling rigid body B_1 with mass m_1 towards the ground plane

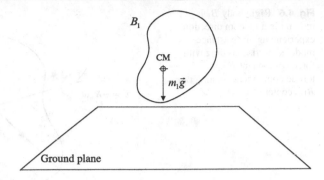

using a fictitious interaction force between the mouse and the selected rigid body is to prevent the introduction of unstable configurations owing to abrupt mouse movements, as explained in Sect. 4.3.4.

4.3.1 Gravity

The force contribution of gravity acting on each rigid body owing to its attraction to the ground is directly obtained from

$$\vec{F} = m\vec{g},$$

where $\vec{g}$ is the gravitational acceleration, m is the rigid body's mass and $\vec{F}$ acts on the body's center of mass (see Fig. 4.5). The gravitational acceleration is in most cases assumed to have constant magnitude equal to 9.81 m/s^2 direction pointing downwards (i.e., towards the ground).

4.3.2 Viscous Drag

The most common use of viscous drag in dynamic simulations of rigid-body systems is to model the air resistance to the body's movement. The goal is to ensure that rigid bodies will eventually come to rest if there are no other external forces acting on them. Figure 4.6 illustrates this. The force component of the viscous drag is computed as

$$\vec{F} = -k_v \vec{v},$$

where $\vec{v}$ is the linear velocity of the rigid body's center of mass and k_v is the linear drag coefficient.

The torque component of the viscous drag is determined using a similar formula given by

$$\vec{\tau} = -k_\omega \vec{\omega},$$

Fig. 4.6 Rigid body B_1 is moving in a random direction experiencing air resistance modeled as viscous drag with force component $\vec{F}$ and torque component $\vec{\tau}$ acting on B_1's center of mass

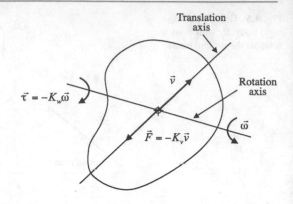

where $\vec{\omega}$ is the angular velocity of the rigid body and k_ω is the angular drag coefficient.

4.3.3   Damped Springs

Springs are mostly used to keep the distance between pairs of rigid bodies at a known value. Whenever the rigid bodies are pushed apart or pulled together, a spring force is applied to both bodies, with same magnitude and opposite direction.

Let B_1 and B_2 be two rigid bodies connected by a spring of resting length r_0. The spring is attached to bodies B_1 and B_2 at points $\vec{p}_1$ and $\vec{p}_2$, respectively. Let $\vec{v}_1$ and $\vec{v}_2$ be the velocities of points $\vec{p}_1$ and $\vec{p}_2$, computed using Eq. (4.6). The spring-force component acting on the center of mass of both rigid bodies is then given by

$$\vec{F}_2 = -\left[k_s \left(|\vec{p}_2 - \vec{p}_1| - r_0 \right) + k_d (\vec{v}_2 - \vec{v}_1) \cdot \frac{(\vec{p}_2 - \vec{p}_1)}{|\vec{p}_2 - \vec{p}_1|} \right] \frac{(\vec{p}_2 - \vec{p}_1)}{|\vec{p}_2 - \vec{p}_1|}$$

$$\vec{F}_1 = -\vec{F}_2, \tag{4.21}$$

with $\vec{F}_i$ being the spring force acting on rigid body B_i for $i \in \{1, 2\}$, k_s being the spring constant and k_d being the damping constant (see Fig. 4.7). Since the spring force is applied to points $\vec{p}_1$ and $\vec{p}_2$, it is substituted for a force-torque pair ($\vec{F}_1$ and $\vec{\tau}_1$) acting on body B_1, and $\vec{F}_2$ and $\vec{\tau}_2$ acting on body B_2, with

$$\vec{\tau}_1 = (\vec{p}_1 - \vec{r}_1) \times \vec{F}_1$$

$$\vec{\tau}_2 = (\vec{p}_2 - \vec{r}_2) \times \vec{F}_2. \tag{4.22}$$

The damping term of Eq. (4.21) is used to prevent oscillation, and does not affect the motion of the center of mass of the connected bodies.

Fig. 4.7 Rigid bodies B_1 and B_2 are connected by a damped spring; (**a**) Bodies at resting position; (**b**) Spring forces exerted on the rigid bodies when they are pushed together

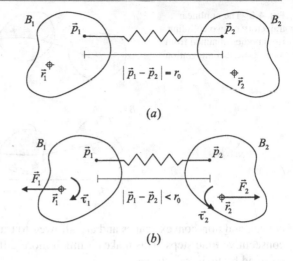

4.3.4   User-Interaction Forces

The user-interaction force is modeled as a damped spring connecting the current mouse position to the position of the rigid body's point being dragged. The idea of using this fictitious spring is to avoid the introduction of unrealistically large external forces acting on the selected body owing to abrupt mouse movements. These large external forces can make the dynamic equations describing the rigid body's motion stiff. Stiff systems are more susceptible to round-off errors and usually require the use of more elaborate and time-consuming numerical-integration methods, such as the implicit Euler method described in Appendix B (Chap. 7).

The main difference between the damped spring described in Sect. 4.3.3 and the fictitious spring used here, is that the resting length of the fictitious spring should be set to zero. A zero resting length means that the selected rigid body will only stabilize its motion when its position is coincident with the mouse position. Therefore, as the user drags the body around, the current mouse position is used to update the actual distance between the rigid body and the mouse. This distance is then used in Eqs. (4.21) and (4.22) to compute the appropriate spring force-torque pair to be applied to the rigid body's center of mass.

4.4   Collision Detection Overview

Accurate collision detection on rigid-body dynamic simulations is much more difficult to achieve than in particle systems because of a fundamental difference in modeling these systems. Particles are usually modeled as simple spherical objects that can translate, but not rotate, during their motion. Their trajectories therefore span a volume in 3D space along straight line segments. Collision detection is then carried out by checking for continuous time intersections between the trajectories of all particles that are potentially colliding. Rigid bodies, on the other hand, have

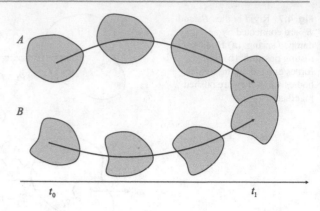

Fig. 4.8 The nonlinear trajectory of two colliding rigid bodies obtained from their numerical integration

convex and non-convex shapes and are allowed to translate and rotate between two consecutive time steps. This makes it much more difficult to determine the volume spanned by their trajectories.

In most applications, collision detection between rigid bodies can be simplified by testing for collisions only at the end of the current time interval. The rigid bodies are said to be colliding whenever there are geometric intersections between their shapes positioned at the end of the current time interval. The actual collision information is obtained from backtracking in time to the point just before their collision occurs. The closest points between the rigid bodies at the collision time are approximated as the collision points, and the collision normal is obtained depending on whether the closest points belong to a vertex–face, face–vertex or edge–edge case. The following summarizes the determination of the collision normal for each case:

1. *Vertex–Face*: unit vector parallel to the face normal.
2. *Face–Vertex*: unit vector parallel to the face normal.
3. *Edge–Edge*: unit vector perpendicular to both edges. Can be computed as the cross-product between the vectors defining the direction of each edge.

In all of the above cases, the actual direction of the collision normal is chosen such that the relative velocity of the rigid bodies at the collision points along the collision normal is negative, indicating that the bodies are moving towards each other. The tangent plane is directly obtained from the collision normal and collision points, as explained in Sect. 6.6 of Appendix A (Chap. 6). Once the collision information is gathered, a collision impulse or contact force of same magnitude and opposite direction is then applied to each colliding body to prevent their interpenetration.

The process of backtracking in time to the moment just before the collision assumes the motion of the rigid bodies is linearized, that is, their actual trajectories are replaced by a simplified one, corresponding to a motion with constant linear and angular velocities (see Figs. 4.8 and 4.9). As explained in Sect. 6.8, the net change in translation and rotation for the colliding rigid bodies can be computed from the difference between their known positions and orientations at t_0 and t_1. We assume this change takes place at a constant rate, thus enabling the computation of the constant linear and angular veloc-

Fig. 4.9 The collision
detection module replaces the
nonlinear trajectory of the
colliding rigid bodies by a
linear trajectory with constant
translation and rotation. The
positions of the rigid bodies
at any time $t \in [t_0, t_1]$ can be
obtained by simple linear
interpolation (see Sect. 6.8 of
Appendix A (Chap. 6) for
more details)

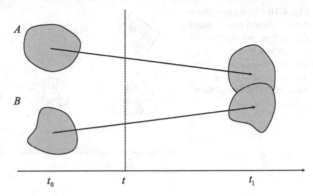

ities for the rigid bodies' motion during the time interval. We can then use
simple linear interpolation to determine the position of the rigid bodies at any
time $t_i \in [t_0, t_1]$. This is an important simplification that helps improve the overall collision detection performance because the backtrack in time is an iterative process that usually requires several iterations to converge to the collision
time.

In the general collision case, the rigid bodies start at a non-colliding state at t_0
and end up colliding at t_1. At each iteration of the backtrack-in-time process, the
current time interval $[t_i, t_{i+1}]$ is split into two sub-intervals $[t_i, t_m]$ and $[t_m, t_{i+1}]$,
and is replaced by the sub-interval that better approximates the collision time. The
closest point information for the selected sub-interval is updated and a new iteration follows. This iterative process continues until the sub-interval converges to
the collision time. The closest-point update can be done using the proximity information if the rigid bodies do not intersect at t_m, or using the intersection regions
when they do intersect at t_m. At the end of each iteration, the updated time interval
$[t_j, t_{j+1}] = [t_i, t_m]$ or $[t_j, t_{j+1}] = [t_m, t_{i+1}]$ is chosen such that the rigid bodies are
not colliding at t_j, but are colliding at t_{j+1}.

Depending on the simulation setup, it is possible that the rigid bodies already
start in a colliding state at t_0. This special case can be handled by executing an extra
intersection test between the rigid bodies positioned at t_0, that is, at the beginning
of the collision detection process for the time interval $[t_0, t_1]$. If the rigid bodies
are already intersecting at t_0, then the collision detection module sets their collision
time to t_0 and computes the collision information from their current intersection
regions.

4.5   Collision Detection Between Non-convex Bodies

Whenever two rigid bodies are checked for collision against each other, the first
thing the collision detection module does is verify that the bodies are either convex,
or decomposed into convex parts. The convex decomposition can in most cases be
computed using the algorithm presented in Appendix F (Chap. 11). However, sometimes the convex-decomposition algorithm is incapable of determining the convex

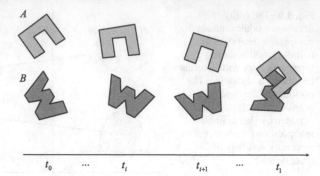

Fig. 4.10 Two non-convex rigid bodies A and B moving for the time interval $[t_0, t_1]$ and intersecting at t_1. The simulation engine backtracks in time using the bisection method to determine their collision time

decomposition of the rigid body, possibly owing to a minimum dihedral angle or cut-face[1] requirement that cannot be satisfied.

When both non-convex bodies are represented by their convex decomposition, the collision-detection module uses the specialized algorithms discussed in Sect. 4.7, which take advantage of the bodies' convexity properties to significantly improve the overall performance. Otherwise, the more general and time-consuming collision-detection algorithm for non-convex rigid bodies is used to compute the collision time and its associated collision points.

As mentioned in the previous section, the backtrack in time is an iterative process. At each iteration, the closest point information between the rigid bodies is updated and the intermediate time interval considered is reduced until it converges to the collision time. In the general non-convex case, this is done by bisecting the current interval $[t_i, t_{i+1}]$ into two halves, namely $[t_i, t_m]$ and $[t_m, t_{i+1}]$ with $t_m = (t_i + t_{i+1})/2$. The rigid bodies are then checked for geometrical intersections at t_m. This test consists of intersecting their hierarchical representations updated with their positions at t_m (see Sect. 2.5.1 for details on intersecting hierarchies). If the bodies don't intersect at t_m, then the collision time is in the sub-interval $[t_m, t_{i+1}]$. Otherwise, the rigid bodies intersect at t_m and the collision time is in the sub-interval $[t_i, t_m]$. In either case, the sub-interval not used is discarded. This iterative process continues until one of the following termination conditions is satisfied:

1. The length $(t_{i+1} - t_i)$ of the current time interval is less than a user-definable threshold value.
2. The current number of iterations has reached a maximum user-definable value.

Upon termination, the collision time is set as t_i and the collision points are set as the closest points between the rigid bodies positioned at t_i.

Unfortunately, the efficient determination of the closest points between non-convex rigid bodies is not as straight-forward as it is for convex bodies. The main reason is that the closest point information can change in a non-monotonic way between consecutive iterations as we backtrack in time to the moment just before

---

[1]The algorithm presented in Appendix F (Chap. 11) limits the set of valid cut faces to simple polygons (without holes or double edges). This, in turn, makes the algorithm unsuitable for decomposing complex geometric shapes.

Fig. 4.11 Intermediate iterations t_{i+1} and t_i of the bisection method used in Fig. 1.4. There is a non-monotonic change in distance to move from closest points $(\vec{a}_1, \vec{b}_1)$ at t_i to closest points $(\vec{a}_5, \vec{b}_7)$ at t_{i+1}

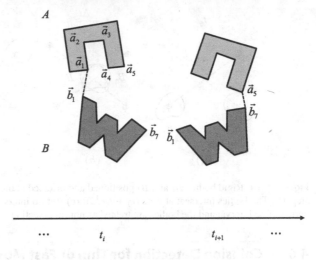

the collision.[2] Figures 4.10 and 4.11 illustrate this case with two non-convex rigid bodies intersecting at t_1.

In this example, as the objects move from t_i to t_{i+1}, their closest points change from vertices $(\vec{a}_1, \vec{b}_1)$ to vertices $(\vec{a}_5, \vec{b}_7)$. In order to reach vertex $\vec{a}_5$ from vertex $\vec{a}_1$ using a geometric search algorithm, we would have to pass through vertices $\vec{a}_2$, $\vec{a}_3$ and $\vec{a}_4$, which are farther away from object B than vertex $\vec{a}_1$, before reaching vertex $\vec{a}_5$, which is closest to object B at t_{i+1}. In other words, starting from the closest points determined at t_i, the geometric search would have to move along directions that increase the closest distance value between the objects, before a new minimum value is reached at vertex $\vec{a}_5$. This increase followed by a decrease in the closest distance makes it impractical to use an effective search direction criteria that is guaranteed to find the closest points at t_{i+1} from the ones already known at t_i.

Because of the possibility of having non-monotonic changes in distance to move between closest points of consecutive iterations, the simulation engine relies instead on the penetration depth calculations to obtain the collision time for non-convex rigid bodies. The penetration depth is computed for each intersection region between the rigid bodies. This computation consists of determining the deepest inside point on each rigid body with respect to the other (i.e., there are two deepest inside points per region, one on each rigid body). The deepest points are set as the collision points and their distance is set as the closest distance for their corresponding intersection region. The collision time is reached when the penetration depths of all intersection regions become less than a user-adjustable threshold. Section 2.5.14 of Chap. 2 presents an efficient algorithm to find the deepest penetration point associated with an intersection region. This algorithm is applied once for each rigid body to determine its deepest point inside the other rigid body.

---

[2]This issue has been already discussed in Sect. 1.4.4 of Chap. 1, but it is revisited here for completeness.

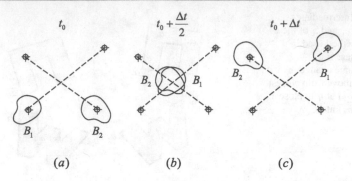

Fig. 4.12 (**a**) Rigid bodies B_1 and B_2 positioned and oriented at the beginning of the current time step; (**b**) The bodies intersect at time $(t_0 + \Delta t/2)$; (**c**) But no intersections occur at the end of the current time interval and the bodies are treated as non-intersecting

4.6   Collision Detection for Thin or Fast Moving Non-convex Bodies

Dealing with thin or fast moving non-convex rigid bodies impose even greater challenges to collision detection. Unfortunately, the usual simplification of testing for collisions only at the end of the current time interval is no longer plausible. Collisions that occur at the beginning of the current time interval have a higher probability of being missed than collisions that occur near the end of the time interval, when the objects are thin or moving fast. This situation is illustrated in Fig. 4.12.

Since the rigid bodies are positioned at the end of the current time interval before any collision-checking is undertaken, intermediate collisions can be missed during simulation. Of course, we could reduce the simulation time interval to catch these collision misses, but this would considerably slow the simulation, defeating the purpose of using the simplification in the first place. Notice that a simple geometric intersection test between the trajectories themselves is not enough to provide robust collision detection either, because the trajectories can overlap at different time instants of the rigid bodies' motion, indicating that they did not actually collide at the point where their trajectories intersected.

In this book, we propose using *continuous collision detection* to handle collisions between thin or fast moving non-convex rigid bodies. The idea is to consider the continuous motion of the rigid bodies for the entire time interval, instead of performing geometric intersection tests between their trajectories without taking time into account.

This continuous collision detection approach requires a few modifications to the data structures used to represent the rigid bodies. The most important modification is on the way the bodies' hierarchical tree representations are updated. In the case of continuous collision detection, the hierarchies need to bound the entire motion of the rigid bodies from t_0 to t_1, instead of just their poses at t_1. This can be efficiently implemented if we refit the hierarchical tree already built at creation time in local-coordinate frame, to bound the primitives' motion in world-coordinate frame from

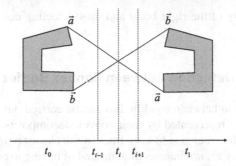

Fig. 4.13 Extreme case for face–face continuous collisions. One of the rigid bodies being tested for collisions undergo a 180° rotation. The in-between motion is continuous but not rigid, as the rigid body compresses at t_{i-1}, almost collapses to a flat shape at t_i, and starts expanding back at t_{i+1}, until it returns to its correct shape at t_1. Collisions detected in such cases are inaccurate because the shape has undergone extreme deformations

t_0 to t_1. The refit process maintains the current parent–child relationship in the tree, and updates the bounding volumes of its nodes to encompass the entire motion of the primitives. Notice that we need to use the bounding rotation spheres instead of the primitives' geometry to compute its bounding volume. This is necessary to bound both the translation and rotation components of the primitive during its motion. That is, the leaf nodes of the hierarchy need to bound the primitives' bounding rotation spheres positioned in world-coordinate frame at t_0 and t_1.

The geometric intersection of the rigid bodies' hierarchical representations results in all primitive–primitive pairs (i.e., triangle–triangle pairs) that have overlapping bounded motions. The fact that their bounded motions overlap doesn't mean that the primitives are actually colliding because the overlap might correspond to different time instants on each trajectory. We need to use the continuous triangle–triangle intersection test discussed in Sect. 2.5.15 to robustly determine whether each primitive–primitive pair collides during their motion. The continuous triangle–triangle intersection test converts the geometric-intersection problem into a root-finding problem for fifteen 3rd degree polynomials in t. The smallest real root between 0 and 1 of such polynomials is set as the collision time between the triangles. The collision time between the non-convex rigid bodies is set as the earliest collision time between their primitives (i.e., triangular faces).

Even though the continuous collision detection between faces is quite effective in practice, it does not give an exact collision time between the rigid bodies. The problem is that the continuous collision detection for faces replaces their translation and rotation by a simple translation defined by straight lines connecting their vertices' positions at t_0 and t_1. Clearly, the in-between motion of the faces is continuous but not necessary rigid, because the faces can deform at intermediate time values $t \in [t_0, t_1]$, depending on the amount of rotation experienced by them. Figure 4.13 shows an extreme case in which a rigid body rotates by 180° during its motion in the time interval. In such cases, the linearized trajectory does not completely bound the original trajectory of the rigid body and thus detecting collisions can become inaccurate.

4.7   Collision Detection Between Convex Bodies

The collision detection between rigid bodies can be carried out significantly faster if they are convex, or represented by their convex decomposition. First of all, it is feasible for the simulation engine to keep track of the closest points between convex rigid bodies when they are *not* intersecting, instead of having to compute the deepest penetration points for each intersection region and use them as an approximation to the collision points, as required in the non-convex case. This is because the distance to move between closest points of consecutive iterations varies monotonically in the convex case. Hence, when a geometric search algorithm moves along the rigid bodies' boundary representation trying to find their closest points at iteration t_{i+1}, it can discard all search directions that correspond to an increase in the current value it has for the closest distance at iteration t_i. Starting from the closest point information at t_i, the geometric search can then quickly converge to the actual closest points between the convex bodies at t_{i+1}.

Second, an upper-bound on the maximum distance traveled by any point of a convex body along a direction vector $\vec{n}$ can be computed for the time interval $[t_i, t_{i+1}]$, provided the convex body is moving at constant translation and rotation for the time interval. Knowing the convex rigid bodies are not intersecting at t_i, the collision detection module can compute an upper-bound to the maximum distance traveled by any point on each convex body along their closest direction,[3] for the time interval $[t_i, t_{i+1}]$. This upper-bound together with the closest distance between the convex objects at t_i is used to estimate a lower-bound on the collision time. Notice that this lower-bound is conservative, that is, it is guaranteed to give a time t_m such that the rigid bodies are closer but not yet colliding at t_m. Clearly, the number of iterations it takes for this conservative time advancement method to converge to the collision time is much less than the number of iterations required using the bisection method. A detailed discussion of the conservative time advancement algorithm and how these upper-bounds are computed is available in Appendix H (Chap. 13).

In this book, we present two extremely efficient algorithms to keep track of the closest point information between convex rigid bodies. Mirtich's *Voronoi Clip* algorithm is the most efficient feature-based algorithm known. The term feature-based refers to the fact that the algorithm is based on geometric operations using the features (i.e., faces, edges and vertices) of the rigid bodies being checked for collision. The *Gilbert–Johnson–Keerthi* (*GJK*) algorithm, on the other hand, is the best performing simplex-based algorithm known to date. The term simplex-based refers to the fact that the algorithm uses only the vertex information of the rigid bodies to construct a sequence of convex hulls. The operations are then carried out on

---

[3]The direction defined by the line connecting the closest points at t_i.

subsets of points (i.e., simplices) that are part of such convex hulls. The Voronoi Clip and GJK algorithms are presented in details in Sects. 4.9 and 4.10, respectively.

4.8   Collision Detection for Thin or Fast Moving Convex Bodies

Fortunately, the conservative time advancement algorithm presented in the previous section is also applicable to the case of thin or fast moving convex rigid bodies. Starting with the initial time interval $[t_0, t_1]$, the collision detection module computes the closest points and closest distance between the rigid bodies at t_0, using either the Voronoi Clip or the GJK algorithm. This information is used by the conservative time advancement algorithm to compute a lower-bound t_m to the collision time between the convex rigid bodies. If the lower-bound to the collision time turns out to be greater than the length of the time interval, that is

$$t_0 + t_m > t_1$$

then the rigid bodies are guaranteed to not collide during their motion. Otherwise, the time interval is shortened to $[t_m, t_1]$, and the closest point information is updated for the rigid bodies positioned at t_m. This iterative process continues until one of the following termination conditions is satisfied.

1. The distance between the closest points becomes less than a user-adjustable threshold value.
2. The distance between the closest points starts to increase. Since we don't know if the rigid bodies intersect or not, it is possible that their closest distance starts to increase at some iteration. This situation corresponds to the case in which the rigid bodies pass by each other during their motion, without intersecting. That is, their closest distance is reduced during their approach, but increases again as soon as they start to move away from each other, without colliding.
3. The size of the current time interval becomes less than a user-adjustable threshold value.
4. The number of iterations executed so far becomes greater than a user-adjustable threshold value.

4.9   The Voronoi Clip Algorithm for Computing Closest Points Between Convex Objects

The basic idea of the Voronoi Clip algorithm is to subdivide the space around a given rigid body into a set of Voronoi regions, each associated with one rigid body's feature. A Voronoi region is defined as the region in space in which any point inside the region is closer to its associated feature than to any other feature of the rigid body. The proximity information encoded in the Voronoi region

Fig. 4.14 Voronoi region of
a vertex

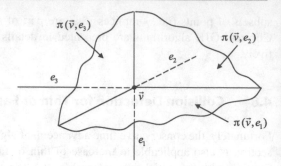

Fig. 4.15 Voronoi region of
an edge

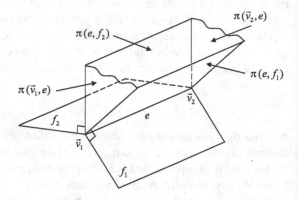

of each rigid body being tested for collision is used to determine the closest features between each pair of rigid bodies. The closest features are then used to estimate the collision frame (i.e., collision point, normal and tangent-plane vectors) if the bodies are not intersecting, or to determine the intersecting features otherwise.

In general, the Voronoi regions are bounded by at most two types of planes: *vertex–edge* and *face–edge* planes. Vertex–edge planes contain the vertex and are normal to an edge incident on the vertex, whereas face–edge planes contain the edge and are parallel to the normal vector of a face that contains the edge. More specifically, the Voronoi region associated with a vertex is bounded by a set of vertex–edge planes, each constructed from the vertex and an edge incident on it. The Voronoi region of an edge, on the other hand, is made of two face–edge planes (one for each face sharing the edge) and two vertex–edge planes (one for each vertex defining the edge). Finally, the Voronoi region of a face is made of the face itself and face–edge planes, each constructed from the face and one of its edges. Figures 4.14, 4.15 and 4.16 show examples of Voronoi regions of a vertex, an edge and a face, respectively.

In Fig. 4.14, vertex $\vec{v}$ has three incident edges, namely e_1, e_2 and e_3. Its associated Voronoi region is therefore made of three vertex–edge planes, that is, planes $\pi(\vec{v}, e_1)$, $\pi(\vec{v}, e_2)$ and $\pi(\vec{v}, e_3)$, where plane $\pi(\vec{v}, e_i)$ contains vertex $\vec{v}$ and is per-

Fig. 4.16 Voronoi region of
a face

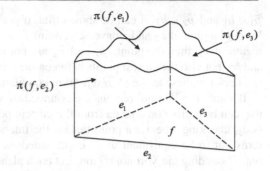

pendicular to edge e_i. The normal vector $\vec{n}_i$ and plane constant d_i corresponding to
each vertex–edge plane $\pi(\vec{v}, e_i)$ are computed as

$$\vec{n}_i = \frac{(\vec{v} - \vec{v}_i)}{|\vec{v} - \vec{v}_i|}$$

$$d_i = \vec{v} \cdot \vec{n}_i,$$

(4.23)

with edge e_i being defined by vertices $\vec{v}$ and $\vec{v}_i$. Notice that the edge direction used in
Eq. (4.23) is not necessarily the edge direction corresponding to an outward normal
of the face containing the edge. Recall that rigid bodies are assumed to be described
by vertices, edges and faces, and the edge direction is such that the normal of the
face containing the edge is pointing from the inside to the outside of the body, using
the right-hand coordinate system.[4]

Figure 4.15 shows the Voronoi region of edge e. Since the edge is made up of
two vertices and is shared by two faces, its corresponding Voronoi region is made of
two face–edge planes ($\pi(f_1, e)$ and $\pi(f_2, e)$) and two vertex–edge planes ($\pi(\vec{v}_1, e)$
and $\pi(\vec{v}_2, e)$). The normal vector $\vec{n}_i$ and plane constant d_i corresponding to each
face–edge plane $\pi(f, e)$ are computed as

$$\vec{n}_i = \vec{n}_f$$

$$d_i = \vec{v} \cdot \vec{n}_i,$$

where $\vec{n}_f$ is the outward normal vector of the face and $\vec{v}$ is one of the two vertices
defining edge e. An example of a Voronoi region associated with a face is shown in
Fig. 4.16. In this case, the face f is triangular and its associated Voronoi region is
bounded by three face–edge planes ($\pi(f, e_1)$, $\pi(f, e_2)$ and $\pi(f, e_3)$) and the face
itself.

Now, suppose we want to check for collisions between two convex rigid bodies
B_1 and B_2. Let b_1 and b_2 be features of these rigid bodies such that $b_1 \in B_1$ and
$b_2 \in B_2$. Also, let $\vec{p}_1$ and $\vec{p}_2$ be the closest points between b_1 and b_2, such that

---

[4]Since an edge is shared by two faces, the underlying implementation data structure representing
the rigid body's face must have its own edge structure because the same edge has one direction for
one of its faces, and the reverse of this direction for the adjacent face.

$\vec{p}_1 \in b_1$ and $\vec{p}_2 \in b_2$. It can be shown that, if point $\vec{p}_1$ is on the interior side of the Voronoi region of b_2 and, conversely, point $\vec{p}_2$ is on the interior side of the Voronoi region of b_1, then the points $\vec{p}_1$ and $\vec{p}_2$ are not only the closest points between b_1 and b_2, but also the closest points between the (convex) rigid bodies B_1 and B_2. We shall refer to these as the *closest feature* conditions.

Because the Voronoi regions are bounded by vertex–edge and face–edge planes that can be easily constructed from the current position and orientation of the rigid body, checking whether a point lies on the interior side of a given Voronoi region turns out to be equivalent to a simple sidedness check of the point against each plane bounding the Voronoi region. Let each plane π bounding a Voronoi region be defined by its normal vector $\vec{n}_\pi$ and a point $\vec{p}_\pi$. Any point $\vec{p} \in \pi$ satisfies the plane equation

$$\vec{p} \cdot \vec{n}_\pi = d_\pi,$$

where d_π is the plane constant obtained from

$$d_\pi = \vec{p}_\pi \cdot \vec{n}_\pi.$$

Let $S_{\vec{p},\pi}$, defined as

$$S_{\vec{p},\pi} = \vec{p} \cdot \vec{n}_\pi - d_\pi, \tag{4.24}$$

be the signed distance between point $\vec{p}$ and plane π. We have that $\vec{p}$ lies on the interior side of the Voronoi region bounded by plane π if

$$S_{\vec{p},\pi} > 0 \tag{4.25}$$

and lies on the exterior side of the Voronoi region bounded by plane π if

$$S_{\vec{p},\pi} < 0. \tag{4.26}$$

So, if point $\vec{p}$ lies in the interior side of *all* planes bounding a Voronoi region, then it is said to be inside the Voronoi region. Otherwise, the point lies outside the Voronoi region (see Fig. 4.17).

The Voronoi Clip algorithm works as follows. We start by arbitrarily selecting one feature of each rigid body being tested for collision. If the features satisfy the closest-feature conditions, then the algorithm terminates and the features are reported as being the ones that contain the closest points between the rigid bodies. However, if the closest-feature conditions are not satisfied, then the algorithm substitutes either one of the features failing the closest-feature conditions for one of its neighboring features. This process is repeated until the closest-feature conditions are satisfied.

In order to prevent cycles and guarantee the termination of the algorithm after a finite number of feature updates, it is necessary to ensure that the inter feature distance does not increase when a feature is substituted for one of its neighbors. It

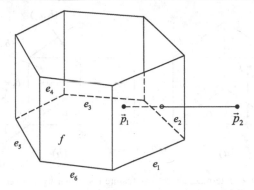

Fig. 4.17 Testing whether points $\vec{p}_1$ and $\vec{p}_2$ lie inside the Voronoi region of face f consists of testing whether the points lie inside all face–edge planes bounding the region. In this particular case, point $\vec{p}_1$ lies on the inside of all planes, meaning it is inside the Voronoi region of f. Point $\vec{p}_2$, on the other hand, lies outside face–edge plane $\pi(f, e_1)$, meaning it is outside the Voronoi region associated with the face

turns out that, if the new feature is of a higher dimension than the current feature being replaced, then the inter feature distance strictly decreases. Such substitutions include changing a vertex for an edge, or an edge for a face. Moreover, if the new feature is of lower dimension than the current feature being replaced, then the inter feature distance remains unchanged. Examples of such substitutions include changing a face for an edge or vertex, and changing an edge for a vertex. Therefore, independent of the feature substitution made at intermediate steps of the algorithm, the inter feature distance will never increase[5] and the algorithm is guaranteed to terminate.

Basically, testing whether the closest-feature conditions are satisfied at each intermediate step of the algorithm consists of solving two instances of the following problem, one for each Voronoi region of the features being considered. Given features $b_1 \in B_1$ and $b_2 \in B_2$, we need to check whether the closest point $\vec{p}_2 \in b_2$ to b_1 lies inside the Voronoi region of b_1. If this is the case, then we repeat the test for the closest point $\vec{p}_1 \in b_1$ to b_2. If not, then we need to update b_1 such that the inter feature distance does not increase. This update consists of substituting b_1 for one of its neighbor features. The difficult part of the problem resides in determining which neighbor feature $(b_1)_{new}$ should replace b_1. We shall examine how this can be done on a case-by-case basis, for each possible combination of (b_1, b_2) features.

4.9.1 Feature b_2 Is a Vertex

In this case, $b_2 = \vec{p}_2$ is a single point. We get the planes associated with the Voronoi region of b_1 and check for sidedness of vertex b_2 using Eqs. (4.25) and (4.26). If b_2

---

[5]This owes to the fact that the bodies have convex shapes. Unfortunately, the same does not apply for the case in which the bodies have non-convex shapes.

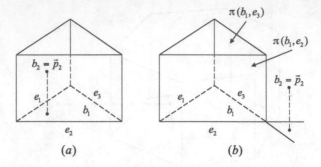

Fig. 4.18 Example of an intermediate closest-feature test when b_2 is a vertex and b_1 is a face. (a) Vertex b_2 is inside all Voronoi planes associated with b_1; (b) Vertex b_2 lies behind Voronoi planes $\pi(f, e_2)$ and $\pi(f, e_3)$. In this case, b_1 should be substituted for either edge e_2 or e_3. Since the edge is of a lower dimension than the face, the inter feature distance remains the same after the substitution

lies on the inside of all planes of the Voronoi region of b_1, then we are done with this intermediate test. Otherwise, there exists at least one plane which b_2 lies on the outside of. We substitute b_1 for the feature associated with one of these violated planes.[6]

Consider the particular example illustrated in Fig. 4.18, with b_1 being a triangular face. Vertex b_2 is tested for sidedness against each of the three face–edge bounding planes, and the face itself. In Fig. 4.18(a), vertex b_2 is on the interior side of all planes and we are done with this intermediate test. In Fig. 4.18(b), vertex b_2 is on the exterior side of bounding planes $\pi(b_1, e_2)$ and $\pi(b_1, e_3)$. In this case, b_1 should be substituted for the feature associated with either one of these planes, namely edges e_2 or e_3.

4.9.2   Feature b_2 Is an Edge

Assume edge b_2 goes from vertex $\vec{v}_1$ to vertex $\vec{v}_2$. In this case, $\vec{p}_2$ can be any point satisfying b_2's edge equation

$$\vec{e}(\lambda) = (1 - \lambda)\vec{v}_1 + \lambda\vec{v}_2, \tag{4.27}$$

with $0 \leq \lambda \leq 1$.[7] The idea is then to clip edge b_2 against all planes defining the Voronoi region of b_1 and check on which side of the clipped edge $\vec{p}_2$ is located.[8] Let $[\lambda_{min}, \lambda_{max}]$ be the portion of edge b_2 that lies inside the Voronoi region of b_1. In other words, edge b_2 intersects two planes π_{min} and π_{max} bounding the Voronoi

---

[6]There is no particular preference for which violated plane should be used in the event that there is more than one.

[7]We shall use the parameter λ to index the points on edge b_2.

[8]Recall that $\vec{p}_2$ is the point on b_2 closest to b_1.

Fig. 4.19 Edge b_2 intersects plane $\pi(b_1, e_2)$ at point $\vec{q}(\lambda_{min})$ and plane $\pi(b_1, e_3)$ at point $\vec{q}(\lambda_{max})$. Therefore, $b_{min} = e_2$ and $b_{max} = e_3$

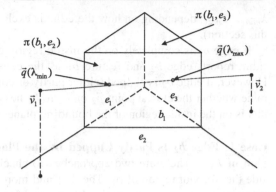

Fig. 4.20 Vertex $\vec{v}_1$ lies inside the Voronoi region of b_1 and so, b_{min} is undefined

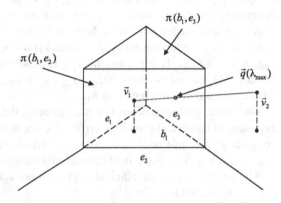

Fig. 4.21 Vertex $\vec{v}_2$ lies inside the Voronoi region of b_1 and so, b_{max} is undefined. Notice that b_{min} and b_{max} are undefined whenever edge b_2 lies completely inside the Voronoi region of b_1

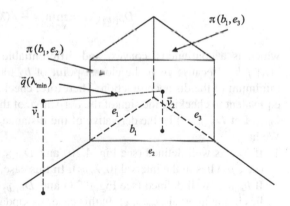

region of b_1 at points $\vec{e}(\lambda_{min})$ and $\vec{e}(\lambda_{max})$, respectively. Also, let b_{min} and b_{max} be the features associated with planes π_{min} and π_{max}. Figures 4.19, 4.20 and 4.21 illustrate possible situations for the case where b_1 is a triangular face.

Edge b_2 can be completely on the inside region of the bounding planes (i.e., $\lambda_{min} = 0$ and $\lambda_{max} = 1$), partially clipped by the bounding planes (i.e., $\lambda_{min} > 0$ or $\lambda_{max} < 1$), or totally clipped by the bounding planes (i.e., $\lambda_{min} = \lambda_{max} = 0$ or

$\lambda_{min} > \lambda_{max}$, depending on how the edge is excluded, as will be explained later in this section).

If edge b_2 is completely on the inside region of the bounding planes, the algorithm reports edge b_2 and feature b_1 as the closest features between the bodies. However, if edge b_2 is clipped (either partly or completely), then we need to determine whether the closest point $\vec{p}_2$ on b_2 to b_1 lies on the part of the clipped edge b_2 that is on the inside region of the bounding planes, and if not, how to update it.

Case 1: Edge b_2 Is Partly Clipped by the Planes Bounding the Voronoi Region of b_1   There are two approaches to check whether point $\vec{p}_2 \in b_2$ lies inside the Voronoi region of b_1. The first and more natural approach is to explicitly compute $\vec{p}_2$. This would entail solving one of the general geometric problems of computing the closest point of an edge to a vertex, an edge to another edge, or an edge to a face, depending on b_1 being a vertex, an edge or a face. Having computed $\vec{p}_2$, we would then proceed by checking whether its associated λ_{p_2} satisfies $\lambda_{min} \leq \lambda_{p_2} \leq \lambda_{max}$. If this is so, then $\vec{p}_2$ is inside the Voronoi region of b_1 and we are done. Otherwise, we have either $0 \leq \lambda_{p_2} < \lambda_{min}$ or $\lambda_{max} < \lambda_{p_2} \leq 1$, that is, $\vec{p}_2$ lies outside the Voronoi region of b_1.

One of the problems of explicitly computing the closest point $\vec{p}_2$ is the possible exposure to numerical round-off errors. Notice that we do not necessarily need to compute $\vec{p}_2$; we just need to determine in which interval $[0, \lambda_{min})$, $[\lambda_{min}, \lambda_{max}]$ or $(\lambda_{max}, 1]$ it lies. This is the fundamental motivation behind the second approach.

The second and more efficient approach considers the distance function from edge b_2 to feature b_1 defined by

$$D_{b_1, b_2}(\lambda) = \min_{x \in b_1} |x - \vec{e}(\lambda)|, \tag{4.28}$$

which is a continuous, convex, and differentiable function of λ, provided that $\vec{e}(\lambda) \notin b_1$. Because $\vec{p}_2$ is the closest point of b_2 to b_1, its associated λ value is a minimum of the distance function. Therefore, checking in which interval $\vec{p}_2$ lies is equivalent to checking the sign of the derivative of the distance function at λ_{min} and λ_{max}. Let $\dot{D}_{b_1, b_2}(\lambda)$ be the derivative of the distance function defined in Eq. (4.28). We have:

1. If b_{min} is well defined (see Fig. 4.20) and $\dot{D}_{b_1, b_2}(\lambda_{min}) > 0$, then the minimum (i.e., $\vec{p}_2$) lies in the interval $[0, \lambda_{min})$. In this case, we update b_1 to b_{min}.
2. If b_{max} is well defined (see Fig. 4.21) and $\dot{D}_{b_1, b_2}(\lambda_{max}) < 0$, then the minimum lies in the interval $(\lambda_{max}, 1]$. In this case, we update b_1 to b_{max}.
3. Else, the minimum lies within the interval $[\lambda_{min}, \lambda_{max}]$ and we are done with this intermediate step.

The computation of the sign of the derivative of the distance function depends on b_1 being a vertex, an edge or a face. If b_1 is a vertex (i.e., $b_1 = \vec{v}$), then the sign of the derivative is immediately obtained from

$$\text{sign}(\dot{D}_{\vec{v}, b_2}(\lambda)) = \text{sign}(\vec{u}_e \cdot (\vec{e}(\lambda) - \vec{v})), \tag{4.29}$$

where $\vec{u}_e$ is the unitary vector defining the direction of edge b_2 given by

$$\vec{u}_e = \frac{(\vec{v}_2 - \vec{v}_1)}{|\vec{v}_2 - \vec{v}_1|}.$$

In the case b_1 is a face (i.e., $b_1 = f$) with unit-normal vector $\vec{n}_f$ (pointing outwards) and plane-constant value d_f, then the sign of the derivative is given by

$$\text{sign}\big(\dot{D}_{f,b_2}(\lambda)\big) = \begin{cases} +\,\text{sign}(\vec{u}_e \cdot \vec{n}_f), & \text{if } S_{\vec{e}(\lambda),f} > 0 \\ -\,\text{sign}(\vec{u}_e \cdot \vec{n}_f), & \text{if } S_{\vec{e}(\lambda),f} < 0. \end{cases} \qquad (4.30)$$

Finally, if b_1 is an edge, then we use its neighboring features b_{min} or b_{max} associated with λ_{min} and λ_{max} to determine the sign of the derivative on the intervals $[0, \lambda_{min})$ and $(\lambda_{max}, 1]$. Notice that, since b_1 is an edge, its neighboring features b_{min} and b_{max} must be a vertex or a face of the body and we can use Eqs. (4.29) and (4.30) to compute the sign of the derivatives.

It is important to notice that the use of the neighboring features is only possible because the distance function is continuous. In other words, the computation of the sign of the derivative with respect to either b_{min} or b_{max} is equal to the sign of the derivative with respect to edge b_1 at the points where b_2 crosses (i.e., enters or leaves) the bounding planes of its Voronoi region, that is, at the points corresponding to λ_{min} and λ_{max} (see Fig. 4.19). The only cases in which the computation of the sign of the derivative fails is when the derivative function itself is undefined. This occurs whenever there exists a $\lambda \in [0, 1]$, such that

$$\vec{e}(\lambda) = b_1 \qquad (4.31)$$

if b_1 is a vertex, or

$$S_{\vec{e}(\lambda),b_1} = 0 \qquad (4.32)$$

if b_1 is a face. The geometric interpretation of being unable to compute the sign of the derivative is that edge b_2 intersects feature b_1. More specifically, Eq. (4.31) is satisfied whenever edge b_2 contains vertex b_1, and Eq. (4.32) is satisfied whenever edge b_2 intersects face b_1. In both cases, the Voronoi Clip algorithm terminates reporting the pair (b_1, b_2) as being interpenetrating.

One last remark on how to clip edge b_2 against the planes bounding the Voronoi region of b_1. If b_1 is a vertex, then all of its bounding planes are vertex–edge planes and we can clip against them in any order. However, if b_1 is an edge, then its Voronoi region is bounded by two vertex–edge and two face–edge planes. We should first clip edge b_2 against the two vertex–edge planes. If no clipping occurs, then we clip against the remaining face–edge planes. Finally, if b_1 is a face, its Voronoi region is bounded by several face–edge planes (one for each edge defining the face) and the face plane itself. In this case, we should first clip edge b_2 against the face–edge planes; if no clipping occurs, then we clip against the face plane.

Fig. 4.22 An example of a
simple exclusion with b_1
being a triangular face

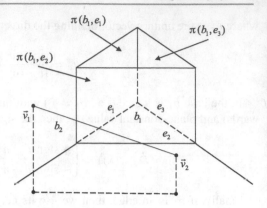

Case 2: Edge b_2 Is Completely Clipped by the Planes Bounding the Voronoi Region of b_1   There are two types of complete exclusion: simple exclusion and compound exclusion. Simple exclusion occurs whenever both vertices defining edge b_2 lie on the outside of a single plane bounding the Voronoi region of feature b_1. Compound exclusion occurs when both vertices defining edge b_2 lie on the outside of different planes bounding the Voronoi region of feature b_1.

Consider, for example, the simple-exclusion case illustrated in Fig. 4.22, with b_1 being a triangular face. Edge b_2 is described by vertices $\vec{v}_1$ and $\vec{v}_2$ corresponding to $\lambda_{min} = 0$ and $\lambda_{max} = 1$, respectively. The inclusion test consists of checking whether edge b_2 is on the interior side of all planes bounding the Voronoi region of b_1. For the case illustrated in Fig. 4.22, the result of the sidedness computation using Eq. (4.24) is

$$S_{\vec{v}_1, \pi(b_1, e_1)} > 0$$

$$S_{\vec{v}_2, \pi(b_1, e_1)} > 0$$

$$S_{\vec{v}_1, \pi(b_1, e_2)} < 0$$

$$S_{\vec{v}_2, \pi(b_1, e_2)} < 0$$

$$S_{\vec{v}_1, \pi(b_1, e_3)} > 0$$

$$S_{\vec{v}_2, \pi(b_1, e_3)} > 0.$$

Analyzing the results, we have that edge b_2 is on the interior side of plane $\pi(b_1, e_1)$ (the signed-distance computations resolve to a positive value), on the exterior side of plane $\pi(b_1, e_2)$, and on the interior side of plane $\pi(b_1, e_3)$. That is, edge b_2 is on the interior side of all bounding planes save $\pi(b_1, e_2)$, indicating the existence of simple exclusion. Feature b_1 is then substituted for the feature associated with plane $\pi(b_1, e_2)$, namely edge e_2. In summary, simple exclusion can be detected whenever the signed-distance computations resolve to a positive value for all bounding planes save one, which has a negative sign. Feature b_1 is then replaced by the feature associated with the violated plane.

Fig. 4.23 An example of a
compound exclusion with b_1
being a vertex with three
incident edges. Points $\vec{q}_2$ and
$\vec{q}_3$ correspond to the
intersections of edge b_2
(defined by points $\vec{v}_1$ and $\vec{v}_2$)
with planes $\pi(b_1, e_2)$ and
$\pi(b_1, e_3)$, respectively

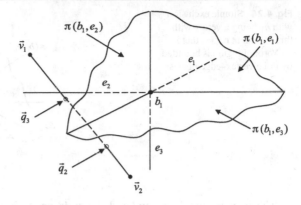

Figure 4.23 illustrates an example of compound exclusion, with b_1 being a vertex
with three incident edges. Again, edge b_2 is described by vertices $\vec{v}_1$ and $\vec{v}_2$ corresponding to $\lambda_{min} = 0$ and $\lambda_{max} = 1$, respectively. Evaluating the signed distance to
plane $\pi(b_1, e_1)$ gives

$$S_{\vec{v}_1, \pi(b_1, e_1)} > 0$$
$$S_{\vec{v}_2, \pi(b_1, e_1)} > 0,$$

indicating that edge b_2 is completely on the interior side of plane $\pi(b_1, e_1)$. Evaluating the signed distance to plane $\pi(b_1, e_2)$ gives

$$S_{\vec{v}_1, \pi(b_1, e_2)} < 0$$
$$S_{\vec{v}_2, \pi(b_1, e_2)} > 0,$$

indicating that edge b_2 intersects plane $\pi(b_1, e_2)$. Because vertex $\vec{v}_1$ lies on the
exterior side of $\pi(b_1, e_2)$, we update $\lambda_{min} = 0$ to $\lambda_{min} = \lambda_2 > 0$ corresponding to
point $\vec{q}_2$. Effectuating the last signed-distance computation to plane $\pi(b_1, e_3)$ gives

$$S_{\vec{v}_1, \pi(b_1, e_3)} > 0$$
$$S_{\vec{v}_2, \pi(b_1, e_3)} < 0,$$

indicating that edge b_2 also intersects plane $\pi(b_1, e_3)$. Because vertex $\vec{v}_2$ lies on
the outside region of $\pi(b_1, e_3)$, we update $\lambda_{max} = 1$ to $\lambda_{max} < 1$ corresponding to
point $\vec{q}_3$. Notice, however, that point $\vec{q}_2$ corresponding to λ_{min} is closer to $\vec{v}_2$ than
point $\vec{q}_3$ corresponding to λ_{max}. That is, $\lambda_{min} > \lambda_{max}$ which is clearly degenerate.
In summary, a compound exclusion can be detected whenever $\lambda_{min} > \lambda_{max}$. Feature
b_1 is then replaced by b_{max} if the last update that caused $\lambda_{min} > \lambda_{max}$ was triggered
by a reduction of λ_{max}. On the other hand, feature b_1 is replaced by b_{min} if the last
update that caused $\lambda_{min} > \lambda_{max}$ was triggered by an increase of λ_{min}.

Fig. 4.24 Simple exclusion
with b_1 being a vertex with
three incident edges, that is,
its Voronoi region is bounded
by three vertex–edge planes

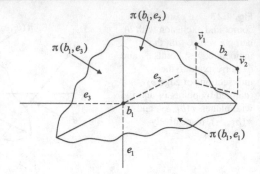

The way feature b_1 is updated depends on b_2 lying on the exterior side of a
vertex–edge or a face–edge plane bounding the Voronoi region of b_1. This in turn
depends on b_1 being a vertex, an edge or a face. In the following paragraphs, we
shall examine all possible combinations and show how b_1 should be updated on
each of them.

Case 2.1: Feature b_1 Is a Vertex and b_2 Is a Simple Exclusion   In this case, the
Voronoi region of b_1 is bounded by vertex–edge planes only, and edge b_2 lies on the
outside region of one of these planes, say plane $\pi(b_1, e_i)$. Vertex b_1 should then be
substituted for the feature associated with $\pi(b_1, e_i)$, that is, edge e_i.

For example, consider the simple-exclusion case shown in Fig. 4.24, with vertex
b_1 having three incident edges.

Evaluating the signed distance of the vertices defining edge b_2 to each of the
bounding planes gives

$$S_{\vec{v}_1, \pi(b_1, e_1)} > 0$$
$$S_{\vec{v}_2, \pi(b_1, e_1)} > 0$$
$$S_{\vec{v}_1, \pi(b_1, e_2)} < 0$$
$$S_{\vec{v}_2, \pi(b_1, e_2)} < 0$$
$$S_{\vec{v}_1, \pi(b_1, e_3)} > 0$$
$$S_{\vec{v}_2, \pi(b_1, e_3)} > 0,$$

indicating that edge b_2 is completely on the exterior side of plane $\pi(b_1, e_2)$. So, we
substitute b_1 for edge e_2, which is the feature associated with $\pi(b_1, e_2)$.

Case 2.2: Feature b_1 Is a Vertex and b_2 Is a Compound Exclusion   Again, the
Voronoi region of b_1 is bounded by vertex–edge planes only, but edge b_2 spans the
exterior side of two of these planes, say planes $\pi(b_1, e_i)$ and $\pi(b_1, e_j)$. We have that

$$0 < \lambda_{max} < \lambda_{min} < 1,$$

indicating that this is a compound exclusion. Assume $\lambda_i = \lambda_{min}$ and $\lambda_j = \lambda_{max}$. In other words, the intersection of edge b_2 with planes $\pi(b_1, e_i)$ and $\pi(b_1, e_j)$ corresponds to points $\vec{q}_i$ and $\vec{q}_j$ associated with λ_{min} and λ_{max}, respectively. Vertex b_1 is then updated as follows.

1. If the minimum lies in the interval $[0, \lambda_{max})$, that is, if

$$\dot{D}_{b_1, b_2}(\lambda_{max}) > 0$$
$$\dot{D}_{b_1, b_2}(\lambda_{min}) > 0,$$

then we substitute b_1 for the feature associated with plane $\pi(b_1, e_i)$, namely edge e_i.

2. If the minimum lies in the interval $(\lambda_{min}, 1]$, that is, if

$$\dot{D}_{b_1, b_2}(\lambda_{max}) < 0$$
$$\dot{D}_{b_1, b_2}(\lambda_{min}) < 0,$$

then we substitute b_1 for the feature associated with plane $\pi(b_1, e_j)$, namely edge e_j.

3. If those tests fail, then the minimum lies in the interval $[\lambda_{max}, \lambda_{min}]$ and we substitute b_1 for e_i if the last update was reducing λ_{max}, or e_j if the last update was increasing λ_{min}.

Figure 4.23 shows an example of a compound exclusion when b_1 is a vertex and b_2 is an edge.

Case 2.3: Feature b_1 Is an Edge and b_2 Is a Simple Exclusion   As mentioned before, the Voronoi region of an edge is bounded by two vertex–edge and two face–edge planes. In both cases, b_1 (i.e., the edge) is substituted for the feature of the plane excluding b_2. More specifically, if b_2 is simply excluded from either vertex–edge planes, then b_1 is replaced by the vertex associated with the plane (see Figs. 4.25 and 4.26).

Otherwise, b_2 is simply excluded from either face–edge planes, and b_1 is substituted for the face associated with the plane (see Figs. 4.27 and 4.28).

Case 2.4: Feature b_1 Is an Edge and b_2 Is a Compound Exclusion   Compound exclusions can occur with one vertex–edge and one face–edge plane, or the two face–edge planes. The compound exclusion cannot occur for the two vertex–edge planes because they are parallel. If the compound exclusion occurs with a vertex–edge and a face–edge plane, then edge b_1 is substituted for the vertex of the vertex–edge plane if the sign of the derivative at the vertex is positive, that is,[9] if

$$\text{sign}(\dot{D}_{\vec{q}_2, b_2}(\lambda)) = \text{sign}(\vec{u}_e \cdot (\vec{e}(\lambda) - \vec{q}_2)) > 0, \tag{4.33}$$

---

[9]Equation (4.33) is the same as Eq. (4.29), and is repeated here for convenience.

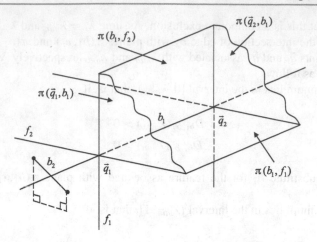

Fig. 4.25 Edge b_2 is simply excluded from vertex–edge plane $\pi(\vec{q}_1, e_1)$ bounding the Voronoi region of edge b_1. In this case, b_1 is substituted for vertex $\vec{q}_1$

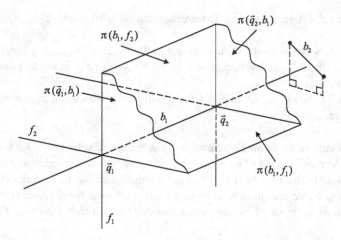

Fig. 4.26 Edge b_2 is simply excluded from vertex–edge plane $\pi(\vec{q}_2, e_1)$ bounding the Voronoi region of edge b_1. In this case, b_1 is substituted for vertex $\vec{q}_2$

where $\vec{u}_e$ is the unitary vector defining the direction of edge b_1 (see Fig. 4.29). Otherwise, b_1 is replaced by the face associated with the face–edge plane.

However, if the compound exclusion occurs with two face–edge planes, say planes $\pi(b_1, f_i)$ and $\pi(b_1, f_j)$, then edge b_1 is replaced by the face of the face–edge plane as follows.

- If b_2 intersects plane $\pi(b_1, f_i)$ at point $\vec{q}_{min}$, then b_1 is substituted for face f_i associated with $\pi(b_1, f_i)$ if the sign of its derivative is negative.
- If b_2 intersects plane $\pi(b_1, f_i)$ at point $\vec{q}_{max}$, then b_1 is substituted for face f_i associated with $\pi(b_1, f_i)$ if the sign of its derivative is positive.
- Otherwise, b_1 is substituted for face f_j associated with plane $\pi(b_1, f_j)$.

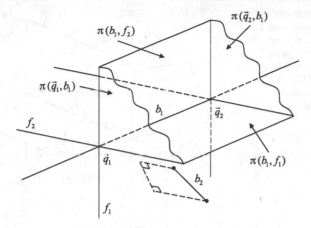

Fig. 4.27 Edge b_2 is simply excluded from face–edge plane $\pi(b_1, f_1)$ bounding the Voronoi region of edge b_1. In this case, b_1 is substituted for face f_1

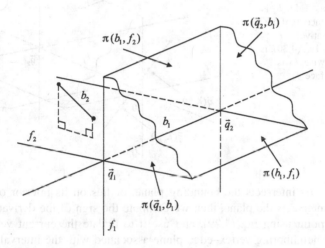

Fig. 4.28 Edge b_2 is simply excluded from face–edge plane $\pi(b_1, f_2)$ bounding Voronoi region of edge b_1. In this case, b_1 is substituted for face f_2

The sign of the derivative at the faces is obtained by substituting f in Eq. (4.30) for the face being considered. Figure 4.30 shows an example of a compound exclusion with two face–edge planes.

Case 2.5: Feature b_1 Is a Face and b_2 Is Either a Simple or Compound Exclusion   This is the most time-consuming update that can occur on the Voronoi Clip algorithm. The problem is that, even if the edge is reported to be a case of simple or compound exclusion, it can still span the exterior side of several face–edge planes bounding the Voronoi region of face b_1, as shown in Fig. 4.31.

In order to overcome this drawback, we need to clip edge b_2 against the vertex–edge planes bounding face b_1. For each vertex–edge plane considered, we check

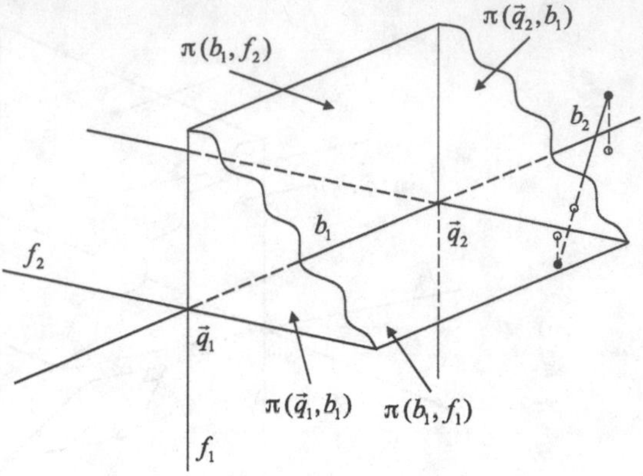

Fig. 4.29 Example of a compound exclusion with a vertex–edge (i.e., π_2) and a face–edge (i.e., π_3) plane. Edge b_1 is substituted for vertex $\vec{q}_2$ if Eq. (4.28) is satisfied. Otherwise, it is substituted for face f_3

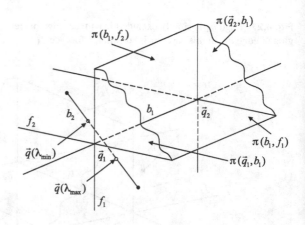

Fig. 4.30 Example of a compound exclusion with two face–edge planes, namely planes π_3 and π_4. Edge b_1 is substituted for face f_3 if the sign of its derivative, evaluated using Eq. (4.30), is positive. Otherwise, b_1 is substituted for face f_4

whether edge b_2 intersects the bounding plane, or lies on its interior or exterior sides. If b_2 intersects the plane, then we compute the sign of the derivative at the intersection point using Eq. (4.29), and use it to update the current vertex–edge plane by the neighboring vertex–edge plane associated with the interval in which the minimum point lies. On the other hand, if b_2 lies on the interior or exterior side of the plane, then we still need to check whether it lies, respectively, on the exterior or interior side of the corresponding neighboring vertex–edge plane. Depending on the result, face b_1 is updated to one of its vertices or edges.

Consider, for example, the situation shown in Fig. 4.31. We start clipping edge b_2 against a randomly selected vertex–edge plane, say plane $\pi(\vec{q}_1, e_n)$ associated with vertex $\vec{q}_1$. Testing b_2 against $\pi(\vec{q}_1, e_n)$ gives

$$S_{\vec{v}_1, \pi(\vec{q}_1, e_n)} < 0$$
$$S_{\vec{v}_2, \pi(\vec{q}_1, e_n)} < 0,$$

indicating that edge b_2 lies completely on the interior side of $\pi(\vec{q}_1, e_n)$. Therefore, we consider clipping b_2 against vertex–edge plane $\pi(\vec{q}_1, e_1)$, which is the neighbor plane on the interior side of $\pi(\vec{q}_1, e_n)$. Clipping b_2 against $\pi(\vec{q}_1, e_1)$ make us find

Fig. 4.31 Edge b_2 is simply excluded from face–edge plane $\pi(e_1, b_1)$ associated with edge e_1. Nonetheless, it spans the vertex–edge planes $\pi(\vec{q}_1, e_1)$, $\pi(\vec{q}_2, e_1)$, $\pi(\vec{q}_2, e_2)$, as well as the face–edge plane $\pi(e_2, b_1)$ (not shown in the figure)

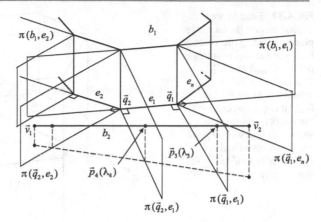

the intersection point $\vec{p}_3(\lambda_3)$ between plane $\pi(\vec{q}_1, e_1)$ and edge b_2. So, we need to compute the sign of the derivative to determine on which interval $[\vec{v}_1, \vec{p}_3]$ (i.e., $[0, \lambda_3]$) or $[\vec{p}_3, \vec{v}_2]$ (i.e., $[\lambda_3, 1]$) the minimum point lies. If the minimum point lies on the interval $[\vec{p}_3, \vec{v}_2]$, that is, if

$$\text{sign } \dot{D}_{\vec{q}_1, b_2}(\lambda_3) = \text{sign}(\vec{u}_{b_2} \cdot (\vec{p}_3 - \vec{q}_1)) < 0,$$

then the closest point on b_2 to b_1 lies somewhere between the bounding planes $\pi(\vec{q}_1, e_n)$ and $\pi(\vec{q}_1, e_1)$. In this case, we substitute face b_1 for vertex $\vec{q}_1$ (see Fig. 4.31). Otherwise, the minimum point lies on the interval $[\vec{v}_1, \vec{p}_3]$, that is

$$\text{sign } \dot{D}_{\vec{q}_1, b_2}(\lambda_3) > 0,$$

and we proceed clipping sub-edge $[\vec{v}_1, \vec{p}_3]$ against vertex-plane $\pi(\vec{q}_2, e_1)$. This, in turn, lets us determine the intersection point $\vec{p}_4(\lambda_4)$ between the sub-edge and plane $\pi(\vec{q}_2, e_1)$. Again, we need to check the sign of the derivative to determine on which interval $[\vec{v}_1, \vec{p}_4]$ or $[\vec{p}_4, \vec{p}_3]$ the minimum lies. If it lies on the interval $[\vec{p}_4, \vec{p}_3]$, that is

$$\text{sign } \ddot{D}_{\vec{q}_2, b_2}(\lambda_3) = \text{sign}(\vec{u}_{b_2} \cdot (\vec{p}_4 - \vec{q}_2)) < 0,$$

then the closest point on b_2 to b_1 lies somewhere between the bounding planes $\pi(\vec{q}_2, e_1)$ and $\pi(\vec{q}_1, e_1)$. Therefore, we substitute face b_1 for edge e_1 (see Fig. 4.31). However, if the minimum lies on the interval $[\vec{v}_1, \vec{p}_4]$, that is

$$\text{sign } \ddot{D}_{\vec{q}_2, b_2}(\lambda_3) = \text{sign}(\vec{u}_{b_2} \cdot (\vec{p}_4 - \vec{q}_2)) > 0,$$

then we need to proceed by clipping sub-edge $[\vec{v}_1, \vec{p}_4]$ against vertex–edge plane $\pi(\vec{q}_2, e_2)$. This is analogous to the previously explained situation where we clipped edge b_2 against vertex–edge plane $\pi(\vec{q}_1, e_1)$. So, we continue clipping for as long as needed until we find the interval on b_2 that contains the point closest to b_1, and substitute b_1 for the closest feature associated with this interval.

Fig. 4.32 Edge b_2 was clipped against the face–edge planes bounding the Voronoi region of face b_1, resulting in points $\vec{v}(\lambda_{min})$ and $\vec{v}(\lambda_{max})$. Before the algorithm substitutes b_1 for b_{min} or b_{max}, it checks whether b_2 intersects b_1. In the case shown, an intersection point $\vec{v}(\lambda_i)$ was found and the bodies are reported as interpenetrating

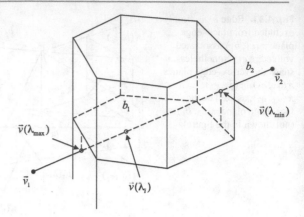

4.9.3   Feature b_2 Is a Face

The way the Voronoi Clip algorithm is set up, it can never compare a face with another face, with the exception of the initial choice of features done at the time the algorithm starts. So, in practice, we can not really select *any* pair b_1 and b_2 of features to start with, but a pair that contains at most one face of either rigid body. Consequently, if the initial selection for b_2 is a face, then b_1 should be either a vertex or an edge. The results of the previous sections are then directly applicable to this case (we just need to replace b_1 for b_2 and vice-versa in the derivations of the equations obtained so far).

4.9.4   Dealing with Interpenetration

Interpenetration of the bodies being tested for collision occurs only when b_1 is a face and b_2 is an edge. Recall that the Voronoi region in this case is bounded by a set of face–edge planes, one associated with each edge, and the face itself. So far, we have shown how to clip edge b_2 against the face–edge planes of b_1. Interpenetration can be detected only when we clip edge b_2 against the face plane itself. If the clip results on the determination of an intersection point between b_2 and the face (i.e., b_1), then the rigid bodies are intersecting and the Voronoi Clip algorithm reports features $b_1 \in B_1$ and $b_2 \in B_2$ as the violating features (see Fig. 4.32).

4.9.5   Avoiding Local Minima

Up till now, we have shown how the Voronoi Clip algorithm updates feature b_1 according to the relative position of feature b_2 with respect to the bounding planes of b_1's Voronoi region. Unfortunately, there is a situation in which the algorithm can find itself trapped in a local minima. This occurs whenever:

Fig. 4.33 Examples of possible local minima. The algorithm reports vertex b_2 and face $b_1 \in B_1$ as closest features: (**a**) The bodies are actually inter penetrating; (**b**) There exists another face b_3 closer to vertex b_2 than face b_1

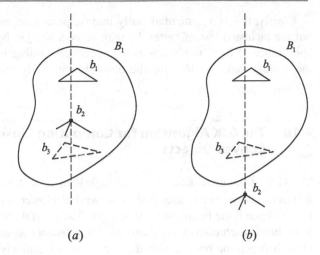

(a)   (b)

- b_1 is a face, and
- b_2 is a vertex inside the Voronoi region of b_1, and
- b_2 lies "below" b_1, and
- all edges connected to b_2 are directed away from b_1.

Here, the algorithm, if implemented as is, reports vertex b_2 and face b_1 as the closest features between the rigid bodies. However, this is not always true, since the bodies can be interpenetrating, or there may exist another face $b_3 \in B_1$ closer to vertex b_2 than face b_1 (see Fig. 4.33).

In order to avoid such local minima, we have to modify the Voronoi Clip algorithm with the following extra steps, applicable whenever b_1 is a face, b_2 is a vertex, and b_2 is in the Voronoi region of b_1:

1. Check whether vertex b_2 lies on the interior side of b_1, that is, if b_2 lies "below" b_1. If so, then move on to the next step. Otherwise, this is not a local minimum situation, and we are done.
2. For each edge e_i connected to vertex b_2, check whether it is directed away from b_1, that is, check whether

$$(\vec{v}_i - b_2) \cdot \vec{n}_{b_1} - d_{b_1} > 0, \tag{4.34}$$

where $\vec{v}_i$ is the other vertex of edge e_i, and $\vec{n}_{b_1}$ and d_{b_1} are the normal vector and plane constant of face b_1.

If both of the above conditions are true, then we are dealing with a potential local minimum. Therefore, we need to test whether vertex b_2 is inside rigid body B_1 by testing whether it is on the interior side of all B_1's faces. If so, then the bodies are interpenetrating and the algorithm terminates. Otherwise, the bodies are not intersecting, hence there exists a face $b_3 \neq b_1$ that is closer to vertex b_2 than b_1 is, and we substitute b_1 for b_3. Notice that b_3 can be obtained as a by-product of the inclusion test provided we also keep track of the face that has the smallest value obtained using Eq. (4.34).

Clearly, this is a computationally intense procedure, especially when we carry out the inclusion test of vertex b_2 with respect to rigid body B_1. Fortunately, the appearance of local minima is rare in practice, leading us to the conclusion that the average running time for the algorithm is rarely affected by this computation.

4.10   The GJK Algorithm for Computing Closest Points Between Convex Objects

The Gilbert–Johnson–Keerthi (GJK) algorithm is used to compute the separation distance between two convex bodies, as well as a lower bound to their interpenetration distance if the bodies are intersecting. The general idea is to randomly select a point inside each convex body and use their distance as an initial value to the distance between the bodies. This distance is then iteratively refined as new pairs of points are found that are closer to each other than the ones already selected. The algorithm continues until there are no more pairs of points closer to each other than the current pair being considered, or a zero distance is found indicating that the bodies are intersecting. The rigid-body features that contain the closest pair of points are then reported back as the closest features between the bodies.

The distance between bodies B_1 and B_2 is defined as

$$d_{B_1, B_2} = \min |b_1 - b_2| \quad \text{with } b_1 \in B_1, \ b_2 \in B_2. \tag{4.35}$$

Let $b_1 = b_1^*$ and $b_2 = b_2^*$ be the values associated with the minimum distance given by Eq. (4.35). In other words, b_1^* and b_2^* are the closest pairs of points between the bodies. The lowest dimensional features containing them are said to be the closest features between the bodies. For instance, if b_1^* lies on an edge of body B_1, then we report the edge as the closest feature associated with B_1, as opposed to reporting one of the faces containing the edge.

Since computing the distance for every possible combination of pairs of points is clearly impractical, the GJK algorithm computes successive approximations to points b_1^* and b_2^*. These approximated points are iteratively refined until their distance differs from a lower bound to the actual distance between the bodies (i.e., lower bound to $|b_1^* - b_2^*|$) by less than a tolerance value.

The mathematical foundation of the approximation algorithm consists of rewriting the distance between the bodies as their Minkowski difference Ψ, defined as

$$\Psi_{B_1, B_2} = \big\{ (b_1 - b_2) \mid b_1 \in B_1 \text{ and } b_2 \in B_2 \big\}.$$

If B_1 and B_2 are convex bodies, it can be shown that their Minkowski difference is also convex. The distance equation (4.35) can then be expressed as

$$d_{B_1, B_2} = \min |\Psi_{B_1, B_2}|. \tag{4.36}$$

From Eq. (4.36), we immediately have that the distance between the bodies is given by the point in the Minkowski difference closest to the origin. In other words, the GJK algorithm transforms the problem of computing the distance between two convex bodies into the problem of finding the point of the Minkowski difference nearest to the origin. Moreover, if the bodies are intersecting, then there exists a point b_I in both bodies such that $b_1 = b_I = b_2$, and the point of the Minkowski difference nearest to the origin is the origin itself.

The main idea behind the approximation algorithm is to construct a sequence of simplexes whose vertices are points of the Minkowski difference, such that at each iteration the current simplex is closer to the origin than any previously computed simplex.

At the first iteration, the initial simplex Q_i is set to empty, reflecting that no points of the Minkowski difference have been selected so far. We then pick an arbitrary point $\vec{p}_i \in \Psi_{B_1, B_2}$ and use it to compute an auxiliary point $\vec{q}_i \in \Psi_{B_1, B_2}$ such that:

$$\vec{q}_i = s_{\Psi_{B_1, B_2}}(-\vec{p}_i), \tag{4.37}$$

where $s_{\Psi_{B_1, B_2}}(-\vec{p}_i)$ is known as the support mapping of Ψ_{B_1, B_2} with respect to point $(-\vec{p}_i)$. It can be shown that the support mapping of the Minkowski difference can be computed as a function of the support mapping of each individual body as

$$s_{\Psi_{B_1, B_2}}(-\vec{p}_i) = s_{B_1}(-\vec{p}_i) - s_{B_2}(\vec{p}_i), \tag{4.38}$$

where $s_B(\vec{p})$, with $B \in \{B_1, B_2\}$ and $\vec{p} = \pm \vec{p}_i$, is defined as

$$s_B(\vec{p}) \in B,$$
$$\vec{p} \cdot s_B(\vec{p}) = \max\{\vec{p} \cdot \vec{x} \mid \vec{x} \in B\}. \tag{4.39}$$

According to Eqs. (4.39), the support mapping $s_B(\vec{p})$ with respect to point $\vec{p}$ is the point on B that has maximum projection along the direction defined by $\vec{p}$. In other words, the support mapping takes a point $\vec{p}$ in B and maps it to another point $s_B(\vec{p})$ also in B, such that its component along $\vec{p}$ is maximum for all points in B (see Fig. 4.34).

There are three important issues that need to be mentioned before we can proceed with the explanation of the GJK algorithm. First, Eq. (4.38) says that there is no need to compute the Minkowski difference between the bodies. The support-mapping computations can be done independently for each body and then merged according to Eq. (4.38). Second, since the support mapping is the maximum projection along $\vec{p}$, it can only be a point on the boundary of the rigid body's shape. Therefore, we can limit our search for the support mapping to the vertices defining the rigid body's boundary, as opposed to looking for candidate points inside that body. Third, because the support mapping is on the rigid body's boundary, the initial point $\vec{p}_i$ in the Minkowski difference can be selected as the difference between any vertex of B_1 and any vertex of B_2. In other words, the determination of the

Fig. 4.34 The support
mapping $s_B(\vec{p})$ is the point
on B with the maximum
projection along $\vec{p}$

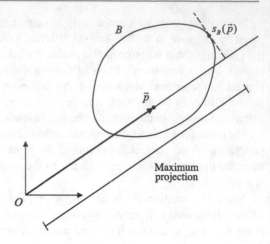

initial point does not require the explicit computation of the Minkowski difference
between the bodies.

Having determined $\vec{p}_i$ and Q_i, as well as the auxiliary point $\vec{q}_i$ at iteration i, we
move on to compute $\vec{p}_{i+1}$ and Q_{i+1} associated with iteration $(i+1)$, such that

$$\vec{p}_{i+1} = \min\{convex(Q_i \cup \{\vec{q}_i\})\},$$
$$Q_{i+1} \subseteq (Q_i \cup \{\vec{q}_i\}); \tag{4.40}$$

Q_{i+1} is chosen as the smallest nonempty set with $\vec{p}_{i+1} \in convex(Q_{i+1})$. In other
words, the simplex Q_{i+1} corresponding to iteration $(i+1)$ is the convex hull of
$(Q_i \cup \{\vec{q}_i\})$, with the added constraint that $\vec{p}_{i+1}$ must be one of its vertices.

The operation $convex(X)$ that appears in Eq. (4.40) is known as the *convex combination* of a finite set of points $\vec{x}_j$ of polyhedron X, and is defined as

$$convex(X) = \sum_{j=1}^{n} \lambda_j \vec{x}_j,$$

with

$$\sum_{j=1}^{n} \lambda_j = 1$$

$$\lambda_j \geq 0, \quad \forall j \in \{1, 2, \ldots, n\}.$$

Another useful operation is the *affine combination* affine(X) of a finite set of
points $\vec{x}_j$ of polyhedron X, expressed as

$$affine(X) = \sum_{j=1}^{n} \lambda_j \vec{x}_j,$$

Fig. 4.35 Visualizing a few
steps of the GJK algorithm
being executed

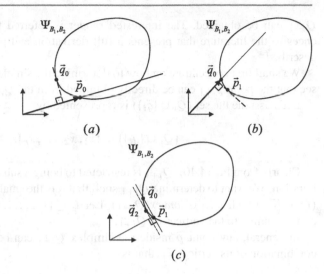

(a)   (b)

(c)

with the restriction

$$\sum_{j=1}^{n} \lambda_j = 1.$$

By definition, the vertices of the simplex Q_{i+1} form a set of affinely independent
points, that is, none of the points in Q_{i+1} can be written as an affine combination
of the other vertices. Moreover, it can be shown that there exists only one Q_{i+1}
satisfying Eq. (4.40). Figure 4.35 illustrates a few steps of the GJK algorithm, with
polyhedron Ψ_{B_1,B_2} being the Minkowski difference of two hypothetical convex bodies (not shown in the figure).

On Fig. 4.35(a), we start with an arbitrary point $\vec{p}_0$ that is the subtraction of a
vertex in B_2 from a vertex in B_1, that is, a point on the boundary of the Minkowski
difference, since both bodies are convex. The initial simplex Q_0 is set to empty.
The next step is then to compute the auxiliary point $\vec{q}_0$ using the support mapping
$s_{\Psi_{B_1,B_2}}(-\vec{p}_0)$ (see Eq. (4.37)). This is done by computing the support mapping for
each individual body and merging the results using Eq. (4.38). Figure 4.35(a) shows
the equivalent of this computation if we had to compute the convex polygon representing the Minkowski difference of the bodies. Point $\vec{q}_0$ is chosen such that it is the
point on the Minkowski difference closest to the origin. It happens that computing
$\vec{q}_0$ is equivalent to finding the point on the Minkowski difference that has minimum
projection along $\vec{p}_0$. Having determined $\vec{p}_0$, $\vec{q}_0$ and Q_0, we use Eq. (4.40) to continue to the next step. In this case, $\vec{p}_1 = \vec{q}_0$ and $Q_1 = \{\vec{q}_0\}$. Figure 4.35(b) and (c)
shows the procedure just explained applied to the next two iterations of the GJK
algorithm.

The only remaining steps that need clarification are how to compute $\vec{p}_{i+1} =$
$\min\{convex(Q_i \cup \{\vec{q}_i\})\}$, and how to construct the simplex $Q_{i+1} \subseteq (Q_i \cup \{\vec{q}_i\})$ such
that $\vec{p}_{i+1} \in convex(Q_{i+1})$. Here, we shall focus on the results of how $\vec{p}_{i+1}$ and

Q_{i+1} can be obtained. The interested reader is referred to Sect. 4.13 for references to the literature that presents a full derivation and proof of the results here described.

We shall first concentrate on how to determine the simplex Q_{i+1}. Later, we shall see that the point $\vec{p}_{i+1}$ can be directly obtained from the Q_{i+1} computations.

Let's assume the set $(Q_i \cup \{\vec{q}_i\})$ is represented by

$$(Q_i \cup \{\vec{q}_i\}) = \{\vec{x}_1, \vec{x}_2, \ldots, \vec{x}_n\}.$$

Clearly from Eq. (4.40), Q_{i+1} is restricted to being a subset of $(Q_i \cup \{\vec{q}_i\})$ at each iteration. We want to determine Q_{i+1} such that it is the smallest nonempty subset of $(Q_i \cup \{\vec{q}_i\})$ with $\vec{p}_{i+1} \in convex(Q_{i+1})$. Let $I_s \subseteq \{1, 2, \ldots, n\}$ be the set of indexes corresponding to the vertices of Q_{i+1}.

In general, any point $\vec{p}$ inside the simplex Q_{i+1} can be described as an affine combination of its vertices $\vec{x}_j$, that is

$$\vec{p} = \sum_{j \in I_s} \lambda_j \vec{x}_j,$$

with

$$\sum_{j \in I_s} \lambda_j = 1.$$

Since we are dealing with three-dimensional spaces, the maximum number of vertices a 3D simplex can have is four. That is, maximum number of vertices in I_s is limited to four, corresponding to Q_{i+1} being a tetrahedron. So, if Q_i already has four vertices, then $(Q_i \cup \{\vec{q}_i\})$ will have five vertices, indicating that one of them can be written as an affine combination of the others. The simplex Q_{i+1} will then be characterized by the affinely independent vertices $\vec{x}_j$ of $(Q_i \cup \{\vec{q}_i\})$, that is, by the vertices $\vec{x}_j$ with $\lambda_j > 0$.

Putting it into equations, we have that Q_{i+1} is defined by the vertices $\vec{x}_j$ satisfying

$$\lambda_j > 0, \quad \forall j \in I_s,$$
$$\lambda_j \le 0, \quad \forall j \notin I_s.$$

In other words, the simplex Q_{i+1} is the convex hull of the affinely independent vertices of $(Q_i \cup \{\vec{q}_i\})$, and point $\vec{p}_{i+1}$ is the point in Q_{i+1} closest to the origin, given by

$$\vec{p}_{i+1} = \sum_{j \in I_s} \lambda_j \vec{x}_j, \qquad (4.41)$$

with

$$\sum_{j \in I_s} \lambda_j = 1. \tag{4.42}$$

Assume I_s has $r \leq n$ vertices, and let $\vec{x}_1, \vec{x}_2, \ldots, \vec{x}_r$ represent an arbitrary ordering of the vertices of I_s. In this context, Eq. (4.42) can be re-written as

$$\lambda_1 = 1 - \sum_{j=2}^{r} \lambda_j.$$

Since we want $\vec{p}_{i+1}$ to be the point closest to the origin, the $\lambda_2, \ldots, \lambda_r$ are computed from the unconstrained minimization of

$$F(\lambda_2, \ldots, \lambda_r) = \left| \vec{x}_1 + \sum_{j=2}^{r} \lambda_j (\vec{x}_j - \vec{x}_1) \right|.$$

Since $F(\lambda_2, \ldots, \lambda_r)$ is a convex function, it is minimized whenever

$$\frac{\partial F(\lambda_2, \ldots, \lambda_r)}{\partial \lambda_j} = 0, \tag{4.43}$$

for $j \in \{2, \ldots, r\}$. Equation (4.43) can then be written in matrix format

$$\mathbf{A_r} \vec{\lambda} = \vec{b},$$

with $\mathbf{A_r} \in \mathbb{R}^{r \times r}$ and $\vec{b} \in \mathbb{R}^r$, such that:

$$\mathbf{A_r} = \begin{pmatrix} 1 & \cdots & 1 \\ (\vec{x}_2 - \vec{x}_1) \cdot \vec{x}_1 & \cdots & (\vec{x}_2 - \vec{x}_1) \cdot \vec{x}_r \\ \vdots & \vdots & \vdots \\ (\vec{x}_r - \vec{x}_1) \cdot \vec{x}_1 & \cdots & (\vec{x}_r - \vec{x}_1) \cdot \vec{x}_r \end{pmatrix} \qquad \vec{b} = \begin{pmatrix} 1 \\ 0 \\ \vdots \\ 0 \end{pmatrix}.$$

Using Cramer's rule, we can compute each λ_j as

$$\lambda_j = \frac{\Delta_j(Q_{i+1})}{\Delta(Q_{i+1})},$$

where

$$\triangle_j(\{\vec{x}_j\}) = 1$$

$$\triangle_m(Q_{i+1} \cup \{\vec{x}_m\}) = \sum_{j \in I_s} \triangle_j(Q_{i+1})(\vec{x}_j \cdot \vec{x}_k - \vec{x}_j \cdot \vec{x}_m) \tag{4.44}$$

$$\triangle(Q_{i+1}) = \sum_{j \in I_s} \triangle_j(Q_{i+1}),$$

with $m \notin I_s$ and k being the minimum index in I_s. It happens that the smallest $Q_{i+1} \subset (Q_i \cup \{\vec{q}_i\})$ is such that

$$\triangle(Q_{i+1}) > 0$$

$$\triangle_j(Q_{i+1}) > 0, \quad \forall j \in I_s \tag{4.45}$$

$$\triangle_m(Q_{i+1} \cup \{\vec{x}_m\}) \le 0, \quad \forall m \notin I_s.$$

Notice that Eqs. (4.44) are solved for each possible instance of I_s, that is, for each possible subset of $(Q_i \cup \{\vec{q}_i\})$. We then select as the solution the subset that satisfies the constraints described in Eqs. (4.45). It can be shown that exactly one solution subset satisfies Eqs. (4.45).

Since the maximum number of vertices n in $(Q_i \cup \{\vec{q}_i\})$ is small (i.e., $n \le 4$), the determination of Q_{i+1} can be done by an exhaustive search among all possible nonempty subsets of $(Q_i \cup \{\vec{q}_i\})$. This translates into searching among

$$\sum_{m=1}^{n} \frac{n!}{m!(n-m)!}$$

candidate subsets that satisfying Eqs. (4.45).

Having determined the subset Q_{i+1} that satisfies Eqs. (4.45), point $\vec{p}_{i+1}$ follows directly from Eq. (4.41), that is

$$\vec{p}_{i+1} = \sum_{j \in I_s} \lambda_j \vec{x}_j.$$

We proceed to iteration $(i+2)$ to determine Q_{i+2} and $\vec{p}_{i+2}$, and so on, until we reach the termination condition explained in Sect. 4.10.1. Let t be the iteration at which the termination conditions are reached. We have

$$\vec{p}_t = \sum_{j \in I_s} \lambda_j \vec{x}_j. \tag{4.46}$$

Each point $\vec{x}_j$ in the Minkowski difference of B_1 and B_2 can then be expressed as

$$\vec{x}_j = (\vec{b}_1)^j - (\vec{b}_2)^j, \tag{4.47}$$

with $(\vec{b}_1)^j \in B_1$ and $(\vec{b}_2)^j \in B_2$. Substituting Eq. (4.47) into (4.46) gives:

$$\vec{p}_t = \sum_{j \in I_s} \lambda_j \left((\vec{b}_1)^j - (\vec{b}_2)^j \right)$$

$$= \sum_{j \in I_s} \lambda_j (\vec{b}_1)^j - \sum_{j \in I_s} \lambda_j (\vec{b}_2)^j$$

$$= \vec{b}_1^* - \vec{b}_2^*.$$

Because B_1 and B_2 are convex, $\vec{b}_1^* \in B_1$ and $\vec{b}_2^* \in B_2$ are the closest points between the bodies.

4.10.1 Termination Condition

Even though it is guaranteed that the GJK algorithm will end in a finite number of iterations whenever bodies B_1 and B_2 are convex polyhedra, the presence of numerical round-off errors in a computer implementation makes it necessary to formulate a termination condition to be checked at the end of each iteration.

The termination condition consists of checking whether point $\vec{p}_i$ obtained at iteration i lies within a tolerance value from the origin. If so, then $\vec{p}_i$ is considered close enough to the origin and the algorithm terminates. The tolerance value used is a lower bound on the module of $\vec{p}_i$ computed as the signed distance of the supporting plane $\pi_{\vec{p}_i, \vec{q}_i}$ to the origin. The supporting plane is defined by its normal vector $\vec{n}_i$ and plane constant d_i as[10]

$$\vec{n}_i = -\vec{p}_i$$

$$d_i = \vec{p}_i \cdot \vec{q}_i.$$

The signed distance of the supporting plane to the origin is then

$$d = \frac{d_i}{|\vec{n}_i|}.$$

Notice that, for $d_i > 0$, the origin lies in the positive half space of $\pi_{\vec{p}_i, \vec{q}_i}$, that is, if we substitute $\vec{x} = \vec{0}$ in the plane equation, we get

$$\vec{n}_i \cdot \vec{x} + d_i = \vec{n}_i \cdot \vec{0} + d_i = d_i > 0,$$

whereas the Minkowski difference always lies in the negative half space of the plane. Therefore, at iteration i we use

$$L_b = \max\{0, d_0, d_1, \ldots, d_i\}$$

----

[10]The plane in this case is defined as $\pi_{\vec{p}_i, \vec{q}_i} = \{\vec{x} : (\vec{n}_i \cdot \vec{x} + d_i) = 0\}$, as opposed to $\{\vec{x} : (\vec{n}_i \cdot \vec{x} - d_i) = 0\}$. The latter is the definition used in all other sections of this book.

Fig. 4.36 Rigid bodies B_1 and B_2 at the moment just before their collision. The relative velocity of the closest points $\vec{p}_1$ and $\vec{p}_2$ is used to determine the direction of the collision normal. Notice that at the exact moment of collision we have $\vec{p}_1 = \vec{p}_2 = \vec{p}_c$

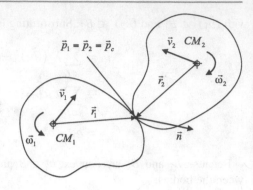

as the lower bound of $|\vec{p}_i|$, and we terminate the algorithm at iteration i whenever

$$|\vec{p}_i| - L_b \leq \mu,$$

with μ being the error-tolerance value.

4.11   Rigid Body–Rigid Body Collision Response

Whenever a rigid body–rigid body collision is detected, the collision-response module is invoked to compute the appropriate collision impulses or contact forces that will prevent interpenetration between the colliding bodies. As explained in Sect. 4.4, the colliding rigid bodies are traced back in time to the moment before their collision. The collision point and normal are then determined from their geometric displacement.

The colliding bodies are arbitrarily assigned indexes 1 and 2, and the normal direction is selected such that the relative velocity $(\vec{v}_1 - \vec{v}_2)$ of the rigid bodies at the collision point along the collision normal is negative just before the collision, that is, we choose $\vec{n}$ such that

$$\big((\vec{v}_1 + \vec{\omega}_1 \times \vec{r}_1) - (\vec{v}_2 + \vec{\omega}_2 \times \vec{r}_2)\big) \cdot \vec{n} < 0 \tag{4.48}$$

is satisfied just before the collision, indicating that the bodies are moving towards each other (see Fig. 4.36). Notice that the velocities at the collision points $\vec{p}_1$ and $\vec{p}_2$ are computed using Eq. (4.6), described in Sect. 4.2.

This index assignment is critical because, from Newton's principle of action and reaction, the collision impulses and contact forces between the rigid bodies have the same magnitude, but opposite directions. Following our convention, a positive impulse should be applied to the rigid body with index 1, whereas a negative impulse should be applied to the rigid body of index 2. Therefore, it is important to keep track of the index assigned to each rigid body, so as to later apply the collision impulses and contact forces on the correct direction (i.e., with the correct sign) to each body. Also, notice that, in the case of multiple rigid body–rigid body collisions, a rigid body might be assigned different indexes for each collision it is involved in.

The difference between a collision and a contact is determined from the module of the relative velocity along the collision normal, at the collision point. If the relative velocity of the rigid bodies at the collision point along the collision normal, at the moment before the collision, is less than a threshold value, then the rigid bodies are said to be in contact and a contact force is computed to prevent their interpenetration. Otherwise, the rigid bodies are said to be colliding and an impulsive force is applied to instantaneously change their direction of motion to avoid the imminent inter penetration.

Also, there may be situations in which several rigid bodies are involved in multiple collisions and contacts. If so, the collision-response module should first resolve all collisions by simultaneously computing all impulsive forces. Having determined all impulsive forces, the collision-response module proceeds by applying the impulses to the appropriate rigid bodies. By the time the impulses are applied, some of the contacts may or may not break, depending on whether the relative acceleration of the rigid bodies at their contact point, along the contact normal, is positive, zero or negative. A contact force is then simultaneously computed for all contacts that have a negative relative acceleration along their contact normal.

4.11.1 Computing Impulsive Forces for a Single Collision

Let's start by examining the case where we have one or more simultaneous collisions, each involving two different rigid bodies. Here, each collision can be dealt with separately and in parallel, since they do not have bodies in common.

Let collision C, involving rigid bodies B_1 and B_2, be defined by its collision normal $\vec{n}$ and tangent axes $\vec{t}$ and $\vec{k}$, as indicated in Fig. 4.37. Let $\vec{v}_1 = ((v_1)_n, (v_1)_t, (v_1)_k)$ and $\vec{\omega}_1 = ((\omega_1)_n, (\omega_1)_t, (\omega_1)_k)$ be the linear and angular velocities of rigid body B_1 just before the collision. Analogously, let $\vec{v}_2 = ((v_2)_n, (v_2)_t, (v_2)_k)$ and $\vec{\omega}_2 = ((\omega_2)_n, (\omega_2)_t, (\omega_2)_k)$ be the linear and angular velocities of rigid body B_2 just before the collision. All these components are known quantities. We need to compute the linear and angular velocities of both bodies just after the collision, namely $\vec{V}_1 = ((V_1)_n, (V_1)_t, (V_1)_k)$, $\vec{\Omega}_1 = ((\Omega_1)_n, (\Omega_1)_t, (\Omega_1)_k)$, $\vec{V}_2 = ((V_2)_n, (V_2)_t, (V_2)_k)$ and $\vec{\Omega}_2 = ((\Omega_2)_n, (\Omega_2)_t, (\Omega_2)_k)$. These, together with the impulsive force $\vec{P} = (P_n, P_t, P_k)$, sums to a total of fifteen unknowns, thus requiring the solution of a system with fifteen equations.

Applying the principle of impulse and linear momentum to each rigid body along the three axes defining the collision frame, we obtain six out of the fifteen equations needed:[11]

$$m_1(\vec{V}_1 - \vec{v}_1) = \vec{P} \tag{4.49}$$

$$m_2(\vec{V}_2 - \vec{v}_2) = -\vec{P}. \tag{4.50}$$

---

[11] We will use the vector-based notation as much as possible to keep the equations concise. However, there are cases in which we do need to rewrite the equations using the individual components of each vector, such as when computing the critical-friction coefficient covered later in this section.

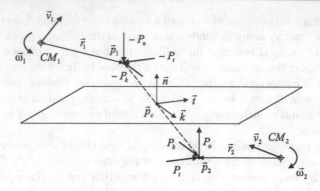

Fig. 4.37 Single rigid-body collision, showing just the closest points $\vec{p}_1$ and $\vec{p}_2$, as well as the location of the center of mass of each colliding body, at the moment just before the collision. A negative and a positive impulse is applied to the body of indexes 2 and 1, respectively. Also, the distance between the closest points is exaggerated to facilitate drawing the tangent plane

Applying the principle of impulse and angular momentum for each rigid body along the three axes defining the collision frame, we obtain another set of six equations:

$$\mathbf{I}_1(\vec{\Omega}_1 - \vec{\omega}_1) = \vec{r}_1 \times \vec{P} = \tilde{r}_1 \vec{P} \tag{4.51}$$

$$\mathbf{I}_2(\vec{\Omega}_2 - \vec{\omega}_2) = -\vec{r}_2 \times \vec{P} = -\tilde{r}_2 \vec{P}, \tag{4.52}$$

where $\tilde{r}_1\vec{P}$ and $\tilde{r}_2\vec{P}$ are the matrix–vector representation of their respective cross-products, as explained in detail in Sect. 6.7 of Appendix A (Chap. 6).

The next equation is obtained by the empirical relation involving the coefficient of restitution and the relative velocity of the rigid bodies at the collision point along the collision normal. Let e denote the coefficient of restitution along the normal direction. We have

$$\big((\vec{V}_1 + \vec{\Omega}_1 \times \vec{r}_1) - (\vec{V}_2 + \vec{\Omega}_2 \times \vec{r}_2)\big) \cdot \vec{n}$$
$$= -e\big((\vec{v}_1 + \vec{\omega}_1 \times \vec{r}_1) - (\vec{v}_2 + \vec{\omega}_2 \times \vec{r}_2)\big) \cdot \vec{n},$$

or equivalently

$$\big((V_1)_n + (r_1)_k(\Omega_1)_t - (r_1)_t(\Omega_1)_k\big)$$
$$- \big((V_2)_n + (r_2)_k(\Omega_2)_t - (r_2)_t(\Omega_2)_k\big)$$
$$= -e\big(((v_1)_n + (r_1)_k(\omega_1)_t - (r_1)_t(\omega_1)_k)$$
$$- ((v_2)_n + (r_2)_k(\omega_2)_t - (r_2)_t(\omega_2)_k)\big). \tag{4.53}$$

The remaining two equations are obtained from the Coulomb friction relations at the collision point. If the relative motion of the rigid bodies at the collision point along $\vec{t}$ and $\vec{k}$ is zero just before the collision, that is, if

$$((\vec{v}_1 + \vec{\omega}_1 \times \vec{r}_1) - (\vec{v}_2 + \vec{\omega}_2 \times \vec{r}_2)) \cdot \vec{t} = 0$$
$$((\vec{v}_1 + \vec{\omega}_1 \times \vec{r}_1) - (\vec{v}_2 + \vec{\omega}_2 \times \vec{r}_2)) \cdot \vec{k} = 0,$$

then their relative motion will remain zero after the collision. More specifically, we use

$$(\vec{V}_1 + \vec{\Omega}_1 \times \vec{r}_1) \cdot \vec{t} = (\vec{V}_2 + \vec{\Omega}_2 \times \vec{r}_2) \cdot \vec{t} \tag{4.54}$$
$$(\vec{V}_1 + \vec{\Omega}_1 \times \vec{r}_1) \cdot \vec{k} = (\vec{V}_2 + \vec{\Omega}_2 \times \vec{r}_2) \cdot \vec{k} \tag{4.55}$$

as the two remaining equations to solve the system. However, if the relative motion is not zero, then the rigid bodies are sliding along $\vec{t}$ and $\vec{k}$ at the collision point. The collision impulse will then act on the opposite direction of motion, trying to prevent the sliding. If it succeeds, then Eqs. (4.54) and (4.55) should be used. Otherwise, the rigid bodies continue sliding throughout the entire collision, and we use

$$P_t = (\mu_d)_t P_n \tag{4.56}$$
$$P_k = (\mu_d)_k P_n \tag{4.57}$$

as the two remaining equations to solve the system. Notice that $(\mu_d)_t$ and $(\mu_d)_k$ are the dynamic Coulomb friction coefficients along the $\vec{t}$ and $\vec{k}$ directions, respectively. Since P_t and P_k are always opposing the sliding motion, the coefficients of friction can be either positive or negative to reflect that condition. The actual signs of the coefficients depend on the relative velocity of the rigid bodies at the collision point along axes $\vec{t}$ and $\vec{k}$, just before the collision. The signs are directly obtained from

$$\text{sign}((\mu_d)_t) = \frac{((\vec{v}_1 + \vec{\omega}_1 \times \vec{r}_1) - (\vec{v}_2 + \vec{\omega}_2 \times \vec{r}_2)) \cdot \vec{t}}{((\vec{v}_1 + \vec{\omega}_1 \times \vec{r}_1) - (\vec{v}_2 + \vec{\omega}_2 \times \vec{r}_2)) \cdot \vec{n}} \tag{4.58}$$
$$\text{sign}((\mu_d)_k) = \frac{((\vec{v}_1 + \vec{\omega}_1 \times \vec{r}_1) - (\vec{v}_2 + \vec{\omega}_2 \times \vec{r}_2)) \cdot \vec{k}}{((\vec{v}_1 + \vec{\omega}_1 \times \vec{r}_1) - (\vec{v}_2 + \vec{\omega}_2 \times \vec{r}_2)) \cdot \vec{n}}. \tag{4.59}$$

As already explained in Chap. 3, this directional-friction model is a generalization of the widely used model of relating the tangential and normal impulses using just one omnidirectional coefficient of friction μ_d, as in

$$P_{tk} = \mu_d P_n, \tag{4.60}$$

where P_{tk} is the impulse on the tangent plane given by

$$P_{tk} = \sqrt{P_t^2 + P_k^2}.$$

For example, if friction is isotropic, that is, independent of direction, then we can write

$$(\mu_d)_t = \mu_d \cos\phi$$

$$(\mu_d)_k = \mu_d \sin\phi$$

for some angle ϕ, and so

$$P_{tk} = \sqrt{P_t^2 + P_k^2}$$
$$= \sqrt{\mu_d^2 P_n^2 \cos\phi^2 + \mu_d^2 P_n^2 \sin\phi^2}$$
$$= \mu_d P_n,$$

which is the same result obtained using the omnidirectional-friction model of Eq. (4.60). The main advantage of using this model is that the non-linear equation:

$$|P_{tk}| = \sqrt{P_t^2 + P_k^2} \le \mu_d P_n$$

that needs to be enforced when the rigid bodies are not sliding at the collision point can be substituted for two linear equations

$$|P_t| \le (\mu_d)_t P_n$$
$$|P_k| \le (\mu_d)_k P_n,$$

which are equivalent to the non-linear equation if friction is isotropic, and most important, are easier to handle in matrix form, as we shall see shortly.

As far as friction is concerned, we have to consider two possible cases. In the first, we assume the rigid bodies continue sliding along the tangent plane after collision, and we use Eqs. (4.49) to (4.53) with Eqs. (4.56) and (4.57) to compute the collision impulse and velocities after the collision. In the second, the rigid bodies are not sliding along the tangent plane after the collision, and we use Eqs. (4.49) to (4.53) with Eqs. (4.54) and (4.55) instead. For now, let's focus on the solution corresponding to the first case. Later, we shall consider the modifications needed to address the second case.

Instead of jumpstart-solving the fifteen-equation system, let's first consider its partitioned block-matrix representation and show how we can use linear-system methods to efficiently resolve the collision. Besides being extremely useful for the single-collision case, the block-matrix representation proves to be invaluable when dealing with multiple simultaneous collisions, as we shall see later in Sect. 4.11.2.

As mentioned, if the rigid bodies continue sliding along the tangent plane after collision, we need to use Eqs. (4.49) to (4.53) with Eqs. (4.56) and (4.57). Here, the fifteen-equation system can be put into the following matrix format:

$$
\begin{bmatrix}
0 & 0 & 0 & 1 & 0 & 0 & 0 & (r_1)_k & -(r_1)_t & -1 & 0 & 0 & 0 & -(r_2)_k & (r_2)_t \\
-(\mu_d)_t & 1 & 0 & 0 & 0 & 0 & 0 & 0 & 0 & 0 & 0 & 0 & 0 & 0 & 0 \\
-(\mu_d)_k & 1 & 0 & 0 & 0 & 0 & 0 & 0 & 0 & 0 & 0 & 0 & 0 & 0 & 0 \\
-1 & 0 & 0 & m_1 & 0 & 0 & 0 & 0 & 0 & 0 & 0 & 0 & 0 & 0 & 0 \\
0 & -1 & 0 & 0 & m_1 & 0 & 0 & 0 & 0 & 0 & 0 & 0 & 0 & 0 & 0 \\
0 & 0 & -1 & 0 & 0 & m_1 & 0 & 0 & 0 & 0 & 0 & 0 & 0 & 0 & 0 \\
0 & (r_1)_k & -(r_1)_t & 0 & 0 & 0 & (I_1)_{nn} & (I_1)_{nt} & (I_1)_{nk} & 0 & 0 & 0 & 0 & 0 & 0 \\
-(r_1)_k & 0 & (r_1)_n & 0 & 0 & 0 & (I_1)_{tn} & (I_1)_{tt} & (I_1)_{tk} & 0 & 0 & 0 & 0 & 0 & 0 \\
(r_1)_t & -(r_1)_n & 0 & 0 & 0 & 0 & (I_1)_{kn} & (I_1)_{kt} & (I_1)_{kk} & 0 & 0 & 0 & 0 & 0 & 0 \\
1 & 0 & 0 & 0 & 0 & 0 & 0 & 0 & 0 & m_2 & 0 & 0 & 0 & 0 & 0 \\
0 & 1 & 0 & 0 & 0 & 0 & 0 & 0 & 0 & 0 & m_2 & 0 & 0 & 0 & 0 \\
0 & 0 & 1 & 0 & 0 & 0 & 0 & 0 & 0 & 0 & 0 & m_2 & 0 & 0 & 0 \\
0 & -(r_2)_k & (r_2)_t & 0 & 0 & 0 & 0 & 0 & 0 & 0 & 0 & 0 & (I_2)_{nn} & (I_2)_{nt} & (I_2)_{nk} \\
(r_2)_k & 0 & -(r_2)_n & 0 & 0 & 0 & 0 & 0 & 0 & 0 & 0 & 0 & (I_2)_{tn} & (I_2)_{tt} & (I_2)_{tk} \\
-(r_2)_t & (r_2)_n & 0 & 0 & 0 & 0 & 0 & 0 & 0 & 0 & 0 & 0 & (I_2)_{kn} & (I_2)_{kt} & (I_2)_{kk}
\end{bmatrix}
\begin{pmatrix}
P_n \\ P_t \\ P_k \\ (V_1)_n \\ (V_1)_t \\ (V_1)_k \\ (\Omega_1)_n \\ (\Omega_1)_t \\ (\Omega_1)_k \\ (V_2)_n \\ (V_2)_t \\ (V_2)_k \\ (\Omega_2)_n \\ (\Omega_2)_t \\ (\Omega_2)_k
\end{pmatrix}
$$

$$
=
\begin{pmatrix}
e((v_1)_n + (r_1)_k(\omega_1)_t - (r_1)_t(\omega_1)_k) \\
\quad - ((v_2)_n + (r_2)_k(\omega_2)_t - (r_2)_t(\omega_2)_k)) \\
0 \\
0 \\
m_1(v_1)_n \\
m_1(v_1)_t \\
m_1(v_1)_k \\
(I_1)_{nn}(w_1)_n + (I_1)_{nt}(w_1)_t + (I_1)_{nk}(w_1)_k \\
(I_1)_{tn}(w_1)_n + (I_1)_{tt}(w_1)_t + (I_1)_{tk}(w_1)_k \\
(I_1)_{kn}(w_1)_n + (I_1)_{kt}(w_1)_t + (I_1)_{kk}(w_1)_k \\
m_2(v_2)_n \\
m_2(v_2)_t \\
m_2(v_2)_k \\
(I_2)_{nn}(w_2)_n + (I_2)_{nt}(w_2)_t + (I_2)_{nk}(w_2)_k \\
(I_2)_{tn}(w_2)_n + (I_2)_{tt}(w_2)_t + (I_2)_{tk}(w_2)_k \\
(I_2)_{kn}(w_2)_n + (I_2)_{kt}(w_2)_t + (I_2)_{kk}(w_2)_k
\end{pmatrix}
\tag{4.61}
$$

where the order in which the equations are laid out in each row is Eq. (4.53) first, then Eqs. (4.56) and (4.57), followed by Eqs. (4.49), (4.51), (4.50) and (4.52). This order is very important, since it simplifies the description of the above system using the partitioned block-matrix representation

$$
\begin{pmatrix}
\mathbf{A}_{1,2} & \mathbf{B}_{1,2} & \mathbf{C}_{1,2} & -\mathbf{B}_{1,2} & \mathbf{E}_{1,2} \\
-\mathbf{I} & m_1\mathbf{I} & \mathbf{0} & \mathbf{0} & \mathbf{0} \\
-\tilde{r}_1 & \mathbf{0} & \mathbf{I}_1 & \mathbf{0} & \mathbf{0} \\
\mathbf{I} & \mathbf{0} & \mathbf{0} & m_2\mathbf{I} & \mathbf{0} \\
\tilde{r}_2 & \mathbf{0} & \mathbf{0} & \mathbf{0} & \mathbf{I}_2
\end{pmatrix}
\begin{pmatrix}
\vec{P}_{1,2} \\
\vec{V}_1 \\
\vec{\Omega}_1 \\
\vec{V}_2 \\
\vec{\Omega}_2
\end{pmatrix}
=
\begin{pmatrix}
\vec{d}_{1,2} \\
m_1\vec{v}_1 \\
\mathbf{I}_1\vec{\omega}_1 \\
m_2\vec{v}_2 \\
\mathbf{I}_2\vec{\omega}_2
\end{pmatrix},
\qquad (4.62)
$$

where $\mathbf{0}$ is the 3×3 zero matrix, $\mathbf{I}$ is the 3×3 identity matrix, and $\vec{P}_{1,2} = \vec{P}$, with the index $(1, 2)$ indicating that the impulse corresponds to the collision between bodies B_1 and B_2.[12] The matrices $\tilde{r}_1$ and $\tilde{r}_2$ are the matrix–vector representations of the cross-products $\vec{r}_1 \times \vec{P}$ and $\vec{r}_2 \times \vec{P}$, respectively. The other matrices are given by

$$
\mathbf{A}_{1,2} =
\begin{pmatrix}
0 & 0 & 0 \\
-(\mu_d)_t & 1 & 0 \\
-(\mu_d)_k & 1 & 0
\end{pmatrix}
\qquad
\mathbf{B}_{1,2} =
\begin{pmatrix}
1 & 0 & 0 \\
0 & 0 & 0 \\
0 & 0 & 0
\end{pmatrix}
$$

$$
\mathbf{C}_{1,2} =
\begin{pmatrix}
0 & (r_1)_k & -(r_1)_t \\
0 & 0 & 0 \\
0 & 0 & 0
\end{pmatrix}
\qquad
\mathbf{E}_{1,2} =
\begin{pmatrix}
0 & -(r_2)_k & (r_2)_t \\
0 & 0 & 0 \\
0 & 0 & 0
\end{pmatrix}
$$

and the vector $\vec{d}_{1,2}$ is computed as

$$
\vec{d}_{1,2} =
\begin{pmatrix}
-e((\vec{v}_1 + \vec{\omega}_1 \times \vec{r}_1) - (\vec{v}_2 + \vec{\omega}_2 \times \vec{r}_2)) \cdot \vec{n} \\
0 \\
0
\end{pmatrix}.
\qquad (4.63)
$$

We can then solve the (often) sparse linear system described in Eq. (4.62) using Gaussian elimination, or a more sophisticated system solver suitable for sparse matrix only. The latter is more difficult to implement, but yields significant efficiency gains over the former method.

Notice that this partitioned-matrix representation is applicable only to the case where the colliding rigid bodies continue sliding throughout the collision. If the bodies are not sliding after collision, either because they were not sliding before the collision or the sliding motion stopped during the collision, then Eqs. (4.54) and (4.55), namely

---

[12]Even though the use of the indexes is not particularly useful for the single-collision case, they will be extensively applied in the block-matrix representation of multiple collisions to distinguish between equations associated with collisions involving different rigid bodies.

$$(\vec{V}_1 + \vec{\Omega}_1 \times \vec{r}_1) \cdot \vec{t} = (\vec{V}_2 + \vec{\Omega}_2 \times \vec{r}_2) \cdot \vec{t}$$
$$(\vec{V}_1 + \vec{\Omega}_1 \times \vec{r}_1) \cdot \vec{k} = (\vec{V}_2 + \vec{\Omega}_2 \times \vec{r}_2) \cdot \vec{k}$$

should be used instead of Eqs. (4.56) and (4.57). This in turn requires modifying the second and third rows of the partitioned-matrix representation, or equivalently, the second and third rows of matrices $\mathbf{A}_{1,2}$, $\mathbf{B}_{1,2}$, $\mathbf{C}_{1,2}$ and $\mathbf{E}_{1,2}$. The modification consists of updating the second row to

$$\begin{pmatrix} 0 & 0 & 0 & 0 & 1 & 0 & -(r_1)_k & 0 & (r_1)_n & (r_2)_k & 0 & -(r_2)_n \end{pmatrix}$$

if there is no sliding motion along the $\vec{t}$ direction, and updating the third row to

$$\begin{pmatrix} 0 & 0 & 0 & 0 & 0 & 1 & (r_1)_t & -(r_1)_n & 0 & -(r_2)_t & (r_2)_n & 0 \end{pmatrix}$$

if the bodies are not sliding along the $\vec{k}$ direction.

Notice that the sliding motion on the tangent plane is directly affected by the coefficients of restitution and friction, as well as by the relative velocities of the rigid bodies just before the collision. Intuitively, for a given coefficient of restitution and relative velocities, the sliding motion will continue if the coefficient of friction is small, or will stop if the coefficient of friction is sufficiently large. Therefore, there exists a critical-coefficient-of-friction value associated with a given coefficient of restitution and relative velocity. If the actual coefficient of friction is less than the critical coefficient of friction, then sliding continues throughout the collision and the system equations associated with the first case should be used. However, if the actual coefficient of friction is greater than or equal to the critical coefficient of friction, then the sliding stops somewhere during the collision and the system equations associated with the second case should be considered instead.[13]

Let's derive an expression for computing the critical coefficients of friction $(\mu_d)^c_t$ and $(\mu_d)^c_k$ along the tangent-plane directions $\vec{t}$ and $\vec{k}$. This will be done by first expressing all velocity components in Eq. (4.53) as a function of the normal-impulse component P_n, and solving for P_n. The computed impulse component P_n will then be substituted back into the expressions for each velocity component. This in turn will give us all velocities as a function of the restitution and friction coefficients, as well as the velocities of the bodies just before their collision.[14] Lastly, we shall substitute these expressions into Eq. (4.54) to determine the critical-coefficient value $(\mu_d)^c_t$ along $\vec{t}$, and into Eq. (4.55) to determine the critical-coefficient value $(\mu_d)^c_k$ along $\vec{k}$.

---

[13]If the actual coefficient of friction is equal to the critical coefficient of friction, then the sliding motion will stop exactly at the instant corresponding to the end of the collision.

[14]Keep in mind that the velocities computed so far assume that the sliding motion continues throughout the collision.

So, from Eqs. (4.49) and (4.50), we can write the linear velocity components as

$$(V_1)_n = \frac{P_n}{m_1} + (v_1)_n \tag{4.64}$$

$$(V_1)_t = \frac{P_t}{m_1} + (v_1)_t \tag{4.65}$$

$$(V_1)_k = \frac{P_k}{m_1} + (v_1)_k \tag{4.66}$$

$$(V_2)_n = -\frac{P_n}{m_2} + (v_2)_n \tag{4.67}$$

$$(V_2)_t = -\frac{P_t}{m_2} + (v_2)_t \tag{4.68}$$

$$(V_2)_k = -\frac{P_k}{m_2} + (v_2)_k. \tag{4.69}$$

Expressing the angular velocities as a function of P_n is a bit more complicated. Using Eqs. (4.51) and (4.52), each angular velocity can be written as

$$\vec{\Omega}_1 = \mathbf{I_1}^{-1} \tilde{r}_1 \vec{P} + \vec{w}_1$$
$$\vec{\Omega}_2 = -\mathbf{I_2}^{-1} \tilde{r}_2 \vec{P} + \vec{w}_2.$$

Let $\mathbf{A_1} = \mathbf{I_1}^{-1} \tilde{r}_1$ and $\mathbf{A_2} = \mathbf{I_2}^{-1} \tilde{r}_2$ be the result of the multiplication of these four known matrices, where

$$\mathbf{A_i} = \left((\vec{A}_i)_n \mid (\vec{A}_i)_t \mid (\vec{A}_i)_k \right) = \begin{pmatrix} (A_i)_{nn} & (A_i)_{nt} & (A_i)_{nk} \\ (A_i)_{tn} & (A_i)_{tt} & (A_i)_{tk} \\ (A_i)_{kn} & (A_i)_{kt} & (A_i)_{kk} \end{pmatrix}$$

for $i \in \{1, 2\}$. Using the fact that $P_t = (\mu_d)_t P_n$ and $P_k = (\mu_d)_k P_n$, after considerable manipulation, we obtain the following expressions for the angular-velocity components.

$$(\Omega_1)_n = \left((A_1)_{nn} + (\mu_d)_t (A_1)_{nt} + (\mu_d)_k (A_1)_{nk} \right) P_n$$
$$+ (\omega_1)_n \tag{4.70}$$

$$(\Omega_1)_t = \left((A_1)_{tn} + (\mu_d)_t (A_1)_{tt} + (\mu_d)_k (A_1)_{tk} \right) P_n$$
$$+ (\omega_1)_t \tag{4.71}$$

$$(\Omega_1)_k = \left((A_1)_{kn} + (\mu_d)_t (A_1)_{kt} + (\mu_d)_k (A_1)_{kk} \right) P_n$$
$$+ (\omega_1)_k \tag{4.72}$$

$$(\Omega_2)_n = -\left((A_2)_{nn} + (\mu_d)_t (A_2)_{nt} + (\mu_d)_k (A_2)_{nk} \right) P_n$$
$$+ (\omega_2)_n \tag{4.73}$$

$$(\Omega_2)_t = -\big((A_2)_{tn} + (\mu_d)_t(A_2)_{tt} + (\mu_d)_k(A_2)_{tk}\big)P_n$$
$$+ (\omega_2)_t \qquad (4.74)$$

$$(\Omega_2)_k = -\big((A_2)_{kn} + (\mu_d)_t(A_2)_{kt} + (\mu_d)_k(A_2)_{kk}\big)P_n$$
$$+ (\omega_2)_k. \qquad (4.75)$$

Substituting Eqs. (4.64), (4.67), (4.71), (4.72), (4.74) and (4.75) into Eq. (4.53), and grouping the terms that have P_n in common, we get

$$P_n\big(\bar{m} + \big((r_1)_k(A_1)_{tn} - (r_1)_t(A_1)_{kn}\big)$$
$$+ \big((r_2)_k(A_2)_{tn} - (r_2)_t(A_2)_{kn}\big) + (\mu_d)_t\big(((r_1)_k(A_1)_{tt} - (r_1)_t(A_1)_{kt})$$
$$+ \big((r_2)_k(A_2)_{tt} - (r_2)_t(A_2)_{kt}\big)\big) + (\mu_d)_k\big(((r_1)_k(A_1)_{tk} - (r_1)_t(A_1)_{kk}\big)$$
$$+ \big((r_2)_k(A_2)_{tk} - (r_2)_t(A_2)_{kk}\big)\big)\big)$$
$$= -(1+e)\big((\vec{v}_1 + \vec{\omega}_1 \times \vec{r}_1) - (\vec{v}_2 + \vec{\omega}_2 \times \vec{r}_2)\big) \cdot \vec{n} \qquad (4.76)$$

where

$$\bar{m} = \left(\frac{1}{m_1} + \frac{1}{m_2}\right).$$

This equation can be further simplified if we observe that

$$(r_i)_k(A_i)_{tn} - (r_i)_t(A_i)_{kn} = \big((\vec{A}_i)_n \times \vec{r}_i\big) \cdot \vec{n}$$
$$(r_i)_k(A_i)_{tt} - (r_i)_t(A_i)_{kt} = \big((\vec{A}_i)_t \times \vec{r}_i\big) \cdot \vec{n} \qquad (4.77)$$
$$(r_i)_k(A_i)_{tk} - (r_i)_t(A_i)_{kk} = \big((\vec{A}_i)_k \times \vec{r}_i\big) \cdot \vec{n}$$

for $i \in \{1, 2\}$. Substituting these equations into (4.76), gives

$$P_n\big(\bar{m} + ((\vec{A}_1)_n \times \vec{r}_1 + (\vec{A}_2)_n \times \vec{r}_2) \cdot \vec{n}$$
$$+ (\mu_d)_t\big((\vec{A}_1)_t \times \vec{r}_1 + (\vec{A}_2)_t \times \vec{r}_2\big) \cdot \vec{n}$$
$$+ (\mu_d)_k\big((\vec{A}_1)_k \times \vec{r}_1 + (\vec{A}_2)_k \times \vec{r}_2\big) \cdot \vec{n}\big)$$
$$= -(1+e)\big((\vec{v}_1 + \vec{\omega}_1 \times \vec{r}_1) - (\vec{v}_2 + \vec{\omega}_2 \times \vec{r}_2)\big) \cdot \vec{n}. \qquad (4.78)$$

Equation (4.78) can be reduced even further if we consider the following constants

$$g_1^{ij} = \big((\vec{A}_1)_i \times \vec{r}_1 + (\vec{A}_2)_i \times \vec{r}_2\big) \cdot \vec{j}$$
$$g_2^{j} = \big((\vec{v}_1 + \vec{\omega}_1 \times \vec{r}_1) - (\vec{v}_2 + \vec{\omega}_2 \times \vec{r}_2)\big) \cdot \vec{j}, \qquad (4.79)$$

with $i, j \in \{n, t, k\}$. Using these constants, Eq. (4.78) can then be rewritten as

$$P_n\big(\bar{m} + g_1^{nn} + (\mu_d)_t g_1^{tn} + (\mu_d)_k g_1^{kn}\big) = -(1+e)g_2^n,$$

which can be solved for P_n, giving

$$P_n = \frac{-(1+e)g_2^n}{\bar{m} + g_1^{nn} + (\mu_d)_t g_1^{tn} + (\mu_d)_k g_1^{kn}}. \tag{4.80}$$

Having computed P_n, we can substitute its value back into Eqs. (4.64) to (4.75) to obtain the values of each velocity component after the collision, for the case where the sliding motion continues throughout the collision. We are now ready to derive the expressions for computing the critical coefficients of friction along the tangent directions $\vec{t}$ and $\vec{k}$.

Let's start by computing $(\mu_d)_t^c$. This coefficient can be obtained if we expand Eq. (4.54) to

$$(\vec{V}_1 + \vec{\Omega}_1 \times \vec{r}_1) \cdot \vec{t} = (\vec{V}_2 + \vec{\Omega}_2 \times \vec{r}_2) \cdot \vec{t}$$

that is

$$(V_1)_t + (\Omega_1)_k (r_1)_n - (\Omega_1)_n (r_1)_k$$
$$= (V_2)_t + (\Omega_2)_k (r_2)_n - (\Omega_2)_n (r_2)_k \tag{4.81}$$

and substitute the value of each velocity component computed as a function of P_n into this equation, giving

$$\frac{P_t}{m_1} + (v_1)_t + (r_1)_n\big((A_1)_{kn} P_n$$
$$+ (A_1)_{kt} P_t + (A_1)_{kk} P_k\big) + (r_1)_n (w_1)_k$$
$$- (r_1)_k\big((A_1)_{nn} P_n + (A_1)_{nt} P_t + (A_1)_{nk} P_k\big) - (r_1)_k (w_1)_n$$
$$= -\frac{P_t}{m_2} + (v_2)_t - (r_2)_n\big((A_2)_{kn} P_n$$
$$+ (A_2)_{kt} P_t + (A_2)_{kk} P_k\big) + (r_2)_n (w_2)_k$$
$$+ (r_2)_k\big((A_2)_{nn} P_n + (A_2)_{nt} P_t + (A_2)_{nk} P_k\big) - (r_2)_k (w_2)_n. \tag{4.82}$$

From $P_t = (\mu_d)_t P_n$ and $P_k = (\mu_d)_k P_n$, we can group the terms of Eq. (4.82) so as to expose the constant values defined in Eqs. (4.79). We have

$$(\mu_d)_t P_n \overbrace{\left(\frac{1}{m_1} + \frac{1}{m_2}\right)}^{\bar{m}} + (\vec{v}_1 + \vec{\omega}_1 \times \vec{r}_1 - \vec{v}_2 - \vec{\omega}_2 \times \vec{r}_2) \cdot \vec{t}$$

$$+ P_n \overbrace{\big((r_1)_n (A_1)_{kn} - (r_1)_k (A_1)_{nn} + (r_2)_n (A_2)_{kn} - (r_2)_k (A_2)_{nn}\big)}^{-((\vec{A}_1)_n \times \vec{r}_1 + (\vec{A}_2)_n \times \vec{r}_2) \cdot \vec{t}}$$

$$\overbrace{-((\vec{A}_1)_t \times \vec{r}_1 + (\vec{A}_2)_t \times \vec{r}_2) \cdot \vec{t}}$$
$$+ (\mu_d)_t P_n \left((r_1)_n (A_1)_{kt} - (r_1)_k (A_1)_{nt} + (r_2)_n (A_2)_{kt} - (r_2)_k (A_2)_{nt}\right)$$

$$\overbrace{-((\vec{A}_1)_k \times \vec{r}_1 + (\vec{A}_2)_k \times \vec{r}_2) \cdot \vec{t}}$$
$$+ (\mu_d)_k P_n \left((r_1)_n (A_1)_{kk} - (r_1)_k (A_1)_{nk} + (r_2)_n (A_2)_{kk} - (r_2)_k (A_2)_{nk}\right) = 0,$$

that is

$$\overbrace{g_2^t}$$
$$(\mu_d)_t P_n \bar{m} + (\vec{v}_1 + \vec{\omega}_1 \times \vec{r}_1 - \vec{v}_2 - \vec{\omega}_2 \times \vec{r}_2) \cdot \vec{t}$$

$$\overbrace{g_1^{nt}}$$
$$- P_n \left((\vec{A}_1)_n \times \vec{r}_1 + (\vec{A}_2)_n \times \vec{r}_2\right) \cdot \vec{t}$$

$$\overbrace{g_1^{tt}}$$
$$- (\mu_d)_t P_n \left((\vec{A}_1)_t \times \vec{r}_1 + (\vec{A}_2)_t \times \vec{r}_2\right) \cdot \vec{t}$$

$$\overbrace{g_1^{kt}}$$
$$- (\mu_d)_k P_n \left((\vec{A}_1)_k \times \vec{r}_1 + (\vec{A}_2)_k \times \vec{r}_2\right) \cdot \vec{t} = 0,$$

which can be written in the condensed form

$$\left((\mu_d)_t \bar{m} - g_1^{nt} - (\mu_d)_t g_1^{tt} - (\mu_d)_k g_1^{kt}\right) P_n = -g_2^t. \tag{4.83}$$

Finally, substituting the value of P_n given in Eq. (4.80) into Eq. (4.83), and solving for $(\mu_d)_t$, we can compute the critical coefficient of friction along the tangent-plane direction $\vec{t}$ as

$$(\mu_d)_t = (\mu_d)_t^c = \frac{g_2^t(\bar{m} + g_1^{nn} + (\mu_d)_k g_1^{kn}) + (1+e)g_2^n(g_1^{nt} + (\mu_d)_k g_1^{kt})}{(\bar{m} - g_1^{tt})(1+e)g_2^n - g_2^t g_1^{tn}}, \tag{4.84}$$

where $(\mu_d)_t^c$ is the critical value of the coefficient of friction along $\vec{t}$ such that the sliding motion stops exactly at the end of the collision.

The derivation of the critical coefficient of friction $(\mu_d)_k^c$ along the tangent-plane direction $\vec{k}$ is very similar to that shown for $(\mu_d)_t^c$. We start by expanding Eq. (4.55) to

$$(V_1)_k + (\Omega_1)_n (r_1)_t - (\Omega_1)_t (r_1)_n$$
$$= (V_2)_k + (\Omega_2)_n (r_2)_t - (\Omega_2)_t (r_2)_n$$

and substitute the velocity-component values obtained from Eqs. (4.66), (4.69) to (4.71), (4.73) and (4.74). We then group the terms in order to expose the constant-value expressions given in Eqs. (4.79). After some manipulation, we get

$$\left((\mu_d)_k \bar{m} + g_1^{nk} + (\mu_d)_t g_1^{tk} + (\mu_d)_k g_1^{kk}\right) P_n = -g_2^k.$$

Finally, substituting the value of P_n obtained from Eq. (4.80) into this expression, and solving for $(\mu_d)_k$, we can compute the critical coefficient of friction along the tangent-plane direction $\vec{k}$ as

$$(\mu_d)_k = (\mu_d)_k^c = \frac{g_2^k(\bar{m} + g_1^{nn} + (\mu_d)_t g_1^{tn}) - (1+e)g_2^n(g_1^{nk} + (\mu_d)_t g_1^{tk})}{(\bar{m} + g_1^{kk})(1+e)g_2^n - g_1^{kn}g_2^k}, \quad (4.85)$$

where $(\mu_d)_k^c$ is the critical value of the coefficient of friction along $\vec{k}$ such that the sliding motion stops exactly at the end of the collision.

We do the following in practice. First, compute the critical coefficients of friction using Eqs. (4.84) and (4.85). Next, compare the actual coefficient of friction $(\mu_d)_t$ and $(\mu_d)_k$ to their associated critical values. If $(\mu_d)_t < (\mu_d)_t^c$, then sliding continues along $\vec{t}$, and we use Eq. (4.56). Else, if $(\mu_d)_t \geq (\mu_d)_t^c$, then sliding along $\vec{t}$ stops during the collision, and we use Eq. (4.54) instead. The same analysis is used for comparing $(\mu_d)_k$ with $(\mu_d)_k^c$ and selecting the appropriate system equation.

As far as the block-matrix representation is concerned, the choice of the equation to use as a function of the critical-coefficient-of-friction values directly affects the rows of matrices $\mathbf{A}_{1,2}$, $\mathbf{B}_{1,2}$, $\mathbf{C}_{1,2}$ and $\mathbf{E}_{1,2}$ being used. We have, therefore, the following four possible cases to consider when building the system matrix:

1. If $(\mu_d)_t < (\mu_d)_t^c$ and $(\mu_d)_k < (\mu_d)_k^c$, then:

$$\mathbf{A}_{1,2} = \begin{pmatrix} 0 & 0 & 0 \\ -(\mu_d)_t & 1 & 0 \\ -(\mu_d)_k & 1 & 0 \end{pmatrix} \qquad \mathbf{B}_{1,2} = \begin{pmatrix} 1 & 0 & 0 \\ 0 & 0 & 0 \\ 0 & 0 & 0 \end{pmatrix}$$

$$\mathbf{C}_{1,2} = \begin{pmatrix} 0 & (r_1)_k & -(r_1)_t \\ 0 & 0 & 0 \\ 0 & 0 & 0 \end{pmatrix} \qquad \mathbf{E}_{1,2} = \begin{pmatrix} 0 & -(r_2)_k & (r_2)_t \\ 0 & 0 & 0 \\ 0 & 0 & 0 \end{pmatrix}.$$

2. If $(\mu_d)_t \geq (\mu_d)_t^c$ and $(\mu_d)_k < (\mu_d)_k^c$, then:

$$\mathbf{A}_{1,2} = \begin{pmatrix} 0 & 0 & 0 \\ 0 & 0 & 0 \\ -(\mu_d)_k & 1 & 0 \end{pmatrix} \qquad \mathbf{B}_{1,2} = \begin{pmatrix} 1 & 0 & 0 \\ 0 & 1 & 0 \\ 0 & 0 & 0 \end{pmatrix}$$

$$\mathbf{C}_{1,2} = \begin{pmatrix} 0 & (r_1)_k & -(r_1)_t \\ -(r_1)_k & 0 & (r_1)_n \\ 0 & 0 & 0 \end{pmatrix}$$

$$\mathbf{E}_{1,2} = \begin{pmatrix} 0 & -(r_2)_k & (r_2)_t \\ (r_2)_k & 0 & -(r_2)_n \\ 0 & 0 & 0 \end{pmatrix}.$$

3. If $(\mu_d)_t < (\mu_d)_t^c$ and $(\mu_d)_k \geq (\mu_d)_k^c$, then:

$$\mathbf{A}_{1,2} = \begin{pmatrix} 0 & 0 & 0 \\ -(\mu_d)_t & 1 & 0 \\ 0 & 0 & 0 \end{pmatrix} \qquad \mathbf{B}_{1,2} = \begin{pmatrix} 1 & 0 & 0 \\ 0 & 0 & 0 \\ 0 & 0 & 1 \end{pmatrix}$$

$$\mathbf{C}_{1,2} = \begin{pmatrix} 0 & (r_1)_k & -(r_1)_t \\ 0 & 0 & 0 \\ (r_1)_t & -(r_1)_n & 0 \end{pmatrix}$$

$$\mathbf{E}_{1,2} = \begin{pmatrix} 0 & -(r_2)_k & (r_2)_t \\ 0 & 0 & 0 \\ -(r_2)_t & (r_2)_n & 0 \end{pmatrix}.$$

4. If $(\mu_d)_t \geq (\mu_d)_t^c$ and $(\mu_d)_k \geq (\mu_d)_k^c$, then:

$$\mathbf{A}_{1,2} = \mathbf{0} \qquad \mathbf{B}_{1,2} = \mathbf{I}$$
$$\mathbf{C}_{1,2} = -\tilde{r}_1 \qquad \mathbf{E}_{1,2} = \tilde{r}_2.$$

Having built the system matrix associated with the collision, we can use Gaussian-elimination or sparse-matrix techniques to solve the linear system of equations and determine the collision impulse, and linear and angular velocities, of the bodies at the moment after their collision.

4.11.2 Computing Impulsive Forces for Multiple Collisions

If three or more rigid bodies are simultaneously colliding with each other, the collision impulse of each individual collision will simultaneously affect the dynamics of the system. Therefore, instead of resolving one collision at a time ignoring the presence of the others, the simulation engine needs to group the rigid bodies into clusters that share at least one collision. The collisions within each cluster can then be simultaneously resolved independent of all other clusters (see Fig. 4.38).

Consider the computation of the collision impulses associated with cluster G_1, as shown in Fig. 4.38. Let collisions C_1 and C_2 be the collisions involving bodies $(B_1 - B_2)$ and $(B_2 - B_3)$, respectively. As far as rigid body B_2 is concerned, the linear- and angular-momentum equations owing to both collisions are

$$m_2(\vec{V}_2 - \vec{v}_2) = -\vec{P}_{1,2} + \vec{P}_{2 \mapsto 1, 3 \mapsto 2}$$
$$I_2(\vec{\Omega}_2 - \vec{\omega}_2) = \tilde{r}_2(-\vec{P}_{1,2} + \vec{P}_{2 \mapsto 1, 3 \mapsto 2}),$$

where $\vec{P}_{2 \mapsto 1, 3 \mapsto 2}$ is the impulse $\vec{P}_{2,3}$ of collision C_2 expressed in the local-coordinate frame[15] associated with collision C_1.

Clearly, the impulse arising from collision C_2 will also affect the computation of the impulse arising from collision C_1, and vice-versa. The correct way to compute the collision impulses is, then, to take both collisions into account when solving the

[15] The local-coordinate frame is defined by the collision normal and tangent plane.

Fig. 4.38 Multiple
rigid-body collisions
separated into three clusters.
Body B_i is added to cluster
G_j if it is colliding with at
least one rigid body already
in G_j. The collision-response
module resolves each cluster
in parallel, since they have no
collisions in common and
therefore can be viewed as
independent groups of
collisions

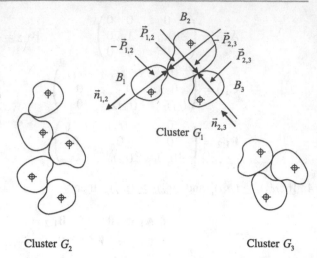

Cluster G_2 Cluster G_3

system equations. Recall from Sect. 4.11.1 that we adopted the convention that a
positive impulse is applied to the rigid body with index 1, and a negative impulse is
applied to the rigid body with index 2. The choice of indexes is related to the relative
velocities of the rigid bodies at the collision point along the collision normal, such
that Eq. (4.48) is satisfied at the moment before the collision.

Whenever a rigid body is involved in multiple collisions, it is possible to have it
assigned to different indexes for each collision. For the particular situation of cluster
G_1, rigid body B_2 has index 2 with respect to its collision with B_1, and index 1
with respect to its collision with B_3. This in turn, affects the choice of sign when
combining the multiple-collision impulses in the system equations. For example, the
minus sign on $\vec{P}_{1,2}$ indicates that rigid body B_2 has index 2 with respect to collision
C_1, whereas the plus sign on $\vec{P}_{2\rightarrow1,3\rightarrow2}$ indicates body B_2 has index 1 with respect
to collision C_2. Moreover, the collision normal and tangent plane are different for
each collision. So, we also need to carry out a change of base between the collision
impulses before combining them.

The best way to deal with multiple collisions is to represent the system equations
associated with each cluster in its block-matrix form

$$\mathbf{A}\vec{x} = \vec{b}$$

where $\vec{x}$ is the state vector containing the variables that need to be determined. In the
single collision case, the state vector is defined by the collision impulse, and the final
linear and angular velocities of the colliding bodies. However, when dealing with
multiple collisions, the state vector can be viewed as the concatenation of several
single-collision state vectors, with the added complexity that no variables should be
accounted for more than once. For instance, Fig. 4.39(a) shows the result of a naive
concatenation of state vectors for the multiple collisions associated with cluster G_1
of Fig. 4.38.

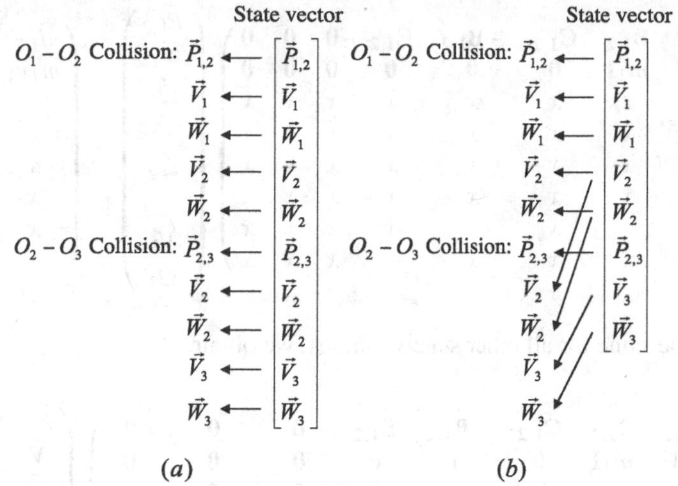

State vector   State vector

$O_1 - O_2$ Collision: $\vec{P}_{1,2}$ ⟵ $\begin{bmatrix} \vec{P}_{1,2} \\ \vec{V}_1 \\ \vec{W}_1 \\ \vec{V}_2 \\ \vec{W}_2 \end{bmatrix}$ $O_1 - O_2$ Collision: $\vec{P}_{1,2}$ ⟵ $\begin{bmatrix} \vec{P}_{1,2} \\ \vec{V}_1 \\ \vec{W}_1 \\ \vec{V}_2 \\ \vec{W}_2 \end{bmatrix}$

$\vec{V}_1$ ⟵
$\vec{W}_1$ ⟵
$\vec{V}_2$ ⟵
$\vec{W}_2$ ⟵

$O_2 - O_3$ Collision: $\vec{P}_{2,3}$ ⟵ $\begin{bmatrix} \vec{P}_{2,3} \\ \vec{V}_2 \\ \vec{W}_2 \\ \vec{V}_3 \\ \vec{W}_3 \end{bmatrix}$ $O_2 - O_3$ Collision: $\vec{P}_{2,3}$ ⟵ $\begin{bmatrix} \vec{P}_{2,3} \\ \vec{V}_3 \\ \vec{W}_3 \end{bmatrix}$

$\vec{V}_2$ ⟵
$\vec{W}_2$ ⟵
$\vec{V}_3$ ⟵
$\vec{W}_3$ ⟵

(a)   (b)

Fig. 4.39 (a) A naive concatenation creates multiple entries for the final linear and angular velocities of all bodies involved in more than one collision; (b) The state-vector variables should have a link back to their collisions. More than one link is used for multiple collisions, as is the case of $\vec{V}_2$ and $\vec{\Omega}_2$

Since rigid body B_2 is involved in both collisions, its final linear and angular velocities $\vec{V}_2$ and $\vec{\Omega}_2$ are accounted twice. The correct way to create the state vector is, then, to keep track of which variables were already added, and mark as "common" the ones added more than once. This is illustrated in Fig. 4.39(b).

Having determined the state vector associated with a cluster, the next step is to fill in the rows of matrix $\mathbf{A}$ and vector $\vec{b}$. This can be done by considering the equation associated with the first link of each variable in the state vector. For example, for the G_1 cluster of Fig. 4.38, the first variable of the state vector is $\vec{P}_{1,2}$. This variable is linked to the $(B_1 - B_2)$ collision. Its associated equations are those involving the coefficient of restitution and friction. Therefore, the first row of matrix $\mathbf{A}$ and vector $\vec{b}$ is:

$$\begin{pmatrix} \mathbf{A}_{1,2} & \mathbf{B}_{1,2} & \mathbf{C}_{1,2} & -\mathbf{B}_{1,2} & \mathbf{E}_{1,2} & \mathbf{0} & \mathbf{0} & \mathbf{0} \\ x & x & x & x & x & x & x & x \\ x & x & x & x & x & x & x & x \\ x & x & x & x & x & x & x & x \\ x & x & x & x & x & x & x & x \\ x & x & x & x & x & x & x & x \\ x & x & x & x & x & x & x & x \\ x & x & x & x & x & x & x & x \end{pmatrix} \begin{pmatrix} \vec{P}_{1,2} \\ \vec{V}_1 \\ \vec{\Omega}_1 \\ \vec{V}_2 \\ \vec{\Omega}_2 \\ \vec{P}_{2,3} \\ \vec{V}_3 \\ \vec{\Omega}_3 \end{pmatrix} = \begin{pmatrix} \vec{d}_{1,2} \\ x \\ x \\ x \\ x \\ x \\ x \\ x \end{pmatrix}.$$

The second variable of the state vector is $\vec{V}_1$. This variable is also linked to the $(B_1 - B_2)$ collision. Its associated equations are the conservation of linear momentum for body B_1. So, the second row of matrix $\mathbf{A}$ and vector $\vec{b}$ is:

$$
\begin{pmatrix}
\mathbf{A}_{1,2} & \mathbf{B}_{1,2} & \mathbf{C}_{1,2} & -\mathbf{B}_{1,2} & \mathbf{E}_{1,2} & 0 & 0 & 0 \\
-\mathbf{I} & m_1\mathbf{I} & 0 & 0 & 0 & 0 & 0 & 0 \\
x & x & x & x & x & x & x & x \\
x & x & x & x & x & x & x & x \\
x & x & x & x & x & x & x & x \\
x & x & x & x & x & x & x & x \\
x & x & x & x & x & x & x & x \\
x & x & x & x & x & x & x & x
\end{pmatrix}
\begin{pmatrix}
\vec{P}_{1,2} \\
\vec{V}_1 \\
\vec{\Omega}_1 \\
\vec{V}_2 \\
\vec{\Omega}_2 \\
\vec{P}_{2,3} \\
\vec{V}_3 \\
\vec{\Omega}_3
\end{pmatrix}
=
\begin{pmatrix}
\vec{d}_{1,2} \\
m_1\vec{v}_1 \\
x \\
x \\
x \\
x \\
x \\
x
\end{pmatrix}.
$$

Doing the same for all other state variables, we obtain:

$$
\begin{pmatrix}
\mathbf{A}_{1,2} & \mathbf{B}_{1,2} & \mathbf{C}_{1,2} & -\mathbf{B}_{1,2} & \mathbf{E}_{1,2} & 0 & 0 & 0 \\
-\mathbf{I} & m_1\mathbf{I} & 0 & 0 & 0 & 0 & 0 & 0 \\
-\tilde{r}_1 & 0 & \mathbf{I}_1 & 0 & 0 & 0 & 0 & 0 \\
\mathbf{I} & 0 & 0 & m_2\mathbf{I} & 0 & 0 & 0 & 0 \\
\tilde{r}_2 & 0 & 0 & 0 & \mathbf{I}_2 & 0 & 0 & 0 \\
0 & 0 & 0 & \mathbf{B}_{2,3} & \mathbf{C}_{2,3} & \mathbf{A}_{2,3} & -\mathbf{B}_{2,3} & \mathbf{E}_{2,3} \\
0 & 0 & 0 & 0 & 0 & \mathbf{I} & m_3\mathbf{I} & 0 \\
0 & 0 & 0 & 0 & 0 & \tilde{r}_3 & 0 & \mathbf{T}_3
\end{pmatrix}
\begin{pmatrix}
\vec{P}_{1,2} \\
\vec{V}_1 \\
\vec{\Omega}_1 \\
\vec{V}_2 \\
\vec{\Omega}_2 \\
\vec{P}_{2,3} \\
\vec{V}_3 \\
\vec{\Omega}_3
\end{pmatrix}
$$

$$
=
\begin{pmatrix}
\vec{d}_{1,2} \\
m_1\vec{v}_1 \\
\mathbf{I}_1\vec{\omega}_1 \\
m_2\vec{v}_2 \\
\mathbf{I}_2\vec{\omega}_2 \\
\vec{d}_{2,3} \\
m_3\vec{v}_3 \\
\mathbf{I}_3\vec{\omega}_3
\end{pmatrix}.
\tag{4.86}
$$

Notice the difference in the order of the matrices displayed on rows 1 and 6 of the system matrix shown in Eq. (4.86). Since $\vec{V}_2$ and $\vec{\Omega}_2$ are common to both $(B_1 - B_2)$ and $(B_2 - B_3)$ collisions, the matrices $\mathbf{A}_{2,3}$, $\mathbf{B}_{2,3}$, $\mathbf{C}_{2,3}$ and $\mathbf{E}_{2,3}$ were rearranged to correctly multiply their associated state vector variables. The correct order is $\mathbf{B}_{2,3}$ multiplying the linear velocity of the body with index 1 (i.e., $\vec{V}_2$), $\mathbf{C}_{2,3}$ multiplying the angular velocity of the body with index 1 (i.e., $\vec{\Omega}_2$), $\mathbf{A}_{2,3}$ multiplying the impulse associated with collision $(B_2 - B_3)$ (i.e., $\vec{P}_{2,3}$), $(-\mathbf{B}_{2,3})$ multiplying the linear velocity of the body with index 2 (i.e., $\vec{V}_3$), and $\mathbf{E}_{2,3}$ multiplying the angular velocity of the body with index 2 (i.e., $\vec{\Omega}_3$.)

Also, notice that Eq. (4.86) was built following *only* the first link of each state-vector variable. We still need to update Eq. (4.86) with the multiple-collision terms. This can be done by considering the state variables that have more than one associated link. The first link was used to define the row. The following links are used to update some elements of this row with the multiple-collision terms.

In general, if body B_i is involved in more than one collision, then the rows associated with $\vec{V}_i$ and $\vec{\Omega}_i$, that is, the rows associated with its final linear and angular velocities, need to be updated. Say, for example, that body B_i has a second link to body B_j. Let $\vec{P}_{i,j}$ designate the state-vector variable corresponding to the impulse associated with this collision. So, the indexes of $\vec{V}_i$ and $\vec{\Omega}_i$ in the state vector define the rows of the system matrix to be updated, and the index of $\vec{P}_{i,j}$ in the state vector defines the column of the system matrix that needs to be updated. Therefore, we need to update the elements

$$[\text{index of } \vec{V}_i][\text{index of } \vec{P}_{i,j}]$$
$$[\text{index of } \vec{\Omega}_i][\text{index of } \vec{P}_{i,j}]$$

of the system matrix given in Eq. (4.86).

The actual update consists of accounting for $\vec{P}_{i,j}$ in the linear- and angular-momentum equations associated with body B_i. This can be done by expressing $\vec{P}_{i,j}$ with respect to the local-coordinate frame of the collision corresponding to the first link of the state variables $\vec{V}_i$ and $\vec{\Omega}_i$.

Say, for example, that the first link of the state variables $\vec{V}_i$ and $\vec{\Omega}_i$ is associated with collision C_m involving bodies B_m and B_i. Let the local-coordinate frame $\mathcal{F}_{m,i}$ of collision $(B_m - B_i)$ be defined by vectors $\vec{n}_{m,i}$, $\vec{t}_{m,i}$ and $\vec{k}_{m,i}$.

Let the second link of the state variables $\vec{V}_i$ and $\vec{\Omega}_i$ be associated with collision C_j involving bodies B_i and B_j. Let the local-coordinate frame $\mathcal{F}_{i,j}$ of collision $(B_i - B_j)$ be defined by vectors $\vec{n}_{i,j}$, $\vec{t}_{i,j}$ and $\vec{k}_{i,j}$. The collision impulse $\vec{P}_{i,j}$ defined in the local frame $\mathcal{F}_{i,j}$ is expressed in the local frame $\mathcal{F}_{m,i}$ as

$$\vec{P}_{i\mapsto m, j\mapsto i} = \mathbf{M}_{i\mapsto m, j\mapsto i}\, \vec{P}_{i,j}$$

with

$$\mathbf{M}_{i\mapsto m, j\mapsto i} = \lambda \begin{pmatrix} \vec{n}_{i,j} \cdot \vec{n}_{m,i} & \vec{n}_{i,j} \cdot \vec{t}_{m,i} & \vec{n}_{i,j} \cdot \vec{k}_{m,i} \\ \vec{t}_{i,j} \cdot \vec{n}_{m,i} & \vec{t}_{i,j} \cdot \vec{t}_{m,i} & \vec{t}_{i,j} \cdot \vec{k}_{m,i} \\ \vec{k}_{i,j} \cdot \vec{n}_{m,i} & \vec{k}_{i,j} \cdot \vec{t}_{m,i} & \vec{k}_{i,j} \cdot \vec{k}_{m,i} \end{pmatrix}.$$

The variable λ can be either 1 or -1, depending on whether body B_i is assigned to index 2 or 1 in collision C_j. The necessary updates are then

$$[\text{index of } \vec{V}_i][\text{index of } \vec{P}_{i,j}] = \vec{P}_{i\mapsto m, j\mapsto i}$$
$$[\text{index of } \vec{\Omega}_i][\text{index of } \vec{P}_{i,j}] = \lambda \tilde{r}_i.$$

As an example, let's apply this multiple-collision-terms update to the G_1 cluster example of Fig. 4.38. In this example, the second link of $\vec{V}_2$ and $\vec{\Omega}_2$ points to the collision between bodies B_2 and B_3. Therefore, we need to update the elements at

$$[\text{index of } \vec{V}_2][\text{index of } \vec{P}_{2,3}] = [4, 6]$$

$$[\text{index of } \vec{\Omega}_2][\text{index of } \vec{P}_{2,3}] = [5, 6]$$

in the system matrix of Eq. (4.86). The actual update will be to substitute the current $\mathbf{0}$ matrix at position $[4, 6]$ for

$$\mathbf{M}_{2 \mapsto 1, 3 \mapsto 2} = \lambda \begin{pmatrix} \vec{n}_{2,3} \cdot \vec{n}_{1,2} & \vec{n}_{2,3} \cdot \vec{t}_{1,2} & \vec{n}_{2,3} \cdot \vec{k}_{1,2} \\ \vec{t}_{2,3} \cdot \vec{n}_{1,2} & \vec{t}_{2,3} \cdot \vec{t}_{1,2} & \vec{t}_{2,3} \cdot \vec{k}_{1,2} \\ \vec{k}_{2,3} \cdot \vec{n}_{1,2} & \vec{k}_{2,3} \cdot \vec{t}_{1,2} & \vec{k}_{2,3} \cdot \vec{k}_{1,2} \end{pmatrix}, \tag{4.87}$$

where frame $\mathcal{F}_{1,2}$ is defined by vectors $\vec{n}_{1,2}$, $\vec{t}_{1,2}$ and $\vec{k}_{1,2}$, and frame $\mathcal{F}_{2,3}$ is defined by vectors $\vec{n}_{2,3}$, $\vec{t}_{2,3}$ and $\vec{k}_{2,3}$. We also need to substitute the element at position $[5, 6]$ for

$$\lambda \tilde{r}_2. \tag{4.88}$$

Also, since body B_2 is assigned to index 1 in its collision with body B_3 (see Fig. 4.38), we should use $\lambda = +1$ in Eqs. (4.87) and (4.88). The final system matrix for this particular example is then:

$$\begin{pmatrix} \mathbf{A}_{1,2} & \mathbf{B}_{1,2} & \mathbf{C}_{1,2} & -\mathbf{B}_{1,2} & \mathbf{E}_{1,2} & \mathbf{0} & \mathbf{0} & \mathbf{0} \\ -\mathbf{I} & m_1\mathbf{I} & \mathbf{0} & \mathbf{0} & \mathbf{0} & \mathbf{0} & \mathbf{0} & \mathbf{0} \\ -\tilde{r}_1 & \mathbf{0} & \mathbf{I}_1 & \mathbf{0} & \mathbf{0} & \mathbf{0} & \mathbf{0} & \mathbf{0} \\ \mathbf{I} & \mathbf{0} & \mathbf{0} & m_2\mathbf{I} & \mathbf{0} & \mathbf{M}_{2 \mapsto 1, 3 \mapsto 2} & \mathbf{0} & \mathbf{0} \\ \tilde{r}_2 & \mathbf{0} & \mathbf{0} & \mathbf{0} & \mathbf{I}_2 & \tilde{r}_2 & \mathbf{0} & \mathbf{0} \\ \mathbf{0} & \mathbf{0} & \mathbf{0} & \mathbf{B}_{2,3} & \mathbf{C}_{2,3} & \mathbf{A}_{2,3} & -\mathbf{B}_{2,3} & \mathbf{E}_{2,3} \\ \mathbf{0} & \mathbf{0} & \mathbf{0} & \mathbf{0} & \mathbf{0} & \mathbf{I} & m_3\mathbf{I} & \mathbf{0} \\ \mathbf{0} & \mathbf{0} & \mathbf{0} & \mathbf{0} & \mathbf{0} & \tilde{r}_3 & \mathbf{0} & \mathbf{T}_3 \end{pmatrix} \begin{pmatrix} \vec{P}_{1,2} \\ \vec{V}_1 \\ \vec{\Omega}_1 \\ \vec{V}_2 \\ \vec{\Omega}_2 \\ \vec{P}_{2,3} \\ \vec{V}_3 \\ \vec{\Omega}_3 \end{pmatrix}$$

$$= \begin{pmatrix} \vec{d}_{1,2} \\ m_1\vec{v}_1 \\ \mathbf{I}_1\vec{\omega}_1 \\ m_2\vec{v}_2 \\ \mathbf{I}_2\vec{\omega}_2 \\ \vec{d}_{2,3} \\ m_3\vec{v}_3 \\ \mathbf{I}_3\vec{\omega}_3 \end{pmatrix}.$$

In summary, for each state-vector variable with more than one link, we need to update the elements of the system matrix corresponding to each of these collisions. When all elements are updated, we solve the resulting linear system using, for example, Gaussian elimination techniques. Another option would be to use specialized methods to solve sparse linear systems, since the system matrix is often sparse. The solution would then give the correct values of the state-vector variables to be used by the collision-response module to prevent the objects from interpenetrating after colliding.

4.11.3 Computing Contact Forces for a Single Contact

Two rigid bodies are said to be in contact whenever their relative velocities along the collision normal is either zero, or less than a threshold value. In such situations, a contact force should be applied, instead of the impulsive force described in Sect. 4.11.1.

In the case of computing impulsive forces for rigid body–rigid body collisions, the system is described by equations of conservation of linear and angular momentum, and the coefficients of friction and restitution. Unfortunately, these equations are no longer valid for the contact-force computation. Therefore, we need to derive other conditions to compute the contact forces, based on the contact geometry[16] and dynamic state of each rigid body. These conditions are exactly the same as those described in Chap. 3 for the particle–particle contact. They are rephrased here for convenience.

The first condition states that the relative acceleration of the rigid bodies at the contact point, along the contact normal, should be greater than or equal to zero, assuming that a negative value indicates that the bodies are accelerating towards each other. In this case, if the computed contact force is such that the relative acceleration at the contact point along the contact normal is zero, then the bodies remain in contact. However, if their relative acceleration is greater than zero, then contact is about to break.

The second condition implies that the contact-force component along the contact normal should be greater than or equal to zero, indicating that the rigid bodies are being pushed away from each other. The contact force is not allowed to have a negative value, that is, is not allowed to keep the bodies connected to each other, preventing their separation.

The third and last condition states that the contact force should be set to zero if the contact between the rigid bodies is about to break. In other words, if the relative acceleration at the contact point, along the contact normal, is greater than zero, then contact is about to break and the contact force should be set to zero.

Let's translate these three conditions into equations that can be used to compute the contact force. Figure 4.40 illustrates a typical situation in which rigid bodies B_1 and B_2 are shown at the moment before contact, in contact, and interpenetrating if a contact force is not applied.

Let $\vec{p}_1(t)$ and $\vec{p}_2(t)$ be the points on bodies B_1 and B_2, respectively, that are about to be in contact. Consider the vector $\vec{q}(t)$ defined as

$$\vec{q}(t) = \begin{pmatrix} q_n(t) \\ q_t(t) \\ q_k(t) \end{pmatrix} = \begin{pmatrix} (\vec{p}_1(t) - \vec{p}_2(t)) \cdot \vec{n}(t) \\ (\vec{p}_1(t) - \vec{p}_2(t)) \cdot \vec{t}(t) \\ (\vec{p}_1(t) - \vec{p}_2(t)) \cdot \vec{k}(t) \end{pmatrix}, \tag{4.89}$$

---

[16]Whenever a collision becomes a contact, the collision normal will be referred to as the contact normal.

Fig. 4.40 (a) Rigid bodies B_1 and B_2 are about to touch each other at points $\vec{p}_1$ and $\vec{p}_2$; (b) Contact is established whenever $\vec{p}_1 = \vec{p}_2$; (c) Interpenetration occurs if $(\vec{p}_1 - \vec{p}_2) \cdot \vec{n} < 0$, where $\vec{n}$ is the contact normal

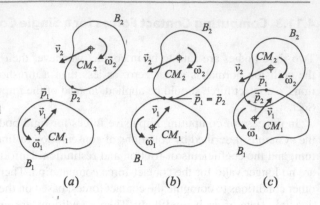

where $\vec{n}(t)$ is the contact normal, pointing from body B_2 to body B_1, and $\vec{t}(t)$ and $\vec{k}(t)$ are vectors defining the tangent plane at the contact. Clearly, $q_n(t)$ defines a distance measure between points $\vec{p}_1(t)$ and $\vec{p}_2(t)$, along the contact normal, as a function of time. We have $q_n(t) > 0$ if the bodies are separated, $q_n(t) = 0$ if the bodies are in contact, and $q_n(t) < 0$ if the bodies are interpenetrating (see Fig. 4.40). Let t_c be the instant at which contact is established, that is

$$\vec{q}(t_c) = \vec{0}.$$

The first condition states that the relative acceleration at the contact point, along the contact normal, should be greater than or equal to zero. This is equivalent to assuring

$$\left. \frac{d^2 q_n(t)}{dt^2} \right|_{t=t_c} \geq 0. \tag{4.90}$$

If we let $\vec{a}(t) = (a_n(t), a_t(t), a_k(t))$ be the relative acceleration at the contact point, we can rewrite Eq. (4.90) as

$$a_n(t_c) \geq 0. \tag{4.91}$$

The components $a_t(t)$ and $a_k(t)$ define the relative acceleration at the contact point on the tangent plane of the contact. They are used only if static or dynamic friction are considered at the contact point, as will be explained later in this section.

The second condition states that the contact-force component along the contact normal should be nonnegative, that is

$$F_n \geq 0, \tag{4.92}$$

where $\vec{F} = (F_n, F_t, F_k)$ is the contact force to be determined. If friction is taken into account, the tangent components F_t and F_k of the contact force are computed according to the Coulomb friction model. To elaborate, if the relative velocity of the points $\vec{p}_1$ and $\vec{p}_2$ along $\vec{t}$ is zero, or less than a threshold value, then there is no sliding at the contact point. In this case, the component F_t will assume values in the range

$$-(\mu_s)_t F_n \leq F_t \leq (\mu_s)_t F_n,$$

depending on the relative acceleration component $a_t(t)$ being positive or negative. In other words, F_t will do its best to prevent the bodies from sliding at the contact point by always opposing the relative acceleration $a_t(t)$.[17] On the other hand, if the relative velocity along $\vec{t}$ is greater than the threshold value, then the bodies are sliding at the contact point and

$$F_t = +(\mu_d)_t F_n \quad \text{or} \quad F_t = -(\mu_d)_t F_n,$$

depending on the relative acceleration $a_t(t)$ being negative or positive. Here, $(\mu_d)_t$ is the dynamic coefficient of friction along direction $\vec{t}$. A similar analysis holds for $\vec{k}$.

The third and last condition states that the contact force is zero if the contact is breaking away, that is, if the relative acceleration along the contact normal is positive. Equivalently, we have

$$F_n a_n(t_c) = 0, \tag{4.93}$$

meaning that, if F_n is greater than zero, then the bodies are in contact and the relative acceleration is zero. Otherwise, if a_n is greater than zero, then the contact is about to break and the contact force should be zero. Putting it all together, we have that the computation of the contact force involves solving the following system of equations:

$$a_n(t_c) \geq 0$$
$$F_n \geq 0 \tag{4.94}$$
$$F_n a_n(t_c) = 0.$$

Here, we adopt the convention that a positive contact force $+\vec{F}$ is applied to the rigid body B_1 (i.e., the body with index 1) and a negative contact force $-\vec{F}$ is applied to the rigid body B_2 (i.e., the body with index 2).

According to Eq. (4.90), the relative acceleration $a_n(t)$, along the contact normal, can be obtained by differentiating Eq. (4.89) twice with respect to time. The first time derivative of Eq. (4.89) gives

$$\frac{dq_n(t)}{dt} = \left(\frac{d\vec{p}_1(t)}{dt} - \frac{d\vec{p}_2(t)}{dt}\right) \cdot \vec{n}(t)$$
$$+ (\vec{p}_1 - \vec{p}_2) \cdot \frac{d\vec{n}(t)}{dt}, \tag{4.95}$$

---

[17]Notice that F_t is zero if $a_t(t)$ is zero.

or equivalently

$$v_n(t) = \left(\vec{v}_{p_1}(t) - \vec{v}_{p_2}(t)\right) \cdot \vec{n}(t)$$
$$+ (\vec{p}_1 - \vec{p}_2) \cdot \frac{d\vec{n}(t)}{dt}, \tag{4.96}$$

where $\vec{v}_{p_1}(t)$ and $\vec{v}_{p_2}(t)$ are the velocity vectors of points $\vec{p}_1(t)$ and $\vec{p}_2(t)$. This gives us an expression for the relative velocity $v_n(t) = dq(t)/dt$ of points $\vec{p}_1(t)$ and $\vec{p}_2(t)$ along the contact normal, as a function of their velocities and collision normal. The time derivative of the collision normal indicates its rate of change in direction as a function of time.

Differentiating Eq. (4.95) once more with respect to time, we obtain

$$\frac{d^2 q(t)}{dt^2} = \left(\frac{d^2 \vec{p}_1(t)}{dt^2} - \frac{d^2 \vec{p}_2(t)}{dt^2}\right) \cdot \vec{n}(t)$$
$$+ 2\left(\frac{d\vec{p}_1(t)}{dt} - \frac{d\vec{p}_2(t)}{dt}\right) \cdot \frac{d\vec{n}(t)}{dt}$$
$$+ (\vec{p}_1 - \vec{p}_2) \cdot \frac{d^2\vec{n}(t)}{dt^2}, \tag{4.97}$$

or equivalently

$$a_n(t) = \left(\vec{a}_{p_1}(t) - \vec{a}_{p_2}(t)\right) \cdot \vec{n}(t) + 2\left(\vec{v}_{p_1}(t) - \vec{v}_{p_2}(t)\right) \cdot \frac{d\vec{n}(t)}{dt}$$
$$+ (\vec{p}_1 - \vec{p}_2) \cdot \frac{d^2\vec{n}(t)}{dt^2}, \tag{4.98}$$

where $\vec{a}_{p_1}(t)$ and $\vec{a}_{p_2}(t)$ are the acceleration vectors of points $\vec{p}_1(t)$ and $\vec{p}_2(t)$. This gives us an expression for the relative acceleration $a_n(t) = d^2q(t)/dt^2$ of points $\vec{p}_1(t)$ and $\vec{p}_2(t)$ along the contact normal, as a function of their accelerations, velocities, contact normal and rate of change in direction of the contact normal.

At the instant of contact $t = t_c$, points $\vec{p}_1(t)$ and $\vec{p}_2(t)$ are coincident, that is

$$\vec{p}_1(t_c) = \vec{p}_2(t_c). \tag{4.99}$$

Substituting Eq. (4.99) into (4.98), we obtain an expression for the relative acceleration along the contact normal at the instant of contact:

$$a_n(t_c) = \left(\vec{a}_{p_1}(t_c) - \vec{a}_{p_2}(t_c)\right) \cdot \vec{n}(t_c)$$
$$+ 2\left(\vec{v}_{p_1}(t_c) - \vec{v}_{p_2}(t_c)\right) \cdot \frac{d\vec{n}(t_c)}{dt}. \tag{4.100}$$

According to Eq. (4.100), the relative acceleration at the instant of contact has two terms. The first depends on the accelerations of the contact points, which in turn are related to the contact force using Newton's law. The second depends on the velocities of the contact points and the rate of change in direction of the collision normal.

For now, let's assume the contact is frictionless, that is

$$\vec{F} = F_n \vec{n}.$$

Later in this section, we shall relax this assumption and show how the system of equations used in the frictionless case can be extended to cope with friction.

If we isolate the terms that depend on the contact force from the terms that do not, we can rewrite Eq. (4.100) as

$$a_n(t_c) = (a_{11})_n F_n + b_1. \qquad (4.101)$$

Substituting Eq. (4.101) into (4.94), we obtain

$$\left((a_{11})_n F_n + b_1 \right) \geq 0$$
$$F_n \geq 0 \qquad (4.102)$$
$$F_n \left((a_{11})_n F_n + b_1 \right) = 0.$$

Thus, the computation of the contact force involves solving the system of equations defined in (4.102), which is quadratic on F_n. One way of doing so is to use quadratic-programming techniques. However, such techniques are difficult to implement, often requiring the use of sophisticated numerical software packages.

Fortunately, the system of equations defined in (4.102) is also formally similar to a numerical programming technique called *linear complementarity*. The implementation using linear-complementarity techniques is significantly easier than the implementation of a quadratic program, and is discussed in detail in Appendix I (Chap. 14). There, we start presenting solution methods for the frictionless case, and show how to modify them to cope with static and dynamic friction at the contacts. These modifications on the solution method require that Eq. (4.102) be expanded to also consider the relation between the relative-acceleration and contact-force components on the tangent plane of the contact.

In the general case where friction is taken into account, the system of equations becomes

$$\begin{pmatrix} a_n(t_c) \\ a_t(t_c) \\ a_k(t_c) \end{pmatrix} = \begin{pmatrix} (a_{11})_n & (a_{12})_t & (a_{13})_k \\ (a_{21})_n & (a_{22})_t & (a_{23})_k \\ (a_{31})_n & (a_{32})_t & (a_{33})_k \end{pmatrix} \begin{pmatrix} F_n \\ F_t \\ F_k \end{pmatrix} + \begin{pmatrix} (b_1)_n \\ (b_1)_t \\ (b_1)_k \end{pmatrix}$$
$$= \mathbf{A}\vec{F} + \vec{b},$$

where

$$a_t(t_c) = \left(\vec{a}_{p_1}(t_c) - \vec{a}_{p_2}(t_c) \right) \cdot \vec{t}(t_c)$$
$$+ 2\left(\vec{v}_{p_1}(t_c) - \vec{v}_{p_2}(t_c) \right) \cdot \frac{d\vec{t}(t_c)}{dt} \qquad (4.103)$$

$$a_k(t_c) = \left(\vec{a}_{p_1}(t_c) - \vec{a}_{p_2}(t_c)\right) \cdot \vec{k}(t_c)$$

$$+ 2\left(\vec{v}_{p_1}(t_c) - \vec{v}_{p_2}(t_c)\right) \cdot \frac{d\vec{k}(t_c)}{dt}. \tag{4.104}$$

The solution method presented in Appendix I (Chap. 14) assumes both matrix **A** and vector $\vec{b}$ are known constants computed from the geometric displacement and dynamic state of the bodies at the instant of contact. Therefore, we need to determine the coefficients of matrix **A** and vector $\vec{b}$, before we can apply the linear-complementarity techniques of Appendix I (Chap. 14).

The first row of matrix **A** and vector $\vec{b}$ is obtained by expressing the normal relative acceleration $a_n(t_c)$ at the instant of contact as a function of the contact-force components F_n, F_t and F_k. This can be done using Eqs. (4.100), (4.103) and (4.104). Let's start by examining the second term of these equations, namely

$$2\left(\vec{v}_{p_1}(t_c) - \vec{v}_{p_2}(t_c)\right) \cdot \frac{d\vec{n}(t_c)}{dt}$$

$$2\left(\vec{v}_{p_1}(t_c) - \vec{v}_{p_2}(t_c)\right) \cdot \frac{d\vec{t}(t_c)}{dt}$$

$$2\left(\vec{v}_{p_1}(t_c) - \vec{v}_{p_2}(t_c)\right) \cdot \frac{d\vec{k}(t_c)}{dt}.$$

The velocities of points $\vec{p}_1$ and $\vec{p}_2$ are known quantities independent of the contact force. We still need to compute the rate of change in direction of the contact normal as a function of time. Section 10.3.2 of Appendix E (Chap. 10) presents a detailed description of how the time derivative of the contact normal for the rigid body–rigid body case can be computed. There are two possible ways of computing the time derivative of the normal vector, depending on the type of contact being a vertex–face or edge–edge contact. In either case, the result of the time derivative of the contact normal is independent of the contact force. So, the contribution of the second term of Eqs. (4.100), (4.103) and (4.104) to matrix **A** is none, and to vector $\vec{b}$ is

$$(b_1)_n = 2\left(\vec{v}_1 + \vec{\omega}_1 \times (\vec{p}_1 - \vec{r}_1) - \vec{v}_2 - \vec{\omega}_2 \times (\vec{p}_2 - \vec{r}_2)\right) \cdot \frac{d\vec{n}}{dt}$$

$$(b_1)_t = 2\left(\vec{v}_1 + \vec{\omega}_1 \times (\vec{p}_1 - \vec{r}_1) - \vec{v}_2 - \vec{\omega}_2 \times (\vec{p}_2 - \vec{r}_2)\right) \cdot \frac{d\vec{t}}{dt} \tag{4.105}$$

$$(b_1)_k = 2\left(\vec{v}_1 + \vec{\omega}_1 \times (\vec{p}_1 - \vec{r}_1) - \vec{v}_2 - \vec{\omega}_2 \times (\vec{p}_2 - \vec{r}_2)\right) \cdot \frac{d\vec{k}}{dt},$$

where $d\vec{t}/dt$ and $d\vec{k}/dt$ are the time derivatives of the tangent-plane directions computed following the techniques presented in Sect. 10.4 of Appendix E (Chap. 10).

Now, let's focus on the first term of Eqs. (4.100), (4.103) and (4.104), namely the terms

$$\left(\vec{a}_{p_1}(t_c) - \vec{a}_{p_2}(t_c)\right) \cdot \vec{n}(t_c)$$
$$\left(\vec{a}_{p_1}(t_c) - \vec{a}_{p_2}(t_c)\right) \cdot \vec{t}(t_c) \tag{4.106}$$
$$\left(\vec{a}_{p_1}(t_c) - \vec{a}_{p_2}(t_c)\right) \cdot \vec{k}(t_c).$$

The acceleration $\vec{a}_{p_1}$ of point $\vec{p}_1$ is obtained directly from Eq. (4.8) as

$$\vec{a}_{p_1} = \vec{\alpha}_1 \times (\vec{p}_1 - \vec{r}_1) + \vec{\omega}_1 \times \left(\vec{\omega}_1 \times (\vec{p}_1 - \vec{r}_1)\right) + \vec{a}_1,$$

where $\vec{\alpha}_1$, $\vec{\omega}_1$ and $\vec{a}_1$ are the angular acceleration, angular velocity and linear acceleration of body B_1 (see Fig. 4.40). Using Eq. (4.11), the linear acceleration $\vec{a}_1$ can be obtained from the net force $(\vec{F}_1)_{net}$ acting at contact point $\vec{p}_1$ as

$$\vec{a}_1 = \frac{(\vec{F}_1)_{net}}{m_1} = \left(\frac{\vec{F} + (\vec{F}_1)_{ext}}{m_1}\right),$$

where $(\vec{F}_1)_{ext}$ is the net external force (such as gravity, spring forces, spatially dependent forces, etc.) acting on body B_1 at $t = t_c$, and $\vec{F}$ is the contact force to be determined. Also, using Eq. (4.18), the angular acceleration $\vec{\alpha}_1$ can be computed from the net torque $(\vec{\tau}_1)_{net}$ acting at contact point $\vec{p}_1$ as

$$\vec{\alpha}_1 = \mathbf{I_1}^{-1}\left((\vec{\tau}_1)_{net} + \vec{H}_1 \times \vec{\omega}_1\right), \tag{4.107}$$

where $\mathbf{I_1}$ and $\vec{H}_1$ are the inertia tensor and angular momentum of body B_1, respectively. The net torque acting on body B_1 is computed by summing the torque induced by all external forces, that is

$$(\vec{\tau}_1)_{net} = (\vec{\tau}_1)_{ext} + \overbrace{(\vec{p}_1 - \vec{r}_1) \times \vec{F}}^{\text{torque resulting from contact force}}, \tag{4.108}$$

where

$$(\vec{\tau}_1)_{ext} = \sum_i (\vec{p}_i - \vec{r}_1) \times (\vec{F}_i)_{ext}$$

with $\vec{p}_i$ being the point on body B_1 at which the external force $(\vec{F}_i)_{ext}$ is being applied. Substituting Eq. (4.108) into (4.107), we obtain

$$\vec{\alpha}_1 = \mathbf{I_1}^{-1}(\vec{p}_1 - \vec{r}_1) \times \vec{F} + \mathbf{I_1}^{-1}\left((\vec{\tau}_1)_{ext} + \vec{H}_1 \times \vec{\omega}_1\right). \tag{4.109}$$

The acceleration $\vec{a}_{p_1}$ of point $\vec{p}_1$ is then

$$\begin{aligned}
\vec{a}_{p_1} = {} & \left(\mathbf{I_1}^{-1}(\vec{p}_1 - \vec{r}_1) \times \vec{F}\right) \times (\vec{p}_1 - \vec{r}_1) \\
& + \left(\mathbf{I_1}^{-1}\left((\vec{\tau}_1)_{ext} + \vec{H}_1 \times \vec{\omega}_1\right)\right) \times (\vec{p}_1 - \vec{r}_1) \\
& + \vec{\omega}_1 \times \left(\vec{\omega}_1 \times (\vec{p}_1 - \vec{r}_1)\right) + \left(\frac{\vec{F} + (\vec{F}_1)_{ext}}{m_1}\right).
\end{aligned} \tag{4.110}$$

Using the general cross-product relations

$$\vec{a} \times \vec{b} = -\vec{b} \times \vec{a}$$
$$\vec{a} \times \vec{b} = \tilde{a}\vec{b}$$

and letting

$$\vec{x}_1 = \vec{p}_1 - \vec{r}_1,$$

we can further simplify the first term of Eq. (4.110) as follows:

$$
\begin{aligned}
\left(\mathbf{I_1}^{-1}(\vec{p}_1 - \vec{r}_1) \times \vec{F}\right) \times (\vec{p}_1 - \vec{r}_1) \\
= \left(\mathbf{I_1}^{-1}\vec{x}_1 \times \vec{F}\right) \times \vec{x}_1 \\
= -\vec{x}_1 \times \left(\mathbf{I_1}^{-1}\vec{x}_1 \times \vec{F}\right) \\
= -\tilde{x}_1 \left(\mathbf{I_1}^{-1}\vec{x}_1 \times \vec{F}\right) \\
= -\left(\tilde{x}_1\mathbf{I_1}^{-1}\right)\vec{x}_1 \times \vec{F} \\
= -\left(\tilde{x}_1\mathbf{I_1}^{-1}\right)\tilde{x}_1\vec{F}.
\end{aligned}
\tag{4.111}
$$

Substituting Eq. (4.111) into (4.110), we have

$$
\begin{aligned}
\vec{a}_{p_1} = \left(\frac{1}{m_1}\mathbf{I} - \tilde{x}_1\mathbf{I_1}^{-1}\tilde{x}_1\right)\vec{F} \\
+ \frac{1}{m_1}(\vec{F}_1)_{ext} + \left(\mathbf{I_1}^{-1}\left((\vec{\tau}_1)_{ext} + \vec{H}_1 \times \vec{\omega}_1\right)\right) \times \vec{x}_1 \\
+ \vec{\omega}_1 \times (\vec{\omega}_1 \times \vec{x}_1),
\end{aligned}
\tag{4.112}
$$

which can be written as

$$\vec{a}_{p_1} = \mathbf{A_1}\vec{F} + \vec{b}_1 \tag{4.113}$$

with

$$\mathbf{A_1} = \left(\frac{1}{m_1}\mathbf{I} - \tilde{x}_1\mathbf{I_1}^{-1}\tilde{x}_1\right)$$
$$\vec{b}_1 = \frac{1}{m_1}(\vec{F}_1)_{ext} + \left(\mathbf{I_1}^{-1}\left((\vec{\tau}_1)_{ext} + \vec{H}_1 \times \vec{\omega}_1\right)\right) \times \vec{x}_1 + \vec{\omega}_1 \times (\vec{\omega}_1 \times \vec{x}_1).$$

Analogously, the acceleration $\vec{a}_2$ of point $\vec{p}_2$ is given by

$$
\begin{aligned}
\vec{a}_{p_2} = \left(\mathbf{I_2}^{-1}(\vec{p}_2 - \vec{r}_2) \times (-\vec{F})\right) \times (\vec{p}_2 - \vec{r}_2) \\
+ \left(\mathbf{I_2}^{-1}\left((\vec{\tau}_2)_{ext} + \vec{H}_2 \times \vec{\omega}_2\right)\right) \times (\vec{p}_2 - \vec{r}_2) \\
+ \vec{\omega}_2 \times (\vec{\omega}_2 \times (\vec{p}_2 - \vec{r}_2)) + \left(\frac{(-\vec{F}) + (\vec{F}_2)_{ext}}{m_2}\right),
\end{aligned}
\tag{4.114}
$$

which can be further simplified to

$$\vec{a}_{p2} = -\mathbf{A_2}\vec{F} + \vec{b}_2 \tag{4.115}$$

with

$$\mathbf{A_2} = \left(\frac{1}{m_2}\mathbf{I} - \tilde{x}_2 \mathbf{I_2}^{-1} \tilde{x}_2 \right)$$

$$\vec{b}_2 = \frac{1}{m_2}(\vec{F}_2)_{ext} + \left(\mathbf{I_2}^{-1}\left((\vec{\tau}_2)_{ext} + \vec{H}_2 \times \vec{\omega}_2 \right) \right) \times \tilde{x}_2$$
$$+ \vec{\omega}_2 \times (\vec{\omega}_2 \times \tilde{x}_2).$$

The relative acceleration at the contact point is therefore

$$(\vec{a}_{p1} - \vec{a}_{p2}) = (\mathbf{A_1} + \mathbf{A_2})\vec{F} + (\vec{b}_1 - \vec{b}_2). \tag{4.116}$$

The final contribution to the elements of vector $\vec{b}$ is obtained by summing the individual contributions of Eqs. (4.105) and (4.116). The matrix $\mathbf{A}$ is obtained by adding up $\mathbf{A_1}$ and $\mathbf{A_2}$, as indicated in Eq. (4.116).

Applying the linear-complementarity techniques of Appendix I (Chap. 14), we can determine the components of the contact-force vector $\vec{F}$. Having $\vec{F}$, we update the dynamic state of each rigid body by applying $+\vec{F}$ on body B_1 and $-\vec{F}$ on body B_2.

4.11.4 Computing Contact Forces for Multiple Contacts

The principle behind the computation of multiple rigid body–rigid body contact forces is the same as that behind the computation of multiple rigid body–rigid body collision impulses. Again, the simulation engine needs to group the rigid bodies into clusters that share at least one contact. The contacts within each cluster can then be simultaneously resolved independent of all other clusters (see Fig. 4.41).

Whenever a rigid body is involved in multiple contacts, it is possible to have it assigned to different indexes for each contact. For the particular situation of cluster G_2 in Fig. 4.41, body B_2 has index 2 with respect to its contact with body B_1, and index 1 with respect to its contact with body B_3. This in turn affects the choice of sign when combining the multiple contact forces in the system equations. Moreover, the contact normal and tangent plane are different for each contact. So, we also need to carry out a change of base between the contact forces before combining them.

In the single rigid body–rigid body contact, the contact-force computation taking friction into account was done using linear-complementarity techniques to solve a system of equations of the form

Fig. 4.41 A multiple rigid body–rigid body contact-force computation. In the situation shown, the rigid bodies are grouped into three clusters that can be resolved in parallel

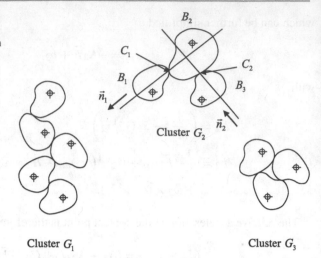

$$a_n(t_c) \geq 0$$

$$F_n \geq 0$$

$$\vec{F}^t(\mathbf{A}\vec{F} + \vec{b}) = 0,$$

where

$$\mathbf{A} = \begin{pmatrix} (a_{11})_n & (a_{12})_t & (a_{13})_k \\ (a_{21})_n & (a_{22})_t & (a_{23})_k \\ (a_{31})_n & (a_{31})_t & (a_{33})_k \end{pmatrix}$$

$$\vec{F} = (F_n, F_t, F_k)^t$$

$$\vec{b} = \big((b_1)_n, (b_1)_t, (b_1)_k\big)^t.$$

This solution method can be extended to the case of multiple-contact-force computations. The main difference between multiple- and single-contact-force computation involving a given body is that the contact force at contact C_i can affect the computation of the contact force at contact C_j. So, instead of solving one contact at a time, we need to simultaneously solve all contacts having a body in common. This in turn has the same effect as merging the several individual systems of equations for each contact into one larger system, and then applying the linear-complementarity techniques to the merged system.

For example, suppose we have a cluster with m simultaneous contacts. Each contact C_i is defined by its contact-normal $(\vec{n})_i$ and tangent-plane vectors $(\vec{t})_i$ and $(\vec{k})_i$. The contact force at contact C_i is then expressed as

$$\vec{F}_i = \big((F_i)_{n_i}, (F_i)_{t_i}, (F_i)_{k_i}\big)^t.$$

The contact-force vector for the multiple-collision system is obtained by concatenating the contact-force vectors for each of the m contacts, that is

$$\vec{F} = \left((F_1)_{n_1}, (F_1)_{t_1}, (F_1)_{k_1}, \ldots, (F_m)_{n_m}, (F_m)_{t_m}, (F_m)_{k_m}\right)^t.$$

The vector $\vec{b}$ becomes

$$\vec{b} = \left((b_1)_n, (b_1)_t, (b_1)_k, \ldots, (b_m)_n, (b_m)_t, (b_m)_k\right)^t$$

and the matrix $\mathbf{A}$ is enlarged to accommodate all contact forces. Its partitioned representation is given by

$$\mathbf{A} = \begin{pmatrix} \mathbf{A}_{11} & \mathbf{A}_{12} & \ldots & \mathbf{A}_{1m} \\ \mathbf{A}_{21} & \mathbf{A}_{22} & \ldots & \mathbf{A}_{2m} \\ & \ldots & & \ldots \\ \mathbf{A}_{m1} & \mathbf{A}_{m2} & \ldots & \mathbf{A}_{mm} \end{pmatrix},$$

where each sub-matrix is given by

$$\mathbf{A}_{ij} = \begin{pmatrix} (a_{ij})_{n_i} & (a_{i(j+1)})_{t_i} & (a_{i(j+2)})_{k_i} \\ (a_{(i+1)j})_{n_i} & (a_{(i+1)(j+1)})_{t_i} & (a_{(i+1)(j+2)})_{k_i} \\ (a_{(i+2)j})_{n_i} & (a_{(i+2)(j+1)})_{t_i} & (a_{(i+2)(j+2)})_{k_i} \end{pmatrix}.$$

If contacts C_i and C_j have no bodies in common, the sub-matrix $\mathbf{A}_{ij}$ is set to $\mathbf{0}$, indicating that their contact forces do not affect each other. However, if contacts C_i and C_j do have a body in common, then the coefficients a_{ij} are the contribution of the contact force at contact C_j to the relative acceleration at contact C_i. More specifically, the coefficient $(a_{ij})_{n_i}$ is the contribution of the contact-force component $(F_j)_{n_j}$ to the relative acceleration at the contact C_i. Analogously, the coefficients $(a_{ij})_{t_i}$ and $(a_{ij})_{k_i}$ are, respectively, the contribution of the contact-force components $(F_j)_{t_j}$ and $(F_j)_{k_j}$ to the relative acceleration at the contact C_i.

Also, notice that the contact force $\vec{F}_j$ is given with respect to the contact frame of C_j, whereas the relative acceleration $\vec{a}_i$ is given with respect to the contact frame of C_i. Therefore, a change of basis is required when computing the coefficients of matrix $\mathbf{A}_{ij}$ and vector $\vec{b}_i$.

Suppose contact C_i involves bodies B_1 and B_2, and contact C_j involves bodies B_2 and B_3, that is, they have body B_2 in common. We want to determine the contribution of the contact force $\vec{F}_j$ of contact C_j to the relative acceleration of contact C_i. This in turn involves determining the coefficients of the sub-matrix $\mathbf{A}_{ij}$ and the components $(b_i)_{n_i}$, $(b_i)_{t_i}$ and $(b_i)_{k_i}$ of vector $\vec{b}$. The relative acceleration at contact C_i between bodies B_1 and B_2 is given by

$$(a_i)_{n_i} = (\vec{a}_1 - \vec{a}_2) \cdot \vec{n}_i + 2(\vec{v}_1 - \vec{v}_2) \cdot \frac{d\vec{n}_i}{dt}$$

$$(a_i)_{t_i} = (\vec{a}_1 - \vec{a}_2) \cdot \vec{t}_i + 2(\vec{v}_1 - \vec{v}_2) \cdot \frac{d\vec{t}_i}{dt} \qquad (4.117)$$

$$(a_i)_{k_i} = (\vec{a}_1 - \vec{a}_2) \cdot \vec{k}_i + 2(\vec{v}_1 - \vec{v}_2) \cdot \frac{d\vec{k}_i}{dt}.$$

As explained in the single-contact case, only the first term of Eqs. (4.117) depends on the forces exerted at contact C_i. The second term depends on the linear and angular velocities, and is added to $(b_i)_{n_i}$, $(b_i)_{t_i}$ and $(b_i)_{k_i}$, as appropriate. Thus, the contribution of the contact force $\vec{F}_j$ of contact C_j does not affect the components of vector $\vec{b}$. In other words, the expressions used to compute vector $\vec{b}$ for the single-contact case are still valid for the multiple-contact case, that is, the components $(b_i)_{n_i}$, $(b_i)_{t_i}$ and $(b_i)_{k_i}$ of vector $\vec{b}$ are given by summing Eqs. (4.105) and (4.116).

Using Eq. (4.61), the contribution of the contact force $\vec{F}_j$ of contact C_j to the acceleration $\vec{a}_1$ of body B_1 involved in collision C_i is

$$\left(\mathbf{I_1}^{-1}(\vec{p}_1 - \vec{r}_1) \times \vec{F}_j\right) \times (\vec{p}_1 - \vec{r}_1) + \frac{\vec{F}}{m_1}.$$

Conversely, the contribution of $\vec{F}_j$ to $\vec{a}_2$ is

$$\left(\mathbf{I_2}^{-1}(\vec{p}_2 - \vec{r}_2) \times (-\vec{F}_j)\right) \times (\vec{p}_2 - \vec{r}_2) - \frac{\vec{F}}{m_2}.$$

The net contribution of $\vec{F}_j$ to the relative acceleration $(\vec{a}_1 - \vec{a}_2)$ at contact C_i is then

$$g_j^i = \left(\mathbf{I_1}^{-1}(\vec{p}_1 - \vec{r}_1) \times \vec{F}_j\right) \times (\vec{p}_1 - \vec{r}_1)$$
$$+ \left(\mathbf{I_2}^{-1}(\vec{p}_2 - \vec{r}_2) \times \vec{F}_j\right) \times (\vec{p}_2 - \vec{r}_2)$$
$$+ \left(\frac{1}{m_1} + \frac{1}{m_2}\right)\vec{F}.$$

Substituting this into the first terms of Eqs. (4.117), we obtain the contributions of $\vec{F}_j$ to each relative-acceleration component at contact C_i as

$$\text{contribution to } (a_i)_{n_i} = g_j^i \cdot \vec{n}_i$$

$$\text{contribution to } (a_i)_{t_i} = g_j^i \cdot \vec{t}_i$$

$$\text{contribution to } (a_i)_{k_i} = g_j^i \cdot \vec{k}_i.$$

Using the fact that the contact force $\vec{F}_j$ is expressed with respect to the contact frame C_j as

$$\vec{F}_j = (F_j)_{n_j} \vec{n}_j + (F_j)_{t_j} \vec{t}_j + (F_j)_{k_j} \vec{k}_j,$$

it can be written with respect to the contact frame C_i as

$$\vec{F}_{j \mapsto i} = \mathbf{M}_{j \mapsto i} \vec{F}_j$$

with

$$\mathbf{M}_{j \mapsto i} = \begin{pmatrix} \vec{n}_j \cdot \vec{n}_i & \vec{t}_j \cdot \vec{n}_i & \vec{k}_j \cdot \vec{n}_i \\ \vec{n}_j \cdot \vec{t}_i & \vec{t}_j \cdot \vec{t}_i & \vec{k}_j \cdot \vec{t}_i \\ \vec{n}_j \cdot \vec{k}_i & \vec{t}_j \cdot \vec{k}_i & \vec{k}_j \cdot \vec{k}_i \end{pmatrix}.$$

Therefore, the coefficients of the sub-matrix $\mathbf{A}_{ij}$ can be immediately obtained after carrying out the matrix multiplication

$$\mathbf{A}_{ij} = (\mathbf{A}_1 + \mathbf{A}_2)\mathbf{M}_{j \mapsto i}. \tag{4.118}$$

Notice that, if $i = j$, then the matrix $\mathbf{M}_{j \mapsto i}$ becomes the identity matrix, and the matrix $\mathbf{A}_{ij}$ in (4.118) is the same as that obtained in Eq. (4.116) for the single-contact case. Also, if friction is not taken into account, the sub-matrix $\mathbf{A}_{ij}$ is reduced to

$$\mathbf{A}_{ij} = (a_{ij})_{n_i},$$

since the contact-force components $(F_j)_{t_j}$ and $(F_j)_{k_j}$ are zero in the frictionless case. This result is also compatible with that obtained for the frictionless single-contact-force computation explained in Sect. 4.11.3.

Having computed the contact force $\vec{F}_i$ for each contact C_i, $1 \leq i \leq m$, we update the dynamic state of each rigid body involved in contact C_i by applying $+\vec{F}_i$ to body B_1 (i.e., the body with index 1) and $-\vec{F}_i$ to body B_2 (i.e., the body with index 2).

When a rigid body is involved in multiple contacts, it is possible to have it assigned to different indexes for each contact. For the particular situation of cluster G_2 in Fig. 4.41, body B_2 has index 2 with respect to its contact C_1 with body B_1, and index 1 with respect to its contact C_2 with body B_3. So, the net contact force actually applied to body B_2 after all contact forces have been computed is

$$(\vec{F}_2 - \vec{F}_1),$$

with $\vec{F}_1$ and $\vec{F}_2$ being the contact forces associated with contacts C_1 and C_2, respectively.

Fig. 4.42 Particle O_1 is colliding with rigid body B_1 at O_2. The velocity $\vec{v}_{p_2}$ and acceleration $\vec{a}_{p_2}$ of point $\vec{p}_2$ are computed using the rigid body's equations of motion

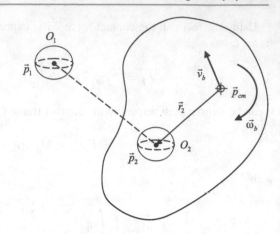

4.12   Particle–Rigid Body Contact Revisited

As mentioned in Sect. 3.6 of Chap. 3, the contact between a particle and a rigid body is modeled as a particle–particle contact between the particle itself and another particle on the rigid body's surface. Modeling the contact in this way has the advantage of letting us use techniques similar to those applied to the particle–particle case. The main differences are:

1. The velocity and acceleration of the particle associated with the rigid body are computed using the rigid-body dynamic equations derived in Sect. 4.2, as opposed to using the particle dynamic equations of Sect. 3.2.
2. The normal and tangent-plane directions are determined from the rigid-body geometry. If the particle on the rigid body lies on a face, edge or vertex, then the contact normal is assigned to the face, edge or vertex normal, respectively. The actual computation of these normals was already covered in Sect. 4.4.

Consider, for example, the particle–rigid body contact illustrated in Fig. 4.42. Assume particle O_1 is in contact with particle O_2 of rigid body B_2.

Let $\vec{p}_1(t)$ and $\vec{p}_2(t)$ be the points representing the particles in contact. Analogously to both particle–particle and rigid body–rigid body single contact cases, we consider the vector $\vec{q}(t)$ defined as

$$\vec{q}(t) = \begin{pmatrix} q_n(t) \\ q_t(t) \\ q_k(t) \end{pmatrix} = \begin{pmatrix} (\vec{p}_1(t) - \vec{p}_2(t)) \cdot \vec{n}(t) \\ (\vec{p}_1(t) - \vec{p}_2(t)) \cdot \vec{t}(t) \\ (\vec{p}_1(t) - \vec{p}_2(t)) \cdot \vec{k}(t) \end{pmatrix}, \qquad (4.119)$$

where $\vec{n}(t)$ is the contact normal, pointing from particle O_2 to particle O_1, and $\vec{t}(t)$ and $\vec{k}(t)$ are vectors defining the tangent plane at the contact. Clearly, $q_n(t)$ defines a distance measure between points $\vec{p}_1(t)$ and $\vec{p}_2(t)$, along the contact normal, as a function of time. We have $q_n(t) > 0$ if the particles are separated, $q_n(t) = 0$ if the particles are in contact, and $q_n(t) < 0$ if the particles are interpenetrating (see Fig. 4.43).

Fig. 4.43 (a) Particles O_1 and $O_2 \in B_2$ are about to touch each other at points $\vec{p}_1$ and $\vec{p}_2$; (b) Contact is established whenever $\vec{p}_1 = \vec{p}_2$. In this case, a positive contact force $\vec{F}$ is applied to particle O_1 and a negative contact force $-\vec{F}$ is applied to particle O_2; (c) Interpenetration occurs if $(\vec{p}_1 - \vec{p}_2) \cdot \vec{n} < 0$, where $\vec{n}$ is the contact normal

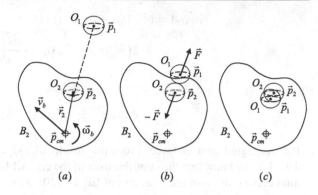

The relative normal acceleration at the contact point is therefore that obtained for the particle–particle single contact, given by

$$a_n(t) = \left(\vec{a}_{p_1}(t) - \vec{a}_{p_2}(t)\right) \cdot \vec{n}(t)$$
$$+ 2\left(\vec{v}_{p_1}(t) - \vec{v}_{p_2}(t)\right) \cdot \frac{d\vec{n}(t)}{dt}. \qquad (4.120)$$

The contact conditions derived in Sect. 3.5.3 still hold here:

$$a_n = \left((a_{11})_n F_n + (b_1)_n\right) \geq 0$$
$$F_n \geq 0$$
$$F_n\left((a_{11})_n F_n + (b_1)_n\right) = 0$$

and the contact force can be computed using the linear-complementarity techniques presented in Appendix I (Chap. 14). The relative acceleration can be written as a linear function of the contact force, that is

$$\dot{a} = \mathbf{A}\vec{F} + \vec{b} \qquad (4.121)$$

and we need to determine the coefficients of matrix $\mathbf{A}$ and vector $\vec{b}$ corresponding to the particle–rigid body contact case. Equation (4.121) can be expanded to

$$\begin{pmatrix} a_n(t_c) \\ a_t(t_c) \\ a_k(t_c) \end{pmatrix} = \begin{pmatrix} (a_{11})_n & (a_{12})_t & (a_{13})_k \\ (a_{21})_n & (a_{22})_t & (a_{23})_k \\ (a_{31})_n & (a_{32})_t & (a_{33})_k \end{pmatrix} \begin{pmatrix} F_n \\ F_t \\ F_k \end{pmatrix} + \begin{pmatrix} (b_1)_n \\ (b_1)_t \\ (b_1)_k \end{pmatrix}$$
$$= \mathbf{A}\vec{F} + \vec{b}, \qquad (4.122)$$

where

$$a_t(t_c) = \left(\vec{a}_{p_1}(t_c) - \vec{a}_{p_2}(t_c)\right) \cdot \vec{t}(t_c)$$
$$+ 2\left(\vec{v}_{p_1}(t_c) - \vec{v}_{p_2}(t_c)\right) \cdot \frac{d\vec{t}(t_c)}{dt} \qquad (4.123)$$

$$a_k(t_c) = \left(\vec{a}_{p_1}(t_c) - \vec{a}_{p_2}(t_c)\right) \cdot \vec{k}(t_c)$$

$$+ 2\left(\vec{v}_{p_1}(t_c) - \vec{v}_{p_2}(t_c)\right) \cdot \frac{d\vec{k}(t_c)}{dt} \tag{4.124}$$

and

$$\vec{F} = (F_n, F_t, F_k)^t$$

is the associated contact force. From the results already obtained in Sects. 3.5.3 and 4.11.3, we know that the contributions of the contact force to the relative acceleration come only from the first term of Eq. (4.120). More specifically, the acceleration of particle O_1 can be expressed as

$$\vec{a}_{p_1} = \frac{(\vec{F}_1)_{net}}{m_1} = \frac{\vec{F}}{m_1} + \frac{(\vec{F}_1)_{ext}}{m_1}, \tag{4.125}$$

where $(\vec{F}_1)_{ext}$ is the sum of all external forces acting on particle O_1. The acceleration of particle O_2 can be determined from the rigid-body motion as

$$\vec{a}_{p_2} = -\mathbf{A_2}\vec{F} + \vec{b}_2,$$

where matrix $\mathbf{A_2}$ and vector $\vec{b}_2$ are obtained from Eq. (4.115). The relative acceleration $(\vec{a}_{p_1} - \vec{a}_{p_2})$ is then

$$\vec{a}_{p_1} - \vec{a}_{p_2} = \frac{1}{m_1}\left(\vec{F} + (\vec{F}_1)_{ext} + \mathbf{A_2}\vec{F} - \vec{b}_2\right)$$

$$= \left(\frac{\mathbf{I}}{m_1} + \mathbf{A_2}\right)\vec{F} + \left(\frac{(\vec{F}_1)_{ext}}{m_1} - \vec{b}_2\right), \tag{4.126}$$

which is already in the desired matrix format of Eq. (4.122).

Now, let's examine the second term of Eqs. (4.120), (4.123) and (4.124), namely:

$$2(\vec{v}_{p_1} - \vec{v}_{p_2}) \cdot \frac{d\vec{n}}{dt}$$

$$2(\vec{v}_{p_1} - \vec{v}_{p_2}) \cdot \frac{d\vec{t}}{dt} \tag{4.127}$$

$$2(\vec{v}_{p_1} - \vec{v}_{p_2}) \cdot \frac{d\vec{k}}{dt}.$$

From the results of Sects. 3.5.3 and 4.11.3, we already know that these terms are independent of the contact force, meaning they only affect the coefficients of vector $\vec{b}$. The computation of the time derivatives of the contact frame, that is, the derivatives of the normal and tangent vectors $\vec{n}$, $\vec{t}$ and $\vec{k}$ is covered in Sects. 10.3.2

and 10.4 of Appendix E (Chap. 10). Therefore, in the following derivations we shall assume these to be known quantities.

The velocity of particle O_2 is computed from the rigid-body motion as

$$\vec{v}_{p2} = \vec{v}_2 + \vec{\omega}_2 \times (\vec{p}_2 - \vec{r}_2). \tag{4.128}$$

Substituting Eq. (4.128) into (4.127), we have that the contribution of the second term of Eqs. (4.120), (4.123) and (4.124) to the coefficients of vector $\vec{b}$ is:

$$(b_1)_n = 2\big(\vec{v}_1 - \vec{v}_2 - \vec{\omega}_2 \times (\vec{p}_2 - \vec{r}_2)\big) \cdot \frac{d\vec{n}}{dt}$$

$$(b_1)_t = 2\big(\vec{v}_1 - \vec{v}_2 - \vec{\omega}_2 \times (\vec{p}_2 - \vec{r}_2)\big) \cdot \frac{d\vec{t}}{dt} \tag{4.129}$$

$$(b_1)_k = 2\big(\vec{v}_1 - \vec{v}_2 - \vec{\omega}_2 \times (\vec{p}_2 - \vec{r}_2)\big) \cdot \frac{d\vec{k}}{dt}.$$

The final coefficients of vector $\vec{b}$ are obtained by summing Eqs. (4.129) with the components of the $\vec{b}$ vector of equation (4.126). Having computed the contact force, we apply $+\vec{F}$ to particle O_1 and $-\vec{F}$ to rigid body B_2 at point $\vec{p}_2$.

4.13 Notes and Comments

Nowadays, there is a substantial number of books and journal articles in the literature that address several aspects of the dynamics of rigid bodies. In this chapter, we used the classic Goldstein [Gol50], and the more recent Beer et al. [BJ77b] and Shabana [Sha10], books as the main references to rigid-body dynamics. Another excellent reference is Baraff et al. [BW98] SIGGRAPH course notes. For example, the derivations of the dynamic state of a rigid body using the position, rotation matrix, linear and angular momenta follows the same line of thought as that presented by Baraff et al. in their course notes.

The collision-detection and response algorithms presented in this chapter assume rigid bodies to be described by their boundary representation, that is, a list of vertices, edges and faces that make up the rigid body's contour. Campagna et al. [CKS98] present a data-structure representation especially tailored for triangle meshes using this boundary representation. It trades memory usage for access time by adding redundant linking information. Using this representation, we can access in constant time every edge and vertex of a given face, every edge incident on a given vertex and every face that contains this vertex, as well as every vertex of a given edge and the faces that share an edge. As far as the collision normal computation is concerned, Thürmer et al. [TW98] present an alternate method for computing vertex normals that reduces the dependence of the normal on the underlying mesh representation. This is achieved by adding weights to the contribution of each face using the angle under which the face is incident to the vertex in question (i.e., it uses the average normal computation weighted by incidence angle).

We also discussed in detail two closest-points algorithms especially tailored for convex bodies, namely the Voronoi Clip and the GJK algorithms. The Voronoi Clip algorithm was developed by Mirtich [Mir97], whereas the GJK algorithm was developed by Gilbert, Johnson and Keerthi [GJK88]. The original references have pointers to implementations of these algorithms provided by their authors. In the case of the GJK algorithm, the work of Bergen [vdB99], Cameron [Cam97] and Ong et al. [OG97] present more robust and efficient implementations than that provided by the original authors. Even though the Minkowski difference is never explicitly computed in the GJK algorithm, the interested reader is referred to Berg et al. [dBvKOS97], Rourke [O'R98] or Skiena [Ski97] for an in-depth description of how the Minkowski sum and difference are computed.

The collision-response module described in this chapter can be sub-divided into two sub-modules: one to compute collision impulses, and another to compute contact forces. Hahn [Hah88] and Mirtich [Mir96b] used the concept of micro-collisions to simulate bodies in contact. That is, contact is simulated as a series of several consecutive collisions. Mirtich went one step further and modeled the relative slipping and sticking of the collision point through the (very short) time interval the bodies are colliding. Another interesting approach to model the relative slipping and sticking of the collision point was developed by Keller [Kel86].

The approach developed in this chapter to deal with friction in collisions is based on the critical-friction-coefficient formulation of Brach [Bra91]. We have extended his work in several ways, however. First, we have explicitly derived the computation of the critical-friction coefficient for single collisions. Second, we present an innovative matrix representation with columns and rows arranged in such way that it can be easily extended to multiple collisions. Last, but not least, our method reduces the multiple-collision problem to the solution of a large sparse linear system (see Duff et al. [DER86] for a comprehensive treatment of sparse matrix methods).

The formulation of the contact-force computation as a quadratic-programming problem was originally introduced by Lötstedt [Löt84]. Baraff (see [Bar92, Bar89, Bar90]) initially modeled the contact-force computation as a quadratic program, but used a heuristic formulation to solve the problem by linear-programming techniques. He then extended his heuristic approach to cope with friction (see Baraff [Bar91]), and later presented other algorithms to solve the quadratic program using the linear-complementarity (see Baraff [Bar94]) formulation.

In this book, we focused our approach to computing contact forces using Baraff's linear-complementarity formulation. We have modified Baraff's formulation to cope with directional friction at the contact points. This in turn required some modification of the linear-complementarity algorithm used to compute the contact forces, described in detail in Appendix I (Chap. 14).

Preliminary results on an alternate contact-force computation technique using singular value decomposition are presented by Mirtich [Mir98]. Another interesting work in applying the linear-complementarity formulation to compute multiple collision impulses with friction was presented by Kawachi et al. [KSK97].

Lastly, the integration of particle and rigid-body systems proposed in this book is at the simulation-engine level, that is, embedding the necessary functionality into a single simulation engine. However, there may be situations in which we want to merge different simulation engines, perhaps developed by different teams. In this case, a simulation-engine level integration may be very difficult, and a higher-level integration technique is needed. Such a technique can be found in Baraff et al. [BW97].

4.14 Exercises

1. The simulation of non-convex rigid bodies is much more inefficient than convex bodies. Usually, it is better to compute the convex decomposition of non-convex objects and use it instead. Lets assume the convex decomposition of a non-convex body yields p convex parts.

   (a) Which approach is more efficient: (1) simulate each convex part as a separate rigid-body glued together by rigid joints, or (2) simulate the non-convex body as a single object and use its convex decomposition only to handle collision detection and response?

   (b) Devise a strategy to cope with numerical rounding errors that may cause the convex parts to separate or interpenetrate during their individual motion, when simulated as separate bodies.

2. Consider a game environment where a given frame-rate must be maintained at all times to ensure a minimum level of playability. The amount of time allocated for the different modules in the game (i.e., the rendering engine, the artificial intelligence engine, the path finding engine, and the simulation engine, to name a few), dynamically varies depending on the user's actions and the game level being played.

   (a) Implement a collision detection algorithm for the game that can stop checking for collisions at a given depth of the hierarchical tree representation of the rigid bodies. For instance, a rigid-body containing 257 faces will have a hierarchy with a depth of $\log_2(2 \times 257 - 1) \approx 9$ (assuming it is a perfectly balanced binary tree). We want to be able to check for collisions down to say, depth 3, such that the lower levels 6 to 9 of the tree are ignored.

   (b) How the collision time and closest point information are obtained in such algorithm? (*Hint*: level of detail.)

   (c) How the collision impulses are applied to the colliding primitives (i.e., triangle faces) if we only have information about the intersecting internal nodes at the collision depth being used?

3. Consider a system that replaces the contact force computation using the LCP approach with a penalty method that uses springs to enforce the non-penetration constraints between colliding objects.

   (a) Implement the algorithm used to compute the spring force between colliding objects. Keep in mind that the objects need to interpenetrate before the penalty force is applied. What rest length should we use for the penalty spring?

   (b) Improve the above algorithm by considering object thickness, that is, the penalty force is also applied if the objects are not intersecting, but are closer to each other by less than their thickness value.

(c) One of the problems with penalty methods is that they can become unstable on rest contact. Depending on the spring stiffness value used, the penalty force can over-push the objects causing vibrations, or under-push the objects making them slowly sink into each other. Devise a strategy to dynamically change the stiffness value of the penalty springs based on the objects' mass, relative velocity and simulation time interval used, such that the above problems are minimized.

4. A practical technique used to improve overall simulation performance when dealing with a large number of rigid bodies stacked on top of each other, is to detect groups of objects that are in contact but not moving relative to each other, and put them in *sleep mode*. Objects in sleep mode are not simulated until they are awaken by a simulation event.

(a) Implement an efficient algorithm capable of detecting disjoint groups of rigid bodies that can be put to sleep at the beginning of a new time interval.

(b) What type of simulation events can awake a sleeping group of rigid bodies?

(c) How do we handle collisions between an active object and a large group of sleeping objects without simultaneously awaken all objects in the group?

References

[Bar89]   Baraff, D.: Analytical methods for dynamic simulation of non-penetrating rigid bodies. Comput. Graph. (Proc. SIGGRAPH) **23**, 223–232 (1989)

[Bar90]   Baraff, D.: Curved surfaces and coherence for non-penetrating rigid body simulations. Comput. Graph. (Proc. SIGGRAPH) **24**, 19–28 (1990)

[Bar91]   Baraff, D.: Coping with friction for non-penetrating rigid body simulation. Comput. Graph. (Proc. SIGGRAPH) **25**, 31–40 (1991)

[Bar92]   Baraff, D.: Dynamic simulation of non-penetrating rigid bodies. PhD Thesis, Cornell University (1992)

[Bar94]   Baraff, D.: Fast contact force computation for non-penetrating rigid bodies. Comput. Graph. (Proc. SIGGRAPH) **28**, 24–29 (1994)

[BJ77b]   Beer, F.P., Johnston, E.R.: Vector Mechanics for Engineers: vol. 2—Dynamics. McGraw-Hill, New York (1977)

[Bra91]   Brach, R.M. (ed.): Mechanical Impact Dynamics: Rigid Body Collisions. Wiley, New York (1991)

[BW97]   Baraff, D., Witkin, A.: Partitioned dynamics. Technical Report CMU-RI-TR-97-33, The Robotics Institute at Carnegie Mellon University (1997)

[BW98]   Baraff, D., Witkin, A.: Physically based modeling. SIGGRAPH Course Notes **13** (1998)

[Cam97]   Cameron, S.: Enhancing GJK: computing minimum and penetration distances between convex polyhedra. In: Proceedings IEEE International Conference on Robotics and Automation, pp. 3112–3117 (1997)

[CKS98]   Campagna, S., Kobbelt, L., Seidel, H.-P.: Directed edges: a scalable representation for triangle meshes. J. Graph. Tools **3**(4), 1–11 (1998)

[dBvKOS97] de Berg, M., van Kreveld, M., Overmars, M., Schwartskopf, O.: Computational Geometry: Algorithms and Applications. Springer, Berlin (1997)

[DER86]   Duff, I.S., Erisman, A.M., Reid, J.K.: Direct Methods for Sparse Matrices. Oxford University Press, London (1986)

[GJK88]   Gilbert, E.G., Johnson, D.W., Keerthi, S.S.: A fast procedure for computing the distance between complex objects in three-dimensional space. IEEE J. Robot. Autom. **4**(2), 193–203 (1988)

[Gol50] Goldstein, H.: Classical Mechanics. Addison-Wesley, Reading (1950)

[Hah88] Hahn, J.K.: Realistic animation of rigid bodies. Comput. Graph. (Proc. SIG-GRAPH), 299–308 (1988)

[Kel86] Keller, J.B.: Impact with friction. Trans. ASME J. Appl. Mech. **53**, 1–4 (1986)

[KSK97] Kawachi, K., Suzuki, H., Kimura, F.: Simulation of rigid body motion with impulsive friction force. In: Proceedings IEEE International Symposium on Assembly and Task Planning, pp. 182–187 (1997)

[Löt84] Lötstedt, P.: Numerical simulation of time-dependent contact friction problems in rigid-body mechanics. SIAM J. Sci. Stat. Comput. **5**(2), 370–393 (1984)

[Mir96b] Mirtich, B.V.: Impulse-based dynamic simulation of rigid body systems. PhD Thesis, University of California, Berkeley (1996)

[Mir97] Mirtich, B.: V-clip: fast and robust polyhedral collision detection. Technical Report TR-97-05, MERL: A Mitsubishi Electric Research Laboratory (1997)

[Mir98] Mirtich, B.: Rigid body contact: collision detection to force computation. Technical Report TR-98-01, MERL: A Mitsubishi Electric Research Laboratory (1998)

[OG97] Ong, C.J., Gilbert, Elmer G.: The Gilbert–Johnson–Keerthi distance algorithm: a fast version for incremental motions. In: Proceedings IEEE International Conference on Robotics and Automation, pp. 1183–1189 (1997)

[O'R98] O'Rourke, J.: Computational Geometry in C. Cambridge University Press, Cambridge (1998)

[Sha10] Shabana, A.A.: Computational Dynamics. Wiley, New York (2010)

[Ski97] Skiena, S.: The Algorithm Design Manual. Springer, Berlin (1997)

[TW98] Thürmer, G., Wüthrich, C.A.: Computing vertex normals from polygonal facets. J. Graph. Tools **3**(1), 43–46 (1998)

[vdB99] van den Bergen, G.: A fast robust GJK implementation for collision detection of convex bodies. J. Graph. Tools **4**(2), 7–25 (1999)

Articulated Rigid-Body Systems

5

5.1   Introduction

The dynamic simulation of rigid-body systems covered in the previous chapter can be further extended to the case of articulated rigid-body systems, where bodies are attached to each other using joints. There are several types of joints that can be used to connect bodies, and they differ from each other by the degree of freedom of the relative motion allowed. Several methods have been proposed to address the dynamics of articulated systems, and most of them fall into one of the following two categories. In the first category, the dynamic equations describing the system's motion are formulated using a reduced set of variables. This is the so called *reduced coordinate* formulation. The reduced set of variables, also known as generalized coordinates, is obtained by removing all degrees of freedom constrained by the joints. The result is a set of parameterized coordinates that fully describes the motion of the entire articulated system while assuring the joint constraints. In the second category, additional constraint forces are introduced in the system to assure the joint constraints throughout motion. This method is known as the *Lagrangian* formulation. The idea is to formulate equations relating the constraint forces (also referred to as the Lagrangian multipliers) with the dynamic state of the articulated system. In the case of articulated rigid-body systems, the formulation consists of building and solving a linear system (often sparse) for the joint forces. Sparsity can then be used advantageously to derive $\mathcal{O}(n)$ algorithms, where n is the total number of articulated bodies being considered.

In this book, we shall direct our analysis to techniques based solely on the Lagrangian formulation. Even though the reduced-coordinate formulation is in some cases more effective than the Lagrangian approach, there are still several reasons for using the Lagrangian formulation as opposed to the reduced-coordinate formulation in a software implementation. The most important reason in our view is modularity, in the sense that, once the joints are specified, their constraints can be formulated in terms of acceleration conditions at the joint points, and a linear system relating the joint forces with the dynamic state of the system is readily obtained from such acceleration conditions. In other words, as soon as the acceleration conditions

M.G. Coutinho, *Guide to Dynamic Simulations of Rigid Bodies and Particle Systems*,   245
Simulation Foundations, Methods and Applications,
DOI 10.1007/978-1-4471-4417-5_5, © Springer-Verlag London 2013

Fig. 5.1 An example of an
articulated body with eight
bodies connected by eight
joints

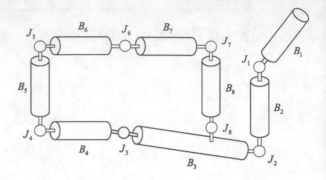

are determined from the type of joints being used, the mathematical framework for computing the joint-constraint forces is exactly the same for all types of joints. Another advantage of formulating the constraints in terms of acceleration conditions is that they can be combined with the computation of contact forces that also rely on acceleration conditions at the contact points, making it easier to simultaneously enforce both joint constraints and contacts during the numerical integration. Equally important is that the acceleration conditions are derived from velocity conditions, which in turn are derived from positional conditions, thus giving us the additional option, if needed, to enforce the constraints at the position-level (via instantaneous change in position) or velocity-level (via impulses applied at the joint).

Most of the notions discussed in Chap. 4 for rigid-body systems can be directly applied to articulated rigid-body systems. The main difference in the mathematical formulation between rigid bodies and articulated rigid bodies consists of enforcing the joint constraints throughout the motion, especially when the articulated body is colliding, or in contact with itself or other articulated bodies.

5.2   Articulated Rigid-Body Dynamics

The dynamic state of an articulated rigid body can always be viewed as the concatenation of the dynamic state of each of its links. Consider the articulated rigid body shown in Fig. 5.1, containing eight links (i.e., eight rigid bodies) and eight joints.

The dynamic state of the articulated rigid body can be expressed as

$$\vec{y}(t) = \left(\vec{y}_1(t), \vec{y}_2(t), \ldots, \vec{y}_8(t)\right)^t, \tag{5.1}$$

where each $\vec{y}_i(t)$ for $i \in \{1, \ldots, 8\}$, represents the dynamic state of body i given by

$$\vec{y}_i(t) = \begin{pmatrix} \vec{r}_i(t) \\ \mathbf{R}_i(t) \\ \vec{L}_i(t) \\ \vec{H}_i(t) \end{pmatrix},$$

with $\vec{r}_i(t)$, $\mathbf{R}_i(t)$, $\vec{L}_i(t)$ and $\vec{H}_i(t)$ being the position and orientation of body B_i's center of mass, and the body's linear and angular momenta, respectively. To numerically integrate the equations of motion of the articulated body, we first need to compute the time derivative of its dynamic state. Deriving Eq. (5.1) with respect to time, we get

$$\frac{d\vec{y}(t)}{dt} = \left(\frac{d\vec{y}_1(t)}{dt}, \frac{d\vec{y}_2(t)}{dt}, \ldots, \frac{d\vec{y}_8(t)}{dt} \right)^t, \qquad (5.2)$$

where each $d\vec{y}_i(t)/dt$ is given by

$$\frac{d\vec{y}_i(t)}{dt} = \begin{pmatrix} \vec{v}_i(t) \\ \vec{\omega}_i(t)\mathbf{R}_i(t) \\ \vec{F}_i(t) \\ \vec{\tau}_i(t) \end{pmatrix}. \qquad (5.3)$$

The variables $\vec{v}_i(t)$, $\vec{\omega}_i(t)$, $\vec{F}_i(t)$ and $\vec{\tau}_i(t)$ in Eq. (5.3) are body B_i's linear velocity, angular velocity, net force and net torque acting on its center of mass.

Clearly from Eqs. (5.2) and (5.3), the numerical integration of the equations of motion can only be carried out if all external forces and torques acting on each body (i.e., each link) are known. In the case of articulated bodies, the motion of the bodies is constrained by the joints attached to them. This constraint is represented by a joint force $\vec{F}_i$ associated with joint J_i, which acts as an external force applied to the connected bodies. So, in order to numerically integrate the equations of motion of an articulated body, we need to first determine the constraint forces associated with each joint in the system. These constraint forces are then summed with all other external forces acting on each interconnected body, thus completely defining the net external force and torque on each link. Having determined the net external force and torque acting on each body, we can proceed with the numerical integration of Eq. (5.2) and determine the position and orientation of each link at the end of the current time interval being considered.

Since the motion of each body influences the motion of all other bodies it is connected to, all constraint forces need to be simultaneously computed to ensure that the connected bodies will remain connected after all external forces and torques are applied to all bodies in the articulation. The goal is then to derive an expression that relates how the dynamics of each interconnected rigid body are affected by the application of the joint force. This expression will then be used to simultaneously compute all joint forces.

As far as notation is concerned, the notation in this section significantly differs from that used in upcoming Sects. 5.6.1 and 5.6.2, for computing impulsive and contact forces between connected links. In those sections, the index of the linked bodies is used to generate the correct index of the impulsive or contact forces associated with each joint. For example, the joint connecting bodies B_i and B_j is referred to as joint J_{ij}, and its associated contact and impulsive forces are $\vec{F}_{ij}$

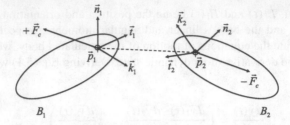

Fig. 5.2 Bodies B_1 and B_2 connected by a generic joint. Points $\vec{p}_1$ and $\vec{p}_2$ are the joint anchor points on bodies B_1 and B_2, respectively. The local-coordinate frame at each anchor point is fixed on the body and is chosen depending on the joint type being used. By convention, a positive joint force $+\vec{F}_c$ is applied to body B_1, whereas a negative joint force $-\vec{F}_c$ is applied to body B_2

and $\vec{P}_{ij}$. In this section, the index of each joint is used to generate the correct index of the linked bodies. For instance, the bodies connected by joint J_i are referred to as bodies $(B_1)_i$ and $(B_2)_i$, and the $\vec{F}_i$ represents the joint force constraining their relative motion.[1] These different notations for computing the dynamics of the articulated system and responding to collisions and contacts requires a redundant underlying representation of the system. More specifically, the software data structures should be such that given a link (i.e., a body) we can efficiently obtain the joints it is connected to, and given a joint we can quickly return the two links attached to it.

For the sake of clarity, we shall first focus on the derivation of the expression relating the joint force and the dynamics of the interconnected bodies for the two-body articulated system shown in Fig. 5.2. Later in this chapter, we shall generalize the derivation for the case of a n-body articulated system.

Typically, a joint is attached to a rigid body at an anchor point. Let $\vec{p}_1(t)$ and $\vec{p}_2(t)$ be the anchor points for a joint attached to bodies B_1 and B_2, respectively. The relative position of the anchor points is used to dictate how the joint affects translation between the rigid bodies. For example, if the joint constraints the anchor points to be coincident throughout their motion, then there can be no relative translation between the bodies at this joint. At each anchor point, there is a local-coordinate frame fixed on the body (see Fig. 5.2). The relative orientation of the local-coordinate frames specifies how the joint constraints the rotation between the rigid bodies. The initial relative orientation of the local-coordinate frames set at the time the joint is created must satisfy the joint constraint and therefore depend on the joint type. During the motion, the joint constraint adjustments maintain the relative orientation of the local-coordinate frames, curbing rotations along constrained directions. Notice that these adjustments are computed with respect to the world-coordinate frame, so a local-to-world transformation is needed (more on this soon).

---

[1]By convention, a positive joint force $+\vec{F}_i$ is applied to body $(B_1)_i$, whereas a negative joint force $-\vec{F}_i$ is applied to body $(B_2)_i$.

Each joint can be represented by a constraint function $\zeta(t)$ that depends on the positions and orientations of the rigid bodies, that is

$$\zeta(t) = \Gamma\big(\vec{p}_1(t), \mathbf{R}_1(t), \vec{p}_2(t), \mathbf{R}_2(t)\big).$$

The first and second time derivatives of the constraint function will therefore depend on the velocities and accelerations of the rigid bodies, respectively. They are represented as

$$\dot{\zeta}(t) = \dot{\Gamma}\big(\vec{v}_1(t), \vec{\omega}_1(t), \vec{v}_2(t), \vec{\omega}_2(t)\big)$$
$$\ddot{\zeta}(t) = \ddot{\Gamma}\big(\vec{a}_1(t), \vec{\alpha}_1(t), \vec{a}_2(t), \vec{\alpha}_2(t)\big).$$

The constraint function $\zeta(t)$ specifies *how* the relative translation and rotation is constrained by the joint. Put another way, it describes the deviation from the desired motion that should be avoided. The joint constraint force is calculated to make the constraint function evaluate to zero, that is, to have a zero deviation from the desired motion.

Let's assume the joint constraint is satisfied at the current time interval, that is:

$$\zeta(t) = 0. \tag{5.4}$$

If the time derivative of the constraint function is also zero, namely

$$\dot{\zeta}(t) = 0, \tag{5.5}$$

then the constraint function will also be satisfied at the next time interval. Specifically, the constraint function $\zeta(t)$ will change to a value other than zero at the next time interval whenever its time derivative $\dot{\zeta}(t)$ becomes non-zero at the current time interval. Likewise, the time derivative of the constraint function will also change to a value other than zero at the next time interval whenever its second time derivative $\ddot{\zeta}(t)$ becomes nonzero at the current time interval. So, provided that the constraint function and its first time derivative are satisfied at creation time, the constraint system only needs to enforce

$$\ddot{\zeta}(t) = 0 \tag{5.6}$$

throughout the entire motion to guaranteed the joint constraint is satisfied. In general, Eqs. (5.4), (5.5) and (5.6) define the three conditions that should be satisfied to enforce joint constraints. However, depending on the type of constraint system used, only a subset of these conditions is actually needed.

In a dynamic simulation engine, there are three types of constraint systems that can be used: position-based, impulse-based and force-based. In a *position-based* constraint system, only the constraint function $\zeta(t)$ is enforced as part of the joint constraint. At any given time interval in which

$$\zeta(t) \neq 0,$$

the constraint system computes the relative translation and rotation corrections needed to enforce Eq. (5.4). The way these corrections are applied depend on the time-stepping scheme used by the numerical integrator being adaptive or fixed. In an adaptive time-stepping scheme, the numerical integrator constantly computes the estimated error and compares it to a user-defined error tolerance value to decide whether the time-step size is appropriate or need to be changed. In such schemes, an abrupt positional adjustment needed to enforce a joint constraint will introduce a discontinuity on the numerical integration, making it unstable. Consequently, whenever the numerical integrator uses an adaptive time-stepping scheme, the positional corrections need to be applied once at the beginning of the current time step, just before the numerical integration starts. The main drawback of this approach is that the joint constraint enforcement is weak, because there are no intermediate corrections applied during the numerical integration itself, and other external forces can push and pull the joint anchor points away from their desired trajectories while processing the integration sub-steps. For this reason, a fixed time-stepping scheme is preferred when using a position-based constraint system. In this case, the positional adjustments can be applied at every sub-step of the numerical integration, providing a framework that strongly enforces joint constraints.

In the case an *impulse-based* constraint system is used, the constraint function and its first time derivative are enforced as part of the joint constraint. The constraint function itself is satisfied at the time the joint is created, so the constraint system just needs to monitor whether

$$\dot{\zeta}(t) \neq 0$$

at the beginning of each time interval and applies the necessary impulses to achieve the required change in velocities needed to enforce Eq. (5.5). Similar to the position-based approach, the impulses can only be applied once at the beginning of the current time interval when the numerical integrator uses an adaptive time-stepping scheme. Therefore, a fixed time-stepping scheme is preferred because it allows impulses to be applied at intermediate sub-steps of the numerical integration, resulting in a stronger enforcement of the joint constraints.

Lastly, in a *force-based* constraint system, the constraint function, and its first and second time derivatives are checked for nonzero values. Usually, both $\zeta(t)$ and $\dot{\zeta}(t)$ are satisfied at the time the joint is created, so the constraint system just needs to monitor whether

$$\ddot{\zeta}(t) \neq 0$$

at the beginning of each time interval, and applies the necessary joint forces to achieve the required change in accelerations needed to enforce Eq. (5.6) throughout the motion. The main advantage of this approach is that the joint constraint force is applied at every sub-step of the numerical integration of the current time interval, independent of the time-stepping scheme being used. Recall that, from the numerical integration standpoint, an adaptive time-stepping scheme is much more efficient than a fixed one. So, a force-based constraint system is more flexible than a position-based or impulse-based system because it simultaneously allows the use of the more efficient adaptive time-stepping scheme and provides a strong enforcement of the joint constraints. Notwithstanding these clear advantages, a force-based constraint system requires the computation of the second time derivatives of the constraint functions, which can result in long and complex expressions to use in software implementations.

In this book, we will focus our discussion on the use of force-based constraint systems to enforce joint constraints. To this end, both constraint function and its first time derivative will have to be computed in order to get to the second time derivative needed for force-based systems. Thus, we will be indirectly addressing the implementation of both position-based and impulse-based systems to some extent. Section 5.7 contains pointers to the literature where additional implementation details of position-based and impulse-based constraint systems can be found.

The main idea behind force-based constraint systems is to use one or more constraint functions to describe the deviation from the desired translational and rotational motions that should be avoided at the joint. Setting these constraint functions to zero and computing their first and second time derivatives yields mathematical expressions relating the accelerations of the joint anchor points that need to be enforced during the motion. These accelerations can be expressed as a function of the (unknown) joint constraint forces as well as all other (known) external forces affecting the rigid-body dynamics. Hence, we can rewrite the second time derivative of the constraint functions in terms of the joint constraint forces, obtaining the following linear system

$$\mathbf{A}\vec{F_c} = \vec{b}. \tag{5.7}$$

In this linear system, we will have one row for each degree of freedom taken away by a joint constraint. For example, consider a single-joint system containing a spherical joint connecting two rigid bodies. The spherical joint will constraint the relative translation between the joint anchor points, forcing them to stay together during their motion. This is equivalent to removing 3 degrees of freedom (i.e., removing their relative translation) out of the 6 possible degrees of freedom (i.e., 3 for relative translation and another 3 for relative rotation). In this case, we will end up with a 3×3 (i.e., square) linear system that can be easily solved for the unknown joint constraint force.

Now, consider another single-joint system containing an universal joint connecting two rigid bodies. The universal joint will not only constraint the relative translation between the joint anchor points but also their relative rotation about one axis. So, the universal joint will remove a total of 4 degrees of freedom, resulting in a 4×3 (i.e., rectangular) linear system to be solved for the unknown joint constraint force (the dimensionality of vector $\vec{b}$ is 4×1 in this case). In order to solve this rectangular linear system, we need to use a technique called *Lagrange multipliers*.

The idea is to transform the rectangular system into a square system by replacing the constraint force with

$$\vec{F}_c = \mathbf{A}^t \vec{\lambda} \tag{5.8}$$

where $\mathbf{A}^t$ is the transpose of $\mathbf{A}$, and $\vec{\lambda}$ is the vector of Lagrange multipliers. In this case, $\vec{\lambda}$ is a 4×1 vector, and $\mathbf{A}^t$ is a 3×4 matrix. Substituting Eq. (5.8) into Eq. (5.7), we obtain a new linear system

$$\mathbf{A}\mathbf{A}^t \vec{\lambda} = \vec{b} \tag{5.9}$$

where the Lagrange multipliers are the unknown. Notice that the combined matrix $(\mathbf{A}\mathbf{A}^t)$ has dimension 4×4, so we can solve this square system for the unknown Lagrange multipliers. Once the Lagrange multipliers are computed, we can substitute their values into Eq. (5.8) to finally obtain the desired joint constraint forces. Having determined the joint constraint forces, we can numerically integrate the rigid bodies' dynamic equations of motion to compute their new trajectories that enforce the joint constraints for the current time interval.

5.3   Single Joint Systems

There are many types of joints that can be used to constraint the motion between two rigid-bodies. Each type yields a different combination of constraint functions used to express the number of degrees of freedom removed from the system. Before we delve into the details of how the constraint functions are specified for each type of joint, lets first derive an expression that relates the accelerations of the joint anchor points with the unknown joint constraint forces. This expression is used to help build the linear system in Eq. (5.7), independent of the type of joint considered.

The acceleration at the anchor point $\vec{p}_1$ attached to rigid-body B_1 can be expressed as a function of the linear and angular accelerations of B_1's center of mass using the rigid-body dynamics' equation (4.8), repeated here for convenience,

$$\vec{a}_{p_1}(t) = \vec{\alpha}_1(t) \times \left(\vec{p}_1(t) - \vec{r}_1(t) \right)$$
$$+ \vec{\omega}_1(t) \times \left(\vec{\omega}_1(t) \times \left(\vec{p}_1(t) - \vec{r}_1(t) \right) \right) + \vec{a}_1(t), \tag{5.10}$$

where $\vec{p}_1(t)$ is the anchor point position and $\vec{r}_1(t)$, $\vec{\omega}_1(t)$, $\vec{\alpha}_1(t)$ and $\vec{a}_1(t)$ are the center of mass position, angular velocity, angular acceleration and linear acceleration of rigid-body B_1, all computed in the world-coordinate frame. A similar expression can be obtained for the anchor point $\vec{p}_2$ on body B_2. In order to simplify the notation in the following derivations, we will omit the reference to time in the variables since they are all evaluated at the beginning of the current time interval.

Using Eq. (4.11), the linear acceleration $\vec{a}_1$ can be obtained from the net force $(\vec{F}_1)_{net}$ acting on the center of mass of body B_1 as

$$\vec{a}_1 = \frac{(\vec{F}_1)_{net}}{m_1} = \left(\frac{\vec{F}_c + (\vec{F}_1)_{ext}}{m_1} \right),$$

where $(\vec{F}_1)_{ext}$ is the net external force (such as gravity, spring forces, spatially dependent forces, etc.) acting on body B_1, and $\vec{F}_c$ is the joint constraint force to be determined. Also, using Eq. (4.18), the angular acceleration $\vec{\alpha}_1$ can be computed from the net torque $(\vec{\tau}_1)_{net}$ acting on B_1's center of mass as

$$\vec{\alpha}_1 = \mathbf{I_1}^{-1}\big((\vec{\tau}_1)_{net} + \vec{H}_1 \times \vec{\omega}_1\big), \qquad (5.11)$$

where $\mathbf{I_1}$ and $\vec{H}_1$ are the inertia tensor and angular momentum of body B_1, respectively. The net torque acting on body B_1 is computed by summing the torque induced by all external forces, that is

$$(\vec{\tau}_1)_{net} = (\vec{\tau}_1)_{ext} + \overbrace{(\vec{p}_1 - \vec{r}_1) \times \vec{F}_c}^{\text{torque resulting from joint constraint force}}, \qquad (5.12)$$

where

$$(\vec{\tau}_1)_{ext} = \sum_i (\vec{p}_i - \vec{r}_1) \times (\vec{F}_i)_{ext}$$

with $\vec{p}_i$ being the point on body B_1 at which the external force $(\vec{F}_i)_{ext}$ is being applied. Substituting Eq. (5.11) into (5.12), we obtain

$$\vec{\alpha}_1 = \mathbf{I_1}^{-1}(\vec{p}_1 - \vec{r}_1) \times \vec{F}_c + \mathbf{I_1}^{-1}\big((\vec{\tau}_1)_{ext} + \vec{H}_1 \times \vec{\omega}_1\big). \qquad (5.13)$$

The acceleration $\vec{a}_{p_1}$ of point $\vec{p}_1$ is then

$$\begin{aligned}
\vec{a}_{p_1} = {} & \big(\mathbf{I_1}^{-1}(\vec{p}_1 - \vec{r}_1) \times \vec{F}_c\big) \times (\vec{p}_1 - \vec{r}_1) \\
& + \big(\mathbf{I_1}^{-1}((\vec{\tau}_1)_{ext} + \vec{H}_1 \times \vec{\omega}_1)\big) \times (\vec{p}_1 - \vec{r}_1) \\
& + \vec{\omega}_1 \times (\vec{\omega}_1 \times (\vec{p}_1 - \vec{r}_1)) + \left(\frac{\vec{F}_c + (\vec{F}_1)_{ext}}{m_1}\right). \qquad (5.14)
\end{aligned}$$

Using the general cross-product relations[2]

$$\vec{a} \times \vec{b} = -\vec{b} \times \vec{a}$$
$$\vec{a} \times \vec{b} = \tilde{a}\vec{b}$$

---

[2] See Sect. 6.7 of Appendix A (Chap. 6) for more details on these expressions.

and the auxiliary variable

$$\vec{x}_1 = \vec{p}_1 - \vec{r}_1,$$

we can further simplify the first term of Eq. (5.14) as follows:

$$
\begin{aligned}
\left(\mathbf{I_1}^{-1}(\vec{p}_1 - \vec{r}_1) \times \vec{F}_c\right) \times (\vec{p}_1 - \vec{r}_1) \\
= \left(\mathbf{I_1}^{-1}\vec{x}_1 \times \vec{F}_c\right) \times \vec{x}_1 \\
= -\vec{x}_1 \times \left(\mathbf{I_1}^{-1}\vec{x}_1 \times \vec{F}_c\right) \\
= -\tilde{x}_1 \left(\mathbf{I_1}^{-1}\vec{x}_1 \times \vec{F}_c\right) \\
= -\left(\tilde{x}_1 \mathbf{I_1}^{-1}\right)\vec{x}_1 \times \vec{F}_c \\
= -\left(\tilde{x}_1 \mathbf{I_1}^{-1}\right)\tilde{x}_1 \vec{F}_c.
\end{aligned}
\tag{5.15}
$$

Substituting Eq. (5.17) into (5.14), we have

$$
\begin{aligned}
\vec{a}_{p1} = \left(\frac{1}{m_1}\mathbf{I} - \tilde{x}_1 \mathbf{I_1}^{-1}\tilde{x}_1\right)\vec{F}_c \\
+ \frac{1}{m_1}(\vec{F}_1)_{ext} + \left(\mathbf{I_1}^{-1}((\vec{\tau}_1)_{ext} + \vec{H}_1 \times \vec{\omega}_1)\right) \times \vec{x}_1 \\
+ \vec{\omega}_1 \times (\vec{\omega}_1 \times \vec{x}_1),
\end{aligned}
\tag{5.16}
$$

which can be written as

$$\vec{a}_{p1} = \mathbf{A_1}\vec{F}_c + \vec{b}_1 \tag{5.17}$$

with

$$
\begin{aligned}
\mathbf{A_1} = \left(\frac{1}{m_1}\mathbf{I} - \tilde{x}_1 \mathbf{I_1}^{-1}\tilde{x}_1\right) \\
\vec{b}_1 = \frac{1}{m_1}(\vec{F}_1)_{ext} + \left(\mathbf{I_1}^{-1}((\vec{\tau}_1)_{ext} + \vec{H}_1 \times \vec{\omega}_1)\right) \times \vec{x}_1 \\
+ \vec{\omega}_1 \times (\vec{\omega}_1 \times \vec{x}_1).
\end{aligned}
$$

Analogously, the acceleration $\vec{a}_2$ of point $\vec{p}_2$ is given by

$$
\begin{aligned}
\vec{a}_{p2} = \left(\mathbf{I_2}^{-1}(\vec{p}_2 - \vec{r}_2) \times (-\vec{F}_c)\right) \times (\vec{p}_2 - \vec{r}_2) \\
+ \left(\mathbf{I_2}^{-1}((\vec{\tau}_2)_{ext} + \vec{H}_2 \times \vec{\omega}_2)\right) \times (\vec{p}_2 - \vec{r}_2) \\
+ \vec{\omega}_2 \times (\vec{\omega}_2 \times (\vec{p}_2 - \vec{r}_2)) + \left(\frac{(-\vec{F}_c) + (\vec{F}_2)_{ext}}{m_2}\right),
\end{aligned}
\tag{5.18}
$$

Fig. 5.3 Bodies B_1 and B_2 connected by a spherical joint. The joint constrains the motion to relative rotations only (relative translations are disallowed)

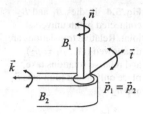

which can be further simplified to

$$\vec{a}_{p2} = -\mathbf{A}_2 \vec{F}_c + \vec{b}_2 \qquad (5.19)$$

with

$$\mathbf{A}_2 = \left(\frac{1}{m_2} \mathbf{I} - \tilde{x}_2 \mathbf{I}_2^{-1} \tilde{x}_2 \right)$$

$$\vec{b}_2 = \frac{1}{m_2} (\vec{F}_2)_{ext} + \left(\mathbf{I}_2^{-1} \left((\vec{\tau}_2)_{ext} + \vec{H}_2 \times \vec{\omega}_2 \right) \right) \times \tilde{x}_2$$
$$+ \vec{\omega}_2 \times (\vec{\omega}_2 \times \tilde{x}_2).$$

Now that we have a way to relate the accelerations of the joint anchor points with the unknown joint constraint forces, we can proceed with the specification of the constraint functions for each type of joint.

5.3.1 Spherical Joint

Also known as *ball-in-socket*, spherical joints do not allow relative translations between the interconnected bodies. Therefore, they have 3 degrees of freedom to rotate the bodies with respect to the coordinate axis defined by the joint's local-coordinate frames. Figure 5.3 shows the schematic representation of a spherical joint.

As previously mentioned, the constraint function $\zeta(t)$ describes the deviation from the desired motion that should be avoided. In this case, the deviation is defined by the relative translation between the joint anchor points, that is,

$$\zeta_1 = \vec{p}_1 - \vec{p}_2 = 0. \qquad (5.20)$$

The first and second time derivatives of this constraint function are given by

$$\dot{\zeta}_1 = \vec{v}_{p1} - \vec{v}_{p2} = 0$$
$$\ddot{\zeta}_1 = \vec{a}_{p1} - \vec{a}_{p2} = 0. \qquad (5.21)$$

Fig. 5.4 Bodies B_1 and B_2 connected by an universal joint. Relative translations are disallowed (i.e., $\vec{p}_1 = \vec{p}_2$), and relative rotations take place only about joint axis $\vec{n}_1$ and $\vec{n}_2$

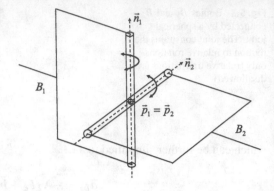

Using Eqs. (5.17) and (5.19), we can replace the anchor points' accelerations $\vec{a}_{p_1}$ and $\vec{a}_{p_2}$ in Eq. (5.21) with expressions relating the joint constraint force, resulting in the following linear system:

$$(\mathbf{A_1}\vec{F}_c + \vec{b}_1) - (-\mathbf{A_2}\vec{F}_c + \vec{b}_2) = 0$$

which can be rearranged to match the form of Eq. (5.7), namely

$$(\mathbf{A_1} + \mathbf{A_2})\vec{F}_c = \vec{b}_2 - \vec{b}_1. \qquad (5.22)$$

This is a 3×3 square system that can be directly solved for the joint constraint forces (i.e., no need to use Lagrange multipliers in this case).

5.3.2 Universal Joint

By definition, universal joints do not allow relative translations between the joint anchor points, as well as relative rotations about a third axis perpendicular to two given joint axis. Figure 5.4 shows the schematic representation of an universal joint.

Let $\vec{n}_1$ and $\vec{n}_2$ be the two world-coordinate joint axis attached to bodies B_1 and B_2, respectively. These define the rotation axis allowed by the joint. They are fixed to their corresponding bodies at the anchor points, and are created perpendicular to each other, that is

$$\vec{n}_1 \cdot \vec{n}_2 = 0.$$

These world-coordinate joint axis can be transformed to their rigid-bodies' local-coordinate frame using

$$(\vec{n}_1)_{local} = \mathbf{R_1}^t \vec{n}_1$$
$$(\vec{n}_2)_{local} = \mathbf{R_2}^t \vec{n}_2 \qquad (5.23)$$

where $\mathbf{R_1}$ and $\mathbf{R_2}$ are the rotation matrices of bodies B_1 and B_2, respectively.

The universal joint needs two constraint functions to describe how it constraints the relative translation and orientation at the anchor points. The relative translation is completely disallowed as in the case of spherical joints, so we can use the exact same constraint function here, namely

$$\zeta_1 = \vec{p}_1 - \vec{p}_2 = 0.$$

The second constraint function needs to constraint the relative rotation between the rigid-bodies, such that the two rotation axis remain perpendicular during their motion (i.e., no rotations about the third axis). This constraint can be mathematically expressed as

$$\zeta_2 = \vec{n}_1 \cdot \vec{n}_2 = 0. \tag{5.24}$$

The next step is to compute the first and second time derivatives of the constraint functions ζ_1 and ζ_2. The ones for the constraint function ζ_1 were already computed in the case of spherical joints. Equation (5.22) describes the final 3×3 linear system obtained from this constraint function. We still need to compute the first and second time derivatives of the second constraint function ζ_2 to obtain the fourth constraint equation. These four equations will be put together to form the linear system

$$\mathbf{A}\vec{F}_c = \vec{b}$$

where $\mathbf{A}$ is a 4×3 matrix, and $\vec{b}$ a 4×1 vector. In order to solve this rectangular system, we will have to use Lagrange multipliers, as previously discussed at the end of Sect. 5.3.

The first time derivative of ζ_2 is given by

$$\dot{\zeta}_2 = \frac{d\vec{n}_1}{dt} \cdot \vec{n}_2 + \vec{n}_1 \cdot \frac{d\vec{n}_2}{dt}. \tag{5.25}$$

According to Sect. 10.2 of Appendix E (Chap. 10), the time derivative of a vector attached to a rigid body is computed as

$$\frac{d\vec{n}_1}{dt} = \vec{\omega}_1 \times \vec{n}_1$$

$$\frac{d\vec{n}_2}{dt} = \vec{\omega}_2 \times \vec{n}_2.$$

Substituting these results into Eq. (5.25), and using the general cross-product relations

$$(\vec{a} \times \vec{b}) \cdot \vec{c} = (\vec{b} \times \vec{c}) \cdot \vec{a}$$
$$(\vec{a} \times \vec{b}) \cdot \vec{c} = -(\vec{a} \times \vec{c}) \cdot \vec{b}$$

we obtain

$$\dot{\zeta}_2 = (\vec{\omega}_1 \times \vec{n}_1) \cdot \vec{n}_2 + \vec{n}_1 \cdot (\vec{\omega}_2 \times \vec{n}_2)$$
$$= (\vec{n}_1 \times \vec{n}_2) \cdot \vec{\omega}_1 - (\vec{n}_1 \times \vec{n}_2) \cdot \vec{\omega}_2$$
$$= (\vec{n}_1 \times \vec{n}_2) \cdot (\vec{\omega}_1 - \vec{\omega}_2) \tag{5.26}$$

A quick inspection of Eq. (5.26) reveals that the equation

$$\dot{\zeta}_2(t) = 0$$

is satisfied whenever the relative angular velocity component along the third joint axis defined by $(\vec{n}_1 \times \vec{n}_2)$ is zero. This validates the condition that rotations are only allowed about the two joint axis $\vec{n}_1$ and $\vec{n}_2$.

Analogous to the first time derivative, the second time derivative of the constraint function is obtained from

$$\ddot{\zeta}_2 = \left(\frac{d\vec{n}_1}{dt} \times \vec{n}_2 + \vec{n}_1 \times \frac{d\vec{n}_2}{dt}\right) \cdot (\vec{\omega}_1 - \vec{\omega}_2) + (\vec{n}_1 \times \vec{n}_2) \cdot (\vec{\alpha}_1 - \vec{\alpha}_2)$$
$$= ((\vec{\omega}_1 \times \vec{n}_1) \times \vec{n}_2 + \vec{n}_1 \times (\vec{\omega}_2 \times \vec{n}_2)) \cdot (\vec{\omega}_1 - \vec{\omega}_2)$$
$$+ (\vec{n}_1 \times \vec{n}_2) \cdot (\vec{\alpha}_1 - \vec{\alpha}_2). \tag{5.27}$$

The only term in Eq. (5.27) that depends on the joint constraint force is the one containing the difference in angular accelerations. All other terms depend only on the dynamic state of the rigid bodies and are readily known. Using Eq. (5.13), the difference in angular accelerations can be expressed as a function of the joint constraint force, that is,

$$(\vec{\alpha}_1 - \vec{\alpha}_2) = \left(\mathbf{I_1}^{-1}\tilde{x}_1 - \mathbf{I_2}^{-1}\tilde{x}_2\right)\vec{F}_c$$
$$+ \mathbf{I_1}^{-1}\left((\vec{\tau}_1)_{ext} + \vec{H}_1 \times \vec{\omega}_1\right)$$
$$- \mathbf{I_2}^{-1}\left((\vec{\tau}_2)_{ext} + \vec{H}_2 \times \vec{\omega}_2\right). \tag{5.28}$$

Replacing Eq. (5.28) into Eq. (5.27), we obtain the fourth row of the linear system

$$\mathbf{A}\vec{F}_c = \vec{b}$$

associated with the universal joint constraint. This is a 4×3 rectangular system, so we need to use Lagrange multipliers to compute the joint constraint force.

5.3.3 Revolute Joint

Also known as *hinge joint* or *pin joint*, revolute joints do not allow relative translation between the joint anchor points, and constraint rotation to be about a single joint axis. They remove a total of 5 degrees of freedom from the relative motion

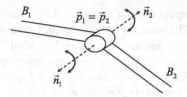

Fig. 5.5 Bodies B_1 and B_2 connected by a revolute joint. Relative translations are disallowed (i.e., $\vec{p}_1 = \vec{p}_2$), and relative rotations take place only about a single joint axis. In this case, the joint axis $\vec{n}_1$ and $\vec{n}_2$ are required to remain parallel throughout the motion

between the rigid bodies at the joint. Figure 5.5 shows the schematic representation of a revolute joint.

Let $\vec{n}_1$ and $\vec{n}_2$ be the two world-coordinate joint axis attached to bodies B_1 and B_2, respectively. They are fixed to their corresponding bodies at the anchor points, and are created parallel to each other, that is

$$\vec{n}_1 \times \vec{n}_2 = 0.$$

The revolute joint needs two constraint functions to describe how it constraints the relative translation and rotation between the rigid-bodies at the joint anchor points. The relative translation is completely disallowed as in the case of spherical and universal joints, so we can use the exact same constraint function here, namely

$$\zeta_1 = \vec{p}_1 - \vec{p}_2 = 0.$$

The second constraint function needs to constraint the relative rotation between the rigid-bodies, such that the two rotation axis remain parallel during their motion (i.e., rotations are allowed only about a single axis). This constraint can be mathematically expressed as

$$\zeta_3 = \vec{n}_1 \times \vec{n}_2 = 0. \tag{5.29}$$

We can avoid computing the time derivatives of the cross-product in Eq. (5.29), by replacing it with 2 scalar products involving the other two local-frame axis perpendicular to $\vec{n}_1$. Hence, enforcing

$$\zeta_3 = 0$$

is equivalent to simultaneously enforcing

$$\zeta_4 = \vec{k}_1 \cdot \vec{n}_2 = 0$$
$$\zeta_5 = \vec{t}_1 \cdot \vec{n}_2 = 0. \tag{5.30}$$

The next step is to compute the first and second time derivatives of the constraint functions ζ_1, ζ_4 and ζ_5. The ones for the constraint function ζ_1 were already computed in the case of spherical and revolute joints. Equation (5.22) describes the final 3×3 linear system obtained from this constraint function. As for the constraint functions ζ_4 and ζ_5, notice the similarities between Eqs. (5.24) and (5.30). They are essentially the same, if we replace $\vec{n}_1$ for $\vec{k}_1$ or $\vec{t}_1$ in ζ_2. Therefore, the first and second time derivatives of ζ_4 are directly obtained from Eqs. (5.26) and (5.27) by replacing $\vec{n}_1$ for $\vec{k}_1$, namely

$$
\begin{aligned}
\dot{\zeta}_4 &= (\vec{\omega}_1 \times \vec{k}_1) \cdot \vec{n}_2 + \vec{k}_1 \cdot (\vec{\omega}_2 \times \vec{n}_2) \\
&= (\vec{k}_1 \times \vec{n}_2) \cdot \vec{\omega}_1 - (\vec{k}_1 \times \vec{n}_2) \cdot \vec{\omega}_2 \\
&= (\vec{k}_1 \times \vec{n}_2) \cdot (\vec{\omega}_1 - \vec{\omega}_2)
\end{aligned}
\tag{5.31}
$$

and

$$
\begin{aligned}
\ddot{\zeta}_4 &= \left(\frac{d\vec{k}_1}{dt} \times \vec{n}_2 + \vec{k}_1 \times \frac{d\vec{n}_2}{dt} \right) \cdot (\vec{\omega}_1 - \vec{\omega}_2) + (\vec{k}_1 \times \vec{n}_2) \cdot (\vec{\alpha}_1 - \vec{\alpha}_2) \\
&= ((\vec{\omega}_1 \times \vec{k}_1) \times \vec{n}_2 + \vec{k}_1 \times (\vec{\omega}_2 \times \vec{n}_2)) \cdot (\vec{\omega}_1 - \vec{\omega}_2) \\
&\quad + (\vec{k}_1 \times \vec{n}_2) \cdot (\vec{\alpha}_1 - \vec{\alpha}_2).
\end{aligned}
\tag{5.32}
$$

In like manner, the first and second time derivatives of ζ_5 are obtained from the first and second time derivatives of ζ_4 by replacing $\vec{k}_1$ for $\vec{t}_1$, that is

$$
\begin{aligned}
\dot{\zeta}_5 &= (\vec{\omega}_1 \times \vec{t}_1) \cdot \vec{n}_2 + \vec{t}_1 \cdot (\vec{\omega}_2 \times \vec{n}_2) \\
&= (\vec{t}_1 \times \vec{n}_2) \cdot \vec{\omega}_1 - (\vec{t}_1 \times \vec{n}_2) \cdot \vec{\omega}_2 \\
&= (\vec{t}_1 \times \vec{n}_2) \cdot (\vec{\omega}_1 - \vec{\omega}_2)
\end{aligned}
\tag{5.33}
$$

and

$$
\begin{aligned}
\ddot{\zeta}_5 &= \left(\frac{d\vec{t}_1}{dt} \times \vec{n}_2 + \vec{t}_1 \times \frac{d\vec{n}_2}{dt} \right) \cdot (\vec{\omega}_1 - \vec{\omega}_2) + (\vec{t}_1 \times \vec{n}_2) \cdot (\vec{\alpha}_1 - \vec{\alpha}_2) \\
&= ((\vec{\omega}_1 \times \vec{t}_1) \times \vec{n}_2 + \vec{t}_1 \times (\vec{\omega}_2 \times \vec{n}_2)) \cdot (\vec{\omega}_1 - \vec{\omega}_2) \\
&\quad + (\vec{t}_1 \times \vec{n}_2) \cdot (\vec{\alpha}_1 - \vec{\alpha}_2).
\end{aligned}
\tag{5.34}
$$

The only term in Eqs. (5.32) and (5.34) that depends on the joint constraint force is the one containing the difference in angular accelerations. All other terms depend only on the dynamic state of the rigid bodies and are readily known. Equation (5.28) specifies the difference in angular accelerations as a function of the joint constraint force. Replacing this equation into Eqs. (5.32) and (5.34), we obtain the fourth and fifth rows of the linear system

$$
\mathbf{A} \vec{F}_c = \vec{b}
$$

Fig. 5.6 Bodies B_1 and B_2
connected by a cylindrical
joint. Relative rotations and
translations are allowed along
a single joint axis

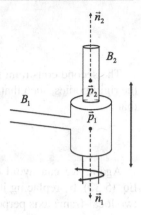

associated with the revolute joint constraint. This is a 5×3 rectangular system, so
we need to use Lagrange multipliers to compute the joint constraint force.

5.3.4   Cylindrical Joint

A cylindrical joint constraints the relative translation and rotation between the rigid-
bodies to be along a single joint axis. They remove a total of 4 degrees of freedom
from the relative motion between the rigid bodies at the joint. Figure 5.6 shows the
schematic representation of a cylindrical joint.

Let $\vec{n}_1$ and $\vec{n}_2$ be the two world-coordinate joint axis attached to bodies B_1
and B_2, respectively. They are fixed to their corresponding bodies at the anchor
points, and are created parallel to each other, that is

$$\vec{n}_1 \times \vec{n}_2 = 0.$$

The cylindrical joint needs two constraint functions to describe how it constraints
the relative translation and rotation between the rigid-bodies at the joint anchor
points. The first constraint function needs to constraint the relative translation between the rigid-bodies to be along the joint axis. This constraint can be mathematically expressed as

$$\zeta_6 = \vec{n}_1 \times (\vec{p}_1 - \vec{p}_2) = 0. \tag{5.35}$$

We can avoid computing the time derivatives of the cross-product in Eq. (5.35),
by replacing it with two scalar products involving the other two local-frame axis
perpendicular to $\vec{n}_1$. Hence, enforcing

$$\zeta_6 = 0$$

is equivalent to simultaneously enforcing

$$\zeta_7 = \vec{k}_1 \cdot (\vec{p}_1 - \vec{p}_2) = 0$$
$$\zeta_8 = \vec{t}_1 \cdot (\vec{p}_1 - \vec{p}_2) = 0. \tag{5.36}$$

The second constraint function needs to constraint the relative rotation between the rigid-bodies, such that the two rotation axis remain parallel during their motion, that is

$$\zeta_3 = \vec{n}_1 \times \vec{n}_2 = 0. \tag{5.37}$$

Again, we can avoid computing the time derivatives of the cross-product in Eq. (5.37), by replacing it with two other constraints ζ_4 and ζ_5 involving the other two local-frame axis perpendicular to $\vec{n}_1$.

The next step is to compute the first and second time derivatives of the constraint functions ζ_7, ζ_8, ζ_4 and ζ_5. The ones for the constraint functions ζ_4 and ζ_5 were already computed in the case of revolute joints. They provide the first two constraint equations associated with cylindrical joints. The third and forth constraint equations are obtained from the second time derivatives of ζ_7 and ζ_8.

The first time derivative of ζ_7 is computed as

$$\dot{\zeta}_7 = (\vec{\omega}_1 \times \vec{k}_1) \cdot (\vec{p}_1 - \vec{p}_2) + \vec{k}_1 \cdot (\vec{v}_{p_1} - \vec{v}_{p_2}). \tag{5.38}$$

The second time derivative is then

$$\ddot{\zeta}_7 = \left((\vec{\alpha}_1 \times \vec{k}_1) + \vec{\omega}_1 \times (\vec{\omega}_1 \times \vec{k}_1) \right) \cdot (\vec{p}_1 - \vec{p}_2)$$
$$+ 2(\vec{\omega}_1 \times \vec{k}_1) \cdot (\vec{v}_{p_1} - \vec{v}_{p_2})$$
$$+ \vec{k}_1 \cdot (\vec{a}_{p_1} - \vec{a}_{p_2}). \tag{5.39}$$

Similar results can be obtained for the first and second time derivatives of ζ_8, if we replace $\vec{k}_1$ for $\vec{t}_1$ in Eqs. (5.38) and (5.39), namely

$$\dot{\zeta}_8 = (\vec{\omega}_1 \times \vec{t}_1) \cdot (\vec{p}_1 - \vec{p}_2) + \vec{t}_1 \cdot (\vec{v}_{p_1} - \vec{v}_{p_2}) \tag{5.40}$$

and

$$\ddot{\zeta}_8 = \left((\vec{\alpha}_1 \times \vec{t}_1) + \vec{\omega}_1 \times (\vec{\omega}_1 \times \vec{t}_1) \right) \cdot (\vec{p}_1 - \vec{p}_2)$$
$$+ 2(\vec{\omega}_1 \times \vec{t}_1) \cdot (\vec{v}_{p_1} - \vec{v}_{p_2})$$
$$+ \vec{t}_1 \cdot (\vec{a}_{p_1} - \vec{a}_{p_2}). \tag{5.41}$$

The only term in Eqs. (5.39) and (5.41) that depends on the joint constraint force is the one containing the difference in accelerations of the joint anchor points. All other terms depend only on the dynamic state of the rigid bodies and are readily known. Using Eqs. (5.17) and (5.19), we can replace the anchor points' accelerations

Fig. 5.7 Bodies B_1 and B_2 connected by a prismatic joint. Relative rotations are disallowed, and relative translations take place only along a single joint axis

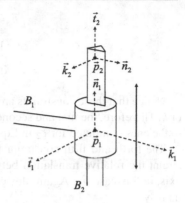

$\vec{a}_{p_1}$ and $\vec{a}_{p_2}$ in Eqs. (5.39) and (5.41) with expressions relating the joint constraint force, that is

$$(\vec{a}_{p_1} - \vec{a}_{p_2}) = (\mathbf{A_1} + \mathbf{A_2})\vec{F}_c + (\vec{b}_1 - \vec{b}_2).$$

Replacing this equation into Eqs. (5.39) and (5.41), we obtain the third and fourth rows of the linear system

$$\mathbf{A}\vec{F}_c = \vec{b}$$

associated with the cylindrical joint constraint. This is a 4×3 rectangular system, so we need to use Lagrange multipliers to compute the joint constraint force.

5.3.5 Prismatic Joint

Also known as *translational joints*, prismatic joints do not allow relative rotations between the joint anchor points and constraint translation to be along the joint axis. They remove a total of 5 degrees of freedom from the relative motion between the rigid bodies at the joint. Figure 5.7 shows the schematic representation of a prismatic joint.

Let $(\vec{n}_1, \vec{t}_1, \vec{k}_1)$ and $(\vec{n}_2, \vec{t}_2, \vec{k}_2)$ be the world-coordinate joint axis attached to bodies B_1 and B_2, respectively. They are fixed to their corresponding bodies at the anchor points, and are created perpendicular to each other, that is

$$\vec{n}_1 \cdot \vec{n}_2 = 0$$
$$\vec{t}_1 \cdot \vec{t}_2 = 0$$
$$\vec{k}_1 \cdot \vec{k}_2 = 0.$$

The prismatic joint needs five constraint functions to describe how it constraints the relative translation and rotation between the rigid-bodies at the joint anchor points. The first three constraint functions are needed to disallow relative rotations between the rigid-bodies. These constraints can be mathematically expressed as

$$\zeta_9 = \vec{n}_1 \cdot \vec{n}_2 = 0$$
$$\zeta_{10} = \vec{t}_1 \cdot \vec{t}_2 = 0 \qquad\qquad (5.42)$$
$$\zeta_{11} = \vec{k}_1 \cdot \vec{k}_2 = 0.$$

Notice that these constraints are identical to ζ_2 in Eq. (5.24), if we replace $\vec{n}$ for $\vec{t}$ or $\vec{k}$. Therefore, the first and second time derivatives of ζ_9, ζ_{10} and ζ_{11} are analogous to the ones computed for ζ_2 in Eqs. (5.26) and (5.27), respectively.

The forth and fifth constraint functions of prismatic joints are needed to constraint the relative translation between the rigid-bodies to be along a single joint axis, in this case $\vec{n}_1$. Again, this constraint is exactly the same as ζ_6 in Eq. (5.35), namely

$$\zeta_6 = \vec{n}_1 \times (\vec{p}_1 - \vec{p}_2) = 0,$$

or, its equivalent

$$\zeta_7 = \vec{k}_1 \cdot (\vec{p}_1 - \vec{p}_2) = 0$$
$$\zeta_8 = \vec{t}_1 \cdot (\vec{p}_1 - \vec{p}_2) = 0.$$

We can then merge together the second time derivative of the five constraint functions to form the linear system

$$\mathbf{A}\vec{F}_c = \vec{b}$$

associated with the prismatic joint constraint. This is a 5×3 rectangular system, so we need to use Lagrange multipliers to compute the joint constraint force.

5.3.6   Rigid Joint

A rigid joint does not allow relative translations and rotations between the rigid bodies at the joint. It removes all 6 degrees of freedom from the relative motion of the bodies.

The framework needed to implement rigid joints has been already covered in previous sections. We can combine the constraint function ζ_1 from spherical joints to prevent relative translations, with the constraint functions ζ_9, ζ_{10} and ζ_{11} from prismatic joints to prevent relative rotations. These constraint functions can be merged together to form the 6×6 linear system

$$\mathbf{A}\vec{F}_c = \vec{b}$$

associated with the rigid joint constraint. This is a square system that can be directly solved for the joint constraint force.

5.4   Multiple Joint Systems

Now, consider the situation in which the articulated system is composed of n bodies connected by q joints. For each joint J_i connecting bodies $(B_1)_i$ and $(B_2)_i$, we will have a linear system relating the accelerations of the joint's anchor points with the joint constraint forces to be determined. In order to simultaneously solve for all joint constraint forces, we merge the individual linear systems into a single one, obtaining a large (and sparse) linear system

$$\mathbf{A}\vec{F} = \vec{b}$$

where the joint constraint force vector is expressed as

$$\vec{F} = \left((\vec{F}_c)_1, (\vec{F}_c)_2, \dots, (\vec{F}_c)_q \right)^t.$$

According to Eq. (5.17), the acceleration of the anchor points $(\vec{a}_{p_1})_i$ and $(\vec{a}_{p_2})_i$ of joint J_i are given by

$$(\vec{a}_{p_1})_i = (\mathbf{A_1})_i (\vec{F}_c)_i + (\vec{b}_1)_i$$
$$(\vec{a}_{p_2})_i = -(\mathbf{A_2})_i (\vec{F}_c)_i + (\vec{b}_2)_i,$$

where, by convention, a negative joint force is applied to the anchor point $\vec{p}_2$. Lets assume another joint J_j is also attached to rigid-body B_1, and that B_1 is arbitrarily assigned to be body $(B_1)_j$ of joint J_j. In this case, a positive constraint force $+(\vec{F}_c)_j$ is applied to B_1 at the anchor point $(\vec{a}_{p_1})_j$. So, the acceleration of the joint anchor point $(\vec{a}_{p_1})_i$ becomes

$$(\vec{a}_{p_1})_i = (\mathbf{A_1})_i (\vec{F}_c)_i + (\mathbf{A_1})_j (\vec{F}_c)_j + (\vec{b}_1)_i$$

creating an off-diagonal entry in the matrix $\mathbf{A}$ at row i and column j. There will also be another entry at row j and column i associated with the effects of the constraint force $(\vec{F}_c)_i$ on the anchor point $(\vec{a}_{p_2})_j$ of joint J_j. In other words, the acceleration of the anchor points of one joint also depend on the constraint forces applied at the other joints attached to the same rigid-body. More specifically, the accelerations at the anchor points will involve as many joint forces as there are joints attached to the body.

To better illustrate this, lets consider the articulated body of Fig. 5.1, repeated in Fig. 5.8 with the body index assignment for each joint. For simplicity, lets assume all 8 joints are spherical joints.[3]

With this arbitrary index assignment, bodies attached to multiple joints may have different indexes associated with each joint. For instance, body B_3 has index 1 with respect to joint J_3 and index 2 with respect to joints J_2 and J_8. Recall that the index

---

[3]The following analysis is still valid for any type of joint used.

Fig. 5.8 For each joint in the system, we assign indexes to the bodies attached to it. Bodies attached to more than one joint are assigned multiple indexes. We then use this assignment to build the linear system containing all joint equations

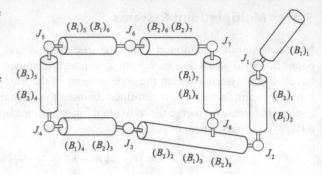

relates the sign of the joint force applied to the body, namely index 1 indicates a positive sign and index 2 indicates a negative sign. So, the constraint equation (5.21), namely

$$\ddot{\zeta}_1 = \vec{a}_{p_1} - \vec{a}_{p_2} = 0$$

applied to joint J_1, gives

$$((\mathbf{A_1})_1^1 \vec{F}_1 + (\vec{b}_1)_1) - (-(\mathbf{A_2})_1^1 \vec{F}_1 + (\mathbf{A_1})_2^1 \vec{F}_2 + (\vec{b}_2)_1) = 0, \qquad (5.43)$$

that is, the acceleration $(\vec{a}_{p_1})_1$ depends only on the joint force $\vec{F}_1$, whereas the acceleration $(\vec{a}_{p_2})_1$ depends on the joint forces $\vec{F}_1$ and $\vec{F}_2$, since body B_2 is attached to joints J_1 and J_2 (see Fig. 5.8). Since body B_2 has index 2 with respect to joint J_1, and index 1 with respect to joint J_2, we use a negative sign preceding $\vec{F}_1$ and a positive sign preceding $\vec{F}_2$ on the second term of Eq. (5.43).

Notice the extra superscript used on all matrices in Eq. (5.43). This superscript indicates the joint point the computation is referring to. For example, matrix $(\mathbf{A_2})_1^1$ is computed as the coefficient matrix of the body with index 2 of joint J_1, applied to the joint point on J_1. Matrix $(\mathbf{A_1})_2^1$, on the other hand, is the coefficient matrix of the body with index 1 of joint J_2, applied to the joint point on J_1.

In general, the terms $(\mathbf{A_i})_j^q \vec{F}_j$ and $(\vec{b}_i)_j$ refer to the coefficients of the body with index $i \in \{1, 2\}$ of joint J_j, applied to the joint point on J_q, and are computed as

$$(\mathbf{A_i})_j^q = \left(\frac{1}{m_i} \mathbf{I} - \tilde{x}_i^q \mathbf{I_i}^{-1} \tilde{x}_i^q \right)$$

$$(\vec{b}_i)_j = \frac{1}{m_i} (\vec{F}_i)_{ext} + \left(\mathbf{I_i}^{-1} ((\vec{\tau}_i)_{ext} + \vec{H}_i \times \vec{\omega}_i) \right) \times \vec{x}_i^i + \vec{\omega}_i \times (\vec{\omega}_i \times \vec{x}_i^i),$$

with

$$\vec{x}_i^q = (\vec{p}_i)_q - \vec{r}_i.$$

Notice that, for the two-body case, we have just one joint, that is, $q = i$ and the superscript index q can be ignored.

Moving all unknown forces to the left side of Eq. (5.43), we can rewrite it as

$$\left((A_1)_1^1 + (A_2)_1^1\right)\vec{F}_1 - (A_1)_2^1 \vec{F}_2 = -(\vec{b}_1)_1 + (\vec{b}_2)_1.$$

Now, applying the constraint equation (5.21) to joint J_2 gives

$$\left(-(A_2)_1^2 \vec{F}_1 + (A_1)_2^2 \vec{F}_2 + (\vec{b}_1)_2\right)$$
$$- \left(-(A_2)_2^2 \vec{F}_2 + (\vec{b}_2)_2 + (A_1)_3^2 \vec{F}_3 - (A_2)_8^2 \vec{F}_8\right) = 0,$$

which can be rearranged as

$$-(A_2)_1^2 \vec{F}_1 + \left((A_1)_2^2 + (A_2)_2^2\right)\vec{F}_2 - (A_1)_3^2 \vec{F}_3 + (A_2)_8^2 \vec{F}_8$$
$$= -(\vec{b}_1)_2 + (\vec{b}_2)_2.$$

Doing the same for all other joints, we can group the eight joint equations into the following linear system:

$$\begin{pmatrix}
(A_1)_1^1 + (A_2)_1^1 & -(A_1)_2^1 & 0 & 0 \\
-(A_2)_1^2 & (A_1)_2^2 + (A_2)_2^2 & -(A_1)_3^2 & 0 \\
0 & -(A_2)_2^3 & (A_1)_3^3 + (A_2)_3^3 & -(A_1)_4^3 \\
0 & 0 & -(A_2)_3^4 & (A_1)_4^4 + (A_2)_4^4 \\
0 & 0 & 0 & (A_2)_4^5 \\
0 & 0 & 0 & 0 \\
0 & 0 & 0 & 0 \\
0 & (A_2)_2^8 & -(A_1)_3^8 & 0
\end{pmatrix}$$

$$\begin{matrix}
0 & 0 & 0 & 0 \\
0 & 0 & 0 & (A_2)_8^2 \\
0 & 0 & 0 & -(A_2)_8^3 \\
(A_2)_5^4 & 0 & 0 & 0 \\
(A_1)_5^5 + (A_2)_5^5 & (A_1)_6^5 & 0 & 0 \\
(A_1)_5^6 & (A_1)_6^6 + (A_2)_6^6 & (A_2)_7^6 & 0 \\
0 & (A_2)_6^7 & (A_1)_7^7 + (A_2)_7^7 & (A_1)_8^7 \\
0 & 0 & (A_1)_7^8 & (A_1)_8^8 + (A_2)_8^8
\end{matrix}
\begin{pmatrix}
\vec{F}_1 \\ \vec{F}_2 \\ \vec{F}_3 \\ \vec{F}_4 \\ \vec{F}_5 \\ \vec{F}_6 \\ \vec{F}_7 \\ \vec{F}_8
\end{pmatrix}$$

$$= \begin{pmatrix}
-(\vec{b}_1)_1 + (\vec{b}_2)_1 \\
-(\vec{b}_1)_2 + (\vec{b}_2)_2 \\
-(\vec{b}_1)_3 + (\vec{b}_2)_3 \\
-(\vec{b}_1)_4 + (\vec{b}_2)_4 \\
-(\vec{b}_1)_5 + (\vec{b}_2)_5 \\
-(\vec{b}_1)_6 + (\vec{b}_2)_6 \\
-(\vec{b}_1)_7 + (\vec{b}_2)_7 \\
-(\vec{b}_1)_8 + (\vec{b}_2)_8
\end{pmatrix}.$$

Fig. 5.9 An articulated body

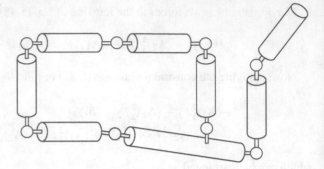

Solving this linear system for the joint forces, we can obtain the constraint forces at each joint and compute the net force and net torque acting on each body. This will let us numerically integrate the articulated system's equation of motion.

5.5   Collision Detection

The collision detection between articulated bodies and other rigid bodies, articulated rigid bodies and particles, can be viewed as an extension of the collision-detection techniques already explained in Chap. 4. Detecting collisions between articulated bodies and other bodies is the roughly same as detecting collisions between each individual link of the articulation and other bodies. Efficiency is achieved by taking advantage of the hierarchical tree representation of each link in the articulation to build a hierarchical tree representation of the articulated system as a whole.

The idea is to use a two-level hierarchical tree representation of the articulated system to efficiently carry out the collision checks. At the first level, each individual link is represented by its own hierarchical tree. The leaves of such trees are the triangular faces defining the geometric boundary of the link. At the second level, the individual hierarchical tree representations of each link are substituted for the root node of their tree, and another hierarchical tree is built having the root nodes of each link as its leaves. In other words, the second-level hierarchical tree is a tree where each of its leaves is a hierarchical tree itself. Figures 5.9, 5.10 and 5.11 show this two-level hierarchical tree representation for a simple articulated body.

The collision check involving articulated rigid bodies is therefore a two-step process. Checking for collisions between two articulated bodies consists of first checking for geometric intersections between their second-level hierarchical tree representations. If no intersections are found, then the articulated bodies are not colliding. Otherwise, the intersecting leaves of their second-level representation are substituted for their corresponding first-level hierarchical tree (recall that each leaf of the second level is a hierarchical tree of itself). The algorithm proceeds checking for collisions between the hierarchical tree representations of the intersecting leaves. If no intersections are found, then the articulated bodies are not colliding. Otherwise, the intersecting leaves of the first level are substituted for the triangular faces they

Fig. 5.10 First-level
hierarchical tree
representation contains the
individual representations of
each link of the articulated
body shown in Fig. 5.9

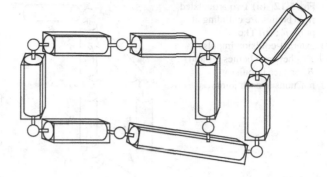

Fig. 5.11 Root node of the
hierarchical tree
representation of each link
obtained in the first level is
used as a leaf of the
hierarchical tree built at the
second level. The root node
of the tree at the second level
contains the entire articulated
structure, as shown here

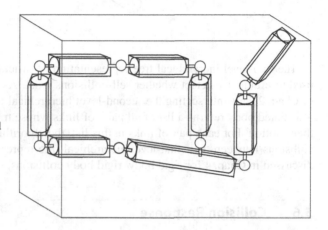

represent. At this point, several triangle–triangle intersection tests are carried out
to detect whether there are pairs of intersecting triangular faces, one on each articulated body being checked for collision. Whenever an intersection is detected, the
articulated bodies are said to be colliding and their trajectories are backtracked in
time to the moment before the most recent collision, that is, just before a pair of
triangular faces intersects for the first time. The geometric displacement of the faces
is then used to compute a collision normal and tangent plane, in the same manner
already explained in Sect. 4.4, for rigid body–rigid body collisions.

Checking for collisions between an articulated body and a single rigid body is
equivalent to checking for collisions between two articulated bodies, with one of
them having just one link and zero joints. Again, we start by checking for geometric intersections between the root node of the hierarchical tree representation of the
rigid body and the second-level hierarchical tree representing the articulated body. If
an intersection is detected, then the leaves of the second-level tree that are intersecting the root node of the single rigid body are further expanded into their corresponding first-level hierarchical trees. The collision detection then proceeds by checking
for intersections between the expanded leaves and the rigid body's hierarchical tree.
The latter is analogous to intersecting two rigid bodies.

Fig. 5.12 (a) Two articulated rigid bodies are colliding at point $\vec{p}_i$; (b) The external-collision impulse $\vec{P}_{1,4}$ between bodies B_1 and B_4 creates impulsive reactions at each joint

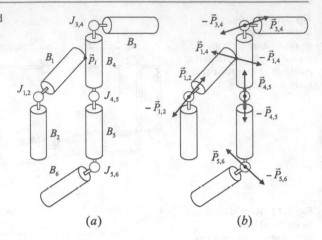

(a) (b)

The two-level hierarchical tree representation of articulated bodies can also be used to efficiently detect whether self-collisions exist. As explained in Sect. 2.5.2 of Chap. 2, self-intersecting the second-level hierarchical tree representation of the articulated body returns a list of all pairs of links whose trajectories overlap during their motion. For each pair of links in this list, the algorithm proceeds checking for collisions between their first-level hierarchical tree representations, the same way discussed in Chap. 4 for rigid body–rigid body collisions.

5.6 Collision Response

Responding to collisions involving articulated bodies is inevitably a multi-collision problem. Whenever a collision is detected with one of the articulated links, the resulting collision impulse propagates its reaction to all other bodies in the articulation through their joint connections. In other words, *external collisions* between the articulated rigid body and other bodies (possibly other articulated rigid bodies as well) create a sequence of *internal collisions* between the links at their connecting joints. The way this sequence of internal collisions is resolved depends on the mathematical model used to describe the collisions.

Consider the situation illustrated by Fig. 5.12(a), where two articulated rigid bodies are colliding at point $\vec{p}_i$. The collision normal and tangent plane at the collision point $\vec{p}_i$ are computed from the bodies' relative geometric displacement just before their collision, using the same techniques discussed in Sect. 4.11, for the case of rigid body–rigid body collisions.

The external-collision impulse $\vec{P}_{1,4}$ generated by this collision will affect the dynamic state of bodies B_1 and B_4, as well as all other bodies attached to them. This modification of the dynamic state of each link is represented by a set of internal-collision impulses, one for each joint of the articulation (see Fig. 5.12(b)). Clearly, one way to solve this multiple-collision problem would be to propagate the impulsive reactions to the external collision as if it were a wave passing through each

Fig. 5.13 Hazardous
situation when incrementally
computing the
internal-collision impulses at
each joint in response to an
external collision. The
existence of closed loops in
the articulated topology
requires all internal impulses
to be computed at once

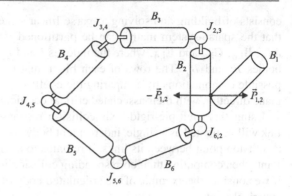

joint. In this case, the joint-impulsive reactions would be incrementally computed
as if they happened at different instants. For example, we would first compute $\vec{P}_{1,4}$
ignoring the internal dynamics of the articulation. Then we would solve for $\vec{P}_{3,4}$ and
$\vec{P}_{4,5}$ on one articulation, and for $\vec{P}_{1,2}$ on the other. Finally, we would compute $\vec{P}_{5,6}$
taking into account that the other impulses have already been applied to the system
(i.e., they occurred at different instants).

There are two fundamental problems with this approach. The first problem is efficiency. In the particular situation shown in Fig. 5.12, we would have to execute the
collision-response module three consecutive times, one for computing $\vec{P}_{1,4}$, another
for $\vec{P}_{3,4}$ and $\vec{P}_{4,5}$, and a third for $\vec{P}_{5,6}$. The second problem has the potential to never
successfully complete the internal-collision-impulse computations, by going to an
infinite-loop mode. This can potentially happen every time one of the articulated
systems has cycles (see Fig. 5.13).

In this book, we shall overlook the propagation time and assume that all internal
collisions happen at the same time as the external collisions generating them. By so
doing, the external-collision impulses will *simultaneously* affect the dynamic state
of all links. Put another way, all collision impulses (external and internal) will be
simultaneously computed by solving a linear system of equations involving the dy
namic state of the bodies and the impulses. Notice, however, that, even though this
assumption produces very good results for articulations containing a small number
of links, it can significantly over simplify the impulse-propagation mechanism for
articulated systems containing a large number of interconnected links.

In the following sections, we shall examine in more detail how the several
collision-response mechanisms discussed in Chap. 4 can be adapted to the case of
articulated systems.

5.6.1 Computing Impulsive Forces for Single or Multiple External Collisions

The simultaneous computation of all internal and external collision impulses can
be done using exactly the same multiple-rigid-body-collision techniques already
developed in Sect. 4.11.2. Recall that the computation of multiple-collision impulses

consists of building and solving a sparse linear system of equations. It was shown that the sparse-system matrix can be partitioned into block matrices of the form $\mathbf{A_{i,q}}$, $\mathbf{B_{i,q}}$, $\mathbf{C_{i,q}}$ and $\mathbf{E_{i,q}}$, where the indexes i and q refer to collision C_{iq} between bodies B_i and B_q. The rows of each block matrix are chosen from a set of four possible combinations by comparing the coefficient of friction along each tangent-plane direction with their associated critical coefficient of friction.[4]

Using this multiple-rigid-body-collision response framework, each individual link will be treated as a single, independent body, and each joint will be dealt with as a collision point between its links. It remains to assure the joint constraints at each joint when computing their corresponding collision impulses. This is best illustrated if we consider the example of the articulated body of Fig. 5.8, where all 8 joints are spherical joints.

In the case of spherical joints, the relative motion of its links is constrained to rotations only. According to Eqs. (5.20) and (5.21), the position, velocity and acceleration of the joint points on each link should coincide throughout the motion. This was used in Sect. 5.3.1 to derive expressions relating the joint forces and the dynamics of their links. Here we use the other two constraints, on position and velocity, to relate the impulses at each joint with the dynamic state of their corresponding links.

Let's start by analyzing the position constraint. Because the positions of the joint points on each link should coincide for the entire motion (see Eq. (5.20)), they cannot slide with respect to each other during a collision. In other words, the use of the critical-coefficient-of-friction value to determine whether the colliding points (i.e., joint anchor points) are sliding or sticking during a collision is no longer necessary. There is no need to compute the value for each joint because we already know that the collision points should stick to each other during a collision.

As for the velocity constraint, the joint points should always remain with the same velocity throughout the motion (see Eq. (5.21)), that is, the links should not separate at their joint points after any collision. This condition can be translated into all joint collisions having a zero coefficient of restitution (inelastic collisions). Therefore, in the particular case of spherical joints, the four possible cases for defining the rows of each block matrix $\mathbf{A_{i,q}}$, $\mathbf{B_{i,q}}$, $\mathbf{C_{i,q}}$ and $\mathbf{E_{i,q}}$, as discussed in Sect. 4.11.2, are reduced to just one case, namely the case in which

$$\mathbf{A_{i,q}} = \mathbf{0} \qquad \mathbf{B_{i,q}} = \mathbf{I} \qquad \mathbf{C_{i,q}} = -\tilde{r}_i \qquad \mathbf{E_{i,q}} = \tilde{r}_q. \tag{5.44}$$

Basically, the coefficient-of-restitution equation should be replaced by the velocity-constraint equation imposed by the type of joint being used. In the case of spherical joints, the velocity-constraint equation is equivalent to forcing the coefficient of restitution to be zero, but this is not always the case for other types of joints, such as the revolute and prismatic joints discussed in Sects. 5.3.3 and 5.3.5, respectively.

---

[4]Refer to Sect. 4.11.1 for a detailed discussion of the techniques used to compute the critical coefficient of friction.

In summary, we build the system matrix containing all internal and external impulses by selecting the appropriate block-matrix representation for each collision. The block-matrix representation associated with all external collisions is selected following the same rules applied to the single-rigid-body-collision case, in which the colliding points can slide or stick to each other during the collision.

5.6.2 Computing Contact Forces for Single or Multiple External Contacts

Whenever one or more links of an articulated body are in contact with each other, or with other bodies in the simulated world, the contact force at the each contact point will affect the dynamics of motion of the entire articulation. This is analogous to the multiple-rigid-body-contact situation described in Sect. 4.11.4. Recall that the simultaneous computation of all contact forces involves building and solving a Linear Complementarity Problem (LCP), with the contact forces and accelerations constrained to non-negative values. Contact points that end with zero relative accelerations remain in contact after the application of the contact forces, whereas contacts with positive accelerations will break up as soon as the contact forces are applied. Contacts having zero contact forces are just touching each other and may or may not break up, depending on the value of their corresponding relative accelerations.

The idea here is to use the exact techniques already described in Sect. 4.11.4. The only modifications needed are those necessary to assure the joint constraints after the contact forces be applied to the system. These modifications should be implemented as part of the LCP solution method described in Appendix I (Chap. 14). According to the results presented in Appendix I (Chap. 14), the LCP solution method incrementally computes the contact force at contact C_i while enforcing the normal- and frictional-contact conditions at all other contacts j (with $j < i$) already considered. This requires bookkeeping the indexes of all contact points already considered such that, at any point during the computation, an index will be in one subset of each of the following three groups.

1. ZA_n or ZF_n, depending on its normal-acceleration and contact-force components along the normal direction $\vec{n}$.
2. ZA_t, $MaxF_t$ or $MinF_t$, depending on its tangential-acceleration and contact-force components along the tangent direction $\vec{t}$.
3. ZA_k, $MaxF_k$ or $MinF_k$, depending on its tangential-acceleration and contact-force components along the tangent direction $\vec{k}$.

Lets again consider the example of the articulated body of Fig. 5.8, where all 8 joints are spherical joints. Because the position of the joint anchor points must coincide throughout the entire motion, it is necessary to assure that the relative acceleration at all joint contacts must always be zero. This requires modifying the LCP solution method to assign all indexes corresponding to a joint contact to groups ZA_n, ZA_t and ZA_k, and never displace them. Doing this guarantees that the relative acceleration at the joint points will be zero after all contact forces are applied, that is, that the links will remain connected at their joint points throughout the entire motion.

According to the LCP solution method discussed in Appendix I (Chap. 14), the contact-point indexes are moved back and forth between different subsets of each of the three main groups, depending on their relative accelerations or contact forces be assigned a negative value. For instance, a contact point with index in ZA_n has a positive normal-contact-force component and zero relative normal acceleration. If in the next iteration of the LCP solution algorithm the normal-contact-force component assumes a negative value, then the system is evolved up to the point at which the normal-contact-force component assumes a zero value, and the index of such a contact point is moved from ZA_n to ZF_n in order to prevent the normal-contact-force component becoming negative. This in turn permits the relative normal acceleration to assume any positive value.

In the case of a spherical joint contact, we need to force the relative acceleration to be always zero. This may require having a negative contact force at the joint, since we cannot move the contact index out of the zero-acceleration subsets. The following modifications are needed for computing contact forces when the contact index refers to a spherical joint contact.

1. The joint contact force can have any value, as opposed to having only non-negative values (as is the case of external contacts). In practice, a negative joint contact force means that the local-coordinate frame used at the joint contact (i.e., the direction of the normal and tangential coordinate axes) is inverted.
2. The tangential components of the joint-contact force can also have any value, as opposed to being limited to μF_n, that is, the normal component multiplied by the coefficient of friction associated with the tangent direction being considered.

In summary, the LCP solution method discussed in Appendix I (Chap. 14) can be modified to deal with joint contact forces by forcing their indexes to be always included in the zero-acceleration subsets, and by letting the joint contact forces assume any finite value. This requires keeping track of which indexes correspond to joint contacts, and adding a conditional statement at the force-computation module to not bother if the contact force of a joint contact becomes negative.

As for implementation, numerical round-off errors can offset the joint anchor points by small values each time the simulation loop is executed. The offset is usually not noticeable at the first few simulation time steps, but can become a problem for simulations that are executed for a substantial amount of time. In these cases, the position of the joint points computed using their corresponding links' dynamic state may no longer coincide with each other, reaching a situation in which their separation is visible on the screen. This is clearly not a "feature" that dynamic-simulation systems want to exhibit. A practical workaround to situations like this consists of adding a fictitious spring with zero resting length connecting the joint points. Whenever the joint points separate from each other owing to round-off errors, the spring force will bring the points together again. The stiffness of the spring to be used depends on the mass of the bodies connected by the joint (the heavier the bodies, the stiffer the spring should be).

5.7   Notes and Comments

In this chapter, we have tried to cover a small but important subset of the several types of techniques applicable to mechanisms commonly used in dynamic simulations of articulated systems. Even though we have concentrated our analysis on rigid bodies connected by commonly used joints, the same techniques can be applied to other types of joints. Different types of joints have different joint constraints to be enforced, thus requiring modifications on the actual constraint equations to be used. However, the general principle of defining the joint constraints and differentiating them twice in time to relate the joint forces and the dynamic state of the articulated system remains unchanged. The differentiation in time may be easier or more difficult to obtain depending on the joint being considered, but the principle remains the same.

As for responding to collisions, independent of the type of joint being used, its velocity constraint should always replace the coefficient-of-restitution equation. The latter is applicable only when the colliding bodies are not interconnected at the collision point. The contact-force computation, on the other hand, may require creating other types of groups on the LCP solution method described in Appendix I (Chap. 14), in order to accommodate the joint constraints. For example, in the case of prismatic joints, the interconnected bodies are constrained to translations along the joint axis only. The relative acceleration of the bodies along the joint axis can be zero, positive or negative, whereas their relative-acceleration components on the contact plane perpendicular to the joint axis should always be zero. This in turn requires creating special-purpose subsets to keep track of the indexes of the prismatic-joint contact forces. For instance, we can think of creating a $ZAany_n$ subset for normal component accelerations that can assume any value.

The joint constraint formulations covered in this book were based on Shabana [Sha10, Sha98], Vondrak et al. [Cas10], Garstenauer et al. [Gar06], Hecker [Hec00a, Hec00b] and Baraff [Bar96]. Other interesting types of constraint formulations can be found in Barzel et al. [BB88]. The use of springs, as well as other techniques, to offset the existence of numerical round-off errors on the position of the joint points can be found in Baumgarte [Bau72] and Barzel et al. [BB88], among others.

Mirtich's [Mir96b] work on constrained rigid-body dynamics is focused on using revolute and prismatic joints to interconnect bodies. His formulation uses spatial-operator algebra (see also Rodriguez et al. [RJKD92]), and extends Featherstone [Fea83, Fea87] to cope with tree-like linkage structures; it further presented some control-systems techniques to kinematically control[5] the motion of articulated bodies. Brach [Bra91] considers chains of rigid bodies interconnected by several types of joints, but limits his analyzes to the two-dimensional case.

---

[5]By kinematical control we mean that the linear and angular position, velocity and acceleration of the bodies are obtained from an animation system, possibly by interpolating their values between two consecutive animation frames.

5.8   Exercises

1. In most cases, it is necessary to impose limits on the motion allowed by joint
   constraints. For example, the amount of relative translation for prismatic joints
   is limited to the actual physical dimension of the hardware used to build the
   joint. Depending on the joint type, there can be limits on translation and rotation
   between the articulated bodies.
   (a) Define a generic joint constraint function that can be used to impose limits
       on the relative translation at the anchor points.
   (b) Define a generic joint constraint function that can be used to impose limits
       on the relative rotation at the anchor points along a joint rotation axis.
   (c) Compute the first and second time derivatives of the joint constraints speci-
       fied in items (a) and (b) above.
   (d) Which one of the following approaches to enforce the joint constraint limits
       is better: a force-based, an impulse-based, a position-based or a combination
       of each? Explain.
2. Fixed joints can be used to simulate fracture in rigid-body dynamics. Usually,
   the rigid body pieces that make up the fractured body are pasted together using
   rigid joints. As the simulation evolves, the force and torque on such joints are
   monitored to check if a user-defined limit has been reached. Once the limit is
   reached, the rigid joint is disabled and the body pieces are allowed to move in
   separate directions as independent bodies.
   (a) How the mass properties of the body can be computed from the mass prop-
       erties of its pieces?
   (b) Should the collision detection module use the entire object as a single entity
       or consider each individual piece as a separate object even when the pieces
       are still connected by rigid joints?
3. Constraint functions can also be used to implement motors to control the relative
   linear and angular velocities of rigid bodies. Lets consider a motor connecting
   rigid bodies B_1 and B_2 at anchor points $\vec{p}_1$ and $\vec{p}_2$, respectively.
   (a) Assume the motor has 3 degrees-of-freedom and is used to control the rela-
       tive linear velocity at the anchor points. More specifically, the motor is used
       to force their relative linear velocity to follow a user-defined function $f(t)$.
       i. Write the velocity-level constraint function for this motor.
       ii. Compute the first derivative of the above constraint function to arrive at
           the acceleration-level constraint function to be used for this motor.
       iii. Repeat the above steps for the case in which the motor is used to control
           the relative angular velocity instead.
   (b) Assume the motor has 1 degree-of-freedom and is used to control the relative
       linear velocity along a local-coordinate axis $\vec{m}_l$ attached to body B_1. Let $\vec{m}$ be
       the world-coordinate frame representation of $\vec{m}_l$.
       i. Compute $\vec{m}$ as a function of the rotation matrix of body B_1.
       ii. Write the velocity-level constraint function for this motor along $\vec{m}$.
       iii. Compute the first derivative of the above constraint function to arrive at
           the acceleration-level constraint function to be used for this motor.

iv. Repeat the above steps for the case in which the motor is used to control the relative angular velocity along $\vec{m}$ instead.

References

[Bar96] Baraff, D.: Linear-time dynamics using Lagrange multipliers. Comput. Graph. (Proc. SIGGRAPH) **30**, 137–146 (1996)

[Bau72] Baumgarte, J.: Stabilization of constraints and integrals of motion in dynamical systems. Comput. Methods Appl. Mech., 1–36 (1972)

[BB88] Barzel, R., Barr, A.H.: A modeling system based on dynamic constraints. Comput. Graph. (Proc. SIGGRAPH) **22**, 179–188 (1988)

[Bra91] Brach, R.M. (ed.): Mechanical Impact Dynamics: Rigid Body Collisions. Wiley, New York (1991)

[Cas10] Casolo, F. (ed.): Motion Control, pp. 1–30. InTech (www.intechopen.com) (2010)

[Fea83] Featherstone, R.: The calculation of robot dynamics using articulated-body inertias. Int. J. Robot. Res. **2**, 13–30 (1983)

[Fea87] Featherstone, R. (ed.): Robot Dynamics Algorithms. Kluwer Academic, Dordrecht (1987)

[Gar06] Garstenauer, H.: A unified framework for rigid body dynamics. Master's Thesis, Johannes Kepler University (2006)

[Hec00a] Hecker, C.: How to simulate a ponytail, part 1. Game Developer Mag., 34–42 (March 2000)

[Hec00b] Hecker, C.: How to simulate a ponytail, part 2. Game Developer Mag., 42–53 (April 2000)

[Mir96b] Mirtich, B.V.: Impulse-based dynamic simulation of rigid body systems. PhD Thesis, University of California, Berkeley (1996)

[RJKD92] Rodriguez, G., Jain, A., Kreutz-Delgado, K.: Spatial operator algebra for multibody system dynamics. J. Astronaut. Sci. **40**, 27–50 (1992)

[Sha98] Shabana, A.A.: Dynamics of Multibody Systems. Cambridge University Press, Cambridge (1998)

[Sha10] Shabana, A.A.: Computational Dynamics. Wiley, New York (2010)

Part II
Mathematical Toolset

The following nine chapters will guide the readers through the details of several mathematical algorithms used as "black box" modules in the implementation of the real-time dynamic simulation engine discussed in Part I. Each of these modules stand alone as a broad and complex topic in itself.

Appendix A: Useful 3D Geometric Constructions

6.1 Introduction

In this appendix, we shall cover some geometrical constructions used as building blocks to implement the several intersection tests that are part of the particle–particle, particle–rigid body and rigid body–rigid body collision-detection algorithms presented in this book. We shall also discuss in Sect. 6.6 how the tangent plane of a collision (or contact) can be determined given the collision (or contact) normal vector.

We shall use the following notation to describe some of these tests. A point P_i in 3D space will be denoted as

$$\vec{p}_i = ((p_i)_x, (p_i)_y, (p_i)_z).$$

A line segment L_s is defined by its two end points $\vec{p}_1$ and $\vec{p}_2$, and is given by

$$\vec{p} = \vec{p}_1 + k(\vec{p}_2 - \vec{p}_1),$$

with $0 \leq k \leq 1$.

The plane β is described by its normal $\vec{n}_\beta$ and a point $\vec{p}_\beta$ in the plane. Any point $\vec{p} \in \beta$ satisfies the equation

$$\vec{p} \cdot \vec{n}_\beta = d_\beta,$$

where d_β is the plane constant obtained from

$$d_\beta = \vec{p}_\beta \cdot \vec{n}_\beta.$$

M.G. Coutinho, *Guide to Dynamic Simulations of Rigid Bodies and Particle Systems*, Simulation Foundations, Methods and Applications, DOI 10.1007/978-1-4471-4417-5_6, © Springer-Verlag London 2013

Fig. 6.1 Projecting $\vec{p}$ on line L

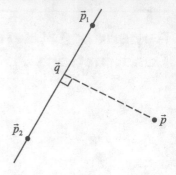

6.2   Projection of a Point on a Line

The projection $\vec{q}$ of point $\vec{p}$ on line L passing through points $\vec{p}_1$ and $\vec{p}_2$ is a point of L (see Fig. 6.1) and therefore satisfies the line equation, that is

$$\vec{q} = \vec{p}_1 + k(\vec{p}_2 - \vec{p}_1), \tag{6.1}$$

where $k \in \mathbb{R}$ is a scalar variable to be determined. Notice also that the vector $(\vec{p} - \vec{q})$ is perpendicular to the line, that is

$$(\vec{p} - \vec{q}) \cdot (\vec{p}_2 - \vec{p}_1) = 0. \tag{6.2}$$

Substituting Eq. (6.1) into (6.2) and solving for k, we have

$$k = \frac{(\vec{p} - \vec{p}_1) \cdot (\vec{p}_2 - \vec{p}_1)}{(\vec{p}_2 - \vec{p}_1) \cdot (\vec{p}_2 - \vec{p}_1)}. \tag{6.3}$$

The projection point $\vec{q}$ is directly obtained by substituting Eq. (6.3) into (6.1). The distance d between $\vec{p}$ and line L is given by

$$d = |\vec{p} - \vec{q}|.$$

6.3   Projection of a Point on a Plane

The projection $\vec{q}$ of a point $\vec{p}$ on a plane β can be computed as follows. The projected point $\vec{q}$ satisfies the plane equation, that is

$$\vec{q} \cdot \vec{n}_\beta = d_\beta. \tag{6.4}$$

Moreover, the vector $(\vec{p} - \vec{q})$ is parallel to the plane normal $\vec{n}_\beta$ (see Fig. 6.2), that is

$$(\vec{p} - \vec{q}) = k\vec{n}_\beta, \tag{6.5}$$

where k is a scalar that needs to be determined.

Fig. 6.2 Projecting $\vec{p}$ on plane β

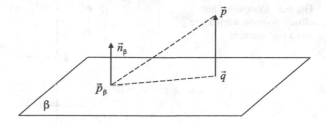

Substituting Eq. (6.5) into (6.4), and solving for k, we obtain

$$k = \frac{\vec{p} \cdot \vec{n}_\beta - d_\beta}{\vec{n}_\beta \cdot \vec{n}_\beta}. \qquad (6.6)$$

Substituting Eq. (6.6) into (6.5), we obtain the projected point $\vec{q}$

$$\vec{q} = \vec{p} - \frac{\vec{p} \cdot \vec{n}_\beta - d_\beta}{\vec{n}_\beta \cdot \vec{n}_\beta} \vec{n}_\beta.$$

The distance d between point $\vec{p}$ and plane β is computed from

$$d = |\vec{p} - \vec{q}| = \left| \frac{\vec{p} \cdot \vec{n}_\beta - d_\beta}{\vec{n}_\beta \cdot \vec{n}_\beta} \right|.$$

6.4 Intersection of a Line Segment and a Plane

The intersection between a line segment and a plane can be the line segment itself (if the line is in the plane), a point or an empty set. Let L be the line segment connecting points $\vec{p}_1$ and $\vec{p}_2$, and let β be the plane with which we want to compute the intersection.

The intersection will be the line itself whenever

$$(\vec{p}_2 - \vec{p}_1) \cdot \vec{n}_\beta = 0,$$

that is, the line is perpendicular to the plane normal, and

$$\vec{p}_1 \cdot \vec{n}_\beta = d_\beta = \vec{p}_2 \cdot \vec{n}_\beta,$$

that is, its points belong to the plane as well.

Now, suppose the line is such that

$$(\vec{p}_2 - \vec{p}_1) \cdot \vec{n}_\beta \neq 0.$$

The idea is then to first intersect the infinite line supporting the line segment with the plane (let's call $\vec{g}$ this intersection point), and then check whether $\vec{g}$ lies between the end points defining the segment. If it does, then $\vec{g}$ is the actual intersection.

Fig. 6.3 Computing the closest point between a line and a line segment

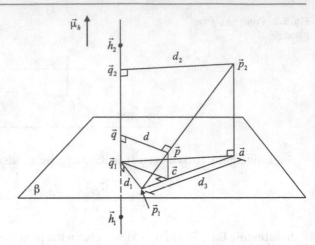

Otherwise, the line segment does not intersect the plane. Let's first compute the intersection point $\vec{g}$. We know $\vec{g}$ lies on the infinite line supporting the line segment, that is

$$\vec{g} = \vec{p}_1 + k_g(\vec{p}_2 - \vec{p}_1),\tag{6.7}$$

where $k_g \in \mathbb{R}$ is a scalar variable to be determined. We also know that the intersection point belongs to the plane, that is

$$\vec{g} \cdot \vec{n}_\beta = d_\beta.\tag{6.8}$$

Substituting Eq. (6.8) into (6.7), and solving for k_g, we obtain

$$k_g = \frac{d_\beta - \vec{p}_1 \cdot \vec{n}_\beta}{(\vec{p}_2 - \vec{p}_1) \cdot \vec{n}_\beta}.$$

If $0 \leq k_g \leq 1$, then the intersection point $\vec{g}$ lies between the end points of the line segment, and the line segment does intersect the plane. Otherwise, the intersection point lies outside the segment and the plane does not intersect the line segment.

6.5   Closest Point Between a Line and a Line Segment

Given a line L passing through points $\vec{h}_1$ and $\vec{h}_2$, and a line segment L_s defined by its two end points $\vec{p}_1$ and $\vec{p}_2$, we want to determine the point $\vec{p} \in L_s$ that is closer to line L than any other point in L_s. This is illustrated in Fig. 6.3.

The closest point $\vec{p}$ belongs to line segment L_s, that is

$$\vec{p} = \vec{p}_1 + k_p(\vec{p}_2 - \vec{p}_1),\tag{6.9}$$

where $0 \leq k_p \leq 1$ is a scalar to be determined. Alternatively, we can rewrite Eq. (6.9) as

$$k_p = \frac{|\vec{p} - \vec{p}_1|}{|\vec{p}_2 - \vec{p}_1|}. \tag{6.10}$$

Let $\vec{q}_1$ and $\vec{q}_2$ be the projections of points $\vec{p}_1$ and $\vec{p}_2$ on line[1] L. We compute d_1 and d_2 as the distance between points $\vec{p}_1$ and $\vec{p}_2$ and their associated projection points.

Now, consider the auxiliary plane β perpendicular to line L and passing through $\vec{p}_1$ (see Fig. 6.3). Let $\vec{a}$ be the projection of point $\vec{p}_2$ on plane β, computed according to Sect. 6.3. We compute the distance d_3 between $\vec{a}$ and $\vec{p}_1$.

Let $\vec{c}$ represent the projection of point $\vec{p}$ (still to be determined) on plane β. By construction, triangles $(\vec{p}_1, \vec{c}, \vec{p})$ and $(\vec{p}_1, \vec{a}, \vec{p}_2)$ are similar, that is

$$\frac{|\vec{c} - \vec{p}_1|}{|\vec{a} - \vec{p}_1|} = \frac{|\vec{p} - \vec{p}_1|}{|\vec{p}_2 - \vec{p}_1|} = k_p, \tag{6.11}$$

where the last equality was obtained using Eq. (6.10). Also, notice that triangles $(\vec{a}, \vec{q}_1, \vec{c})$ and $(\vec{p}_1, \vec{c}, \vec{q}_1)$ are rectangular on $\vec{c}$, and

$$|\vec{q}_1 - \vec{a}| = |\vec{q}_2 - \vec{p}_2| = d_2.$$

Applying the Pythagorean theorem to each triangle, we obtain

$$d_1^2 = |\vec{c} - \vec{q}_1|^2 + |\vec{c} - \vec{p}_1|^2$$
$$d_2^2 = |\vec{c} - \vec{q}_1|^2 + |\vec{a} - \vec{c}|^2.$$

Eliminating $|\vec{c} - \vec{q}_1|^2$ from the above equations, we have

$$d_1^2 - d_2^2 = |\vec{c} - \vec{p}_1|^2 - |\vec{a} - \vec{c}|^2. \tag{6.12}$$

Factoring out the right-hand side of Eq. (6.12):

$$d_1^2 - d_2^2 = (|\vec{c} - \vec{p}_1| + |\vec{a} - \vec{c}|)(|\vec{c} - \vec{p}_1| - |\vec{a} - \vec{c}|). \tag{6.13}$$

From Fig. 6.3, we immediately have

$$|\vec{c} - \vec{p}_1| + |\vec{a} - \vec{c}| = d_3. \tag{6.14}$$

Substituting Eq. (6.14) into (6.13):

$$|\vec{c} - \vec{p}_1| - |\vec{a} - \vec{c}| = \frac{(d_1^2 - d_2^2)}{d_3}. \tag{6.15}$$

---

[1]The projection of a point on a line was already discussed in Sect. 6.2.

Solving Eqs. (6.15) and (6.14) for $|\vec{c} - \vec{p}_1|$, we obtain

$$|\vec{c} - \vec{p}_1| = \frac{(d_1^2 - d_2^2 + d_3^2)}{2d_3}. \tag{6.16}$$

Finally, substituting Eqs. (6.16) and (6.14) into (6.11) we compute the scalar k_p as

$$k_p = \frac{(d_1^2 - d_2^2 + d_3^2)}{2d_3^2}.$$

If $0 < k_p < 1$, then the closest point $\vec{p}$ lies inside the line segment L_s and is obtained directly from Eq. (6.9). If $k_p \leq 0$, then we set $\vec{p} = \vec{p}_1$. Otherwise, $k_p \geq 1$ and we set $\vec{p} = \vec{p}_2$.

6.6   Computing the Collision- or Contact-Local Frame from the Collision- or Contact-Normal Vector

The relative displacement of the colliding particles or rigid bodies is used to determine the collision normal at the collision point. The actual computation of the collision normal is slightly different depending on whether we are considering particle–particle, particle–rigid body or rigid body–rigid body collisions. Assume that the collision- or contact-normal vector is given by $\vec{n}$, and that the tangent plane is defined by two vectors $\vec{t}$ and $\vec{k}$, mutually perpendicular and perpendicular to $\vec{n}$ as well. Together, they form the local-coordinate system, usually referred to as the *collision frame*, with origin at the collision (or contact) point. The computation of the tangent plane is done after the collision normal is determined, and depends strictly on it.

All impulsive and contact forces are computed with respect to their local collision frames. Assuming $\vec{n}$ is known, the question is how we can determine the other vectors $\vec{t}$ and $\vec{k}$? The answer is simple: there are several ways we can generate the other two vectors from the normal vector. In this book, however, we shall use the following approach.

Let the collision normal be given as $\vec{n} = (n_x, n_y, n_z)$. The vector $\vec{t} = (t_x, t_y, t_z)$ is perpendicular to $\vec{n}$, that is

$$\vec{t} \cdot \vec{n} = t_x n_x + t_y n_y + t_z n_z = 0. \tag{6.17}$$

Clearly, we have just one equation and three variables, namely t_x, t_y and t_z. The idea is then to establish some rules to assign values to the variables so that Eq. (6.17) can be satisfied. To that end, we undertake the following steps. Compute the absolute value of each component of the normal vector $\vec{n}$, and compare them such that:

1. If $|n_x| \leq |n_y|$ and $|n_x| \leq |n_z|$, then set the auxiliary vector $\vec{a}$ to

$$\vec{a} = (0, n_z, -n_y).$$

2. If $|n_y| \le |n_x|$ and $|n_y| \le |n_z|$, then set the auxiliary vector $\vec{a}$ to

$$\vec{a} = (-n_z, 0, n_x).$$

3. Otherwise, set the auxiliary vector $\vec{a}$ to

$$\vec{a} = (n_y, -n_x, 0).$$

The tangent vector $\vec{t}$ will then be given by

$$\vec{t} = \frac{\vec{a}}{|\vec{a}|}.$$

The other vector $\vec{k}$ is immediately obtained as

$$\vec{k} = \vec{n} \times \vec{t},$$

since it is perpendicular to both $\vec{n}$ and $\vec{t}$. Notice that this choice for $\vec{a}$ forms a positively oriented basis $(\vec{n}, \vec{t}, \vec{k})$ following the right-hand rule for the local-coordinate frame at the collision or contact point.

6.7   Representing Cross-Products as Matrix–Vector Multiplication

Sometimes it is useful to represent a cross-product as a matrix–vector multiplication. Consider the cross-product between vectors $\vec{a} = (a_x, a_y, a_z)$ and $\vec{b} = (b_x, b_y, b_z)$, namely

$$\vec{a} \times \vec{b} = \begin{pmatrix} a_y b_z - b_y a_z \\ -a_x b_z + b_x a_z \\ a_x b_y - b_x a_y \end{pmatrix}. \tag{6.18}$$

Now, let's define the matrix $\tilde{a}$ obtained from vector $\vec{a}$ as

$$\tilde{a} = \begin{pmatrix} 0 & -a_z & a_y \\ a_z & 0 & -a_x \\ -a_y & a_x & 0 \end{pmatrix}. \tag{6.19}$$

If we multiply $\vec{b}$ by the matrix $\tilde{a}$, we obtain

$$\tilde{a}\vec{b} = \begin{pmatrix} 0 & -a_z & a_y \\ a_z & 0 & -a_x \\ -a_y & a_x & 0 \end{pmatrix} \begin{pmatrix} b_x \\ b_y \\ b_z \end{pmatrix} = \begin{pmatrix} a_y b_z - b_y a_z \\ -a_x b_z + b_x a_z \\ a_x b_y - b_x a_y \end{pmatrix}. \tag{6.20}$$

Comparing Eqs. (6.18) and (6.20), we immediately conclude that

$$\vec{a} \times \vec{b} = \tilde{\mathbf{a}}\vec{b}. \tag{6.21}$$

Equation (6.21) is known as the matrix–vector representation of the cross-product between vectors $\vec{a}$ and $\vec{b}$, where the matrix $\tilde{\mathbf{a}}$ is constructed from vector $\vec{a}$ as indicated in Eq. (6.19).

6.8   Interpolating Positions and Orientations

In the context of collision detection, the object's non-linear motion from t_0 to t_1 obtained from the numerical integration of its dynamic state is replaced by a linear motion with constant translation and rotation.

Let the position and orientation of the object at time instant t_0 be represented by the vector $\vec{p}_0$ and the rotation matrix $\mathbf{R}_0$, respectively. Similarly, let the position and orientation of the object at time instant t_1 be represented by $\vec{p}_1$ and $\mathbf{R}_1$, respectively.

The constant linear and angular velocities $\vec{v}$ and $\vec{\omega}$ associated with the linearized version of the motion, are computed as follow:

$$\vec{v} = \frac{(\vec{p}_1 - \vec{p}_0)}{(t_1 - t_0)}$$

$$\vec{\omega} = \frac{\alpha \vec{r}}{(t_1 - t_0)},$$

where $\vec{r}$ and α are the rotation axis and angle of the delta rotation matrix

$$\triangle \mathbf{R} = \mathbf{R}_1 \mathbf{R}_0^t.$$

As discussed in Appendix C (Chap. 8), the rotation of an object can be represented by either a rotation matrix or a unit quaternion. Let $\vec{q}_0$ be the unit quaternion representation of the rotation matrix $\mathbf{R}_0$. The position and orientation of the object at any time t, with $t_0 \leq t \leq t_1$, can be obtained using linear interpolation as follow:

$$\vec{p}(t) = \vec{p}_0 + (t - t_0)\vec{v}$$

$$\vec{q}(t) = \vec{q}_0 + \frac{(t - t_0)}{2} \vec{\omega}\vec{q}_0 \tag{6.22}$$

with $\vec{q}(t)$ being the quaternion representation of the rotation matrix $\mathbf{R}(t)$. Notice that $\vec{q}(t)$ needs to be normalized (i.e., turned into a unit quaternion) before it can be converted to its rotation matrix representation $\mathbf{R}(t)$. Also, the angular velocity vector $\vec{\omega}$ in Eq. (6.22) needs to be converted to a pure quaternion before it gets multiplied by $\vec{q}_0$. Section 8.3 of Appendix C (Chap. 8) describes how any arbitrary vector $\vec{v} \in \mathbb{R}^3$ can be represented as a pure quaternion.

6.9   Suggested Readings

Most of the geometric constructions presented in this appendix are standard and can be found in almost all computer graphics books. In this appendix, we decided to use the same notation and solution methods presented by Glassner [Gla90], excepting both the computation of the closest point between a line and a line segment (obtained from Karabassi et al. [KPTB99]), and the determination of the tangent plane given the normal vector (obtained from Stark [Sta09] and Hughes et al. [HM99]).

References

[Gla90] Glassner, A.: Useful 3D geometry. In: Graphics Gems I, pp. 297–300 (1990)

[HM99] Hughes, J.F., Möller, T.: Building an orthonormal basis from a unit vector. J. Graph. Tools **4**(4), 33–35 (1999)

[KPTB99] Karabassi, E.-A., Papaioannou, G., Theoharis, T., Boehm, A.: Intersection test for collision detection in particle systems. J. Graph. Tools **4**(1), 25–37 (1999)

[Sta09] Stark, M.M.: Efficient construction of perpendicular vectors without branching. J. Graph. Tools **14**(1), 55–62 (2009)

Appendix B: Numerical Solution of Ordinary Differential Equations of Motion

7

7.1 Introduction

The simulation engine is constantly required to compute the dynamic state of all rigid bodies and particles in the scene,[1] owing to the net torque and net force being exerted on them. In the case of rigid bodies, this computation requires numerically solving four first-order ordinary differential equations (ODEs) of motion: two coupled equations for the linear momentum and linear position of the body, and two coupled equations for the angular momentum and angular position of the body. The four ODEs of motion are:

$$\frac{d\vec{x}(t)}{dt} = \vec{v}(t) = f_x(t, \vec{x})$$

$$\frac{d\vec{L}(t)}{dt} = \vec{F}(t) = f_L(t, \vec{L})$$

$$\frac{d\mathbf{R}(t)}{dt} = \tilde{\omega}(t)\mathbf{R}(t) = f_R(t, \mathbf{R})$$

$$\frac{d\vec{H}(t)}{dt} = \vec{\tau}(t) = f_H(t, \vec{H})$$

(7.1)

where $\vec{x}(t)$, $\vec{v}(t)$, $\vec{L}(t)$, $\tilde{\omega}(t)$ and $\vec{H}(t)$ are the linear position, linear velocity, linear momentum, angular velocity and angular momentum, respectively, of the body being moved. The optional function-style representation of the time derivatives in Eq. (7.1) is used to simplify the notation and make the equations in this appendix more readable.

---

[1]In this appendix, the word scene refers to the simulated world containing all bodies being simulated.

M.G. Coutinho, *Guide to Dynamic Simulations of Rigid Bodies and Particle Systems*, 291
Simulation Foundations, Methods and Applications,
DOI 10.1007/978-1-4471-4417-5_7, © Springer-Verlag London 2013

Recall from Chap. 4 that the linear and angular momentum are computed as

$$\vec{L}(t) = m\vec{v}(t)$$
$$\vec{H}(t) = \mathbf{I}(t)\vec{\omega}(t),$$

with m and $\mathbf{I}(t)$ being the mass and inertia tensor of the body at time t. The inertia tensor of the body is computed relative to the world (fixed) frame, and is given by

$$\mathbf{I}(t) = \mathbf{R}(t)\mathbf{I}_b\mathbf{R}^{-1}(t),$$

where $\mathbf{I}_b$ is the (constant) inertia tensor relative to the body's frame.[2] The remaining variables in Eq. (7.1) are the rotation matrix $\mathbf{R}(t)$ representing the angular position of the body at time t, the net force $\vec{F}(t)$ acting on the center of mass of the body, and the net torque $\vec{\tau}(t)$ computed from

$$\vec{\tau}(t) = \sum_{i=1}^{n}\left(\vec{x}_i(t) - \vec{x}_{cm}(t)\right) \times \vec{F}_i(t),$$

where n is the total number of external forces acting on the body at time t, $\vec{F}_i(t)$ is the ith external force, $\vec{x}_i$ is the point on the body at which force $\vec{F}_i(t)$ is being applied, and $\vec{x}_{cm}(t)$ is the current position of the body's center of mass.

In the case of particle-systems simulation, the angular-momentum and angular-position equations in (7.1) are not applicable, and the ODEs of motion are reduced to the two coupled equations involving the linear momentum and linear position of the particle. Here, we shall represent the dynamic equations as a single state vector $\vec{Y}(t)$, given by

$$\vec{Y}(t) = \begin{pmatrix} \vec{x}(t) \\ \vec{L}(t) \end{pmatrix} \qquad \frac{d\vec{Y}(t)}{dt} = \begin{pmatrix} \vec{v}(t) \\ \vec{F}(t) \end{pmatrix} \qquad (7.2)$$

for particles, or

$$\vec{Y}(t) = \begin{pmatrix} \vec{x}(t) \\ \mathbf{R}(t) \\ \vec{L}(t) \\ \vec{H}(t) \end{pmatrix} \qquad \frac{d\vec{Y}(t)}{dt} = \begin{pmatrix} \vec{v}(t) \\ \vec{\omega}(t)\mathbf{R}(t) \\ \vec{F}(t) \\ \vec{\tau}(t) \end{pmatrix} \qquad (7.3)$$

for rigid bodies. Most of the formulas presented in this appendix are expressed in terms of this single state vector representation, also referred to as the dynamic-state vector of a particle or rigid body in Chaps. 3 and 4, respectively. Since the ODEs for

---

[2]See Appendix D (Chap. 9) for details on how to compute the inertia tensor $\mathbf{I}_b$ in body-frame coordinates.

particles are a subset of the ODEs for rigid bodies, we shall focus on the solution equations for the latter.

The numerical integration of the ODEs of motion consists of starting at an initial configuration where all positions and momenta are known, and gradually increase the independent variable t (time) through finite steps h (time step), computing the *approximate* value of the linear and angular positions and momenta of the body being moved that best match the Taylor series expansion of their *exact* solution. The Taylor series expansion of the exact solution $\vec{Y}(t)$ at $t = (t_i + h)$, when the values of $\vec{Y}(t_i)$ (the initial condition) and h are known, is given by the infinite sum

$$\vec{Y}(t_i + h) = \sum_{n=0}^{\infty} \frac{h^n}{n!} \frac{\partial^n \vec{Y}(t_i)}{\partial t^n} = \vec{Y}(t_i) + h \frac{\partial \vec{Y}(t_i)}{\partial t} + \frac{h^2}{2!} \frac{\partial^2 \vec{Y}(t_i)}{\partial t^2} + \cdots. \qquad (7.4)$$

The degree to which the approximate solution matches the exact solution depends on how close it matches the Taylor series expansion of the exact solution. In other words, the approximate solution is usually a truncation of the Taylor series expansion and the omitted terms reflect the error between the exact and approximate solutions. The point at which the truncation takes place depends on the integration method being used.

In general, the numerical solution of Eqs. (7.2) and (7.3) for time $t = (t_i + h)$ requires the complete knowledge of the state of the system at time $t = t_i$. Starting at the very first time step $t = t_0$, the simulation engine knows the initial state of the system, that is, it knows the linear and angular positions and momenta of each body in the scene. In most cases, the initial linear and angular momenta are set to zero, but nothing prevents us from assigning any finite value to them. At each subsequent time step, the simulation engine computes the net force and torque acting on each body in the scene, and numerically solves Eqs. (7.2) and (7.3) for these values.

It is important to recognize that, independent of the numerical method being used, the simulation engine will always be required to compute the net torque and net force acting on each body at the time interval being considered. Simple numerical methods usually require just one computation at the beginning of each time step. However, as will be shown in Sect. 7.3, there are numerical methods that require computing the net force and net torque acting on the body not only at the beginning of the time interval, but also at some intermediate time values along the current time step. These methods usually combine such intermediate information to obtain the approximate solution for the entire time step. In these cases, the simulation engine needs to temporarily position the bodies at these intermediate time values before it can compute the net torque and net force acting on them.

It is also clear from Eq. (7.4) that the choice of time step h directly affects the efficiency and stability of the numerical method being used. Too big a step, and the approximate solution may no longer resemble the exact solution; too short a step, and the efficiency can be unnecessarily dragged to unbearable levels. This is true for all methods presented in this appendix, and the problem of estimating the error

Fig. 7.1 The exact solution is approximated by a straight line segment. The slope of the line is determined at time t_i and is assumed to be constant over the entire time step h

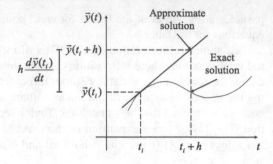

and determining the right time step h to be used in order to keep the error below a threshold value is discussed in detail in Sect. 7.4. For now, let's consider each integration method assuming that the time step h is adequate to keep the numerical error under control.

7.2   Euler Method

The Euler method is by far the simplest, and least accurate, of all methods presented in this appendix. Nonetheless, it is important to understand it because other methods are constructed on top of the basic ideas presented here.

7.2.1   Explicit Euler

The explicit Euler method, also known as the *forward Euler* method, approximates the Taylor series expansion up to its first order, that is, it approximates the infinite sum given in Eq. (7.4) by a straight line. The approximate solution $\vec{Y}(t_i + h)$ is then obtained from

$$\vec{Y}(t_i + h) = \vec{Y}(t_i) + h \frac{d\vec{Y}(t_i)}{dt} + O\left(h^2\right)$$

$$= \vec{Y}(t_i) + h f_Y(t_i, \vec{Y}) + O\left(h^2\right), \tag{7.5}$$

with $O(h^2)$ representing the order of the error obtained from truncating Eq. (7.4) at its second term. Figure 7.1 illustrates the basic idea behind the explicit Euler method. The slope of the curve is computed once at time t_i, and is assumed to be constant for the entire time step (remember that this is a straight-line approximation).

The explicit Euler method can be used to numerically integrate our ODEs of motion given in Eqs. (7.2) and (7.3) for any body that is being moved in the scene, as follows. We have the initial time t_0 and the time step h being used. We know the body's linear and angular positions and momenta at time t_0, namely

$$\vec{Y}(t_0) = \begin{pmatrix} \vec{x}(t_0) \\ \mathbf{R}(t_0) \\ \vec{L}(t_0) \\ \vec{H}(t_0) \end{pmatrix}, \tag{7.6}$$

where

$$\vec{L}(t_0) = m\vec{v}(t_0)$$
$$\vec{H}(t_0) = \mathbf{I}(t_0)\vec{\omega}(t_0).$$

According to Eq. (7.5), the time derivative of the dynamic state of the body is computed once at time t_0. This computation consists of first determining the net force $\vec{F}(t_0)$ and net torque $\vec{\tau}(t_0)$ acting on the center of mass of the body at time t_0, and then substituting this information into Eq. (7.3) to get

$$\frac{d\vec{Y}(t_0)}{dt} = \begin{pmatrix} \vec{v}(t_0) \\ \vec{\omega}(t_0)\mathbf{R}(t_0) \\ \vec{F}(t_0) \\ \vec{\tau}(t_0) \end{pmatrix}. \tag{7.7}$$

Therefore, the numerical solution using the explicit Euler method is given by

$$\vec{Y}(t_0 + h) = \vec{Y}(t_0) + h\frac{d\vec{Y}(t_0)}{dt} = \begin{pmatrix} \vec{x}(t_0) + h\vec{v}(t_0) \\ \mathbf{R}(t_0) + h\vec{\omega}(t_0)\mathbf{R}(t_0) \\ m\vec{v}(t_0) + h\vec{F}(t_0) \\ \mathbf{I}(t_0)\vec{\omega}(t_0) + h\vec{\tau}(t_0) \end{pmatrix}.$$

7.2.2 Implicit Euler

Depending on the type of external forces acting on the body, the net torque and net force computations can sometimes introduce a linear, or even a non-linear, relation between the accelerations and the positions and velocities of the bodies in the scene. This dependence introduces linear (or nonlinear) coefficients in the ODEs of motion that can considerably complicate their numerical integration. For example, if two bodies are connected by a spring, the net torque and net force acting on them will have a contribution from the spring force, which in turn depends on the relative displacement of the bodies. The same spring can be pulling the bodies together in one time step, and pushing the bodies apart in another, subsequent, time step. In this case, the position dependence of the spring force introduces linear coefficients on the ODEs of motion.

In the more general case where there is dependence between the net force, and positions and velocities of the body, Eq. (7.1) can be rewritten as

$$\frac{d\vec{x}(t)}{dt} = -\left(\vec{c}_x(t)\right)^t \vec{v}(t)$$

$$\frac{d\vec{L}(t)}{dt} = -\left(\vec{c}_L(t)\right)^t \vec{F}(t)$$

$$\frac{d\mathbf{R}(t)}{dt} = -\left(\vec{c}_R(t)\right)^t \vec{\omega}(t)\mathbf{R}(t)$$

$$\frac{d\vec{H}(t)}{dt} = -\left(\vec{c}_H(t)\right)^t \vec{\tau}(t),$$

(7.8)

where $(\vec{c}_x(t))^t$, $(\vec{c}_L(t))^t$, $(\vec{c}_R(t))^t$ and $(\vec{c}_H(t))^t$ are positive variables that can be either linear or nonlinear. In the following paragraphs, we shall restrict our discussion to the case where all $\vec{c}$ are linear coefficients with a constant value in the time interval being considered.[3] All interaction forces covered in this book fall into this category.

A practical issue that is of special concern when such coefficients exist is the numerical stability of the solution method being applied. Clearly, the numerical stability of Eqs. (7.8) is closely related to the time step h being used. If the time step is too big, the numerical solution may significantly differ from the exact solution, and, as the integration evolves, may no longer follow the exact solution. In extreme cases, the numerical integration becomes unstable, oscillating with increasing amplitudes and moving further away from the exact solution.

The maximum time step h that can be used in the numerical integration of Eqs. (7.8), still producing a stable result, is directly related to the magnitudes of the coefficients $\vec{c}(t)$. If their magnitudes differ by a significant degree (i.e., one is orders of magnitude greater than the others), the maximum time step h will be limited by the inverse of the largest magnitude value. Notice that this limitation is for purposes of stability rather than accuracy. As will be explained in more detail in Sect. 7.4, even though the numerical error analysis may indicate that we can safely increase the current time step h being used, the stability analysis may say that we should not increase the time step if we want to keep the numerical integration stable. Since the maximum time step h is limited by the inverse of the largest magnitude value, there may be cases when the maximum time step h needed to be used to guarantee numerical stability is so small that efficiency is severely impaired, and the simulation seems to be not moving forward in time anymore. When situations like that occur, we say that Eqs. (7.8) are *stiff*.

---

[3]They may have different constant values for different time intervals, but their value is constant within the same time interval.

The implicit Euler method, also known as the *backwards Euler* method, is generally used when the ODEs of motion form a set of *stiff* equations. This method gives us a way of using larger time steps h when we have stiff equations, at the expense of being less accurate; this is a good trade-off considering that we were not moving forward using the smaller time steps anyway. Therefore, in the implicit Euler method, we care more for stability than accuracy.[4] The basic idea is to use a similar Euler approximation technique to compute $\vec{Y}(t_0 + h)$ as in Eq. (7.5). The difference here is that, instead of computing the time derivative at the beginning of the time interval, we compute it at the end of the time interval, that is

$$\vec{Y}(t_i + h) = \vec{Y}(t_i) + h\frac{d\vec{Y}(t_i + h)}{dt}. \tag{7.9}$$

From Eqs. (7.8), we know that

$$\frac{d\vec{Y}(t_i + h)}{dt} = -(\vec{c}_Y)^t \vec{Y}(t_i + h),$$

where

$$(\vec{c}_Y)^t = \left(\vec{c}_x(t), \vec{c}_L(t), \vec{c}_R(t), \vec{c}_H(t)\right)^t.$$

Substituting this information into Eq. (7.9), we have

$$\left(1 + h(\vec{c}_Y)^t\right)\vec{Y}(t_i + h) = \vec{Y}(t_i), \tag{7.10}$$

which we can solve for $\vec{Y}(t_i + h)$. Even though the derivation of Eq. (7.10) considered only the single-variable case, we can in fact combine all linear and angular equations associated with a rigid body into a linear system of the form

$$(\mathbf{I} + h\mathbf{C})\vec{Y}(t_i + h) = \vec{Y}(t_i), \tag{7.11}$$

where $\mathbf{C}$ is the positive definite coefficient matrix. In practice, the linear system in Eq. (7.11) is often sparse, depending on the type of force interactions between the bodies in the scene. This means that, instead of using a general $O(n^3)$ linear equation solver to determine the solution of a n dimensional system, we can take advantage of specialized sparse-matrix solvers that can compute a solution for Eq. (7.11) in $O(n)$.

---

[4]Stability analysis of this method indicates that the numerical solution is stable for *all* time-step sizes.

7.3   Runge–Kutta Method

The Runge–Kutta method extends the basic idea of the explicit Euler method of computing the time derivative at the beginning of the time interval by computing intermediate values of the time derivatives throughout the time interval, and combining these values to match the Taylor series expansion up to some truncation term. The coefficients (or weights) of each of the terms being combined are carefully chosen to cancel out as many low-order derivative terms of the infinite sum in Eq. (7.4) as possible, leaving the higher-order derivatives not canceled out as part of the truncation error. The number of intermediate values used depends on the order of the Runge–Kutta method being applied.

7.3.1   Second-Order Runge–Kutta Method

The second-order Runge–Kutta method, also known as *midpoint* method, combines the information of two "Euler like" steps to approximate the Taylor series expansion up to its third term. The approximate solution $\vec{Y}(t_i + h)$ is then determined from

$$\vec{k}_1 = h f_Y(t_i, \vec{Y}), \tag{7.12}$$

$$\vec{k}_2 = h f_Y\left(t_i + \frac{h}{2}, \vec{Y} + \frac{\vec{k}_1}{2}\right), \tag{7.13}$$

$$\vec{Y}(t_0 + h) = \vec{Y}(t_0) + \vec{k}_2 + O\left(h^3\right). \tag{7.14}$$

Figure 7.2 illustrates the basic idea behind this method. The time derivative is evaluated once at time t_0 to get a first estimative of the slope of the curve. This estimative is used to determine the midpoint of the curve at time $t = (t_0 + h/2)$. Another time derivative is then evaluated to determine the slope of the curve at the midpoint, which is then used as a linear approximation of the slope of the curve for the entire time step, as is illustrated in Fig. 7.2(b). The numerical integration of the ODEs of motion using the second-order Runge–Kutta method can be determined from the following procedure.

As in the explicit Euler method, we have the initial time t_0 and the time step h. We also know the body's linear and angular positions and momenta at time t_0, namely

$$\vec{Y}(t_0) = \begin{pmatrix} \vec{x}(t_0) \\ \mathbf{R}(t_0) \\ \vec{L}(t_0) \\ \vec{H}(t_0) \end{pmatrix}, \tag{7.15}$$

where

$$\begin{aligned} \vec{L}(t_0) &= m\vec{v}(t_0) \\ \vec{H}(t_0) &= \mathbf{I}(t_0)\vec{\omega}(t_0). \end{aligned} \tag{7.16}$$

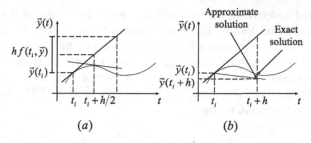

Fig. 7.2 (a) A Euler-like step is computed using the information at time t_i to determine the first estimative $f_y(t_0, \vec{y})$ of the slope of the curve. The result is then used to compute the slope of the curve at its midpoint, that is, $f_y(t_0 + h/2, \vec{y} + \vec{k}_1/2)$. (b) The slope of the midpoint approximates the slope of the curve for the entire time step. Notice that the straight line approximating the curve is parallel to the tangent to the curve at the midpoint shown in (a), that is, has the same slope as $f_y(t_0 + h/2, \vec{y} + \vec{k}_1/2)$

Again, we can compute the net force $\vec{F}(t_0)$ and net torque $\vec{\tau}(t_0)$ acting on the body at time t_0. Substituting these values into Eq. (7.12), we can compute the $\vec{k}_1$'s for the linear and angular positions and momenta of the body. Using the function-style notation for the time derivatives, we have:

$$\vec{k}_1 = \begin{pmatrix} \vec{k}_{1x} \\ \vec{k}_{1R} \\ \vec{k}_{1L} \\ \vec{k}_{1H} \end{pmatrix} = \begin{pmatrix} hf_x(t_0, \vec{x}) \\ hf_R(t_0, \mathbf{R}) \\ hf_L(t_0, \vec{L}) \\ hf_H(t_0, \vec{H}) \end{pmatrix} = \begin{pmatrix} h\vec{v}(t_0) \\ h\vec{\omega}(t_0)\mathbf{R}(t_0) \\ h\vec{F}(t_0) \\ h\vec{\tau}(t_0) \end{pmatrix}. \qquad (7.17)$$

Now, according to Eq. (7.13), we need to use these estimates to evaluate the linear and angular accelerations of the body at the midpoint. We need to compute:

$$\vec{k}_2 = \begin{pmatrix} hf_x(t_0 + h/2, \vec{x} + \vec{k}_{1x}/2) \\ hf_R(t_0 + h/2, \mathbf{R} + \vec{k}_{1R}/2) \\ hf_L(t_0 + h/2, \vec{L} + \vec{k}_{1L}/2) \\ hf_H(t_0 + h/2, \vec{H} + \vec{k}_{1H}/2) \end{pmatrix}. \qquad (7.18)$$

In plain English, Eq. (7.18) says that, at the midpoint, the body will be positioned at $(\vec{x} + \vec{k}_{1x}/2)$, oriented by $(\mathbf{R} + \vec{k}_{1R}/2)$, with linear and angular momenta given by $(\vec{L} + \vec{k}_{1L}/2)$ and $(\vec{H} + \vec{k}_{1H}/2)$, respectively. In other words, the second arguments of the f functions in Eq. (7.18) are in fact the initial conditions at the midpoint, namely:

$$\vec{Y}\left(t_0 + \frac{h}{2}\right) = \begin{pmatrix} \vec{x}(t_0 + h/2) \\ \mathbf{R}(t_0 + h/2) \\ \vec{L}(t_0 + h/2) \\ \vec{H}(t_0 + h/2) \end{pmatrix} = \begin{pmatrix} \vec{x}(t_0) + (h/2)\vec{v}(t_0) \\ \mathbf{R}(t_0) + (h/2)\vec{\omega}(t_0)\mathbf{R}(t_0) \\ \vec{L}(t_0) + (h/2)\vec{F}(t_0) \\ \vec{H}(t_0) + (h/2)\vec{\tau}(t_0) \end{pmatrix}.$$

We still need to determine the net force and net torque acting on the body at the midpoint. This can be done by first positioning the body at $\vec{x}(t_0 + h/2)$ with orientation $\mathbf{R}(t_0 + h/2)$, then setting its linear and angular momenta to $\vec{L}(t_0 + h/2)$ and $\vec{H}(t_0 + h/2)$, respectively. Now that the body is correctly positioned and oriented at the midpoint, we can compute the net force $\vec{F}(t_0 + h/2)$ and net torque $\vec{\tau}(t_0 + h/2)$ acting on it. Substituting this information into Eq. (7.18) and expanding the function-style notation, we have:

$$\vec{k}_2 = \begin{pmatrix} h\vec{v}(t_0 + h/2) \\ h\vec{\omega}(t_0 + h/2)\mathbf{R}(t_0 + h/2) \\ h\vec{F}(t_0 + h/2) \\ h\vec{\tau}(t_0 + h/2) \end{pmatrix} = \begin{pmatrix} h\frac{\vec{L}(t_0+h/2)}{m} \\ h\frac{\vec{H}(t_0+h/2)}{\mathbf{I}(t_0+h/2)} \\ h\vec{F}(t_0 + h/2) \\ h\vec{\tau}(t_0 + h/2) \end{pmatrix}. \tag{7.19}$$

We can then substitute Eqs. (7.15) and (7.19) back into Eq. (7.14) to obtain the approximate linear and angular positions and momenta of the body using the second-order Runge–Kutta method.

7.3.2 Forth-Order Runge–Kutta Method

The forth-order Runge–Kutta method combines the information of four "Euler like" steps to approximate the Taylor-series expansion up to its fifth term. The approximate solution $\vec{Y}(t_0 + h)$ is then determined from:

$$\vec{k}_1 = hf_Y(t_0, \vec{Y}), \tag{7.20}$$

$$\vec{k}_2 = hf_Y\left(t_0 + \frac{h}{2}, \vec{Y} + \frac{\vec{k}_1}{2}\right), \tag{7.21}$$

$$\vec{k}_3 = hf_Y\left(t_0 + \frac{h}{2}, \vec{Y} + \frac{\vec{k}_2}{2}\right), \tag{7.22}$$

$$\vec{k}_4 = hf_Y(t_0 + h, \vec{Y} + \vec{k}_3), \tag{7.23}$$

$$\vec{Y}(t_0 + h) = \vec{Y}(t_0) + \frac{\vec{k}_1}{6} + \frac{\vec{k}_2}{3} + \frac{\vec{k}_3}{3} + \frac{\vec{k}_4}{6} + O\left(h^5\right). \tag{7.24}$$

Figure 7.3 illustrates how this method extends the second-order Runge–Kutta method by computing one more time derivative at the mid-point, and another time derivative at the endpoint of the time interval being considered. The (1/3) and (1/6) coefficients used in Eq. (7.24) were chosen to cancel out the lower order time derivative terms, making the approximate solution differ by $O(h^5)$ from the exact solution.

The computation of the time derivatives at each of the three intermediate values requires positioning, orienting and setting the dynamic state of the body according to the second arguments of the f functions in Eqs. (7.20) to (7.24). Only then we can compute the net force and torque acting on the body at the time interval being considered.

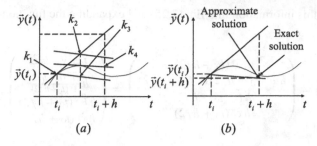

(a) (b)

Fig. 7.3 (a) Four time derivatives are computed: one at the beginning, two at the middle, and one at the end of the time interval. The label of the points indicate which $\vec{k}$ was used to compute it. (b) The combination of all intermediate values results in a linear approximation that differs only by $O(h^5)$ from the exact solution

The time-derivative vectors $\vec{k}_1$ and $\vec{k}_2$ are computed the same way as the second-order Runge–Kutta method. We can continue applying the same techniques we used for computing $\vec{k}_2$ to obtain the time-derivative vectors $\vec{k}_3$ and $\vec{k}_4$ given in Eqs. (7.22) and (7.23), respectively. Let's first consider the computation of $\vec{k}_3$, namely:

$$
\vec{k}_3 = \begin{pmatrix} h f_x (t_0 + h/2, \vec{x} + \vec{k}_{2x}/2) \\ h f_R (t_0 + h/2, \mathbf{R} + \vec{k}_{2R}/2) \\ h f_L (t_0 + h/2, \vec{L} + \vec{k}_{2L}/2) \\ h f_H (t_0 + h/2, \vec{H} + \vec{k}_{2H}/2) \end{pmatrix}.
$$

(7.25)

Equation (7.25) says that, at time $t = (t_0 + h/2)$, the body will be positioned at $(\vec{x} + \vec{k}_{2x}/2)$, oriented by $(\mathbf{R} + \vec{k}_{2R}/2)$, with linear and angular momenta given by $(\vec{L} + \vec{k}_{2L}/2)$ and $(\vec{H} + \vec{k}_{2H}/2)$, respectively. In other words, the second arguments of the f functions in Eq. (7.25) are the initial conditions at time $t = (t_0 + h/2)$, namely:[5]

$$
\vec{Y}^*(t_0 + h/2) = \begin{pmatrix} \vec{x}^*(t_0 + h/2) \\ \mathbf{R}^*(t_0 + h/2) \\ \vec{L}^*(t_0 + h/2) \\ \vec{H}^*(t_0 + h/2) \end{pmatrix} = \begin{pmatrix} \vec{x}(t_0) + (h/2)\frac{\vec{L}(t_0+h/2)}{m} \\ \mathbf{R}(t_0) + (h/2)\frac{\vec{H}(t_0+h/2)}{\mathbf{I}(t_0+h/2)} \\ \vec{L}(t_0) + (h/2)\vec{F}(t_0 + h/2) \\ \vec{H}(t_0) + (h/2)\vec{\tau}(t_0 + h/2) \end{pmatrix}.
$$

The net force $\vec{F}^*(t_0 + h/2)$ and net torque $\vec{\tau}^*(t_0 + h/2)$ are computed after the body is correctly positioned at $\vec{x}^*(t_0 + h/2)$ with orientation $\mathbf{R}^*(t_0 + h/2)$, and its linear and angular momenta are set to $\vec{L}^*(t_0 + h/2)$ and $\vec{H}^*(t_0 + h/2)$, respectively.

---

[5]The superscript $*$ is used to differentiate the $\vec{k}_3$ time-derivative estimate from the $\vec{k}_2$ estimate, since both refer to the same time $t = (t_0 + h/2)$.

Substituting this information into Eq. (7.25) and expanding the function-style notation we get:

$$
\vec{k}_3 = \begin{pmatrix} h\vec{v}^*(t_0 + h/2) \\ h\vec{\omega}^*(t_0 + h/2)\mathbf{R}^*(t_0 + h/2) \\ h\vec{F}^*(t_0 + h/2) \\ h\vec{\tau}^*(t_0 + h/2) \end{pmatrix} = \begin{pmatrix} h\frac{\vec{L}^*(t_0+h/2)}{m} \\ h\frac{\vec{H}^*(t_0+h/2)}{\mathbf{I}^*(t_0+h/2)} \\ h\vec{F}^*(t_0 + h/2) \\ h\vec{\tau}^*(t_0 + h/2) \end{pmatrix}, \qquad (7.26)
$$

where

$$
\mathbf{I}^*(t_0 + h/2) = \mathbf{R}^*(t_0 + h/2)\mathbf{I}_b\big(\mathbf{R}^*(t_0 + h/2)\big)^{-1}.
$$

The time-derivative vector:

$$
\vec{k}_4 = \begin{pmatrix} hf_x(t_0 + h, \vec{x} + \vec{k}_{3x}/2) \\ hf_R(t_0 + h, \mathbf{R} + \vec{k}_{3R}/2) \\ hf_L(t_0 + h, \vec{L} + \vec{k}_{3L}/2) \\ hf_H(t_0 + h, \vec{H} + \vec{k}_{3H}/2) \end{pmatrix} \qquad (7.27)
$$

is computed by first setting the dynamic state of the body to:

$$
\vec{Y}(t_0 + h) = \begin{pmatrix} \vec{x}(t_0 + h) \\ \mathbf{R}(t_0 + h) \\ \vec{L}(t_0 + h) \\ \vec{H}(t_0 + h) \end{pmatrix} = \begin{pmatrix} \vec{x}(t_0) + h\frac{\vec{L}^*(t_0+h/2)}{m} \\ \mathbf{R}(t_0) + h\frac{\vec{H}^*(t_0+h/2)}{\mathbf{I}^*(t_0+h/2)} \\ \vec{L}(t_0) + h\vec{F}^*(t_0 + h/2) \\ \vec{H}(t_0) + h\vec{\tau}^*(t_0 + h/2) \end{pmatrix},
$$

then determining the net force $\vec{F}(t_0 + h)$ and net torque $\vec{\tau}(t_0 + h)$ acting on the body at time $t = (t + h)$, and lastly substituting this information into Eq. (7.27) to obtain:

$$
\vec{k}_4 = \begin{pmatrix} h\vec{v}(t_0 + h) \\ h\vec{\omega}(t_0 + h)\mathbf{R}(t_0 + h) \\ h\vec{F}(t_0 + h) \\ h\vec{\tau}(t_0 + h) \end{pmatrix} = \begin{pmatrix} h\frac{\vec{L}(t_0+h)}{m} \\ h\frac{\vec{H}(t_0+h)}{\mathbf{I}(t_0+h)} \\ h\vec{F}(t_0 + h) \\ h\vec{\tau}(t_0 + h) \end{pmatrix}. \qquad (7.28)
$$

By combining all $\vec{k}$'s computed in Eqs. (7.17), (7.19), (7.6) and (7.28) into Eq. (7.24), we have the approximate linear and angular positions and momenta of the body using the forth-order Runge–Kutta method.

7.4   Using Adaptive Time-Step Sizes to Speed Computations

As mentioned earlier, the choice of the time step h directly affects the efficiency and stability of the numerical method being used. If the time step h is too big, then the approximate solution may significantly differ from the exact solution, and the numerical integration is meaningless. On the other hand, if the time step h is too small, then the approximate solution may follow more closely the exact solution, but at the expense of moving forward slowly in time, possibly slower than necessary. The best choice of h depends on the equations being solved, and on their initial conditions. It is clear that, as the system evolves, the initial conditions for each time step change, and so the choice of h to be used.

Ideally, we should be able to pick the right time step h depending on the system being solved at each time step. The right time step would be one allowing the numerical integrator to move forward in time as fast as it can, still keeping the error difference between the approximate and exact solutions less than a desired threshold value. We should be able to increase or decrease the value of the time step at run-time if the error is smaller or larger than the maximum-allowed threshold value, respectively.

We already know from the previous sections that the error between the approximate and exact solutions for both explicit Euler and Runge–Kutta methods can always be expressed as being proportional to a power of h. What we still need to know is how to compute this error and take advantage of this relation with h to adaptively adjust its value as the simulation evolves.

One technique commonly used to estimate the truncation error is called *step doubling*. As its name implies, the idea is to compute the linear and angular positions and momenta using the step size h, and then compute them again using two steps of size $(h/2)$. Even though the final time step size is h in both cases, the result obtained using the two steps of size $(h/2)$ is more accurate than that using the single step size h. Their difference can therefore be used as an estimate of the truncation error, which in turn is proportional to a power of h.

To illustrate this idea, let $\vec{Y}(t_0 + h)$ and $\vec{Y}(t_0 + h/2 + h/2)$ be the approximate values computed through the numerical integration of Eq. (7.1), using one time step h and two time steps $(h/2)$, respectively. The difference between these value is given by

$$\Delta_Y = \vec{Y}(t_0 + h/2 + h/2) - \vec{Y}(t_0 + h).$$

We already know this difference is proportional to a power of h, that is

$$|\Delta_Y| \approx h^p, \tag{7.29}$$

where the value of p depends on the numerical method being applied. Table 7.1 shows the values of p for the numerical methods presented in this appendix.

So far, we have computed the difference $\Delta_Y(t_0 + h)$, and have determined its relation with the time step h being used. Now, we need to ascertain how to use this information to adjust the time step h so that the error will be less than a desired threshold value.

Table 7.1 The value of p to be used depending on the numerical method applied

Integration method	Value of p
Explicit Euler	2
Implicit Euler	N/A
Second-order Runge–Kutta	3
Fourth-order Runge–Kutta	5

Let $\triangle_d$ be the desired (user-definable) threshold value, and let h_d be its associated time step, that is, the time step that should be used to give an error equal to $\triangle_d$, we know that

$$|\triangle_d| \approx h_d^p. \tag{7.30}$$

Since Eqs. (7.29) and (7.30) refer to the same ODEs, their constant of proportionality is the same. Therefore, if we divide one by the other we can cancel out their constant of proportionality, obtaining

$$\left|\frac{\triangle_Y}{\triangle_d}\right| = \left(\frac{h}{h_d}\right)^p.$$

We have the difference $\triangle_y$, the time step h being used, and the desired threshold error value $\triangle_d$. Solving for the unknown h_d, gives

$$h_d = h \left|\frac{\triangle_d}{\triangle_y}\right|^{\frac{1}{p}}. \tag{7.31}$$

Equation (7.31) shows how we can adjust the time step h using the step-doubling technique. If the computed error $\triangle_y$ is greater than the desired threshold error value $\triangle_d$, then $|\triangle_d/\triangle_y| < 1$ and h_d will be less than h, that is, the current time step h should be decreased to h_d. In this case, the integrator needs to "undo" its computations and start all over again for the new (reduced) time-step value. On the other hand, if the computed error $\triangle_y$ is smaller than the desired threshold error value $\triangle_d$, then $|\triangle_d/\triangle_y| > 1$ and h_d will be greater than h, that is, the next time step h should be increased to h_d.

In practice, because reducing the value of h is such an expensive operation (we need to redo all computations for the new value), it is important to exercise caution when we have room to increase the value of h. Keep in mind that Eq. (7.31) gives an estimate of how much we can increase or decrease the time step h depending on the error difference found. If we have room to increase, but increase too much, then in the next time step we may find the error is greater than the threshold error value, and we shall be forced to reduce the time step, undo the current operation and start the computations all over again. So, the gain of increasing the time step to move faster in time immediately turns out to be a considerable loss. Therefore, it is strongly advisable to increase the time step only by a percentage of the actual value computed using Eq. (7.31). For instance, instead of increasing h to h_d, we could increase it to $(0.8h_d)$, leaving a 20 % safety margin.

7.5 Suggested Readings

There are several other numerical methods in the literature that are applicable to our ODEs of motion, but are not so popular as the Euler and Runge–Kutta methods covered in this appendix. For example, Press et al. [PTVF96] present other methods such as the Bulirsch–Stoer and the fifth-order Runge–Kutta that are as effective as those presented here. In the case of the fifth-order Runge–Kutta method, the estimation of the truncation error can be done without using step doubling. This comes from the fact that the fifth-order Runge–Kutta has an embedded fourth-order Runge–Kutta on it, such that it can use the same time step to evaluate the results of two Runge–Kutta methods and compare them to estimate the integration error. Sharp et al. [SV94] present a general formulation for determining pairs of embedded Runge–Kutta integrators.

A more in-depth explanation of the implicit Euler method, and how the coefficients relate to the time step being used, can also be found in Press et al. [PTVF96], as well as in Baraff and Witkin's SIGGRAPH 98 course notes [BW98].

References

[BW98]   Baraff, D., Witkin, A.: Physically based modeling. SIGGRAPH Course Notes **13** (1998)

[PTVF96]   Press, W.H., Teukolsky, S.A., Vetterling, W.T., Flannery, B.P.: Numerical Recipes in C: The Art of Scientific Computing. Cambridge University Press, Cambridge (1996)

[SV94]   Sharp, P.W., Verner, J.H.: Completely embedded Runge–Kutta pairs. SIAM J. Numer. Anal. **31**, 1169–1190 (1994)

Appendix C: Quaternions

8

8.1 Introduction

Quaternions are mathematical structures from algebraic geometry that are widely used in computer graphics as an alternate way of representing 3D rotations of objects and their orientation in a scene. Quaternions use a four-dimensional notation to represent 3×3 rotation matrices that is more efficient to manipulate, and more robust with respect to numerical round-off errors observed when combining rotation matrices.

The four-dimensional space of quaternions is composed of a real axis, and three orthogonal axes $\vec{i}, \vec{j}, \vec{k}$ known as *principal imaginaries*. We can think of the principal imaginary axis as an extension of complex numbers, since they have the same basic complex number characteristic of satisfying

$$\vec{i}^2 = \vec{j}^2 = \vec{k}^2 = -1.$$

Being four-dimensional structures, quaternions can be represented as a quadruplet of real numbers, namely

$$q = s + x\vec{i} + y\vec{j} + z\vec{k}$$
$$= s + \vec{v}, \tag{8.1}$$

consisting of a real part s and a pure imaginary part $\vec{v}$ given by

$$\vec{v} = \begin{pmatrix} x \\ y \\ z \end{pmatrix} = x\vec{i} + y\vec{j} + z\vec{k}.$$

M.G. Coutinho, *Guide to Dynamic Simulations of Rigid Bodies and Particle Systems*, 307
Simulation Foundations, Methods and Applications,
DOI 10.1007/978-1-4471-4417-5_8, © Springer-Verlag London 2013

8.2   Basic Quaternion Operations

Quaternions can be combined and manipulated in a way similar to complex numbers, where the real and imaginary parts are dealt with separately. Given two quaternions $q_1 = s_1 + \vec{v}_1$ and $q_2 = s_2 + \vec{v}_2$, the following basic rules define the most common set of operations used with quaternions.

8.2.1   Addition

The addition of two quaternions is similar to the addition of two complex numbers, and is given by

$$q_1 + q_2 = (s_1 + s_2) + (\vec{v}_1 + \vec{v}_2),$$

where $(s_1 + s_2)$ is the real part of the result (notice that all summands are scalar) and $(\vec{v}_1 + \vec{v}_2)$ is the imaginary part of the result (notice that all summands are vectors). The result of the addition is a quaternion.

8.2.2   Dot product

The dot product of two quaternions is equivalent to the addition of the dot products of their real (scalar) and imaginary (vector) parts, namely

$$q_1 \cdot q_2 = s_1 s_2 + \vec{v}_1 \cdot \vec{v}_2,$$

where $\vec{v}_1 \cdot \vec{v}_2$ is the usual dot product of two vectors[1] in $\mathbb{R}^3$. Notice that the result of a dot product is a scalar.

8.2.3   Multiplication

The multiplication of two quaternions can be computed as if we were multiplying two complex numbers, with the added complexity of having the imaginary part being a vector. In this case, the multiplication of the imaginary axes $\vec{i}$, $\vec{j}$ and $\vec{k}$ obeys the following basic rules:

$$
\begin{aligned}
\vec{j}\vec{i} &= -\vec{k} & \vec{k}\vec{j} &= -\vec{i} & \vec{i}\vec{k} &= -\vec{j} \\
\vec{k}\vec{i} &= +\vec{j} & \vec{i}\vec{j} &= +\vec{k} & \vec{j}\vec{k} &= +\vec{i} \\
& & \vec{i}\vec{j}\vec{k} &= -1.
\end{aligned}
\tag{8.2}
$$

---

[1] Unless otherwise stated, whenever we mention $\mathbb{R}^n$, we are referring to the n-dimensional Euclidean space and its associated properties.

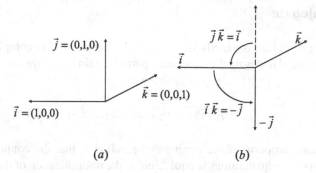

(a)   (b)

Fig. 8.1 (a) The three orthogonal principal imaginary axes viewed as a canonical basis of a 3D Euclidean space; (b) Multiplication on the right by $\vec{k}$ causes a clockwise 90 degree rotation in four-dimensional space around the $\vec{k}$ axis, rotating the $\vec{i}$ axis into the $-\vec{j}$ axis (from $\vec{i}\vec{k} = -\vec{j}$ in (8.2)), and rotating the $\vec{j}$ axis into the $\vec{i}$ axis (from $\vec{j}\vec{k} = \vec{i}$ in (8.2)). This can also be verified by applying the right-hand rule for rotating vectors represented in the right-hand coordinate system

We can alternatively visualize the multiplication of one imaginary axis by another as a 3D rotation (see Fig. 8.1(a)). For example, the multiplication on the right by $\vec{k}$ can be visualized by applying the right-hand rule for rotating axis $\vec{i}$ and $\vec{j}$ in Fig. 8.1(b).

In order to compute an algebraic expression for the multiplication of two quaternions, we have to expand their imaginary parts and use Eq. (8.2) to compute the multiplication of the imaginary axes among themselves, that is

$$
\begin{aligned}
q_1 q_2 &= (s_1 + \vec{v}_1)(s_2 + \vec{v}_2) \\
&= (s_1 + v_{1x}\vec{i} + v_{1y}\vec{j} + v_{1z}\vec{k})(s_2 + v_{2x}\vec{i} + v_{2y}\vec{j} + v_{2z}\vec{k}) \\
&= (s_1 s_2 - v_{1x} v_{2x} - v_{1y} v_{2y} - v_{1z} v_{2z}) \\
&\quad + s_1(v_{2x}\vec{i} + v_{2y}\vec{j} + v_{2z}\vec{k}) + s_2(v_{1x}\vec{i} + v_{1y}\vec{j} + v_{1z}\vec{k}) \\
&\quad + (v_{1y} v_{2z} - v_{1z} v_{2y})\vec{i} + (v_{1z} v_{2x} - v_{1x} v_{2z})\vec{j} \\
&\quad + (v_{1x} v_{2y} - v_{1y} v_{2x})\vec{k} \\
&= (s_1 s_2 - \vec{v}_1 \cdot \vec{v}_2) + (s_1 \vec{v}_2 + s_2 \vec{v}_1 + \vec{v}_1 \times \vec{v}_2).
\end{aligned}
$$

Notice that the multiplication of quaternions is not commutative. This should not come as a surprise, since multiplication of quaternions is equivalent to a 3D rotation, which itself does not enjoy the commutative property with respect to the multiplication operation.

8.2.4 Conjugate

The conjugate operation is exactly the same as its counterpart in complex number theory. We just need to negate the imaginary part to obtain the conjugate of a quaternion, that is

$$\bar{q_1} = \overline{s_1 + \vec{v}_1} = s_1 - \vec{v}_1. \tag{8.3}$$

Another basic property of the conjugate operation is that the conjugate of the multiplication of two quaternions is equivalent to the multiplication of the conjugate of each quaternion, that is

$$\begin{aligned}
\bar{q_1}\bar{q_2} &= (s_1 - \vec{v}_1)(s_2 - \vec{v}_2) \\
&= (s_1 s_2 - \vec{v}_1 \cdot \vec{v}_2) + \left(-s_1 \vec{v}_2 - s_2 \vec{v}_1 + (-\vec{v}_1) \times (-\vec{v}_2)\right) \\
&= (s_1 s_2 - \vec{v}_1 \cdot \vec{v}_2) - (s_1 \vec{v}_2 + s_2 \vec{v}_1 + \vec{v}_2 \times \vec{v}_1) \\
&= \overline{q_1 q_2}.
\end{aligned}$$

8.2.5 Module

The module, also known as magnitude, is computed as the dot product between the quaternion and its conjugate, and is given by

$$|q_1|^2 = q_1 \cdot \bar{q_1} = \bar{q_1} \cdot q_1 = s_1^2 + \vec{v}_1 \cdot \vec{v}_1 = s_1^2 + v_{1x}^2 + v_{1y}^2 + v_{1z}^2.$$

The module of the multiplication of two quaternions is the same as the multiplication of the modules of each quaternion, since

$$\begin{aligned}
|q_1 q_2|^2 &= (q_1 q_2)(\overline{q_1 q_2}) = (q_1 q_2)(\bar{q_2}\bar{q_1}) \\
&= q_1 (q_2 \bar{q_2}) \bar{q_1} = q_1 |q_2|^2 \bar{q_1} \\
&= |q_2|^2 q_1 \bar{q_1} = |q_1|^2 |q_2|^2.
\end{aligned}$$

8.2.6 Inverse

The inverse of a quaternion can be directly derived from the expression used to compute its module, resulting in

$$q_1^{-1} = \frac{\bar{q_1}}{|q_1|^2}. \tag{8.4}$$

8.3 Unit Quaternions

Another commonly used representation for a quaternion $q = s + \vec{v}$ is to write it as $q = s + a\vec{u}$, where the imaginary part $\vec{u}$ is a unitary vector (i.e., $|\vec{u}| = 1$). We can compute a and $\vec{u}$ from $\vec{v}$ as follows:

$$\vec{u} = \begin{pmatrix} x/a \\ y/a \\ z/a \end{pmatrix} = \frac{x}{|\vec{v}|}\vec{i} + \frac{y}{|\vec{v}|}\vec{j} + \frac{z}{|\vec{v}|}\vec{k}.$$

A quaternion with zero real part (i.e., $s = 0$) is called a *pure quaternion*. Any arbitrary vector $\vec{v} \in \mathbb{R}^3$ can be represented as a pure quaternion:

$$q = 0 + \vec{v} \tag{8.5}$$

using the notation in (8.1). A quaternion with module equal to one is called a *unit quaternion*, also known as *unit-magnitude quaternion*. A pure unit quaternion is then a quaternion with zero real part and module equal to one. Since any arbitrary vector in $\mathbb{R}^3$ can be represented as a pure quaternion, any unitary vector in $\mathbb{R}^3$ (i.e., any normalized vector) can be represented as a pure unit quaternion.

The family of all unit quaternions (i.e., all q such that $|q| = 1$) form an hyper sphere of radius 1 in the four-dimensional space of quaternions. Because a unit quaternion q always satisfies the condition $|q| = 1$, from Eq. (8.4), we can directly conclude that:

$$q^{-1} = \frac{\bar{q}}{|q|^2} = \bar{q}, \tag{8.6}$$

that is, the inverse of a unit quaternion is equal to its conjugate, which in turn can be computed by negating its imaginary part (see Eq. (8.3)).

8.3.1 Rotation-Matrix Representation Using Unit Quaternions

Unit quaternions play an important role in computer graphics because they can be used as an equivalent representation of 3×3 rotation matrices. In this section, we shall briefly go over all transformations required to switch back and forth between unit quaternions and rotation-matrix representations for right-handed coordinate systems.

The 3×3 rotation-matrix representation of a rotation of an angle of θ degrees about the unit-magnitude axis $\vec{u}$ that passes through the origin is given by:

$$\mathbf{R} = \begin{pmatrix} tu_x^2 + \cos\theta & tu_xu_y + u_z\sin\theta & tu_xu_z - u_y\sin\theta \\ tu_xu_y - u_z\sin\theta & tu_y^2 + \cos\theta & tu_yu_z + u_x\sin\theta \\ tu_xu_z + u_y\sin\theta & tu_yu_z - u_x\sin\theta & tu_z^2 + \cos\theta \end{pmatrix}, \tag{8.7}$$

where u_x, u_y and u_z are the components of the unit-magnitude vector $\vec{u}$ and $t = (1 - \cos\theta)$. This rotation can, in turn, be represented by the unit quaternion

$$q = \cos\frac{\theta}{2} + \sin\frac{\theta}{2}\vec{u}. \tag{8.8}$$

Conversely, given a unit quaternion $q = s + \vec{v}$, the rotation axis $\vec{u}$ and the rotation angle θ represented by the quaternion can be computed as

$$\cos\theta = 2s^2 - 1$$
$$\sin\theta = 2s\sqrt{1 - s^2} \tag{8.9}$$

and

$$\vec{u} = \frac{\vec{v}}{\sqrt{1 - s^2}}. \tag{8.10}$$

If we are using the 3×3 matrix representation, the rotation axis $\vec{u}$ and rotation angle θ can be determined from:

$$\cos\theta = \frac{R_{xx} + R_{yy} + R_{zz} - 1}{2} \tag{8.11}$$

and

$$u_x = \frac{R_{yz} - R_{zy}}{2\sin\theta}$$
$$u_y = \frac{R_{zx} - R_{xz}}{2\sin\theta} \tag{8.12}$$
$$u_z = \frac{R_{xy} - R_{yx}}{2\sin\theta},$$

with the constraint that $\sin\theta \neq 0$. If this constraint is not met, then the rotation axis is undetermined.

Lastly, given a unit quaternion $q = s + \vec{v}$, its equivalent 3×3 rotation matrix representation can be directly computed by substituting Eqs. (8.9) and (8.10) into Eq. (8.7). The matrix representation of the unit quaternion is then:

$$\mathbf{R} = 2\begin{pmatrix} s^2 + v_x^2 - \frac{1}{2} & v_x v_y - s v_z & v_x v_z + s v_y \\ v_x v_y + s v_z & s^2 + v_y^2 - \frac{1}{2} & v_y v_z - s v_x \\ v_x v_z - s v_y & v_y v_z + s v_x & s^2 + v_z^2 - \frac{1}{2} \end{pmatrix}, \tag{8.13}$$

where v_x, v_y and v_z are the components of the imaginary part $\vec{v}$, of the unit quaternion q.

At this point, we can easily switch back and forth between the quaternion and the 3×3 matrix representation of a rotation of θ degrees about the unit-magnitude axis $\vec{u}$ using Eqs. (8.7) to (8.13). The only remaining question is how to rotate an arbitrary vector $\vec{p} \in \mathbb{R}^3$ using these representations. If we are using the 3×3 matrix representation, then we can rotate $\vec{p}$ simply by computing

$$\vec{p}_r = \mathbf{R}\vec{p}, \tag{8.14}$$

where $\mathbf{R}$ is the rotation matrix and $\vec{p}_r$ is the rotated vector.

If we are using the quaternion representation, the vector $\vec{p} \in \mathbb{R}^3$ can be represented by the pure quaternion $q_p = 0 + \vec{p}$ (see Eq. (8.5)), and the rotation can then be computed as a quaternion multiplication given by

$$\begin{aligned} q_{p_r} = q q_p \bar{q} &= (s + \vec{u})(0 + \vec{p})(s - \vec{u}) \\ &= 0 + \left((s^2 - \vec{u} \cdot \vec{u})\vec{p} + 2(\vec{p} \cdot \vec{u})\vec{u} + 2s(\vec{u} \times \vec{p}) \right) \\ &= 0 + \vec{p}_r, \end{aligned} \tag{8.15}$$

where q_{p_r} is the pure quaternion representing the rotated vector $\vec{p}_r$.

8.3.2 Advantages of Using Unit Quaternions

There are several advantages of using quaternion representation instead of the 3×3 matrix representation for rotations. Here, we will focus on the most important ones.

The immediate advantage is that quaternions encode rotations by four real numbers, whereas the representation of these transformations as 3×3 matrices requires nine. This may save significant space for complex scenes with a large number of objects being simulated.

Besides the extra space needed, another problem of requiring more parameters to encode rotation matrices is that they are also prone to "drifting" when multiplied by one another. The drifting is caused by the fact that the "sin" and "cos" computations for a rotation round an arbitrary axis introduce round-off errors into the nine elements needed to encode the 3×3 rotation matrix. When multiplied by another rotation matrix, the result matrix may no longer be a rotation matrix. The round-off errors can be such that the determinant of the result matrix differs from one by a small amount. If the determinant is not equal to one, then the result matrix is no longer orthogonal, and therefore not a rotation matrix. Subsequent multiplications by other rotation matrices will rapidly increase the error to a noticeable level, such that the object being "rotated" will in fact be rotated *and* distorted or arbitrarily scaled when rendered in the scene.

A common way of solving the drifting problem for the matrix representation of rotations is to use the Gram–Schmidt orthogonalization algorithm for keeping the

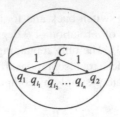

Fig. 8.2 The hyper sphere of radii 1 in the four-dimensional space of quaternions. The intermediate interpolated quaternions $q_{i_1}, \ldots, q_{i_n}$ lie on the smallest great hyper arc of the great hyper circle that contains q_1 and q_2 (the quaternions being interpolated)

result matrix orthogonal. The idea is to every so often check whether the determinant of the result matrix differs from one by an amount greater than a tolerance level, and if so apply the algorithm to decompose the result matrix into an orthogonal matrix times an upper triangular matrix. This decomposition is known as the QR decomposition. The result matrix can then be substituted for the orthogonal matrix, and the upper triangular matrix can be used to estimate the round-off error introduced so far. The practical problem of using this scheme to correct inevitable round-off errors when combining rotation matrices is that it is time consuming, and may not be appropriate for use in simulation engines with stringent operational requirements.

With the unit quaternion representation, the drifting problem arising from the "sin" and "cos" computations and the round-off errors introduced when two unit quaternions are multiplied still exists. In these cases, the result quaternion may no longer have module equal to one, and therefore no longer represents a rotation matrix. However, with the quaternion representation, the drift problem can be easily fixed by re-normalizing the result quaternion. If we think of the unit quaternion as being constrained to the surface of a four-dimensional hyper sphere of radius one, then the drift can be visualized as the quaternion being moved in or out of the surface owing to round-off errors. The re-normalization is equivalent to projecting the quaternion back to another location on the surface close to the correct location the quaternion was supposed to be if drift had not occurred.

Lastly, one of the main reasons most graphics packages use quaternions is the ability to easily interpolate between unit quaternions representing an object orientation in two consecutive animation frames. Again, if we think of the unit quaternion as being constrained to the surface of a four-dimensional hyper sphere of radius one, the intermediate interpolated unit quaternions will lie on the smallest great hyper arc that connects the unit quaternions being interpolated (see Fig. 8.2).

The same is not true if we are using rotation matrix representation. It is usually very hard to interpolate rotations between two orientations using the rotation matrix representation, and still get a smooth transition (i.e., one without jerkiness) between the orientations as the scene is animated.

8.4 Suggested Readings

Quaternions were originally developed as a way of rotating a 3D vector by multiplying it by another 3D vector. The method of specifying rotations and orientations of coordinate systems via unit quaternions was formally introduced to the computer graphics industry by Shoemake [Sho85]. There you can find a more detailed explanation of why the rotation of a vector $\vec{p} \in \mathbb{R}^3$ by the unit quaternion q can be computed using Eq. (8.15), as well as the derivation of a more sophisticated method to interpolate a set of quaternions using Bézier curves. For readers interested in quaternion visualization techniques, we strongly recommend the work of Hart et al. [HFK94], wherein is presented an alternate exponential notation for representing unit quaternions.

The derivation of Eq. (8.7), that is, the determination of the 3×3 rotation-matrix representation given the angle and axis of rotation, can be found in Craig [Cra89], Pique [Piq90] and in several other books in the fields of mechanics, robotics or computer graphics. An in-depth explanation of general 3D transformations, and how to convert between right-handed and left-handed coordinate systems, is given in Foley et al. [FvDFH96].

Lastly, the Gram–Schmidt algorithm used for correcting the drifting problem observed when multiplying several rotation matrices can be found in Strang [Str91], Golub et al. [GL96] and Horn et al. [HJ91].

References

[Cra89] Craig, J.J.: Introduction to Robotics, Mechanics and Control. Addison-Wesley, Reading (1989)

[FvDFH96] Foley, J.D., van Dam, A., Feiner, S.K., Hughes, J.F.: Computer Graphics Principles and Practice. Addison-Wesley, Reading (1996)

[GL96] Golub, G.H., Van Loan, C.F.: Matrix Computations. Johns Hopkins University Press, Baltimore (1996)

[HFK94] Hart, J.C., Francis, G.K., Kauffman, L.H.: Visualizing quaternion rotation. ACM Trans. Graph. 13(3), 256–276 (1994)

[HJ91] Horn, R.A., Johnson, C.R.: Matrix Analysis. Cambridge University Press, Cambridge (1991)

[Piq90] Pique, M.E.: Rotation tools. In: Graphics Gems I, pp. 465–469 (1990)

[Sho85] Shoemake, K.: Animating rotation with quaternion curves. Comput. Graph. (Proc. SIGGRAPH) 19, 245–254 (1985)

[Str91] Strang, G.: Linear Algebra and Its Applications. Academic Press, San Diego (1991)

Appendix D: Rigid-Body Mass Properties

9.1   Introduction

The way rigid bodies interact with each other in a dynamic simulation depends a great deal on their mass distribution. As was shown in Appendix B (Chap. 7), the rigid body's total mass, center of mass and inertia tensor directly affect the computation of the net force and net torque acting on it, which in turn are used to solve the differential equations of motion. These quantities, namely total mass, center of mass and inertia tensor, are commonly known as the body's mass properties, and depend on the rigid body's shape and density.

Several algorithms have been proposed so far in the computer graphics and simulation and modeling literature to compute the mass properties of a given rigid body object. They usually fall into one of the two high-level classes of algorithms. The first class of algorithms is frequently used in computer solid modeling. Algorithms of this class decompose the original solid-modeling representation of the object into small cells, and compute the approximate value of the object's mass properties by summing the mass properties of each cell. The degree to which the approximate value matches the exact value depends on the granularity of the cell decomposition. However, independent of how fine-grained the decomposition is, the mass properties computed using this class of algorithms are always an approximation of their exact value because of inevitable mismatches between the object's volume and the volume occupied by the cells in the decomposition.

The second class of algorithms assumes the boundary representation of the object is given, that is, the object's polygonal faces, vertices and their neighboring information, and compute the object's mass properties directly from it. Some of these algorithms are specifically designed for the case in which the object's faces are triangles. In this case, the triangular faces are connected to the origin of the coordinate system, forming several tetrahedra. The mass properties of the object are computed by combining the mass properties of each tetrahedron. The drawback to using this method is that some of the tetrahedra can be thin and tall, introducing numerical errors into the computations that can degrade the final result.

M.G. Coutinho, *Guide to Dynamic Simulations of Rigid Bodies and Particle Systems,*   317
Simulation Foundations, Methods and Applications,
DOI 10.1007/978-1-4471-4417-5_9, © Springer-Verlag London 2013

In this appendix, we present Mirtich's algorithm for computing the *exact* values of the mass properties of rigid body objects from their boundary representation. The objects are assumed to be composed by a set of homogeneous polyhedra, each with its own constant density value. The mass properties are computed by incrementally simplifying the initial volume integrals to surface integrals over the faces of the object, then to surface integrals over the faces projected to one of the coordinate planes, and finally to line integrals along the edges of each projected face, which can then be computed directly from its vertices. Despite its complex derivation, the algorithm presented here is surprisingly fast, varying linearly with respect to the total number of faces, edges and vertices of the object.

9.2   Mirtich's Algorithm

The computation of the mass properties involves computing the center of mass, total mass and inertia tensor of the object, from the center of mass, total mass and inertia tensor of each of its homogeneous polyhedra. Assuming the object is represented by n_p homogeneous polyhedra, its total mass can be directly determined from

$$M = \sum_{i=1}^{n_p} \rho_i V_i, \tag{9.1}$$

where ρ_i and V_i are the density and volume of polyhedron i, respectively. The density values are assumed to be given, so that the volume of each polyhedron can be computed from its shape as

$$V_i = \int dV. \tag{9.2}$$

Assuming, for the time being, that we know how to compute the volume integral in (9.2), we can determine the volume of each polyhedron, and use this information in (9.1) to compute the total mass of the object. Knowing the total mass of the object, we can compute the coordinates of its center of mass C as

$$C_x = \frac{1}{M} \sum_{i=1}^{n_p} \int_{V_i} x \, dM = \frac{1}{M} \sum_{i=1}^{n_p} \rho_i \int_{V_i} x \, dV$$

$$C_y = \frac{1}{M} \sum_{i=1}^{n_p} \int_{V_i} y \, dM = \frac{1}{M} \sum_{i=1}^{n_p} \rho_i \int_{V_i} y \, dV \tag{9.3}$$

$$C_z = \frac{1}{M} \sum_{i=1}^{n_p} \int_{V_i} z \, dM = \frac{1}{M} \sum_{i=1}^{n_p} \rho_i \int_{V_i} z \, dV.$$

In Eqs. (9.3), the homogeneity assumption of the polyhedra is used to convert the mass integrals into volume integrals, since $dM = \rho_i \, dV$ for each polyhedron i.

Having derived formulas to compute the total mass and center of mass of the object, the remaining mass property that needs to be determined is the inertia tensor. The inertia tensor is a 3×3 matrix that contains the moments and products of inertia about the center of mass of the object. In other words, it express how the mass of the object is distributed relative to its center of mass.

The computation of the inertia tensor involves determining the nine elements of its 3×3 matrix representation, given by

$$\mathbf{I} = \begin{pmatrix} I_{xx} & -I_{xy} & -I_{xz} \\ -I_{yx} & I_{yy} & -I_{yz} \\ -I_{zx} & -I_{zy} & I_{zz} \end{pmatrix}, \tag{9.4}$$

where I_{xx}, I_{yy} and I_{zz} are the moments of inertia about axes x, y and z, respectively, and I_{xy}, I_{yx}, I_{xz}, I_{zx}, I_{zy} and I_{yz} are the products of inertia between the axes. A well-known property of inertia tensors found in the mechanical engineering literature is that the inertia tensor $\mathbf{I}$ is a real symmetric matrix, that is

$$I_{xy} = I_{yx}$$
$$I_{xz} = I_{zx}$$
$$I_{zy} = I_{yz},$$

so we only need to worry about six out of the nine elements in (9.4). Another useful property of inertia tensors is that it is always possible to find a body-frame coordinate system in which all products of inertia are zero. This body-frame has its origin at the center of mass and coordinate axis aligned with the principal axis of inertia. In this case, $\mathbf{I}$ is diagonal and we just need to keep track of its three diagonal elements.

It is also important to notice that, if the mass distribution of the object doesn't change over time, its inertia tensor relative to its body frame is constant. However, it is constant only in the body-frame coordinate system, but not in the world-frame coordinate system because, as the simulation evolves, the object changes position and orientation and its mass distribution relative to the world frame changes as well. If $\mathbf{I}$ is the inertia tensor relative to the body frame, and $\mathbf{R}$ is the rotation that takes the body frame to the world frame, then the inertia tensor $\mathbf{I}^w$ relative to the world frame is given by

$$\mathbf{I}^w = \mathbf{R}\mathbf{I}\mathbf{R}^{-1} = \mathbf{R}\mathbf{I}\mathbf{R}^t. \tag{9.5}$$

The moments and products of inertia of the object relative to the world frame can be individually determined from the following set of equations.

$$I_{xx}^w = \sum_{i=1}^{n_p} \rho_i \int_{V_i} \left(y^2 + z^2\right) dV$$

$$I_{yy}^w = \sum_{i=1}^{n_p} \rho_i \int_{V_i} \left(z^2 + x^2\right) dV$$

$$I_{zz}^w = \sum_{i=1}^{n_p} \rho_i \int_{V_i} \left(x^2 + y^2\right) dV$$

$$I_{xy}^w = I_{yx}^w = \sum_{i=1}^{n_p} \rho_i \int_{V_i} xy\, dV \tag{9.6}$$

$$I_{yz}^w = I_{zy}^w = \sum_{i=1}^{n_p} \rho_i \int_{V_i} yz\, dV$$

$$I_{zx}^w = I_{xz}^w = \sum_{i=1}^{n_p} \rho_i \int_{V_i} zx\, dV.$$

We can use the *parallel axis* theorem from mechanical engineering to compute the inertia tensor relative to a body frame parallel to the world frame, but with its origin translated to the object's center of mass. The new moments and products of inertia for this new frame set forth below.

$$I_{xx} = I_{xx}^w - M\left(C_y^2 + C_z^2\right)$$

$$I_{yy} = I_{yy}^w - M\left(C_z^2 + C_x^2\right)$$

$$I_{zz} = I_{zz}^w - M\left(C_x^2 + C_y^2\right) \tag{9.7}$$

$$I_{xy} = I_{yx} = I_{xy}^w - M C_x C_y$$

$$I_{yz} = I_{zy} = I_{yz}^w - M C_y C_z$$

$$I_{zx} = I_{xz} = I_{zx}^w - M C_z C_x.$$

Equations (9.7) give us a way of computing the constant inertia tensor relative to a body frame that is parallel to the world frame, but with its origin at the object's center of mass.

A closer look at Eqs. (9.2), (9.3), (9.6) and (9.7), quickly reveals that, in order to compute the object's mass properties, we need to be able to evaluate the following volume integrals defined over each polyhedron of the object

$$T_x = \int_f x\, dV \qquad T_{x^2} = \int_f x^2\, dV$$

$$T_y = \int_f y\, dV \qquad T_{y^2} = \int_f y^2\, dV$$

$$T_z = \int_f z\, dV \qquad T_{z^2} = \int_f z^2\, dV \tag{9.8}$$

$$T_1 = \int_f dV \qquad T_{xy} = \int_f xy\, dV$$

$$T_{yz} = \int_f yz\, dV \qquad T_{zx} = \int_f zx\, dV.$$

The basic idea to solve the volume integrals in (9.8) is to gradually reduce their complexity from volume integrals to surface integrals, then from surface integrals to projected surface integrals, then from projected surface integrals to line integrals, and lastly to evaluate the line integrals from the object's vertex coordinates. These reductions are achieved using well known theorems from advanced calculus.

9.2.1 Volume-Integral to Surface-Integral

The very first step is to reduce the volume integrals in (9.8) to surface integrals over the faces of the object. The volume-to-surface reduction is achieved through the use of the *divergence* theorem. The divergence theorem states that, given a bounded volume V in space and its outward normal (i.e., the normal that points from the inside to the outside of V), then for any continuous vector field $\vec{F}$ defined on V, we have

$$\int_V \nabla \cdot \vec{F}\, dV = \int_{\partial V} \vec{F} \cdot \vec{n}\, dA, \tag{9.9}$$

where ∂V is the boundary of V and ∇ is the divergence operator given by

$$\nabla \cdot \vec{F} = \frac{\partial \vec{F}}{\partial x} + \frac{\partial \vec{F}}{\partial y} + \frac{\partial \vec{F}}{\partial z}. \tag{9.10}$$

Equation (9.9) explicitly shows the way to convert the volume integrals to surface integrals. The volume integrals in (9.8) can be reduced to surface integrals by choosing a continuous force field for each of them. A guess can certainly be used, but we prefer one that simplifies the surface-integral computation. For example, let's examine what would be a suitable choice of force field for the volume integral

$$T_x = \int_V x\, dV.$$

We have to find a force field $\vec{F}$ that satisfies

$$\nabla \cdot \vec{F} = \frac{\partial \vec{F}}{\partial x} + \frac{\partial \vec{F}}{\partial y} + \frac{\partial \vec{F}}{\partial z} = x.$$

There are many force fields that we can choose from for this given case, but a suitable guess would be one that makes the right-hand side of Eq. (9.9) as straightforward as possible to compute. In this context, we shall pick a force field that turns the dot product of the right-hand side of Eq. (9.9) into a simple scalar multiplication, or

$$\vec{F} = \left(\frac{x^2}{2}, 0, 0 \right)^t.$$

Substituting this into Eq. (9.9) gives

$$T_x = \int_V x \, dV = \int_{\partial V} \vec{F} \cdot \vec{n} \, dA = \sum_{f \in \partial V} \int_f \left(\frac{n_x x^2}{2} \right) dA, \qquad (9.11)$$

where the surface integrals are computed for each face of the object. Because in our case each polygonal face has constant normal, we can pull the normal component out of the integral in (9.11), further simplifying the expression to

$$T_x = \sum_{f \in \partial V} \frac{n_x}{2} \int_f x^2 \, dA.$$

The same procedure can be applied for all volume integrals in (9.8), and the result is summarized in Table 9.1. This table shows the appropriate force-field choice and the equivalent surface integral for each volume integral in (9.8).

Having computed the surface integral associated with each volume integral in (9.8), we are ready to proceed to the next step of the integration, which consists of reducing the surface integrals to line integrals. However, before we do that, we shall "standardize" this reduction by first projecting each face of the polyhedron onto one of the coordinate planes.

9.2.2   Surface-Integral to Projected-Surface-Integral

The surface to projected-surface reduction is achieved by projecting each face of the polyhedron onto one of the coordinate planes xy, yz or zx. The choice of the coordinate plane to which the face will be projected depends on the relative orientation of the face with respect to the coordinate plane, that is, it depends on the values of the components n_x, n_y and n_z of the face normal.

Table 9.1 Volume- to surface-integral reduction for each volume integral in (9.8). Even though there are many possible choices of force fields that can be used, the chosen ones significantly simplify the surface-integral computations

Index i	Volume integral T_i	Force field $\vec{F}_i$	Equivalent surface integral
1	$\int_V 1\,dV$	$(x,0,0)^t$	$\sum_{f\in\partial V} n_x \int_f x\,dA$
x	$\int_V x\,dV$	$(\frac{x^2}{2},0,0)^t$	$\sum_{f\in\partial V} \frac{n_x}{2} \int_f x^2\,dA$
y	$\int_V y\,dV$	$(0,\frac{y^2}{2},0)^t$	$\sum_{f\in\partial V} \frac{n_y}{2} \int_f y^2\,dA$
z	$\int_V z\,dV$	$(0,0,\frac{z^2}{2})^t$	$\sum_{f\in\partial V} \frac{n_z}{2} \int_f z^2\,dA$
x^2	$\int_V x^2\,dV$	$(\frac{x^3}{3},0,0)^t$	$\sum_{f\in\partial V} \frac{n_x}{3} \int_f x^3\,dA$
y^2	$\int_V y^2\,dV$	$(0,\frac{y^3}{3},0)^t$	$\sum_{f\in\partial V} \frac{n_y}{3} \int_f y^3\,dA$
z^2	$\int_V z^2\,dV$	$(0,0,\frac{z^3}{3})^t$	$\sum_{f\in\partial V} \frac{n_z}{3} \int_f z^3\,dA$
xy	$\int_V xy\,dV$	$(\frac{x^2y}{2},0,0)^t$	$\sum_{f\in\partial V} \frac{n_x}{2} \int_f x^2y\,dA$
yz	$\int_V yz\,dV$	$(0,\frac{y^2z}{2},0)^t$	$\sum_{f\in\partial V} \frac{n_y}{2} \int_f y^2z\,dA$
zx	$\int_V zx\,dV$	$(0,0,\frac{z^2x}{2})^t$	$\sum_{f\in\partial V} \frac{n_z}{2} \int_f z^2x\,dA$

The surface integral over the face f can be related to the surface integral over its projection f_p as follows. Let the plane equation of face $f \in \partial V$ be given by

$$n_x\vec{x} + n_y\vec{y} + n_z\vec{z} + d = 0,$$

where the scalar constant d can be obtained from

$$d = -\vec{n} \cdot \vec{p}$$

for any point $\vec{p} \in f$. Then, the surface integral over the face f can be computed from the surface integral over the projected face f_p as

$$\int_f g(\alpha,\beta,\gamma)\,dA = \frac{1}{|n_\gamma|}\int_{f_p} g(\alpha,\beta,h(\alpha,\beta))\,d\alpha\,d\beta, \qquad (9.12)$$

where $g(\alpha,\beta,\gamma)$ is any polynomial function of α, β and γ, and $h(\alpha,\beta)$ is given by

$$h(\alpha,\beta) = -\frac{1}{n_\gamma}(n_\alpha\alpha + n_\beta\beta + d). \qquad (9.13)$$

The use of α, β and γ instead of x, y and z in Eqs. (9.12) and (9.13) emphasizes the fact that the face-projection plane is selected at run-time depending on the choice that maximizes n_γ, that is, the choice that maximizes the area of the projected face (see Fig. 9.1). Possible combination values for (α,β,γ) are (x,y,z), (y,z,x) and (z,x,y).

Fig. 9.1 At run-time, the
largest component of the face
normal is selected as n_γ and
the α, β and γ axes are
mapped to the x, y and z axes
according to this selection.
For the cubic object shown
here, the largest component of
the normal $\vec{n}$ of face f is n_z,
and therefore γ is associated
with z given the combination
$(\alpha, \beta, \gamma) = (x, y, z)$

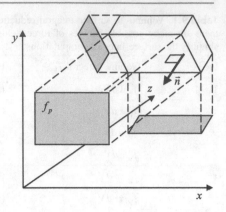

Independent of the combination used, the computation of the surface integrals in
Table 9.1 can always be reduced to the computation of surface integrals of the form:

$$\int_f \alpha \, dA \qquad \int_f \alpha^2 \, dA \qquad \int_f \alpha^3 \, dA \qquad \int_f \alpha^2 \beta \, dA$$

$$\int_f \beta \, dA \qquad \int_f \beta^2 \, dA \qquad \int_f \beta^3 \, dA \qquad \int_f \beta^2 \gamma \, dA \qquad (9.14)$$

$$\int_f \gamma \, dA \qquad \int_f \gamma^2 \, dA \qquad \int_f \gamma^3 \, dA \qquad \int_f \gamma^2 \alpha \, dA.$$

This convenient representation is possible because the surface integrals in Table 9.1 have terms of the form α, α^2, α^3 and $\alpha^2 \beta$, for any of the three possible combination values of (α, β, γ). Since the actual combination value can only be determined at run-time, we shall compute the projected surface integrals of each face as a function of α, β and γ. This we do by substituting Eqs. (9.12) and (9.13) into each surface integral in (9.14).

The surface integrals for each face of the object as a function of its projected surface integral are then given by:

$$\int_f \alpha \, dA = \frac{1}{|n_\gamma|} P_\alpha, \qquad (9.15)$$

$$\int_f \alpha^2 \, dA = \frac{1}{|n_\gamma|} P_{\alpha^2}, \qquad (9.16)$$

$$\int_f \alpha^3 \, dA = \frac{1}{|n_\gamma|} P_{\alpha^3}, \qquad (9.17)$$

$$\int_f \alpha^2 \beta \, dA = \frac{1}{|n_\gamma|} P_{\alpha^2 \beta}, \qquad (9.18)$$

$$\int_f \beta \, dA = \frac{1}{|n_\gamma|} P_\beta, \qquad (9.19)$$

$$\int_f \beta^2 \, dA = \frac{1}{|n_\gamma|} P_{\beta^2},$$ (9.20)

$$\int_f \beta^3 \, dA = \frac{1}{|n_\gamma|} P_{\beta^3},$$ (9.21)

$$\int_f \beta^2 \gamma \, dA = -\frac{1}{|n_\gamma| n_\gamma} (n_\alpha P_{\alpha \beta^2} + n_\beta P_{\beta^3} + d P_{\beta^2}),$$ (9.22)

$$\int_f \gamma \, dA = -\frac{1}{|n_\gamma| n_\gamma} (n_\alpha P_\alpha + n_\beta P_\beta + d P_1),$$ (9.23)

$$\int_f \gamma^2 \, dA = \frac{1}{|n_\gamma| n_\gamma^2} (n_\alpha^2 P_{\alpha^2} + 2 n_\alpha n_\beta P_{\alpha\beta} + n_\beta^2 P_{\beta^2}$$
$$+ 2 d n_\alpha P_\alpha + 2 d n_\beta P_\beta + d^2 P_1),$$ (9.24)

$$\int_f \gamma^3 \, dA = -\frac{1}{|n_\gamma| n_\gamma^3} (n_\alpha^3 P_{\alpha^3} + 3 n_\alpha^2 n_\beta P_{\alpha^2 \beta} + 3 n_\alpha n_\beta^2 P_{\alpha \beta^2}$$
$$+ n_\beta^3 P_{\beta^3} + 3 d n_\alpha^2 P_{\alpha^2} + 6 d n_\alpha n_\beta P_{\alpha\beta} + 3 d n_\beta^2 P_{\beta^2}$$
$$+ 3 d^2 n_\alpha P_\alpha + 3 d^2 n_\beta P_\beta + d^3 P_1),$$ (9.25)

$$\int_f \gamma^2 \alpha \, dA = \frac{1}{|n_\gamma| n_\gamma^2} (n_\alpha^2 P_{\alpha^3} + 2 n_\alpha n_\beta P_{\alpha^2 \beta} + n_\beta^2 P_{\alpha \beta^2}$$
$$+ 2 d n_\alpha P_{\alpha^2} + 2 d n_\beta P_{\alpha\beta} + d^2 P_\alpha),$$ (9.26)

where the projected surface integral $P_{\alpha^u \beta^v}$ is computed as

$$P_{\alpha^u \beta^v} = \int_{f_p} \alpha^u \beta^v \, dA.$$ (9.27)

Having determined the surface integrals as a function of the projected surface integrals, we can then proceed to the next step, which consists of reducing the projected surface integrals to line integrals along each edge of the projected face.

9.2.3 Projected-Surface-Integral to Line-Integral

The projected surface integral is reduced to a line integral using the *Green's* theorem. The Green's theorem can be envisage as the 2D case of the divergence theorem presented in Sect. 9.2.1. It states that, given a planar surface f_p, a continuous force field $\vec{H}$ defined over f_p, and the outward normal $\vec{m}$ along the boundary ∂f_p of f_p, the surface integral is then equivalent to the line integral

$$\int_{f_p} \Delta \cdot \vec{H} \, dA = \oint_{\partial f_p} \vec{H} \cdot \vec{m} \, ds,$$ (9.28)

Fig. 9.2 The projected surface integral is reduced to a line integral over the edges of the projected face f_p. The line integral traverses each edge $e \in f_p$ in a counterclockwise direction

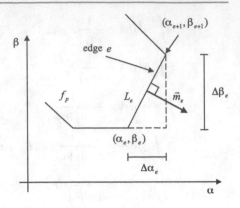

Table 9.2 The line integrals along each edge of the projected face f_p in terms of the α and β components selected at run-time. The change of variable $ds = L_e\, d\lambda$, with L_e being the length of edge e, is used to simplify the integral to vary from 0 to 1

Index i	Proj. surf. integral P_i	Force field $\vec{H}_i$	Equivalent line integral
α	$\int_{P_i} \alpha\, dA$	$(\frac{\alpha^2}{2}, 0)^t$	$\frac{\text{sign}(n_\gamma)}{2} \sum_{e=1}^{n_e} \Delta\beta_e \int_0^1 \alpha^2(L_e\lambda)\, d\lambda$
α^2	$\int_{P_i} \alpha^2\, dA$	$(\frac{\alpha^3}{3}, 0)^t$	$\frac{\text{sign}(n_\gamma)}{3} \sum_{e=1}^{n_e} \Delta\beta_e \int_0^1 \alpha^3(L_e\lambda)\, d\lambda$
α^3	$\int_{P_i} \alpha^3\, dA$	$(\frac{\alpha^4}{4}, 0)^t$	$\frac{\text{sign}(n_\gamma)}{4} \sum_{e=1}^{n_e} \Delta\beta_e \int_0^1 \alpha^4(L_e\lambda)\, d\lambda$
β	$\int_{P_i} \beta\, dA$	$(0, \frac{\beta^2}{2})^t$	$-\frac{\text{sign}(n_\gamma)}{2} \sum_{e=1}^{n_e} \Delta\alpha_e \int_0^1 \beta^2(L_e\lambda)\, d\lambda$
β^2	$\int_{P_i} \beta^2\, dA$	$(0, \frac{\beta^3}{3})^t$	$-\frac{\text{sign}(n_\gamma)}{3} \sum_{e=1}^{n_e} \Delta\alpha_e \int_0^1 \beta^3(L_e\lambda)\, d\lambda$
β^3	$\int_{P_i} \beta^3\, dA$	$(0, \frac{\beta^4}{4})^t$	$-\frac{\text{sign}(n_\gamma)}{4} \sum_{e=1}^{n_e} \Delta\alpha_e \int_0^1 \beta^4(L_e\lambda)\, d\lambda$
$\alpha\beta$	$\int_{P_i} \alpha\beta\, dA$	$(\frac{\alpha^2\beta}{2}, 0)^t$	$\frac{\text{sign}(n_\gamma)}{2} \sum_{e=1}^{n_e} \Delta\beta_e \int_0^1 \alpha^2(L_e\lambda)\beta(L_e\lambda)\, d\lambda$
$\alpha^2\beta$	$\int_{P_i} \alpha^2\beta\, dA$	$(\frac{\alpha^3\beta}{3}, 0)^t$	$\frac{\text{sign}(n_\gamma)}{3} \sum_{e=1}^{n_e} \Delta\beta_e \int_0^1 \alpha^3(L_e\lambda)\beta(L_e\lambda)\, d\lambda$
$\alpha\beta^2$	$\int_{P_i} \alpha\beta^2\, dA$	$(0, \frac{\alpha\beta^3}{3})^t$	$\frac{\text{sign}(n_\gamma)}{3} \sum_{e=1}^{n_e} \Delta\beta_e \int_0^1 \alpha(L_e\lambda)\beta^3(L_e\lambda)\, d\lambda$

where the circular line integral traverses *counterclockwise* the boundary of f_p (see Fig. 9.2). Again, we need to choose a suitable force field $\vec{H}$ such that the right-hand side of Eq. (9.28) is simplified as much as possible for the following line integral computations.

The selection process is identical to that described in Sect. 9.2.1. We shall pick a force field $\vec{H}$ that turns the dot product of the right-hand side of Eq. (9.28) into a simple scalar multiplication. We shall also break the line integral into smaller pieces along each edge of the projected face, since each edge has a constant outward normal that can be extracted from the integration. Table 9.2 shows the selected force fields for each projected surface integral that appears in Eqs. (9.15) to (9.26).

At this point, we have successfully reduced the volume integrals to line integrals over each edge of each projected face of each polyhedron that composes the object. Now, we need to address the last remaining part of the algorithm, which is to com-

Table 9.3 Vertex-based computation of each line integral in Table 9.2

Line integral	Equivalent vertex-based computation
$\int_0^1 \alpha^2(L_e\lambda)\,d\lambda$	$\frac{1}{3}\sum_{i=0}^2 \alpha_{e+1}^i \alpha_e^{2-i}$
$\int_0^1 \alpha^3(L_e\lambda)\,d\lambda$	$\frac{1}{4}\sum_{i=0}^3 \alpha_{e+1}^i \alpha_e^{3-i}$
$\int_0^1 \alpha^4(L_e\lambda)\,d\lambda$	$\frac{1}{5}\sum_{i=0}^4 \alpha_{e+1}^i \alpha_e^{4-i}$
$\int_0^1 \beta^2(L_e\lambda)\,d\lambda$	$\frac{1}{3}\sum_{j=0}^2 \beta_{e+1}^j \beta_e^{2-j}$
$\int_0^1 \beta^3(L_e\lambda)\,d\lambda$	$\frac{1}{4}\sum_{j=0}^3 \beta_{e+1}^j \beta_e^{3-j}$
$\int_0^1 \beta^4(L_e\lambda)\,d\lambda$	$\frac{1}{5}\sum_{j=0}^4 \beta_{e+1}^j \beta_e^{4-j}$
$\int_0^1 \alpha^2(L_e\lambda)\beta(L_e\lambda)\,d\lambda$	$\frac{1}{12}\left(\beta_{e+1}\sum_{i=0}^2 (i+1)\alpha_{e+1}^i \alpha_e^{2-i} + \beta_e \sum_{i=0}^2 (3-i)\alpha_{e+1}^i \alpha_e^{2-i}\right)$
$\int_0^1 \alpha^3(L_e\lambda)\beta(L_e\lambda)\,d\lambda$	$\frac{1}{20}\left(\beta_{e+1}\sum_{i=0}^3 (i+1)\alpha_{e+1}^i \alpha_e^{3-i} + \beta_e \sum_{i=0}^3 (4-i)\alpha_{e+1}^i \alpha_e^{3-i}\right)$
$\int_0^1 \alpha(L_e\lambda)\beta^3(L_e\lambda)\,d\lambda$	$\frac{1}{20}\left(\alpha_{e+1}\sum_{j=0}^3 (j+1)\beta_{e+1}^j \beta_e^{3-j} + \alpha_e \sum_{j=0}^3 (4-j)\beta_{e+1}^j \beta_e^{3-j}\right)$

pute the line integrals given in Table 9.2 as a function of the vertex coordinates of each edge.

9.2.4 Computing Line Integrals from Vertex Coordinates

The line integrals given in Table 9.2 are all of the form

$$\int_0^1 \alpha^p(L_e\lambda)\beta^q(L_e\lambda)\,d\lambda,$$

where L_e is the length of the edge e being considered in the integration, and $0 \le p \le 4$ and $0 \le q \le 4$ are the coefficients of α and β, respectively.

Evaluating the line integrals from the vertex coordinates consists of computing the following expression for each edge being integrated:

$$\int_0^1 \alpha^p(L_e\lambda)\beta^q(L_e\lambda)\,d\lambda = \frac{1}{k_{pq}}\sum_{i=0}^p \sum_{j=0}^q \frac{\binom{p}{i}\binom{q}{j}}{\binom{p+q}{i+j}} \alpha_{e+1}^i \alpha_e^{p-i} \beta_{e+1}^j \beta_e^{q-j},$$

where $k_{pq} = (p+q+1)$ and

$$\binom{p}{i} = \frac{p!}{i!(p-i)!}.$$

Table 9.3 shows the vertex-based computation for each line integral in Table 9.2. We use the vertex coordinates to compute the line integrals, and substitute the result into Table 9.2 to compute the projected surface integrals. The surface integrals are computed from the projected surface integrals using Eqs. (9.15) to (9.26), and their values are substituted back into Table 9.1 to compute all volume integrals. Finally, the mass properties are evaluated from the volume integrals using Eqs. (9.2), (9.3), (9.6) and (9.7).

9.3   Suggested Readings

The algorithm presented in this appendix was developed by Mirtich [Mir96a, Mir96b]. Despite its complex derivation and endless expressions relating volume to surface integrals, surface to line integrals, and line to vertex computations, the implementation is fairly straightforward. All volume integrals can be computed in a single pass through the polyhedron's faces, edges and vertices, resulting in a fast practical algorithm. Kallay [Kal06] presents an alternate method specialized for triangulated meshes.

A comprehensive survey of the various types of algorithms used to compute the mass properties of objects can be found in Lee et al. [LR82a]. The approximate cell-decomposition methods mentioned in the introduction can also be found in Lee et al. [LR82a, LR82b]. The other boundary-representation method specially designed for polyhedra with triangular faces was developed by Lien et al. [LK84].

Lastly, the derivation and analysis of the inertia tensor formulas, as well as the parallel-axis theorem, can be found in Beer et al. [BJ77a], Alonso et al. [AF67], and many other mechanical engineering books that deal with the dynamics of mechanical parts.

References

[AF67]   Alonso, M., Finn, E.J.: Fundamental University Physics. Addison-Wesley, Reading (1967)

[BJ77a] Beer, F.P., Johnston, E.R.: Vector Mechanics for Engineers: vol. 1—Statics. McGraw-Hill, New York (1977)

[Kal06] Kallay, M.: Computing the moment of inertia of a solid defined by a triangle mesh. J. Graph. Tools **11**(2), 51–58 (2006)

[LK84]   Lien, S.-L., Kajiya, J.T.: A symbolic method for calculating the integral properties of arbitrary non-convex polyhedra. IEEE Comput. Graph. Appl. **4**(10), 34–41 (1984)

[LR82a] Lee, Y.T., Requicha, A.A.G.: Algorithms for computing the volume and other integral properties of solids. (1) Known methods and open issues. Commun. ACM **25**(9), 635–641 (1982)

[LR82b] Lee, Y.T., Requicha, A.A.G.: Algorithms for computing the volume and other integral properties of solids. (2) A family of algorithms based on representation conversion and cellular approximation. Commun. ACM **25**(9), 642–650 (1982)

[Mir96a] Mirtich, B.V.: Fast and accurate computation of polyhedral mass properties. J. Graph. Tools **1**(2), 31–50 (1996)

[Mir96b] Mirtich, B.V.: Impulse-based dynamic simulation of rigid body systems. PhD Thesis, University of California, Berkeley (1996)

Appendix E: Useful Time Derivatives

10

10.1 Introduction

In this appendix, we shall present a detailed description of how the time derivatives of a normal vector, a rotation matrix and a quaternion are computed. These time derivatives are used extensively in Chaps. 4 and 5 to describe the dynamic equations of a rigid body.

10.2 Computing the Time Derivative of a Vector Attached to a Rigid Body

The time derivative of a vector attached to a rigid body is used as a auxiliary result to most of the following sections in this appendix. Let points $\vec{p}_1(t)$ and $\vec{p}_2(t)$ of a rigid body B define a general vector $\vec{p}(t)$ given by

$$\vec{p}(t) = \vec{p}_1(t) - \vec{p}_2(t), \tag{10.1}$$

that is, the general vector $\vec{p}(t)$ is attached to the rigid body, so that its linear and angular velocities can be computed as a function of the rigid body's linear and angular velocities. The time derivative of the general vector $\vec{p}(t)$ is then

$$\frac{d\vec{p}(t)}{dt} = \frac{d\vec{p}_1(t)}{dt} - \frac{d\vec{p}_2(t)}{dt}. \tag{10.2}$$

Assume that at time instant t the rigid body is moving with a linear velocity $\vec{v}(t)$ and an angular velocity $\vec{\omega}(t)$. Since $\vec{p}_1$ and $\vec{p}_2$ are points on the rigid body, the time derivatives of their positions is directly obtained as:

$$\frac{d\vec{p}_1(t)}{dt} = \vec{v}(t) + \vec{\omega}(t) \times \vec{p}_1$$

$$\frac{d\vec{p}_2(t)}{dt} = \vec{v}(t) + \vec{\omega}(t) \times \vec{p}_2. \tag{10.3}$$

M.G. Coutinho, *Guide to Dynamic Simulations of Rigid Bodies and Particle Systems*, Simulation Foundations, Methods and Applications, DOI 10.1007/978-1-4471-4417-5_10, © Springer-Verlag London 2013

Substituting Eqs. (10.3) into (10.2), we have

$$\frac{d\vec{p}(t)}{dt} = \vec{\omega}(t) \times \vec{p}_1 - \vec{\omega}(t) \times \vec{p}_2$$

$$= \vec{\omega}(t) \times (\vec{p}_1 - \vec{p}_2).$$

Using Eq. (10.1), we immediately have that the time derivative of a general vector attached to a rigid body is computed as:

$$\frac{d\vec{p}(t)}{dt} = \vec{\omega}(t) \times \vec{p}(t).$$

10.3   Computing the Time Derivative of a Contact-Normal Vector

Whenever particles or rigid bodies are in contact, the determination of the contact force necessary to prevent their interpenetration requires the computation of the time derivative of their contact normal. This computation is done slightly differently depending on whether we have a particle–particle, particle–rigid body or rigid body–rigid body contact.

10.3.1 Particle–Particle Contact

In the particle–particle case, the contact-normal direction is defined as the vector connecting the contacting particles O_1 and O_2, that is

$$\vec{n}(t) = \vec{p}_1(t) - \vec{p}_2(t).$$

The time derivative of the normal vector direction is obtained as

$$\frac{d\vec{n}(t)}{dt} = \frac{d\vec{p}_1(t)}{dt} - \frac{d\vec{p}_2(t)}{dt},$$

$$= \vec{v}_1 - \vec{v}_2 \tag{10.4}$$

where $\vec{p}_1$ and $\vec{p}_2$ are the velocities of particles O_1 and O_2, respectively. The actual derivative of the normal vector is obtained by normalizing Eq. (10.4), that is

$$\frac{d\vec{n}(t)}{dt} = \frac{(\vec{v}_1 - \vec{v}_2)}{|\vec{v}_1 - \vec{v}_2|}.$$

10.3.2 Rigid Body–Rigid Body Contact

There are two possible ways the contact-normal direction can be computed for a rigid body–rigid body contact. If the contact is between a vertex or an edge of rigid body B_1 with a face of rigid body B_2, then the contact-normal direction is given by the face-normal direction, that is

$$\vec{n}(t) = \vec{a}(t) \times \vec{b}(t), \tag{10.5}$$

where $\vec{a}(t)$ and $\vec{b}(t)$ are two edges of the face used to compute the face normal. However, if the contact is between an edge of B_1 with an edge of B_2, then the contact-normal direction is given by

$$\vec{n}(t) = \vec{e}_1(t) \times \vec{e}_2(t), \tag{10.6}$$

where $\vec{e}_1(t)$ is the edge of B_1 and $\vec{e}_2(t)$ is the edge of B_2.

Let's start by examining the time derivative of Eq. (10.6), namely

$$\frac{d\vec{n}(t)}{dt} = \frac{d\vec{e}_1(t)}{dt} \times \vec{e}_2(t) + \vec{e}_1(t) \times \frac{d\vec{e}_2(t)}{dt}. \tag{10.7}$$

If we think of edge $\vec{e}_1(t)$ as a general vector attached to rigid body B_1, then using the results of Sect. 10.2 we obtain

$$\frac{d\vec{e}_1(t)}{dt} = \vec{\omega}_1(t) \times \vec{e}_1(t), \tag{10.8}$$

where $\vec{\omega}_1(t)$ is the angular velocity of rigid body B_1. Conversely, we have

$$\frac{d\vec{e}_2(t)}{dt} = \vec{\omega}_2(t) \times \vec{e}_2(t), \tag{10.9}$$

where $\vec{\omega}_2(t)$ is the angular velocity of rigid body B_2. Substituting Eqs. (10.8) and (10.9) into Eq. (10.7), we get

$$\frac{d\vec{n}(t)}{dt} = \left(\vec{\omega}_1(t) \times \vec{e}_1(t)\right) \times \vec{e}_2(t) + \vec{e}_1(t) \times \left(\vec{\omega}_2(t) \times \vec{e}_2(t)\right). \tag{10.10}$$

Using the general cross-product relation

$$\vec{a} \times (\vec{b} \times \vec{c}) = -(\vec{b} \times \vec{c}) \times \vec{a}$$

in the first cross-product term of Eq. (10.10), we obtain

$$\frac{d\vec{n}(t)}{dt} = \vec{e}_1(t) \times \left(\vec{\omega}_2(t) \times \vec{e}_2(t)\right) - \vec{e}_2(t) \times \left(\vec{\omega}_1(t) \times \vec{e}_1(t)\right). \tag{10.11}$$

Using yet another general cross-product relation

$$\vec{a} \times (\vec{b} \times \vec{c}) = (\vec{a} \cdot \vec{c})\vec{b} - (\vec{a} \cdot \vec{b})\vec{c}, \qquad (10.12)$$

we can substitute both cross-product terms of Eq. (10.11) by

$$\frac{d\vec{n}(t)}{dt} = \left(\vec{e}_1(t) \cdot \vec{e}_2(t)\right)\vec{\omega}_2(t) - \left(\vec{e}_1(t) \cdot \vec{\omega}_2(t)\right)\vec{e}_2(t)$$
$$- \left(\left(\vec{e}_2(t) \cdot \vec{e}_1(t)\right)\vec{\omega}_1(t) - \left(\vec{e}_2(t) \cdot \vec{\omega}_1(t)\right)\vec{e}_1(t)\right).$$

Merging similar terms, we have that the time derivative of the contact-normal direction for edge–edge contact is given by

$$\frac{d\vec{n}(t)}{dt} = \left(\vec{e}_1(t) \cdot \vec{e}_2(t)\right)\left(\vec{\omega}_2(t) - \vec{\omega}_1(t)\right) + \left(\vec{e}_2(t) \cdot \vec{\omega}_1(t)\right)\vec{e}_1(t)$$
$$- \left(\vec{e}_1(t) \cdot \vec{\omega}_1(t)\right)\vec{e}_2(t). \qquad (10.13)$$

The derivations for vertex–face contact, represented by Eq. (10.5), are almost the same as the derivations for edge–edge contact, represented by Eq. (10.5), that is

$$\frac{d\vec{n}(t)}{dt} = \left(\vec{a}(t) \cdot \vec{b}(t)\right)\left(\vec{\omega}_b(t) - \vec{\omega}_a(t)\right) + \left(\vec{b}(t) \cdot \vec{\omega}_a(t)\right)\vec{a}(t)$$
$$- \left(\vec{a}(t) \cdot \vec{\omega}_a(t)\right)\vec{b}(t). \qquad (10.14)$$

The only difference is that, since the normal in the vertex–face contact is computed as the cross-product of two edges belonging to the same face (i.e., the same rigid body), their angular velocities are the same. In other words

$$\vec{\omega}_a(t) = \vec{\omega}_b(t) = \vec{\omega}(t), \qquad (10.15)$$

where $\vec{\omega}(t)$ is the angular velocity of the rigid body the face belongs to. Substituting Eq. (10.15) into Eq. (10.14), we get

$$\frac{d\vec{n}(t)}{dt} = \left(\vec{a}(t) \cdot \vec{b}(t)\right)\left(\vec{\omega}(t) - \vec{\omega}(t)\right) + \left(\vec{b}(t) \cdot \vec{\omega}(t)\right)\vec{a}(t)$$
$$- \left(\vec{a}(t) \cdot \vec{\omega}(t)\right)\vec{b}(t)$$
$$= \left(\vec{b}(t) \cdot \vec{\omega}(t)\right)\vec{a}(t) - \left(\vec{a}(t) \cdot \vec{\omega}(t)\right)\vec{b}(t). \qquad (10.16)$$

Using the general cross-product relation described in Eq. (10.12), we obtain

$$\frac{d\vec{n}(t)}{dt} = \vec{\omega}(t)\left(\vec{a}(t) \times \vec{b}(t)\right) = \vec{\omega}(t) \times \vec{n}(t), \qquad (10.17)$$

which is compatible with the expression obtained for the time derivative of a general vector attached to a rigid body.

The actual time derivative of the contact normal for both situations is then obtained by normalizing Eqs. (10.13) and (10.17), that is, by computing

$$\left(\frac{d\vec{n}(t)}{dt}\right) \Big/ \left|\frac{d\vec{n}(t)}{dt}\right|.$$

10.4 Computing the Time Derivative of the Tangent Plane

Following the convention described in Sect. 6.6 of Appendix A (Chap. 6), the tangent plane direction $\vec{t}(t)$ is directly obtained from the normal vector direction $\vec{n}(t) = (n_x(t), n_y(t), n_z(t))$ by setting to zero its component with the smallest absolute value, swapping the remaining two components and multiplying one of them by -1. We use an auxiliary vector $\vec{a}$ as follows.

1. If $|n_x| \le |n_y|$ and $|n_x| \le |n_z|$, then set the auxiliary vector $\vec{a}$ to

$$\vec{a} = (0, n_z, -n_y). \tag{10.18}$$

2. If $|n_y| \le |n_x|$ and $|n_y| \le |n_z|$, then set the auxiliary vector $\vec{a}$ to

$$\vec{a} = (-n_z, 0, n_x). \tag{10.19}$$

3. If $|n_z| \le |n_x|$ and $|n_z| \le |n_z|$, then set the auxiliary vector $\vec{a}$ to:

$$\vec{a} = (n_y, -n_x, 0). \tag{10.20}$$

The tangent vector $\vec{t}$ is then set to

$$\vec{t} = \frac{\vec{a}}{|\vec{a}|}.$$

The time derivative of the tangent vector $\vec{t}$ is computed as a function of the time derivative of the auxiliary vector, namely

$$\frac{d\vec{t}}{dt} = \left(\frac{d\vec{a}}{dt}\right) \Big/ \left|\frac{d\vec{a}}{dt}\right|,$$

where:
1. If $\vec{a} = (0, n_z, -n_y)$, then

$$\frac{d\vec{a}}{dt} = \left(0, \frac{dn_z(t)}{dt}, -\frac{dn_y(t)}{dt}\right).$$

2. If $\vec{a} = (-n_z, 0, n_x)$, then

$$\frac{d\vec{a}}{dt} = \left(-\frac{dn_z(t)}{dt}, 0, \frac{dn_x(t)}{dt}\right).$$

3. If $\vec{a} = (n_y, -n_x, 0)$, then

$$\frac{d\vec{a}}{dt} = \left(\frac{dn_y(t)}{dt}, -\frac{dn_x(t)}{dt}, 0 \right).$$

The tangent-plane direction $\vec{k}(t)$ is computed as the cross-product of $\vec{n}(t)$ and $\vec{t}(t)$, that is

$$\vec{k} = \vec{n} \times \vec{t}.$$

Therefore, its time derivative can be obtained as

$$\frac{d\vec{k}}{dt} = \frac{d\vec{n}}{dt} \times \vec{t} + \vec{n} \times \frac{d\vec{t}}{dt}$$

after the result is normalized.

10.5   Computing the Time Derivative of a Rotation Matrix

A rotation matrix $\mathbf{R}(t)$ can be viewed as a transformation between a coordinate frame[1] $\mathcal{F}_1$ and the canonical coordinate frame $\mathcal{F}_0$, with the origin of $\mathcal{F}_1$ being coincident with the origin of $\mathcal{F}_0$. Let $\mathcal{F}_1$ be defined by the coordinate vectors $\vec{x}_1$, $\vec{y}_1$ and $\vec{z}_1$, and let the canonical vectors be $\vec{x}_0 = (1, 0, 0)^t$, $\vec{y}_0 = (0, 1, 0)^t$ and $\vec{z}_0 = (0, 0, 1)^t$. Then, a point $\vec{p}_1$ in the coordinate frame $\mathcal{F}_1$ is transformed to a point $\vec{p}_0$ in the canonical frame $\mathcal{F}_0$ by applying the rotation matrix

$$\vec{p}_0 = \mathbf{R}(t)\vec{p}_1.$$

Viewed as a "change of basis" transformation, it is natural to describe the rotation matrix $\mathbf{R}(t)$ using its column-vector representation:

$$\mathbf{R}(t) = \left(\vec{c}_1(t) \mid \vec{c}_2(t) \mid \vec{c}_3(t) \right), \tag{10.21}$$

where the column vectors $\vec{c}_1$, $\vec{c}_2$ and $\vec{c}_3$ represent the coordinate axes $\vec{x}_1$, $\vec{y}_1$ and $\vec{z}_1$ expressed in canonical-frame coordinates.

The time derivative of the rotation matrix is then computed as

$$\frac{d\mathbf{R}(t)}{dt} = \left(d\vec{c}_1(t)/dt \mid d\vec{c}_2(t)/dt \mid d\vec{c}_3(t)/dt \right). \tag{10.22}$$

Let $\vec{\omega}(t)$ be the angular velocity of frame $\mathcal{F}_1$ expressed in canonical-frame coordinates. Using the results obtained in Sect. 10.2, we have that the time derivative of each column vector can be obtained as

---

[1] In the rigid-body case, the coordinate frame $\mathcal{F}_1$ is the body frame.

$$\frac{d\vec{c}_1(t)}{dt} = \vec{\omega}(t) \times \vec{c}_1(t)$$

$$\frac{d\vec{c}_2(t)}{dt} = \vec{\omega}(t) \times \vec{c}_2(t) \qquad\qquad (10.23)$$

$$\frac{d\vec{c}_3(t)}{dt} = \vec{\omega}(t) \times \vec{c}_3(t).$$

Substituting Eqs. (10.23) into (10.22), we have

$$\frac{d\mathbf{R}(t)}{dt} = \left(\vec{\omega}(t) \times \vec{c}_1(t) \mid \vec{\omega}(t) \times \vec{c}_2(t) \mid \vec{\omega}(t) \times \vec{c}_3(t) \right).$$

Using the matrix–vector representation of a cross-product as described in Sect. 6.7, we get

$$\frac{d\mathbf{R}(t)}{dt} = \left(\tilde{\omega}(t)\vec{c}_1(t) \mid \tilde{\omega}(t)\vec{c}_2(t) \mid \tilde{\omega}(t)\vec{c}_3(t) \right), \qquad (10.24)$$

where $\vec{\omega} = (\omega_x, \omega_y, \omega_z)$ and

$$\tilde{\omega}(t) = \begin{pmatrix} 0 & -\omega_z & \omega_y \\ \omega_z & 0 & -\omega_x \\ -\omega_y & \omega_x & 0 \end{pmatrix}.$$

Equation (10.24) can then be written as

$$\frac{d\mathbf{R}(t)}{dt} = \tilde{\omega}(t)\left(\vec{c}_1(t) \mid \vec{c}_2(t) \mid \vec{c}_3(t) \right).$$

Thus, the time derivative of a rotation matrix $\mathbf{R}(t)$ is given by

$$\frac{d\mathbf{R}(t)}{dt} = \tilde{\omega}(t)\mathbf{R}(t). \qquad\qquad (10.25)$$

10.6   Computing the Time Derivative of a Unit Quaternion

The time derivative of a unit quaternion $q = s + \vec{v}$ will be computed using the results already obtained for the time derivative of a rotation matrix. Recall from Appendix C (Chap. 8) that the rotation-matrix representation of a unit quaternion is given by

$$\mathbf{R} = 2 \begin{pmatrix} s^2 + v_x^2 - \frac{1}{2} & v_x v_y - s v_z & v_x v_z + s v_y \\ v_x v_y + s v_z & s^2 + v_y^2 - \frac{1}{2} & v_y v_z - s v_x \\ v_x v_z - s v_y & v_y v_z + s v_x & s^2 + v_z^2 - \frac{1}{2} \end{pmatrix}, \qquad (10.26)$$

where v_x, v_y and v_z are the components of the imaginary part $\vec{v}$ of the unit quaternion q. The time derivative of this rotation matrix is then[2]

$$\frac{d\mathbf{R}}{dt} = 2 \begin{pmatrix} 2(s\dot{s} + v_x\dot{v}_x) & \dot{v}_x v_y + v_x\dot{v}_y - \dot{s}v_z - s\dot{v}_z & \dot{v}_x v_z + v_x\dot{v}_z + \dot{s}v_y + s\dot{v}_y \\ \dot{v}_x v_y + v_x\dot{v}_y + \dot{s}v_z + s\dot{v}_z & 2(s\dot{s} + v_y\dot{v}_y) & \dot{v}_y v_z + v_y\dot{v}_z - \dot{s}v_x - s\dot{v}_x \\ \dot{v}_x v_z + v_x\dot{v}_z - \dot{s}v_y - s\dot{v}_y & \dot{v}_y v_z + v_y\dot{v}_z + \dot{s}v_x + s\dot{v}_x & 2(s\dot{s} + v_z\dot{v}_z) \end{pmatrix}.$$

$$(10.27)$$

As mentioned in Sect. 10.5, the rotation matrix $\mathbf{R}(t)$ can be viewed as a transformation between the body frame and the canonical frame. Let $\tilde{\omega}(t)$ be the angular velocity of the body frame expressed in canonical-frame coordinates. Using Eq. (10.25), we have that the time derivative of the rotation matrix is computed as

$$\frac{d\mathbf{R}(t)}{dt} = \tilde{\omega}(t)\mathbf{R}(t), \tag{10.28}$$

where $\vec{\omega} = (\omega_x, \omega_y, \omega_z)$ and

$$\tilde{\omega}(t) = \begin{pmatrix} 0 & -\omega_z & \omega_y \\ \omega_z & 0 & -\omega_x \\ -\omega_y & \omega_x & 0 \end{pmatrix}. \tag{10.29}$$

Right multiplying both sides of Eq. (10.28) by $\mathbf{R}^{-1}(t) = \mathbf{R}^t(t)$ gives

$$\tilde{\omega}(t) = \frac{d\mathbf{R}(t)}{dt}\mathbf{R}^t(t). \tag{10.30}$$

Substituting Eqs. (10.26), (10.27) and (10.29) into Eq. (10.30), we obtain a linear system that can be solved for ω_x, ω_y and ω_z as follows.

Inspecting Eq. (10.29), we have that ω_x is obtained by multiplying the third row of $d\mathbf{R}(t)/dt$ by the second column of $\mathbf{R}^t(t)$, that is

$$\frac{\omega_x}{4} = (\dot{v}_x v_z + \dot{v}_z v_x - \dot{v}_y s - \dot{s}v_y)(v_x v_y + v_z s)$$

$$+ (\dot{v}_y v_z + \dot{v}_z v_y + \dot{v}_x s + \dot{s}v_x)\left(s^2 + v_y^2 - \frac{1}{2}\right)$$

$$+ 2(\dot{s}s + \dot{v}_z v_z)(\dot{v}_y v_z - \dot{v}_x s).$$

Grouping the terms with common derivatives, we get

$$\frac{\omega_x}{4} = \dot{v}_x\left(v_x v_y v_z + s\left(v_z^2 + s^2 + v_y^2 - \frac{1}{2}\right)\right)$$

$$+ \dot{v}_y\left(v_z\left(v_y^2 - \frac{1}{2}\right) - v_x v_y v_z\right)$$

---

[2]To simplify the notation, we shall use $\dot{a}$ to represent the time derivative $\frac{da}{dt}$.

$$+ \dot{v}_z \left(v_y \left(v_x^2 + v_y^2 + v_z^2 + s^2 - \frac{1}{2} \right) + v_y v_z^2 - v_x v_z s \right)$$

$$+ \dot{s} \left(s v_y v_z - v_x \left(s^2 + \frac{1}{2} \right) \right). \tag{10.31}$$

Since $q = s + \vec{v}$ is a unit quaternion, it must satisfy

$$v_x^2 + v_y^2 + v_z^2 + s^2 = 1 \tag{10.32}$$

$$\dot{v}_x v_x + \dot{v}_y v_y + \dot{v}_z v_z + \dot{s} s = 0. \tag{10.33}$$

Using Eq. (10.32) into (10.31), we have

$$\frac{\omega_x}{4} = \dot{v}_x \left(v_x v_y v_z + s \left(\overbrace{v_z^2 + s^2 + v_y^2}^{1-v_x^2} - \frac{1}{2} \right) \right)$$

$$+ \dot{v}_y \left(v_z \left(v_y^2 - \frac{1}{2} \right) - v_x v_y v_z \right)$$

$$+ \dot{v}_z \left(v_y \left(\overbrace{v_x^2 + v_y^2 + v_z^2 + s^2}^{1} - \frac{1}{2} \right) + v_y v_z^2 - v_x v_z s \right)$$

$$+ \dot{s} \left(s v_y v_z - v_x \left(s^2 + \frac{1}{2} \right) \right)$$

$$= \dot{v}_x \left(v_x v_y v_z + s \left(\frac{1}{2} - v_x^2 \right) \right)$$

$$+ \dot{v}_y \left(v_z \left(v_y^2 - \frac{1}{2} \right) - v_x v_y v_z \right)$$

$$+ \dot{v}_z \left(v_y \left(\frac{1}{2} + v_z^2 \right) + v_y v_z^2 - v_x v_z s \right)$$

$$+ \dot{s} \left(s v_y v_z - v_x \left(s^2 + \frac{1}{2} \right) \right).$$

Regrouping the terms and using Eq. (10.33), we have

$$\frac{\omega_x}{4} = \left(\overbrace{\dot{v}_x v_x + \dot{s} s}^{-\dot{v}_y v_y - \dot{v}_z v_z} \right) v_y v_z - \left(\overbrace{\dot{v}_y v_y + \dot{v}_z v_z}^{-\dot{v}_x v_x - \dot{s} s} \right) v_x s$$

$$+ \dot{v}_x s \left(\frac{1}{2} - v_x^2 \right) + \dot{v}_y v_z \left(v_y^2 - \frac{1}{2} \right)$$

$$+ \dot{v}_z v_y \left(\frac{1}{2} + v_z^2 \right) - \dot{s} v_x \left(\frac{1}{2} + s^2 \right)$$

$$= \frac{s}{2} \dot{v}_x - \frac{v_z}{2} \dot{v}_y + \frac{v_y}{2} \dot{v}_z - \frac{v_x}{2} \dot{s},$$

that is

$$\omega_x = 2s\dot{v}_x - 2v_z\dot{v}_y + 2v_y\dot{v}_z - 2v_x\dot{s}. \tag{10.34}$$

Inspecting Eq. (10.29) one more time, we have that ω_y is obtained by multiplying the first row of $d\mathbf{R}(t)/dt$ by the third column of $\mathbf{R}^t(t)$, that is

$$\frac{\omega_y}{4} = 2(\dot{s}s + \dot{v}_x v_x)(v_z v_x - v_y s)$$
$$+ (\dot{v}_y v_x + \dot{v}_x v_y - \dot{v}_z s - \dot{s}v_z)(v_z v_y + v_x s)$$
$$+ (\dot{v}_z v_x + \dot{v}_x v_z + \dot{v}_y s + \dot{s}v_y)\left(s^2 + v_z^2 - \frac{1}{2}\right).$$

Doing groupings and substitutions similar to those we employed when computing ω_x, we obtain

$$\omega_y = 2v_z\dot{v}_x + 2s\dot{v}_y - 2v_x\dot{v}_z - 2v_y\dot{s}. \tag{10.35}$$

Finally, inspecting Eq. (10.29) one last time, we have that ω_z is obtained by multiplying the second row of $d\mathbf{R}(t)/dt$ by the first column of $\mathbf{R}^t(t)$, that is

$$\frac{\omega_z}{4} = (\dot{v}_x v_y + \dot{v}_y v_x + \dot{v}_z s + \dot{s}v_z)\left(s^2 + v_x^2 - \frac{1}{2}\right)$$
$$+ 2(\dot{s}s + \dot{v}_y v_y)(v_x v_y - s v_z)$$
$$+ (\dot{v}_z v_y + \dot{v}_y v_z - \dot{v}_x s - \dot{s}v_x)(v_x v_z + v_y s).$$

Again, doing groupings and substitutions similar to those we employed when computing ω_x, we obtain

$$\omega_z = -2v_y\dot{v}_x + 2v_x\dot{v}_y + 2s\dot{v}_z - 2v_z\dot{s}. \tag{10.36}$$

Equations (10.34), (10.35) and (10.36) form a linear system:

$$\begin{pmatrix} \omega_x \\ \omega_y \\ \omega_z \\ 0 \end{pmatrix} = 2 \begin{pmatrix} s & -v_z & v_y & -v_x \\ v_z & s & -v_x & -v_y \\ -v_y & v_x & s & -v_z \\ v_x & v_y & v_z & s \end{pmatrix} \begin{pmatrix} \dot{v}_x \\ \dot{v}_y \\ \dot{v}_z \\ \dot{s} \end{pmatrix}, \tag{10.37}$$

where Eq. (10.33) was used in the last row to make the matrix square. Because the determinant of this matrix is -1, the matrix is always invertible. Inverting the system in Eq. (10.37), we obtain

$$\begin{pmatrix} \dot{v}_x \\ \dot{v}_y \\ \dot{v}_z \\ \dot{s} \end{pmatrix} = \frac{1}{2} \begin{pmatrix} s & v_z & -v_y & v_x \\ -v_z & s & v_x & v_y \\ v_y & -v_x & s & v_z \\ -v_x & -v_y & -v_z & s \end{pmatrix} \begin{pmatrix} \omega_x \\ \omega_y \\ \omega_z \\ 0 \end{pmatrix}, \tag{10.38}$$

which gives the time derivative of the unit quaternion as a function of the angular-velocity components.

10.7 Suggested Readings

Most of the derivations in this appendix were either directly obtained, or inspired, from Baraff et al. [BW98] and Mirtich's [Mir96b] work. The main difference in the derivations presented here from their work is in the computation of the time derivative of a unit quaternion. Mirtich assumed the angular velocity of a rigid body is expressed in the body-frame coordinates, instead of being given in the canonical-frame coordinates as used in this book. For that reason, the results obtained in Sect. 10.6 are different from Mirtich's final equations.

Baraff et al., on the other hand, presented a totally different approach to compute the time derivative of a unit quaternion. They represented the angular velocity $\vec{\omega}(t)$ as a rotation about the $(\vec{\omega}(t)/|\vec{\omega}(t)|)$ axis with magnitude $|\vec{\omega}(t)|$. A unit quaternion $q(t)$ can then be built from this rotation axis and rotation angle as

$$q(t) = \cos\left(\frac{|\vec{\omega}(t)|t}{2}\right) + \sin\left(\frac{|\vec{\omega}(t)|t}{2}\right)\frac{\vec{\omega}(t)}{|\vec{\omega}(t)|}.$$

The time derivative of the quaternion is then, after some manipulation, given by

$$\frac{dq(t)}{dt} = \frac{1}{2}q_{\omega}(t)q(t),$$

where $q_{\omega}(t) = 0 + \vec{\omega}(t)$ is the pure quaternion representing the angular velocity.

Lastly, the general cross-product relations were obtained from Gardshteyn et al. [GR80].

References

[BW98] Baraff, D., Witkin, A.: Physically based modeling. SIGGRAPH Course Notes **13** (1998)

[GR80] Gradshteyn, I.S., Ryzhik, I.M.: Table of Integrals, Series and Products. Academic Press, San Diego (1980)

[Mir96b] Mirtich, B.V.: Impulse-based dynamic simulation of rigid body systems. PhD Thesis, University of California, Berkeley (1996)

Appendix F: Convex Decomposition of 3D Polyhedra

11

11.1 Introduction

Most algorithms presented in this book are specially tailored for convex objects. The assumption that the objects being manipulated are convex guarantees faster solutions and much more efficient implementations that take full advantage of the nice properties of convex polyhedra. Nevertheless, most interesting dynamic-simulation scenarios contain at least one non-convex object, making it necessary to pre-process non-convex objects into a set of convex polyhedra before applying most of the algorithms described in this book.

The general convex decomposition problem of partitioning a non-convex 3D polyhedron into a minimum number of convex parts is a rather complex one, known to be NP-hard. There is a significant amount of work in the computational-geometry literature establishing worst-case bounds on the time complexity of convex decomposition algorithms, as well as lower bounds on the total number of convex polyhedra found in the decomposition. However, in the context of dynamic simulations, we are more concerned with the quality of the convex decomposition than the actual number of convex parts it comprises. We want a convex decomposition of "good" quality, tolerant to numerical round-off errors that may be introduced during the computations. We want a convex partition that is suitable for computing hierarchical decompositions of the object (such as those presented in Chap. 2), for checking geometrical intersections between objects to detect the existence of collisions, and for accurately computing the normal vector at the collision point between two objects.

In this appendix, we shall present a simplified version of Joe's algorithm, a convex-decomposition algorithm developed in the context of mesh generation for finite element analysis of complex 3D shapes. The algorithm decomposes non-convex 3D polyhedra into a "good" quality set of convex parts. By "good" quality we mean that the algorithm avoids long and skinny convex parts, as well as unnecessarily short edges and narrow subregions in the convex decomposition. In the case of finite-element analysis, this means that the tetrahedral mesh created from the convex decomposition contains tetrahedra of about the same size and shape. In the context

Fig. 11.1 An example of a special case that is not handled by the algorithm: a polyhedron made of two tetrahedra connected by a single vertex v_0

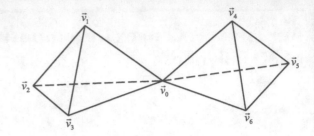

of dynamic simulation, this means that the convex decomposition can be effectively used to produce high-quality hierarchical decompositions of the non-convex object.

There are a few restrictions, though, to the type of 3D polyhedra the algorithm can handle. The original algorithm is restricted to decomposing *simple* non-convex polyhedra, that is, polyhedra that satisfy the following five conditions.

1. The polyhedron has no interior holes.
2. The faces of the polyhedron may have holes. These holes can either stop somewhere inside the polyhedron, or go through the polyhedron from one face to another.
3. The polyhedron is not self-intersecting.
4. Each edge is incident on exactly two faces.
5. The faces surrounding each vertex form a simple circuit.

The last condition states that, for each vertex of the non-convex polyhedron, if we construct a double linked-list of neighbor faces in which a face is linked to another if they share a common edge that has the given vertex as one of its extreme points, then all faces are reachable from any other face in the list. This condition is necessary to avoid special cases wherein the polyhedron can be separated into two parts that share only a single vertex (see Fig. 11.1).

The simplified version presented in this appendix restricts even further the simple-polyhedron assumption stated in the original algorithm. Besides being simple, the polyhedra being decomposed must also satisfy the following two conditions.

6. The faces of the polyhedron have no holes.
7. The faces are convex polygons.

Even though condition 6 limits the polyhedron faces to be simple polygons themselves, this does not prevent the non-convex polyhedron from having exterior holes. Figure 11.2 shows the difference between a face having a hole, and the polyhedron itself having an exterior hole. Exterior holes are allowed, provided that they don't go through the interior of any face.

These extra assumptions have no effect on the main body of Joe's algorithm itself. However, they will be useful to restrict the types of non-convex polyhedra that can be handled, simplify the occurrence of special cases, and reduce the complexity of a software implementation. An example of special cases that are avoided in the simplified version is the creation of double-occurring faces after the non-convex polyhedron is split by a cut plane (see Fig. 11.3).

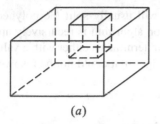 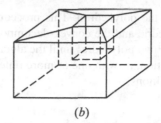

(a) (b)

Fig. 11.2 (a) The face has an interior hole that stops somewhere inside the polyhedron; (b) The faces have no interior holes. Nonetheless, the polyhedron itself has an exterior hole with the same depth as (a)

Fig. 11.3 Double-occurring faces may appear in the original Joe's algorithm, where faces are allowed to have internal holes. In this case, the cut face f_c sub-divides the original non-convex polyhedron in a simply connected polyhedron with face f_c occurring twice

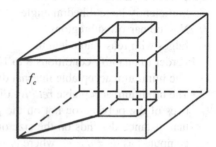

11.2 Joe's Algorithm

The algorithm that computes the convex decomposition of a 3D polyhedron that satisfies conditions 1 to 7 above is simple to state, but much more complicated to implement. The basic idea is to go through the list of edges of the polyhedron and compute the dihedral angle associated with each edge (see Sect. 2.2.4 of Chap. 2). The dihedral angle is the internal angle formed by the faces that share the edge. If the dihedral angle is less than or equal to π, then the polyhedron is convex at the edge. Otherwise, the polyhedron is non-convex at the edge, and the edge is said to be a *reflex* edge. It is clear that the polyhedron will be non-convex if and only if it has at least one reflex edge.

Having determined all reflex edges of the non-convex polyhedron, the algorithm proceeds by recursively resolving each reflex edge. The process of resolving reflex edges consists of splitting their dihedral angle into sub-angles less than or equal to π. The way the dihedral angle is split depends on the conditions that need to be met to obtain a "good" quality convex partition. In our case, we want to avoid small dihedral angles, short edges and narrow subregions when resolving a reflex edge. In other words, the selection of a cut plane that split the dihedral angle of a reflex edge is a process of accepting (or rejecting) cut-plane candidates that are computed from a set of conditions that need to be satisfied to obtain our "good" quality convex partition.

Once a cut plane that satisfies the conditions is obtained, a cut face associated with the cut plane is traced. The cut face is computed by intersecting the cut plane with the faces of the polyhedron, such that the interior of the cut face lies in the interior of the polyhedron. This procedure will usually split the polyhedron into two polyhedra, and the convex-decomposition algorithm is recursively applied for each of the two polyhedra[1] until the algorithm terminates either with a valid convex decomposition, or with one or more reflex edges that could not be resolved for the given conditions.

11.2.1 Determining Candidate Cut Planes

Candidate cut planes are determined for each reflex edge being resolved, according to the set of conditions that we want to meet.

8. Sufficiently large dihedral angles.
9. Not too narrow subregions.
10. Edges with reasonable length.

In order to quantify conditions 8 to 10, we use the following variables.

11. The minimum acceptable internal dihedral angle, denoted by θ_{acc}.
12. The minimum acceptable *relative* distance between the cut plane and other vertices of the polyhedron not on the plane, denoted by d_{acc}. Notice that the actual distance depends on the size of the polyhedron being decomposed and is computed as $d_i = d_{acc}\bar{e}_i$, where $\bar{e}_i$ is the average length of the edges of polyhedron P_i.

The minimum acceptable dihedral angle variable in 11 is used to address condition 8 in avoiding long and skinny convex parts, whereas the minimum acceptable relative distance variable in 12 is used to address conditions 9 and 10 in avoiding both short edges and narrow convex regions.

Another important variable to be considered is the total number of candidate cut planes n_c considered for each reflex edge. This variable is used to limit the amount of execution time spent trying to resolve each reflex edge, and restrict the set of candidate cut planes to those that are most likely to be accepted. Therefore, for each reflex edge, up to n_c candidate cut planes are computed and tested against the desired conditions 8 to 10.

The actual list of candidate cut planes is constructed for each reflex edge as follows. Let e_r be a reflex edge of the non-convex polyhedron P_i. Let faces f_1 and f_2 be incident on edge e_r, and let $\theta_e > \pi$ be its associated dihedral angle.

Naturally, the first two choices of candidate cut planes are those forming a dihedral angle of $\theta = \theta_e - \pi$ with faces f_1 and f_2, respectively (see Fig. 11.4). These choices are added to the list of candidate cut planes only if their dihedral angle θ satisfies the minimum acceptable dihedral angle condition 11, that is, only if

$$\theta \geq \theta_{acc}. \tag{11.1}$$

---

[1]This is true provided the cut face turns out to be a simple polygon. However, there are cases where the cut face can be either a multiply connected polygon with the reflex edge lying on the outer boundary or the inner boundary of a hole, or a simply connected, but non-simple, polygon.

Fig. 11.4 First two choices of candidate cut planes that form an angle of $\theta_e - \pi$ with each of the faces f_1 and f_2 incident on the reflex edge e_r. The angles θ_1 and θ_2 must be tested against the minimum dihedral angle condition of Eq. (11.1) before they can be added to the list of candidate cut planes

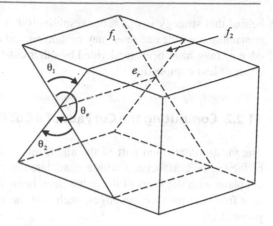

The next choices of candidate cut planes are those that contain the reflex edge e_r and another polyhedron edge sharing a vertex with e_r. Again, these choices will be added to the list of candidate cut planes only if their corresponding dihedral angles satisfy Eq. (11.1).

If the list of candidate cut planes obtained so far has not yet achieved the limit of n_c cut planes, then we continue choosing candidate cut planes that bisect the internal dihedral angle θ_e forming angles θ with face f_1, that satisfy Eq. (11.1) and are of the form

$$\theta = \rho \theta_e,$$

with $\rho \in \{0.25, 0.5, 0.75, 0.375, 0.625\}$. The actual number of candidate cut planes added in this last step depends on the value of θ_e, and on the number of candidate cut planes selected.

Having determined the list of candidate cut planes for the reflex edge e_r, we are ready to compute a cut face associated with each candidate cut plane. As each edge of the cut face is being traced, conditions 8 to 10 are constantly checked to verify whether the candidate cut plane should be rejected.

A candidate cut plane is rejected if one of the following occurs.

13. The minimum dihedral-angle condition is not satisfied. In this case, we have found an edge of the cut face that forms an internal dihedral angle θ that does not satisfy Eq. (11.1).

14. The minimum acceptable relative-distance condition is not satisfied. In this case, there exists at least one vertex of the polyhedron that does not lie on the cut plane and is distant from the plane by an amount less than or equal to the minimum acceptable distance $d = d_{acc}\bar{e}$, where $\bar{e}$ is the average length of the edges of the polyhedron.

15. The cut face is not a simple polygon, that is, it contains one or more holes.

If none of the candidate cut planes in the list satisfies the above criteria, then the reflex edge e_r cannot be resolved at this time, and the algorithm proceeds to another reflex edge, leaving the unresolved one to be addressed again later. The rationale behind this strategy is that, after resolving other reflex edges, the sub-polyhedron containing the reflex edge e_r may be smaller and easier to decompose, or the reflex edge e_r may have been subdivided by other cut faces into two or more reflex sub-edges of less complexity.

11.2.2 Computing the Cut Face of a Cut Plane

The most complicated part of the algorithm is undoubtedly computing the edges of the cut face associated with a candidate cut plane. The idea is to intersect the cut plane with the faces of the polyhedron being decomposed and construct the cut face from the intersection edges, such that the cut face lies in the interior of the polyhedron.

Starting with the reflex edge e_r, we trace the cut face, one edge at a time, moving along the direction corresponding to the normal vector of the cut plane, such that the interior of the polyhedron being cut is to the left of the boundary of the cut face. In most cases, this direction is counter-clockwise, but it can be clockwise as well, and we should keep track of the relative direction of the faces in each sub-polyhedra as they are cut by the cut planes.

One advantage of tracing the cut face one edge at a time is that the internal dihedral angle of each new edge can be immediately computed and tested using Eq. (11.1). The candidate cut plane is rejected if the internal dihedral angle of the new edge is less than the minimum acceptable value. Also, as new edges of the cut face are traced, if a duplicate vertex other than the first vertex is found, then the cut face is at least simply connected, and the candidate cut plane is rejected as well.

The cut face associated with a candidate cut plane is determined as follows. Let P be the non-convex polyhedron to which we are applying the convex decomposition algorithm. Let f_c be the cut face associated with the cut plane α passing through e_r, and let $\vec{v}_0, \vec{v}_1, \ldots, \vec{v}_i$ be the cut-face vertices traced so far. Assume that the last-computed edge $(\vec{v}_{i-1}, \vec{v}_i)$ of the cut face f_c lies on face $f_k \in P$. The next vertex v_{i+1} of the cut face is computed according to one of the following two possible situations.

In the first situation considered, the last-computed vertex v_i lies in the interior of an edge $e_k \in P$ (see Fig. 11.5).

In this case, the direction $\vec{d}_{next}$ of the next edge $(\vec{v}_i, \vec{v}_{i+1})$ of the cut face f_c is unique, and can be determined from the cross-product of the normal vector $\vec{n}_\alpha$ of the cut plane α, and the normal vector $\vec{n}_f$ of the polyhedron face f_j (the other face incident on e_r). Since the next vertex $\vec{v}_{i+1}$ of the cut face f_c lies on an edge of the polyhedron face f_j, and we know the direction $\vec{d}_{next}$ of the edge $(\vec{v}_i, \vec{v}_{i+1})$, the next vertex $\vec{v}_{i+1}$ can be found as the first intersection of the ray $(\vec{v}_i + t\vec{d}_{next})$, for $t > 0$, with the edges of f_j that are also intersected by the cut plane.[2]

---

[2]In our simplified version of the algorithm, the faces of the polyhedron are assumed to be convex, and therefore there is only one edge of the convex face f_j that intersects the cut plane α.

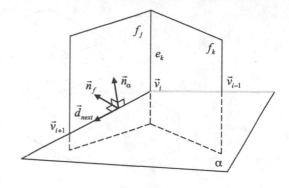

Fig. 11.5 Case when the last-computed vertex v_i lies in the interior of a polyhedron edge e_k. Here, there is only one way to compute the direction of the next edge $(\vec{v}_i, \vec{v}_{i+1})$ of the cut face f_c

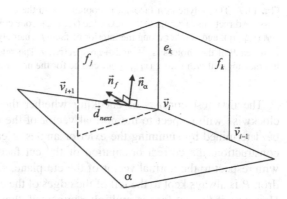

Fig. 11.6 If the polyhedron being decomposed has no coplanar faces with the cut plane α that contain the last edge $(\vec{v}_{i-1}, \vec{v}_i)$, then the direction that minimizes the internal angle at $\vec{v}_i$ is unique. In this case, the procedure used to compute the next vertex $\vec{v}_{i+1}$ is identical to that illustrated in Fig. 11.5

In the second possible situation, the last-computed vertex v_i is a vertex of an edge $e_k \in P$ (see Fig. 11.6).

Hence, the direction $\vec{d}_{next}$ of the next edge $(\vec{v}_i, \vec{v}_{i+1})$ of the cut face f_c may not be unique. In fact, if the polyhedron being decomposed has faces coplanar to the cut plane α that contain the last edge $(\vec{v}_{i-1}, \vec{v}_i)$ of the cut face f_c, then any edge of these faces can be the next edge. Therefore, the next vertex $\vec{v}_{i+1}$ may either lie in the interior of an edge of f_j (see Fig. 11.6), or be a vertex of the polyhedron P (see Fig. 11.7).

The way to resolve this ambiguity is to remember that, by construction, we are always keeping the interior of the polyhedron P to the left of the cut face f_c, that is, to the left of the directed sub-chain $(\vec{v}_{i-1}, \vec{v}_i, \vec{v}_{i+1})$ defining the two consecutive edges $(\vec{v}_{i-1}, \vec{v}_i)$ and $(\vec{v}_i, \vec{v}_{i+1})$ of f_c. Because of this, the direction we should pick to determine the next vertex $\vec{v}_{i+1}$ from the set of candidate directions must be the one that minimizes the interior angle at vertex $\vec{v}_i$. If the direction that minimizes the interior angle at vertex $\vec{v}_i$ coincides with the direction of an edge of f_j, then the next vertex $\vec{v}_{i+1}$ is the other vertex of the edge. Otherwise, the next vertex v_{i+1} lies in the interior of an edge of f_j and can be computed as before.

After determining all edges of the cut face f_c, we still need to carry out two more tests before accepting f_c as a valid cut face that meets all desired conditions 8 to 10.

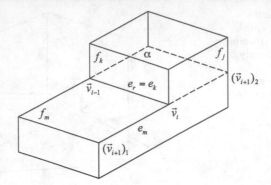

Fig. 11.7 The polyhedron face f_m is coplanar with the cut plane α. In this case, there are two possible directions to compute the next edge $(\vec{v}_i, \vec{v}_{i+1})$, one coincident with edge e_m of f_m, namely $(\vec{v}_i, (\vec{v}_{i+1})_1)$, and another along the interior of face f_j, namely $(\vec{v}_i, (\vec{v}_{i+1})_2)$. The internal angle at $\vec{v}_i$ for each of the choices is $\frac{3\pi}{2}$ and $\frac{\pi}{2}$, respectively. The selected direction should minimize the internal angle at $\vec{v}_i$, making $(\vec{v}_{i+1})_2$ our choice for the next vertex $\vec{v}_{i+1}$

The first test consists of checking whether the cut face is oriented counter-clockwise with respect to the normal vector of the cut plane. The orientation can be determined by summing the exterior angles at each vertex of the cut face. By construction, the correct orientation of the cut face should be counter-clockwise with respect to the normal vector of the cut plane, since the interior of the polyhedron P is always kept to the left of the edges of the cut face, as they are discovered. However, if the cut face is multiply connected, then the orientation will be clockwise instead of counter-clockwise. In this case, the cut plane associated with this cut face is rejected.

The second test consists of checking whether the cut face has interior holes. This is done as follows. Initially, we consider the set of edges of the polyhedron P that intersect the cut plane α. From this set, we remove any edge that contains a vertex of the cut face, either in its interior or as a vertex of the edge itself. Finally, for each edge left in the set, we compute its intersection with the cut plane α. If the intersection point lies inside the cut face, then the cut face has holes and its associated cut plane is rejected.

11.2.3 Termination Conditions

It is clear that there may be cases where one or more reflex edges cannot be successfully resolved for the given minimum internal-dihedral-angle and relative-distance values. A workaround for these cases is to reduce the minimum acceptable values and execute the algorithm one more time, not on the original non-convex polyhedron, but on the convex decomposition of the polyhedron found so far.

Even though this strategy considerably improves the chances of resolving all reflex edges, there may be still cases wherein some reflex edges may not be resolved. For these cases, a more sophisticated algorithm must be used, such as one that extends the original Joe's algorithm to allow the creation of simply connected or multiply connected cut faces.

11.3   Suggested Readings

The algorithm presented in this appendix is part of a tetrahedral mesh-generation algorithm for convex and non-convex polyhedra developed by Joe [Joe94, Joe91]. The original algorithm is itself a modification of Chazelle's algorithm [Cha84], which resolves each reflex edge by a cut face without taking into account the quality of the convex partition produced. Bajaj et al. [BD92] developed an extension to Chazelle's algorithm capable of handling internal holes on the non-convex polyhedra.

As far as triangulating the faces of the resulting convex decomposition, several algorithms can be used depending on the faces being convex or non-convex polygons. If the faces are convex, then we suggest computing the Delaunay triangulation of each face using the algorithm presented in Joe [Joe86]. Otherwise, we suggest using more sophisticated triangulation algorithms for convex and non-convex polygons, such as those described in Joe [JS86] and Keil [Kei96].

References

[BD92] Bajaj, C.L., Dey, T.K.: Convex decomposition of polyhedra and robustness. SIAM J. Comput. **21**(2), 339–364 (1992)

[Cha84] Chazelle, B.: Convex partitions of polyhedra: a lower bound and worst-case optimal algorithm. SIAM J. Comput. **13**(3), 488–507 (1984)

[Joe86] Joe, B.: Delaunay triangular meshes in convex polygons. SIAM J. Sci. Stat. Comput. **7**, 514–539 (1986)

[Joe91] Joe, B.: Delaunay versus max–min solid angle triangulations for three-dimensional mesh generation. Int. J. Numer. Methods Eng. **31**, 987–997 (1991)

[Joe94] Joe, B.: Tetrahedral mesh generation in polyhedral regions based on convex polyhedron decompositions. Int. J. Numer. Methods Eng. **37**, 693–713 (1994)

[JS86] Joe, B., Simpson, R.B.: Triangular meshes for regions of complicated shape. Int. J. Numer. Methods Eng. **23**, 751–778 (1986)

[Kei96] Keil, M.: Polygon decomposition. In: Handbook of Computational Geometry. Elsevier, Amsterdam (1996)

Appendix G: Constructing Signed Distance Fields for 3D Polyhedra

12

12.1 Introduction

In this appendix, we shall discuss the construction of signed distance fields for 3D polyhedra in the context of collision detection. Basically, a signed distance field is a continuous representation of distances to the zero iso-contour of the 3D polyhedra, that is, distances to its boundary surface. The sign is used to differentiate between points inside and outside the object. By convention, points that are outside the object are assigned a positive distance value, points on the object's surface have zero distance value, and points that are inside are assigned a negative value. Usually, a signed distance field is built by superimposing a grid over the object, large enough to bound its volume, and have each grid vertex store the signed distance to its closest point on the object's surface. The signed distance of a generic point in the grid other than a grid vertex is obtained by first locating the grid cell that contains the point, and then using trilinear interpolation on the grid cell vertices to determine the signed distance of the point to the object's surface.

The quality of the signed distance field directly depends on the relation between the grid resolution and the mesh resolution used to represent the object's surface. In general, a low-resolution mesh representation has few surface details and as so, a low-resolution grid representation of the signed distance field often suffices to provide good quality distance values. As the mesh resolution increases, so does the need to increase the grid resolution of the signed distance field in order to capture accurate distance values to the higher resolution surface. A low-resolution grid superimposed on a high-resolution mesh will often smooth out mesh details, creating a simplified representation of the original mesh. This simplified mesh representation can be used as a replacement in the simulation engine of the original high-resolution object in order to improve the simulation speed and still obtain quality results.

The *marching cubes* is the standard algorithm used to create a new mesh representation of the object's surface from its signed distance field. The basic idea of this algorithm is to loop through (i.e., march) all grid cells (i.e., cubes) detecting the ones that cross the object's surface. A grid cell is considered to be crossing the object's surface whenever the signed distance values at its vertices don't have the same sign, that is, some of its vertices are inside while others are outside the object. In the marching cubes algorithm, grid vertices with a zero signed distance value are tagged as inside vertices even though they are in fact on the object's surface. There are a total of 256 possible different configurations of sign assignment to a grid cell. This is because a grid cell has 8 vertices, each being tagged as either inside or outside the object, resulting in $2^8 = 256$ combinations. Look-up tables are used to encode the appropriate tiling to be used for a grid cell depending on its configuration. More details on the marching cubes algorithm can be found in the references listed in Sect. 12.5, including recent work on modifying and extending the look-up tables to make topological guarantees to the newly constructed mesh, such that it doesn't have holes.

12.2   A Memory Efficient Signed Distance Field

The naive approach to build signed distance fields uses a dense grid representation, that is, it allocates memory for the entire grid. It then loops through each grid vertex computing the distance to its closest point on the object's surface. The sign of the closest distance is then chosen depending on the grid vertex be inside or outside the object.[1] In terms of memory requirements, the naive approach uses $O(n^3)$ memory for a uniform grid with n subdivisions along each axis.

In the context of collision detection, we are mostly interested in having high-quality distance values for the grid vertices that are *inside* the object. These distance values are used to interpolate the penetration depth and the gradient direction vector at a generic point inside in the grid. The gradient direction is used to move from the given point's location towards its closest point on the zero iso-contour of the object, that is, the closest point on the object's surface. Outside points are not colliding with the object, so their distance computation doesn't need to be as accurate as the one for inside points. In fact, it is best if outside points are detected and discarded as early as possible in the collision detection check to avoid unnecessary computations.

In this book, we present a new signed distance field representation of objects that is memory efficient and specially tailored for collision detection. It uses an order of magnitude less memory than that required for a dense grid making it possible to use grid resolutions on the order of thousands of cells and still be manageable and efficient.

The main idea behind this new representation is to view the grid not as a collection of grid vertices, but rather as a set of scanlines along each of the three coordinate planes XY, YZ and ZX. These scanlines may intersect or not the object's surface. When intersections occur, the intersection points always come in pairs, one for entering and the other for exiting the object. Since we know the 3D coordinates of the begin and end points of each scanline, we can represent their intersection points using scalar values varying from 0 to 1, with 0 being coincident with the begin point of

---

[1]This point-in-object test is covered in details in Sect. 2.5.13 of Chap. 2.

the scanline and 1 with the end point of the scanline. This simplified representation is key to achieve memory efficiency, because we no longer need to store the actual 3D coordinates of each intersection point. Instead we use a single scalar value to replace the three scalar values making up the 3D coordinate of an intersection point.

The memory savings are best illustrated if we consider the particular case of convex objects. In the convex object case, there can be at most two intersection points per scanline. Since a uniform grid with n subdivisions along each axis has $O(n^2)$ scanlines for each coordinate plane XY, YZ and ZX, there are a total of $O(3n^2)$ scanlines to be considered. Let's assume all scanlines intersect the convex object, that is, we have a $2 \times O(3n^2) = O(6n^2)$ intersection points, each represented by a scalar value. Therefore, we need $O(6n^2) \approx O(n^2)$ memory to store the signed distance for all intersections. Compare this result with the memory requirements of $O(n^3)$ for a dense grid to store the signed distance at all grid vertices, and we have an order of magnitude gain over the dense grid representation.

As far as the scanline intersections are concerned, it is possible that the entry and exit points be coincident, for example, when the scanline intersects the object exactly at a corner vertex. In these cases, the intersection is ignored because the region of the scanline inside the object is empty, that is, the distance between the entry and exit points is zero.

12.2.1 Computing the Grid Cell Size

The grid cell size can be determined from the axis-aligned bounding volume representation of the object. Let (b_x, b_y, b_z) define the extent along each coordinate axis of the axis-aligned box bounding the object, and without loss of generality, lets assume b_x is the largest one, that is

$$b_x \geq b_y$$
$$b_x \geq b_z.$$

Let the user-defined parameter R be the desired resolution along the axis with maximum extent, in this case, the x-axis. The size of each cell along the x-axis is then

$$n_x = \frac{b_x}{R}.$$

Since it is best to use grid cells of uniform size, the size of each cell along the y- and z-axis is made the same as the one used for the x-axis, that is

$$n_y = n_x$$
$$n_z = n_x.$$

The grid resolution on each axis is then

$$r_x = R$$
$$r_y = \left\lceil \frac{b_y}{n_y} \right\rceil$$
$$r_z = \left\lceil \frac{b_z}{n_z} \right\rceil,$$

rounded to the nearest integer value. As will be discussed in Sect. 12.2.5, the gradient calculations require look ahead one cell on each direction along the coordinate axis from the point at which it is being computed. So, we need to extend the object's bounding volume by at least one cell in each direction to enable gradient calculations on points near its boundary. Therefore, the actual number of cells along each axis becomes

$$r_x = r_x + 2$$
$$r_y = r_y + 2$$
$$r_z = r_z + 2,$$

with the axis-aligned bounding box representation of the object being extended by

$$\vec{n}_{ext} = (n_x, n_y, n_z)$$

to include an extra cell on each direction, that is

$$\vec{B}_{min} = \vec{B}_{min} - \vec{n}_{ext}$$
$$\vec{B}_{max} = \vec{B}_{max} + \vec{n}_{ext},$$

where $\vec{B}_{min}$ and $\vec{B}_{max}$ are the lower and upper corner points defining the axis-aligned bounding box of the object, respectively. Figure. 12.1 illustrates this bounding box extension to include the extra cells.

12.2.2 Scanline Rasterization

The rasterization process consists of intersecting the scanlines along planes XY, YZ and ZX, with the object's geometry. There are $r_x r_y$ scanlines along the XY plane, $r_y r_z$ scanlines along the YZ plane, and $r_z r_x$ scanlines along the ZX plane. The scanlines along XY are parallel to the z-axis, the ones along the YZ are parallel to the x-axis and the ones along ZX are parallel to the y-axis. Each scanline will store its intersection information as a vector sorted by increasing intersection values. Recall that the number of entries in this vector is either zero or even because the intersections come in pairs of entry and exit points. As far as performance is

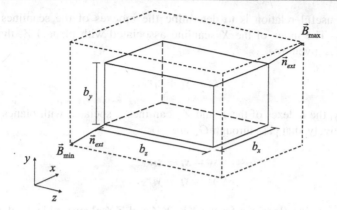

Fig. 12.1 The original axis-aligned bounding box is extended by one cell on each direction to allow gradient calculations on faces near its boundary

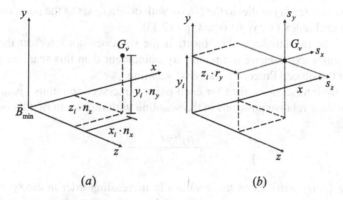

(a)   (b)

Fig. 12.2 (a) The 3D coordinates of a grid vertex G_v can be obtained from its grid index (i.e., specifies how many cells it is away from $\vec{B}_{min}$ along each axis) and the grid cell size. (b) Scanlines passing through G_v. Their integer indexes can be obtained from G_v's grid indexes and the resolution along each axis

concerned, the scanline-object intersection tests can be greatly optimized because the ray representing the scanline is always parallel to a coordinate axis.

Before we delve into the details of the rasterization algorithm, lets consider a couple of definitions that are used throughout this appendix. These are illustrated in Fig. 12.2. First, the 3D coordinate of a grid vertex G_v defined by its grid indexes (x_i, y_i, z_i) is computed as

$$x = (\vec{B}_{min})_x + x_i n_x$$
$$y = (\vec{B}_{min})_y + y_i n_y \qquad (12.1)$$
$$z = (\vec{B}_{min})_z + z_i n_z.$$

Another useful relation is to determine the indexes of the scanlines passing through G_v. The index of the X scanline associated with plane YZ, that passes through G_v is given by

$$s_x = y_i + z_i r_y. \tag{12.2}$$

Similarly, the indexes of the Y and Z scanlines associated with planes ZX and XY, respectively, that pass through G_v are

$$\begin{aligned} s_y &= x_i + z_i r_x \\ s_z &= x_i + y_i r_x. \end{aligned} \tag{12.3}$$

The rasterization algorithm for the XY, YZ and ZX planes is identical, provided that the indexing of the scanlines used is changed accordingly. For example, lets consider the rasterization of the XY plane.

1. For each $x_i \in [0, r_x]$ and for each $y_i \in [0, r_y]$, build the ray representing this scanline. This ray is parallel to the z-axis with origin $\vec{r}_0$ set as the point associated with the grid index $(x_i, y_i, 0)$ (use Eq. (12.1)).
2. Check if the ray intersects the object. If the ray does not intersect the object, or if all entry-exit intersection points are coincident then this scanline does not intersect the object. Proceed to the next scanline.
3. If there are intersections, then for each pair of intersection points $(\vec{p}_{entry}, \vec{p}_{exit})$, compute their relative positions in the scanline with respect to $\vec{r}_0$, that is

$$\frac{(\vec{p}_j - \vec{r}_0)_z}{(\vec{B}_{max} - \vec{B}_{min})_z}$$

with $j \in \{entry, exit\}$. Store these values in increasing order in the vector of intersection results associated with this scanline. Proceed to the next scanline.

Upon completion, the rasterization process will generate three vectors of scanlines, one for each coordinate plane XY, YZ and ZX, with each element of these vectors being a vector itself containing the sorted relative position values of the scanline intersections with the object. Notice that the scanline intersection computation can be parallelized because there is no memory access overlap or synchronization requirements between the intersection calculations for each plane.

12.2.3 Computing the Signed Distance at a Grid Vertex

Let G_v be a grid vertex defined by its grid indexes (x_i, y_i, z_i). Using Eqs. (12.2) and (12.3), we can compute the indexes s_x, s_y and s_z of the 3 scanlines passing through it. Let d_x, d_y and d_z be the signed distance values at G_v along scanlines s_x, s_y and s_z, respectively. The final signed distance value d_g at G_v is set as the smallest absolute value of the signed distances among the 3 scanlines passing through it, that is

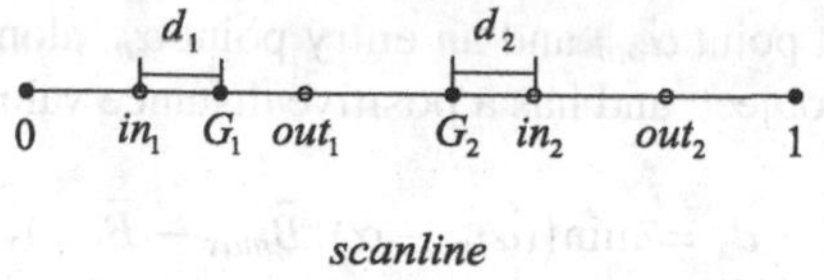

scanline

Fig. 12.3 Scanline with intersection points sorted in increasing order of distances to the starting point 0. Grid vertex G_1 lies inside the object between intersection points in_1 and out_1. Since it is closer to in_1 than out_1, the absolute value of its signed distance is d_1. At the same time, grid vertex G_2 lies outside the object between intersection points out_1 and in_2. The absolute value of its signed distance is d_2 because it is closer to in_2 than out_1

1. If $|d_x| \le |d_y|$ and $|d_x| \le |d_z|$, then $d_g = d_x$.
2. If $|d_y| \le |d_x|$ and $|d_y| \le |d_z|$, then $d_g = d_y$.
3. If $|d_z| \le |d_x|$ and $|d_z| \le |d_y|$, then $d_g = d_z$.

The signed distances d_x, d_y and d_z of G_v are computed from the relative position of the grid vertex with respect to the intersection points on each scanline. For instance, if the grid vertex lies between an entry and exit intersection point on the scanline, then the grid vertex is inside the object along the scanline. In this case, the grid vertex will have a negative signed distance with absolute value equal to the smallest distance between itself and the entry and exit points. Otherwise, the grid vertex is considered to be outside the object along the scanline. Figure 12.3 illustrates these cases for a single scanline.

To illustrate, lets examine in details the algorithm used to compute the signed distance value d_x for the scanline s_x passing through G_v. A similar algorithm can be used to determine the signed distance values d_y and d_z associated with scanlines s_y and s_z, respectively.

1. Use Eq. (12.1) to compute the position (x, y, z) of the grid vertex G_v.
2. Compute the relative position of G_v along s_x, that is

$$\alpha = \frac{x - (\vec{B}_{min})_x}{(\vec{B}_{max} - \vec{B}_{min})_x}.$$

3. Loop through the intersection vector associated with s_x and determine whether the relative position of the grid vertex lies:
   (a) Before the first entry point located at α_0. In this case, G_v lies outside the object along s_x, and has a positive distance value of

$$d_x = (\alpha_0 - \alpha)(\vec{B}_{max} - \vec{B}_{min})_x.$$

   (b) Between an entry point α_{in} and an exit point α_{out} along s_x. In this case, G_v lies inside the object, and has a negative distance value of

$$d_x = -\min\big((\alpha - \alpha_{in})(\vec{B}_{max} - \vec{B}_{min})_x,$$
$$(\alpha_{out} - \alpha)(\vec{B}_{max} - \vec{B}_{min})_x\big).$$

(c) Between an exit point α_{out} and an entry point α_{in} along s_x. In this case, G_v lies outside the object, and has a positive distance value of

$$d_x = \min\big((\alpha_{in} - \alpha)(\vec{B}_{max} - \vec{B}_{min})_x,$$
$$(\alpha - \alpha_{out})(\vec{B}_{max} - \vec{B}_{min})_x\big).$$

(d) After the last exit point α_1. In this case, the grid vertex lies outside the object along s_x, and has a positive distance value of

$$d_x = (\alpha - \alpha_1)(\vec{B}_{max} - \vec{B}_{min})_x.$$

4. If the intersection vector associated with s_x is empty, then G_v lies outside the object and its distance value is assigned to an arbitrarily large positive value, such as the maximum extent of the axis-aligned box bounding the object.

12.2.4 Computing the Signed Distance at a Point

The computation of the signed distance at a generic point inside the grid is much more involving than the one at a grid vertex. First, we need to determine the grid cell that contains the point. Second, we need to compute the signed distance at each of the 8 grid vertices defining this cell, and finally we need to use trilinear interpolation to determine the signed distance value at the point location.

Let $\vec{p} = (p_x, p_y, p_z)$ be a generic point inside the grid. Its relative position with respect to the lower end point of the grid is given by

$$t_x = \big(p_x - (\vec{B}_{min})_x\big)/n_x$$
$$t_y = \big(p_y - (\vec{B}_{min})_y\big)/n_y$$
$$t_z = \big(p_z - (\vec{B}_{min})_z\big)/n_z$$

which corresponds to the grid cell

$$c_x = \lfloor t_x \rfloor$$
$$c_y = \lfloor t_y \rfloor$$
$$c_z = \lfloor t_z \rfloor.$$

The position of the point relative to the lower end point of its grid cell is then

$$t_x = t_x - c_x$$
$$t_y = t_y - c_y$$
$$t_z = t_z - c_z.$$

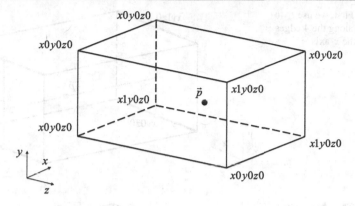

Fig. 12.4 The signed distance value at $\vec{p}$ can be computed from the signed distance values at the grid vertices using trilinear interpolation

Using the results from Sect. 12.2.3, we can compute the signed distance value at each of the 8 grid vertices of the grid cell (c_x, c_y, c_z) which contains the point. More specifically, we need to compute the signed distances at the following 8 grid vertices:

$$x0y0z0 = d_g(c_x, c_y, c_z)$$
$$x1y0z0 = d_g(c_x + 1, c_y, c_z)$$
$$x0y1z0 = d_g(c_x, c_y + 1, c_z)$$
$$x1y1z0 = d_g(c_x + 1, c_y + 1, c_z)$$
$$x0y0z1 = d_g(c_x, c_y, c_z + 1)$$
$$x1y0z1 = d_g(c_x + 1, c_y, c_z + 1)$$
$$x0y1z1 = d_g(c_x, c_y + 1, c_z + 1)$$
$$x1y1z1 = d_g(c_x + 1, c_y + 1, c_z + 1)$$

with $d_g(x_i, y_i, z_i)$ being the signed distance at the grid vertex defined by grid indexes (x_i, y_i, z_i).

Figure 12.4 shows a grid cell containing the point $\vec{p}$. The signed distance value at $\vec{p}$ can be computed from the signed distance values at the grid vertices using trilinear interpolation. First, we linear interpolate along the x-axis using t_x to obtain 4 points out of the initial 8 points making up the grid cell (see Fig. 12.5). Then, we linear interpolate those 4 points along the y-axis using t_y to obtain 2 new points (see Fig. 12.6). Finally, we linear interpolate those 2 points along the z-axis using t_z to get to the final distance value $d(p_x, p_y, p_z)$ (see Fig. 12.7), that is:

$$xy0z0 = x0y0z0 + (x1y0z0 - x0y0z0)t_x$$
$$xy1z0 = x0y1z0 + (x1y1z0 - x0y1z0)t_x$$
$$xy0z1 = x0y0z1 + (x1y0z1 - x0y0z1)t_x$$

Fig. 12.5 First, we use t_x to interpolate along the 4 edges parallel to the x-axis

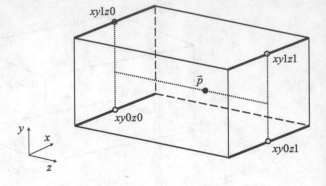

Fig. 12.6 Then, we use t_y to interpolate along the 2 edges parallel to the y-axis, connecting the 4 results of the first interpolation

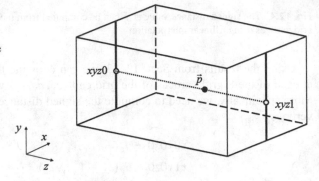

$$xy1z1 = x0y1z1 + (x1y1z1 - x0y1z1)t_x$$
$$xyz0 = xy0z0 + (xy1z0 - xy0z0)t_y$$
$$xyz1 = xy0z1 + (xy1z1 - xy0z1)t_y$$
$$xyz = xyz0 + (xyz1 - xyz0)t_z.$$

12.2.5 Computing the Gradient at a Point

The gradient at a generic point inside the grid can be computed using central differencing. The main idea is to look ahead and behind one grid cell from the point location and compute the variation of the signed distance values along each axis. This variation is combined into a normalized vector to define the gradient at the point.

Let $\vec{p} = (p_x, p_y, p_z)$ be the point location at which we want to compute the gradient of the signed distance field. Using central differencing, we obtain

$$g_x = (d(p_x + n_x, p_y, p_z) - d(p_x - n_x, p_y, p_z))/(2n_x)$$
$$g_y = (d(p_y, p_y + n_y, p_z) - d(p_x, p_y - n_y, p_z))/(2n_y)$$
$$g_z = (d(p_z, p_y, p_z + n_z) - d(p_x, p_y, p_z - n_z))/(2n_z)$$

Fig. 12.7 Finally, we use t_z to interpolate the previous 2 results forming a line parallel to the z-axis

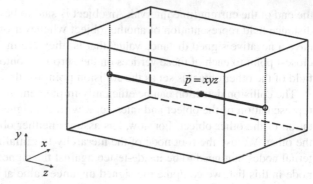

with $d(i, j, k)$ being the signed distance at the generic point (i, j, k). The vector $\vec{g} = (g_x, g_y, g_z)$ is set as the gradient at $\vec{p}$ after it is normalized.

12.2.6 Computing the Closest Point on the Zero Iso-contour

The computation of the point on the zero iso-contour that is closest to a generic point inside the grid is an iterative process. Starting at the given point $\vec{p}$, we first compute both its signed distance and gradient vector. Then, we keep moving the point by its signed distance along its gradient direction until it reaches the zero iso-contour (i.e., the object's surface). The termination condition at each iteration consists of checking if the absolute value of the signed distance becomes less than a user-defined tolerance value. Optionally, we can also use a second termination condition that compares the number of iterations executed so far with a user-definable limit, after which, the algorithm returns whatever intermediate point it has as the final result.

The following steps summarize each iteration of the algorithm.

1. Compute the signed distance d at the current point $\vec{p}$.
2. If the absolute value of the signed distance is less than a user-defined tolerance, then return the current point location as the closest point.
3. If the current number of iterations have reached a user-defined limit, then return the current point location as the closest point.
4. Compute the gradient $\vec{g}$ at the current point.
5. Update the current point location to $\vec{p}_{new} = \vec{p} - d\vec{g}$, and proceed to the next iteration.

12.3 Detecting Collisions

Collision detection with signed distance field representations usually consider the geometric positioning of the objects at the end of the current time interval associated with the motion. The backtracking in time to determine the actual collision time when the objects are about to collide is not executed in this case. Instead, an approximation of the collision information is obtained from the intersecting state at the end of the current time interval. An object is said to be colliding with the signed distance field representation of another object whenever one or more of its vertices have a negative signed distance value, that is, they are inside the other object. The closest point to each of these vertices on the zero iso-contour of the signed distance field of the other object is set as the collision point for the vertex.

The collision detection can be efficiently implemented if we use the hierarchical representation of the object and intersect it with the signed distance field representation of the other object. For now, lets assume neither object is completely inside the other. We use the root node of the hierarchy to initialize an auxiliary list of internal nodes that need to be inside-tested against the signed distance field. For each node in this list, we compute the signed distance value at the corner vertices of its bounding volume.[2] At this point, there are three cases to consider. First, if the signed distance value of all vertices is positive, then the internal node is completely outside the signed distance field and is discarded. Second, if the signed distance value of all vertices is negative, then the internal node is completely inside the signed distance field. In this case, we recursively visit its children internal nodes until we reach all its children leaf nodes. The primitive associated with each leaf node is guaranteed to be inside the signed distance field, and so we compute the signed distance value, gradient and closest point on the zero iso-contour for each of its vertices. Lastly, if the signed distance values at the corner vertices have different signs, then the internal node crosses the zero iso-contour. In this case, we add its children nodes to the auxiliary list of internal nodes that need to be tested for inclusion. If the children nodes are in fact leaf nodes, then we compute the signed distance value of each primitive's vertex of each leaf node, to determine whether the vertex is inside the signed distance field. At the end, the auxiliary list of internal nodes is empty and we have determined all inside vertices, if any.

Unfortunately, the above algorithm can fail if the signed distance field region lies completely inside the root bounding volume of the hierarchy. We can avoid this pitfall by first testing if the grid representing the signed distance field is completely inside the root bounding volume of the hierarchy. If this is this case, then we need to invert the order in which the objects are being tested for collisions, that is, we need to test the second object against the signed distance field representation of the first object.

12.4   Resolving Collisions

Since no backtracking in time is performed when colliding with signed distance field representations, we use the current set of inside vertices and their corresponding closest points as an approximation to the actual collisions. The idea is to process each inside vertex and its closest point as a separate collision between the objects

---

[2]In the particular case of using a bounding-sphere representation for the object, we need to use the corner vertices of the axis-aligned box bounding the sphere.

and merge their individual contributions to determine the net linear and angular velocities of the objects after these multiple simultaneous collisions occur. The merge can be an average of the individual contributions weighted by their penetration distances, that is, deeper vertices will have their collision response affect the motion of the objects more than shallow vertices. A more detailed explanation of this process follows.

Each inside vertex of the first object is assumed to have collided with its corresponding closest point on the second object. We use the rigid body dynamic equations described in Sect. 4.2 to calculate the velocities of the objects at these points. The collision impulse, and new linear and angular velocities of the center of mass of the objects are determined using the framework for computing impulsive forces for a single collision between rigid bodies as explained in details in Sect. 4.11.1. These new velocities computed for each inside vertex collision are averaged using the penetration depth of the vertex as its weight. The net linear and angular velocities of the objects computed from this averaging process are used to update the objects' motions for the current time interval. The problem at this point is we don't know the actual collision time between the objects because no backtracking in time was performed. So we don't know at which point in time we need to replace the current objects' velocities with the new ones needed to resolve collisions, in order to correctly update the objects' motion for the remaining time until the end of the current time interval. The workaround proposed in this book, is to assume all collisions take place at the beginning of the current time interval, so that the numerical integration using the new dynamic state of the colliding objects just after the collision is restarted for the entire time interval. The final position and orientation of the colliding objects is then updated to reflect the changes introduced by the collision. Because these changes affect the path of the objects for the time-step, the simulation engine needs to check again for new collisions.

In theory, this iterative process continues until all collisions are resolved. In practice, the simulation engine performs a user-defined number of collision iterations before it overrides the physical parameters of each colliding object to use inelastic collisions between them (i.e., zero coefficient of restitution) in all future iterations. The goal is to significantly reduce the number of newly introduced collisions in future iterations as the objects no longer bounce off of each other during collisions, as is the case in standard elastic collisions.

The main difficulty in using signed distance fields for collision handling is that point-inside tests are usually not enough to detect all collisions between objects. For instance, edge–face collisions can be missed if the vertices defining the edge have a positive signed distance value (i.e., are outside) but the edge itself is piercing through the object. In these cases, robustness can be improved if the objects have adequate mesh resolution, but higher resolution models can negatively affect the overall performance of the simulation engine (i.e., larger hierarchies and more point-inside tests needed to detect collisions).

In this book, we prefer using geometric intersections over signed distance fields for detecting object collisions in most cases, because they can better handle thin and fast moving objects, and have optimized algorithms for convex shapes (signed distance fields make no distinction between convex and non-convex shapes). The only exception would be handling collision with a large static environment, for instance, a terrain or the uneven walls of a room bounding the simulation world. The objects used to bound these environments tend to have infinite thickness, that is, any other object inside these objects, no matter how deep they are, need to be pushed back into the simulated world. In such cases, the point-inside collision tests are usually robust enough to process all collisions.

12.5   Suggested Readings

The memory efficient signed distance algorithm presented in this appendix was developed by Coutinho et al. [CM]. Baerentzen et al. [BA02] discuss an alternative approach using a dense grid representation and geometrically computing the closest distances to the mesh using angle weighted normals to guarantee correctness of inside and outside queries. The use of signed distance fields in the context of level sets is discussed in Sethian [Set96, Set99] and Velho et al. [VGdF02]. There are many great references to the marching cubes algorithm used to construct triangulated meshes from signed distance fields. We refer the readers to Lorensen et al. [LC87], Bloomenthal [Blo94] and Lewiner et al. [LLVT03] as a starting point.

Finally, Guendelam et al. [GBF03] present an alternate collision response algorithm using signed distance fields that can be also applied to the memory efficient representation discussed in this book.

References

[BA02]   Baerentzen, J.A., Aanaes, H.: Generating signed distance fields from triangle meshes. Technical Report IMM-TR-2002-21, Technical University of Denmark (2002)

[Blo94]   Bloomenthal, J.: An implicit surface polygonizer. In: Graphics Gems IV, pp. 324–349 (1994)

[CM]   Coutinho, M., Marino, S.: Systems and Methods for Representing Signed Distance Functions. US Patent 7,555,163. Sony Pictures Imageworks

[GBF03]   Guendelman, E., Bridson, R., Fedkiw, R.: Nonconvex rigid bodies with stacking. Comput. Graph. (Proc. SIGGRAPH) **22**, 871–878 (2003)

[LC87]   Lorensen, W.E., Cline, H.E.: Marching cubes: a high resolution 3D surface construction algorithm. Comput. Graph. (Proc. SIGGRAPH) **21**(4) (1987)

[LLVT03] Lewiner, T., Lopes, H., Vieira, A.W., Tavares, G.: Efficient implementation of marching cubes cases with topological guarantees. J. Graph. Tools **8**(2), 1–18 (2003)

[Set96]   Sethian, J.A.: A fast marching level set method for monotonically advancing fronts. Proc. Natl. Acad. Sci. **93**(4), 1591–1595 (1996)

[Set99]   Sethian, J.A.: Level Set Methods and Fast Marching Methods. Cambridge University, Cambridge (1999)

[VGdF02] Velho, L., Gomes, J., de Figueiredo, L.H.: Implicit Objects in Computer Graphics. Springer, Berlin (2002)

Appendix H: Conservative Time Advancement for Convex Objects

13

13.1   Introduction

The collision time between two convex objects moving for the time interval $[t_0, t_1]$ at constant translation and rotation can be exactly determined up to a user-defined tolerance. This is possible because the change in value of the distance between the objects' closest points is monotonic for convex objects, that is, if they intersect at $t_c \leq t_1$ then this distance must only decrease as we move from t_0 to t_c.

Usually, the motion obtained from the numerical integration is non-linear. For collision detection purposes, this nonlinear motion is approximated by a linear one with constant translation and rotation. Section 6.8 of Appendix A (Chap. 6) describes how the object's position and orientation at t_0 and t_1 can be used to compute the constant linear and angular velocities for the time interval.

Figure 13.1 shows two convex objects separated by a distance $|\vec{d}|$ at t_0. We want to determine whether the objects intersect during their motion for the time interval $[t_0, t_1]$, and if so, we want to find out their collision time t_c up to a user-defined tolerance.

Let $\vec{p}_1$ and $\vec{p}_2$ be the objects' closest points at t_0, and let $\vec{d}$ be the vector connecting them, that is

$$\vec{d} = \vec{p}_2 - \vec{p}_1.$$

Let α_1 and α_2 be the planes perpendicular to vector $\vec{d}$ passing through points $\vec{p}_1$ and $\vec{p}_2$, respectively. Let $\vec{n}$ be defined as the direction of vector $\vec{d}$, that is

$$\vec{n} = \frac{\vec{d}}{|\vec{d}|}.$$

Since points $\vec{p}_1$ and $\vec{p}_2$ are the closest points between the convex objects at t_0, it is guaranteed that no other points of the objects lie in the region between the planes α_1 and α_2. This means the actual collision points $\vec{p}_{c_1}$ and $\vec{p}_{c_2}$ to be determined at collision time t_c are distant from each other by at least $|\vec{d}|$ at time t_0, along

M.G. Coutinho, *Guide to Dynamic Simulations of Rigid Bodies and Particle Systems*, Simulation Foundations, Methods and Applications, DOI 10.1007/978-1-4471-4417-5_13, © Springer-Verlag London 2013

Fig. 13.1 (a) Position and orientation of the convex objects at t_0; the closest points are $\vec{p}_1$ and $\vec{p}_2$; (b) The objects at collision time t_c; the collision points are $\vec{p}_{c_1}$ and $\vec{p}_{c_2}$

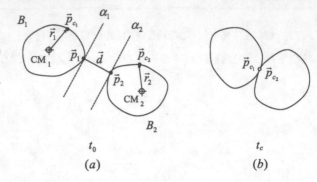

t_0

(a)

t_c

(b)

the direction $\vec{n}$. So, if we move the objects closer to each other by $|\vec{d}|$ along $\vec{n}$, we are guaranteed to not have reached their collision time t_c, because the distance between the actual collision points is greater than the distance the objects were moved. This simple, yet clever observation defines the main idea behind *conservative time advancement*. The algorithm iteratively moves the objects by their closest distance along the direction defined by the vector connecting their closest points, until either their closest distance is less than a user-defined tolerance or the objects are identified to not be colliding during the time interval.

13.2 Computing the Conservative Time Advancement

Let $D_1(\Delta t)$ be the distance traveled by point $\vec{p}_1$ for a time period Δt, along the direction $\vec{n}$. Similarly, let $D_2(\Delta t)$ be the distance traveled by point $\vec{p}_2$ for the same time period Δt, along the direction $-\vec{n}$. The conservative time estimate Δt of how far the objects can be moved without passing their intersection time t_c, is computed from

$$D_1(\Delta t) + D_2(\Delta t) = |\vec{d}|, \qquad (13.1)$$

that is, Δt is the time it takes for the objects to move by their current closest point's distance along $\vec{n}$. In order to solve this equation for Δt, we must first compute the time-dependent functions $D_1(t)$ and $D_2(t)$.

According to Eq. (4.6) in Chap. 4, the velocity of a point $\vec{p}_{c_1}$ on rigid body B_1 at time t_0, is expressed as

$$\vec{v}_{p_{c_1}}(t) = \vec{v}_1(t) + \vec{\omega}_1(t) \times \vec{r}_1, \qquad (13.2)$$

where $\vec{v}_1$ and $\vec{\omega}_1$ are the linear and angular velocities of object B_1, and $\vec{r}_1$ is the distance between $\vec{p}_{c_1}$ and B_1's center of mass. As mentioned earlier, the objects are moving at constant translation and rotation, that is, at constant linear and angular velocities. So, the time dependency in Eq. (13.2) is linear on t, that is

$$\vec{v}_{p_{c_1}}(t) = (\vec{v}_1 + \vec{\omega}_1 \times \vec{r}_1)t. \qquad (13.3)$$

The distance traveled along the direction $\vec{n}$ is then

$$D_1(t) = \vec{v}_{p_{c_1}} \cdot \vec{n}$$
$$= (\vec{v}_1 + \vec{\omega}_1 \times \vec{r}_1)t \cdot \vec{n}$$
$$= (\vec{v}_1 \cdot \vec{n} + (\vec{\omega}_1 \times \vec{r}_1) \cdot \vec{n})t. \qquad (13.4)$$

An upper bound on the motion owing to the angular term in Eq. (13.4) is obtained when $\vec{\omega}_1$ is perpendicular to $\vec{r}_1$, and their cross-product is aligned with $\vec{n}$, resulting in

$$(\vec{\omega}_1 \times \vec{r}_1) \cdot \vec{n} \le |\vec{\omega}_1||\vec{r}_1|. \qquad (13.5)$$

If we compute the distance between the vertices of object B_1 and its center of mass, and set its maximum value to $(r_1)_{max}$,[1] then we can use $(r_1)_{max}$ as an upper bound to $|\vec{r}_1|$ in Eq. (13.5), that is

$$(\vec{\omega}_1 \times \vec{r}_1) \cdot \vec{n} \le |\vec{\omega}_1|(r_1)_{max}.$$

Substituting this result back into Eq. (13.4), we obtain an upper bound to the maximum distance traveled by $\vec{p}_{c_1}$, that is

$$D_1(t) \le (\vec{v}_1 \cdot \vec{n} + |\vec{\omega}_1|(r_1)_{max})t. \qquad (13.6)$$

Doing a similar analysis for point $\vec{p}_{c_2}$ of object B_2, and keeping in mind its motion is along $-\vec{n}$, we obtain

$$D_2(t) \le (-\vec{v}_2 \cdot \vec{n} + |\vec{\omega}_2|(r_2)_{max})t. \qquad (13.7)$$

Substituting Eqs. (13.6) and (13.7) into Eq. (13.1), we get an upper bound to the distance the objects can travel along $\vec{n}$ without colliding, namely

$$((\vec{v}_1 - \vec{v}_2) \cdot \vec{n} + |\vec{\omega}_1|(r_1)_{max} + |\vec{\omega}_2|(r_2)_{max})t \le |\vec{d}|.$$

The conservative time advancement, that is, the maximum time we can move the objects without reaching their collision time t_c is then

$$\Delta t = \frac{|\vec{d}|}{(\vec{v}_1 - \vec{v}_2) \cdot \vec{n} + |\vec{\omega}_1|(r_1)_{max} + |\vec{\omega}_2|(r_2)_{max}}. \qquad (13.8)$$

The following summarizes the algorithm used for conservative time advancement. Notice that time is normalized, that is, values of 0 and 1 correspond to times t_0 and t_1, respectively. The algorithm starts at $t_c = 0$.

---

[1]This can be done once when the object is registered with the simulation engine, as explained in Sect. 1.4.1 of Chap. 1.

1. Compute the closest points between the objects at t_c using either the Voronoi Clip or the GJK algorithms presented in Chap. 4. Check if the closest distance is less than the user-defined tolerance and if so, report the objects as colliding at the current t_c. Also, account for numerical rounding errors by checking if the closest distance is negative, that is, the interpolation went too far and passed the actual collision time and the objects are now intersecting at the current t_c. In this case, report the objects as colliding at the previous t_c (i.e., when they were not intersecting yet), or if $t_c = 0$, report the objects as colliding at the beginning of the time interval.
2. Compute Δt in Eq. (13.8). If the denominator is zero, then the objects are not moving relative to each other and we can discard this collision.
3. If $\Delta t < 0$, then the objects are moving away from each other and we can discard this collision as well.
4. Update the current collision time value $t_c = t_c + \Delta t$.
5. There are two termination conditions to be considered at this point:
   (a) If $t_c > 1$, then the objects are not colliding during the time interval $[t_0, t_1]$ and we can discard this collision.
   (b) If the number of iterations executed so far have reached a user-defined maximum value, then the objects are reported as colliding at the current t_c.
6. Compute the objects' position and orientation at the updated t_c value. Section 6.8 of Appendix A (Chap. 6) describes how the objects are repositioned at t_c using simple linear interpolation.
7. Proceed to the next iteration going back to item 1 above.

13.3   Suggested Readings

The conservative time advancement technique was first introduced by Mirtich [Mir96b] to bound the motion of convex rigid bodies. In his work, the distances $D_1(t)$ and $D_2(t)$ were bound by ballistic motion, assuming gravity is the only external force acting on the object. In this appendix, we presented Coumans [Cou12, Cou05] extension to Mirtich's work, which includes the more practical case when objects are moving with constant linear and angular velocities for the time interval being considered.

References

[Cou05] Coumans, E.: Continuous collision detection and physics. Technical Report, Sony Computer Entertainment (2005)
[Cou12] Coumans, E.: Bullet Software Package. AMD (2012). Game Physics Simulation web site http://www.bulletphysics.org/
[Mir96b] Mirtich, B.V.: Impulse-based dynamic simulation of rigid body systems. PhD Thesis, University of California, Berkeley (1996)

Appendix I: The Linear-Complementarity Problem

14

14.1 Introduction

As explained in Chaps. 3 and 4, there exists a linear relation between the relative acceleration $\vec{a}_i$ between two contacting bodies and the contact force $\vec{F}_i$ at contact point C_i, expressed by

$$
\vec{a}_i = \begin{pmatrix} (a_i)_n \\ (a_i)_t \\ (a_i)_k \end{pmatrix} = \begin{pmatrix} (a_{ii})_n & (a_{i(i+1)})_t & (a_{i(i+2)})_k \\ (a_{(i+1)i})_n & (a_{(i+1)(i+1)})_t & (a_{(i+1)(i+2)})_k \\ (a_{(i+2)i})_n & (a_{(i+2)(i+1)})_t & (a_{(i+2)(i+2)})_k \end{pmatrix} \begin{pmatrix} (F_i)_n \\ (F_i)_t \\ (F_i)_k \end{pmatrix}
$$
$$
+ \begin{pmatrix} (b_i)_n \\ (b_i)_t \\ (b_i)_k \end{pmatrix} = \mathbf{A}_i \vec{F}_i + \vec{b}_i, \tag{14.1}
$$

where the index n indicates the component along the contact-normal direction, and the indexes t and k indicate the components along the contact-tangent plane (i.e., the plane passing through the contact point with normal vector parallel to the contact normal). The coefficients of matrix $\mathbf{A}_i$ and vector $\vec{b}_i$ are computed from the mass properties and relative geometrical displacement of the contacting objects at contact C_i. For example, coefficient $(a_{ii})_n$ relates the normal contact-force component $(F_i)_n$ with the normal relative-acceleration component $(a_i)_n$ at contact C_i. Analogously, coefficients $(a_{i(i+1)})_t$ and $(a_{i(i+2)})_k$ relate the force components $(F_i)_t$ and $(F_i)_k$ with the acceleration[1] components $(a_i)_t$ and $(a_i)_t$ along the tangent plane. As for vector $\vec{b}_i$, it can be shown that it is a vector in the column space of $\mathbf{A}_i$, that is, there exists a nonzero vector $\vec{z}$ such that $\vec{b}_i = \mathbf{A}_i \vec{z}$. As we shall see later in this appendix, the fact that $\vec{b}$ lies in the column space of $\mathbf{A}_i$ turns out to be a fundamental result to the analysis of the existence of valid contact forces, since it guarantees that a solution to the system of equations always exists for frictionless contacts.

---

[1]Unless otherwise stated, the term acceleration used in this appendix means the relative acceleration between the contacting bodies at a contact point.

M.G. Coutinho, *Guide to Dynamic Simulations of Rigid Bodies and Particle Systems,*   369
Simulation Foundations, Methods and Applications,
DOI 10.1007/978-1-4471-4417-5_14, © Springer-Verlag London 2013

In the case of multiple simultaneous contacts, the accelerations and contact forces at each individual contact point are merged into a system-wide acceleration and contact-force vector

$$\vec{a} = (\vec{a}_1, \vec{a}_2, \ldots, \vec{a}_m)^t$$
$$\vec{F} = (\vec{F}_1, \vec{F}_2, \ldots, \vec{F}_m)^t, \tag{14.2}$$

with m being the total number of simultaneous contacts. In the context of simultaneous contacts, Eq. (14.1) is replaced by

$$
\begin{aligned}
\dot{\vec{a}} &= \mathbf{A}\vec{F} + \vec{b} \\
&= \begin{pmatrix}
\mathbf{A}_{11} & \mathbf{A}_{12} & \mathbf{A}_{13} & \cdots & \mathbf{A}_{1m} \\
\mathbf{A}_{12}^t & \mathbf{A}_{22} & \mathbf{A}_{23} & \cdots & \mathbf{A}_{2m} \\
\mathbf{A}_{13}^t & \mathbf{A}_{23}^t & \mathbf{A}_{33} & \cdots & \mathbf{A}_{3m} \\
\cdots & \cdots & \cdots & \cdots & \cdots \\
\mathbf{A}_{1m}^t & \mathbf{A}_{2m}^t & \mathbf{A}_{3m}^t & \cdots & \mathbf{A}_{mm}
\end{pmatrix} \vec{F} + \begin{pmatrix} b_1 \\ b_2 \\ b_3 \\ \vdots \\ b_m \end{pmatrix},
\end{aligned} \tag{14.3}
$$

where each sub-matrix $\mathbf{A}_{ij}$ is a 3×3 matrix of the same form as matrix $\mathbf{A}_i$ in Eq. (14.1). For instance, sub-matrix $\mathbf{A}_{23}$ relates the contact force $\vec{F}_3 = ((F_3)_n, (F_3)_t, (F_3)_k)^t$ of contact C_3 with the acceleration $\vec{a}_2 = ((a_2)_n, (a_2)_t, (a_2)_k)^t$ of contact C_2.

According to the contact-force derivations presented in Chaps. 3 and 4, the contact force at each contact point C_i is said to be valid if it satisfies the *non-interpenetration conditions* (also referred to as *normal conditions*) at C_i, namely

$$(F_i)_n (a_i)_n = 0$$
$$(a_i)_n \geq 0 \tag{14.4}$$
$$(F_i)_n \geq 0,$$

that is, either the contact-force or the acceleration components along the contact normal can be greater than zero, but never both of them simultaneously.

The actual derivation of Eq. (14.4), as well as how the coefficients of matrix $\mathbf{A}$ and vector $\vec{b}$ are computed for a given contact configuration, were already covered in detail in Chaps. 3 and 4. Here, we shall focus on how the system of equations is actually solved.

It happens that the formulation presented in Eqs. (14.4) and (14.3) fits the well-known Linear Complementarity Problem (LCP) formulation of linear programming theory. The approach indicated depends on whether friction is being considered. There are three possible cases to be addressed: frictionless contacts, contacts with static friction only, and the more general case of contacts with dynamic friction. In the following sections, we shall present approaches to the LCP problem associated with each of these three possible cases.

14.2   Dantzig's Algorithm: The Frictionless Case

Dantzig's algorithm works by incrementally computing intermediate solutions for instances of the problem defined by Eqs. (14.4) and (14.3), where each instance takes into account one more contact point than the previous instance. At instance i, the algorithm computes the contact force for the ith contact point without violating the non-interpenetration conditions for the $(i-1)$ contact points already resolved at instance $(i-1)$. Assuming we have m simultaneous contact points, the solution of the LCP problem is immediately obtained after solving each of the m instances.

In the frictionless case, the direction of the contact force is the same as the direction of the contact normal, that is, the contact force has no tangential components. Therefore, the system of equations is formulated using only the normal components of the contact-force and acceleration vectors given in Eq. (14.2). In other words, for each frictionless contact C_i we have

$$\vec{a}_i = \big((a_i)_n, (a_i)_t, (a_i)_k\big)^t = \big((a_i)_n, 0, 0\big)^t$$
$$\vec{F}_i = \big((F_i)_n, (F_i)_t, (F_i)_k\big)^t = \big((F_1)_n, 0, 0\big)^t,$$

and the system-wide vectors representing the accelerations and contact forces can then be written using the shorthand format

$$\vec{a} = \big((a_1)_n, \ldots, (a_i)_n, \ldots, (a_m)_n\big)^t$$
$$\vec{F} = \big((F_1)_n, \ldots, (F_i)_n, \ldots, (F_m)_n\big)^t,$$

omitting the tangential components. This significantly simplifies the computation of matrix $\mathbf{A_i}$ and vector $\vec{b}_i$ associated with contact C_i, since there is no need to compute the coefficients related to the tangential components. Therefore, for the frictionless case, $\mathbf{A_i}$ and vector $\vec{b}_i$ are reduced to

$$\mathbf{A_i} = \big((a_{ii})_n\big)$$
$$\vec{b} = \big((b_i)_n\big),$$

that is, they become scalars.

According to Eq. (14.4), a solution is achieved whenever either the contact force or the relative acceleration along the contact normal of each contact point is zero. As shown in Fig. 14.1, a positive relative normal acceleration $(a_i)_n > 0$ indicates that the contacting bodies are moving away from each other at contact point C_i, and the contact is about to break. In this situation, the contact force $(F_i)_n$ in Eq. (14.4) should be set to zero to enforce

$$(F_i)_n (a_i)_n = 0.$$

If the normal acceleration $(a_i)_n$ is zero (see Fig. 14.2), contact between the bodies is maintained, and any nonnegative contact force $(F_i)_n$ can be used in Eq. (14.4). The problem arises when the normal acceleration $(a_i)_n$ is negative, as shown in

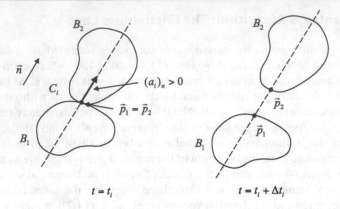

Fig. 14.1 The relative-acceleration component $(a_i)_n$ along the contact-normal direction is positive and the contact force f_i is zero (contact is about to break at $t = (t_i + \triangle t_i)$)

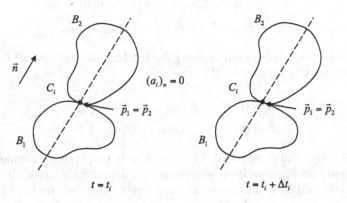

Fig. 14.2 The relative-acceleration component $(a_i)_n$ along the contact-normal direction is zero, and the contact force can be any nonnegative value (bodies remain in contact)

Fig. 14.3. Here, the bodies are accelerating towards each other at the contact point, indicating that they are about to interpenetrate. A sufficiently powerful positive contact force $(F_i)_n$ should then be applied to make the negative normal acceleration become zero. Clearly, the contact points we need to worry about are those having negative normal acceleration.

As mentioned before, the main idea of Dantzig's algorithm is to assure the non-interpenetration conditions at each new contact point while maintaining these conditions at the contact points already resolved. For example, at the first instance, the algorithm ignores all contact points save one.[2] This has the same effect as setting all contact forces to zero, and solving Eqs. (14.4) and (14.3) for just one contact point, that is, solving

---

[2] The order in which the contact points are resolved is irrelevant.

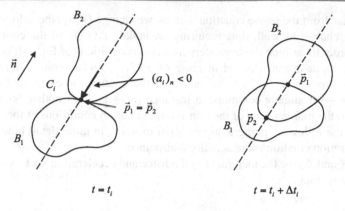

$t = t_i$ $t = t_i + \Delta t_i$

Fig. 14.3 The relative-acceleration component $(a_i)_n$ along the contact-normal direction is negative, and the contact force should be large enough to reduce it to zero to prevent interpenetration

$$(a_1)_n = ((a_{11})_n (F_1)_n + (b_1)_n) \geq 0$$

$$(F_1)_n (a_1)_n = (F_1)_n ((a_{11})_n (F_1)_n + (b_1)_n) = 0 \qquad (14.5)$$

$$(F_1)_n \geq 0.$$

For this contact point, the algorithm checks whether the normal acceleration $(a_1)_n$ is positive, zero or negative, and makes the necessary adjustment to the contact force $(F_1)_n$ in the latter case so as to prevent interpenetration of the contacting bodies at the contact point. At the end of the first instance of the algorithm, the contact-force vector will have the intermediate value

$$\vec{F} = ((F_1)_n, 0, 0, \ldots, 0)^t,$$

with

$$(F_1)_n \geq 0.$$

At the second instance, the algorithm computes the contact force $(F_2)_n$ so that the normal acceleration $(a_2)_n$ is nonnegative. This should be done without violating the non-interpenetration conditions along the normal direction of the contact point already resolved on the first instance. So, at the second instance, Eqs. (14.4) and (14.3) are reduced to:

$$\begin{pmatrix} (a_1)_n \\ (a_2)_n \end{pmatrix} = \left(\begin{pmatrix} (a_{11})_n & (a_{12})_n \\ (a_{21})_n & (a_{22})_n \end{pmatrix} \begin{pmatrix} (F_1)_n \\ (F_2)_n \end{pmatrix} + \begin{pmatrix} (b_1)_n \\ (b_2)_n \end{pmatrix} \right) \geq \begin{pmatrix} 0 \\ 0 \end{pmatrix}$$

$$\begin{pmatrix} (F_1)_n \\ (F_2)_n \end{pmatrix}^t \left(\begin{pmatrix} (a_{11})_n & (a_{12})_n \\ (a_{21})_n & (a_{22})_n \end{pmatrix} \begin{pmatrix} f_1 \\ f_2 \end{pmatrix} + \begin{pmatrix} (b_1)_n \\ (b_2)_n \end{pmatrix} \right) = \begin{pmatrix} 0 \\ 0 \end{pmatrix}$$

$$\begin{pmatrix} (F_1)_n \\ (F_2)_n \end{pmatrix} \geq \begin{pmatrix} 0 \\ 0 \end{pmatrix}.$$

It is clear from the above equation that, as we change $(F_2)_n$, the values of $(a_2)_n$ *and* $(a_1)_n$ change as well, thus requiring an update $\triangle(F_1)_n$ to the contact force $(F_1)_n$ in order to enforce the non-interpenetration conditions of Eq. (14.5).

In general, at instance m, an increase of $\triangle(F_m)_n$ on the contact force $(F_m)_n$ requires an update $\triangle(F_i)_n$ on the values of the contact forces $(F_i)_n$ for all $i \in \{1, \ldots, (m-1)\}$ already computed at instance $(m-1)$. This update is absolutely essential to the maintenance of the non-interpenetration conditions at these contact points. In the following paragraphs, we shall examine in more detail how the non-interpenetration conditions are actually maintained.

Let $\triangle\vec{F}$ and $\triangle\vec{a}$ be the increment to the force and acceleration vectors computed at instance m, that is

$$\triangle\vec{F} = \big(\triangle(F_1)_n, \triangle(F_2)_n, \ldots, \triangle(F_m)_n\big)^t$$

$$\triangle\vec{a} = \big(\triangle(a_1)_n, \triangle(a_2)_n, \ldots, \triangle(a_m)_n\big).$$

The updated force and acceleration vectors are then given by

$$\vec{F}_{new} = \vec{F} + \triangle\vec{F}$$

$$\vec{a}_{new} = \vec{a} + \triangle\vec{a}. \tag{14.6}$$

Substituting Eq. (14.3) into (14.6), we get

$$\triangle\vec{a} = \vec{a}_{new} - \vec{a}$$
$$= (\mathbf{A}\vec{F}_{new} + \vec{b}) - (\mathbf{A}\vec{F} + \vec{b})$$
$$= \big(\mathbf{A}(\vec{F} + \triangle\vec{F}) + b\big) - (\mathbf{A}\vec{F} + \vec{b})$$
$$= \mathbf{A}\triangle\vec{F}. \tag{14.7}$$

So, as we increase $(F_m)_n$ by $\triangle(F_m)_n$, some $(a_i)_n$'s and $(F_j)_n$'s will increase or decrease according to Eq. (14.7), depending on the values of the coefficients of matrix $\mathbf{A}$. Clearly, the problem arises when the adjustments associated with contact point C_m violate the non-interpenetration conditions for one or more contact points C_i with $i \in \{1, 2, \ldots, (m-1)\}$.

As stated in Eq. (14.4), the non-interpenetration conditions are achieved at the contact point C_i whenever the collision force $(F_i)_n$ is zero and $(a_i)_n > 0$ (i.e., we need to maintain the condition $(F_i)_n = 0$), or the relative acceleration $(a_i)_n$ is zero and $(F_i)_n \geq 0$ (i.e., we need to maintain the condition $(a_i)_n = 0$). Therefore, there are only two ways the non-interpenetration conditions at contact point C_i can be violated.

1. If $(F_i)_n = 0$ and an increase in $(F_m)_n$ by $\triangle(F_m)_n$ forces $(a_i)_n$ to assume a negative value.
2. If $(a_i)_n = 0$ and an increase in $(F_m)_n$ by $\triangle(F_m)_n$ forces $(F_i)_n$ to assume a negative value.

If the non-interpenetration conditions at contact point C_i were achieved with $(F_i)_n = 0$, then we need to check whether condition (1) is valid after each increase in $(F_m)_n$. On the other hand, if the non-interpenetration conditions were achieved with $(a_i)_n = 0$, then we need to check whether condition (2) is valid. In other words, we need to keep track of which case the contact point falls into (either zero contact force or zero acceleration) before we can decide the condition in need of verification. This can be efficiently implemented as follows.

At the beginning of instance m, we sub-divide the contact points into two groups. The first group, called ZA (zero acceleration), contains the indexes of all contact points C_i with $i < m$ that have $(a_i)_n = 0$. Because instance $(m - 1)$ was already resolved, the contact force for each contact point in ZA is guaranteed to have $(F_i)_n \geq 0$, that is

$$ZA = \{(1 \leq i < m) : (a_i)_n = 0 \text{ and } (F_i)_n \geq 0\}.$$

The second group, called ZF (zero force), contains the indexes of all contact points C_i with $i < m$ that have $(F_i)_n = 0$. Again, since instance $(m - 1)$ was already resolved, the normal acceleration for these contact points is guaranteed to be $(a_i)_n > 0$, that is

$$ZF = \{(1 \leq i < m) : (F_i)_n = 0 \text{ and } (a_i)_n > 0\}.$$

As we increase $(F_m)_n$ by $\triangle(F_m)_n$, the algorithm tries to keep $(a_i)_n = 0$ for all $i \in ZA$, and to keep $(F_j)_n = 0$ for all $j \in ZF$, while updating the contact forces and normal accelerations using Eq. (14.7). The idea is then to set $\triangle(a_i)_n = 0$ for all $i \in ZA$, such that $(a_i)_n$ remains the same, then set $\triangle(F_j)_n = 0$ for all $j \in ZF$, such that $(F_j)_n$ remains the same, and lastly solve Eq. (14.7) for the unknowns $\triangle(F_i)_n$ for $i \in ZA$. If while solving Eq. (14.7) we detect that some $(F_i)_n$ with $i \subset ZA$ has decreased to zero, then we temporarily stop the computations and move contact point C_i from ZA to ZF. By so doing, we prevent $(F_i)_n$ from decreasing even further and end up assuming a negative value. On the other hand, if we detect that some $(a_i)_n$ with $i \in ZF$ has decreased to zero, then we temporarily stop the computations and move contact point C_i from ZF to ZA to prevent $(a_i)_n$ from assuming a negative value. In both cases, Eq. (14.7) is rearranged according to the index update of the contact points in both ZA and ZF groups, and the computation continues until we have increased $(F_m)_n$ enough to make $(a_m)_n = 0$. Figure 14.4 shows a finite-state machine representation of the possible group changes that contact point C_i can make while solving Eq. (14.7).

Let's examine in more detail how Eq. (14.7) is actually solved for the unknowns $\triangle(F_i)_n$ for $i \in ZA$. Because the order in which the contact points are numbered is irrelevant, let's assume that $ZA = \{1, 2, \ldots, k\}$ and $ZF = \{(k + 1), (k + 2), \ldots, (m - 1)\}$, and that we have $(a_m)_n < 0$.[3] The matrix $\mathbf{A}$ and increment vector $\triangle \vec{F}$ can

---

[3]If $(a_m)_n \geq 0$, then we can immediately solve instance m by setting $(F_m)_n = 0$.

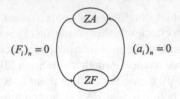

$(F_i)_n = 0$ $(a_i)_n = 0$

Fig. 14.4 At any instant during the solution of Eq. (14.7), a contact point C_i can be in one of two states, namely ZA and ZF. The *arrows* show the direction of the possible movements, together with the condition that needs to be satisfied to trigger the movement

then be partitioned such that the first k columns correspond to contact points in ZA, and the remaining columns to contact points in ZF. By so doing, we have

$$\mathbf{A} = \begin{pmatrix} \mathbf{A_{11}} & \mathbf{A_{12}} & \vec{v}_1 \\ \mathbf{A_{12}}^t & \mathbf{A_{22}} & \vec{v}_2 \\ \vec{v}_1^t & \vec{v}_2^t & c \end{pmatrix} \tag{14.8}$$

and

$$\Delta \vec{F} = \begin{pmatrix} \vec{x} \\ \vec{0} \\ \Delta(F_m)_n \end{pmatrix}, \tag{14.9}$$

where $\mathbf{A_{11}} \in \mathbb{R}^{k \times k}$ and $\mathbf{A_{22}} \in \mathbb{R}^{(m-1-k) \times (m-1-k)}$ are square symmetric matrices, $\vec{v}_1 \in \mathbb{R}^k$ and $\vec{v}_2 \in \mathbb{R}^{(m-1-k)}$ are vectors, c is a scalar and $\vec{x} \in \mathbb{R}^k$ is the unknown contact-force increment we want to determine. Substituting Eqs. (14.8) and (14.9) into Eq. (14.7), we obtain

$$\Delta \vec{a} = \mathbf{A} \Delta \vec{F} = \mathbf{A} \begin{pmatrix} \vec{x} \\ \vec{0} \\ \Delta(F_m)_n \end{pmatrix} = \begin{pmatrix} \mathbf{A_{11}}\vec{x} + \vec{v}_1 \Delta(F_m)_n \\ \mathbf{A_{12}^t}\vec{x} + \vec{v}_2 \Delta(F_m)_n \\ \vec{v}_1^t \vec{x} + c \Delta(F_m)_n \end{pmatrix}. \tag{14.10}$$

We can then rearrange $\Delta \vec{a}$ in the same way we did for $\Delta \vec{F}$, that is

$$\Delta \vec{a} = \begin{pmatrix} \vec{0} \\ \vec{w} \end{pmatrix}, \tag{14.11}$$

where $\vec{0} \in \mathbb{R}^{k \times k}$. Combining Eqs. (14.10) and (14.11), we have

$$\mathbf{A_{11}}\vec{x} + \vec{v}_1 \Delta(F_m)_n = \vec{0},$$

that is, we need to solve the linear system

$$\mathbf{A_{11}}\vec{x} = -\vec{v}_1 \Delta(F_m)_n \tag{14.12}$$

for the unknown contact force increment $\vec{x}$. Since we don't know in advance which increment $\Delta(F_m)_n$ should be used in order to increase $(a_m)_n$ to zero, we initially solve for

$$\Delta(F_m)_n = 1$$

and then adjust the solution by computing the smallest positive scalar s such that, when we increase $\vec{F}$ by $s\Delta\vec{F}$, we have either $(a_m)_n = 0$, or some contact point moved between ZA and ZF. In other words, the scalar s is used to limit how much we can increase $(F_m)_n$ without violating the non-interpenetration conditions for the remaining contact points.

There are three situations to consider when computing the scalar s. If $\Delta(a_m)_n > 0$, then the normal acceleration at contact point C_m is increasing. Because we want to increase $(a_m)_n < 0$ up to the point at which it becomes zero, then the maximum allowed step size s that does not make $(a_m)_n > 0$ is

$$s = -\frac{(a_m)_n}{\Delta(a_m)_n}. \tag{14.13}$$

The second situation occurs whenever $\Delta(F_i)_n < 0$ for $i \in ZA$, that is, the contact force at contact point C_i is decreasing. Because we want to enforce $(F_i)_n \geq 0$ for $i \in ZA$, the maximum allowed step size s that does not make $(F_i)_n$ negative is

$$s \leq -\frac{(F_i)_n}{\Delta(F_i)_n}, \quad \forall i \in ZA \quad \text{with } \Delta(F_i)_n < 0. \tag{14.14}$$

The third and last situation occurs when we have $\Delta(a_i)_n < 0$ for $i \in ZF$, that is, the normal acceleration at contact point C_i is decreasing. Because we want to enforce that $(a_i)_n > 0$ for $i \in ZA$, the maximum allowed step size s that does not make $(a_i)_n$ negative is

$$s \leq -\frac{(a_i)_n}{\Delta(a_i)_n}, \quad \forall i \in ZF \quad \text{with } \Delta(a_i)_n < 0. \tag{14.15}$$

The goal is to select the smallest s satisfying Eqs. (14.13), (14.14) and (14.15). Having determined s, we update $\vec{F}$ and $\vec{a}$ by

$$\vec{F}_{new} = \vec{F} + (s\Delta\vec{F})$$

$$\vec{a}_{new} = \vec{a} + (s\Delta\vec{a}).$$

If the smallest s was obtained from Eq. (14.13), then $(a_m)_n = 0$ after the update, and the non-interpenetration conditions at contact point C_m are satisfied. In this case, contact point C_m is moved into ZA and the mth instance of the algorithm is completed.

However, if the smallest s was obtained from Eq. (14.14), then there exists a contact point C_i with $i \in ZA$ that had its force $(F_i)_n$ decreased to zero before we could reach $(a_m)_n = 0$. In this case, we need to move index i from ZA to ZF to prevent the force from becoming negative. The partition of matrix A is then updated to account for the contact point moved, and the algorithm loops back to continue increasing $(F_m)_n$ until $(a_m)_n = 0$.

A similar update happens if the smallest s was obtained from Eq. (14.15). In this case, there exists a contact point C_i with $i \in ZF$ that had its acceleration $(a_i)_n$ decreased to zero before we could reach $(a_m)_n = 0$. This makes it necessary to move index i from ZF to ZA to prevent the acceleration from becoming negative. Again, the partition of matrix A is rearranged to account for the contact point moved, and the algorithm loops back to continue increasing $(F_m)_n$ until $(a_m)_n = 0$.

14.2.1 Termination Conditions

There are two critical assumptions in the frictionless algorithm described in the previous section that have the potential of being invalid, meaning they can compromise the existence of a solution. The first critical assumption is the existence of a solution $\vec{x}$ to the linear system defined by Eq. (14.12) with $\Delta(F_m)_n = 1$, that is, the existence of a solution to

$$\mathbf{A_{11}}\vec{x} = -\vec{v}_1. \tag{14.16}$$

Fortunately, it can be shown that the vector $\vec{v}_1$ is always in the column space of $\mathbf{A_{11}}$ for all possible combinations of indexes in ZA and ZF. Therefore, the linear system in Eq. (14.16) is well conditioned and a solution $\vec{x}$ is guaranteed to always exist.

The second critical assumption is that an increase in $(F_m)_n$ will also cause an increase in $(a_m)_n$ by a positive amount, such that $(a_m)_n$ will eventually reach the desired zero value. If we substitute $(s\Delta\vec{F})$ back into Eq. (14.10), we have that $(a_m)_n$ increases by

$$s\big((\vec{v}_1)^t\vec{x} + c\big) = s\Delta(a_m)_n.$$

In this case, it can be shown that, if $\mathbf{A}$ is positive definite, then both $((\vec{v}_1)^t\vec{x} + c)$ and step size s are always positive. This in turn means that $(a_m)_n$ will always increase by a positive amount at the end of each step, that is, the algorithm is guaranteed to terminate after a finite number of steps.

The interested reader is referred to Sect. 14.4 for pointers to the literature containing formal proofs of these assumptions.

14.3 Baraff's Algorithm: Coping with Friction

Baraff's extension to Dantzig's algorithm addresses the friction problem in much the same way as the normal conditions were addressed in the frictionless case. Again, the idea is to incrementally compute intermediate solutions for instances of the problem defined by Eqs. (14.4) and (14.3), where each instance takes into account one more contact point than the previous instance. At instance i, the algorithm computes the contact force for the ith contact point without violating the normal *and* friction conditions for the $(i-1)$ contact points already resolved at instance $(i-1)$. The actual friction conditions to be satisfied at each contact point depend on the contact's being static or dynamic.

Respecting friction, the contact force will have a normal component *and* a tangential component, the latter owing to the friction force acting at the contact point. Clearly, the relation between the normal and tangential contact-force components depends on the contact model adopted.

In this book, we use the Coulomb friction model to relate the tangential and normal contact-force components. More specifically, we use a directional-friction model to compute the tangential contact-force components.[4] Let $\vec{F_i}$ be the contact force associated with contact C_i, that is

$$\vec{F_i} = \left((F_i)_n, (F_i)_t, (F_i)_k \right)^t.$$

Using the directional-friction model, the contact-force components on the tangent plane are obtained from the contact-force component along the normal direction using

$$(F_i)_t = \mu_t (F_i)_n$$
$$(F_i)_k = \mu_k (F_i)_n,$$

where μ_t and μ_k are the coefficients of friction along the tangent-plane directions $\vec{t}$ and $\vec{k}$.

It is important to notice that the directional-friction model is a generalization of the widely used model of relating the tangential and normal contact-force components using just one omnidirectional coefficient of friction μ, as in

$$(F_i)_{tk} = \mu (F_i)_n. \tag{14.17}$$

In Eq. (14.17), the term $(F_i)_{tk}$ refers to the net contact-force component on the tangent plane given by

$$(F_i)_{tk} = \sqrt{(F_i)_t^2 + (F_i)_k^2}.$$

---

[4]This is the same model used in Chaps. 3 and 4.

For example, if friction is isotropic, that is, independent of direction, we can write

$$\mu_t = \mu \cos \phi$$
$$\mu_k = \mu \sin \phi$$

for some angle ϕ, and so

$$(F_i)_{tk} = \sqrt{(F_i)_t^2 + (F_i)_k^2}$$
$$= \sqrt{\mu^2 (F_i)_n^2 \cos \phi^2 + \mu^2 (F_i)_n^2 \sin \phi^2}$$
$$= \mu (F_i)_n,$$

which is the same result obtained using the omnidirectional friction model of Eq. (14.17). The main advantage of using the directional-friction model is that the nonlinear equation

$$\left| (F_i)_{tk} \right| = \sqrt{(F_i)_t^2 + (F_i)_k^2} \le \mu (F_i)_n$$

that needs to be enforced when the contacting bodies are not sliding at the contact point (i.e., static friction) can be substituted for two linear equations

$$\left| (F_i)_t \right| \le \mu_t (F_i)_n$$
$$\left| (F_i)_k \right| \le \mu_k (F_i)_n,$$

which are equivalent to the nonlinear equation if friction is isotropic, and, most important, can be independently resolved.

The way the normal and tangential contact-force components are related in the Coulomb friction model depends on the contact's being static or dynamic. A contact is said to be static if the net relative velocity along its tangent plane is zero, or less than a threshold value. Otherwise, the contact is said to be dynamic. In either case, the system-wide contact-force and relative-acceleration-vector components for m simultaneous contacts are expressed as

$$\vec{a} = \left((a_1)_n, (a_1)_t, (a_1)_k, \ldots, (a_m)_n, (a_m)_t, (a_m)_k \right)^t, \qquad (14.18)$$
$$\vec{F} = \left((F_1)_n, (F_1)_t, (F_1)_k, \ldots, (F_m)_n, (F_m)_t, (F_m)_k \right)^t, \qquad (14.19)$$

that is, the tangential contact-force components are no longer omitted, as in the frictionless case (see Eq. (14.5)). Therefore, the frictional contact-force computation requires solving the following system (which is the same as that shown in Eq. (14.3), but repeated here for convenience):

$$\vec{a} = \mathbf{A}\vec{F} + \vec{b} = \begin{pmatrix} \mathbf{A_{11}} & \mathbf{A_{12}} & \mathbf{A_{13}} & \cdots & \mathbf{A_{1m}} \\ \mathbf{A_{12}}^t & \mathbf{A_{22}} & \mathbf{A_{23}} & \cdots & \mathbf{A_{2m}} \\ \mathbf{A_{13}}^t & \mathbf{A_{23}}^t & \mathbf{A_{33}} & \cdots & \mathbf{A_{3m}} \\ \cdots & \cdots & \cdots & \cdots & \cdots \\ \mathbf{A_{1m}}^t & \mathbf{A_{2m}}^t & \mathbf{A_{3m}}^t & \cdots & \mathbf{A_{mm}} \end{pmatrix} \vec{F} + \begin{pmatrix} b_1 \\ b_2 \\ b_3 \\ \vdots \\ b_m \end{pmatrix}, \qquad (14.20)$$

where $\vec{a}$ and $\vec{F}$ are given by Eqs. (14.18) and (14.19), and each sub-matrix $\mathbf{A_{ij}}$ is a 3×3 matrix relating the relative acceleration at contact C_i with the contact force at contact C_j. Clearly from Eq. (14.20), an increment of

$$\Delta \vec{F} = \left(\Delta(F_1)_n, \Delta(F_1)_t, \Delta(F_1)_k, \ldots, \Delta(F_m)_n, \Delta(F_m)_t, \Delta(F_m)_k \right)^t$$

to the contact-force components will cause a variation of

$$\vec{a} = \left(\Delta(a_1)_n, \Delta(a_1)_t, \Delta(a_1)_k, \ldots, \Delta(a_m)_n, \Delta(a_m)_t, \Delta(a_m)_k \right)^t$$

to the acceleration components obtained from

$$\Delta \vec{a} = \mathbf{A} \Delta \vec{F}. \qquad (14.21)$$

The problem is that, depending on the values of the coefficients of matrix $\mathbf{A}$, an increment of $\Delta(F_m)_n$ to the normal contact-force component of contact C_m at the mth iteration can increase or decrease the contact-force and acceleration components of other contacts already resolved in one of the previous iterations. Not only that, an increment of $\Delta(F_m)_t$ or $\Delta(F_m)_k$ to the tangential-force components of contact C_m can not only affect the normal and friction conditions already established for the previous $(m-1)$ contacts, but can also increase or decrease the normal components $(F_m)_n$ and $(a_m)_n$ associated with contact C_m. Another important issue is that, because we are adopting the Coulomb friction model, the tangential contact-force components and their increments are computed as a function of the normal-force component and its increment. This in turn, requires that we first resolve the normal conditions at contact C_m, and only then resolve the friction conditions while enforcing the normal conditions just obtained.

Therefore, enforcing the normal and friction conditions at the mth iteration is a two-step process. We need to first resolve the normal conditions at contact C_m, assuming $\Delta(F_m)_t$ and $\Delta(F_m)_k$ are zero, while maintaining the normal and friction conditions for the previous $(m-1)$ contact points. We need then to adjust $\Delta(F_m)_t$ and $\Delta(F_m)_k$ to assure the friction conditions along the tangent-plane directions $\vec{t}$ and $\vec{k}$, while maintaining the normal and friction conditions for the previous $(m-1)$ contact points, as well as the normal condition for contact C_m. At the end of the mth iteration, we have assured both normal and friction conditions for all m contacts.

In the following sections, we shall apply this solution scheme to both static and dynamic friction, and study the termination conditions for each case.

14.3.1 Static-Friction Conditions

In the static-friction case, the relation between the normal and tangential contact-force components depends on the value of the relative tangential acceleration. Let $\vec{a}_i$ and $\vec{F}_i$ be, respectively, the relative acceleration and contact force at contact C_i, that is

$$\vec{a}_i = \left((a_i)_n, (a_i)_n, (a_i)_n\right)$$
$$\vec{F}_i = \left((F_i)_n, (F_i)_n, (F_i)_n\right).$$

If the relative tangential acceleration is zero, then the tangential components of the contact force are constrained within a range proportional to the value of the normal component. Since we are using the directional-friction model, this condition translates into assuring

$$\begin{aligned}
\left|(F_i)_t\right| &\le \mu_t(F_i)_n, \quad \text{if } (a_i)_t = 0 \\
\left|(F_i)_k\right| &\le \mu_k(F_i)_n, \quad \text{if } (a_i)_k = 0,
\end{aligned} \tag{14.22}$$

as opposed to assuring the commonly used condition

$$\left|(F_i)_t^2 + (F_i)_k^2\right| \le \mu(F_i)_n$$

that arises when the anisotropic-friction model is considered. Notice that the coefficients μ_t and μ_k in Eq. (14.22) are the static-friction coefficients along the tangent-plane directions $\vec{t}$ and $\vec{k}$, respectively.

If on the other hand the relative tangential acceleration is not zero, then the tangent components of the contact force will have maximum magnitude

$$\begin{aligned}
\left|(F_i)_t\right| &= \mu_t(F_i)_n, \quad \text{if } (a_i)_t \ne 0 \\
\left|(F_i)_k\right| &= \mu_k(F_i)_n, \quad \text{if } (a_i)_k \ne 0
\end{aligned}$$

and opposite direction with respect to the relative tangential acceleration, that is, the contact force and relative acceleration must have opposite signs:

$$\begin{aligned}
(F_i)_t(a_i)_t &< 0 \\
(F_i)_k(a_i)_k &< 0.
\end{aligned}$$

Therefore, the static friction conditions that need to be assured at each contact point C_i are

$$\left|(F_i)_t\right| \le \mu_t(F_i)_n$$
$$(a_i)_t(F_i)_t \le 0 \tag{14.23}$$
$$(a_i)_t\left(\mu_t(F_i)_n - \left|(F_i)_t\right|\right) = 0$$

and

$$|(F_i)_k| \le \mu_k(F_i)_n$$

$$(a_i)_k(F_i)_k \le 0 \qquad (14.24)$$

$$(a_i)_k\big(\mu_k(F_i)_n - |(F_i)_k|\big) = 0.$$

The last condition in Eqs. (14.23) and (14.24) assures that $(F_i)_t$ and $(F_i)_k$ will have maximum magnitude $\mu_t(F_i)_n$ and $\mu_k(F_i)_n$ whenever $(a_i)_t \ne 0$ and $(a_i)_k \ne 0$, respectively.

As mentioned, the way the static-friction conditions are assured is very similar to that used to assure the normal conditions. In the frictionless case, we created two groups of indexes, namely ZA and ZF, and used them to partition the contact-force and acceleration vectors $\Delta \vec{F}$ and $\Delta \vec{a}$ such that the first rows are filled in with contact points with index in ZA, the next rows are filled in with contact points with index in ZF, and the last row is filled in with $\Delta(F_m)_n$ and $\Delta(a_m)_n$ associated with contact C_m. The partition results in

$$\Delta \vec{F} = \begin{pmatrix} \vec{x} \\ \vec{0} \\ \Delta(F_m)_n \end{pmatrix} \qquad \Delta \vec{a} = \begin{pmatrix} \vec{0} \\ \vec{y} \\ \Delta(a_m)_n \end{pmatrix}, \qquad (14.25)$$

where $\vec{F}$ and $\vec{a}$ are related by

$$\Delta \vec{a} = \mathbf{A} \Delta \vec{F}. \qquad (14.26)$$

We then made $\Delta(F_m)_n = 1$ and solved a sub-system of Eq. (14.26) of the form

$$\mathbf{A}_{11}\vec{x} = -\vec{v}_1$$

for $\vec{x}$, that is, for the force increments $\Delta(F_i)_n$ with $i \in ZA$ (see Sect. 14.2 for details on how this sub-system is constructed from Eq. (14.26)). We substitute $\vec{x}$ and $\Delta(F_m)_n = 1$ back into Eq. (14.25) to obtain all components of $\Delta \vec{F}$, and use Eq. (14.26) again to obtain all components of $\Delta \vec{a}$. Finally, we compute the minimum scalar s to be used in

$$\vec{a} = \vec{a} + s\Delta \vec{a}$$
$$\vec{F} = \vec{F} + s\Delta \vec{F}$$

such that, either the normal conditions are met to contact C_m, or a change in the index sets ZA or ZF is required, in which case we need to loop back and re-partition vectors $\Delta \vec{F}$ and $\Delta \vec{a}$ according to the updated groups and solve the updated system.

Following the same principles used to resolve the normal conditions for the frictionless case, we shall create eight groups to manage the indexes of the contact points. The first two groups are identical to the frictionless case, namely groups ZA_n (zero normal acceleration) and ZF_n (zero normal contact force). These groups are used to assure the normal conditions for static contacts.

The next three groups are ZA_t, $MaxF_t$ and $MinF_t$. They are used to classify the contact points with respect to their static-friction conditions along the tangent-plane direction $\vec{t}$. The ZA_t (zero acceleration) group is used to keep track of the contact points that have zero tangential acceleration along $\vec{t}$, that is

$$ZA_t = \left\{ (1 \leq i < m) : (a_i)_t = 0 \text{ and } \left| (F_i)_t \right| \leq \mu_t (F_i)_n \right\}, \tag{14.27}$$

whereas the $MaxF_t$ (maximum friction force) and $MinF_t$ (minimum friction force) groups are used to keep track of the contact points that have non-zero tangential acceleration along $\vec{t}$, that is

$$MaxF_t = \left\{ (1 \leq i < m) : (a_i)_t < 0 \text{ and } (F_i)_t = \mu_t (F_i)_n \right\}$$
$$MinF_t = \left\{ (1 \leq i < m) : (a_i)_t > 0 \text{ and } (F_i)_t = -\mu_t (F_i)_n \right\}. \tag{14.28}$$

Notice that, by construction, the contact-force components $(F_i)_n$ are always non-negative. The last three groups are ZA_k, $MaxF_k$ and $MinF_k$. They are used to classify the contact points with respect to their static-friction conditions along the tangent-plane direction $\vec{k}$. Their descriptions are analogous to those given to groups ZA_t, $MaxF_t$ and $MinF_t$, that is:

$$ZA_k = \left\{ (1 \leq i < m) : (a_i)_k = 0 \text{ and } \left| (F_i)_k \right| \leq \mu_k (F_i)_n \right\}$$
$$MaxF_k = \left\{ (1 \leq i < m) : (a_i)_k < 0 \text{ and } (F_i)_k = \mu_k (F_i)_n \right\} \tag{14.29}$$
$$MinF_k = \left\{ (1 \leq i < m) : (a_i)_k > 0 \text{ and } (F_i)_k = -\mu_k (F_i)_n \right\}.$$

Let's examine how these eight groups are used at the mth iteration to assure the normal and static-friction conditions for all other $(m - 1)$ contact points already resolved at iteration $(m - 1)$. At any point in the algorithm, the index i of each contact point C_i appears in three out of the eight groups above described. More specifically, we assure the normal conditions at contact C_i with $i \leq m$ by setting:
- $i \in ZA_n$ if $(a_i)_n = 0$ and $(F_i)_n \geq 0$, or
- $i \in ZF_n$ if $(f_i)_n = 0$ and $(a_i)_n \geq 0$.

We assure the static-friction conditions along the tangent-plane direction $\vec{t}$ by setting:
- $i \in ZA_t$ if $(a_i)_t = 0$ and $-\mu_t (F_i)_n \leq (F_i)_t \leq \mu_t (F_i)_n$, or
- $i \in MinF_t$ if $(F_i)_t = -\mu_t (F_i)_n$ and $(a_i)_t > 0$, or
- $i \in MaxF_t$ if $(F_i)_t = \mu_t (F_i)_n$ and $(a_i)_t < 0$.

Finally, we assure the static-friction conditions along the tangent-plane direction $\vec{k}$ by setting:
- $i \in ZA_k$ if $(a_i)_k = 0$ and $-\mu_t (F_i)_n \leq (F_i)_k \leq \mu_t (F_i)_n$, or
- $i \in MinF_k$ if $(F_i)_k = -\mu_t (F_i)_n$ and $(a_i)_k > 0$, or
- $i \in MaxF_k$ if $(F_i)_k = \mu_t (F_i)_n$ and $(a_i)_k < 0$.

The first step at the mth iteration is to assure the normal conditions at C_m. This can be done by partitioning the vectors $\Delta \vec{F}$ and $\Delta \vec{a}$ such that the first rows are filled in with contact points with index in ZA_n, the next rows are filled in with contact points with index in ZF_n, and the last row is filled in with $\Delta\vec{F}_m$ and $\Delta\vec{a}_m$ associated with contact C_m. The partition results in

$$\Delta\vec{F} = \begin{pmatrix} \vec{x} \\ \vec{0} \\ \Delta(F_m)_n \\ \Delta(F_m)_t \\ \Delta(F_m)_k \end{pmatrix} \qquad \Delta\vec{a} = \begin{pmatrix} \vec{0} \\ \vec{y} \\ \Delta(a_m)_n \\ \Delta(a_m)_t \\ \Delta(a_m)_k \end{pmatrix}, \qquad (14.30)$$

where $\vec{F}$ and $\vec{a}$ are related by Eq. (14.26). Notice that $\vec{x}$ and $\vec{y}$ in Eq. (14.30) are of the form:

$$\vec{x} = \left(\Delta(F_1)_n, \Delta(F_1)_t, \Delta(F_1)_k, \ldots, \Delta(F_j)_n, \Delta(F_j)_t, \Delta(F_j)_k\right)^t$$
$$\vec{y} = \left(\Delta(a_{j+1})_n, \Delta(a_{j+1})_t, \Delta(a_{j+1})_k, \ldots, \Delta(a_{m-1})_n, \Delta(a_{m-1})_t, \Delta(a_{m-1})_k\right)^t,$$

assuming $ZA_n = \{1, 2, \ldots, j\}$ and $ZF_n = \{(j + 1), (j + 2), \ldots, (m - 1)\}$. Because we are assuring the normal conditions first, we set

$$\Delta(F_i)_t = \Delta(F_i)_k = 0 \quad \forall i$$
$$\Delta(a_i)_t = \Delta(a_i)_k = 0 \quad \forall i$$
$$\Delta(F_m)_n = 1$$
$$\Delta(F_m)_t = 0$$
$$\Delta(F_m)_k = 0$$

and solve a sub-system of the form of Eq. (14.30) for $\vec{x}$, that is, for the force increments $\Delta(F_i)_n$ with $i \in ZA_n$. The matrix $\mathbf{A_{11}}$ and vector $\vec{v}_1$ defining the sub-system are constructed exactly as described in Sect. 14.2. Having computed $\vec{x}$, we substitute its value back into $\Delta\vec{F}$ and use Eq. (14.26) again to obtain all components of $\Delta\vec{a}$. Lastly, we compute the minimum scalar s to be used in

$$\vec{a} = \vec{a} + s\Delta\vec{a}$$
$$\vec{F} = \vec{F} + s\Delta\vec{F}$$

such that, either the normal conditions are met to contact C_m, or a change in the index sets ZA_n or ZF_n is required, in which case we need to loop back and repartition vectors $\Delta\vec{F}$ and $\Delta\vec{a}$ according to the updated groups and solve the updated system. The scalar s is determined as follows.

• If $i \in ZA_n$ and $\Delta(F_i)_n < 0$, then

$$s \le -\frac{(F_i)_n}{\Delta(F_i)_n}. \qquad (14.31)$$

- If $i \in ZF_n$ and $\Delta(a_i)_n < 0$, then

$$s \le -\frac{(a_i)_n}{\Delta(a_i)_n}. \tag{14.32}$$

- As long as $(a_m)_n < 0$, we want to force it to zero in order to satisfy the normal conditions at contact C_m. So, if $\Delta(a_m)_n > 0$, then

$$s \le -\frac{(a_m)_n}{\Delta(a_m)_n}. \tag{14.33}$$

If the minimum scalar s comes from Eq. (14.33), then the normal conditions are established at contact point C_m. If it comes from Eq. (14.32), then we need to move its associated index i from ZF_n to ZA_n. Lastly, if the scalar s comes from Eq. (14.31), then we need to move its associated index i from ZA_n to ZF_n. Notice that, in both cases where the index sets are modified, we need to loop back and repartition the force and acceleration vectors until Eq. (14.33) is satisfied.

Having resolved the normal conditions at contact C_m, the next step consists of resolving its static-friction conditions. If the normal contact-force component $(F_m)_n$ obtained after assuring the normal conditions at contact C_m is zero, then the static-friction conditions are satisfied by setting $(F_m)_t = (F_m)_k = 0$, and we are done with the mth iteration. Also, if $m \in ZA_n$, that is if $(a_m)_n = 0$ after the normal conditions are assured, then setting $(F_m)_t = (F_m)_k = 0$ also assures the static friction conditions because

$$(F_m)_t = 0 < \mu_t (F_m)_n$$
$$(F_m)_k = 0 < \mu_k (F_m)_n.$$

If none of the above conditions is satisfied, then, whenever $(a_m)_t$ or $(a_m)_k$ are negative, we resolve the static-friction conditions by applying a solution method identical to that used for the normal conditions. The solution method consists of solving Eq. (14.26) by first partitioning it in a way that the first rows correspond to zero-acceleration increments, and the next rows correspond to zero-force increments. The partition is computed after setting:

$$\Delta(F_i)_t = \mu_t \Delta(F_i)_n, \quad \forall i \in MaxF_t$$
$$\Delta(F_i)_t = -\mu_t \Delta(F_i)_n, \quad \forall i \in MinF_t$$
$$\Delta(F_i)_k = \mu_k \Delta(F_i)_n, \quad \forall i \in MaxF_k$$
$$\Delta(F_i)_k = -\mu_k \Delta(F_i)_n, \quad \forall i \in MinF_k \tag{14.34}$$
$$\Delta(a_i)_t = 0, \quad \forall i \in ZA_t$$
$$\Delta(a_i)_k = 0, \quad \forall i \in ZA_k$$
$$\Delta(F_m)_n = 1.$$

The components $\Delta(F_m)_t$ and $\Delta(F_m)_k$ are set according to the following:[5]

$$\Delta(F_m)_t = \mu_t \overbrace{\Delta(F_m)_n}^{1} = \mu_t, \quad \text{if } (a_m)_t < 0$$

$$\Delta(F_m)_t = -\mu_t \overbrace{\Delta(F_m)_n}^{1} = -\mu_t, \quad \text{if } (a_m)_t > 0$$

$$\hspace{9cm} (14.35)$$

$$\Delta(F_m)_k = \mu_k \overbrace{\Delta(F_m)_n}^{1} = \mu_k, \quad \text{if } (a_m)_k < 0$$

$$\Delta(F_m)_k = -\mu_k \overbrace{\Delta(F_m)_n}^{1} = -\mu_k, \quad \text{if } (a_m)_k > 0.$$

After the assignments described by Eqs. (14.34) and (14.35) are completed, we partition the original system such that:

- The first rows are filled with the rows of the original system that have zero acceleration.
- The next rows are filled with the rows of the original system that have zero force.
- The last three rows correspond to the normal and tangential equations defined by contact C_m.

Notice that the original system given by Eq. (14.26) is laid out such that each contact corresponds to three consecutive rows of the system, one for the normal and two for the tangential contact directions. This may no longer be the case after the above-mentioned partition is carried out. In other words, the system to be solved is partitioned, not with respect to the contact points in the sense that their three corresponding equations are always kept together (i.e., laid out consecutively in the system), but with respect to which rows have zero force or acceleration assigned to them. The partition result is shown in Eq. (14.30).

Another fact worth mentioning is that, when $\Delta(F_i)_t = \pm\mu_t\Delta(F_i)_t$ and $i \notin ZF_n$ (i.e., $\Delta(F_i)_n \neq 0$), then we need to merge this row with the row corresponding to $\Delta(F_i)_n$. We then do a substitution of variable

$$\Delta(q_i)_n = (1 \pm \mu_t)\Delta(F_i)_n$$

to solve the system for $\Delta(q_i)_n$ and use its value to compute $\Delta(F_i)_n$ and $\Delta(F_i)_t$. The same applies for $\Delta(F_i)_k$.

Having partitioned the system according to Eq. (14.30), we solve for the subsystem containing the rows associated with zero-acceleration increments. This will give us the complete vector $\Delta\vec{F}$, which can be substituted back again into Eq. (14.26) to compute $\Delta\vec{a}$. Lastly, we compute the minimum scalar s to be used in

---

[5]Notice that, if $(a_m)_t = 0$, then we the static-friction condition is immediately satisfied by setting $(F_m)_t = 0$. The same applies to $(F_m)_k$ if $(a_m)_k = 0$.

$$\vec{a} = \vec{a} + s\Delta\vec{a}$$
$$\vec{F} = \vec{F} + s\Delta\vec{F}$$

such that, either the static-friction conditions are met for contact C_m, or a change in the index sets is required, in which case we need to loop back and re-partition vectors $\Delta\vec{F}$ and $\Delta\vec{a}$ according to the updated groups and solve the updated system. The minimum scalar $s \geq 0$ is determined as follows

- If $i \in ZA_n$ and $\Delta(F_i)_n < 0$, then

$$s \leq -\frac{(F_i)_n}{\Delta(F_i)_n}. \tag{14.36}$$

- If $i \in ZF_n$ and $\Delta(a_i)_n < 0$, then

$$s \leq -\frac{(a_i)_n}{\Delta(a_i)_n}. \tag{14.37}$$

- If $i \in ZA_t$ and $\Delta(a_i)_t \neq 0$, then we set

$$s = 0. \tag{14.38}$$

- If $i \in MaxF_t$ and $\Delta(a_i)_t < 0$, then

$$s \leq -\frac{(a_i)_t}{\Delta(a_i)_t}. \tag{14.39}$$

- If $i \in MinF_t$ and $\Delta(a_i)_t > 0$, then

$$s \leq -\frac{(a_i)_t}{\Delta(a_i)_t}. \tag{14.40}$$

- If $i \in ZA_k$ and $\Delta(a_i)_k \neq 0$, then we set

$$s = 0. \tag{14.41}$$

- If $i \in MaxF_k$ and $\Delta(a_i)_k < 0$, then

$$s \leq -\frac{(a_i)_k}{\Delta(a_i)_k}. \tag{14.42}$$

- If $i \in MinF_k$ and $\Delta(a_i)_k > 0$, then

$$s \leq -\frac{(a_i)_k}{\Delta(a_i)_k}. \tag{14.43}$$

- If $i = m$, then,

– If $(a_m)_t > 0$ and $\triangle(a_m)_t < 0$, then

$$s \leq -\frac{(a_m)_t}{\triangle(a_m)_t}. \tag{14.44}$$

– If $(a_m)_t < 0$ and $\triangle(a_m)_t > 0$, then

$$s \leq -\frac{(a_m)_t}{\triangle(a_m)_t} \tag{14.45}$$

– If $(a_m)_t = 0$ and $\triangle(F_m)_t \neq 0$, then

$$s \leq \frac{(\mu_t(F_m)_n - (F_m)_t)}{\triangle(F_m)_t}. \tag{14.46}$$

– If $(a_m)_k > 0$ and $\triangle(a_m)_k < 0$, then

$$s \leq -\frac{(a_m)_k}{\triangle(a_m)_k}. \tag{14.47}$$

– If $(a_m)_k < 0$ and $\triangle(a_m)_k > 0$, then

$$s \leq -\frac{(a_m)_k}{\triangle(a_m)_k}. \tag{14.48}$$

– If $(a_m)_k = 0$ and $\triangle(F_m)_k \neq 0$, then

$$s \leq \frac{(\mu_k(F_m)_n - (F_m)_k)}{\triangle(F_m)_k}. \tag{14.49}$$

If the minimum s comes from one of Eqs. (14.44) to (14.49), then the static-friction conditions are met at least in one of the tangent directions. We can carry out a quick test to determine whether they are met on both directions, and if so the mth iteration is completed. However, if the minimum s comes from any other equation, then we need to update the groups accordingly and loop back to repartition the system and solve it again. There are several cases to be considered when carrying out the update.

- If minimum s comes from Eq. (14.36), then move its associated index i from ZA_n to ZF_n.
- If minimum s comes from Eq. (14.37), then move its associated index i from ZF_n to ZA_n.
- If minimum s comes from Eq. (14.38), then move its associated index i from ZA_t to $MaxF_t$ if $\triangle(a_i)_t < 0$, or $MinF_t$ otherwise.
- If minimum s comes from Eq. (14.39), then move its associated index i from $MaxF_t$ to ZA_t.
- If minimum s comes from Eq. (14.40), then move its associated index i from $MinF_t$ to ZA_t.

Fig. 14.5 At any instant during the solution of Eq. (14.26), a contact point C_i can appear in three out of eight possible states. The *arrows* show the direction of the possible movements, together with the condition that needs to be satisfied to trigger the movement

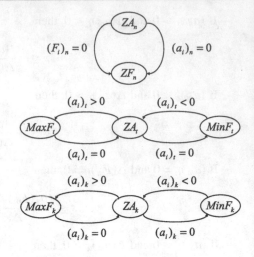

- If minimum s comes from Eq. (14.41), then move its associated index i from ZA_k to $MaxF_k$ if $\Delta(a_i)_k < 0$, or $MinF_k$ otherwise.
- If minimum s comes from Eq. (14.42), then move its associated index i from $MaxF_k$ to ZA_k.
- If minimum s comes from Eq. (14.43), then move its associated index i from $MinF_k$ to ZA_k.

  Figure 14.5 illustrates the possible state transitions between group indexes.

14.3.2 Dynamic Friction

Dynamic friction occurs whenever the relative tangential velocity at contact C_i differs from zero. In this case, the magnitude of the tangential contact-force components are always maximum, that is

$$(F_i)_t = \pm\mu_t(F_i)_n$$
$$(F_i)_k = \pm\mu_k(F_i)_n. \tag{14.50}$$

The sign in Eqs. (14.50) is chosen such that the contact force is pointing in the opposite direction of the tangential velocity, that is

$$\mathrm{sign}\big((F_i)_t\big) = -\,\mathrm{sign}\big((\vec{v}_r)_i \cdot \vec{t}\,\big)$$
$$\mathrm{sign}\big((F_i)_k\big) = -\,\mathrm{sign}\big((\vec{v}_r)_i \cdot \vec{k}\,\big),$$

where $(\vec{v}_r)_i$ represents the relative tangential velocity at contact point i.

Since the magnitude of the dynamic contact-force components is fixed and linearly proportional to the normal contact-force component, we can merge the three rows associated with contact C_i in Eq. (14.26) and make the following substitution of variable

$$\Delta(q_i)_n = (1 \pm \mu_t \pm \mu_k)\Delta(F_i)_n,$$

solve the system for $\Delta(q_i)_n$, and use its value to compute $\Delta(F_i)_n$, $\Delta(F_i)_t$ and $\Delta(F_i)_k$. In other words, we can use the same algorithm proposed in Sect. 14.3.1 for the static-friction case to enforce the dynamic-friction conditions at contact C_m.

At the m-iteration, we make the variable substitution and compute the appropriate $\Delta\vec{F}$ that enforces the normal conditions at all contact points, including C_m. Having done so, the tangential contact-force components are computed using Eqs. (14.50). Lastly, index m is assigned to the following groups.

- If $(a_m)_n = 0$, then add m to ZA_n.
- If $(F_m)_n = 0$, then add m to ZF_n.
- If $(a_m)_t = 0$, then add m to ZA_t.
- If $(a_m)_t \neq 0$, then add m to $MaxF_t$ if $\text{sign}(F_m)_t > 0$, or to $MinF_t$ otherwise.
- If $(a_m)_k = 0$, then add m to ZA_k.
- If $(a_m)_k \neq 0$, then add m to $MaxF_k$ if $\text{sign}(F_m)_k > 0$, or to $MinF_k$ otherwise.

14.3.3 Termination Conditions

Most of the termination-condition properties discussed for the frictionless case are still valid for the static-friction case, save the one that guarantees the existence of a positive scalar s. It can be shown that, for the frictionless case, the existence of a positive scalar $s > 0$ guarantees that the algorithm will always progress and will eventually terminate. However, in the static-friction case, there can be situations wherein the scalar s is zero.

Consider the case wherein the contact point C_i is initially assigned to ZA_n, and $(F_i)_n$ decreases to zero after some steps $s\Delta(F_i)_n$. In this case, the algorithm temporarily stops and moves index i from ZA_n to ZF_n, and adjusts the corresponding columns of matrix $\mathbf{A}$. The algorithm then proceeds to the next iteration, and we may find that $(a_i)_n$ immediately assumes a negative value. Again, the algorithm temporarily stops and moves index i from ZF_n to ZA_n, and adjusts the corresponding columns of matrix $\mathbf{A}$. Clearly, the algorithm is locked in an infinite loop with index i moving back and forth groups ZA_n and ZF_n.

Steps of size zero, such as the one just described, can be detected during program execution by keeping track of the group the index i just came from in the previous step, if any. If the group the index i is moving to is the same as the group it came from in the previous step, then the contact C_i is oscillating. The way to deal with this is to temporarily give up trying to assure both normal and static conditions at contact C_i. This has the effect of postponing the assurance of such conditions at C_i to a later time during the algorithm's execution. The rationale behind this strategy is that, when the algorithm comes back to contact C_i, more contacts have been assured and the conditions that created the loop may no longer be the current conditions of the problem. Unfortunately, the bottom line is that it can't be proved whether the algorithm will always terminate when static friction is considered.

In the dynamic-friction case, the situation gets even worse because the system matrix $\mathbf{A}$ is no longer symmetric, and is possibly indefinite. In this context, several properties that were used to guarantee the existence of a solution in the frictionless case no longer apply. Here, it is possible to have a situation in which, either the normal force component $(F_i)_n$, or the tangential force components $(F_i)_t$ and $(F_i)_k$, will indefinitely increase without driving $(a_i)_n$, $(a_i)_t$ or $(a_i)_k$ to zero. Another possible situation is that increasing the contact force components may not necessarily trigger a change in the index set of the groups ZA_n, ZF_n, ZA_t, $MaxF_t$, $MinF_t$, ZAk, $MaxF_k$ or $MinF_k$.

As for implementation, these cases correspond to finding an unbounded scalar[6] $s = \infty$. The way to deal with this is to treat as collisions all contacts C_i that are generating an unbounded scalar s, and apply the multiple-collision techniques presented in Chaps. 3 and 4 to resolve them. In summary, we resolve all contact first, and treat the remaining contacts that are generating unbounded scalars s as collisions.

14.4   Suggested Readings

The determination of the existence of a solution for a general LCP problem is known to be NP-hard, whereas finding the solution itself is a NP-complete problem. However, there are some special cases of the coefficient matrix $\mathbf{A}$ in which the LCP problem becomes convex, that is, the existence and actual computation of a solution can be done in polynomial time, with worst-case exponential time complexity. Such cases are addressed in detail in Cottle et al. [CPS92].

In the context of frictionless contact-force computations, the matrix $\mathbf{A}$ is symmetric and positive semi-definite (PSD), and the vector $\vec{b}$ lies in the column space of $\mathbf{A}$. Fortunately, this is one of the cases when a polynomial time algorithm can be used, such as Dantzig's algorithm described in Cottle et al. [CD68]. Baraff [Bar94, Bar93] presented a modification of Dantzig's pivot-based method to cope with both static and dynamic friction. In the latter case, the matrix $\mathbf{A}$ is not symmetric and possibly indefinite, and a solution may or may not be found. If a solution is not found, then Baraff's algorithm is capable of detecting such a situation, and indicates the contacts that should be dealt with as collisions in order to resolve the inconsistencies.

Other inconsistencies may also occur whenever vector $\vec{b}$ does not lie in the column space of $\mathbf{A}$. Such situations can happen when the contact geometry represents an unsatisfiable combination of kinematic constraints of the system. A more sophisticated implementation could use this to check for inconsistencies on user-definable configurations where some objects are attached to others by joints. Since in most

---

[6]Before computing s, we initialize it to ∞, such that we can detect at the end of the iteration whether $s = \infty$.

cases users have the freedom to attach joints to whichever objects they deem appropriate, inconsistencies may arise from an inattentive selection of joint attachments.

Usually, the linear system defined by Eq. (14.16) can be solved using standard Gaussian elimination techniques readily available from several books on linear algebra and matrix theory, such as Strang [Str91], Golub et al. [GL96] and Horn et al. [HJ91]. However, efficacy can be boosted if we use techniques that take into account the fact that consecutive invocations of the linear system differ by a few rows and columns from the previous invocation. Such techniques would incrementally update the LU decomposition of matrix $\mathbf{A}$ already computed in the previous step, as opposed to computing the decomposition from scratch. This has the effect of reducing the computational cost from $\mathcal{O}(n^3)$ to $\mathcal{O}(n^2)$. Gill et al. [GMSW87] discuss in detail an incremental factorization technique that maintains LU factors for general sparse matrices.

Another commonly used formulation of the contact-force computation states the problem as a quadratic programming problem (QP), that is

$$\min_f \left(f^t \mathbf{A} f - b^t f \right) \quad \text{subjected to} \quad \left\{ \begin{matrix} \mathbf{A}f \geq b \\ f \geq 0 \end{matrix} \right\}.$$

Lötstedt [Löt84] originally proposed this approach based on a simplification of the Coulomb friction model used to avoid the non-linear constraint:

$$\left| (f_i)_F \right| = \sqrt{(f_i)^2_{F_x} + (f_i)^2_{F_y}} \leq \mu(f_i)_N.$$

In this case, the LCP problem is transformed into a LQP optimization problem. Gill et al. [GM78] and Lawson et al. [LH74] present some numerically stable techniques that can be used to solve the LQP problem.

Finally, the proof of the termination conditions discussed in Sects. 14.2.1 and 14.3.3 can be found in Baraff [Bar94].

References

[Bar93] Baraff, D.: Issues in computing contact forces for non-penetrating rigid bodies. Algorithmica **10**, 292–352 (1993)

[Bar94] Baraff, D.: Fast contact force computation for non-penetrating rigid bodies. Comput. Graph. (Proc. SIGGRAPH) **28**, 24–29 (1994)

[CD68] Cottle, R.W., Dantzig, G.B.: Complementary pivot theory of mathematical programming. Linear Algebra Appl. **1**, 103–125 (1968)

[CPS92] Cottle, R.W., Pang, J.-S., Stone, R.E.: The Linear Complementarity Problem. Academic Press, San Diego (1992)

[GL96] Golub, G.H., Van Loan, C.F.: Matrix Computations. Johns Hopkins University Press, Baltimore (1996)

[GM78] Gill, P.E., Murray, W.: Numerically stable methods for quadratic programming. J. Math. Program. **14**, 349–372 (1978)

[GMSW87] Gill, P.E., Murray, W., Saunders, M.A., Wright, M.H.: Maintaining LU factors of a general sparse matrix. Linear Algebra Appl. **88/89**, 239–270 (1987)

[HJ91] Horn, R.A., Johnson, C.R.: Matrix Analysis. Cambridge University Press, Cambridge (1991)

[LH74] Lawson, C.L., Hanson, R.J.: Solving Least Squares Problems. Prentice-Hall, New York (1974)

[Löt84] Lötstedt, P.: Numerical simulation of time-dependent contact friction problems in rigid-body mechanics. SIAM J. Sci. Stat. Comput. 5(2), 370–393 (1984)

[Str91] Strang, G.: Linear Algebra and Its Applications. Academic Press, San Diego (1991)

Index